Alan Simpson's Windows® XP Bible

Alan Simpson's Windows® XP Bible

Alan Simpson with Brian Underdahl

Hungry Minds™

Best-Selling Books • Digital Downloads • e-Books • Answer Networks • e-Newsletters • Branded Web Sites • e-Learning

New York, NY ✦ Cleveland, OH ✦ Indianapolis, IN

Alan Simpson's Windows® XP Bible

Published by
Hungry Minds, Inc.
909 Third Avenue
New York, NY 10022
www.hungryminds.com

Library of Congress Control Number: 2001092883

ISBN: 0-7645-4860-3

Printed in the United States of America

10 9 8 7 6 5 4 3 2 1

1B/QU/QZ/QR/IN

Distributed in the United States by Hungry Minds, Inc.

Distributed by CDG Books Canada Inc. for Canada; by Transworld Publishers Limited in the United Kingdom; by IDG Norge Books for Norway; by IDG Sweden Books for Sweden; by IDG Books Australia Publishing Corporation Pty. Ltd. for Australia and New Zealand; by TransQuest Publishers Pte Ltd. for Singapore, Malaysia, Thailand, Indonesia, and Hong Kong; by Gotop Information Inc. for Taiwan; by ICG Muse, Inc. for Japan; by Intersoft for South Africa; by Eyrolles for France; by International Thomson Publishing for Germany, Austria, and Switzerland; by Distribuidora Cuspide for Argentina; by LR International for Brazil; by Galileo Libros for Chile; by Ediciones ZETA S.C.R. Ltda. for Peru; by WS Computer Publishing Corporation, Inc., for the Philippines; by Contemporanea de Ediciones for Venezuela; by Express Computer Distributors for the Caribbean and West Indies; by Micronesia Media Distributor, Inc. for Micronesia; by Chips Computadoras S.A. de C.V. for Mexico; by Editorial Norma de Panama S.A. for Panama; by American Bookshops for Finland.

For general information on Hungry Minds' products and services please contact our Customer Care department within the U.S. at 800-762-2974, outside the U.S. at 317-572-3993 or fax 317-572-4002.

For sales inquiries and reseller information, including discounts, premium and bulk quantity sales, and foreign-language translations, please contact our Customer Care department at 800-434-3422, fax 317-572-4002 or write to Hungry Minds, Inc., Attn: Customer Care Department, 10475 Crosspoint Boulevard, Indianapolis, IN 46256.

For information on licensing foreign or domestic rights, please contact our Sub-Rights Customer Care department at 212-884-5000.

For information on using Hungry Minds' products and services in the classroom or for ordering examination copies, please contact our Educational Sales department at 800-434-2086 or fax 317-572-4005.

For press review copies, author interviews, or other publicity information, please contact our Public Relations department at 317-572-3168 or fax 317-572-4168.

For authorization to photocopy items for corporate, personal, or educational use, please contact Copyright Clearance Center, 222 Rosewood Drive, Danvers, MA 01923, or fax 978-750-4470.

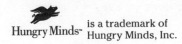

Hungry Minds™ is a trademark of Hungry Minds, Inc.

About the Author

Alan Simpson is a freelance computer/Internet consultant and veteran author of digilit (digital literature). He's the author of more than 80 computer books, published in many languages throughout the world. Alan is best known for his light, conversational writing style and clear jargon-free approach to dealing with technical topics. Prior to writing books full time, Alan taught introductory and advanced computer programming courses at San Diego State University and University of California, San Diego Extension. He also worked as a freelance programmer and computer consultant. He maintains the www.coolnerds.com Web site (when time permits), and can be reached at alan@coolnerds.com.

Brian Underdahl is the best-selling author of more than 50 computer books, including several current titles from IDG Books Worldwide: *Pocket PCs For Dummies*, *Opera Web Browser For Dummies*, *Windows 98 One Step at a Time*, *Internet Bible*, 2nd Edition, *Teach Yourself Office 2000*, *Teach Yourself Windows 2000 Professional*, and *Teach Yourself Windows Me*. Brian spends most of his time at the keyboard, writing about personal computing. When he finds the time, he enjoys taking in the view from the home he and his wife, Darlene, built in the mountains 2,000 feet above Reno, Nevada. He tries to find the time to attend Mensa meetings whenever possible, and he has become a fairly decent gourmet cook in the recent years, too.

Credits

Acquisitions Editor
Terri Varveris

Project Editor
Keith Cline

Technical Editor
Greg Guntle

Editorial Manager
Kyle Looper

Project Coordinator
Nancee Reeves

Graphics and Production Specialists
Jackie Nicholas, Jill Piscitelli,
Kendra Span, Erin Zeltner

Quality Control Technicians
Carl W. Pierce, Marianne Santy,
Robert Springer

Proofreading and Indexing
TECHBOOKS Production Services

To Susan, Ashley, and Alec, as always

Preface

Welcome to Alan Simpson's Windows XP Bible.

Professional Edition versus Home Edition

Microsoft Windows XP is the latest version of the widely used Windows operating system. This book covers both the Professional edition and Home edition of Windows XP. On the surface, the two editions are virtually identical. Skills you learn on one edition will carry right over to the other edition. The Professional edition offers some extra tools that are of interest to professional corporate system administrators and network administrators. The Professional edition is the only one to support the use of multiple monitors, however, which might be of interest to home and small business users as well. If you're wondering which version to buy, you might want to review Chapter 34, which covers the features of the Professional edition that aren't available in the Home edition.

Who Should Read This Book

This book is written for people who are *not* professional computer programmers or corporate administrators. It's written for that enormous class of people commonly referred to as *users* in the computer biz. These are people whose job requires them to *use* a computer as an adjunct to their "real job," which isn't necessarily computer science. I think it's safe to say that about 99 percent of the jobs in this world fall into that non-computer science category.

Of course, plenty of people just enjoy using their PCs at home. Or, at least, would like to *start* enjoying that PC at home. This book is certainly not "all work and no play." You can do tons of fun and creative things with Windows XP. And this book covers them all in considerable depth. So if you're just looking to get the most from your home PC, you've definitely come to the right place.

No Experience Required

This book is not an "upgrade" book for people who already know some earlier version of Windows by heart. Even if you're new computers and don't know a megabyte from a turtle dove, you'll do just fine.

Features of This Book

Like most books, this one has the standard table of contents in the front and an index at the back to help you find information on an as-needed basis. Within chapters, lots of pictures and step-by-step instructions are provided to speed your learning and help you get the most from your PC as quickly as possible. The chapters are grouped into parts dealing with specific features, as follows:

Part I: Know This or Suffer

This part covers all the basics of opening and closing things, finding stuff, navigating your computer, getting instant help, creating shortcuts, and more. If you're a newbie, this is the stuff you *really* need to know to get started.

Part II: Becoming an Internet Guru

The first chapter in this part tells you everything you need to get online and start using the Internet. Then you learn to use all the most popular features of the Internet, including the World Wide Web, e-mail, newsgroups, conferencing, gaming, and instant messages.

Part III: Have It Your Way

In this part, you learn how to customize your work environment to suit your needs. Some important basic skills covered here include creating folders; moving, copying, and deleting files; and personalizing Windows XP to your tastes, and using the new speech and handwriting recognition features.

Part IV: Growth, Maintenance, and General Tweaking

This part helps you perform routine maintenance tasks to keep your PC running at maximum speed. You also learn how to install new programs and eliminate old ones, protect your computer, keep Windows up-to-date, create and manage user accounts, and take advantage of a notebook computer.

Part V: Work and Play

In this part, you discover general techniques for working with text, numbers, and graphic images (pictures), music, video, movies, and DVD. Create your own custom audio CDs and movies, get pictures from digital cameras and scanners, and so forth.

Part VI: Local Area Networks

Here, you find out how to set up a local area network using the Home Networking Wizard. Learn how to share a single Internet connection and account, as well as share disk drives, printers, files, and folders. If you're already a member of a network, you'll learn how to take advantage of its features here.

Part VII: Advanced Stuff

This part covers some of the more advanced topics that may not be relevant to everyone. Also, I go deeper into some of the more technical stuff that normally stays hidden behind the scenes — such as the Registry, file associations, and advanced features of Windows XP Professional.

The book also has some margin icons:

Tip icons indicate a useful trick, technique, or other tidbit worth calling special attention to so that you don't miss it.

Caution icons point out a technique you need to think about before you act. Tread carefully because if you make a mistake, it'll be difficult — or impossible — to undo.

Cross-reference icons refer to a source of additional information on a topic (just in case I didn't already tell you enough to bore you to tears).

Note icons identify a piece of information that's especially noteworthy for some reason.

New Feature icons point out something that's "new" in Windows XP. Of course, how "new" a feature is depends on where you're coming from, so I've had to wing it a bit. As a general rule, if a feature wasn't available in Windows 2000 or Windows Millennium Edition, I've flagged it as "new."

Acknowledgments

Even though only the authors' names appear on the cover, every book is actually a team effort. Many people were involved in the creation of this book. My sincere thanks to all the people whose skills and talents helped to make this book a reality.

First of all, many, many thanks to everyone at Hungry Minds, Inc. who made this book happen. You were all very supportive, very professional, and very patient. In particular, I'd like to thank Kyle Looper (Editorial Manager), Terri Varveris (Acquisitions Editor), Keith Cline (Project Editor), and Nancee Reeves (Production Coordinator).

Many thanks to everyone at Microsoft for helping me get an early start on this great product and for all the support and answers provided along the way.

To Matt Wagner and everyone at Waterside: Thanks for getting this opportunity to me and for making the deal happen.

And, of course, to my family: Thank you, thank you, thank you for your patience and understanding. I really had to concentrate on this one and I appreciate all of your support.

—Alan Simpson

Many special thanks to Walt Bruce, Andy Cummings, and David Mayhew at Hungry Minds, Inc. for keeping me busy.

—Brian Underdahl

Contents at a Glance

Contents

Part III: Have It Your Way   315

Chapter 12: General Housekeeping (Copying, Deleting, and So On)   317

Part IV: Growth, Maintenance, and General Tweaking   441

Part V: Work and Play   555

Part VII: Advanced Stuff   719

Know This or Suffer

As the title of this part implies, these chapters cover all the "basic skills" you'll need to use Windows XP successfully. These skills apply to using your computer in general, and will also apply to virtually everything you ever do at your computer. No matter what your long-term goal is — be it to work with photographs, create a Web site, become a programmer, manage your business, or just have fun — the essential skills you'll learn here in Part I will provide the foundation on which you'll build your more advanced skills.

What Is Windows XP?

Hello, and welcome to *Alan Simpson's Windows XP Bible*. The goal of this book, as mentioned in the Introduction (which, if you're like me, you probably skipped), is to teach both beginners and experienced users alike how to really put Windows XP to work. Because this is a book for all levels of users, this chapter starts off with the absolute basics. And therefore, I suppose, a good starting point is to answer the question, "What is Windows XP?"

What Is Windows XP?

Windows XP is the latest and greatest version of the ubiquitous Windows operating system. The *XP* stands for experience (as in "The Jimi Hendrix . . ." for those of you who were around back then). This version of Windows is certainly going to offer a new experience for those of you coming from earlier versions of Windows. Part of Microsoft's goal in this new version was to create a smoother, frictionless work environment. After many weeks of using this new product, I think it's safe to say that they've accomplished that goal. It's difficult to isolate any one new feature that provides for this new experience. It's really about the new interface in general, and how easy it is to tweak things to be as you want them to be.

 If you're an experienced Windows user and want some specifics on what's new in Windows XP, see Appendix B.

For those of you who are new to the game, let's start by pointing out that Microsoft Windows XP is a computer program. Specifically, it's a type of program known as an *operating system*, often abbreviated OS. You may have heard of some of the other operating systems out there, such as DOS, the Mac OS used on Macintosh computers, and Linux and UNIX, used mainly in large businesses.

One thing that makes the OS different from all other programs available for PCs is that an OS is *required* to make your system work. A computer without an OS is like a car without an engine. Turning on a computer that has no operating system installed leads to nothing but a message on the screen telling you there is no operating system installed.

One reason that an operating system is required on all computers is that it plays the important role of making all the things that make up a computer system — the screen, mouse, keyboard, the programs you use, the hard disk, and all that other stuff — work in harmony. And thankfully, it does all that in the background, without your even being aware of it. And without your having to know how it does it.

The operating system also provides the user interface for the computer. That is, it determines what you see on your screen and how you interact with those things. To that extent, learning to use your computer is really a matter of learning to use its operating system. In fact, learning Windows XP is probably the most important first step in learning to use your computer. That's partly because you need to learn to use Windows just to start any other programs you plan to use. In addition, many of the skills you acquire while learning to use Windows will apply to just about anything you do with your computer, be that word processing, making custom CDs, working with digital photographs, creating Web pages . . . whatever. So every moment spent learning Windows is actually an investment in learning to use your entire computer and all the amazing things that it is capable of doing.

You might be aware that Windows XP comes in several different flavors, two of which are *client-side* products: the Windows XP Home Edition, and the Windows XP Professional Edition. This book covers both those products. The differences between these two products are so few, they're barely noticeable. When they do arise during the course of this book, however, I'll be sure to point them out.

The other versions are *server-side* products, named Windows XP Server and Windows XP Advanced Server. This book doesn't address those products specifically, because they're not the kinds of products the typical computer user would ever get involved with. Rather, they're products that corporate network administrators and other highly technical computer professions use to build *servers* for the Internet and large networks.

If you're a newbie, and if I've already gotten ahead of you here with this client/server business, I apologize for that. Frankly, it's not terribly important anyway. All that matters at this point is that you understand that this book is for people using either Windows XP Home Edition or Windows XP Professional Edition. With that out of the way, we can get back to the absolute basics.

Hardware and Software Basics

For those of you who are new to computers, this section discusses some basic terminology. Computer *hardware* is the stuff you can see and touch; if you throw it off the roof of a building, it will probably break. Your basic PC consists of the hardware components shown in Figure 1-1. Each component plays some role in helping you use the computer:

✦ **Monitor:** The big TV-like thing. Probably has its own on/off switch as well as brightness, contrast, and other buttons for fine-tuning the onscreen display.

✦ **Screen:** The part of the monitor where all the action takes place — similar to a TV set screen.

✦ **System unit:** The main body of the computer. Houses the main on/off switch plus access to the floppy disk and CD-ROM drives.

✦ **Mouse:** Your main tool for navigating (getting around) and for making the computer do what you want it to do. I'll talk about mice in more detail in a moment.

✦ **Keyboard:** Laid out like a standard typewriter, the keyboard is used for typing and, in some cases, can also be used as an alternative to the mouse.

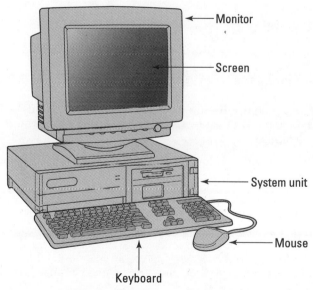

Figure 1-1: Basic PC hardware

Computer *software* refers to the somewhat invisible stuff that makes the computer do whatever it is you want it to do. Any program that you purchase or download, as well as any pictures, music, or other stuff you put "in your computer" is software. Software is information that's recorded to some kind of disk, such as a floppy disk, CD-ROM, or the hard disk that resides permanently inside your computer.

So with the basic concepts of hardware and software covered, let's start talking about how you use that stuff.

Mouse Basics

The one piece of hardware you need to get comfy with right off the bat is the mouse. To use the mouse, rest your hand comfortably on it, with your index finger resting (but not pressing) on the left mouse button, as shown in Figure 1-2. When the computer is on, you'll see a little arrow, called the mouse pointer, on the screen. As you roll the mouse around on a mouse pad or on your desktop, the mouse pointer moves in the same direction as you move the mouse.

 Figure 1-2: Rest your hand comfortably on the mouse, with your index finger near the button on the left.

The following list explains basic mouse terminology you need to know:

✦ **Mouse button (or primary mouse button):** Usually the mouse button on the left—the one that rests comfortably under your index finger when you rest your right hand on the mouse.

✦ **Right mouse button (or secondary mouse button):** The mouse button on the right.

✦ **Point:** To move the mouse so that the mouse pointer is touching, or "hovering over," some object on the screen.

✦ **Click:** To point to an item and then press and release the primary mouse button.

✦ **Double-click:** To point to an item and then click the primary mouse button twice in rapid succession—click click!

✦ **Right-click:** To point to an item and then press and release the secondary mouse button.

✦ **Drag:** To hold down the primary mouse button while moving the mouse.

✦ **Right-drag:** To hold down the secondary mouse button while moving the mouse.

Windows XP is geared toward two-button mouse operation. If your mouse has a little wheel in the middle, you can use that for scrolling, as discussed in Chapter 2. If your mouse has three buttons on it, you can ignore the button in the middle for now. I'll show you how you can get some hands-on experience using your mouse in a moment.

If you're a lefty, you can configure a mouse for left-hand use. Doing so makes the button on the right the primary mouse button and the button on the left the secondary mouse button (so your index finger is still over the primary mouse button). Chapter 15 provides instructions for switching your mouse buttons around for left-handed use.

Starting Windows XP

If Windows XP is already installed on your PC, starting Windows XP is a simple task. Follow these steps:

Caution   If Windows XP has not been installed on your PC already, refer to the instructions that came with your Windows XP package (or Appendix A in this book) for installation instructions.

1. If your computer has a floppy disk drive, check to make sure no disk is in that drive (see Figure 1-3). If you think a disk is in that drive, push the little button on the front of the drive to pop out the disk.

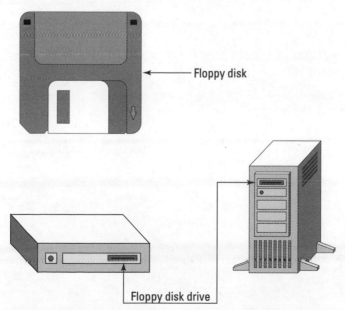

Floppy disk

Floppy disk drive

Figure 1-3: Remove any floppy disks from the floppy disk drive before turning on your computer.

2. Turn on all peripherals attached to your PC, such as your monitor and printer, and any other connected device that has its own on/off switch.

3. Turn on the main power on the system unit.

4. To ensure that your computer doesn't attempt to boot from a CD-ROM, open the CD-ROM drive and remove any CD that might be in there.

5. Wait a minute or so for your computer to boot up (start itself and load Windows XP for you).

You might see some weird, highly technical information whiz by on the screen. That phase of the startup is called the Power-On Self-Test (POST), and you can pretty much ignore it. What happens next depends on how your copy of Windows XP is set up. So just continue to read along and ignore anything that doesn't appear on your own screen.

Logging on

If your computer is set up to support multiple users, you'll first come to the Welcome screen, which looks something like the example shown in Figure 1-4. Just click your user name (or Guest, if you don't have an account on this computer) to proceed.

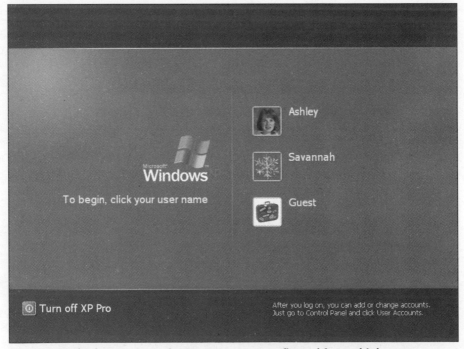

Figure 1-4: The logon screen for XP computers configured for multiple users

Why No Floppy Disk?

Floppy disks and CD-ROMs are used to transport software, like CDs and cassette tapes are used to transport music, from the factory to your PC. Software that you use all the time, such as Windows XP, is stored on the *hard disk* inside your computer. You never see this hard disk directly because it cannot be removed from the computer.

When you first turn on a computer, it may check to see whether a floppy disk is in drive A (the floppy drive). If there is a disk in that drive, the PC attempts to boot up (load the operating system) from that floppy. If the floppy doesn't contain an operating system, the PC won't start. Instead, some message such as `Non-System disk or disk error.` `Replace and press any key when ready` **appears onscreen.**

If that happens, remove the floppy disk from the floppy disk drive. On most computers, just push the little button on the front of the drive and the disk will pop out (if a disk is in the floppy drive). Then press any key on the keyboard (such as the spacebar, the Enter key, or some letter) to resume startup. Your PC will then automatically go to your hard drive (drive C, as it's called) and load the operating system from that drive.

If you then see a prompt requesting a password, go ahead and type your password. Note that passwords are *case-sensitive*. So if your company network administrator gave you a password, be sure to type it using exactly the same upper- and lower-case letters provided. Be aware that whenever you type a password, the letters you type won't appear onscreen. Instead, you'll just see a dot or asterisk for each character you type. The purpose of the dots or asterisks is to prevent someone from peeking over your shoulder to learn your password (technically known as shoulder surfing).

If this is the first time you've started Windows on this computer, and you don't want to assign yourself a password, you can leave the password box empty. If you do assign yourself a password, be sure to write that password down on a piece of paper and keep it in a secure place, using the same upper- and lowercase letters you use to type in the password. It would be a shame to forget your own password and then be locked out of your own computer!

 Note If you work in a company that requires a user name and password to log on, contact your company's network administrator to get an account.

To the desktop

Once you get past the logon procedure (and any other little gizmos that your computer manufacturer might have added to the mix), you'll get to the Windows XP *desktop*. I can't even tell you, for certain, exactly how that will look. When you get to the screen that has the Start button in the lower-left corner, and some icons (little pictures) on the screen, like the example shown in Figure 1-5, you'll know you're at the desktop.

Figure 1-5: The Windows XP desktop, from which all your journeys begin.

The desktop will be your home base for everything you do on the computer. Any other programs you start might temporarily cover the desktop. When you exit such a program, however, you'll be taken right back to the desktop. The desktop is *always* there, even if it's currently covered by something else.

The desktop gets its name from the fact that it plays the same role as your "real" desktop. If your real desktop looks anything like mine, it might be so covered with junk that you can hardly even see it. But that doesn't mean your desk has ceased to exist. Once you clear off some of the junk and put away some of the papers, your real desktop will still be there. The same holds true for the Windows desktop that's now (hopefully) visible on your screen.

The Windows XP Desktop

Throughout the rest of this book, we'll be showing the Windows desktop with a simple gray background rather than any fancy pictures. The reason being that the pictures in this book are quite a bit smaller than your screen, not to mention grayscale (black and white). So a plain gray background will make it easier to see the pictures in this book.

You can easily adjust the look and feel of your own Windows XP desktop to your liking, as you'll learn in Chapter 14.

With that in mind, take a look at Figure 1-6. This figure shows the names of the various doodads that appear on the Windows desktop. Becoming familiar with those names is a good idea, as you'll come across them constantly in your work with Windows XP. The sections that follow describe each item in some detail.

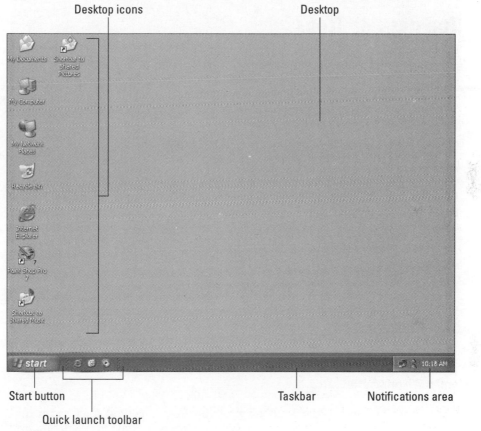

Figure 1-6: Names of things on the Windows XP desktop

The desktop

The desktop, proper, is the large area of the screen. Everything else you see on the screen is actually resting on top of this virtual desktop. As mentioned, from the moment you start your computer, to the moment you turn it off, the desktop is always there — when it's completely covered by some large program window.

The mouse pointer

The mouse pointer is the little indicator that moves when you move the mouse. As mentioned, to point to something, you rest this mouse pointer on it. Sometimes the mouse pointer appears as a hollow arrow. Other times, it has a different shape, depending on where it's currently resting. When the computer is busy doing something, the mouse pointer turns to a little hourglass symbol. That means "Wait — the computer is doing something." Wait until the mouse pointer changes back to a little arrow (or some other symbol) before you try clicking anything else on-screen.

The desktop icons

Each little picture on the desktop is an *icon*. Each icon, in turn, represents some program you can run, or some location on your computer where things are stored. The desktop icons on your computer probably won't match the ones shown in the figure, because different computers have different programs installed. And all Windows users (including you) can easily add new desktop icons, and delete unused ones, to their liking.

To open an icon, you either click or double-click it, depending on how your copy of Windows XP is currently configured. If you click a desktop icon and it doesn't open up into a window, your computer is set up for double-clicking. You'll have to double-click icons to open them for the time being. The section "To Single-Click or Double-Click" later in this chapter shows you how to choose one method or the other.

The taskbar

The *taskbar* is the colored strip along the bottom of the desktop. In a sense, the taskbar is like the center desk drawer of a real desk. It provides quick access to frequently used programs and features of Windows. Even when some large program window is covering the Windows desktop and its icons, the taskbar can remain visible on the screen so that you can get to the things if offers. As discussed in the sections that follow, the taskbar contains the Start button, the Quick Launch toolbar, and the Notifications area.

If you don't see the taskbar at all, it's probably hidden (out of the way for the moment). Typically, to bring the taskbar into view, you must move the mouse pointer down to the very bottom of the screen. If the taskbar doesn't slide into view automatically, you may have to drag it up. To do so, move the mouse button to the very bottom of the screen, hold down the primary (left) mouse button, drag the mouse pointer upward a half inch or so, and then release the mouse button. Chapter 13 explains how you can customize the appearance and behavior of the taskbar.

The Start button

The *Start button*, as the name implies, is where you can start any program on your computer. When you click the Start button, the Start menu opens (see Figure 1-7). The Start menu is divided into two sections. The left half of the menu provides access to frequently used programs. The right side provides access to frequently used *folders* (places where things that are "in your computer" are stored), as well as access to Help and Support and other features of Windows. Your Start menu won't look exactly like the one in the figure. Again, that's because it provides options, programs, and features that might be unique to your computer. Furthermore, you can easily customize the Start button to your liking, as discussed in Chapter 13.

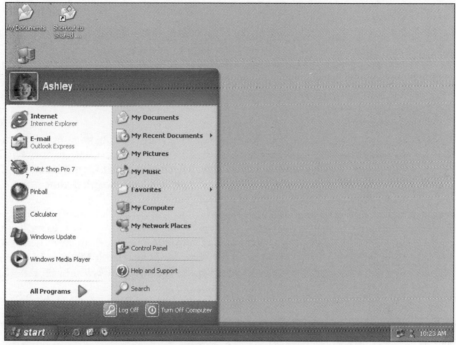

Figure 1-7: Click the Start button to open the Start menu.

As mentioned, the left half of the Start menu provides access to frequently used programs. To gain access to all the programs installed on your computer, click the All Programs button on the Start menu.

The Quick Launch toolbar

The Quick Launch toolbar (also called the *application launcher*) provides one-click access to commonly used programs. It provides an alternative to going through the Start menu to start these programs (and can be handy when your desktop icons are covered by some large program window). When you point to an icon in the Quick Launch toolbar, you'll see the name of the program or service that the icon represents.

The Show Desktop icon on the Quick Launch toolbar provides a service I wish I had on my real desktop. When you click it, all open windows on the desktop are instantly swept out of view, so you can see your desktop again. Clicking that button a second time brings all the clutter back onto the desktop. As discussed later, you can also bring items back onto the desktop one at a time, by clicking their taskbar buttons, which will be visible whenever you have programs open on the desktop.

The Notifications area

The Notifications area contains the clock, and icons that keep you posted as to the status of various programs or services running on your computer. Pointing to the current time reveals the current date. Double-clicking the current time brings up a *dialog box* that lets you set the current date, in case it's wrong. (As you'll learn, a dialog box is a window that pops up on the screen and provides options from which you can choose.)

When you point to an icon in the Notifications area, a brief message displays describing what the icon means. Although this varies from one program to the next, clicking an icon in the Notifications area will display options for that item. Double-clicking the icon will display more information and options for that item.

You also might see an occasional message pop up from the Notifications area. Sometimes these are messages from Windows and inform you of some feature you might have overlooked. If your computer is connected to the Internet, you also might receive messages regarding updates that are available at Microsoft's Web site, to keep your system up-to-date. These messages are always self-explanatory—you just have to follow the instructions provided by the message.

You're Not Helpless

Most beginners need to overcome two major hurdles to really start using their computers. The first is the sheer anxiety that comes from fear of the unknown. "Am I going to do the wrong thing and ruin the computer?" "Am I going to find out I'm too stupid to work this thing?" The answer to both questions is definitely no. There is no secret "ruin this computer" button that you can accidentally click. In fact, if you sat blindfolded at the computer for hours and just clicked away and pounded the keyboard at random, you would probably do no harm whatsoever.

If you're thinking you're too stupid, you're dead wrong, The very fact that you can read these words proves that you're smart enough. Unlike the olden days of computing, when you practically had to be an electrical engineer just to use the darn thing, modern-day computing is a simple matter of pointing and clicking. Granted, you weren't just *born* knowing how to work a computer. But neither was anyone else. If Albert Einstein came back to life and was placed in front of a computer, he wouldn't have a *clue* as to how to work it either. We all have to learn the things we weren't just born knowing—which is pretty much, everything!

The second big bugaboo that plagues newbies is the feeling of helplessness that comes from not knowing what to do next. "If only there were someone sitting right here to answer all my questions." Well, paying someone to sit there and answer all your questions can be a bit expensive—and also quite unnecessary, because there are lots of ways to get help and information as you go. The sections provide all the proof that you're really not as helpless as you may feel from time to time.

Backing out of jams

Sometimes, especially as a beginner, you might open some item and then not know what to do with it. In this case, you'll probably want to back out of that selection until you get to more familiar territory. When you find yourself in unfamiliar territory, try any of these techniques to back out of your current situation gracefully:

✦ Click somewhere on the desktop, or some other neutral looking area of the screen. Doing so will often undo whatever your last click did.

✦ Press the Escape key (labeled Esc or Cancel) on the keyboard. This key is so named because it enables you to escape from unfamiliar territory. And it's a darn good key to become familiar with.

✦ Look for any of the buttons shown in Figure 1-8. If you see one, click it. You'll be taken back to wherever you were before without a hitch.

Figure 1-8: The Escape key, and any of these buttons, will help you back out of unfamiliar territory.

✦ If all else fails, press Alt+F4. (On the keyboard, hold down the key labeled Alt, press and release the key labeled F4, and then release the Alt key.) This key combination closes whatever window is currently open.

If you can remember these techniques, you should be able to back your way out of any jam, no matter how lost you feel. If you really, really, really get stuck and none of the previous techniques work, and the computer appears to be *hung* (not responding normally to your keystrokes and mouse clicks), you might have to use the Windows Task Manager to locate and kill the offending task. This is the least desirable approach because it doesn't give you a chance to save any work you've completed. If all else fails, however, it might be your last resort.

To get to the Windows Task Manager, right-click the taskbar and choose Task Manager from the menu that appears. Alternatively, press Ctrl+Alt+Del (hold down the Ctrl key, hold down the Alt key, hold down the Delete keys simultaneously for a moment), and then release all three keys. The Windows Task Manager opens (see Figure 1-9).

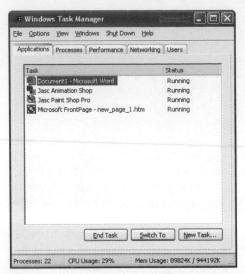

Figure 1-9: The Windows Task Manager

The Task Manager will list all running programs. The hung program (if any) will have the words not responding after the program name in the Status column of the display. Click the name of that errant program, and then click the End Task button. The program should close, and things should return to normal. To close the Windows Task Manager, click the Close (large red X) button in its upper-right corner.

Again, only use the Windows Task Manager as a last resort. As you'll learn later, there are far better and safer ways to end "normally" running programs.

Using the Help and Support Center

Windows XP offers a wide range of Help and Support options. You can see what's available by doing either of the following:

✦ Click the Start button, and then click Help and Support.

✦ Press the Help key (labeled F1 near the upper-left corner of your keyboard).

Tip   The Help key (F1) is almost universal. You can press it in just about any program to get help for whatever program you're working with at the moment.

The Help and Support Center will open (see Figure 1-10). Some options on the screen are updated automatically from time to time, via the Internet. So yours may not look exactly like the one shown. To use this, just click any blue text that looks interesting. The Windows basics help topic provides instructions for specific tasks (although not in any particular order).

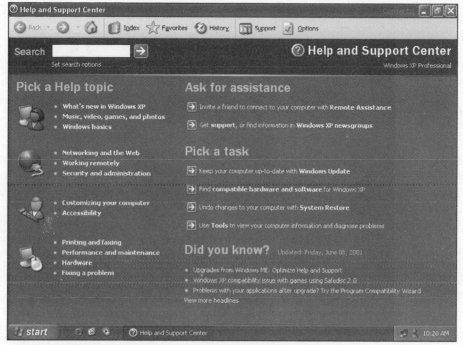

Figure 1-10: Windows XP Help and Support Center window

Tip To see whether an item is clickable, point to it. If the mouse pointer changes to a little pointing hand, go ahead and click. Of course, you can always just click, and perhaps double-click the item. If nothing happens, you know it's not clickable.

Buttons across the top of the Help and Support Center window help you get around within Help, as follows:

✦ **Back:** After you go to a new page, you can press the Back button to return you to the page you just left.

✦ **Forward (right-pointing arrow):** The forward-pointing arrow to the right of the Back button enables you to return to the page that you just backed out of (if any.)

✦ **Home:** Takes you back to the first page of Help and Support Center, shown in Figure 1-10.

✦ **Index:** Takes you to the Help system index, which is the same as the index at the back of a book. For more information, see the section "Using Help's Search and Index features" later in this chapter.

✦ **Favorites:** Lists Help topics you have added to your list of favorites, as discussed in the section "Using Help's Search and Index features."

✦ **History:** Displays a list of Help pages you have already visited.

✦ **Support:** Provides an overview of Support options available from Microsoft.

Those buttons alone will enable you to explore the Help system on your own. When looking for help with specific questions, however, the Search and Index features will be your best bet.

Using Help's search and index features

The Search box is always available in the Help and Support Center window. To use it, just click the text box titled Search. If there's already some text in that box that you want to get rid if, just drag the mouse pointer through that text. Whatever you type replaces that selected text. Type in a word or phrase that describes what you need help with, and then click the button just to the right of where you typed the word or phrase. In Figure 1-11, for example, I typed **Make a CD** and then clicked the button. The Help window splits into two panes. The left pane displays topics relevant to my search. To see the help for any of those listed topics, just click the topic. The right pane will display the help.

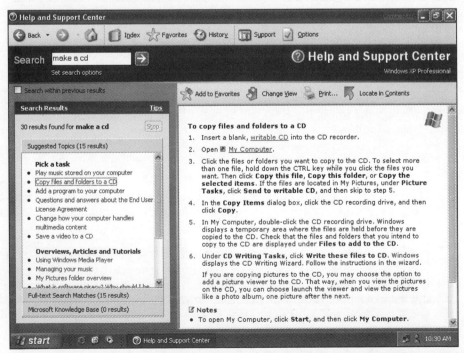

Figure 1-11: Results of searching for "Make a CD" and clicking the Copy files and folders to a CD topic

What's with the Internet Connection Wizard?

Some of the choices within the Help system will attempt to access the Internet to provide you with the most current information. If your computer isn't connected to the Internet, you'll end up at an Internet Connection Wizard dialog box rather than at the appropriate Internet page. As discussed in Chapter 5, you need some kind of modem and an account with an *Internet service provider* (ISP) to get beyond the Internet Connection Wizard to the Help page you were actually supposed to see. Part II of this book tells you everything you need to know. For now, if you just want to close the Internet Connection Wizard without setting up an account, click the Cancel button near the lower-right corner of the Internet Connection Wizard dialog box.

The right pane offers help on the topic you clicked, usually in the form of step-by-step instructions. To see the definition of any green underlined term, just click the term. Buttons above the right pane offer the following:

✦ **Add to Favorites:** Adds the Help topic to your list of favorites. At any time in the future, you can quickly jump back to this topic by clicking the Favorites button near the top of the screen.

✦ **Change View:** Removes the left pane so that you can see more of what's behind the window. Clicking that button a second time restores the left pane.

✦ **Print:** Prints the current Help page.

If the amount of text available in the window is longer than what can display on the Help screen, a scroll bar will appear to the right of the text. You can scroll through the text by clicking the buttons at the top and bottom of the scroll bar. Or, if your mouse has a wheel, click anywhere within the text and spin the wheel on your mouse to scroll up or down.

Tip   You'll learn more about using scroll bars in Chapter 2.

The Help index, which appears when you click the Index button near the top of the page, displays an index to the Help system, similar to the index at the back of a book. You can scroll through the index using the scroll bar at its right edge. Optionally, click in the text box below `Type in the keyword to find` and start typing some word that best describes the information you're looking for. As you type, you'll automatically be taken to the part of the index that matches what you have typed so far. If you locate an index entry that matches what you're looking for, click it. Then click the Display button below the index. If several topics are available, a Topics Found dialog box displays. Click whichever topic in that dialog box best describes what you're looking for, and then click the Display button.

Figure 1-12 shows an example where I searched for the word *volume*. When I got to that section of the index, I chose `adjusting speaker volume` to display the help you see in the right pane.

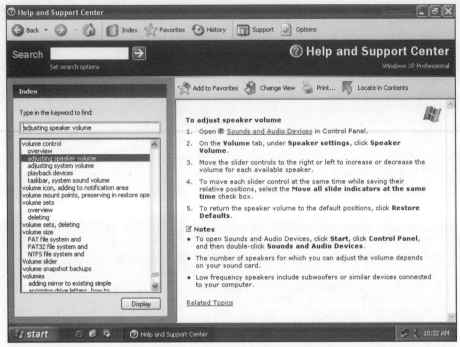

Figure 1-12: The Help index in the left pane of Window's Help and Support window

Whether you use Search or the Help index to get help on specific topics is entirely up to you. I do recommend trying Search first, however, as it's easier and often produces better results. If you can't find what you're looking for using Search, then try the Help index.

Closing Help

The Windows Help and Support Center window is like any other window. You can size it and move it like any other. You'll learn specific techniques for doing so in Chapter 2. But one thing you'll want to learn right now is that you can close *any* open window on the screen by clicking the Close (X) button in the upper-right corner of the window. So when you're done with Help and want to close its window, to uncover the desktop once again, just go ahead and click the Close button.

Tip   For an overview of Windows XP, click the Start button and choose Tour Windows XP. Alternatively, if you don't see that option on the Start menu, click the All Programs option and choose Accessories, and then choose Tour Windows XP from the menu.

ToolTips, right-clicks, and the "What's This?" button

Although the Help system provides extensive help, you can get to a couple of simple "quick and dirty" types of help without going through the Help system. For starters, be aware that just about everything you see on your screen has a small hidden *ToolTip*. This is really no more than the name of the item in most cases. However, when you cannot figure out what the heck some icon is supposed to represent, you can just point to the item for a moment to reveal its tiny ToolTip.

Most items also offer shortcut menus. If you're not quite sure what's going to happen when you click an icon, or want a quick overview of the options available for an icon, try right-clicking, rather than clicking, the item. Usually you'll see a little shortcut menu of options. In Figure 1-13, for example, I right-clicked directly on the desktop. You can see the shortcut menu that appeared after I did so.

If the item you right-clicked can be customized in any way, shape, or form, you'll see a Properties option in the menu. An item's *properties* are its characteristics, such as color, size, shape, and so forth. Choosing the Properties option will take you to the dialog box for changing that item's properties.

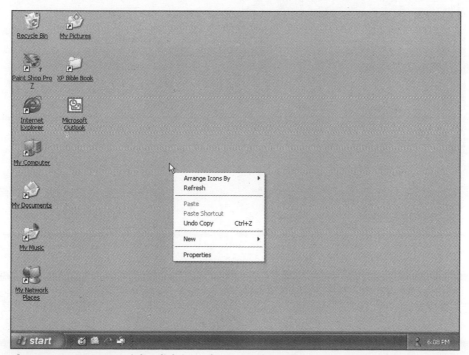

Figure 1-13: You can right-click just about anything on the screen to see a menu of options relevant to that item.

If the item you right-clicked can be moved, renamed, deleted, and so forth, you'll see appropriate options. You can never do any harm by right-clicking an item, so don't be afraid to try it. If, for whatever reason, the item you right-clicked has no shortcut menu, nothing will happen when you right-click. If you right-click an item, and then decide not to make a selection from the shortcut menu, just click some neutral area outside the shortcut menu, or press the trusty Escape key, to close the menu without making a selection.

Caution   Never, ever delete something just because you don't know what it is! You should delete only items you recognize and are sure you want to get rid of. Otherwise, you might delete a file that's important to the proper functioning of Windows, which would make your computer perform erratically, or not at all!

Finally, if you're in a program or dialog box, look to the upper-right corner of its window to see whether there's a button with a question mark on it. For example, the Date and Time Properties dialog box shown in Figure 1-14 has one. (To open the dialog box, I double-clicked the current time in the lower-right corner of the screen.)

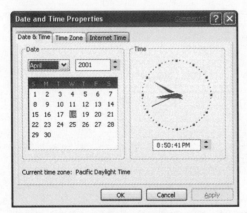

Figure 1-14: A "What's This?" button, identified by a question mark (?), is available in this sample dialog box.

The button with the question mark is called the What's This? button. As the name implies, it answers the question "What the heck is *that* thing?" that's likely to pop into your mind from time to time. To use the button, click it. The mouse pointer gains a question mark. Next, within the dialog box, click the item you're wondering about. An extra large ToolTip appears, giving you more information about the item.

Unfortunately, the What's This? button isn't universally available. And not all items that you click will have Help text associated with them. When the button is available, however, it can certainly come in handy!

To Single-Click or Double-Click

Before we close this chapter, I want to take you through your first complete practical use of the Start menu, a dialog box, and some other features discussed in this chapter. Here you'll decide whether you want to click or double-click icons to open them. To give it a whirl, follow these steps:

1. Click the Start button in the lower-left corner of the screen.

2. Click the Control Panel option. The Control Panel opens, looking something like Figure 1-15.

 Note

If you see a bunch of icons in your Control Panel, rather than the categories shown in the figure, click Switch to Category View in the left pane of the window.

3. Click Appearance and Themes.

4. Click Folder Options near the bottom of the window that opens. The Folder Options dialog box displays (see Figure 1-16).

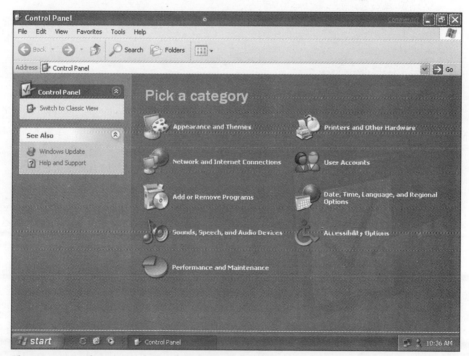

Figure 1-15: The Control Panel, in Category view

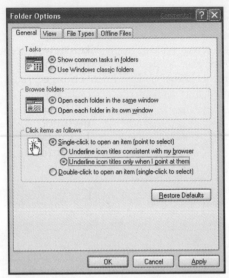

Figure 1-16: The Folder Options dialog box

5. To make sure your open windows resemble the ones shown in this book, click Show Common Tasks in Folders to select that option (as in the figure).

6. Under Click Items As Follows, choose either the Single-Click To Open . . . or Double-Click To Open option, depending on which you prefer. (I always use single click).

7. If you opted for single-clicking, you can choose to have clickable items underlined all the time (consistent with your Web browser), or only when you point to them.

8. Click the OK button at the bottom of the dialog box. Your selections are saved and the dialog box closes. You're back at the Control Panel window.

Caution   Clicking the Close (X) button at the top of a dialog box closes the box without saving your changes. To apply the selections you've made in a dialog box, click its OK button. More on dialog boxes coming up in Chapter 2.

9. To close the Control Panel window, click the Close (X) button in its upper-right corner. You're back at the desktop now.

To test your selection, click any desktop icon. If it opens, you've selected single-clicking. If it doesn't open, you must have selected double-clicking. In that case, try double-clicking any icon to open it. To close whatever window the icon opens, do the usual thing. Click the Close (X) button in the upper-right corner of the window.

Logging Off, Shutting Down

Your computer is not a TV. One of the most common mistakes newbies make when using a PC is simply to turn off the PC when they're done. This is not good because it doesn't give you, or your computer, a chance to save any changes you made or any work you accomplished. The first thing you want to do when you plan to shut down your computer—or even just plan to walk away from it for a while—is save any work in progress. In this chapter, you haven't created anything, so there's nothing to save. But for future reference, bear in mind that anything left unsaved on your screen is likely to go bye-bye forever if you don't remember to save your work before shutting down your computer.

Tip As you'll learn in Chapter 3, you can easily save your work at any time. In fact, it's a good idea to save your work every few minutes, just to make sure you don't accidentally lose it.

You can end your session at the computer a few different ways. If you share this computer with others, and want to leave it on for them, you can just log off. Doing so will allow others to log on immediately, but they won't be able to see or change any of your stuff. To log off, follow these steps:

1. Click the Start button.

2. Click the Log Off button near the bottom of the menu.

3. Click the Log Off button that appears.

The Welcome screen shown back near the beginning of this chapter reappears. The computer is still running, so another user can log on simply by clicking his or her user name.

To shut down the computer altogether, or put it to sleep so to speak, so that it consumes little or no electricity, follow these steps:

1. Click the Start button.

2. Click the Turn Off Computer button near the bottom of the menu. The Turn Off Computer dialog box displays (see Figure 1-17, although your options may vary)

Figure 1-17: The Turn Off Computer dialog box

3. Choose one of the following options (as available):

- **Hibernate:** Saves everything on the screen and puts the computer into a minimal power-consumption state. When you restart the computer, the desktop will look exactly as you left it (hopefully).

- **Standby (if available):** Puts the computer into a minimal power-consumption state, but does not save current settings. Restart will be quicker than if you had turned off. But you'll be returned to an empty desktop.

- **Turn Off:** Turns the computer all the way off. Nothing is saved, no power is consumed while the computer is off, and restarting will be from scratch. (The computer will go through the POST again at restart.)

- **Restart:** Briefly shuts off the computer, and then instantly restarts it. Also known as *rebooting*. Required after certain kinds of hardware and software installations, and also after a serious "crash" when something has caused your computer to start acting weird.

Your computer might show additional instructions at this point. Most likely, however, the computer will just shut down (or go to sleep.) Note that if you selected Turn Off, chances are your computer will indeed shut itself off. So you don't need to press the Power button on the system unit to finish the job. However, some older computers don't have this capability, in which case you will need to press the main Power button to complete the shutdown procedure. As a safety device, to prevent accidental shutdown, some computers require that you press the Power button and hold it there for four or five seconds before the computer actually shuts down.

Summary

In this chapter, you learned the most important of Windows XP basic skills. My goal in this chapter has been to help those of you who are new to this program become comfortable with using the mouse and get a sense for the way things work. Chapter 2 rounds out what you have learned here and hopefully answers any questions that might have popped into your mind as you read this chapter. Here's a quick recap of the important points covered in this chapter:

✦ Windows XP is an operating system—the mandatory program that makes everything work behind the scenes, and also determines how you, the user, will interact with the computer to get things done.

✦ To start Windows XP, just turn on your computer. (First make sure there is no floppy disk in the floppy drive.)

✦ After Windows XP has successfully started, you are taken to the Windows desktop, your "home base" from which you'll start all projects, and where you'll end up when you've finished.

✦ To point to an item (or hover over an item) means to move the mouse pointer (using your mouse) so that it's touching the item.

✦ To click an item means to point to it and then press and release the primary (left) mouse button. Double-click means to do the same, but you press and release the primary mouse button twice in rapid succession.

✦ To right-click an item means to point to it and then press and release the secondary (mouse) button.

✦ If you find yourself in unfamiliar territory, try clicking some neutral area of the desktop, or pressing the trusty Escape key (sometimes labeled Esc or Cancel on your keyboard) to back out of the situation.

✦ To get help in Windows, press the F1 key or click the Start button and choose Help and Support.

✦ To close any window that's taking up space on your screen, click its Close button (marked with an X and always in the upper-right corner of the window.)

✦ Before leaving your PC for any length of time, you should either log off or shut down the computer using options available at the bottom of the Start menu.

✦ If you're asked about saving any work in progress while logging off or shutting down, choose Yes unless you're sure you haven't completed any work worth saving.

✦ ✦ ✦

Getting Around Like a Pro

A big part of learning to use a computer is knowing where, and how, to find stuff. This holds true regardless of how you plan to use your computer, be it for writing, math, photography, art, music, the Internet — you name it. The easy, yet important, skills you learn in this chapter will apply to everything you do with your computer. Like the basic skills covered in Chapter 1, the Windows XP skills covered in this chapter are really skills you need to use your computer effectively, regardless of what you plan to do with it.

Managing Icons

Imagine a desk with all the usual accoutrements: telephone, calculator, calendar, pens and pencils, the documents you're using, and a big stack of bills. Now imagine you have the power to touch any one of those objects and shrink it to the size of a pea, just to get it out of the way temporarily. That power would certainly help unclutter your desktop. When you need to use one of those pea-sized objects, you could tap it with your finger, and bingo: The object would open in its natural size.

Of course, no real-world desktop works this way. The Windows XP desktop, however, works exactly that way. You can make things grow and shrink, appear and disappear, just by clicking them with your mouse.

A pea-sized object on your computer screen is called an *icon*. As you saw back in Chapter 1, there are probably some icons right on top of your desktop, as well as some smaller icons in the Quick Launch toolbar and Notifications area of the taskbar. Icons also appear within many of the program windows you open on your desktop.

The appearance of an icon often gives you some clue about what kind of stuff is inside the icon and what is likely to appear when you open the icon. The following list summarizes the main types of icons you'll come across:

✦ **Folder icon:** Represents a folder, a place on the computer where files are stored. Opening a folder icon displays the contents of that folder. For example, in Figure 2-1 the My Documents, My Music, My Pictures, XP Bible on Max, and 01Chap desktop icons are all folder icons. Two of those folders, My Pictures and 01Chap are currently open in the desktop. Each of those folders contains still more icons.

✦ **Program icon:** Represents a program. When you open a program icon, you start the program it represents. For example, opening the Internet Explorer icon launches the Microsoft Internet Explorer program. There's no real consistency to program icons. Each is just a "logo" of the underlying program.

✦ **Document icon:** Represents a document; typically this is something you can change and print. The icon usually has a little dog-ear fold in the upper-right corner to resemble a paper document. For example, inside the 01Chap window in the lower-right corner of Figure 2-1, many of the icons represent Microsoft Word documents (hence the letter W in the icon). The Grandmom icon in the upper My Pictures window is also a document icon. It represents a picture stored on disk. I'm currently viewing the contents of that folder in Thumbnails view, which, as you'll learn later, displays a small thumbnail-sized image of the actual photo, as opposed to some generic icon.

✦ **Shortcut icon:** The little arrow in the lower-left corner of an icon identifies that icon as a shortcut to some program, document, folder, or Web site. Unlike most icons, which generally represent an actual file or location on your disk, shortcut icons just provide quick access to things. Several of the desktop icons in Figure 2-1 are shortcuts. You'll learn how to create and use shortcuts in Chapter 4.

You also will come across icons that don't fall into any of these categories. Some icons represent disk drives, printers, help files, settings, and so on. Don't worry, however, you can manipulate virtually all icons by using the set of basic skills in the following list:

✦ As you know, you can open any icon by double-clicking it. If you've opted to switch to the single-click approach, you also can open the icon with a single-click. Whatever the icon represents will open in a *window* atop the desktop, as discussed in a moment.

✦ To move an icon, drag it to any new location on the screen. To move a bunch of icons, first select the icons you want to move by dragging the mouse pointer. Then drag the whole selection to a new place on the screen.

Tip   Remember, to drag something means to rest the mouse pointer on the item you want to move, and then to hold down the mouse button as you move the mouse pointer to the new location. To drop the item at the new location, just release the mouse button.

Figure 2-1: Various icons displayed on the Windows desktop, and within a couple of open windows

✦ To see all the options available for an icon, right-click the icon to open its shortcut menu.

✦ To organize all the icons on the desktop, right-click an empty part of the desktop and choose Arrange Icons By on the shortcut menu that appears. Then click whichever option you prefer (Name, Type, and so forth). Choosing Name will arrange the icons into (roughly) alphabetic order (although some icons, such as My Documents, My Computer, and Recycle Bin, tend to stay near the upper-left corner of the screen).

✦ To have Windows XP automatically arrange icons for you, right-click an empty part of the desktop or the window and choose Arrange Icons By from the menu, and then choose Auto Arrange from the submenu that appears. After you have done this, however, you cannot move icons, because they will immediately jump back into their original place. To turn off the automatic arrangement, repeat this step. When Auto Arrange has a check mark next to it, that feature is currently turned on.

✦ If you prefer to put icons into your own order, and want them neatly arranged, choose Arrange Icons By ⇨ Align to Grid. After you do so, the icons will align on an invisible grid, creating a neater appearance.

As mentioned, when you open an icon, a window appears. Learning how to work those windows is an important part of using your PC. As you learn in the next section, you have quite a bit of control over the size and shape of every window that appears on your screen.

Managing Open Windows

In the olden days of computers, when you ran a program, that program took over the entire screen. To use a different program, you had to exit the one you were in and then start the other program. That program, in turn, hogged the entire screen. With WindowsXP, you can pretty much run as many programs as you want. Instead of hogging the entire screen, each program occupies only a *window* on the screen. That's where the name *Windows* comes from in Microsoft Windows. In Figure 2-2, for example, I currently have two open windows on the screen: one titled My Computer, the other titled Windows Media Player. You can see the title (name) of each window in its upper-left corner.

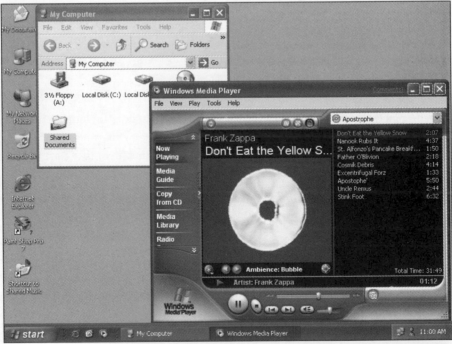

Figure 2-2: Two open windows on the desktop: My Computer and Windows Media Player

What's with the ⇨ ?

Throughout this book, I use the symbol ⇨ to separate options you choose in a series. For example, "Click the Start button and choose All Programs ⇨ Accessories ⇨ Notepad" is a shortcut way of saying "Click the Start button, choose the All Programs option, choose the Accessories option, and then click the Notepad option."

Window dressing

Every window that you open on your desktop will have certain elements in common. What's *inside* the window will vary a lot, because all programs display within windows. If you look closely, however, you may notice the frames surrounding those windows are similar. The reason for this similarity is simple: All the tools you use to manage the window are in this frame. Because of this arrangement, you need to learn only one set of skills to manage windows. Those skills then apply to any and all open windows. Figure 2-3 points out the tools that are common to most windows.

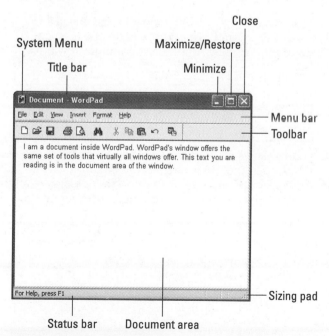

Figure 2-3: Features available on most windows that open on your desktop

Most windows have all the tools shown in Figure 2-3. The following sections describe how you work with each tool. (If you want to open the WordPad window on your own screen, click the Start button and choose All Programs ⇨ Accessories ⇨ WordPad.)

Title bar

The title bar shows the System Menu icon, the title of the window or name of the program being run in the window, and the buttons for resizing and closing the window. The title bar alone offers some handy features:

✦ To expand a window to full-screen size or to shrink it back to its original size, double-click its title bar.

✦ To move a window to some new location on the screen, drag the window by its title bar.

Tip Remember, to *drag* something means to put the mouse pointer on it and then to hold down the mouse button while moving the mouse. You can move a window only if it's smaller than the entire screen.

Minimize button

When you click the Minimize button, the window disappears and shrinks to a button in the taskbar. Doing so gets the window out of the way for the moment so that you can see the desktop behind that window. To reopen a minimized window, click its button in the taskbar.

Every open window has a button in the taskbar associated with it. As an alternative to using the Minimize button to hide/show a window, you can just click that button in the taskbar.

To instantly minimize all open windows on your screen, thereby showing the desktop, click the Show Desktop button in the Quick Launch toolbar. Doing so instantly clears all the clutter from your desktop, but only by hiding—not closing—all the open windows. To redisplay all open windows, click that button a second time.

Tip As an alternative to using the Show Desktop button, you can right-click some neutral area of the taskbar, perhaps just to the left of the Notifications area. Then choose Show the Desktop from the menu that appears. To restore the windows to their previous size, right-click the same area again and choose Show Open Windows.

Maximize/Restore button

Clicking the Maximize button expands the window to full-screen size (a quick way to hide other windows that may be distracting you). When the window is full-screen size, the Maximize button turns into the Restore button. To return the window to its previous size, click the Restore button.

Closing versus Minimizing a Window

Think of minimizing a window as taking some document on a real desktop and sliding it into a desk drawer. The document is not cluttering your desk anymore, but it is within easy reach. Just click the document's taskbar button, and you're back in action. Closing a window, on the other hand, is more like putting a real folder back in the file cabinet. You still can get back to the document when you want it, but you'll need to restart the program from scratch, at which point it opens up with no document. Then you need to open the document you want to work with using options on the program's File menu, as discussed in Chapter 3.

From a technical standpoint, closing a window has two advantages: It frees the memory (RAM) the program was using, and it gives you an opportunity to save your work. Minimizing a window does neither of those; it just shrinks the window to a taskbar button to get it out of the way for the moment.

Tip   You also can double-click an open window's title bar to maximize or restore it.

Close button

Clicking the Close button closes the window, taking it off the screen and out of the taskbar as well. To restart the program in the future, you'll need to go through whatever procedure you usually perform to start that program.

Caution   When you start creating your own documents, be aware that closing a program closes the document as well. If you don't *save* your work before closing the program, all that work will be lost! You'll learn about creating and saving documents in Chapter 3.

Sizing pad

The sizing pad in the lower-right corner of the window enables you to size the window. Just point to the sizing pad, and then drag it outward to enlarge the window, or inward to shrink the window. You can actually size a window by dragging any edge or any corner of the window. The sizing pad just provides for a slightly larger target on which to rest the mouse pointer.

Menu bar

Many windows that you open will have a menu bar across the top. The menu bar offers access to all the features that the program within the window has to offer. When you click on a menu option, a menu drops down (as in the example shown in Figure 2-4, where I've clicked the File menu option in the WordPad program).

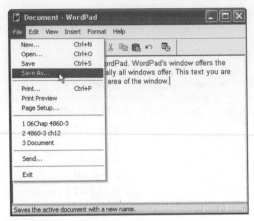

Figure 2-4: Sample open menu

After you've opened a menu, you can point to any item on the menu to highlight it, or to display any submenus that might be available. If a menu option has a sub-menu to offer, you'll see a right-pointing triangle at the right edge of the option. Pointing to the option will instantly display the submenu. If ever you open a menu by accident, or change your mind after the fact, you can back out gracefully by pressing the trusty Esc key, or by clicking some neutral area outside the menu.

To select an option on the menu, click it. After you've opened a menu, you also can move the cursor across the menu bar (without holding down any mouse buttons) to open those menus.

Shortcut Keys (*Key+Key*)

Many keyboard shortcuts are actually combination keystrokes, expressed as *Key+Key*. These involve holding down the first key, tapping the second key, and then releasing the first key. For example, Ctrl+A means hold down the Ctrl key, press and release the letter *A*, and then release the Ctrl key. Shift+F1 means hold down the Shift key, press and release the function key labeled F1, and then release the Shift key. Alt+Enter means hold down the Alt key, press and release the Enter key, and then release the Alt key.

As you'll eventually discover, most combination keystrokes start with one of the following special keys: Ctrl (Control), Alt (Alternate), or Shift. That's partly because those keys never actually type any characters on the screen. Most keys offer Ctrl, Alt, and Del keys on both the left and right side of the keyboard, so you can use either hand to press the combination keystroke.

Many menu options display *shortcut keys*. These are keystrokes you can use as an alternative to going through the menus. If you look to the right of the Save option in the File menu shown in Figure 2-4, for example, you'll notice the shortcut option Ctrl+S. So let's say you're working on a document and you want to save your work. Your hands are on the keyboard rather than on the mouse. Instead of going through the menu and choosing File ⇨ Save, you can just press Ctrl+S on the keyboard if you prefer.

If you don't know the shortcut key for performing a task, but would still prefer to use the keyboard rather than the mouse, you can work the menus right from the keyboard. Just press and release the Alt key. You'll notice that each option in the menu suddenly sports one underlined letter. After you press the Alt key, for example, the letter *F* in the File option will be underlined. After the underline appears, you can just type that underlined letter to open the corresponding menu.

When the menu is open, you can use the ←, →, ↑, and ↓ arrow keys on the keyboard to move the selection highlight about the menus. To choose the currently highlighted option, press Enter. Optionally, you can just type the underlined letter of the option you want.

Tip   Remember, shortcut keys and other keyboard alternatives are *just* an alternative for people who prefer the keyboard to the mouse. You can always use the mouse to work the menus.

Occasionally, you will come across a menu option that acts as a *toggle*, which is to say the option represents some feature that can be turned on, or turned off. If you open the View menu in WordPad, for instance, you might notice that some of its items have check marks next to them, as in Figure 2-5. Choosing an option that has a check mark next to it turns the toggle off and removes the check mark. If you choose the currently checked Toolbar option in WordPad's View menu, for example, the Toolbar option is turned off, which makes the toolbar disappear from the screen. To turn the toolbar back on, choose View ⇨ Toolbar again to switch that option back on.

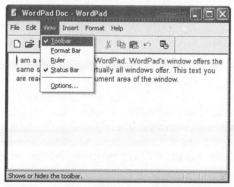

Figure 2-5: The View menu in WordPad is open.

Toolbar

Some windows also have a toolbar just below the menu bar. The toolbar provides one-click access to the most frequently used menu commands. Most toolbars provide ToolTips, a brief description that appears on the screen after you rest the mouse pointer on the button for a few seconds. Other programs, including WordPad, might show the descriptive text for the button you're pointing to down in the status bar.

Toolbars are optional in most programs. You can turn them on and off using options from that program's View menu. Some programs even offer customizable toolbars (although WordPad isn't one of them). If a toolbar can be customized, right-clicking the toolbar and choosing Customize from its shortcut menu will take you to the options for customizing the toolbar. For future reference, keep in mind that if you're looking to learn more about the toolbars in a specific program, you can open that program's help system and search for the word *toolbar*.

Status bar

The status bar along the bottom of a window plays different roles in different programs. However, a common role is to display helpful information. For example, the status bar at the bottom of the WordPad window often displays the helpful message `For Help, press F1` to let you know that help is available for the program. When you point to a toolbar button in WordPad, the status bar message changes to describe the purpose of that button.

Tip   Virtually any program you use will also offer a Help option in its menu bar, which you can choose to get help with that particular program.

Like toolbars, a program's status bar is often optional. You can usually turn it on and off by choosing View ➪ Status Bar from the program's menus.

Document area

Programs designed to help you create and edit things generally offer a large *document area* where your work appears. The document might be a photograph, drawing, spreadsheet, written text . . . whatever. It all depends on what the specific program you're using at the moment is designed to do. We'll get deeper into the concepts of working with documents in Chapter 3. For now, let's continue to look at tools and techniques for managing open windows on your desktop.

System menu

The System menu enables you to move, size, and close the window by using the keyboard rather than the mouse. You might find this handy if you do a lot of typing and prefer not to take your hands off the keyboard to manage a window. To open the System menu, press Alt+Spacebar (hold down the Alt key, press and release the spacebar, and then release the Alt key) or click the System menu icon in the upper-left corner of the window. When the System menu is open, you can choose options in the usual manner. Click the option you want. Alternatively, on the keyboard, type the underlined letter of the option you want; for example, type the letter *N* to choose the Minimize option.

Moving a window without the title bar

As mentioned earlier, you can move a window about the screen by dragging its title bar. (Unless the window is already maximized, in which case you need to shrink the window down a bit first.) Every now and then, however, you might run into a situation where the title bar of the window isn't visible onscreen. This is often the case when some free Internet service places some irritating banner ad on your screen that cannot be covered by any open windows.

Not to fear, however; there is a solution. Even without being able to see the title bar, you can move the window by following these steps:

1. Click anywhere on the window you want to move, just to make sure it's the *active window* (the one capable of accepting input from the keyboard).

2. Press Alt+Spacebar to open that window's system menu. (Don't worry if you can't see that menu.)

3. Type the letter *M* to choose <u>M</u>ove from the system menu.

4. Press the ↓ (down-arrow key) several times to move the window downward.

If it doesn't work, it may be because the window is currently maximized and therefore cannot be moved. In that case, repeat Steps 1 and 2. Then type the letter *R* to choose <u>R</u>estore (thereby shrinking the window a bit). Then proceed with Steps 3 and 4.

Arranging Open Windows

Essentially, no limit restricts the number of windows you can open on your desktop. You can stack windows one atop the other, in exactly the same manner you can stack sheets of paper one atop the other on your real desk. And just like on your real desktop, you can quickly make a disorganized mess of things. In Figure 2-6, for example, I have opened quite a few programs, including Solitaire, Calculator, WordPad, and Windows Explorer (which is deeply buried behind the other windows). This section discusses ways you can manage multiple windows on the desktop, starting with the important concept of the active window.

Tip

The programs shown in Figure 2-6 are all Windows components — programs that come with Windows XP. You can probably see Calculator, WordPad, and Windows Explorer on the Accessories submenu in All Programs. Solitaire is usually found under All Programs ⇨ Games. You'll learn how to install and remove these optional Windows components in Chapter 16.

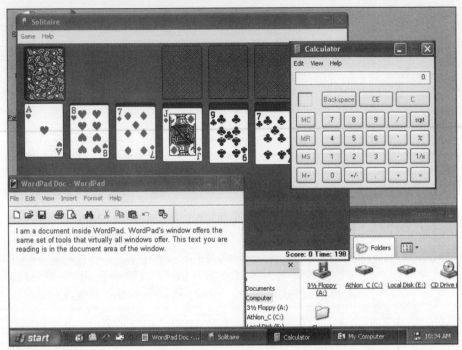

Figure 2-6: Several open windows stacked up on the Windows desktop

The active window

When you have two or more windows open on the desktop, only one window is the *active window*. If you use the keyboard at all, it's important to know which of those windows is currently the active window, because that's the only window that can accept keyboard input. If I were to try to type text into the WordPad document shown in Figure 2-6 right now, no text would appear in the window. Why? Because currently the Calculator program is in the active window, and only the program in the active window will respond to input from the keyboard. The problem is easily solved. Just click anywhere on WordPad's window to make it the active window, and start typing.

If you look at the taskbar in Figure 2-6, you'll notice that it now contains four new buttons labeled WordPad Doc, Solitaire, Calculator, and My Computer (which actually represents the Windows Explorer program, as discussed later). The taskbar always displays a button for each "running task"—that is, each open program on the desktop. You can usually tell, at a glance, which window on the desktop is currently the active window by the following clues:

✦ The taskbar button for the active window is colored a little differently, and appears "pushed in."

✦ The title bar for the active window is a little brighter than the title bars of the inactive windows.

✦ The active window is always at the "top of the stack." That is, no other windows overlap the active window.

Now here are two ways in which you can make any open window the active window, with just a click of the mouse:

✦ Click on any visible portion of the window that you want to make active.

✦ Alternatively, click the toolbar button for the window you want to make active (very handy if that window is completely covered by other windows on the desktop!).

Instantly, the window pops to the top of the stack, no longer obscured by other windows. You then can use the keyboard to work within that window if you like.

You also can use the keyboard, if you want, to make any open window the active window. Just hold down the Alt key, and press the Tab key. A small box containing an icon for each open window appears. Without releasing the Alt key, press the Tab key repeatedly until the title of the window you want to make active displays. Then release the Alt key.

Tip The buttons in the taskbar will get smaller and smaller as you open more windows. If you cannot read a toolbar button's label, just point to the button. The full label will appear in a ToolTip.

The bottom line is this: If you do something at the keyboard, and nothing happens (or something unexpected happens), there's a good chance that you weren't paying attention to which window was the active window at the moment. You can easily make any open window the active window by clicking anywhere on that window, or by clicking the window's toolbar button.

Cascading and tiling open windows

You can instantly arrange all the open windows on the desktop with just a couple of mouse clicks. Just to the left of the Notifications area in the taskbar is a neutral area that never gets covered by buttons. Right-clicking that neutral area displays the menu shown near that area in Figure 2-7. Options on that menu for arranging open windows are summarized in the following list:

✦ **Cascade:** Stacks open programs from the upper-left corner of the desktop with just their title bars showing, as in Figure 2-7.

✦ **Tile Windows Horizontally:** Sizes windows equally (if possible) and presents them as tiles with no overlap. If there are only two or three windows open, each is stretched lengthwise across the screen.

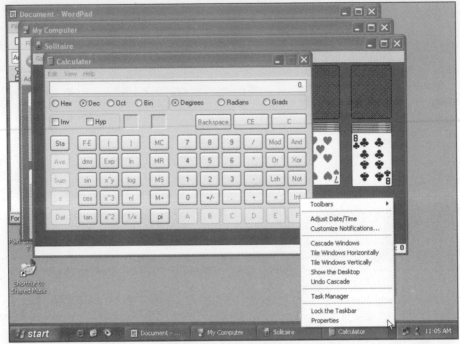

Figure 2-7: The taskbar's right-click menu revealed near the Notifications area of the taskbar. Open windows on this desktop are cascaded.

✦ **Tile Windows Vertically:** As above, but windows are stretched to the height of the screen.

✦ **Show the Desktop:** Hides all open windows, leaving only their taskbar buttons visible (same as clicking the Show Desktop button in the Quick Launch toolbar).

✦ **Undo:** Undoes whichever option you last selected.

Note   Calculator is unique in that its window cannot be resized. The reason that the Calculator window is as large as it is in Figure 2-7 is because I switched to the Scientific calculator by choosing View ➪ Scientific from the Calculator's toolbar.

When the desktop is crowded, consider minimizing all the open windows. Then click the taskbar button for the program you want to work with, to open only its window on the desktop.

Taskbar Tips

As mentioned earlier, clicking an open window's taskbar button is a quick and easy way to make it the active window (bringing it to the top of the stack). However, you can do other things with the buttons as well:

✦ You can minimize an open window just by clicking its taskbar button. Clicking the button a second time brings it back into view.

✦ To see the options for a particular window, right-click its taskbar button.

 Note   Some of the options below require that the taskbar be unlocked. If you have any problems, right-click the neutral area of the taskbar and select the Lock the Taskbar option to turn it off.

✦ To size the taskbar (to make it thinner or thicker), drag its inner edge (the edge nearest the center of the screen) up or down.

✦ To move the taskbar to some other edge of the screen, drag the neutral area to some other edge of the screen. If it won't go, try widening it first.

✦ To size a toolbar within the taskbar (such as the Quick Launch toolbar), drag the dotted lines at the edge of the taskbar to the left or right.

✦ To add toolbars to, or remove toolbars from, the taskbar, right-click its neutral area and choose Toolbars. Then choose any toolbar to display or hide.

✦ To turn a taskbar toolbar into a free-floating toolbar that you can place anywhere on the screen, drag the dots at the edge of the toolbar out onto the desktop.

✦ To put a floating toolbar back into the taskbar, drag it back into the taskbar.

✦ To rearrange items in the toolbar, drag the dots nearest the Start button to the right, past any item that you want to put to the left of the current item.

✦ To resize an item within the toolbar, drag its dots to the left, right, up, or down.

You can further personalize the taskbar in a variety of ways to suit your own work style and environment. Chapter 13 describes some of those more advanced techniques. If you want to take a quick look at the Properties dialog box that offers those additional options, just right-click the neutral area of the taskbar and choose and choose Properties.

For the moment, I think our time is better spent on more basic skills. In particular, it's time to talk about those dialog boxes that come up from time to time, and how you operate the various controls they offer.

Using Dialog Boxes

A dialog box is sort of like a window. Instead of representing an entire program, however, a dialog box generally contains some simple settings from which you can choose. The term *dialog box* comes from the fact that you carry on a kind of "dialogue" with the box by making selections from the options it presents. Controls within a dialog box are similar to the controls on any other kind of machine, be it a car, dishwasher, or stereo. Controls enable you to control how a program behaves and looks.

As you may recall, many objects on your screen have *properties*, characteristics such as size, color, and so forth that you can change. If an object does offer properties that you can change, right-clicking the object and choosing Properties from the shortcut menu will take you directly to the Properties dialog box for that particular object. For example, the desktop itself has properties that you can alter. If you right-click the desktop "proper" (not the taskbar, not an icon, not an open window) and choose Properties, you'll come to the Display Properties dialog box shown in Figure 2-8.

Tip

> The Properties dialog boxes for many objects also are available in the Control Panel, which you can get to by choosing the Control Panel option from the Start menu.

Figure 2-8: The Display Properties dialog box

Within the dialog box, you see examples of some common controls. The following sections explain how to work all the different kinds of controls you may come across in your daily use of Windows. The sample Display Properties dialog box doesn't offer all the controls discussed here. But trust me, you will eventually come across all the controls described in the next few sections.

Tabs

Some dialog boxes contain more controls than can actually fit into the box. In this case, options are split into two or more tabs. For example, the Display Properties dialog box contains the tabs shown in Figure 2-9. To view the options offered by a tab, click the tab you want. Alternatively, you can hold down the Ctrl key while pressing the Tab key to move from one tab to the next. Pressing Ctrl+Shift+Tab moves through the tabs in the opposite order, from right to left.

Figure 2-9: An example of tabs

Buttons

Buttons are simple. You click them with your mouse. If a button has an underlined letter in its label, you can optionally hold down the Alt key and press the key that represents the underlined letter. For example, as an alternative to clicking a button labeled <u>P</u>attern, you can press Alt+P.

You might notice one button in a group has a slightly darker appearance than the others, such as the OK button shown in Figure 2-10. That button is called the *default button* and, as an alternative to clicking directly on that button, you can press the Enter key. Many dialog boxes also have a Cancel button, which enables you to escape gracefully from the dialog box without saving any changes. As an alternative to clicking the Cancel button, you can press the Esc key or click the Close (X) button in the upper-right corner of the dialog box.

Figure 2-10: An example of buttons

If your hands happen to be on the keyboard rather than the mouse and you want to choose a button, you can press the Tab key to move forward from one control to the next, or you can press Shift+Tab to move backward through the controls until the button you want to press is highlighted with a dotted line. Then press Enter to push that highlighted button.

The buttons play an important role in dialog boxes. Keeping them straight is important. Remember these important points:

✦ The Apply button (if available and enabled) applies your selection right now, without closing the dialog box.

✦ The OK button applies your selection(s) and then closes the dialog box.

✦ The Cancel button (or pressing the Esc key) closes the dialog box without applying or saving any options you selected. However, it does not undo any selections you have already applied!

✦ Any button that appears to be dim is currently *disabled*, and clicking it will do you no good. The button will become enabled again once it can serve some purpose. For example, the Apply button will be enabled only after you make some selection that you *can* apply.

Don't forget the handy Help (?) button displayed near the top of many dialog boxes. You can click this button and then click any option within the dialog box to learn more about that option.

Dimmed (disabled) controls

Buttons aren't the only controls that might be dimmed and disabled. At any given time, any control in a dialog box, as well as any option on a menu, might be dimmed. This doesn't mean something is broken. It means that the control is not relevant or meaningful at the moment. Therefore, there's no point in selecting it. When you first open a dialog box, for example, the Apply button will be disabled, because you haven't yet made any selections to apply. As soon as the situation changes (for instance, you make a selection that can be applied) and the control becomes meaningful, it will automatically be *enabled* (undimmed).

Tip   I've actually seen people click away repeatedly at a disabled control, as though doing so will some how "wake up" that control. Trust me on this. It won't.

Option buttons

Option buttons (also called radio buttons) are a set of two or more mutually exclusive options. The name radio button comes from the buttons on old-fashioned car radios, where pushing a button to select a station automatically unpushed whatever button was previously pressed. Figure 2-11 shows a couple option buttons available on the Start Menu tab of the Taskbar and Start Menu Properties dialog box (which opens when you right-click the Start button and choose Properties).

Choosing an option button is simple, just click it. Often you can click the text next to the radio button, which provides a larger target. Choosing radio buttons with the keyboard is a little trickier. Within the dialog box, you need to press the Tab or Shift+Tab keys until one of the radio button options is selected (has a little gray border around it or its label). Then you can use the arrow keys to move that gray border to the option you want. To move out of the radio button group, press the Tab or Shift+Tab keys.

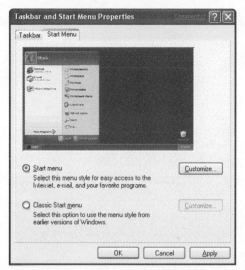

Figure 2-11: The Start menu and Classic Start menu options here are mutually exclusive, as indicated by the option buttons. You can select one or the other, but not both.

Preview area

Some dialog boxes offer a preview area, which is an area of the dialog box that gives you a preview of how the applied selection will affect the object. For example, the Taskbar and Start Menu Properties dialog box shown in Figure 2-11 contains a preview of the Start menu. Choosing one of the option buttons below the preview area shows you how your selection will change the appearance of the Start menu. Therefore, if you don't like what you see in the preview area, you can switch back to the other option before you actually apply the change to the real Start menu.

Check boxes

Check boxes, like the examples shown in the in Figure 2-12, enable you to turn some option on or off. (That figure is showing the Taskbar tab of the Taskbar and Start Menu Properties dialog box.) Unlike option buttons, check boxes are not mutually exclusive. You can select any combination of check boxes you want. When a check box is selected (contains an X or a check mark), the option is turned on. When the check box is empty (clear), the option is turned off. If the check box is gray in the middle, that usually means that some, but not all, of a subset of options is selected. (Don't worry about that right now.) To select — or clear — a check box, click it. Often you can click the text to the right of a check box to turn it on and off.

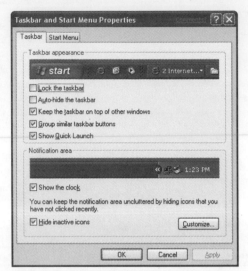

Figure 2-12: Check boxes in this dialog box
enable you to control the appearance and
behavior or the taskbar.

Although the mouse is the simplest way to turn a check box on or off, you also can
do so with the keyboard. Press Tab or Shift+Tab until the option you want has a gray
border around it. Then press the spacebar to select and deselect the check box.

Sliders

Sliders enable you to adjust a setting along some ruler. For example, the Screen
Resolution option on the Settings tab of the Display Properties dialog box, shown in
Figure 2-13, enables you to adjust the screen resolution by dragging the slider left
and right across the bar. If you must use the keyboard, you need to press the Tab
key until the slider control is selected. Then you can use the ← and → keys to move
the slider left and right.

Drop-down lists

A drop-down list (also called a combo box) is a small control containing some text
and a button with a little "v" shape or down-pointing arrow on it. Clicking that
down-pointing arrow opens a list of choices. In Figure 2-14, for example, I have
opened the drop-down list for the Screen Saver option on the Screen Saver tab of
the Display Properties dialog box. To make a selection from the drop-down list, just
click whatever option you want.

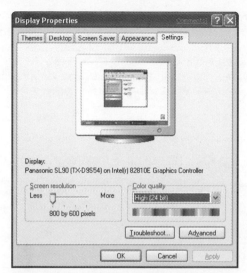

Figure 2-13: The Screen resolution control in this dialog box is an example of a slider.

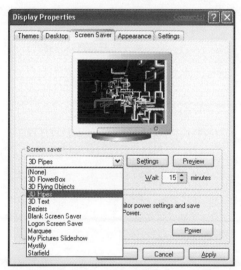

Figure 2-14: The Screen Saver control in this dialog box is an example of a drop-down list.

If the drop-down list contains more options than can fit in the drop-down menu, the list displays a scroll bar that enables you to scroll additional options into view (as discussed later in this chapter).

Like other controls, it is possible to work a drop-down list via the keyboard. The trick is to press Tab or Shift+Tab until the blinking cursor is inside the control you want. To display the drop-down list, press Alt+↓ (hold down the Alt key, press the down-arrow key on the keyboard, and then release both keys). When the list is open, you can select an option by moving the highlighter up and down using the up- and down-arrow keys. When the option you want is highlighted, press Alt+Enter.

Spin buttons

If a text box displays a number, a date, or a time, the text box may have a pair of little spin buttons attached to it, such as the Wait option in Figure 2-14. Click the up button to increase the number, or the down button to decrease the number. Optionally, you can just drag the mouse pointer through the contents of the box, and type in a new number.

Lists

A list or list box is a list of alternative options. It's similar to a drop-down list, except the list is already open — you don't need to click any button to view the list. In Figure 2-15, the Background control presents a list of backgrounds from which to choose. There are more items in the list than are currently visible, as indicated by the scroll bar to the right of the list.

Figure 2-15: The Background control here is an example of a list.

To choose an option from a list, click it. If the list has a scroll bar, you can use any of the techniques described in the next section to scroll through the list and view additional options.

You also can make selections from a list box using the keyboard. Press Tab or
Shift+Tab until the focus (the gray frame) is inside the list box. Then use the up- and
down-arrow keys to move the highlighter to the option you want and press Enter.

Scroll bars

Scroll bars, as mentioned, enable you to scroll through lengthy lists of items. They
usually appear to the right of a lengthy list. However, scroll bars aren't limited to
dialog boxes. They appear any time there's more information that can be seen at
the moment. In Figure 2-16, for example, I'm viewing the contents of my My Music
folder, using the Windows Explorer program (which isn't a dialog box at all!). The
scroll bar near the middle of the window is actually attached to the Explorer bar on
the left side of the window. Which tells me that there's more information below in
the Explorer bar.

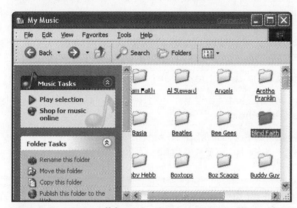

Figure 2-16: Scroll bars in this window indicate that's
there more than can be seen at the moment.

Vertical and horizontal scroll bars in the right pane tell me that there are more
icons to view both below, and to the right, which I can scroll into view. All scroll
bars consist of a slider box, a slider bar, and a couple of buttons at the ends, as
illustrated in Figure 2-17.

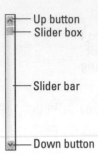

— Up button
— Slider box

Figure 2-17: The anatomy of a scroll bar

— Slider bar

— Down button

The size of the slider box relative to the size of the slider bar gives you a sense of how much additional information is available. If the slider box is about 10 percent of the size of the slider bar, about 90 percent of the available information is currently scrolled out of view. You can use any of the following techniques to scroll through the additional information:

✦ To move up or down a little bit at a time, click the up- or down-arrow button at the end of the taskbar.

✦ To move more quickly than that, drag the slider box through the slider bar.

✦ To jump to a specific part of the list, click within the slider bar at about where you want to position the slider box.

✦ If your mouse has a wheel, you may be able to scroll vertically by spinning the mouse wheel. (I say *may* be able to, because the wheel doesn't work in all programs.)

Tip   If your wheel doesn't work right off the bat, click the scroll bar, or just to the left of the scroll bar. Then try again. It might work this time.

If your hands are super-glued to the keyboard and don't want to use the mouse, you can use the ↓, ↑, Page Up (PgUP), Page Down (PgDn) keys to scroll vertically. To jump to the top of the list, press the Home key. To jump to the end of the list, press the End key. If a horizontal scroll bar is available as well, you can use the → and ← keys to scroll left and right.

Text boxes

Text boxes appear wherever you need to type in some information. Before you can type in a text box, however, the blinking cursor needs to be in the text box. To move the cursor into the text box, just click the text box. Alternatively, press the Tab or Shift+Tab keys to move through the available controls until the cursor lands in the text box. Then start typing.

Changing text

Several general rules apply to typing and editing (changing) text in text boxes, as well as most forms of text in general. To make simple changes or corrections, you can position the blinking cursor where you want to make a change, either by clicking the spot or by using the arrow keys. Then:

✦ To delete the character to the right of the cursor, press the Delete (Del) key.

✦ To delete the character to the left of the cursor, press the Backspace key.

✦ To insert new text, start typing.

✦ To choose between Insert and Overwrite mode, press the Insert (Ins) key.

Let me explain the difference between Insert mode and Overwrite mode. Let's say a text box already contains this text:

```
Wanda Starr
```

Next, you place the cursor just to the left of the *S* in Starr. If you then type **Bea** and a space, in Insert mode, the new text is inserted, like this:

```
Wanda Bea Starr
```

If you were to type **Bea** followed by a blank space in Overwrite mode, the new text would replace existing text, like this:

```
Wanda Bea r
```

In the preceding example, the new letters *Bea* and the blank space that follows have replaced the letters *Star*.

Selecting text

To change or delete a chunk of text, you also can select that text first. To select text, do one of the following:

✦ Drag the mouse pointer through the text you want to select.

✦ Position the blinking cursor to the start or end of the text you want to select and then hold down the Shift key while you press the arrow keys to extend the selection.

✦ In some cases, you can select all the text in a text box by clicking the label next to the text box.

✦ Select a single word by double-clicking that word.

The selected text will be highlighted somehow, typically as white letters against a blue background. Once you select a chunk of text, you can

✦ Press Delete (Del) to delete the selected text.

✦ Or, start typing new text.

When you type new text, whatever you type replaces what was previously selected.

Knowing these simple techniques can actually save you quite a bit of time. When you're browsing the World Wide Web with Microsoft Internet Explorer, for example, you often need to type in some fairly lengthy URLs, such as `http://www.microsoft.com`. Because so many URLs are alike, however, you can save a lot of time by selecting just the text you want to change. To change that Microsoft URL to `http://www.coolnerds.com`, for example, you could just drag the mouse pointer through *microsoft* to select that chunk of text. Then type **coolnerds** to replace the selected text, ending up with `http://www.coolnerds.com`.

Copying text and pictures

The ability to cut and paste into text boxes is also a huge timesaver. If the information that you need to type into a text box is visible just about anywhere on the screen or available someplace where you can get it to the screen, there's never any need to retype it. Just select the text that you want to copy into the text box by dragging the mouse pointer through that text. Then, press Ctrl+C to copy the selected text to the Windows Clipboard (which is an invisible placeholder for cut and copied text). Then click in the text box into which you need to type the text, so it gets the blinking cursor, and press Ctrl+V. The text lands in the text box.

The Ctrl+C (Copy) shortcut, and Ctrl+V (Paste) shortcut are supported universally throughout Windows and Windows programs. You can use these keys to copy just about anything to just about anything else. If you're not sure, don't be afraid to try it out. You cannot do any harm by trying! The same technique works for pictures as well. To select a picture, however, you don't drag the mouse pointer. Instead, you just click the picture to select it, and then press Ctrl+C. To paste the picture into a graphics program or word processing document, click at about where you want to place the picture, and then press Ctrl+V.

Often you can even do it without even touching the keyboard. Just drag the mouse pointer through the text you want to copy, or click the picture you want to copy. Then right-click the selected text or picture and choose Copy. Then right-click where you want to paste and choose Paste.

Tip   If, for whatever reason, you cannot copy a picture on the screen into the Clipboard, you can always take a snapshot of the screen and paste that into your word processing document or graphics program. The section titled "Screenshots" in Chapter 24 explains how.

Exploring Your Computer

Now that you have the basic skills to work in the Windows desktop, as well as any dialog boxes that pop up, it's time to turn our attention to the one Windows program you're likely to use more than any other. Its name is Windows Explorer (or just Explorer, for short). As its name implies, its purpose is to enable you to explore the contents of your computer.

There are lots of ways to start Explorer, as you'll learn. For starters, either of these methods will do:

✦ Click the Start button and choose My Documents.

✦ Or, click the Start button and choose All Programs ➪ Accessories ➪ Windows Explorer.

Either way, Explorer will open, looking something like Figure 2-18. Like all windows, Explorer has a title bar with Minimize, Maximize/Restore, and Close buttons, a menu bar, toolbar, and so forth. Unlike most programs, however, Explorer doesn't display its own name in its title bar. Instead, it displays whatever it is that you're exploring at the moment. In Figure 2-18, for example, Explorer's title bar shows the contents of the folder named My Documents. As you'll learn shortly, My Documents is a folder on your computer's hard disk where you'll store all your personal files.

The New Explorer Bar

The Explorer window, shown in Figure 2-18, is currently divided into two panes. The left pane is called the Explorer bar. The Explorer bar contains three drop-down bars, as described in the following list.

✦ **Tasks:** Provides quick access to tasks you might want to perform at the moment. The tasks available to you will change as you make different selections from the rightmost pane. Clicking an option will start the selected task.

✦ **Other Places:** Lists other places on your computer that you can jump to within Explorer. When you click one of those options, the right pane changes to show the contents of that new location. The Back button in the toolbar takes you back to wherever you just left.

✦ **Details:** Shows detailed information about the current location, or the selected file or folder in the right pane.

You can open or close the Tasks, Other Places, or Details portion of the bar by clicking the small button to the right of the title.

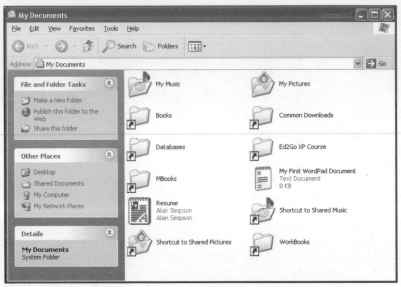

Figure 2-18: Windows Explorer currently showing the contents of the My Documents folder, as indicated in its title bar

A couple of good things to know about the Explorer bar, right off the bat. . . . First, if you resize the Explorer window, the Explorer bar automatically disappears (which is helpful if you get to a point when leaving it open would prevent the contents of the right pane from being displayed). Second, the Explorer bar is optional and may not be visible at all if someone else has disabled it. If you can't see the Explorer bar, no matter how large you make the window, you can turn it back on by following these steps:

1. Choose Tools ➪ Folder Options from the Explorer menu bar.

2. On the General tab, choose Show Common Tasks in Folders.

3. Click the OK button to close the Folder Options dialog box.

The rightmost pane displays the contents of whatever it is you're exploring at the moment. In Figure 2-18, for example, I can see that my My Documents folder currently contains several additional folders, including My Music and My Pictures. There also are a couple of documents in there, named Resume and My First WordPad Document. Note that the folders all have icons that look like manila file folders. Documents will have other icons. As you know, you can open any icon just by clicking or double-clicking the icon. If you open a folder icon, you'll see the contents of that folder within Explorer. The Explorer title bar will then display the name of the currently open folder. To return to My Documents, click the Back button on the Explorer toolbar.

If you open a document icon, the document will open in whatever program is *associated* with the type of document you opened. For example, opening the My First WordPad Document icon in the figure opens that document in Microsoft Word (if it's installed) or the Windows WordPad program (if Microsoft Word isn't available). The program's window covers (or overlaps) the Explorer window. From within the open program, you can then edit, print, or do whatever else the program enables you to do. After you have finished working with the document, you can close the program (by clicking its Close button).

Cross-Reference Chapter 3 covers working with programs and documents in more detail.

Umpteen ways to view files and folders

Explorer offers many different ways to view the icons in its right pane. Choosing one view over another is just a matter of what's convenient at the moment. To change the view, you can click the Views button in the toolbar and make your selection from the menu that appears. Alternatively, choose View from the Explorer menu bar and select a view from the menu that opens. Your have the following choices:

✦ **Thumbnails:** Displays the contents of any pictures in the current folder as small thumbnail-sized images. Folders and files that don't contain pictures just appear as large icons.

✦ **Tiles:** Shows information about each file and folder (as available) beneath the item's name, as in the example shown in Figure 2-18.

✦ **Icons:** Shows just an icon and name for each file and folder.

✦ **List:** Reduces the size of the icons to about the same size as corresponding text, and presents the information in a list.

✦ **Details:** Shows detailed information about each icon, including its size (except in the case of folders), type, and the date and time the item was last modified. Although as discussed later, you can choose for yourself what you want the Details view to display.

The Thumbnails and Details views offer some extra unique options, discussed in the sections that follow.

Fun with Thumbnails view

Thumbnails view is great for viewing any folder that contains pictures stored as files on your hard disk. For example, Figure 2-19 shows the contents of my My Pictures folder in Thumbnails view. The icons for files that contain pictures are actually small thumbnail-sized views of the images themselves. Folders within my My Pictures folder show up as large folder icons, with an even tinier view of some of the pictures within those folders.

Figure 2-19: The contents of my My Pictures folder in Thumbnails view

Notice that the Tasks options in the Explorer bar (now showing as Picture Tasks) offers some unique options. The Order Prints Online and Print Pictures options start up wizards that will help you do as they say. Note that, unless you *select* specific files before you choose one of these options, you'll end up with prints of all the pictures in the folder. The section "Select, Then Do" in Chapter 12 explains the many ways in which you can select file icons in Windows Explorer.

Tip   Your My Music folder also offers a couple of unique tasks, including the option to buy music off the Internet, and to play all the songs in the folder. If you choose the Play All task, Windows Media Player opens to play the songs (as discussed in Chapter 25).

Picture slide shows

The View as Slide Show option enables you to view each of the pictures in the folder in a slide show manner. Each picture—including those in subfolders within the My Pictures folder—appears full size on the screen for a few seconds. If you move the mouse as the slide show is going by, a toolbar will appear on the screen, enabling you to pause, restart, or close the slide show, as well as to scroll back to the preceding picture, or forward to the next picture.

Filmstrip view

A new option, titled Filmstrip, is available when you choose View from the Explorer menu bar. Selecting that view adds a picture preview screen to the pane, and presents icons for the pictures in a horizontal strip along the bottom of the pane, like a filmstrip. A horizontal scroll bar appears along the bottom of the filmstrip to help you scroll through the pictures. Clicking a thumbnail displays a larger view of the picture in the upper pane, as in Figure 2-20.

Figure 2-20: The Filmstrip view of my My Pictures folders

Buttons in the upper pane enable you to move to the next or preceding picture, zoom in on any part of the picture, and zoom back out, choose between "best fit" and "actual size" for sizing the picture, as well as to rotate the picture clockwise and counterclockwise. To leave the Filmstrip view, just choose any other option from the Views button or View menu.

Choosing details to view

As mentioned, the Details view shows details about each icon in the folder you're viewing at the moment, as in the example shown in Figure 2-21.

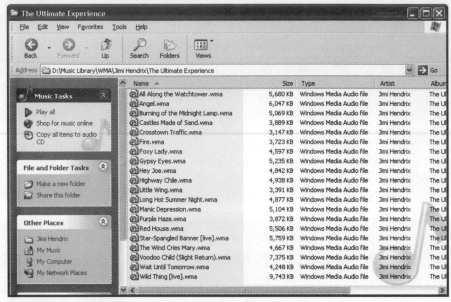

Figure 2-21: A folder's contents displayed in Details view

You can custom design the Details view for the folder you're viewing at the moment by following these steps:

1. Choose View ➪ Choose Details from the Explorer menu bar to open the Choose Details dialog box shown in Figure 2-22.

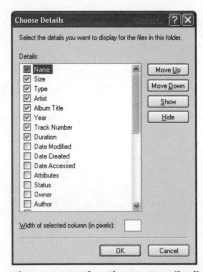

Figure 2-22: The Choose Details dialog box

2. Choose which information you want the Details view to display via the check boxes provided, or by clicking an option and then clicking the Show or Hide button.

3. To set a default width for the currently selected column, enter a measurement in pixels in the Width box. Alternatively, leave the setting at zero to allow Windows to size the column automatically.

Tip A pixel is only one tiny, lighted dot on the screen, too small to even see with the naked eye. Therefore, when setting a column width, use at least 20 pixels

4. You can reorder the options by using the Move Up and Move Down buttons to move the current item.

5. To change the order of items in the Details view, click any item you want to move and then use the Move Up and Move Down buttons to reposition the item.

6. Click the OK button when you finish.

Tip Because the Details view settings apply to the current folder only, you can choose different details for different types of folders. For example, the details you select for your My Pictures folder might differ from the details you select for your My Music folder.

If you're not already viewing icons in Details view, just choose Details from the View menu or Views button. The display will now contain all the columns you specified in the Choose Details dialog box. If necessary, you can scroll left and right using the horizontal scroll bar that appears beneath the list. To change the width of a column, drag the bar that separates one column heading from the next left or right. To rearrange columns, drag any column heading to the left or right.

You also can sort (that is, alphabetize) the list by the contents of any column. Just click the column heading of the column you want to sort. To switch from ascending order to descending order, or vice-versa, click the column heading again.

Most of a file's details are managed automatically by Windows. However, some details items are up to you. To view, and optionally change, the details for a single file, right-click the file and choose Properties. The Properties dialog box for that one file will open. The General tab will contain factual information about the file, with only a few settings that you can actually change. To fill in personal details about the file, click the Summary tab. Use the button near the bottom of the dialog box to choose between a Simple or Advanced view of the information. Figure 2-23 shows both views.

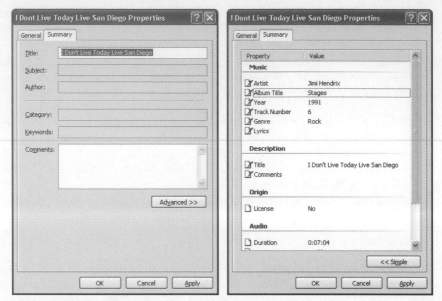

Figure 2-23: The Summary tab of a file's properties in Simple and Advanced views

You can fill in the blanks for any missing information you want. Then click OK after you have finished.

Note   If Windows won't let you change the file's properties, clear the Read-only check box on the General tab.

Arranging Explorer icons

You can choose how icons in the right pane of the Explorer window are arranged by choosing View ➪ Arrange Icons By from the menu bar. You have the following options:

✦ **Name:** Displays icons with folders in alphabetic order, followed by files in alphabetic order.

✦ **Size:** Files are listed in smallest to largest order.

✦ **Type:** Files are presented in groups by type.

✦ **Modified:** Displays icons based on the date they were last modified.

These four options are pretty universal. When viewing the contents of your My Pictures or My Music folder, you'll also be given options for arranging icons relative to those file types. In My Pictures, for example, you'll have the option to arrange icons by the date the picture was taken, and the dimensions (size) or the pictures. In My Music, for example, you'll be able to arrange icons based on artist, album, length, and so forth.

Grouping icons

To group icons in the display, choose View ➪ Arrange Icons By ➪ Show in Groups. This option acts as a toggle and, once selected, is automatically applied to whichever option you selected from the Arrange Icons By menu. For example, Figure 2-24 shows the folders in my My Music folder arranged by name, and displayed in groups. To turn off the grouping, choose View ➪ Arrange Icons By ➪ Show in Groups again.

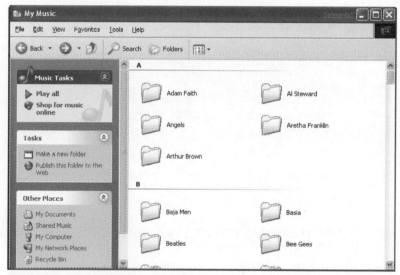

Figure 2-24: Icons arranged by name, and shown in groups

The Folders list and other bars

The Folders list available in Explorer provides a quick and easy way to jump to specific areas of your computer and to folders on your hard disk. To open the Folders list, just click the Folders button on the toolbar, or choose View ➪ Explorer Bar ➪ Toolbar from the menu. Figure 2-25 shows an example of the Folders list on the left side of the Explorer window.

You can expand and contract items in the list by clicking the plus sign (+, to expand) or the minus sign (–, to contract) to the left of the item. The Folders list provides a quick alternative to "drilling down" through folders to get to a specific subfolder. For example, the computer represented in Figure 2-25 has a folder named Art Parts within a folder named Clip Art, which in turn is contained within the My Pictures folder of My Documents. Without the Folders list open, I would have to work my way down to that folder. Which is to say, that in My Documents I'd need to open My Pictures. Then in that folder I would need to open Clip Art, and then finally Art Parts. In the Folders list, however, I can just click the Art Parts folder to jump to it directly, no matter where I happen to be at the moment.

Figure 2-25: The Folders list open on one of my computers

Cross-Reference Chapter 13 will teach you ways to create your own folders and subfolders, as well as ways in which you can customize your folders

Other bars accessible after you choose View ➪ Explorer Bar from the menu include the following:

✦ **Search:** Displays the Search Companion described under "Searching for Lost Files" a little later in this chapter.

✦ **Favorites:** Displays your list of favorites—things you visit frequently. Chapter 13 discusses ways to create and manage Favorites in more detail.

✦ **Media:** Opens a "player" frame for playing multimedia files, such as music and video. If your computer is connected to the Internet, it takes you to the Microsoft site WindowsMedia.com, where you can select music and videos to play in Windows Media Player (as discussed in Chapter 25).

✦ **History:** Displays a list of Web sites and folders you've visited recently, organized and grouped by day, Web site, and so forth. As in the Folders bar, you can expand and contract items by clicking them, and jump to a location by clicking its name in the list.

✦ **Tip of the Day:** Displays a Tip of the Day, and a Next Tip link, at the bottom of the Explorer window. Tips are downloaded from the Microsoft Web site.

Locking, unlocking, moving, and resizing toolbars

You can add and remove various toolbars in Explorer, as you can in most Windows programs. You also can move toolbars around. However, you must unlock the toolbars first, if they're locked. To lock, as well as to unlock the toolbars, choose View ➪ Toolbars ➪ Lock the Toolbars. When the toolbars are locked, Lock the Toolbars option has a check mark next to it. The little dots at the left of the toolbars, which you can drag to move the toolbars, disappear when the toolbars are locked. To combine, split, and move toolbars, do the following:

✦ To combine two toolbars into one, drag the lower toolbar into the upper toolbar.

✦ To size combined toolbars, drag the dots to the left or right.

✦ To switch the left/right positions of combined toolbars, drag the dots of the leftmost toolbar all the way to the right.

✦ To split combined toolbars into the two separate bars, drag the dots of the rightmost toolbar down below the current toolbar.

Standard Buttons toolbar

The Standard Buttons toolbar, which is visible in all the sample Explorer windows in this chapter, provides quick access to commonly used features of Explorer. You can show or hide that toolbar by choosing View ➪ Toolbars ➪ Standard Buttons.

The Address bar

The optional Address bar, visible beneath the Standard Buttons toolbar in Figure 2-26, shows the name of the location you're viewing at the moment. It also provides a drop-down list of other commonly accessed locations on your computer. You can jump to a new location by choosing it from the drop-down list.

Figure 2-26: An Explorer window with all the trimmings

You also can type the name of a new location to visit into the Address bar. After you've finished typing, just press Enter or click the Go button to go to that location. Note that if you have Internet access, you can type the URL of any Web site into the Address bar. For example, typing www.coolnerds.com and pressing Enter, or clicking the Go button, takes you to my Web site. Clicking the Back button takes you back to wherever you left from on your own computer. Although this is handy for quick visits to Web sites, you'll probably want to use the Internet Explorer program, discussed in Chapter 6, for most of your Web browsing.

The Links bar

The optional Links bar, shown below the Address bar in Figure 2-26, provides quick links to commonly visited Web sites or locations on your own computer. The icons that initially appear within the Links bar are just examples. You can easily add your own links, and remove any you don't want.

Tip   If you have Internet access, clicking the Customize Links icon in the Links bar will take you to a Web page that provides more detailed instructions about how to customize your links.

To add a link, first go to the folder or Web site to which you want to add a link. If the Address bar isn't already open, open it. Then drag the tiny icon that appears within the Address bar onto the Links bar and drop it between any existing links in the Links bar.

It's possible that your Links bar won't be large enough to display all available links. When that occurs, you can click the >> arrows at the right of the Links bar to view remaining links.

To rename a link, right click its icon in the Links bar and choose Rename. Enter a new name (or edit the existing name) in the dialog box that appears. To remove a link, just click its icon in the bar and choose Delete.

The Status bar

The optional Status bar in Explorer provides brief information about whatever you're viewing in Explorer at the moment. It also offers the standard sizing pad, which you can drag to resize the window. You can see an example along the bottom of the Explorer window shown in Figure 2-26. Choose View ➪ Status Bar from the Explorer menu bar to hide or display the Status bar.

Searching for Lost Files

It's not unusual, especially among beginners, to lose files on a hard disk. You might download a file from the Internet or create and save some document without paying much attention to where you put it or what you named it. Or, you may be digging around for some document you created ages ago, and have long since lost track of its name and/or location. The Explorer Search Companion will help you find it.

 Cross-Reference   Newbies take note. Chapter 3 teaches you all about creating and saving documents. Chapter 6 explains how to download files from the Internet.

To open the Search Companion:

✦ If you're already in Windows Explorer, just click the Search button in the Standard Buttons toolbar.

✦ Or, choose View ⇨ Explorer Bar ⇨ Search.

✦ Or, press Ctrl+E.

✦ Or, if you're not in Windows Explorer, click the Start button and choose Search.

The first time the Search Companion opens, you'll see a prompt asking whether you want to search with, or without, an animated screen character. This is a one-time question, so you might not see it at all. Frankly, it makes little difference which you choose, unless you happen to be fond of animated dogs. You can change your mind at any time by choosing Change Preferences within the Search bar.

The first set of options to appear in the Search Companion bar, shown in Figure 2-27, are as follows:

✦ **Pictures, music, or video:** This option limits the results of the search to those types of files.

✦ **Documents:** This option limits the search to document files that go with specific programs, such as Word documents, Excel documents, and so forth.

✦ **All files and folders:** This option returns search results with all types of files.

✦ **Computers or people:** This option enables you to search for computers in a local network, people in your address book, or the Internet.

✦ **Information in Help and Support Center:** This option plays the same role as the Search option in Windows Help.

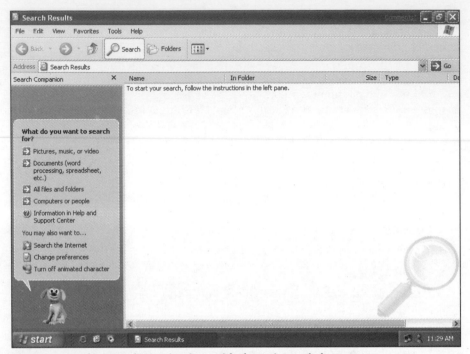

Figure 2-27: The Search Companion, with the animated character

The options that appear next depend on what you select. To see the full range of searching options, you need to click Use Advanced Search Options. You can fill in any information you do know about the file. If you don't know a specific piece of information about a file (such as its size), leave that option blank. Staying with the example of searching for lost files or folders, you'll likely be given the following options:

✦ **All or part of filename:** If you know anything about the name of the file, you can enter that here. For music, videos, and other media files, you can even add information that's not specifically in the file name, but elsewhere in the file's properties. For example, searching for "Hendrix" in music and sound files will find files with *Hendrix* in the file name, the artist name, album name, and so forth.

✦ **A word or phrase in the file:** If you don't remember the name of the file, but remember something about its contents, you can enter that here. If you're searching for a letter written to Jack Jones, for example, and are pretty sure the letter contains "Dear Jack" or "Dear Mr. Jones," you can enter **Jack** or **Jones** as the content to search for.

✦ **Look in:** This option enables you to expand or narrow the search to certain drives or folders. If you know the file is in My Documents or one of the folders contained within My Documents, for instance, you can choose My Documents as the place to look in. This speeds up the search, because only that folder (and its subfolders) are searched.

✦ **When was it modified:** If all you remember about the file is that you created or modified it yesterday, last week, or within some other time frame, you can choose this option and specify a range of dates.

✦ **What size is it:** In the unlikely event that you happen to remember only the approximate size of the file, you can choose this option to search for files within a range of sizes.

✦ **More advanced options:** As the name implies, choosing More Advanced Options enables you to narrow things down even further, including the following:

- **Search system folders:** If selected, searches "system folders" outside of My Documents, including the folders where Windows XP stores its own files.

- **Search hidden files and folders:** If selected, files and folders that are normally hidden from view are included in the search. Any file or folder can be hidden or unhidden by right-clicking its icon, choosing Properties, and then selecting or clearing the Hidden option on the General tab.

- **Case sensitive:** If selected, only files that match the exact upper/lower-case letters in whatever word or phrase you're searching for are included in the results of the search.

- **Search tape backup:** If you use a tape backup device to make backups of your files, choosing this option enables you to search the tape backups.

In most cases, it won't be necessary to provide anything other than part of the file name, or perhaps something about the contents of the file. So don't let all the searching options throw you for a loop. As an example, suppose that after clicking the Start button and choosing Search, I choose Pictures, Music, or Video from the Search Explorer bar. Then I choose Music and Sound, and enter **Hendrix** as all or part of the file name, as in Figure 2-28.

After I click the Search button and wait for a few seconds, the right pane shows a bunch of files. Even though the name *Hendrix* doesn't appear in each file's specific file name, Search was clever enough to include files that have *Hendrix* in the artist's name, as in Figure 2-29. (There I'm in Details view and have chosen to include Artist in that view via Choose Details, as described earlier.)

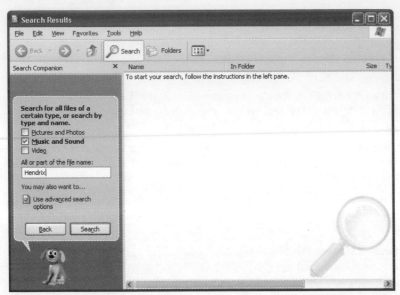

Figure 2-28: About to search for Music and Sound files containing *Hendrix*

Figure 2-29: The results of a search for music and sound files that have *Hendrix* in the file name include files that have *Hendrix* in the artist's name.

The Search bar remains open after the search is complete. Therefore, if you don't find what you're looking for on the first search (or end up with too many items), you can choose an option under No, Refine this Search, and then take another shot at it. When you're happy with the results of the search, choose Yes, Finished Searching to bring back the normal Explorer bar.

Keep in mind that even though the title of the Explorer window reads Search Results when the search is complete, you are still in Windows Explorer. And hence, you use all the techniques described earlier in this chapter to view and arrange the icons to your liking. Likewise, you can open any icon by clicking, or double-clicking it.

 In some cases, you might want to see the contents of the entire folder in which a found file is located. To do that, right-click any icon in the right pane and choose Open Containing Folder.

Good Places to Know

So far, this discussion about using Windows Explorer has pretty much focused on the hard disk, drive C:. There are no doubt other disk drives. In this section, you'll learn how to access those drives using My Computer. You also will learn about some key folders on your hard disk, including My Documents and Shared Documents.

Introducing My Computer

Contrary to what the heading implies, I'm not going to introduce you to my personal computer. My Computer, in this context, refers to the view of the available disk drives offered by the Windows My Computer option on a computer. I used that folder as an example quite often in the preceding section. However, I didn't mention that you can quickly view the contents of that folder in three different ways:

✦ Click the Start button and choose My Computer.

✦ Or, if you see a My Computer icon on your Windows desktop, open it (by clicking or double-clicking it).

 To add a My Computer icon to your desktop, right-click the desktop and choose Properties. Click the Desktop tab, and then click the Customize Desktop button. Under Desktop Icons, choose My Computer. Then click each open dialog box's OK button.

✦ Or, if you're already in Windows Explorer, click My Computer under Other Places in the Explorer bar.

Figure 2-30 shows the locations of the various options for launching My Computer. It doesn't matter which one you use—just choose whichever is most convenient at the moment.

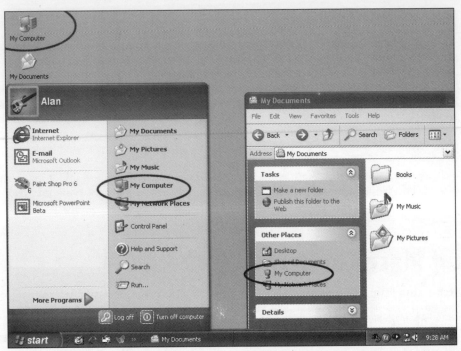

Figure 2-30: Three ways to get to the My Computer view of your computer's disk drives

Tip   Yet a fourth way to quickly view the contents of My Computer is to click its name in the Folders list of Explorer.

Explorer displays an icon for each drive in your computer. Exactly what you see when My Computer opens depends on the drives that your system has. Just about every computer has a local hard drive named C:, as well a floppy drive named A: and a CD-ROM or DVD drive named D:, as in the example shown in Figure 2-31.

You may notice some folder icons in My Computer as well, particularly one named Shared Documents. That item isn't really a disk drive — it's a *virtual disk drive* that is discussed a bit later in this chapter. For now, let's focus on the actual drives.

To view the contents of a drive, click (or double-click) its icon. The contents of the drive will most likely display as folder and file icons. Folders are just groups of files that somehow go together. Folders are always represented by manila file folder icons. The icon for a file will vary with the type of information the file contains, as well as the specific view you're using in Explorer at the moment, as discussed later in this chapter.

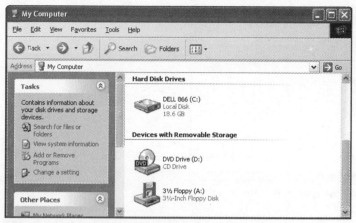

Figure 2-31: Sample contents of a My Computer view.

If you open the icon for the C: drive, for example, you'll probably see at least three folders named Documents and Settings, Programs Files, and WINDOWS as in Figure 2-32. (If instead you see a message saying that the files are hidden, choose Show the Contents of This Drive under System Tasks to display the contents of the drive.) I don't recommend that you mess with the contents of any of these folders. The only "safe" place for a beginner to work with files on the hard disk is in the folder named My Documents, discussed in a moment. Just for your basic knowledge, however, here's what's stored in those folders:

✦ **Documents and Settings:** Contains folders and files that are unique to you, the current user of this computer. Your My Documents folder is contained within this folder. But there are faster and easier ways to get to that folder as opposed to "drilling down" from this level.

✦ **Program Files:** Any programs that you install on your computer will most likely put their files in a subfolder within this Program Files folder. Unless you *really* know what you're doing, you'd be wise to stay out of this folder and let Windows manage it for you behind the scenes. You can start any program that's installed on your computer from the Start menu, or the All Programs option available on that menu.

✦ **WINDOWS:** The files that make up your Windows operating system are stored within this folder. This is another folder you'll want to stay out of, unless you're an expert who has some reason to be working directly with Windows files.

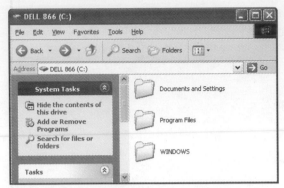

Figure 2-32: Viewing the contents of the C: drive
on one of my computers

To return to the My Computer view of things, click the Back button on Explorer's
toolbar.

Your hard disk is nonremovable, in the sense that you can't take it out of its drive.
So you can always open that icon to view the hard drive's contents. Obviously, you
can insert and remove disks from drives that support removable disks, such as
your floppy (A:) and CD-ROM or DVD (D:) drive. To view the contents of such a
disk, insert the disk into its drive. Then open the drive's icon in My Computer.
Explorer will display the contents of that drive as file and folder icons as well.

What Happened to My Documents?

If you're an experienced Windows user, you might wonder why the traditional My Documents
folder isn't visible when you first view the contents of your C: drive. The My Documents folder
now exists as a subfolder within Documents and Settings. If you open that folder, you'll see a
folder for each user who has an account on this computer, as well as a few other folders. If
you open the folder that bears your user name, you'll see your My Documents folder within
that folder.

The reason for the change has to do with the improved support for multiple users that XP
provides. Each user has her own My Documents folder, which prevents multiple users from
overcrowding a single My Documents folders. Each user also has his own desktop, and Start
menu settings, Favorites, and so forth, and these too are stored within the user's folder.

These changes are pretty transparent when you're working in Windows. Normally there's
really no need for you to ever dig around in any subfolders within Documents and Settings.
You can get to your own My Documents folder from many places on the desktop and within
Explorer. There's really no need to "drill down" to the folder via the Documents and Settings
folder.

Note   If you attempt to view the contents of such a drive while it's empty, you'll just see a little message asking you to put a disk into the drive. When you insert the disk, the message disappears and Explorer displays the contents of the disk.

You rarely need to use My Computer to use a CD-ROM or DVD disk. Most of these have an autostart capability. Just insert the disk into its drive and wait a few seconds for something to appear on-screen. If nothing happens, you can open the icon for the drive in My Computer. Be aware, however, that doing so might automatically start some program on the CD, in which case you won't be taken to the traditional view of the drive's contents.

If you do get to a traditional view of the drive's contents, and you're looking to install a program that's on that CD, you can probably just click (or double-click) the icon for the file named SETUP.EXE on that disk. Refer to Chapter 16 for detailed information in installing new programs.

Introducing My Documents

Even though most of the folders on your hard disk contain still more folders and files that you probably don't want to mess with, there is one folder on your hard disk that's especially reserved for you and your personal files. Its name is My Documents, and you can quickly get to it using any of the following methods, as illustrated in Figure 2-33:

✦ Click the Start button and choose My Documents.

✦ Or, if you're already in an Explorer window, choose My Documents from Other Places in the Explorer bar at the left side of that window.

✦ Or, if you see a My Documents icon on your desktop, just open that icon.

Tip   To add a My Documents icon to your desktop, right-click the desktop and choose Properties. Click the Desktop tab, and then click on the Customize Desktop button. Under Desktop Icons, choose My Documents. Then click each open dialog box's OK button.

Windows Explorer opens and displays the contents of your My Documents folder. That folder might contain still more folders, such as My Music and My Pictures. And it might contain some documents, such as the Things to Do document in Figure 2-34.

Keep in mind that the My Documents folder is yours, and yours alone. Other people who use this same computer and who log on with their own user names will have their own My Documents folders. Any files that users of this computer can share will be in the Shared Documents folder.

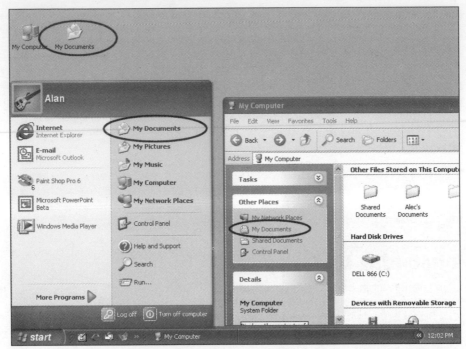

Figure 2-33: Various places from which you can open your My Documents folder

Introducing Shared Documents

As the name implies, the Shared Documents folder contains files and folders that all users of this computer can access. You can open Shared Documents by choosing that option under Other Places in the Explorer bar. You also can find its icon in My Computer. As always, you'll see the folders and files contained within the Shared Documents folder. And you can open anything in that file or folder by clicking or double-clicking it.

Tip   To create a shortcut to Shared Documents on your desktop, open My Computer as described earlier. Then drag the Shared Documents icon out to the desktop and drop it there. More on creating shortcuts in Chapter 4.

The main thing to keep in mind is that shared items don't appear within your My Documents folder — even though other people are willing to share. You must specifically go to the Shared Documents folder to find those shared items.

If you want to share items from your My Documents folder, or any of its subfolders, you must move or copy those items from their current location to the Shared Documents folder (or one of its subdocuments). Keep in mind that once you *move* an item to Shared Documents, it is no longer available via My Documents. If someone else deletes that shared item, it's gone for good. If someone else changes the item, you're stuck with those changes.

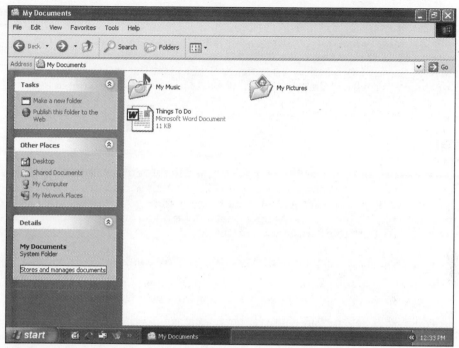

Figure 2-34: Contents of a sample My Documents folder

On the other hand, if you *copy* items to Shared Documents, you retain your own copy in your My Documents folder. So there's no loss if someone else deletes it. Likewise, if someone changes the Shared Documents item, those changes won't be reflected in the copy that's in your My Documents folder. If you prefer the changed copy, and want that one in your My Documents folder, you must copy the changed version from Shared Documents to My Documents.

Chapter 12 discusses moving and copying files and folders in detail. If you're just looking to *move* something from My Documents to Shared Documents, however, the procedure is simple enough:

1. Open My Documents.

2. Drag the item you want to move from the right pane of the Explorer window to the Shared Documents option under Other Places in the Explorer bar, and drop it there.

The item disappears from My Documents. If you switch to Shared Documents by clicking that option under Other Places, you'll see that the item is now in that folder.

Tip   As you'll learn in Chapter 4, you can add to your My Documents folder shortcuts to anything you've moved into Shared Documents. That way, those items will still be just one click away whenever you're in your My Documents folder.

The same basic technique works the other way around. Be aware, however, that once you move something from Shared Documents to My Documents, the item is no longer shared (which might irritate your fellow computer users). If you're sure you want to do this, however, open Shared Documents and drag the item you want to move to the My Documents option under Other Places. If you then click My Documents, you'll see that the item now exists in your My Documents folder.

Summary

The concepts and basic skills you have learned in this chapter are important, and most of them you'll use in your day-to-day interaction with your computer. Of course, they won't become second nature to you until you've had some hands-on practice. Still, it's important to know what can be done, and how to do it. Here's a quick recap of the topics discussed in this chapter:

✦ An icon is a small picture that opens into a full window.

✦ To close an open window, reducing it once again to an icon, click the Close (X) button in the upper-right corner of that window.

✦ Dialog boxes present controls that enable you to choose among various options a particular program or device offers.

✦ Windows Explorer is a good program to know, because it enables you to explore and access the various disk drives, folders, and files in your computer.

✦ The Search Companion offered by Explorer helps you find lost folders and files.

✦ The My Computer location within Explorer gives you access to all your computer's disk drives.

✦ The My Documents folder gives each user his own place on the hard disk in which to store his own, unshared documents.

✦ The Shared Documents folder holds folders and files that all users of your computer can access.

✦   ✦   ✦

Opening Programs and Documents

Just about everything you do on a computer involves using some program. As you probably know, thousands of programs are available for Windows computers, ranging from games for toddlers to advanced programming languages. Windows XP comes with many programs built right in. The larger programs, such as Windows Media Player, Microsoft Internet Explorer, and so forth, are described in a later chapter in this book. Some of the smaller, simpler programs, such as Calculator and WordPad, are covered here in this chapter.

Using Programs

The term *program* generally refers to something you buy to use on your computer. There are programs to do just about anything imaginable on your PC. All programs are, of course, *software*. Programs also are known as *application programs*, or *applications*, or even just *apps* for short. Small simple programs, such as the Calculator and WordPad programs that come with Windows XP, are often referred to as *applets*.

Many programs enable you to create, edit (change), print, or play *documents*. For example, you might use WordPad or Microsoft Word to create, edit, and print typewritten documents. You might use a graphics program to create drawings, or to edit digital photographs, as well as to print them. A program such as Windows Media Player enables you to play multimedia documents such as music and video.

Opening programs

To use a program, you need to start it on your system. There are lots of different words for "starting" a program. For example, the terms *launch* a program, *open* a program, *run* a program, *execute* a program, and *fire up* a program all mean the same as *start* a program. Each program you start will generally appear in its own window on the Windows desktop.

The typical scenario for starting any program in Windows XP is as follows:

1. Click the Start button.
2. If you see an icon for the program you want to start in the left half of the menu, click its icon and skip the remaining steps.
3. Click All Programs to see a more complete list of programs on your computer.
4. Click the icon for the program you want to start. Alternatively, if necessary, click the option that provides the submenu for the program you want. Then click the icon.

As an example of the last step, the icon for the Calculator program is inside the Accessories submenu. Therefore, to start Calculator, you must point to Accessories, and then click the Calculator option, as in Figure 3-1.

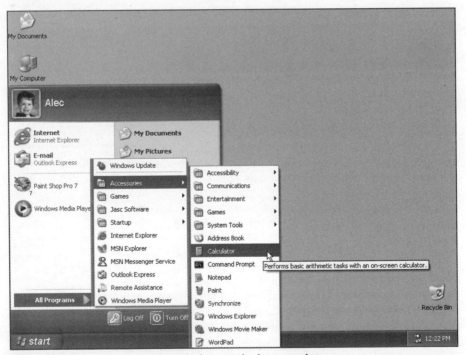

Figure 3-1: About to open the Windows Calculator applet

If your Windows desktop or taskbar sports an icon for the program you want to start, you can, of course, just click (or double-click) that icon. No need to go through the menus in that case.

Cross-Reference

In Chapter 4, you'll learn how to create your own shortcuts to favorite programs. Chapter 13 shows you how to customize your Start menu for easy access to favorite programs.

Getting help in programs

Most programs come with their own online help, similar to Windows online help. The help a program offers, however, is geared toward that particular program rather than toward Windows XP. To get to a program's online help, while you're in that program, try either of these methods:

✦ Choose Help ⇨ Help Topics (or some similar option) from that program's menu bar.

✦ Or, just press the Help key (F1) on your keyboard.

The Help window that appears will be about the program you're currently using. Typically, the left pane initially shows a table of contents titled "Contents" on its tab. In the Contents view, you can click any item that has a book icon to "open the book" and see the "pages" within. Clicking an item that sports a "page" icon opens that page in help. In Figure 3-2, for example, I opened the book named Calculator, and then clicked Perform a Simple Calculation to view the help in the right pane.

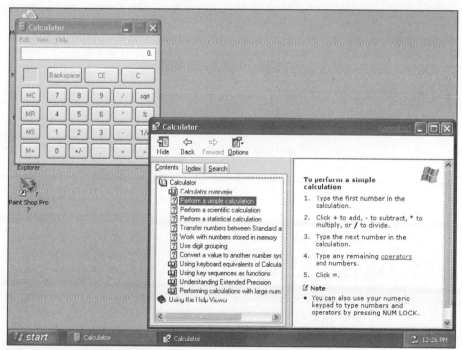

Figure 3-2: Viewing the "Perform a Simple Calculation" page in Calculator's help

Many programs' help windows also offer an Index and Search option in the left pane. For example, you can see tabs with those titles above the list of contents shown in Figure 3-2. Click the tab to look up specific information within the program's help.

Because the help usually appears in a window that's separate from the program's window, you can move and size the windows to give you the best possible view of both. If the windows overlap, you can click either window or its taskbar button to make it the active window. As discussed in Chapter 2, the active window is always on the top of the stack and also is the only window capable of accepting keyboard input.

You also can reduce the size of the help window by closing the Topics list. Click the Hide button in the help window's toolbar to hide the list. Click the Show button to reopen it. To close the help window, click its Close (X) button, just as you'd close any other window.

Using the program

Every program is different, so no hard-and-fast rules apply to all programs. However, most programs do share some common themes. For example, most programs provide access to their features via *menu commands*, which you can get to by clicking the options in the menu bar near the top of the window. Many programs offer toolbars, which just provide simple one-click access to the more commonly used menu commands.

Even though all programs are different, and therefore offer different commands, many programs' menu bars offer the options in this list:

✦ **File:** Use this menu to open, save, and close documents, as well as to print the document currently shown within the program's document area.

✦ **Edit:** Use this menu to access basic editing commands, as well as Cut, Copy, and Paste, for copying and moving items within a document, or from one document to another.

✦ **View:** Use this menu to hide and display toolbars and to choose different ways to view the document you're working on.

✦ **Format:** Use this menu to *format* (change something about the appearance of) something within the document.

✦ **Tools:** This menu contains any special tools that the program offers. It also might offer an Options or Preferences option, which enables you to better tailor certain features of the program to your own needs.

✦ **Window:** If the program you're using enables you to have several documents open at the same time, the Window menu will provide options for arranging the document windows, and for easily jumping from one window to the next.

✦ **Help:** As you know, this menu provides help for the program.

Most programs that enable you to edit documents work on a "select, then do" basis. First select the item within the document that you want to change, move, edit, delete, or whatever. To select text, drag the mouse pointer through it. To select a picture, click the picture. After you've made a selection, you'll typically find the commands for working with the selected item on the Edit or Format menu.

Closing a program

When you finish using a program, you should close it. Use whichever of the following techniques is most convenient at the moment:

✦ Click the Close (X) button in the upper-right corner of the program's window.

✦ Or, choose File ➪ Exit from the program's menu bar.

✦ Or, right-click the program's taskbar button and choose Close.

✦ Or, press Alt+F4.

After you've closed a program, its taskbar button will disappear. To reopen the program in the future, you need to go through the Start button again. Alternatively, if the program has a shortcut icon on the desktop or in Quick Launch toolbar, click (or double-click) that icon.

Starting Programs Not on the Menu

Typically, once you install a program, you can find the icon needed to start that program in your All Programs menu. Sometimes, however, you might need to run programs that haven't been installed. In fact, usually to install a program, you need to run its SETUP.EXE program!

Chapter 16 provides all the details about installing programs. For now, these quick pointers will cover all the most likely scenarios:

✦ If you downloaded the program from the Internet, just clicking the icon for the downloaded program should either start the program or begin the program installation procedure.

✦ If you recently purchased a program, and it's on a CD-ROM, just insert that disk into your CD-ROM drive and wait for instructions to appear on-screen.

✦ If you need to install a program from a floppy disk or other disk (including a CD-ROM that won't autostart), use My Computer to display the contents of the disk. Then click (or double-click) the SETUP.EXE file that will likely appear on that disk.

If all else fails, you may need to read the instructions. (Bummer, I know.) If you don't have any printed instructions, you'll probably find them in a file named README.TXT on the same disk that the program is stored on. Alternatively, in the case of a program you downloaded from the Internet, the instructions should appear on the Web page from which you downloaded the file.

Working with Documents

Unlike a program, which is something you generally purchase, a document is usually something you create on your own. Or, it might be something that you downloaded from the Internet or received as an e-mail attachment. You use programs to create, edit, view, open, print, and save documents.

You might be tempted to think of documents as being like "real-world" documents, such as typewritten letters, memos, and such. Although those things certainly are documents, the term has a much broader meaning in computers. Whereas a program is something you "run" on your computer, a document is anything you create, edit, print, or view from within some program. Hence, photographs, music files, videos, Web pages, and so forth are all documents in the computer sense of the term.

Creating a document

If you've never created, saved, or opened a document before and you want to try it, you can use the following steps, right now, to create a simple document using the WordPad program that comes with Windows XP. Here we go:

1. Click the Windows Start button and choose All Programs ➪ Accessories ➪ WordPad. The WordPad program opens on your screen as in Figure 3-3 (although initially the document area will be all white).

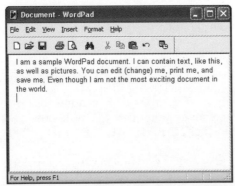

Figure 3-3: WordPad open in the desktop

2. Type some text. Whatever you type automatically appears within the large document area of WordPad's open window, as in Figure 3-3.

> **Tip**
>
> Unlike a typewriter, you don't want to press the carriage return (that is, the Enter key) at the end of each line when typing in a program. Text will automatically *word wrap* (break between two words) to the next line as appropriate. Press Enter only to end very short lines, or entire paragraphs.

So now you have a tiny document you created with WordPad. Your document has not been saved yet, however, and it has no file name. Let's discuss general techniques for saving any kind of document, using this little WordPad document as an example.

Editing and formatting a document

Nothing in a document is ever carved in granite. You can make changes at any time. Although tools and techniques vary from one program to the next, any program that enables you to type text will probably let you do the following:

✦ To add new text, click at about where you want the inserted text to appear, to move the blinking cursor to that spot. Then just type your text.

✦ To delete the character to the left of the cursor, press the Backspace key. To delete the character to the right of the cursor, press the Delete (Del) key.

✦ To select a chunk of text to format or delete, drag the mouse pointer through that text.

✦ To format the selected text, make a selection from the Format menu.

✦ To move the selected text, choose Edit ➪ Cut from the menu bar, or press Ctrl+X. Then click where you want to place the (now invisible) text, and choose Edit ➪ Paste or press Ctrl+V.

✦ To copy the selected text, choose Edit ➪ Copy from the menu bar, or press Ctrl+C. Then click where you want to place the copied text and choose Edit ➪ Paste or press Ctrl+V.

> **Tip**
>
> The Ctrl+C (Copy) and Ctrl+V (Paste) shortcut keys are virtually universal throughout Windows and programs that run on Windows. You can often use them in situations where there is no Edit menu from which to choose those options. You can even use Ctrl+C to copy something from one program's document, and then use Ctrl+V to paste that item into another program's document.

✦ To delete the selected text, press the Delete (Del) key or choose Edit ➪ Clear from the menu bar.

Of course, for more detailed instructions on using a program, you need to refer to that program's written documentation or help.

Printing a document

In most programs, you can print the document you're working on by choosing File ➪ Print from that program's menu bar. When the Print dialog box opens, just click its OK button. In many programs you can press Ctrl+P to print, as opposed to going through the menu. Alternatively, if the program's toolbar shows a printer icon or button, just click that.

Saving a document

One thing definitely applies to all documents, and to all programs. And it's a very important thing, so I'm going to express it loud and clear here:

Any work you do is not saved until you specifically save it!

This is important because many beginners spend considerable time creating a document and then, unwittingly, they close the program or turn off the computer unaware that, in doing so, they just lost all the work they finished. That sort of defeats the purpose of having a computer in the first place.

Saving a document is easy. The only trick is to *remember* to do it once in a while. Anyway, here's how you save a document:

1. Choose File ➪ Save from the program's menu bar. The Save As dialog box appears, as in Figure 3-4.

2. Typically, the Save In drop-down list in the dialog box will suggest your My Documents folder as the place to save the document. If it doesn't, you can choose My Documents from that drop-down list, or from the buttons at the left side of the dialog box, or from the list of folders shown below the Save In dialog box (if it's available here).

 Tip   Remember, documents that you save in My Documents aren't accessible to other people who use this computer. If you want to share this document with others, choose Shared Documents from the Save In drop-down list.

3. Next to File Name, type in a name for the document. Try to think of a name that will make it easy to identify the document later. Try to limit the name to three or four words, maximum, so you don't end up with extremely long file names cluttering up your Windows Explorer window in the future.

4. Click the Save button.

The Save As dialog box closes and you're returned to your program and document. You might notice the title bar of the program now shows the name of the document on which you're working.

Figure 3-4: The ever-important Save As dialog box

When you save a document, you save all work you've done up until the moment you save. If you change or add to the document, you must specifically save the document again to save those changes or additions. To save a document that already has a file name, choose File ➪ Save from the program's menu bar once again. Alternatively, you can click the little Save button in the toolbar (if any), or press Ctrl+S. You won't be prompted to enter a file name again because you already gave the document a file name the first time you saved it. However, rest assured that the copy of the document that's safely stored on your disk exactly matches the copy you're now viewing on your screen.

Tip

Many programs offer an "autosave" feature that will automatically save your work from time to time. This is a great safety device. To see whether a program offers this feature, search its help for the term *autosave*.

If you ever want to save the current version of a document under a new name, so that you don't alter the original copy, choose File ➪ Save As from the program's menu bar. There you can enter a new name for this copy. Your original copy will remain unchanged, with the file name you originally gave to it.

Closing a document

You can close a document in many ways. If you want to close a document and the program you used to create the document, close the program using any method described under "Closing a Program" earlier in this chapter.

Some programs (although WordPad isn't one of them) enable you to close a document without closing the program. Such programs provide a File ⇨ Close option on their menu bar to perform this task. Programs that enable you to edit several documents simultaneously will generally display each open document in its own window. That window, in turn, will have Minimize, Maximize/Restore, and Close (X) buttons. Clicking the Close button on the document's window closes just that document — not the entire program.

Tip   Closing the program that you're working in will automatically close all open documents within that program as well. You will have a chance to save any unsaved work.

If you see a dialog box that looks something like Figure 3-5, that means you've changed the document since the last time you saved it. Click whichever button best describes what you want to do:

✦ **Yes:** Saves your document in its current state, and then closes it.

✦ **No:** Closes the document *without* saving your changes. Choose this option only if you made a mess of things or have ended up with something really weird on your screen that you don't want to save.

✦ **Cancel:** Closes the current dialog box without closing (or saving) your document. You're exactly where you were before you opted to close the document.

Figure 3-5: Last chance to save the current document before closing it

Opening Documents

Opening documents is one of those tasks that virtually all computer users do several times a day. So naturally, Windows offers umpteen different ways to do it. Of course, there is no wrong way or right way. It's all just a matter of using whichever method is most convenient at the moment. Note that it's rarely necessary to open the program first. If you just open the document from Windows, the appropriate program for working with that document will open automatically we well.

From the Start menu

The My Recent Documents option on the Start menu keeps track of documents you've worked with lately. So one quick and easy way to open a document is to click the Start button and then point to or click My Recent Documents, as in Figure 3-6. If you see the name of the document you want to open, just click its name.

If you don't see a My Recent Documents option on your Start menu, but would like to have one, right-click the Start button and choose Properties. Click the Customize button next to Start Menu, and then click the Advanced tab. Then choose the Show Most Recently Used Documents check box near the bottom of the dialog box. Close both open dialog boxes, as usual, by clicking their OK buttons.

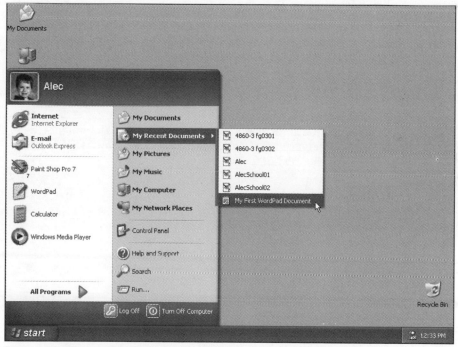

Figure 3-6: The My Recent Documents menu, off of the Start menu

From Explorer

As you know from Chapter 2, Windows Explorer enables you to view the contents of any disk, and any folder that's in a disk. You can open any document by navigating to its folder in Explorer and then clicking (or double-clicking) the document's file name or icon. To open a document you saved in My Documents, for example, you can click the Start button and choose to go straight to that folder. Then click the icon for the document you want to open.

If the document isn't in My Documents, you can navigate to the folder that does contain the document from within Explorer. If the document is in Shared Documents, but you're currently viewing My Documents in Explorer, for example, just click Shared Documents under Other Places in the Explorer bar. Explorer will then show the contents of the Shared Documents folder, and you can click (or double-click) the document's icon there.

From a program

Yet another way to open a document is to use the File menu inside the program you want to use to edit the document. Although the exact steps may vary a little from program to program, this procedure does work in most programs:

1. If you haven't already done so, start the program you want to use to edit the document you want to open.

2. From this program's menu bar, choose File.

3. Often the File menu will display a list of recently saved documents, as in the example shown in Figure 3-7. If you see the document you want to open, click its name and skip the rest of the steps.

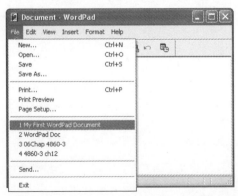

Figure 3-7: Many programs list recently edited documents right on the File menu. Here they're numbered 1–4.

4. Choose Open to get to the Open dialog box. In most programs, the Open dialog box will automatically display the contents of the My Documents folder, as in Figure 3-8.

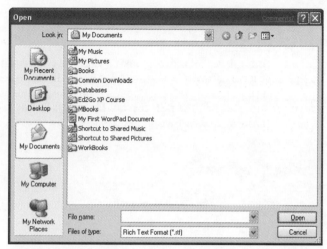

Figure 3-8: The Open dialog box enables you to locate and open a document from within a program.

5. If your document isn't in the current folder, navigate to the appropriate folder using the Look in drop-down list, or by opening the appropriate folder from the list of folder and file names, or by clicking on an option in the left pane.

6. When you do get to the appropriate folder, click (or double-click) the icon for the file you want to open.

If the program you're using enables you to open multiple documents, and you want to open several from the current folder, you can hold down the Ctrl key as you point to or click the names of the files you want to open. Then click the Open button to open them all.

If, for whatever reason, you're unable to locate the icon for the document you want to open, remember you can always use the Search Companion to track it down, as discussed under "Searching for Lost Files" in Chapter 2.

When Documents Get Weird

When you open a document icon, Windows decides which program to use to display that document by looking at the document's *file name extension*. Although usually invisible to you, the extension is a period followed by one or more letters at the end of the file name. For example, WordPad (and Microsoft Word) documents all have a .DOC extension, which is to say that Windows *associates* different types of documents with different programs based on the document's filename extension. Sometimes the association won't exist, or won't be what you want, as discussed next.

Windows cannot open a file

If you attempt to open a document that Windows hasn't yet associated with a program, you'll come to the dialog box shown in Figure 3-9. As the dialog box indicates, you can attempt to go online (if you have Internet access) and look up the needed information. Alternatively, you can click the Select from List button and select a program from the Open With dialog box shown in Figure 3-10.

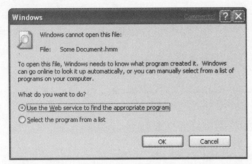

Figure 3-9: This dialog box appears when Windows can't associate a document with a program.

If you know enough about the document you're attempting to open, you can enter a description of the type of document it is in the dialog box. You can then choose which of the listed programs you want to use to open the program. If you like, you can set up a permanent association between documents that have this file name extension and the selected program by choosing the Always use check box. If you're not sure, however, you would be wise not to select that check box!

If you take a wild guess, and the program you chose can't open the document, you'll just see a message to that effect, and no harm done. Then again, the program you chose might open the document and take its best shot at displaying it. When that happens, you're likely to end up with a mess. For example, Figure 3-11 shows a photograph that I opened in the Notepad program. Because Notepad doesn't have a clue as to how to display a photo, it just displays the meaningless mess shown in the figure.

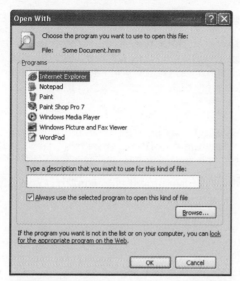

Figure 3-10: The Open With dialog box enables you to select a program with which to open a document.

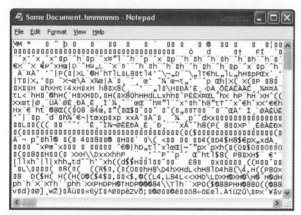

Figure 3-11: The Notepad applet making a vain attempt to display a photograph

It's important to understand that when you see a mess like this, you *do not* want to save the document! If you do, you may never be able to open it in *any* program in the future! You need to close the program. If asked whether you want to save the document, be sure you choose No!

That's not the program I wanted

The associations that Windows makes between documents and programs might not always be what you want them to be. For example, you might want to edit a picture in some graphics program such as Paint Shop Pro. When you click the document's icon, however, the picture opens in an entirely different program. There are a couple of solutions to this problem:

✦ Open the program you want to use, and then choose File ➪ Open from that program's menu bar and open the document normally from the Open dialog box that appears.

✦ Or, in Explorer, right-click the icon for the document you want to open, and choose Open With from the menu that appears. Select the program you want to use to open the file.

The section "Expanding Your Open With Menu" in Chapter 4 provides more information on using the Open With menu. For now, we need to focus on one other type of program—the ones that aren't very compatible with Windows XP.

Dealing with Troublesome Programs

Not all programs run perfectly in Windows XP. Some programs just won't run at all. Others may run poorly or require you to change some settings to get the program to look right on the screen. Windows XP offers a new *Compatibility mode* that can greatly simplify the task of getting these errant programs to run correctly. To use the Compatibility mode, follow these steps:

1. Click the Start button and navigate normally to the menu option that you normally use to start the program. But don't click on the option for starting the program. Instead . . .

2. Right-click the option for starting the program and choose Properties from the menu that appears.

3. Click the Compatibility tab in the Properties dialog box that opens to get to the options shown in Figure 3-12.

If you know that the program ran properly in some earlier version of Windows, select the Run this program using compatibility mode option, and then choose the appropriate earlier version of Windows that the program ran under, such as Windows 95. Optionally, you also can choose any combination of the following options:

✦ **Run in 256 colors:** Allows older programs designed to run on 256-color displays to run properly (and more quickly) in Windows XP.

✦ **Run in 640x480 screen resolution:** If an older full-screen program's window fills only a portion of your screen, select this option to allow the program to run in true full-screen size.

✦ **Disable visual themes:** If fancy screen features of Windows XP make your older program look weird on the screen, select this option to disable those features while the program is running.

After making your selections, click the OK button and try running the program again. You may have to experiment with different combinations of settings to get the program to run to your liking.

Tip
You can run a program's installation program in Compatibility mode as well. Just right-click the installation program's icon, choose Properties, and click the Compatibility tab. See Chapter 16 for information about how to locate those icons.

If the program still refuses to run, you may be able to get some information or updated drivers from the Internet. Assuming you've already set up your Internet connection, follow these steps:

1. Click the Start button and choose Help and Support.

2. Click Find compatible hardware and software for Windows XP.

You can use options in the left pane, such as Software Lists, About Compatible Hardware and Software, and Program Compatibility Wizard to look for appropriate information. If all else fails, you may need to contact the program's publisher and ask what's needed to make the program run on Microsoft Windows XP.

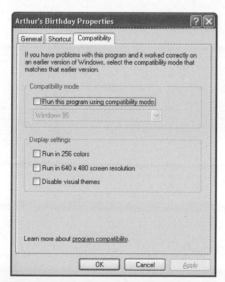

Figure 3-12: The Compatibility tab of a program's Properties dialog box

Summary

What you've learned in this chapter should help you to run any program on your system. You'll also be able to open any document, whether it's something you created yourself or one you downloaded or received as an e-mail attachment. Remember these main points:

✦ To start any program that's installed on your computer, click the Start button. If you don't see the program's icon on the Start menu, check the All Programs menu.

✦ You can get help in just about any program by selecting Help from its menu bar.

✦ When you use a program to create or edit a document, it's important to remember to save your work before closing the program or shutting down your computer.

✦ To print a document, choose File ⇨ Print from the program's menu bar.

✦ To You can open documents via the My Recent Documents item on the Start menu, Windows Explorer, or the File option on the program's menu bar.

✦   ✦   ✦

Shortcuts and Other Cool Tricks

With all the knowledge you have gained so far, you will be able to get around in Windows, as well as in many different programs you will use. With practice, you will be able to find and use anything you need, when you need it. You might eventually discover that you're going through a fairly long series of clicks to perform routine tasks. This chapter shows you ways to reduce the process to a single a click by creating shortcuts.

What Is a Shortcut?

A *shortcut* is an icon that provides easy access to any program, document, folder, or nearly any other resource on your computer. A shortcut icon looks like the original icon, but it has a small arrow in the lower-left corner. If the shortcut is in a folder, and you're currently viewing that folder in the Tiles view, the word *shortcut* appears beneath the file name, as shown in Figure 4-1.

Figure 4-1: The Shared Documents icon on the left, and a shortcut to Shared Documents on the right

Clicking (or double-clicking) the shortcut has the same result as clicking the original icon — it opens the program, folder, or document that the icon represents. However, you can place the shortcut anywhere you want. The Windows desktop and the Quick Launch toolbar are prime candidates because they are so readily accessible at all times.

One important technical difference exists between the original icons and any short-cuts you create. The original icon represents the actual underlying file or folder. So when you delete *that* icon, you delete what it represents. You don't ever want to do this by accident, because you'll lose whatever the icon represents. If you were to delete the original Shared Documents icon—which is visible within My Computer—you delete the entire Shared Documents folder and every file and folder within it. Not good!

The shortcut icon, on the other hand, just contains the *location* of the actual under-lying file or folder. So when you delete the shortcut icon, you're simply deleting the icon itself. The file or folder that the icon represents is not deleted or altered in any way.

Incidentally, you might notice that the size of the shortcut icon back in Figure 4-1 is 1K. In reality, it's probably much smaller than that—Windows just tends to round sizes off to the nearest kilobyte. The Shared Documents folder itself might be huge, containing many megabytes of information. But because a shortcut contains infor-mation only about the *location* of the Shared Documents folder, it is always tiny, no matter how much information is actually in the Shared Documents folder.

Adding Desktop Shortcuts

The desktop, of course, is always a handy place to put a shortcut. To add a shortcut to a file, folder, or other location to your Windows desktop, use Windows Explorer to get to the original folder or file icon to which you want to create a shortcut. To create a shortcut to My Pictures or My Music, for example, open My Documents to view the original icons. To create a shortcut to Shared Documents or a particular drive on your computer, open My Computer.

When you can see the icon to which you want to create a shortcut, make sure the Explorer window is small enough so that you can at least see some portion of the desktop. Then, using the secondary (right) mouse button, drag the icon out to the desktop and drop it there. From the menu that appears, choose Create Shortcuts Here. A new icon titled "Shortcut to" followed by the original icon name appears. The new name is already selected, so you can enter a new name if you like. For example, I usually delete the "Shortcut to" part of the name, because I can already tell the item is a shortcut by the little curved arrow.

Tip   You can rename a shortcut icon at any time by right-clicking the icon and choosing Rename.

Remember, you can always tidy the desktop icons by right-clicking the desktop and choosing Arrange Icons By ⇨ Name.

As is typical of Windows, you can create desktop shortcuts in other ways as well. And as usual, choosing one method or another is simply a matter of personal pref-erence or convenience. For instance, you can right-click the desktop and choose

New ⇨ Shortcut. A Create Shortcut Wizard appears, with a Browse button that you can use to locate the item to which you want to create the shortcut. Within Explorer, you can right-click on any icon and choose Send To ⇨ Desktop (create shortcut).

Tip If you haven't already done so, you can create desktop icons for My Computer and My Documents by right-clicking the desktop and choosing Properties. In the Display Properties dialog box that opens, click the Desktop tab, and then click the Customize Desktop button. Under Desktop Icons, choose My Documents and/or My Computer.

If you get tired of going through the Start menu to launch a favorite program, you can easily put a shortcut to that program right on your desktop. In some cases, however, you might not know the exact name and location of the file needed to start the program. If so, instead of using Windows Explorer, follow these steps:

1. Click the Start button, choose All Programs, and work your way to the option that enables you to start the program to which you want to create a shortcut. However, don't click that option. Instead . . .

2. Right-click the menu option and choose Send To ⇨ Desktop (create shortcut).

The Start menu might cover the new icon. If so, close it by clicking any neutral portion of the desktop, or by pressing the Esc key.

Removing Desktop Shortcuts

To keep your desktop from getting too cluttered, you might occasionally want to remove shortcuts that you're not using much any more. This is simple to do. Just right-click the shortcut icon and choose Delete. A dialog box displays asking for confirmation. To complete the job, simply click the Yes button.

If you ever do this by accident, and you catch the error right away, you can undo the deletion by right-clicking the desktop and choosing Undo Delete. If it's too late for that, you can recover the shortcut icon from the Recycle Bin, as discussed under "Using the Recycle Bin" in Chapter 12.

Adding Shortcuts to the Quick Launch Toolbar

Although the desktop is a handy place for shortcuts, it does have one drawback. The desktop is often covered by whatever you're working on at the moment. To reveal the desktop, you need to click the Show Desktop button down in the Quick Launch toolbar. If you don't want to be bothered with that, you can place the shortcut right on the Quick Launch toolbar. As you may recall, that's the toolbar that usually displays just to the right of the Start button, as shown in Figure 4-2. That way, it will always be visible on your screen — at least whenever the Quick Launch toolbar is visible.

Figure 4-2: The Quick Launch toolbar includes the Show Desktop icon, plus any other shortcuts you care to add to it.

The Quick Launch toolbar needs to be visible, and the taskbar unlocked, before you can add shortcuts. So, to get started, follow these steps:

1. Right-click the taskbar and, if Lock the Taskbar is selected, choose that option to unlock the taskbar.

2. If the Quick Launch toolbar isn't visible in your taskbar, right-click the taskbar and choose Toolbars ⇨ Quick Launch.

To copy a shortcut from your desktop onto the Quick Launch toolbar, just drag the shortcut icon from the desktop and drop it anywhere on the Quick Launch toolbar. If you want to move, rather than copy, the desktop shortcut icon onto the Quick Launch toolbar, right-drag the icon to the toolbar and choose Move Here after you release the right mouse button.

To create a Quick Launch icon from an icon within Windows Explorer, drag the icon from Explorer and drop it onto the Quick Launch toolbar. I have gotten mixed results when dragging program icons from the All Programs menu into the Quick Launch toolbar. Occasionally, it *moves* the icon to the toolbar, thereby removing it from the menu. The simple solution, however, is to create a desktop shortcut to the program, as described earlier. Then just move or copy that new shortcut icon from the desktop onto the Quick Launch toolbar.

Using the Quick Launch toolbar

While we're on the subject of the Quick Launch toolbar, you might find handy a few facts about it:

✦ If the toolbar contains more icons than currently visible, click the >> arrow at the right edge of the toolbar to scroll other items into view.

✦ To widen or narrow the Quick Launch toolbar, drag the dots at its right edge to the left or right.

Note   If you don't see little dots at the edge of the Quick Launch toolbar, the taskbar is locked. Right-click the taskbar and choose Lock the Taskbar to clear the check mark and unlock the taskbar.

✦ To reposition an icon in the Quick Launch toolbar, just drag the item to the left or right. A black bar displays, showing you where the icon will land when you release the mouse button.

✦ To display an icon's name, just point to the icon in the Quick Launch toolbar.

✦ To show large or small icons in the Quick Launch toolbar, right-click the toolbar itself (not an icon within the toolbar), and then choose View and an icon size.

✦ To display icon names in the Quick Launch toolbar, right-click the toolbar and choose Show Text.

✦ To view the name of the Quick Launch toolbar within the toolbar, right-click the toolbar and choose Show Title.

✦ To separate the Quick Launch toolbar from the taskbar, drag the dots at the left edge of the toolbar out to the desktop, and drop them there.

✦ To move the Quick Launch toolbar back onto the taskbar, drag the Quick Launch window's title bar back onto the taskbar, and drop it there.

✦ To reposition the Quick Launch toolbar on the taskbar, drag the buttons at the left edge of the toolbar left or right. If you can't get the toolbar back over to the Start button, drag the dots nearest the Start button over to the right of the Quick Launch toolbar.

✦ To change the height of the entire taskbar, drag its upper edge up or down slightly.

With regard to that last item, it is possible to make the taskbar so narrow that it becomes virtually invisible. When that happens, just move the mouse pointer all the way to the bottom of the screen. Then drag upward to widen the taskbar. You can control the behavior of the taskbar in other ways as well, as discussed under "Personalizing the Taskbar" in Chapter 13.

Deleting Quick Launch icons

If you want to remove any unused shortcut icons from your Quick Launch toolbar, simply right-click the icon you want to remove and choose Delete. Choose Delete Shortcut from the confirmation dialog box that appears.

My Documents shortcuts to shared documents

If you have some folders and documents in your My Documents folder, and others within the Shared Documents folder, you'll probably get tired of switching between the two folders to open and save documents. The simple solution is to add a shortcut to your My Documents folder for every folder and icon you place in Shared Documents. For starters, open and size both folders so that you can see their contents. You can use your choice of method, but the following steps do work just fine:

1. Open My Documents, and then click Shared Documents under Other Places in the Explorer bar.

2. Reduce the size of the Shared Documents folder to about half the screen.

3. Open My Documents from the Start menu, desktop, or anyplace else other than from within the Shared Documents folder.

4. Size and position the My Documents folder to about half the screen so that you can see the contents of both My Documents and Shared Documents.

Tip   To create a new folder within My Documents, open My Documents normally. Then choose File ⇨ New ⇨ Folder from Explorer's menu bar. Type a name for the folder and press Enter. For details and other ways to create folders, see "About Folders" in Chapter 13.

If you want to move (not copy) a folder or document from My Documents to Shared Documents, just drag its icon from the My Documents folder into the Shared Documents folder and drop it there. After you move an item into Shared Documents, use the secondary (right) mouse button to drag its icon back into My Documents. When you release the mouse button, choose Create Shortcuts Here. Figure 4-3 shows an example in which I moved the folders named Common Downloads, Databases, Ed2Go XP Course, and MBooks into Shared Documents. Then I created shortcuts to each of those within My Documents. You can tell which icons in My Documents are shortcuts by the little shortcut arrows on those icons.

Figure 4-3: Shortcuts to Shared Documents folders within My Documents

After you have finished the job, you'll find it much easier to work with documents from both folders, because you won't need to be navigating to Shared Documents all the time. When you open My Documents, you just have to click the folder (or file's) shortcut icon within My Documents to open it.

Furthermore, you will find it easier to work with Shared Documents in programs' Open and Save As dialog boxes. Most programs automatically set these dialog boxes to open My Documents by default. And those dialog boxes also display the shortcuts to your shared documents, as shown in Figure 4-4. You won't need to navigate to Shared Documents using the drop-down list in those dialog boxes anymore. Just click the appropriate shortcut icon within the Open or Save As dialog box to get to the shared items. Very handy!

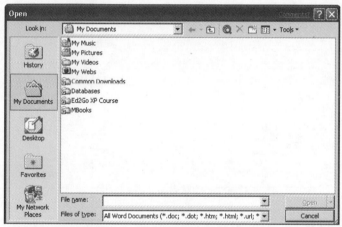

Figure 4-4: Shortcuts to Shared Documents are visible in many programs' Open and Save As dialog boxes.

Expanding Your Open With Menu

As you learned in Chapter 3, you can usually click (or double-click) any document icon to open that document in whatever program is associated with that type of document. For example, opening an icon named My Letter.doc would cause that document, My Letter, to open in the Microsoft Word program (if you have it), or the smaller WordPad program that comes with Windows XP.

In some cases, however, you may want the flexibility to send a particular type of document to any one of several programs. Suppose you create your own Web pages for publishing on the Internet's World Wide Web. Web page documents generally have the file name extension .htm or .html. When you open such a file, it appears within your Web browser, usually Microsoft Internet Explorer. If you create your own Web pages, you might want to see how the page will look in other Web browsers, such as Netscape Navigator. Or, you might want to open the Web page in a text editor such as Notepad, which enables you to work directly with the HTML that defines the appearance of the page.

To see which installed programs you can currently use to open a specific document, right-click the icon for the document you want to open, and point to or click Open With. Your options display on a submenu. In the example in Figure 4-5, for instance, I right-clicked a file named index.htm and chose Open With. The submenu lists the programs that can currently be used to open that program: Internet Explorer, Notepad, and WordPad.

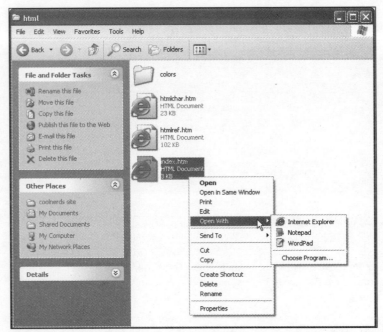

Figure 4-5: The Open With submenu for a document file with an .htm file name extension

Tip   File name extensions are usually hidden. To bring them out of hiding, choose Tools ⇨ Folder Options from Explorer's menu bar. On the View tab, clear the Hide Extensions for Known File Types check box.

If the program you want to use doesn't appear on the submenu, you can select the Choose Program option to view more programs. Doing so opens the Open With dialog box, shown in Figure 4-6, where you can do the following:

✦ Select the program you want to use to open the file from any of those listed in the dialog box.

✦ If you want to make the selected program the default for opening the document, choose the Always use the selected program to open this kind of file check box. Choosing this option defines the program used to open the document when you click or double-click its icon. But you can still right-click and choose Open With in the future to choose some other program.

✦ Optionally, click the Browse button to find some other installed program to open the file. (You need to know the program's exact location and file name, as discussed in a moment.)

✦ If you don't know which program is needed to open this type of file, and you have an Internet connection, click the `Look for the appropriate program on the Web` link for suggestions.

Choose OK after making your selection.

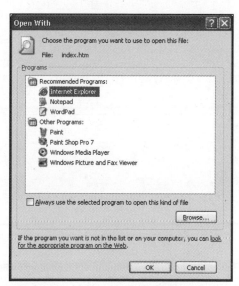

Figure 4-6: The Open With dialog box.

Windows XP is pretty good at keeping the Open With submenu up-to-date with programs currently installed on your computer. Be aware, however, it isn't always perfect. Suppose, for example, that you install Netscape Navigator so that you can use it to preview your Web pages. However, that program might not be on your Open With submenu. You can add the program to your Open With menu if you want. As mentioned, you need to know the exact location of the program's file. Typically this is a path name in the following format:

```
C:\Program Files\foldername\filename.exe
```

Foldername is the name of the folder that the program file is stored in, and *filename* is the actual program file's name. You might not know this off the top of your head, but you can find out by checking the properties of any shortcut to the program. If there's a shortcut on your desktop that enables you to start the program, right-click that icon and choose Properties. Alternatively, click the Start button and work your way to the menu option used to start the program. But don't click that option. Instead, right-click the option and choose Properties.

The section "About Paths" in Chapter 13 describes paths in more depth.

In the Properties dialog box that opens, the Target text box on the Shortcut tab displays the full path to the program. The full path might not be visible. Typically, however, it is selected, so you can just press Ctrl+C to copy the path to the Windows Clipboard. Open Notepad (click the Start button and choose All Programs ➪ Accessories ➪ Notepad). Then choose Edit ➪ Paste from its menu bar to paste in the path. Figure 4-7 shows an example where I have pasted the path to the Netscape 6 program into Notepad.

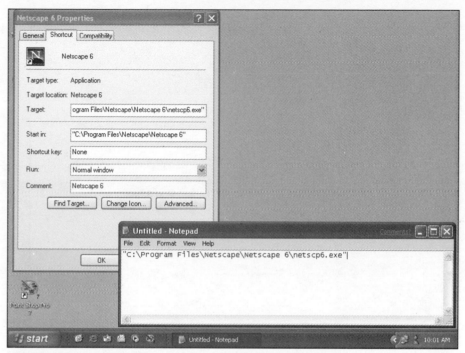

Figure 4-7: My Netscape 6 program path pasted into Notepad

Armed with that knowledge, you can now add the program to your list of Open With programs. To do so, follow these steps:

1. Right-click the icon for the document file that you want to be able to open in some other program.

2. Choose Open With ➪ Choose Program.

3. Click the Browse button. Initially you are taken to the C:\Program Files folder.

4. Open the folder(s) that contains the program you want to add to the list (for instance, first the Netscape folder, and then the Netscape 6 folder in my example).

5. Click (or double-click) the program's name (for example, netscp6 or netscp6.exe in my example).

6. If you want the selected program to be the default for opening this type of document, choose the Always use the select program check box.

7. Click the OK button.

The program will open in the selected program. In the future, whenever you right-click the icon for any program that has the same file name extension, the new program will display on the Open With menu. In the example shown in Figure 4-8, for instance, I right-clicked a file with an .html file name extension, and now my Open With list includes an icon for the Netscape 6 program.

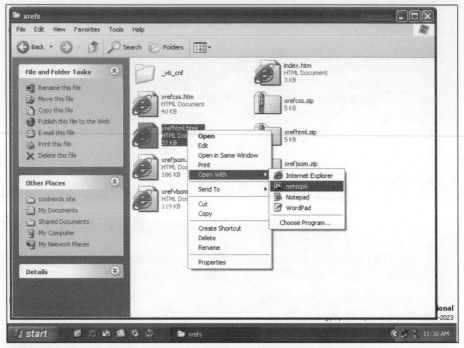

Figure 4-8: Icon for Netscape 6 now added to my Open With menu

Autostarting Favorite Programs

You can have Windows XP automatically start any program after you turn on your PC and Windows has started. Shortcuts to your autostart programs are in your Startup option that appears in All Programs when you open the menu. To autostart a program from your More Program menu, open All Programs and get to the icon for starting the program that you want to autostart. Then right-drag that icon onto the Startup option but don't release the mouse button yet. Wait for the Startup submenu to open, drag the mouse pointer over to the submenu, and then release the mouse button and choose Copy Here.

The next time you shut down and then restart your computer, the program will appear, open on the desktop and ready for use.

Should you ever change your mind and no longer want to autostart the program, click the Start button, open All Programs, and then point to the Startup option. In the submenu that appears, right-click the item you no longer want to autostart and choose Delete. Choose Yes when asked for confirmation.

If that's difficult, you can optionally open the All Programs menu, right-click the Startup option, and then choose Open. A folder named Startup will open in Explorer. You can create shortcut icons for any programs you want to autostart within that folder. For example, you can right-drag any program's shortcut icon from the desktop or All Programs into the Startup folder. Then release the mouse button and choose Copy Here.

Summary

This chapter ends Part I of the book. I focused mainly on "basic skills" required to use Windows. Admittedly, however, I have gone beyond the basics to more advanced techniques for creating shortcuts and such. In fact, if you have been reading along since Chapter 1, you probably now know more about Windows than the vast majority of people using it! Here are the main points to remember from this chapter:

✦ To create a shortcut from the desktop to any program, folder, or document on your computer, right-drag the item's icon onto the desktop, release the mouse button, and choose Create Shortcuts Here.

✦ To move or copy a desktop shortcut onto the Quick Launch toolbar, right-drag the icon onto the toolbar, release the mouse button, and choose Copy Here or Move Here.

✦ To quickly access various programs on your computer that you might want to use to view or edit a document file, right-click an icon and choose Open With.

✦ To have a program start automatically when Windows starts, create a shortcut to the icon within the Startup submenu on the All Programs menu.

✦   ✦   ✦

Becoming an Internet Guru

Windows XP provides all the programs and tools you need to take full advantage of everything the Internet has to offer. In this part, you'll learn how to connect your computer to the Internet. You'll also learn how to do e-mail, work with e-mail attachments, browse the World Wide Web, download files, participate in newsgroups, communicate in real time using the new Windows Messenger, and even hold online conferences. If your computer has speakers, a microphone, or Web cam attached, you'll also learn how to use those devices to turn your computer into a high-tech videophone.

Connecting to the Internet

You've undoubtedly heard of the Internet — the huge network that connects millions of computers from around the world. I'm sure many of you are already connected to the Internet. This chapter is for those of you who have no access to the Internet yet. Here, you'll learn all the different options for getting online and the step-by-step procedures needed to create a dial-up connection to the Internet from your own PC.

When to Ignore This Chapter

Before you dig into the many options and complexities of connecting your computer to the Internet, you should be aware that the vast majority of Internet service providers (ISPs) offer programs that you can run to set up your connection in an instant. This is especially true of the newer *broadband* connections, such as cable and DSL connections. But even the more common dial-up connections discussed in this chapter have largely been automated by most ISPs.

Therefore, after you've chosen your ISP and received account information and instructions from them, you should definitely follow all their instructions before you even look at this chapter. Chances are, by the time you've finished following their instructions, your connection will work just fine and everything that follows in this chapter will be largely irrelevant. You'll need to use this chapter only if your ISP doesn't provide any sort of installation or setup instructions at all.

Are you already connected?

Some of you may already have access to the Internet and not know it. If you have an account with one of the large commercial online services such as CompuServe, America Online, Prodigy, or the Microsoft Network (MSN), for example, you already have access to the Internet through that service. To get to the Internet, hunt for the word *Internet* within that service for more information. Then you can skip the rest of this chapter because you already have access to the Internet.

If you work for a large organization, you may be able to access the Internet through your computer at work. If you're in doubt, ask your network administrator, or whoever is in charge of granting network access to workers.

Will you use Internet Connection Sharing?

Windows XP comes with a feature called Internet Connection Sharing, in which several computers that are connected together in a network can share a single modem and Internet account. If you plan to use that feature, you need set your Internet connection in only one computer in your network. It doesn't really matter which computer you use, so long as you use the computer to which you've attached your modem. Other computers in the network won't need their own modems. Once you get that Internet connection working, you can set up your user accounts as discussed in Part VI of this book

Choosing a Modem

To connect to the Internet, your computer will need a *modem*. A modem is a device that connects your computer to the a phone line, cable, or satellite. Although there are hundreds of makes and models of modems to choose from, they break down into two main categories:

✦ **Dial-up (56K):** Connects your computer to a standard telephone line. Many computers come with this type of modem already built in.

✦ **Broadband:** High-speed cable and DSL connections to the Internet require specialized modems that connect to a cable TV outlet or DSL phone line.

Most ISPs that offer broadband services, such as cable or DSL, will provide a modem with the service, or give you a list of compatible modems to choose from. If you won't be going with such a service, but plan to use a "standard" dial-up connection instead, you'll need a dial-up modem. There are three basic types of dial-up modems from which to choose:

✦ **Internal:** The modem is built in to the computer, only the plugs for connecting to a phone line (and perhaps a telephone) are visible outside the computer.

✦ **External:** The modem is outside the computer. You'll need to connect one cable from the modem to the computer, another from the modem to the phone line, and perhaps another to the telephone if you use the same phone line for both voice calls and your Internet connection. Most likely, you'll need to plug the modem into a power outlet on the wall as well.

✦ **PC card (PCMCIA):** A small credit-card-sized modem that fits into the PCMCIA slot found on most notebook computers.

If your computer came with a modem built in, the modem is probably ready to go. You just need to connect the "Line" jack to your telephone line. Optionally, if you'll be using one phone line for both voice calls and your Internet connection, you'll also need to connect the "Phone" jack on the computer to your telephone.

If your computer doesn't have a modem built in, you need to purchase a modem that's compatible with Windows XP as well as with your Internet service provider. Virtually all ISPs support 56K modems that support the V.90 standard, and there are literally hundreds of those to choose from on the market.

Note   If you can get Internet access through some other computer, you might want to change the Windows XP hardware compatibility list (www.microsoft.com/hcl) for modems that have been tested and certified to run on Window XP.

After you've purchased a modem, you need to install it as per the manufacturer's instructions. If you purchase a used modem and don't have any instructions, you can probably just follow the generic steps for installing the modem, as discussed in Chapter 17.

Setting Up an Internet Account

Once your modem is hooked up and installed, you're ready to set an your account with an ISP. There are thousands of ISPs to choose from. If you plan on setting up a dial-up account with a traditional modem and phone line, it's important to find an ISP that can provide a *local access number* that you can dial for free. The local access number is the phone number your modem will dial to connect to the Internet. You want to make sure that number is within the area code and range of dialing prefixes for which there are no tolls whatsoever. Check your local telephone directory for a list of dialing prefixes you can dial free. Then check out your potential ISP's list of local access numbers to ensure they have one that will be toll free for you.

Caution   Don't take lightly the issue of a local access number within your "free" dialing area. If the number you dial has any toll charges, you may get slapped with some pretty horrific phone bills!

If you haven't given any thought to choosing an ISP, here are some resources you can use to search for a service that meets your needs:

✦ Go to the section titled "Using the New Connection Wizard" later in this chapter. When using the wizard, select Choose from a list of Internet service providers (ISPs) when prompted.

✦ Check your local Yellow Pages (under Internet) or newspaper for local Internet services.

✦ Call your local cable TV or phone company and ask whether they offer a service.

✦ If you have access to the Internet through work or a friend, visit ISP FIND at http://www.ispfinder.com.

Many ISPs will provide a disk or CD for setting up your account. If you have such a disk, you can use it to set up your account as per your ISP's instructions. Chances are, that's all you'll need to do. If, instead, your ISP just gives you a bunch of account information, you can use the New Connection Wizard described later in this chapter to set up your account. Make sure you keep that information in a safe place where you can always find it. You'll need it to set up your account. And, in case some mishap messes up your account at some time in the future, you'll need that information again to repair or re-create your account.

As a convenience, Table 5-1 lists the types of information your ISP might provide. I've left the second column in this table blank so that you can jot down whatever information you get from your ISP. Don't be alarmed if your ISP doesn't provide all the items listed in the table. Just jot down whatever information you have.

Table 5-1 Information Provided by My ISP	
Information	*Fill In Your Info*
Your IP address	
Your subnet mask	
Your gateway IP address	
Your computer's user host name	
Your ISP's domain name	
Your ISP's primary DNS server IP address	
Your ISP's secondary DNS server IP address (if any)	
Your ISP's domain suffix	
Your ISP's telephone number	
Your login name	
Your password	

Caution For obvious security reasons, you may not want to write your password in Table 5-1, especially if other people might be peeking at your answers. But you could put in a hint—a word or phrase that will remind you of the password.

Using the New Connection Wizard

The New Connection Wizard, which comes with Windows XP, is a handy program for setting up your Internet account. The wizard poses questions for you to answer and gives you blanks to fill in. To start the New Connection Wizard, follow these steps:

1. Click the Start button and choose All Programs ⇨ Accessories ⇨ Communications ⇨ New Connection Wizard.

2. From the first wizard screen, click the Next button.

3. Choose Connect To the Internet from the second wizard screen and then click the Next button.

4. The third wizard screen, shown in Figure 5-1, asks how you want to set up your account. Choose whichever option best describes what you want to do. For clarification, here's what they mean:

   - **Choose from a list of Internet service providers (ISPs):** Select this option only if you've never contacted an ISP or set up an account and you want to purchase an account right now.

   - **Set up my connection manually:** If you've set up an account with an ISP and have a user name and password (and perhaps some other information from Table 5-1), choose this option.

   - **Use the CD I got from an ISP:** If you purchased an account already and your ISP has provided you with a CD, choose this option.

5. After making your choice, click the Next button and follow the instructions on the screen.

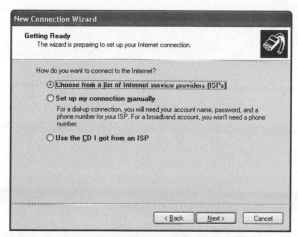

Figure 5-1: Three ways to set up an Internet account in the New Connection Wizard

If you chose the first or third option, it's all just a matter of doing what the wizard tells you to do. I cannot take you step-by-step through those options because how you progress through the wizard depends on how you answer the questions. It's important, however, to pay attention to the following warning.

Caution   User names and passwords are usually case-sensitive. Any time the New Connection Wizard asks you to type a user name or password, make sure you type it using the *exact* upper/lowercase letters provided by your ISP.

If you chose the second option, Set up my connection manually, you'll be presented with questions about your account. Remember, you must enter the requested information *exactly* as provided by your ISP. The slightest typographical error will prevent your account from working properly. Because many of you will be setting up a dial-up account, I'll use that type of an account as an example of the types of questions you're likely to see and appropriate answers to those questions. The first screen for setting up a connection manually, shown in Figure 5-2, asks how you want to connect.

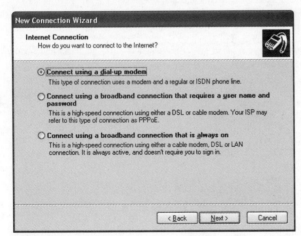

Figure 5-2: Choose how you want to connect to the Internet.

Assuming you're setting up a traditional dial-up account (or ISDN account), choose the first option and click the Next button. The next page asks for the ISP's name. This is just a name used to describe the ISP, so you can type it in however you want. Click the Next button. You'll then be prompted for a phone number as in Figure 5-3. This will be the local access number provided by your ISP. Be sure to type it in exactly as specified by your ISP, and follow any dialing rules of your area. If you live in an area that requires 10-digit dialing, for instance, include the area code. As the wizard suggests, you might want to dial the number with your telephone and listen for a modem sound, to verify that you've dialed the number correctly. Click Next after typing in the local access number.

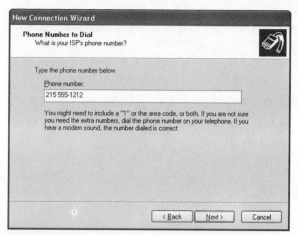

Figure 5-3: Enter your local access number in this wizard screen.

The next wizard screen, shown in Figure 5-4, asks for your user name and password. These must be typed *exactly* as provided by your ISP. Note that if you've gotten separate user names and passwords for logging on and e-mail, you want to enter your logon account name and password here. You won't be using your e-mail user name or password until you set up your e-mail account (as discussed in Chapter 8).

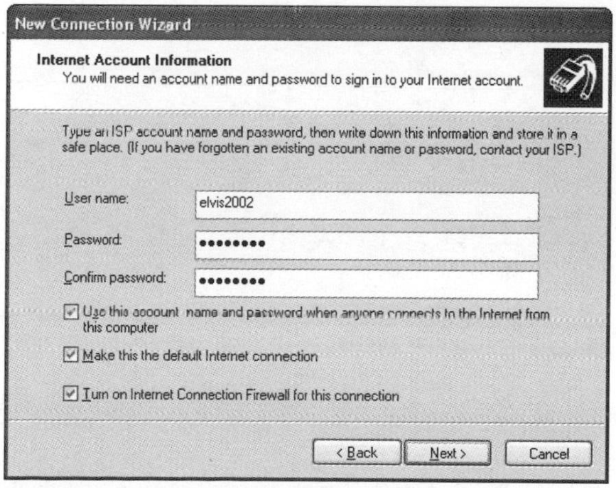

Figure 5-4: The Internet Account Information Wizard screen

Options at the bottom of the screen are summarized here:

✦ **Use this account name and password when anyone connects:** Choose this option if you've set up multiple user accounts on this computer and want all users to use this account to access the Internet.

✦ **Make this the default Internet connection:** If this is your only account or is your "main" account for accessing the Internet, choose this option.

✦ **Turn on the Internet Connection Firewall:** A firewall protects your computer from unauthorized users (hackers) trying to access your computer through the Internet. Go ahead and select this option, if it's available.

The last wizard screen tells you that you've completed all the necessary steps. To make it easy to get to the connection's icon, you may want to select the Add a shortcut check box as in Figure 5-5. Then click the Finish button. If any more instructions appear on-screen, be sure to follow them carefully. At this point, you're ready to try out the connection.

Figure 5-5: The New Connection Wizard successfully completed

Making the connection

If you have set up an "always on" broadband account, you should be connected to the Internet and ready to go at this point. To test your connection, just open Microsoft Internet Explorer as discussed in Chapter 6.

If you set up a dial-up account, you might need to connect "manually." There are many ways to do that. If you opted to add a shortcut icon to your desktop, you can just click (or double-click) that icon to get started. If you didn't set up a desktop shortcut, you'll need to get to the connection's icon (sometimes called a *connectoid*) in the Network Connections window. To open that window, follow these steps:

1. Click the Start button.

2. Choose All Programs ➪ Accessories ➪ Communications ➪ Network Connections.

3. Click (or double-click) the icon for your Internet account. For example, the My ISP icon in Figure 5-6 is a dial-up connection for my Internet account.

Tip   If you want to create an easy shortcut to your connectoid, right-drag its icon out of the Network Connections folder onto the desktop or Quick Launch toolbar (see Chapter 4). When you release the right mouse button, choose Create Shortcuts Here.

Figure 5-6: The My ISP icon in this example represents a dial-up connection to an ISP.

Adding Network Connections to Your Start Menu

You can add a Network Connections option to your Start menu, so that you don't have to dig through All Programs ➪ Accessories to get there. Right-click the Start button and choose Properties. Then, click on the Customize button and click on the Advanced tab. Under Show Menu Items, scroll down to the Network Connections option. You'll have two choices for displaying that option.

If you choose Display as Connect to Menu, the Start menu will gain an option titled Connect To. Clicking that option will display a submenu of all available Internet connections. If you select Link to Network Connection Folder instead, your Start menu will gain a Network Connections option. Clicking that option will take you to the full Network Connections window shown in Figure 5-7.

The Connect dialog box appears (see Figure 5-7). If you filled out all the questions correctly in the New Connection Wizard, all the information you need to log on will already be filled in. Otherwise, you'll need to fill in the user name, password, and local access number provided by your ISP. Then click the Dial button to make your connection.

Figure 5-7: The Connect dialog box

You should see a small dialog box that keeps you informed of what's going on (dialing, connecting, and so forth). When you're connected, you might see a small network icon (two monitors) in the Notifications area. Pointing to this icon shows some information about the connection. Double-clicking this little icon shows more information, as shown in Figure 5-8. If you don't see the tiny icon in the Notifications area, don't worry about it. You can activate it later as discussed under "Troubleshooting a Connectoid" later in this chapter.

When you're connected, you'll stay connected until you specifically break the connection. If you now open some Internet program, such as Microsoft Internet Explorer (Chapter 6), you should be taken to some home page

If you have any problems connecting, don't panic just yet! The default "assumptions" that Windows XP makes about your connection may not be appropriate for your area. You will learn about the potential problems, and fixes, under "Troubleshooting a Connectoid" later in this chapter.

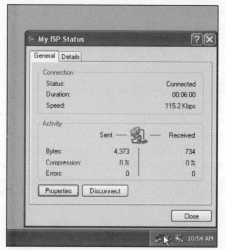

Figure 5-8: The "connected" icon near the mouse pointer, and the Status dialog box that opens when you click that icon

Ending the connection

If you have a dial-up account, remember that you're connected until you specifically disconnect. This means that if you use the same telephone line for both voice and Internet connectivity, anybody who attempts to call you will get a busy signal while you're connected. As long as that little two-monitor icon is visible in the taskbar, you are connected to your ISP. When you're done cruising the Internet, you should always disconnect, using whichever of the following methods you prefer:

✦ Right-click the little two-monitor icon and choose Disconnect.

✦ Double-click the little two-monitor icon on the taskbar and then click the Disconnect button in the dialog box that appears.

✦ Open Network Connections as described earlier, right-click the connectoid's icon, and choose Disconnect.

If you use your voice telephone line for your Internet connection, the line will be freed up for normal phone conversations.

Troubleshooting a Connectoid

The New Connection Wizard is pretty good at setting up an Internet account, but it's not always perfect. If you have any problems connecting, your first step should be to try one of the built-in Windows XP troubleshooters. To do so, follow these steps:

1. Click the Start button and choose Help and Support.

2. Choose Fixing a Problem on the first page of the Help and Support Center window.

3. Choose Networking Problems.

4. Choose Modem Troubleshooter and follow the instructions presented on the screen.

If you complete the troubleshooter and continue to have connection problems, you might need to dig in pretty deeply to get to and repair some faulty settings. Be aware, however, that only your ISP knows what's appropriate for the service they provide. So your best bet is to use their written documentation or tech support to get the information you need to connect properly. You also need to know how to get to the many settings that are available to you. Just about all the settings for connecting to your ISP are in the connectoid's Properties dialog box. To get there, follow these steps:

1. Open Network Connections. (If it's not on your Start menu yet, choose All Programs ➪ Accessories ➪ Communications ➪ Network Connections.)

2. Right-click the icon that represents your Internet connection, and choose Properties.

Initially you're taken to the General tab of the connection's Properties dialog box. The example shown in Figure 5-9 is for a dial-up account. As you progress through the various options in the sections that follow, you'll find that other types of accounts offer some of the same options.

Figure 5-9: The General tab of a dial-up connectoid's properties

To ensure that the Notifications area of that taskbar displays an icon when you're connected to the Internet, be sure that the last option, Show icon in the notification area when connected, is selected.

Modem options

If you have multiple modems connected to your computer, use the Connect Using drop-down list in the Properties dialog box to choose the modem you want to use for this connection. If your ISP recommends that you enable or disable any modem features, such as error control or compression, click the Configure button to get to the options shown in Figure 5-10.

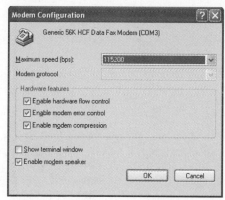

Figure 5-10: Modem configuration options for a dial-up connection to the Internet

Setting up alternate dialing numbers

The Phone Number area of the General tab gives you several options for dialing into your ISP. The most important, of course, is your local access number, which should be entered exactly as provided by your ISP. If your ISP has provided several numbers, you can list several numbers. That way, if a particular access number is busy when you dial in, Windows will automatically dial an alternate number to gain access. Just remember to make sure all the numbers you enter are within your toll-free dialing region if you want to avoid ghastly phone bills. To enter multiple phone numbers, click the Alternates button to get to the options shown in Figure 5-11.

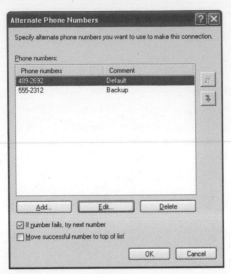

Figure 5-11: The Alternate Phone
Numbers dialog box

Use the Add, Edit, and Delete buttons to add, change, and delete alternate phone
numbers. Obviously, you'll want to choose the first check box to have Windows try
alternate numbers when a specific number doesn't work. You can have Windows
automatically move the successful number to the top of the list as well.

Defining dialing rules

The Dialing Rules option is an important one and the cause for many faulty Internet
connections. Dialing rules vary from one location to the next, so you want to make
sure you set the rules properly for your area. Click the Dialing Rules button to get
started. Click the location you're dialing from (or New Location, if that's the only
option) and then click the Edit button.

Tip   If you're setting up a connection on a portable computer and need to dial from
multiple locations, see "Managing Multiple Dial-Up Connections" in Chapter 21 for
information about creating multiple "dial from" locations.

On the General tab shown in Figure 5-12, make sure all the options are correct. If
you need to dial a number to access an outside line, for example, enter that number
under Dialing Rules. If you suspect that call waiting is interfering with your Internet
connection, choose the To disable call waitin, dial option and then type in the number you need to dial to disable call waiting.

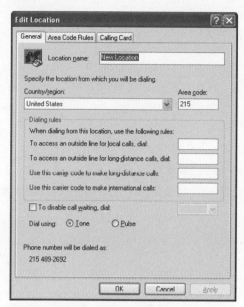

Figure 5-12: The General tab of a dial from location's Properties dialog box

Area code rules also vary from one location to the next, so you want to make sure to set the rules to match where you're dialing from and where you're dialing to. Click the Area Code Rules tab and then click the New button. To define a rule, specify the area code you'll be dialing *to* in the Area Code box. Under Prefixes, choose whether the rule will apply to all prefixes within that area code, or just specific prefixes. Then choose whether to dial a 1 and/or to dial the area code when dialing to that area code. In Figure 5-13, for example, I have set up a 10-digit dialing rule for my area code. Which is to say, when dialing the 215 area code, I need to dial the area code (but not a 1) prior to dialing the number. You can set up different rules for different area codes, if necessary.

Finally, if you're not able to dial for free and want to put phone charges on a calling card, click the Calling Card tab to get to the options shown in Figure 5-14. Choose your card from the list provided or click the New button to add a new card. Then enter your account number, PIN, and any other information relevant to your calling card account.

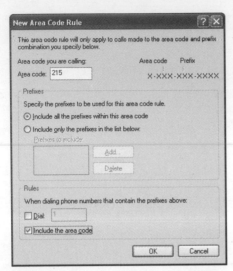

Figure 5-13: The new Area Code Rules dialog box

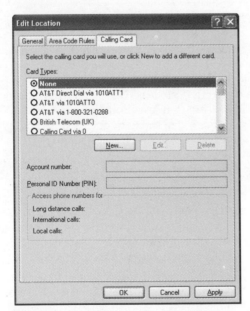

Figure 5-14: Calling card options for a dial-up Internet account

Auto-dial and hang up options

The Options tab for a connectoid's properties, shown in Figure 5-15, enables you to choose how to dial. If you always dial into the same account, for example, you can clear the two Prompt check boxes, as in Figure 5-15, to have the connectoid dial without displaying the Connect dialog box. If your ISP's line is often busy, you can set the Redialing options to have Windows keep trying the number until a successful connection is made.

Figure 5-15: Dial, redial, and hang up options

If you're concerned that you might leave your Internet connection on by mistake — long after you've stopped using it — set the Idle time before hanging up option to any duration you want. You also can have Windows automatically redial the connection in the event that the connection is dropped accidentally.

X.25 accounts

X.25 is a relatively new networking protocol that bypasses traditional telephone lines. This service needs to be purchased separately and requires special hardware. The "phone number" you use to dial is called an X.121 address. If you have an X.25 account, click the X.25 button on the Options tab to set it up. In the X.25 Logon Settings dialog box that opens, choose your service provider under Network and enter the X.121 address to which you'll be dialing (see Figure 5-16). If appropriate for your account, you also can enter user data and facilities information.

Figure 5-16: The X.25 Logon Settings dialog box

Networking options

The Networking tab, shown in Figure 5-17, provides a world of options that apply to all your network connections. For Internet connections, the first option is the most important. The vast majority of Internet connections support PPP connections, which is the option currently selected in the figure. The other option available from that drop-down list, SLIP: Unix Connection, isn't as widely used. If your ISP requires SLIP, however, you need to select that option as opposed to the PPP option.

Figure 5-17: The Networking tab of a dial-up account's Properties dialog box

When PPP is selected, the Settings button is available. Clicking that button presents the options shown in Figure 5-18. As obscure as the settings are, even these can prevent a successful Internet connection. If you're having any problems connecting to your ISP, you may want to disable those options to see whether that helps. To get it right, however, you should really ask your ISP for the appropriate settings.

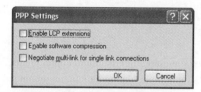

Figure 5-18: The PPP settings dialog box

TCP/IP settings

Another common cause of faulty Internet connections centers on TCP/IP (Transmission Control Protocol/Internet Protocol) settings. To check, and possibly correct those, you need to click Internet Protocol (TCP/IP) as in Figure 5-19, and then click the Properties button. If your ISP gave you a specific IP address and/or DNS server addresses, you need to select the appropriate options and fill in the correct addresses. Figure 5-18 shows an example using some hypothetical addresses, just so you can see what they might look like.

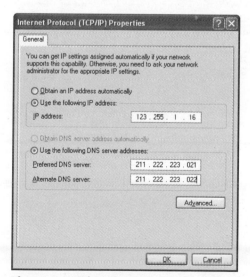

Figure 5-19: The Internet Protocol (TCP/IP) Properties dialog box

Even more advanced TCP/IP options are available from the Advanced button. It's very unlikely that an ISP would require that you tweak any of those more advanced options. They're really more for large corporate networks with their own domain name servers, Dynamic Host Configuration Protocol (DHCP), LMHOSTS lookup, and so forth. If you're a corporate network administrator who needs access to such advanced settings, the Advanced button will take you to them.

The Security and Advanced tabs of the connectoid's Properties dialog box provide options that, as a rule, won't affect your ability to connect to your ISP. If you've made any changes or corrections to any of the options discussed in this section, be sure to close all open dialog boxes by clicking their OK buttons. Then try connecting to your ISP through your connectoid again normally.

Cross-Reference Internet connection sharing is covered in Chapter 26. Internet security and firewalls are discussed in Chapter 29.

More Connection Automation

If you want your computer to dial in to the Internet as soon as you open Microsoft Internet Explorer, follow these steps:

1. Click the Start button and choose Control Panel. If Control Panel opens in Category view, click Network and Internet Connections.

2. Open the Internet Options icon.

3. Click the Connections tab.

4. If you have more than one connection defined, click the one that you'll use as the default and then click the Set Default button (if it's available).

5. Choose Always dial my default connection, as in Figure 5-20.

6. Click the OK button.

From this point, you should be able to browse the Web at any time, just by opening your Microsoft Internet Explorer program. More on browsing the Web in Chapter 6.

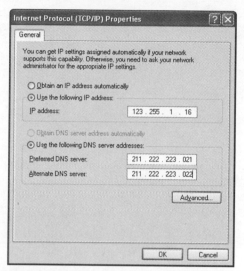

Figure 5-20: Internet Explorer set up to connect automatically

Summary

To connect to the Internet, you basically need two things: some type of modem and an account with an Internet service provider. This chapter has covered all the options and techniques required to get started. Here's a quick recap of the important points covered in this chapter:

✦ If you have an account with one of the large online services, such as AOL, CompuServe, MSN, or Prodigy, you already have Internet access. Go to that service and look for information about using the Internet.

✦ You can find an Internet service provider in the New Connection Wizard, through your local newspaper or Yellow Pages, or at the www.ispfinder.com Web site.

✦ Unless your ISP provides a disk to set up your Internet account automatically, you'll probably need to run the New Connection Wizard to set up your account (Start ➪ All Programs ➪ Accessories ➪ Communications ➪ New Connection Wizard).

✦ If you set up a dial-up account to connect to the Internet, use the "connectoid" icon on the desktop or in the Network Connections window to connect to the Internet.

✦ If you have any problems making a connection with your ISP, see the troubleshooting sections in this chapter.

✦   ✦   ✦

Browsing the World Wide Web

The Internet offers many services, including the wildly popular Word Wide Web (a.k.a. the Web). The Web provides an easy point-and-click interface to a vast amount of information, free software, technical support, and just plain fun. Even if you haven't actually been on the Internet yet, you've undoubtedly seen Web site addresses — those www.whatever.com things — in ads, letterheads, or elsewhere. In this chapter, you'll learn how to get to those addresses and much more about using the Web.

Getting on the Web

Getting on to the World Wide Web is easy. The exact way you go about it, however, depends on your Internet connection and your Internet service provider (ISP). If you work for a company that provides a permanent connection to the Internet, for example, you may have to log on to your company's network and then start your Web browser. If you're going through one of the big online services, such as America Online, CompuServe, or Prodigy, you'll probably need to start the browsing software those services come with and then click a Connect to the Internet button. If you have a dial-up connection of the sort discussed in Chapter 5, you may need to open the connectold to your ISP first.

As a general rule, however, you probably can get right on to the World Wide Web by opening Microsoft Internet Explorer. You can do this in three different ways. Use whichever method is most convenient:

✦ Open the Internet Explorer icon on your desktop.

✦ Click the Launch Internet Explorer Browser icon in the Quick Launch toolbar.

✦ Choose Start ➪ Internet Explorer.

If an Internet Connection Wizard dialog box appears, read it carefully and follow its instructions to set up your Internet connection. (You'll only need to do this step the first time you start your browser.)

Most browsers, including Internet Explorer, automatically prompt you to connect to the Internet if you're not connected already. This means you can start your browser without bothering to connect first. If you are prompted to connect, just click the Connect button that appears.

Your Web browser will start and connect to its *default home page*. That page will fill the large document area within Internet Explorer, as in the example shown in Figure 6-1. That figure shows the home page at www.idg.com (the publishers of this book), although your default home page is likely to be www.msn.com, the home page for the Microsoft Network.

Don't be alarmed if you end up at a completely different Web site. It's easy to change your default home page.

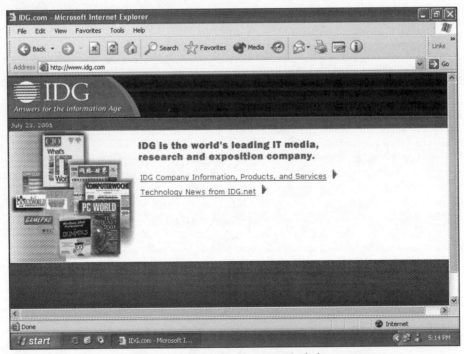

Figure 6-1: Internet Explorer, showing the Hungry Minds home page

Choosing Your Own Home Page

You're not stuck with using the Internet Explorer default home page. In fact, you can specify any starting page you want, use the page you're currently viewing, or start with a blank one. To do this, choose Tools ⇨ Internet Options from the Internet Explorer menu bar. Click the General tab. Next, fill in the Address text box in the Home Page area with the address of your favorite starting Web page or click the Use Current button to select the current page you're browsing as your home page. Click the Use Default button to revert to Microsoft's site as the home page. Alternatively, click the Use Blank button to save a few seconds when you fire up Internet Explorer. If you do this, Explorer won't go looking for your home page. Finally, click OK to save your changes.

Visiting a Web Site

Every Web site has its own unique address, or Uniform Resource Locator (URL). Most start with `http://www` (for Hypertext Transfer Protocol, World Wide Web). Most also end with a three-letter extension that tells you a bit about who owns the site. For example, commercial sites end in .com, educational institutions end in .edu, government sites end in .gov, and non-profit organizations end in .org. For example, my personal Web site's URL is `http://www.coolnerds.com`. (Feel free to stop by and see whether I have any new tips for you!)

To visit a Web site, *point* your Web browser to that site by entering the site's URL into the Address text box of your Web browser. Here are the exact steps:

1. Click the URL currently in the Address bar (`http://www.msn.com` in this example). The current URL will be selected (highlighted).

Tip

If you don't see the Address bar, choose View ⇨ Toolbars ⇨ Address Bar from the Internet Explorer menu bar. If no text box appears next to the Address bar toolbar, double-click the vertical bar to the left of the word *Address* and the text box will appear.

2. Replace the address currently shown with the address to which you want to go. You can type over the highlighted address or use standard text-editing techniques to change the current URL to the URL you want.

3. Press Enter.

4. Wait for the page to appear.

While you're waiting, the icon near the upper-right corner will spin to let you know the browser is working. The status bar at the bottom of the screen will present messages to inform you of the browser's progress. When the `Done` message appears in the left side of the status bar, the entire page has been downloaded to your PC. Figure 6-2 shows the Web site that appeared after I entered the URL `http://www.dummies.com` into the Address box.

Figure 6-2: Now viewing the page at `http://www.dummies.com`

Note

In case you're wondering whether there's some kind of tie-in here, the publisher of this book, Hungry Minds Inc., is also the publisher of the For Dummies series of books.

If you don't see a status bar at the bottom of the Web browser window, choose View ➪ Status Bar from the Internet Explorer menu bar. (When the status bar is visible, the View ➪ Status Bar option has a check mark next to it.)

Tip

Because most Web sites start with `http://www`, it's not really necessary to type that part of the URL. In fact, if you just type the main name (for instance, `coolnerds` rather than `http://www.coolnerds.com`), most of the time Internet Explorer will still take you to the correct site. Saves a lot of typing!

Internet Explorer keeps track of sites you visit and tries to fill in the blanks of any partial Web site addresses you type. This feature is called AutoComplete. Suppose, for example, that you visited my site at `www.coolnerds.com` in the past and now you want to revisit this site. You could click whatever URL is currently shown in the Address box to select that entire address and then start typing www.cool. . . . Chances are, by the time you've typed that much, Internet Explorer will finish typing the rest of the URL, at which point you can press Enter to go there. If Internet Explorer tries to complete the address for you, but gets the wrong address, don't worry. Keep typing the address you want. If you end up with some extra stuff to the right of the address you typed, press Delete (Del) as needed to delete it.

Pictures, Sounds, and Movies

If a Web page displays a large photo or picture, the picture will be resized to fit within the current Explorer window size. If you rest the mouse pointer on the picture for a few seconds, you'll see a button with arrows at all four corners. Clicking that button will switch the picture between full size and the smaller size needed to fit within your browser window. You'll also see a small menu bar that enables you to save the picture to your own computer, print it, or e-mail it to someone.

When you click a link to a video or audio file, you'll be given the option to play the file in Internet Explorer. If you choose Yes, the Media Explorer bar will open, and you can continue browsing while the file is being downloaded. However, you won't be able to save a copy of the file to your own PC. If you choose No, the file will (usually) open in Windows Media Player, where you can save a copy to your own computer.

For more information on using multimedia files in Internet Explorer, choose Help ➪ Contents and Index from the Internet Explorer menu bar. Then click the Search tab, type **media options**, and then click List Topics. You also can find many settings for customizing how multimedia files are played by choosing Tools ➪ Internet Options from the Internet Explorer menu bar. On the Advanced tab, scroll down to the Multimedia category to view your options. For more information about an option, click the ? button in the upper-right corner of the Internet Options dialog box, and then click the option for which you need help.

The AutoComplete feature is entirely optional. To turn it on or off, choose Tools ➪ Internet Options from the Internet Explorer menu bar. Click the Advanced tab. Under the Browsing category in the list that appears, click the check box next to Use Inline AutoComplete to turn this feature on (checked) or off (no check mark).

Using hyperlinks

One of the best features of the Web is its use of hyperlinks — hot spots on the screen — which, when clicked, take you to images, videos, audio clips, or other Web pages. Most hyperlinks appear as underlined text; but any text, or even part of a picture, can be a hyperlink. When the mouse pointer is touching a hyperlink, it changes to the little pointing hand. A ToolTip showing a description of the hyperlink or the address to which the hyperlink will take you also may appear near the mouse pointer. The status bar typically will show the hyperlink's address. To follow the link to its destination, click the left mouse button and wait for the new page to appear on your screen.

While you cruise the Web, Internet Explorer may occasionally display Security Alert dialog boxes. These alert you to the possible security risks of carrying out an action. The message is really more a disclaimer than a warning of an actual threat. You can customize the security options, as explained in "Personalizing Your Browser," later in this chapter.

You'll learn more about Internet security in Chapter 29.

Printing a Web page

You can easily print a copy of whatever Web page you're viewing at the moment by clicking the Print button on the Internet Explorer toolbar. Alternatively, just choose File ➪ Print from the Internet Explorer menu bar, or click the Print button on the toolbar. If the page you're viewing is divided into separate frames, you can right-click within the frame you want to print and choose Print from the menu that appears.

Creating a Favorites list

As you follow links and explore the Web, you're sure to find sites you'll want to revisit. You can make the return trip easier by adding the site to your Favorites while you're there. To add a site to your Favorites list, follow these steps:

1. While viewing the page you want to add, choose Favorites ➪ Add to Favorites from the Internet Explorer menu bar. The Add Favorite dialog box displays, as shown in Figure 6-3.

2. Type in a name for this favorite item or accept the suggested name.

3. Click the OK button.

As a shortcut, you can go to the page you want to add to Favorites and then press Ctrl+D. Internet Explorer adds the page to your Favorites list without displaying the Add Favorite dialog box.

Figure 6-3: The Add Favorite dialog box

Revisiting a Favorite page

When you want to revisit this site, you needn't type its address. Instead, follow these steps:

1. Click the Favorites menu in the Internet Explorer menu bar.

2. If your favorite page is stored in a subcategory (or folder) on the Favorites menu, point to or click that folder.

3. Click the name of the site you want to revisit.

You'll be whisked back to the favorite page you chose. Later in this chapter, you'll learn how to organize your Favorites list into subcategories — such as Cooking, Stock Investments, or Pets — so that you can find your favorite places more easily.

Using other navigation tools

The Standard Buttons toolbar across the top of the Internet Explorer window provides some additional, simple navigation buttons (refer back to Figures 6-1 and 6-2). You also can navigate by using shortcut keys or menu options, if you prefer.

If the Standard Buttons toolbar isn't visible, choose View ➪ Toolbars ➪ Standard Buttons from the Internet Explorer menu bar. If you don't see text descriptions on each button (as shown in Figures 6-1 and 6-2) and you want to, choose View ➪ Toolbars ➪ Customize and select Show text labels in the Text options list box to turn them on. Click Close to close the Customize Toolbar dialog box. You'll learn more about the Internet Explorer toolbars under "Clever Bar Tricks," later in this chapter.

You can use the following navigation buttons, shortcuts, and menu options:

✦ **Back:** Returns to the previous page you visited during this browsing session, if any (same as pressing Alt+left arrow, backspace, or choosing View ➪ Go To ➪ Back from the menu bar).

✦ **Forward:** Goes to the page from which you just backed up during this browsing session, if any (same as pressing Alt+right arrow or choosing View ➪ Go To ➪ Forward from the menu bar).

✦ **Stop:** Ends the download (useful if you find that a download is taking too long). This frees the browser, enabling you to visit elsewhere (same as pressing Esc or choosing View ➪ Stop from the menu bar).

✦ **Refresh:** Ensures you are viewing the absolute latest version of the current page (same as pressing F5 or choosing View ➪ Refresh from the menu bar).

✦ **Home:** Returns to your default home page (same as choosing View ➪ Go To ➪ Home Page from the menu bar).

✦ **Media Bar:** Displays the Media bar in the left pane of the screen (same as choosing View ➪ Explorer Bar ➪ Media). This frame includes a pane you can use to search the Web for multimedia (that is, music and videos) and includes controls for playing media files.

✦ **Search:** Displays a Search Explorer bar in the left frame of the screen (same as choosing View ➪ Explorer Bar ➪ Search or pressing Ctrl+E). This frame enables you to search the Internet for all kinds of good stuff, as explained later in this chapter.

✦ **Favorites:** Displays the Favorites Explorer bar in the left frame of the screen (same as choosing View ➪ Explorer Bar ➪ Favorites from the menu bar or pressing Ctrl+I). Like the Favorites menu, this frame enables you to jump quickly to your favorite Web sites. I'll explain more about working with the Favorites Explorer bar later in this chapter.

✦ **History:** Displays the History Explorer bar in the left frame of the screen. (same as choosing View ➪ Explorer Bar ➪ History from the menu bar or pressing Ctrl+H). You can use the History frame to revisit places you've been before, even if they aren't your favorites. I'll give you a History lesson later in this chapter.

Tip

Choosing View ➪ Go To from the menu bar also displays a brief list of recently visited Web pages. Click any page listed on the menu to revisit. The small arrows attached to the Back and Forward buttons in the Standard toolbar also provide lists of recently visited pages.

✦ **Mail:** Takes you to Internet e-mail, as discussed in Chapter 8.

✦ **Print:** As mentioned, prints the Web page you're viewing (same as choosing File ➪ Print from the menu bar or pressing Ctrl+P).

✦ **Tip of the Day:** Choosing View ➪ Explorer Bar ➪ Tip of the Day displays a daily "tip" in a bar along the bottom of the window.

All the Explorer bars have a Close (X) button at the upper-right corner, which you can click to close the bar. The Tip of the Day bar's Close button is in its upper-left corner.

Every Web site you visit is bound to have hyperlinks to take you to other sites in which you're interested. So the few skills you've learned so far will enable you to explore the Web forever! At some point, however, you may get tired of being led around the Web, and you might start asking, "How do I find information on such and such?" The *such-and-such* part can be any topic that interests you. And I do mean any topic, because the Web is loaded with millions of pages of information. The next section explains how to find just about everything, from apples to zoonoses, on the Internet.

Searching the Web

Internet Explorer offers you several ways to search for information on the Internet. Perhaps the handiest is the built-in Search Explorer bar. To use it, click the Search button on the Standard Buttons toolbar, or choose View ➪ Explorer Bar ➪ Search from the menu bar. The viewing area splits into two frames, as in the example shown in Figure 6-4. Whatever page you were viewing scoots over to the frame on the right. The new frame on the left acts as your Search browser.

Figure 6-4: Click the Search button to open the Search Explorer bar on the left side of the screen.

Now, to search for your topic on the Internet, follow these steps:

1. If you want, choose the search options by clicking Change preferences on the Search bar.

2. Type your question, such as **Where can I find San Diego weather forecasts?** into the text box, and then click the Search button or press Enter.

Tip You really don't need to type the entire question. A key word or phrase, such as *San Diego weather*, will do.

3. If the search is successful, you will see a list of hyperlinks that satisfy your search. (Be sure to scroll up and down through the entire frame to see what's available and look for any Next Page or Previous Page hyperlinks that take you to additional matches for your search.) Now, click the hyperlink of the item you want to explore.

Soon a list of Web sites dealing with your question will appear to the right of the Search bar. Click any blue underlined link to visit the referenced page. Use the Back button on the toolbar to return to the list. You'll be amazed at how quickly you can home in on the information you seek. If you want to view a page without the Search bar taking up space, click the Search button on the toolbar again. To reopen the Search bar, click that Search button again.

If you don't find what you're looking for, you can repeat Steps 1 through 3. For example, start with step 1 and try another search query, or click the Back button and then click a different hyperlink. Very convenient!

Caution   Remember, just because you read something on the Web doesn't make it so! When doing online research, always try to get corroboration from several sources and use your own common sense before you believe any "facts" you find.

Searching from a Web page

You can search the Internet from the Web site for a specific search engine if you want. For example, you can go straight to the Yahoo! Web site by entering www.yahoo.com into the Address box. Or, visit the Lycos search engine at www.lycos.com. Other popular search engines can be found at www.excite.com (Excite) and www.infoseek.com (Infoseek).

What's a Search Engine, Anyway?

A *search engine* is a special type of Web site that helps you find resources on the Internet, including Web pages, newsgroups, and more. When you start a search, the engine looks through an existing database of Web pages, not the Internet itself. This is good, because it would take an extremely long time to actually visit all the millions of pages on the World Wide Web. The only downside being that, the results of your search might be somewhat outdated. For example, Web sites come and go, so some of the links that appear might lead to Web sites that no longer exist (leaving you with a 404 Page not found error. If that happens, just click the Back button to try another page on the list.

Different search engines use different methods to keep their databases up-to-date. Some engines index frequently appearing keywords on Web pages. Others rely on submissions by people who want their own Web sites listed. And still others are updated manually by people who actually scour the Web for sites of interest. And of course, some engines use a combination of these methods. Therefore, if a particular search engine doesn't help you find what you're looking for, you might consider performing the same search using a different search engine.

Most search engines enable you to enter complex search criteria, such as zoonoses *and* rabbits. Unfortunately, the methods for performing these fancier searches depend on the engine you choose. Luckily, most search engines offer Help buttons or hyperlinks you can click for more details and examples, but you may need to visit the search engine's Web site to get this help.

Tip For an even better way to search, visit www.copernic.com and download a copy of Copernic. This application automatically submits your query to a number of search engines simultaneously, and then consolidates and ranks the results to help you perform more efficient Web searches. You can even tell Copernic to check each of the hyperlinks and then remove any that are no longer valid. You'll find several different versions of Copernic available, including a free, ad-supported version.

Searching from the Address bar

In a hurry? Then why not do an *autosearch* right from the Address bar? It's as easy as following these steps:

1. Click the Address text box.

2. Type **go** or **find** followed by a space.

3. Type the topic you seek.

4. Press Enter.

For example, type **go llamas** or **find llamas** or **? llamas** and press Enter. This will fire up the Internet Explorer MSN search engine and begin searching the Web for the topic you entered.

Going Places You've Gone Before (History 101)

Maybe history wasn't your best subject in school, but it can be a lifesaver when you're cruising the Internet. Let's say you've been quite the Internet butterfly, flitting from site to site as you visit the Internet's most interesting spots. Now further suppose that you want to return to a page you visited yesterday or the day before, but you forgot to add this page to your Favorites list. Are you stuck? Of course not! Returning to this page is no sweat if you use the History list, which Internet Explorer updates for you automatically.

Note The History list is a special folder on your hard drive (\Documents and Settings*yourusername*\Local Settings\History). The History bar, discussed next, makes it easy for you to work with the History list.

Opening the History bar

The first step in working with the History list is to open the History bar. To do this, click the History button on the Standard Buttons toolbar or choose View ➪ Explorer Bar ➪ History from the Internet Explorer menu bar. The screen will split into two frames, with the left frame showing the History bar and the right frame showing whatever Web page you're currently viewing. Figure 6-5 shows an example containing several days of history information.

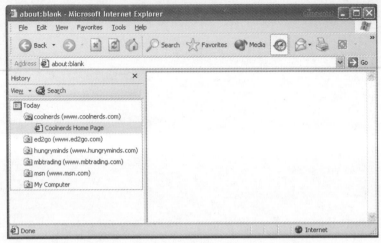

Figure 6-5: Viewing your place in history with the History bar

When the History bar is open, jumping to a previously visited page is easy. To do so, just follow these steps:

1. Click the hyperlink for the day you want to revisit. For example, in Figure 6-5, I clicked the hyperlink for Today. (If several weeks of history exist, click the hyperlink for the week you want, and then click the hyperlink for the desired day.)

2. Click the hyperlink for the site you want to revisit. (Sites are marked with a folder icon.) A list of pages you visited at this site will appear below the folder in the History bar.

3. Click the page you want to revisit. The page is marked with a globe and paper icon.

That's all there is to it! The page you chose to revisit will appear in the right frame, ready for you to explore. (If you really like this page, adding it to your Favorites list is a good idea, as explained earlier.)

You can repeat the preceding three steps to revisit any of the pages for any date in the History Explorer bar. When you finish using the History Explorer bar, you can hide it again by clicking the History button on the toolbar.

Finding What You Found

Every so often, your searches will retrieve a page that doesn't seem to belong there. Say, for example, you're looking for Mikhail Baryshnikov and up pops a page about football. You can't for the life of you figure out what Baryshnikov and football have in common. When you visit the page, you still have no idea. This is where the faithful Find feature comes in handy. Choose Edit ➪ Find (on this page) from the Internet Explorer menu bar (or press Ctrl+F), type the specific word you're looking for (in this case, *Baryshnikov*), and click the Find Next button. The Find feature will try to locate the word you're looking for on the current Web page.

In the case of the ballet-football mystery, I had done a Find for Barysh (just part of the word will often do), and discovered the sports writer said the quarterback "leapt with the grace of Baryshnikov." Mystery solved! There's nothing a search engine can do about synonyms, homonyms, and creative metaphors, but at least now we know what our pal Mikhail was doing in the end zone.

Rewriting History

Internet Explorer updates the History list each time you visit another page on the Internet. This happens automatically whether or not the History Explorer bar is visible. You can customize the History list in several ways, including the following:

✦ To delete an item from the History list, right-click it in the History Explorer bar and choose Delete from the pop-up menu.

✦ To empty the History list, choose Tools ➪ Internet Options from the Internet Explorer menu bar, choose the General tab, click the Clear History button and then click Yes.

✦ To view or change the number of days pages are kept in the History list, choose Tools ➪ Internet Options from the Internet Explorer menu bar, choose the General tab and then look at or change the Days to keep pages in History option.

Getting the Most from Your Favorites List

You've already seen how the Search and History Explorer bars and the Favorites menu can help you navigate the Internet more quickly. There's also a Favorites Explorer bar to speed your visits to favorite spots on the Net. To display it, click the Favorites button on the Standard Buttons toolbar or choose View ➪ Explorer Bar ➪ Favorites from the menu bar. As usual when you choose an Explorer bar, your screen will split into two frames, with the Favorites Explorer bar on the left and the current Web page on the right, as shown in Figure 6-6.

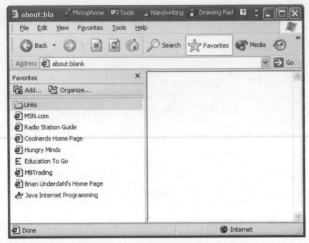

Figure 6-6: The Favorites Explorer bar makes quick work of jumping to your favorite Web pages.

Choosing a favorite page from the Favorites Explorer bar is a lot like revisiting a page in the Favorites menu:

1. If your favorite page is stored in a subcategory (or folder), click that folder in the Favorites Explorer bar. Folders are listed alphabetically, which makes them easy to find.

2. Click the name of the site you want to revisit.

As usual, the page you chose will appear in the right-hand frame. When you're ready to hide the Favorites Explorer bar, click the Favorites button on the toolbar.

Adding folders to your Favorites list

You can organize your Favorites list into subcategories (or folders), just as you group your computer files into folders. Suppose, for example, that you discover a bunch of great cooking sites and you want to add them to a Cooking category in your Favorites list. Grouping the cooking links this way is much more convenient than scattering them all over your Favorites list.

Several ways exist to create new folders in your Favorites list. Perhaps the easiest is to set up the folder when you add a Web page to your Favorites list. Here's how:

1. Go to the page you want to add, and then choose Favorites ➪ Add to Favorites from the Internet Explorer menu bar. You'll see the Add Favorite dialog box, shown earlier in Figure 6-3.

2. Type a name for this favorite item or accept the suggested name.

3. Click the Create in button. The Add Favorite dialog box will expand, as shown in Figure 6-7.

4. If you want the new folder to appear below one of the existing folders in the Favorites list, click that folder name.

5. Click the New Folder button, type a name for your new folder, and then click OK. Your new folder will appear in the Create in list and it will be selected automatically. (When a folder is selected, its icon appears open.)

6. Be sure the folder in which you want to store your favorite page is selected. If it isn't, click it.

7. Click the OK button to add your favorite page to the selected folder.

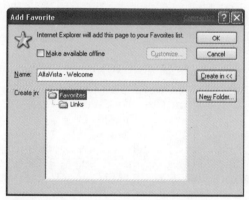

Figure 6-7: Click the Create in button to choose (or create) folders for organizing your favorite pages.

Adding Favorite items to existing folders

If the Favorites folder in which you want to store a favorite item already exists, your job is even easier. Just complete Steps 1, 2, 3, 6, and 7 from the preceding section (skip Steps 4 and 5).

If drag-and-drop is more your style, you'll love this trick for adding new items to the Favorites list:

1. Open the Favorites Explorer bar.

2. Go to the page you want to add to Favorites or to any page that offers a hyperlink to the page you want to add.

3. If you're currently viewing the page you want to add, position the mouse pointer on the tiny icon just to the left of the URL in the Address box. If you're viewing a page that offers a hyperlink to the page you want to add, position the mouse on the hyperlink.

4. Drag the icon or hyperlink to the appropriate folder in the Favorites Explorer bar. When the black horizontal marker appears at the place where you want the new favorite item, release the mouse button.

Reorganizing your Favorites list

You may want to reorganize your Favorites list or clean it up occasionally. For example, you might want to move some favorite pages from one folder to another, delete old favorites you no longer want, or change a folder name so that it's more descriptive. You can do all this from the Organize Favorites dialog box or by using drag-and-drop and other file management techniques.

Using the Organize Favorites dialog box

To use the Organize Favorites dialog box, choose Favorites ➪ Organize Favorites from the Internet Explorer menu bar. You'll see the Organize Favorites dialog box, as shown in Figure 6-8.

How you organize your Favorites list is up to you. If you're already comfortable with the file management techniques covered in Chapter 2, you'll quickly realize that using the Organize Favorites dialog box is much like using My Computer, although it's a tad more friendly. Try these tricks for starters:

✦ To open a folder, click the folder. The folder you opened will appear in the list along the right of the Organize Favorites dialog box.

✦ To create a new folder inside whatever folder is shown in the folder list, click the Create Folder button, type a new folder name and press Enter.

✦ To delete a folder or a favorite item, select it (by clicking it) and then click the Delete button or press your Delete key. Click Yes when asked about moving the item to the Recycle Bin.

✦ To move a folder or a favorite item, select it and then click the Move to Folder button. When prompted to browse, click the folder in which the selected item belongs and then choose OK.

✦ To rename a folder or a favorite item, select it and then click the Rename button. Type a new name and then press Enter.

When you finish using the Organize Favorites dialog box, click its Close (X) button.

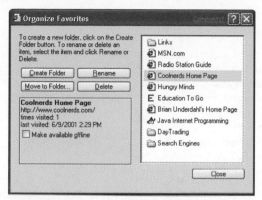

Figure 6-8: You can use the Organize Favorites dialog box to set up your Favorites list any way you like.

Using file management techniques

The Favorites folder is just another folder on your computer, which means you can use all the standard file management tricks to reorganize items when the Organize Favorites dialog box or Favorites Explorer bar is open. For example, you can right-click items and choose options from the pop-up menu and you can use drag-and-drop to move and copy items. You also can use My Computer or Windows Explorer to organize the Favorites list if you want.

Speaking of kids, you can find some real lifesavers for the seemingly endless barrage of homework that kids get these days at the following sites: www. dictionary.com, www.encyclopedia.com, www.bigchalk.com, www.school. discovery.com, and http://encarta.msn.com/homework (to name just a few).

Kid Safe Surfing

As you may know, the Internet is not censored, and there are a lot of Web sites out there that contain content that is not at all appropriate for children. If you're a parent who's concerned about having Internet access in the home, be sure to visit www.smarparent.com where you can stay up-to-date with all the tools and techniques available to keep kids safe online.

Also, be aware that even an innocent Web search can produce links to not-so-innocent Web sites. For example, a search for *Escort* (as in the car from Ford) will turn up links to sites offering "escort services." Some search engines, such as Ask Jeeves for Kids (www. ajkids.com), do an admirable job of weeding out such links before they get to your kids' computer screens.

Clever Bar Tricks

I have already mentioned several ways to use the various bars in Internet Explorer. In this section, I'll summarize the basics, in case you feel like looking them up in one place. The browser has three types of bars: toolbars, the status bar, and Explorer bars. To display or hide one of these bars, just choose the appropriate option from the View menu, as described here:

✦ To display or hide one of the toolbars, choose View ➪ Toolbars and then either Standard Buttons, Address Bar, or Links.

✦ To display or hide text labels on the Standard Buttons toolbar, choose View ➪ Toolbars ➪ Customize and select Show text labels from the Text Options drop-down list. Then click the Close button.

✦ To display or hide the status bar, choose View ➪ Status Bar.

✦ To display or hide an Explorer bar, choose View ➪ Explorer Bar and then choose the Explorer bar you want. (You also can click the Search, Favorites, or History buttons on the Standard Buttons toolbar.)

Remember, if a toolbar's option is checked on the View menu, that bar will be visible. If it isn't checked, you won't see that bar.

The Links toolbar offers buttons that can take you to handy places on the Internet, and it contains the same entries as the Links folder in your Favorites list. The initial items are set up as a gift to you from Microsoft, but you can update them if you want. To add an item, drag a Web page hyperlink or the icon next to the URL in the Address box to the place in the Links bar or Links folder where you want the new item to appear. To delete an item, right-click the item and choose Delete. To change the URL of the item, right-click the item and choose Properties.

Clever toolbar tricks

You can reposition the toolbars if you want. To reposition a toolbar, move your mouse to the dotted line at the left side of the toolbar. (If you don't see the dotted line, choose View ➪ Toolbars, and select Lock the toolbars to clear its check mark and unlock the bars.) Then, drag the bar up, down, left, or right. (As you drag, the mouse pointer changes to a four-headed arrow.) When the bar pops into place, release the mouse button.

Tip To prevent the toolbars from being moved accidentally, you can choose View ➪ Toolbars ➪ Lock the Toolbars to reselect that option.

When the toolbars are unlocked, you can also resize them, making them narrower (to show fewer buttons) or wider (to show more buttons). To resize a toolbar, drag the dotted vertical line at the left of the toolbar to the left or to the right. (This line won't appear if the toolbars are locked.) The mouse pointer changes to a two-headed arrow when it's safe to drag. If you want to shrink or expand the toolbar quickly, double-click the vertical line instead.

> **Tip**   To display or hide a toolbar quickly, right-click in any visible toolbar and then click the name of the toolbar you want to show or hide.

Most of the figures in this chapter show the Internet Explorer title bar, menu bar, and some of the toolbars along the top of the window. Figure 6-9 shows the Internet Explorer window after unlocking the toolbars and moving the Links toolbar to the top row.

Clever Explorer bar tricks

As you know, when you open an Explorer bar, the left frame shows the bar and the right frame shows the current Web page. Now, here are some ways to put any Explorer bar through its paces:

✦ To hide the Explorer bar, click the same button on the Standard Buttons toolbar you clicked to display it originally. Alternatively, click the Close (X) button on the Explorer bar's upper-right corner.

✦ To narrow or widen an Explorer bar, move your mouse pointer to the border on the right side of the bar until the pointer changes to a two-headed arrow. Then drag the border to the left or to the right.

Clever full-screen tricks

When you choose View ➪ Full Screen, or press the F11 key, the current Web page displays without the added clutter of the status bar, menu bar, Address bar, or Links toolbar (see Figure 6-10). You can quickly toggle between the normal display shown in earlier figures and the full-screen display by pressing F11.

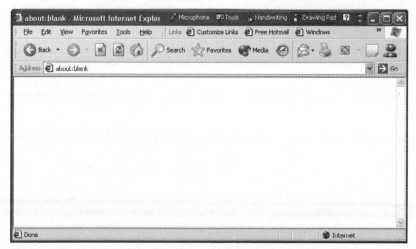

Figure 6-9: Here are the menu bar and the Standard Buttons, Address bar, and Links toolbars after unlocking and then moving and resizing some of them.

You can customize full-screen view in several ways:

✦ To display or hide bars in full-screen view, right-click any visible toolbar and choose Menu Bar, Address Bar, or Links (as appropriate).

✦ If the menu bar, Address bar, or Links toolbar are visible, you can resize or move them as described earlier. Note, however, that you can move them to the left or right only.

✦ To toggle the Auto-Hide feature for the Standard Buttons toolbar, right-click the toolbar and choose Auto-Hide. When Auto-Hide is on, the Standard Buttons toolbar is invisible until you point your mouse to the top of the screen, where the toolbar magically reappears. When Auto-Hide is off, the Standard Buttons toolbar is always visible in full-screen view.

To turn off the Auto-Hide feature, bring the toolbar back into view, right-click some empty area, and choose Auto-Hide again.

When viewing Internet Explorer full-screen, you can click the Restore button near its upper-right corner, or press the F11 key, to return to the normal windowed view.

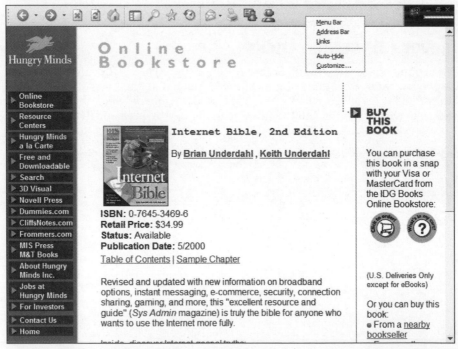

Figure 6-10: This is Internet Explorer in full-screen view. In this example, I right-clicked the Standard Buttons toolbar.

Browsing without Your Browser

Practically everything in Windows XP is capable of connecting you to the Internet, whether you've fired up Internet Explorer or another browser first. When you open Windows Explorer, or the Address toolbar on the taskbar, for example, you can type a URL into the Address text box and press Enter, just as you do in Internet Explorer. Instantly the window will have all the basic features of Internet Explorer, and you can surf the Net as usual.

If you don't see an Address bar in Windows Explorer, choose View ➪ Toolbars ➪ Address Bar from its menu bar. To view an Address bar on the taskbar, right-click some neutral area of the taskbar and choose Toolbars ➪ Address. To move or size the Address bar in the taskbar, right-click the taskbar and clear the check mark next to Lock the Taskbar. The Address bar in the taskbar will gain the dotted vertical line. You can drag that line left or right to size the bar, or up onto the screen to reposition it. Figure 6-11 shows an example with the Address bar displayed in Windows Explorer (under the toolbar in the My Computer window). The free-floating Address bar on the desktop was dragged off of the taskbar.

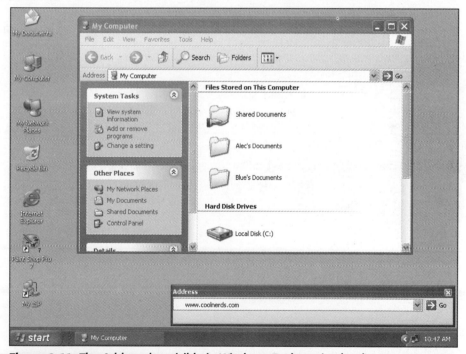

Figure 6-11: The Address bar visible in Windows Explorer (under the My Computer toolbar) and free-floating on the desktop

You also can choose options on the View or Favorites menus in My Computer or Windows Explorer to use the toolbars, Explorer bars, and Favorites lists you learned about in this chapter. And, anytime you click a hyperlink *anywhere* — on your desktop, in a document, or on a button — the Internet features will kick in exactly as you'd expect. This Internet-awareness in Windows XP is a huge bonus because you never have to plan your Internet travels ahead of time. Just do what's convenient and Windows XP will handle the rest.

Adding Internet Links to the Desktop

Windows XP offers tons of ways to integrate the Internet with your desktop. I'll dive deeper into those features in Chapter 7. To whet your appetite for what's to come, I want to explain a few quick ways to create links to the Internet right on your Windows desktop. To begin, go to the Web page you want to add to your desktop or go to a Web page *containing* a hyperlink you want to add. Now, do any of the following steps to add a hyperlink to your desktop:

✦ To add a link to the current page, choose File ➪ Send ➪ Shortcut to Desktop from the Internet Explorer menus.

✦ To drag-and-drop a link to the current page, be sure you can see the desktop. (Click the Refresh button in your browser if you need to.) Then drag the little icon shown next to the URL in the Address box to your desktop and release the mouse button (see Figure 6-12).

✦ To drag-and-drop a link that's somewhere on the current Web page, point to the link so that the mouse pointer changes to a pointing hand. Then drag the link to your desktop and release the mouse button (see Figure 6-13).

Figure 6-12: Start dragging the mouse pointer to create a desktop hyperlinkto the current page

Figure 6-13: Start dragging at the mouse pointer to create a desktop hyperlinkto a hyperlink contained on the current page.

A shortcut to the Internet hyperlink will appear on your desktop. Now you can open it as you would open any shortcut on your desktop (for example, by double-clicking or clicking it), and the Web page you linked to will open in your browser.

Of course, what goes on the desktop can easily be swept off it. If you no longer want the desktop shortcut, just drag it to the Recycle Bin.

Tip You can drag-and-drop Internet shortcuts to the Start button, to the Favorites Explorer bar, or to any toolbar on the taskbar.

Downloading from the Web

Downloading means to copy a file from the Internet to your own PC. Tons of things exist on the Web for you to download—mostly in the form of free programs, updates to existing programs, and shareware (try-before-you-buy) programs. Downloading from the Web is remarkably easy, almost effortless. Typically, you'll find a link to the program or file you want to download, as in the example shown in Figure 6-14. The links shown are available at www.microsoft.com/downloads.

If you see instructions for using the downloaded file, you might want to print those so that you have them handy when the download is complete. Just choose File ⇨ Print from the Internet Explorer menu bar to print whatever page you're viewing at the moment.

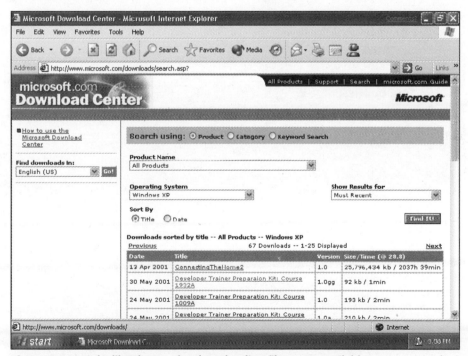

Figure 6-14: Links like these—for downloading files—are available on many Web sites.

Downloading when a link exists

To perform the download when a link exists, follow these steps:

1. Click the link that offers to download the file. If necessary, read any instructions that appear, and keep on clicking links as needed until you see a dialog box like the one shown in Figure 6-15.

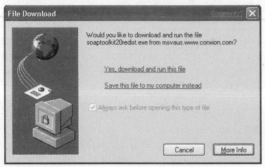

Figure 6-15: This dialog box asks what you want to do with a Web file.

2. Choose Save this file to disk and then click the OK button. The Save As dialog box appears, as shown in Figure 6-16.

Figure 6-16: Tell Internet Explorer where to put the file you're downloading.

3. In the Save As dialog box, choose the disk drive and folder in which you want to store the file you're downloading. Take a quick look at the file name, too, so you'll remember what file to look for later.

Tip Beginners often forget to choose a folder for the file they're downloading, and then have problems finding the downloaded file later. If you want to make sure the downloaded file will be easy to find, choose Desktop from the Save In drop-down list in the Save As dialog box. That will put the icon for the downloaded file right on your Windows desktop, where it will be plainly visible.

4. Click the Save button.

The download will begin and you'll see a progress meter. You can do other work while waiting for the download to complete; but if you interact with the Internet a lot, you'll slow down the download. If you can find something to do locally (on your own PC rather than on the Internet), you won't compete with the download. Of course, if the file you're downloading is a large one, going out to lunch isn't a bad idea!

Downloading when no link exists

In some cases, you might see a picture in a Web page, or some other item that offers no real download option. Chances are, you can download a copy of that item right to your own PC by following these steps:

1. Right-click the link or the item you want to download to your own PC.

2. From the pop-up menu that appears, choose Save Target As or Save Picture As (or whichever option implies you can save the item you just right-clicked).

3. When the Save dialog box appears, choose the disk drive and folder in which you want to store the file and remember to take a quick look at the file name.

4. Click the Save button to begin the download.

As with any download, you'll see a dialog box keeping you informed of the download's progress. When the download is complete, that dialog box disappears from the screen.

Caution Of course, you should *never* steal any Web page, pictures, sounds, or videos without permission. *Always* treat everything on the Web as copyrighted material, unless you're given explicit swiping rights in writing.

As with any download, the downloaded item will appear as an icon in whichever folder you selected in step 3. Clicking (or double-clicking) that icon will open the file.

Inoculating Your Computer Against Viruses

Occasionally, high-tech vandals sneak nasty little programs, called *viruses*, into files. If you download a file containing a virus, you probably won't know it until the virus starts doing damage (or playing little tricks, if it's not an overly hostile virus). As discussed in Chapter 29, e-mail attachments are the main culprits for transmitting viruses. You can take steps within Outlook Express to minimize your exposure to such viruses. For full-scale virus protection, however, a third-party virus scanning and elimination program might be your best bet.

Before you purchase anti-virus software, be sure to check for products that are compatible with Windows XP. You can do so by clicking the Start button, choosing Help and Support, and then clicking on Find compatible hardware and software for Windows XP in the Help and Support Center. You can purchase products at any computer store (brick-and-mortar or online). For more information, visit the Web sites of these anti-virus software publishers: McAfee Network Security and Management at www.mcafee.com, or Symantec at www.symantec.com/avcenter. For a broader overview of viruses, go to a search engine such as www.lycos.com and search for virus or anti-virus software.

Saving a Web page

You can save an entire Web page, which is handy if you want to design a page similar to an existing page on the Web. To save the page, choose File ⇨ Save As from the Internet Explorer menus. From the Save as Type drop-down list, choose one of the following options:

✦ **Web Page, complete (*.htm,*.html):** Saves the Web page and any graphics that go along with it. But graphics and text are stored in separate files.

✦ **Web Archive, single file (*.mht):** Saves the Web page and its graphic images in a single file with the .mht extension.

✦ **Web Page, HTML only (*.htm,*.html):** Saves only the text and HTML (formatting) codes, but no graphics.

✦ **Text File (*.txt):** Saves only the text with no graphics or HTML formatting.

Then enter a name for the page, and click the Save button.

Using downloaded files

Once the download (or Save As) is finished, an icon representing the downloaded files will appear in whatever folder you selected as the Save In destination in the Save As dialog box. If you selected Desktop from the Save In drop-down list, the icon will appear right on your Windows desktop. And at that point, the file is not different from any other on your hard disk. So to open the downloaded file, you can just click (or double-click) its icon.

If the file you downloaded is a program (as opposed to a document), it (the program or its installation procedure) should start right up. If you printed out instructions for installing or using the downloaded file, refer to those for more information, if necessary. If the file you downloaded is some kind of document, such as text, a picture, music, or whatever, that document should open in an appropriate program automatically.

If opening the downloaded file takes you to the Open With dialog box, as discussed under "Opening a Document" back in Chapter 3, you most likely don't have a program that's suitable for opening that type of document. Your best bet for finding out what kind of program might be appropriate would be to return to the Web site from which you downloaded the file and see whether that site offers any recommendations.

Keep in mind that you can tell what type of file an icon represents by the file name extension. For example, program files usually have the extension .exe. Sound files have file name extensions such as .wav, .mpe, and .au. Graphic images come in countless different formats, some common ones being .gif, .jpeg, .bmp, and .png. Compressed files often have the extension .zip. If you can't see the file name extension, you'll need to "unhide" file name extensions via the Folder Options icon in the Control Panel, as discussed under "Viewing and Hiding File Info" in Chapter 2.

Tip You need Adobe Acrobat Reader to open the popular Portable Document Format (.pdf) files. You can download the reader from `www.adobe.com`.

Copying off the Web

It isn't really necessary to download an entire page of the Web if you're just looking to copy some text into a word processing program, or a picture into a graphics program. A simple cut-and-paste procedure will do the trick there. To copy text, for example, open any text editor such as WordPad, which comes with Windows XP (click the Start button and choose All Programs ➪ Accessories ➪ WordPad. Or open any word processing program, such as Microsoft Word.

Back in Internet Explorer, just select the text you want to copy by dragging the mouse pointer through it. Then press Ctrl+C or choose Edit ➪ Copy from the Internet Explorer menu bar to copy the selection to the Windows Clipboard.

Next, switch to your text editor or word processing program, position the cursor to where you want to place the selection, and press Ctrl+V or choose Edit ➪ Paste from that program's menu bar.

The procedure differs only slightly for copying pictures. Open a graphics program, such as Paint (click the Start button and choose All Programs ➪ Accessories ➪ Paint) or some other, more complete program such as Paint Shop Pro or PhotoShop.

A Note on Zip Files

Some of the files available for download on the Web are compressed (or *zipped*), so they'll download more quickly. These files typically have the extension .zip on their file names. Before you can use such a file, you must decompress (or *unzip*) it. To do this, you can use the Compressed Folders tool discussed in Chapter 12. For a more in-depth discussion of how file name extensions associate documents with programs, see Chapter 33.

Optionally, you can use a third-party Zip tool, such as WinZip (available from www.winzip.com). Be aware, however, that if you install a third-party zip program, you lose the built-in capability to handle zip files as compressed folders. You can find alternative "freebie" zip programs at any of the Web sites offering shareware and freeware programs, such as MSN Computing Central Forum at http://computingcentral.msn.com/software or Tucows at www.tucows.com. This type of program is generally categorized as a *utility* at such sites. Although if the site offers a search capability, searching for the word *zip* will probably turn up lots of programs that will do the trick.

In Internet Explorer, right-click the picture you want to copy and then press Ctrl+C, or choose Edit ➪ Copy from the Internet Explorer menu bar. That will copy the picture to the Windows Clipboard. Next, switch to your graphics program and press Ctrl+V or choose Edit ➪ Paste from its menu bar.

Once the copied text or picture is in your program, choose File ➪ Save from that program's menu bar to save the item to your own hard disk. When the Save As dialog box appears, choose any folder on your local hard disk from the Save In drop-down list or navigator below that box. Then enter a file name and click Save, just as you would with any other document.

Of course, just because you can copy things this easily doesn't mean you have full rights to the content. You still need to abide by all the applicable laws if the material you copied is copyrighted.

Clip art, sound, and more for Microsoft Office

If you're a Microsoft Office user, be sure to visit Office Online for help, updates, templates, and other freebies to go along with your favorite Office programs. Just choose Help ➪ Office on the Web from your favorite Office 2000 or Office XP program's menu bar. Internet Explorer will start up automatically, and you'll be taken to a Web page that's dedicated to the program from which you started. You also can get to Office on the Web by typing the URL www.officeupdate.microsoft.com directly into your Internet Explorer Address bar.

If you use the Microsoft Office Clip Art Gallery, you can add pictures to it via the Web as well. Go to any Office 2000 or XP program and choose Insert ➪ Picture ➪ Clip Art. When the Clip Art Gallery opens, choose Clips Online. Internet Explorer will open and you'll be taken to Design Gallery Live. There you can search for specific images, sounds, and movies, or just browse through current offerings. Follow the instructions presented on the page you're viewing to select items to download and begin the installation process.

When download is complete, the items you downloaded will be organized into your Clip Art Gallery automatically. You don't need to mess around with individual files or import them into the gallery manually. Just use the Clip Art Gallery as you always have and you'll find the new clips within appropriate categories, ready to use.

Personalizing Your Browser

Part III of this book explains many ways to personalize your Windows XP system. As you might expect, your browser and Internet settings are fully customizable, too, and you may want to look at your options if things aren't working exactly as you'd like. You can get started in either of two ways:

✦ Choose Start ⇨ Control Panel from the Windows taskbar. If Control Panel opens in Category view, click Network and Internet Connections. Then open the Internet Options icon.

✦ Choose Tools ⇨ Internet Options from the Internet Explorer menu bar.

You'll see the Internet Options dialog box, shown in Figure 6-17. Like most dialog boxes that enable you to customize stuff in Windows XP, this one offers several tabs at the top, which you can click to choose various categories of settings. The basic drill goes like this:

1. Choose the tab containing the settings you want to change. (Figure 6-17 shows the General tab.)

2. Change the settings as needed. (If you need help with a particular setting, click the question mark (?) button at the upper-right corner of the dialog box, and then click the setting about which you want to know more.)

3. Repeat Steps 1 and 2 as needed.

4. When you finish making changes, click OK as needed to save your changes and close the dialog box. Alternatively, click Cancel to discard the changes and close the dialog box. Or, click Apply to save your changes and stay in the dialog box.

The following list offers a quick summary of each tab:

✦ **General:** Enables you to choose your home page, to delete or change settings for temporary Internet files the browser stores in a special cache so that you can view them more quickly, and to adjust your History folder settings. You also can choose colors, fonts, languages, and other formatting (accessibility) options.

✦ **Security:** Enables you to set the security level for various zones of Web content you visit on the Internet.

✦ **Privacy:** Enables you to set the privacy level you prefer while browsing the Web.

✦ **Content:** Enables you to control the Internet content that can be viewed on your computer; to use security certificates to identify sites, publishers, and yourself; and to adjust personal information and the Microsoft Wallet used for Internet shopping.

✦ **Connections:** Enables you to change your Internet connection settings using an automated wizard or manual options to specify a corporate proxy server, or to use automatic configuration settings stored on a network server.

✦ **Programs:** Enables you to specify the default programs to use for mail, news, and Internet phone calls, as well as your calendar and contact list. You also can have Internet Explorer check to see whether it is the default browser.

✦ **Advanced:** Enables you to customize advanced options for accessibility, browsing, multimedia, security, Java VM, printing, searching, toolbars, and HTTP 1.1.

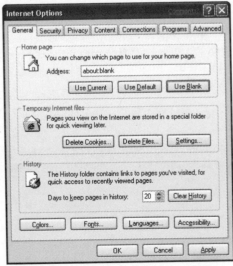

Figure 6-17: Use the General tab of the Internet Options dialog box to customize your Internet settings.

Getting Support Online

When you're feeling helpless and in need of a quick answer to a specific question, the built-in Help system may be able to provide what you need. After you have an Internet connection and know the basics of browsing the Web, however, the help that's available to you expands greatly. A good place to start your search for information is Microsoft's Online Support site, which you can get to by choosing Help ⇨ Online Support from the Internet Explorer menu bar. You'll be taken to Microsoft's support area, which will look something like Figure 6-18. (Because this is something that is on the Internet, however, there's no telling exactly how it will look when you visit.)

The Support site consists of several key areas you can familiarize yourself with by browsing around, clicking hyperlinks, choosing items from drop-down lists, typing text into search boxes, and clicking buttons as needed. But here's a quick summary of what is likely to be available:

✦ **FAQs by product:** (a. k. a. Frequently Asked Questions and Tasks) Provides quick answers to the most common questions on Windows, the Internet, e-mail, Microsoft Office, Games, and more.

✦ **Newsgroups:** The best way to get specific answers to specific questions from real live human beings.

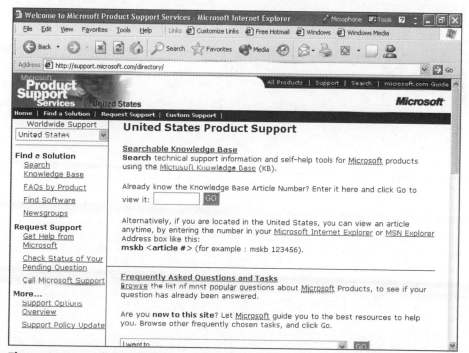

Figure 6-18: You'll find an array of choices for technical support at Microsoft's Support page.

✦ **Get Help from Microsoft:** Not always free, but does enable you to get answers to specific questions from experts.

✦ **Find Software:** Search for updates to your existing programs.

✦ **Search Knowledge Base:** Enables you to search an enormous database of information about Microsoft products, including very advanced technical information.

✦ **Support Options Overview:** As the name implies, a summary of still more support options offered by Microsoft.

Disconnecting from the Web

Even if you pay next to nothing for your Internet connection, disconnecting from your dial-up line when you're not actively surfing the Internet is a good idea. This way, you don't tie up your own line or the one owned by your ISP. Disconnecting is easy to do and, because your browser usually reconnects whenever it needs to, you have nothing to lose by disconnecting.

Here are some ways to disconnect your dial-up connection:

✦ Choose Disconnect Now if a Disconnect dialog box asks whether you want to close the connection to your ISP. This dialog box usually pops up when you close Internet Explorer and other programs that connect to the Internet automatically.

✦ Double-click the little connection icon in the lower-right corner of the taskbar and click the Disconnect button in the dialog box that appears. (The connection icon shows two computers tied together.)

✦ Right-click the little connection icon in the lower-right corner of the taskbar and choose Disconnect from the pop-up menu.

Summary

This chapter has been something of a whirlwind tour of the World Wide Web and the Internet Explorer browser that comes with Windows XP. The techniques presented here represent the most important everyday skills you need to use the Web successfully. Here's a quick recap of the important points covered in this chapter:

✦ To browse the World Wide Web, connect to the Internet and then start your Web browser program.

✦ Every site on the World Wide Web has a unique address, or URL, often in the format www.*whatever*.com.

✦ To go to a specific Web site, type its address (URL) into the Address text box near the top of the Web browser window and then press Enter.

✦ You can browse the Web by clicking *hyperlinks* — hot spots that appear on the various pages you visit.

✦ To keep track of your favorite Web pages, add them to your Favorites list. That is, visit the Web page and then choose Favorites ⇨ Add to Favorites from the menu bar.

✦ To revisit a favorite page at any time, open the Favorites menu and click the name of your favorite page.

✦ To search for specific information on the Web, use a search engine. Click the Search button on the Standard Buttons toolbar to begin your search.

✦ To download a file means to copy it from the Internet to your own PC.

✦ To download a file from the Web, click the download link and choose Save this file to disk in the dialog box. Or, right-click the link or item you want to download and choose the Save As option from the pop-up menu.

✦ ✦ ✦

Maximum Web

Windows XP and the Microsoft Internet Explorer Version 6.0 that comes with it provide some features designed to make your use of the Internet, and the time you spend browsing the Web, more productive and entertaining. In this chapter, you'll learn about those features, including offline browsing, Active Desktop, and automatic updates. First we'll take a look behind the scenes at how the Web *really* works, so you can better understand *why* some of the techniques described in this chapter work.

How the Web Really Works

When you're browsing the Web, you may get the impression it's like TV. For instance, when you go to a URL such as www.microsoft.com, you see what's on the Web site — sort of like your Web browser is a telescope peering at pages far away, although, technically, that's not exactly how it works.

Actually, when you browse to a URL, your screen doesn't just show the contents of that distant computer. Instead, your Web browser just tells that distant computer to send files from its hard disk to your computer's hard disk. After the files have been downloaded to your PC, your Web browser shows them to you. So the browser is actually showing you files on your screen that are on your *own* PC, not files on the remote (distant) computer!

If you have standard modem/dial-up access to the Internet, you may have noticed the first time you visit a page it takes quite a while for the page to show on your screen. That delay is the amount of time it takes to copy files from the remote computer's hard disk to your own hard disk. But subsequent visits using the Back button, History list, or whatever, are much faster. That's because whenever you point your Web browser to a URL, the first thing Internet Explorer does is check to see whether the materials of this URL have already been downloaded to your PC. If they have, your Web browser reads the material from your local hard disks, which is much, much faster than downloading from the Web site.

This approach is good because it makes your Web browsing go much faster, and it helps keep traffic on the Internet to a minimum. It also means, however, that when you view a Web page, you may be viewing it as it looked a while ago and not as it really looks right now. Suppose, for example, that I point my Web browser to www.coolnerds.com. Then I cruise around some other sites for 15 minutes or so, and then I return to the coolnerds Web site. The page I'm viewing at that moment is the one I downloaded 15 minutes ago. If the author of the coolnerds page made any changes in the past 15 minutes, I wouldn't see those changes.

Fortunately, this is not a big issue because few Web sites update their content that frequently. Furthermore, you can always force your Web browser to download the latest version of a page by clicking the Refresh button in the Web browser's toolbar. Finally, with *offline browsing*, discussed a little later in this chapter, you can control exactly when all the time-consuming downloads take place.

Managing Temporary Internet Files

Files downloaded from Web sites are stored on your hard drive in your Internet *cache* (pronounced like *cash*). You're probably unaware of it because it's hidden behind the scenes. However, you can control both the size of the cache and how often pages are updated. To do so, follow these steps:

1. Start Microsoft Internet Explorer.

2. Choose Tools ⇨ Internet Options to open the Internet Options page. In the General tab, you'll see some options under Temporary Internet Files, as shown in Figure 7-1.

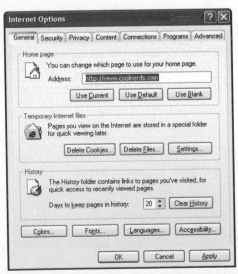

Figure 7-1: The General tab of the Internet Options dialog box

3. Click the Settings button in the Temporary Internet Files pane to get to the dialog box shown in Figure 7-2.

Figure 7-2: The Settings dialog box for Temporary Internet Files

The Settings dialog box provides several options for controlling how these temporary Internet files are handled. You can choose how often the temporary files are updated. For a detailed explanation of an option, click the Help (question mark) button that's just to the left of the Close button. Then click the option you want more information about. Here's a quick summary:

✦ **Every visit to the page:** Ensures every visit to a Web site is fresh, but can make browsing very slow indeed.

✦ **Every time you start Internet Explorer:** Faster than the preceding option, this option checks only for updates if you've closed Internet Explorer since your last visit. Definitely speeds up browsing through pages you've visited in your current Internet Explorer session.

✦ **Automatically:** Windows handles updates and downloading for you, to maximize your productivity while browsing the Web.

✦ **Never:** Always takes material from the Internet cache (if possible). The only way to ensure you're getting fresh material is to click the Refresh button when you get to a page.

You can use the slider bar to decide how much disk space you want to sacrifice to the Internet cache. The larger the cache, the more pages can be stored and the faster your browsing goes. A small cache saves disk space but doesn't allow for many temporary Internet files to be stored locally. This, in turn, may slow down your browsing because only enough room exists to store information from, say, the last two or three sites you visited.

Covering Your Tracks

The fact that Internet Explorer stores temporary Internet files on your hard disk means that anyone who can access the folder can browse around and see where you've been on the Internet. If you're concerned about privacy, you may want to delete those files. To do so, click the Delete Files button under Temporary Internet Files in the Internet Options dialog box. For reasons described a little later, I don't recommend deleting cookies! However, you may want to delete *some* cookies, as discussed under "About Cookies," in this chapter.

Be aware that the History bar also keeps track of where you've been. You can clear out your History bar by clicking the Clear History button in the Internet Options dialog box. Finally, be aware that some sites will automatically add themselves to your list of favorites. To get rid of any of those, choose Favorites from Internet Explorer's menu bar. Right-click any item on the menu that you want to get rid of, and choose Delete.

The default folder used for the Internet cache is `C:\Documents and Settings\your user name\Temporary Internet Files` (where *your user name* is the user name you log on with). If, for whatever reason, you want to move that, click the Move folder button and browse to a new location. This might be useful if you have a second hard disk drive on which you want to place your temporary files (thereby freeing up the disk space the folder takes up on your C: drive).

About cookies

Cookies are tiny text files that a Web site can store on your computer. That information is then used on your next visit to the site to identify you. If you regularly shop at a site, for example, that site might put your account number into a cookie on your hard disk. When you return in the future, it pulls your account number out of the cookie and "knows" who you are. So when you make a purchase, you don't need to go through the whole process of entering your billing address, shipping address, and so forth. Sites that enable you to create your own home page within the site also use cookies to identify you on return visits.

Because the cookie can contain only brief, simple text, you needn't worry about people sneaking any viruses or other harmful programs onto your computer through cookies. So I do not recommend deleting cookies through the Internet Options dialog box.

On the other hand, some sites do use cookies in less-than-scrupulous ways. For example, they might keep track of what sites you've visited and how often, and then sell your e-mail address to junk e-mailers.

If you want to check for, and get rid of, any of those cookies, I *don't* recommend deleting all your cookies, because you'll lose the convenient ones as well. Instead, click the Settings button in the Internet Options dialog box to get to the Settings dialog box. Then click View Files. The contents of your Temporary Internet Cache display in Windows Explorer.

You can easily identify cookies, because the file name will start with "Cookie:" If you sort the files into alphabetic order by clicking the Name column, all the cookie files will be clumped together under the letter *C* in the list, as shown in Figure 7-3. You can then get some idea of who placed the cooking on your system, based on the cookie's file name.

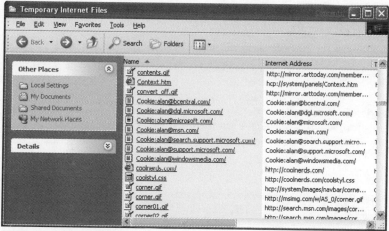

Figure 7-3: Windows Explorer displaying the contents of my Temporary Internet Files folder

For example, the cookie `alan@dgl.microsoft.com` is clearly from Microsoft, and they're not about to go using the information in unsavory ways (partly because it would be embarrassing to get caught; partly because they're not that desperate for income!). If you see a cookie that looks suspicious, such as those that belong to a Web site you don't recognize, you can delete it by right-clicking its icon and choosing Delete. After you have finished, just close the Explorer window by clicking its Close (X) button.

Cookies and privacy

Depending on your Internet Security settings, many Web sites may automatically be prevented from adding cookies to your computer. If you peek down at Internet Explorer's status bar while you're browsing the Web, you might see a tiny icon with an International "No" symbol on it. If you double-click that tiny icon, a Privacy Report dialog box opens. A list of cookies appears in the dialog box. Any cookies that Internet Explorer rejected will be marked as `Blocked`. If you click on the `Learn more about privacy` link within that dialog box, you can learn more about how and why Internet Explorer blocks certain cookies, and how to control which sites can, and cannot, add cookies to your computer.

Cross-Reference   See "Beefing Up Internet Security" in Chapter 29 for more information on protecting your computer from potentially hazardous files on the Web.

As I write this chapter, the whole issue of privacy on the Internet is still in its infancy. There are bound to be many changes to how privacy is enforced over the coming months and years. The Federal Trade Commission (www.ftc.gov) maintains information on privacy initiatives and includes an option for filing complaints online. To keep abreast of Microsoft's role in privacy issues, go to http://search.microsoft.com and search for the phrase "Internet privacy."

About downloaded objects

The View Objects button in the Settings dialog box shown back in Figure 7-2 enables you to view, and optionally delete, any downloaded objects. An object is generally some kind of "player" or other plug-in that provides access to special features, such as 3D animations offered by some Web sites. As a rule, you probably don't want to delete those either, because you'll just have to redownload them if you ever need them again. If you ever want to just take a peek to see what's there, however, click the View Objects button. Explorer displays the contents of your Downloaded Program Files folder, where those items are stored.

A Simple Way to Avoid the Wait

Here's a simple way to avoid waiting some of the time involved in downloading Web pages. It works during normal, everyday browsing and doesn't involve offline browsing at all. Here's how it works. Suppose you come to a Web page that has several interesting looking links. Before you start reading the current page, you can right-click any link that looks interesting and choose Open in New Window. The new page will start to appear in a separate browser window. You can minimize that window by clicking its Minimize button to get it out of the way during the download. You can do that for as many links as you want. Then just continue reading the page that's still open on your desktop. Or, do any other work that needs to be done on your computer.

It still may take a while for the download to complete. The more links you open in new windows, the longer it takes to download all the pages. After you have finished viewing the current page, click any Internet Explorer icon in the taskbar to open the minimized page. If the download was completed while the window was minimized, you won't have to wait to view its full content.

You will end up with several copies of Internet Explorer open, each in its own window. You can close any window by clicking its Close button, as usual. Alternatively, right-click the window's taskbar button and choose Close. The taskbar button for the page you're viewing at the moment will have the "pushed-in" appearance on the taskbar. If you open more windows than there is room for on the taskbar, the buttons are joined into a single Inter Explorer button. Click that button to display a menu of all open pages. Click any menu option to view that open page.

Avoiding the Wait with Offline Browsing

Offline browsing offers a way to control when time-consuming downloads take place so that you can make the time you spend on the Web more productive. Essentially, offline browsing enables you to update your favorite Web content during off-hours (such as when you're asleep) so that when you do come back to review your favorite Web pages, they will have already been downloaded to your computer and will appear instantly as you go through their links. In fact, because you don't even need to be online to view the pages, you could review them on a laptop on your way to work or whatever (assuming you're not driving a car at the time!).

Pages that can be downloaded during off-hours are called *offline favorites* in Internet Explorer jargon. Creating an offline favorite is simple and works with any Web site. While you're in Internet Explorer and viewing a page that you want to add to your offline favorites, just follow these steps:

1. Choose Favorites ➪ Add to Favorites from the Internet Explorer menu bar. The dialog box shown in Figure 7-4 opens.

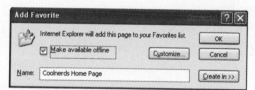

Figure 7-4: The Add Favorite dialog box

2. Choose Make Available Offline. (Optionally, you can click the Customize button to get to the Offline Favorite Wizard, discussed under the section with that title later in this chapter.)

3. Click the OK button.

If you have already built up a list of favorite Web sites, and want to convert some of those to offline favorites, follow these steps:

1. In Internet Explorer, click the Favorites button in the toolbar, or choose View ➪ Explorer Bar ➪ Favorites, to open your list of favorites.

2. Right-click any Web item that you want to convert to an offline favorite and choose Make Available Offline.

   The Offline Favorite Wizard, discussed next, will start automatically.

The Offline Favorite Wizard

The first page of the Offline Favorite Wizard (after the optional Introductory page), shown in Figure 7-5, enables you to choose how much content you want downloaded while you're away. If you choose Yes, you can choose how many links "deep" you want the download to go. If you set that value to 1, for instance, the page that the favorite refers to and all the pages that are accessible via hyperlinks from that page will be downloaded. If you set that value to 2, pages that are available from hyperlinks on the first level of pages will also be downloaded, and so forth. Click the Next button after you have made your selection.

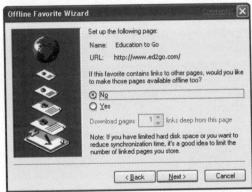

Figure 7-5: First page of the Offline Favorite Wizard

The second page of the wizard enables you to choose between manual updating of all offline pages, and downloading while you're away. Choose the second option, I would like to create a new schedule to schedule the downloads for off-hours. Click the Next button to display the third page of the wizard, shown in Figure 7-6. Here you can determine how often you want pages downloaded. The default setting, 1, downloads pages daily.

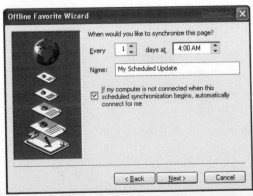

Figure 7-6: Third page of the Offline Favorite Wizard

You also can select a time for the download to occur. For example, I set mine to 4 a.m. in this example, because I'm (hopefully) not in the office at that time. You also can name the schedule and opt to have your computer connect to the Internet if it isn't already connected. (This is required if you have a dial-up connection as opposed to a full-time connection such as cable or DSL.) Click the Next button to reveal the page shown in Figure 7-7.

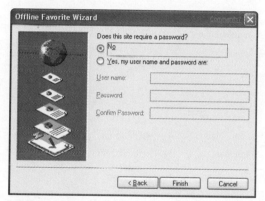

Figure 7-7: Fourth page of the Offline Favorite Wizard

In most cases, you can choose No, because few Web sites require a user name and password to log on. In the event that the favorite you're working with now does require you to log on, choose the Yes option and enter whatever user name and password you normally enter to gain access to the site. Click the Finish button, and you're done.

Allowing for the automatic download

Keep in mind one important point regarding these automatic downloads. Your computer needs to be "on" when the scheduled time arrives. Likewise, if you access the Internet through an external modem, the modem needs to be turned on as well. You can turn off the monitor, however, because it is not needed for automatic downloads.

Tip Some network cards support a Wake On LAN capability, which automatically wakes up a hibernating computer when the request to access the Internet arises. See your computer documentation to see whether it has this capability.

Browsing offline

Whenever you want to view the downloaded pages on your PC, open Internet Explorer in the usual manner. Then choose File ➪ Work Offline from the menu bar. Doing so prevents Internet Explorer from attempting to download the offline favorite from the Internet. Then open your Favorites bar and click any favorite that you've designated as an offline favorite. Internet Explorer shows you the copy of the page that has already been downloaded, so there's no need to wait.

While working offline, you won't have access to pages that require you to be online. If you click a link that requires that you to be connected to the Internet, the dialog box shown in Figure 7-8 appears. You can either choose Stay Offline to continue browsing your offline favorites or you can click the Connect button to go online and browse the page normally.

Figure 7-8: This dialog box appears when you attempt to access a Web page that hasn't been downloaded as an offline favorite.

Updating pages manually

If you ever want to update all your offline favorites on the spur of the moment, get online and choose Tools ➪ Synchronize from the Internet Explorer menu bar. Then click Offline Web Pages at the top of the list of pages and click the Synchronize button. You must wait for the downloads, of course. After the download has completed, the pages in your Internet cache will indeed be in sync with the latest pages on those favorite Web sites.

Managing download schedules

You can change how often or at what time Windows downloads your offline favorites. In Internet Explorer, choose Tools ➪ Synchronize. Then click Offline Web Pages and click the Setup button. The Synchronization Settings dialog box shown in Figure 7-9 opens. The three tabs across the top of the dialog box provide many different ways to control how and when offline favorites are synchronized, as follows:

   ✦ **Logon/LogOff:** Enables you to synchronize selected items automatically when you log on or log off of the computer

   ✦ **On Idle:** Enables you to synchronize selected items while the computer is idle but still connected to the Internet

   ✦ **Scheduled:** Enables you to create your own schedules for synchronizing offline favorites

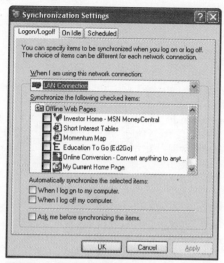

Figure 7-9: The Synchronization Settings
dialog box for offline favorites

On the Scheduled tab, you can click the Add button to create a schedule based on
time. For example, you could create a schedule that updates offline favorites every
day at 6 a.m. Note that regardless of the type of schedule you create, you will
always see a list of offline favorites with check boxes next to them. Only pages that
you select (by filling their check boxes) will be updated according to the schedule
you create.

Removing offline favorites

To convert an offline favorite to a regular favorite, open the Favorites bar again in
Internet Explorer. Right-click any listed page in the bar and choose Make Available
Offline again to clear the check mark next to that menu option. You are asked for
confirmation. Just click the Yes button.

The Little Bar that Appears with Internet Explorer

When Internet Explorer starts, or when you click in a field on a form, the *Language
bar* shown in Figure 7-10 pops up on-screen. That bar is telling you that the cursor
is positioned at a place where you can use voice or handwriting, as opposed to the
keyboard, for input. However, it works only if you set up speech recognition or
handwriting recognition, as discussed in Chapter 15.

`Microphone  Tools  Handwriting  Drawing Pad`

Figure 7-10: The Language bar above the Internet Explorer title bar

The Language bar disappears as suddenly as it appeared whenever the cursor is positioned someplace where speech and handwriting are not supported. When you click the Internet Explorer Address bar, for example, the Language bar goes into hiding (because you cannot use voice or handwriting to type a URL into version 6.0 of Internet Explorer). However, that might change with future versions. Time will tell.

Using the Active Desktop

Active Desktop is a feature of Windows that enables you to place "live" objects on your screen that can constantly receive data from the Internet. For example, you could put a stock ticker on your Windows desktop, which in turn would show you the current price of any stocks you're following. To add an Active Desktop item to the desktop, follow these steps:

Note   Actually, stock quotes described here are delayed 20 minutes, which I guess doesn't quite constitute a live "real-time" feed.

1. Right-click any neutral area on the desktop and choose Properties.

2. Click the Desktop tab.

3. Click the Customize Desktop button.

4. Click the Web tab to get to the options shown in Figure 7-11.

5. Click the New button.

6. To find Active Desktop items available from Microsoft, click the Visit Gallery button. Internet Explorer opens and you are taken to the Microsoft Desktop Gallery page.

7. Choose a desktop item to add by clicking the Add to Active Desktop button that appears with each example. For the current example, I am using the Microsoft Investor item.

8. Follow the onscreen instructions. (If in doubt, just choose the default answer to any questions that appear.)

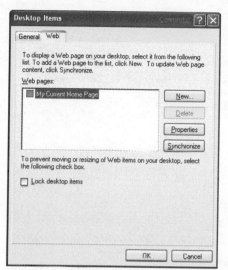

Figure 7-11: The Web tab enables you to find and add active items to your desktop.

You need to wait as the item downloads to your computer. After the download has finished, close Internet Explorer to see your desktop item. Although there may be some differences among desktop items, most items can be positioned on the desktop by pointing to them to display a small title bar. You can then drag that title bar to place the item anywhere on your desktop.

You also can customize most desktop items to suit your own needs. To customize the Microsoft Investment stock ticker, for example, click the Custom option on the ticker. A dialog box appears. Make your selections from the options provided. In Figure 7-12, for example, I've selected a list of stocks to track in Microsoft Investor.

Different desktop items offer different options. As a general rule, however, most enable you to decide how often the information in the ticker is updated. If you find that a desktop item is eating up too much bandwidth (that is, slowing down your other Internet access), you can close it by pointing to it and then clicking its Close button. When you want to bring the item back to the desktop, return to the Web tab shown back in Figure 7-11. Then choose the item by clicking its check box.

Tip

> If you prefer not to have the ticker right on your desktop, you can add it to the Web page at `http://moneycentral.msn.com/investor` instead.

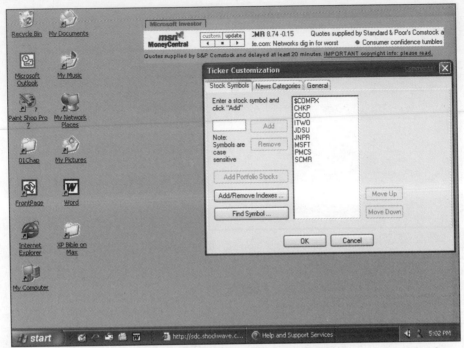

Figure 7-12: Microsoft Investor stock ticker, and the dialog box for customizing it

Automatic Updates

The Windows Update feature provides quick access to changes, enhancements, and bug fixes in Windows XP, without your making an effort to find them. This feature, of course, requires a connection to the Internet, because that's where the updates are stored.

You may already be aware of this feature from the notifications that pop up from the Automatic Updates icon in the Notifications area of the taskbar, like the example shown in Figure 7-13.

Figure 7-13: A sample Automatic Updates notification

When you see such a message, you just need to click it. A wizard displays to help you decide what to do. For example, the first time you click the option, you might come to a wizard that enables you to choose how updates are handled. The second page of that wizard, shown in Figure 7-14, enables you to choose how you want automatic updates to be handled.

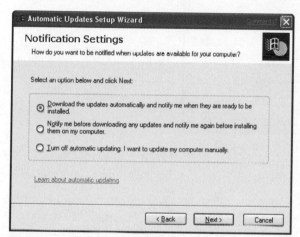

Figure 7-14: This wizard enables you to decide how automatic updates are handled.

Although the explanations are pretty self-explanatory, here's what the options mean:

✦ **Download the updates automatically:** This first option downloads updates as they become available to you. You might not even be aware of the download. However, the download won't be installed automatically. Instead, you see a notification message that you can click to install the downloaded files.

✦ **Notify me before downloading:** Updates are not downloaded to your computer behind the scenes. Instead, you are notified when a download is ready. You can then choose when you want to start the download.

✦ **Turn off automatic updating:** Choosing this option disables automatic updating altogether. But you can update manually at any time using Windows Update, described in Chapter 18.

If you choose the first option (which is probably the most convenient), you receive notification after any updates have been downloaded to your computer and are ready to be installed. Click the notification to open a simple wizard, like the example shown in Figure 7-15. As instructed by the wizard, if you plan on installing the update now, you would do well to close all open programs and save any work in progress first. That's because the update might require restarting your computer. If you restart while you have unsaved documents open on the desktop, you'll lose all unsaved work.

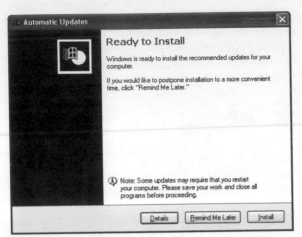

Figure 7-15: An update has been downloaded and is ready to be installed.

Chances are, you won't even notice any difference in Windows when the update is complete. Many of the updates are just minor bug fixes, or "patches" to security holes that have been uncovered since the original release of Windows XP.

Changing your automatic update settings

If you change your mind about how you want automatic updates to be handled, follow these steps to change your settings:

1. Click the Start button and select Control Panel.

Note If you can't find Control Panel on your Start menu, right-click the Start button and choose Properties. Click the Customize button next to the Start Menu option. Then on the Advanced tab, choose Display as Link under Control Panel in the Start Menu Items list.

2. If you get to the Categories view, choose Switch to Classic View.

3. Open the System icon and click the Automatic Updates tab to get to the options shown in Figure 7-16.

4. Make your selection from the Notification Settings and then click the OK button.

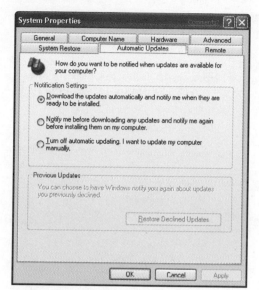

Figure 7-16: The Automatic Updates tab of
System Properties

Finding declined updates

If you ever decline an update, and then want to get back to it in the future, repeat
Steps 1 and 2 in the preceding section to get to the Automatic Updates tab in
System Properties. Click the Restore Declined Updates button. The items will be
available when you click the Automatic Updates icon in the Notifications area.

Summary

In this chapter, you have learned how the Internet works behind the scenes and
some good tricks for getting the best out of your Internet time with Windows XP
and Internet Explorer 6.0. Surprisingly, there's quite a bit more to Internet Explorer
that we haven't been able to address in these last two chapters. After all, this is a
book about Windows, not Internet Explorer! You can learn more about other features within Internet Explorer from its Help, from the Internet Explorer Web site, or
from any book dedicated to that program. In this chapter, you learned the following:

✦ Any Web content you view is actually on your computer by the time you see
it, stored inside a folder known as the Internet cache.

✦ Offline browsing enables you to predownload Web pages at off-hours so that
when you're ready to view them, you don't have to wait for the downloads.

✦ Active Desktop items present "live" information from the Internet while your computer is connected to the Internet.

✦ Automatic updates keep you posted when new programs for Windows XP become available. Use the Automatic Updates icon in the Control Panel to enable or disable these updates. Use Windows Setup to perform manual updates.

✦   ✦   ✦

Internet E-Mail

Perhaps the busiest feature of the Internet is electronic mail, e-mail for short. And no wonder: Unlike regular snail mail, which takes days to reach its destination, e-mail usually takes only a few seconds, no matter how far the message has to travel. And unlike phone calls, which require that you stop what you're doing to talk and aren't easily recorded, you can attend to your e-mail messages when convenient. And you can also file them away for future reference, so you have a record of your communications.

In the e-mail world, every person has a unique address. You've probably seen dozens of Internet e-mail addresses, which all tend to look something like `someone@someplace.com`. For example, my e-mail address is `alan@coolnerds.com`. In this chapter, you learn to send and receive Internet e-mail messages using Microsoft Outlook Express. This program is built into Windows XP and the Internet Explorer program.

About E-Mail

Before we begin this foray into e-mail, you need to understand a couple of things. For one, the Outlook Express program described in this chapter is not required for e-mail services. For example, if you have an America Online account, you can handle your e-mail from the screen that opens as soon as you log in. If you have a Web mail type service (also called HTTP mail), you can do your e-mail through Internet Explorer. Exactly how you send and receive e-mail depends on your service, and only your e-mail service provider can give you the information you need. You *can* create an Outlook Express e-mail account for HTTP mail, but you do not have to.

Outlook Express is really designed for use with traditional POP3 (Post Office Protocol, Version 3) e-mail accounts, although it can also be used with IMAP (Internet Access Message Protocol), and HTTP (Hypertext Transfer Protocol) accounts. To set up an e-mail account, you need to know some basic information about your account, such as your e-mail address, the type of account, the name of the server (or servers), and so forth. Only your e-mail service provider, or company network administrator, can provide that information. For convenience, you may want to jot down any information that you have about your account in the right column of Table 8-1.

Tip   If you used a program provided by your ISP to set up your Internet account, you e-mail account may already be working. If this is the case, you only need to know your own e-mail address to get started with e-mail.

Table 8-1 **Information You Need from Your ISP to Send and Receive E-mail**	
Information to Get	*Write It in This Column*
Outgoing (SMTP) mail server address	
Incoming mail server type (POP3 or IMAP)	
Incoming mail server address	
Your e-mail address	
Your e-mail account name	
Your e-mail password	

If you don't have an e-mail address and would like to obtain one, you can set up a Microsoft Hotmail account for free. Here's how:

1. Choose Start ⇨ Control Panel.

2. Open the User Accounts icon and click on your account name or picture.

3. Choose "Set up my account to use a .NET Passport" and follow the instructions presented by the Wizard to create a new Hotmail account. If you do set up a Hotmail account, you'll have two options for managing your e-mail:

   • **Open Internet Explorer and go to www.msn.com.** Under Message Center at the right side of the screen, click on the Envelope icon under E-mail.

   • **Optionally, you can use Outlook Express to create a new mail account.** When you get to the wizard page that asks for the type of account to create, as described in a moment, choose HTTP as your account type.

Should you decide to use Outlook Express to manage your hotmail e-mail, you need only know your own e-mail address. The Wizard will take care of the rest.

Starting Outlook Express

You can start Microsoft Outlook Express in any of several ways. Use whichever method is most convenient:

✦ Click the Start button and choose E-Mail (Outlook Express) if available.

✦ Open the Outlook Express icon on your desktop (if available).

✦ Click the Start button and choose All Programs ⇨ Outlook Express.

✦ If you're in Internet Explorer, click the Mail button on the Standard Buttons toolbar and then click the Read Mail option.

✦ If you're in Internet Explorer, choose Tools ⇨ Mail and News ⇨ Read Mail from the Internet Explorer menu bar.

✦ Click the Launch Outlook Express button on the Quick Launch toolbar (if it's visible on your taskbar).

The first time you start Outlook Express on a computer (assuming no e-mail account has been created yet), a wizard asks you a series of questions about your e-mail account. You should just follow the instructions presented by the wizard to create your account. When you get to the Wizard page that asks for your E-mail Server Names, shown in Figure 8-1, you need to choose your incoming mail server type and fill in the incoming and outgoing mail server names carefully. You must type in the information exactly as provided by your ISP. In the example shown in the figure, I've selected the POP3 server type and provided (hypothetical) server names in the format that most server names follow. If you choose HTTP as the incoming server type, you need only know the incoming mail server name. (Or, if you're setting up a hotmail account, you can choose Hotmail from the "My HTTP mail service provider is" option that appears on the screen.)

After filling in the blanks and clicking the Next> button, the wizard prompts you for your mail logon information, as shown in Figure 8-2. Note that this will be the user name and password for using e-mail, which won't necessarily be the same as the user name and password you use to log onto your Internet account. You must enter the information exactly as provided by your ISP. Be sure to use the exact upper/lowercase letters provided by your ISP, as these items are case-sensitive.

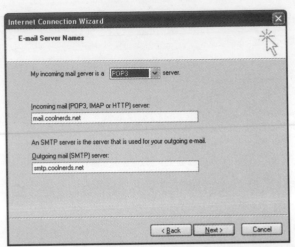

Figure 8-1: The Internet Connection Wizard page for setting up your E-mail account server type and names

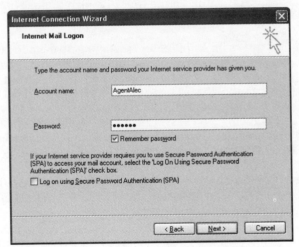

Figure 8-2: The Internet Connection Wizard page for providing your account name, password, and other options

If you choose the Remember Password option, you won't need to enter a password each time you check your e-mail. But of course, anyone with whom you share this computer will also be able to check your mail if you choose this option. Do not select the last option on the page unless your ISP specifically requires Secure Password Authentication. Click the Next button to complete the wizard. Then click the Finish button on the last wizard page.

After you complete the wizard, Outlook Express starts. Any e-mail messages that are waiting for you show up in your Inbox. You can your Inbox by clicking on the Inbox item under "Local Folders" in the Folders list at the left side of the Outlook Express window, as shown in Figure 8-3. To find out if any messages are waiting for you on your e-mail server, click the Send/Receive button in the toolbar.

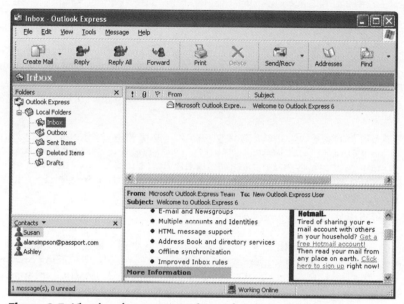

Figure 8-3: Viewing the contents of my Inbox in Outlook Express

If you don't get an error message, then you've set up your account properly and you can skip to the section titled "Composing a Message," later in this chapter. If you do get some sort of error message, you'll need to go in and make some corrections to your account, as discussed in the next section.

Tip
When it comes to hiding/displaying toolbars and Explorer bars, Outlook Express is different from most programs. See "Choosing what appears in the window," later in this chapter, for details.

Creating and Changing E-Mail Accounts

The wizard that appears the first time you start Outlook Express isn't the only way to create an e-mail account. If you have any problems with your account, or want to set up multiple accounts, you can do so through the Internet Accounts dialog box. To get there, follow these steps:

1. Choose Tools ➪ Accounts from the Outlook Express menu bar.

2. Click on the Mail tab.

3. To change an existing account, click on the account name and then click the Properties button.

Tip

To create a new e-mail account, click the Add button and choose Mail. The Wizard will appear to help you set up your new account.

4. In the account Properties dialog box that appears, check the following settings:

   • On the General tab, make sure the "Include this account when receiving mail or synchronizing" option is selected. Also, make sure you've typed your own e-mail address correctly.

   • On the Servers tab, make sure your incoming and outgoing mail server names and account name are correct. Retype your password if you think you might have typed it incorrectly the first time. Verify that you've selected authentication options as per your Internet Service Provider (or company network administrator.)

5. Click the OK button after you finish.

Tip

Anytime you need help with one of the options in an Outlook Express dialog box, click the question mark (?) button at the upper-right corner of the dialog box and then click the field or option that's puzzling you. A pop-up description appears near the mouse pointer. Press the Esc key to hide the description again.

Try clicking the Send/Recv button again to see if your account is working properly. If problems persist, you may need to contact your Internet Service Provider or company's network administrator for additional support.

Composing a Message

After you start Outlook Express, typing an e-mail message is easy. Try any of these three ways to begin:

   ✦ Click the Create Mail button on the Outlook Express toolbar.

   ✦ Choose Message ➪ New ➪ Mail Message from the Outlook Express menu bar.

   ✦ Press Ctrl+N when a mail folder is open.

Regardless of how you start, the New Message window for composing your e-mail message will appear onscreen, looking something like Figure 8-4. To compose your message, first fill in the address portion of the window as explained in the following steps.

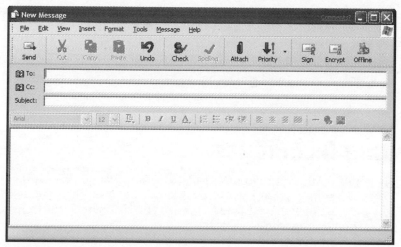

Figure 8-4: The New Message window for composing a new e-mail message

1. In the To: box, type the complete mailing address of each recipient. For example, typing **alan@coolnerds.com** addresses the message to me. To send the message to multiple recipients, type in each e-mail address separated by a semicolon (;).

Tip

Instead of typing in an e-mail address, you can choose one from your Address Book by clicking the little Rolodex card icon. You'll find more about this topic under "Using the Address Book" later in this chapter. (By the way, sending messages to yourself when you're trying new features in your e-mail program is a good idea.)

2. In the Cc: box, type the e-mail address of anyone to whom you want to send a carbon copy of this message. Again, you can type multiple recipients as long as you place a semicolon between each address.

3. In the Bcc: box, type the e-mail addresses of anyone who is to receive blind carbon copies. Separate multiple addresses by a semicolon.

Tip

If the Bcc: box is not visible, you can display it by selecting View ⇨ All Headers. A carbon copy of an e-mail address shows the recipient who also received a copy of the message. A blind carbon copy does not display the names of its recipients, so the other recipients don't know who else received this message.

4. In the Subject: box, type a brief subject description. This part of the message appears in the recipient's Inbox and is visible prior to opening the message.

5. If you want to set the priority or importance of the message, choose Message ⇨ Set Priority from the New Message toolbar and then choose High, Normal, or Low. Or, click the Priority icon just above the address area and

choose the priority you want. If you choose high or low priority, a message line appears above the address area to reflect the priority you chose. The default priority is Normal.

6. Type your message in the larger editing window below the address portion. Next we'll look at some tools and techniques you can use to compose and edit your message.

Basic Editing Techniques

If you know how to use Microsoft Word, WordPerfect, WordPad, or some other Windows word processing program, you already know the basic skills you need to type and edit a message in Outlook Express. In case you're unfamiliar with word processing, you should know a few key facts.

First, the text will automatically wrap to the next line when the insertion point (or cursor) reaches the right edge of the editing window. So when you type a paragraph, press Enter only to end the paragraph or to end a short line. When you press Enter, the insertion point will move to the next line.

Tip   Outlook Express can create messages in either HTML format (the default "looks like a Web page" format) or plain text format. See "Formatting your messages," later in this chapter, for more information.

As you type, you can use the buttons in the Formatting toolbar (shown just above the message) to format your text, insert a horizontal line, or add a picture to your e-mail. More on these topics under "Formatting your messages" a little later in this chapter.

If you need to change the text in your message, use either of the following techniques:

✦ Position the insertion point where you want to make the change (for example, click your mouse or press the arrow keys on your keyboard). Then type new text, press Backspace or Delete to delete text, or press Enter to break the paragraph or line in two.

✦ Select a chunk of text (for example, drag the mouse pointer through it). Then, delete the chunk by pressing Backspace or Delete, or format it by choosing buttons on the Formatting toolbar. (If you select the wrong chunk of text, click the mouse outside the selection or press an arrow key to deselect it.)

Tip   To select all the text in the message, choose Edit ⇨ Select All from the New Message window menu bar or press Ctrl+A.

You can use standard Windows Clipboard techniques or drag-and-drop to copy or move text and objects in the message. To begin, select the chunk of text or click an object you want to move or copy. Then do any of the following:

✦ To copy the selection using the Windows Clipboard, choose Edit ⇨ Copy (or press Ctrl+C, or click the Copy button on the toolbar). Position the insertion point where the copied item should appear and choose Edit ⇨ Paste (or press Ctrl+V, or click the Paste button on the toolbar).

✦ To move the selection using the Windows Clipboard, choose Edit ⇨ Cut (or press Ctrl+X, or click the Cut button on the toolbar). Position the insertion point where the moved item should appear and choose Edit ⇨ Paste (or press Ctrl+V, or click the Paste button on the toolbar).

✦ To copy the selection with drag-and-drop, hold down the Ctrl key while dragging your selection to a new place in the message.

✦ To move the selection with drag-and-drop, drag your selection to a new place in the message without pressing any keys.

Suffice it to say, nothing you type in your message is final until you actually send the message. As you learn in a moment, there's quite a bit more that you can do to "fancy up" your message. But, assuming your typed your message, you're probably ready to send it, as discussed next.

Sending an E-Mail Message

Figure 8-5 shows an example of a completed e-mail message. Note that the title of the New Message window changes to reflect whatever you typed into the Subject line of your message. I still refer to it as the New Message window here though, so don't let that confuse you. Anyway, sending the completed message is easy. Do whichever of the following in most convenient at the moment:

✦ Click the Send button in the New Message window toolbar.

✦ Press Alt+S

✦ Choose File ⇨ Send Message from the New Message window menu bar.

The New Message window will close. If you see a message like the example in Figure 8-6, it just means that the message is being placed in your Outlook Express Outbox rather than being send immediately. Just click the OK button. Clicking the Send/Recv button in Outlook Express's toolbar will send any messages that are currently stored in your Outbox.

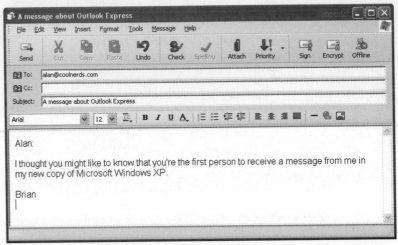

Figure 8-5: A completed e-mail message in the New Message window

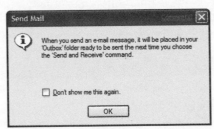

Figure 8-6: This reminder appears if e-mail sent e-mail messages are stored in your Outbox prior to actually being sent.

You can easily choose whether you want messages to be sent immediately when you click the Send button or to be placed in your Outbox so you can send groups of messages at a time. Choose Tools ➪ Options from Outlook Express's menu bar and then click the Send tab. To send messages immediately, choose "Send messages immediately." To place sent messages in your Outbox for sending later, clear that check box.

Attaching Files to E-Mail Messages

While you're composing an e-mail message in the New Message window, you can attach one or more files to the message. The attachment won't appear in the body of the message. Rather, the recipient will just see a little paper clip icon in their

Inbox indicating that a file is attached to the message. But to play it safe, you should always mention the attachment in the body of your message, just to ensure that the recipient is aware that there's a file attached to the message. The attachment can be virtually any kind of file on your PC — a word processing document, a graphic image, a program, whatever.

 Tip

If the attachment is large, you may want to compress the file(s) using the Compressed Folders feature (see Chapter 12) or a Zip program such as WinZip (available at http://www.winzip.com). Doing so shrinks the files so that they transfer more quickly and with less chance of damage during the transfer.

To attach one or more files to your e-mail message, click the Attach File toolbar button (the little paperclip) or choose Insert ⇨ File Attachment from the New Message window menu bar. When the Insert Attachment dialog box appears, browse to the file you want to attach and then click the filename and click the Attach button (or double-click the filename). You can attach as many files as you wish. Each attached file will be represented by an icon at the bottom of the address area, as in the example shown in Figure 8-7.

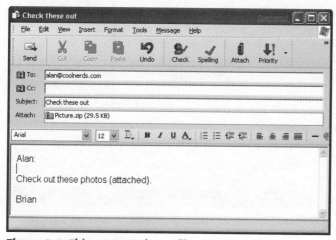

Figure 8-7: This message has a file named Picture.zip attached.

 Tip

If you change your mind about an attachment, you can click its icon and press the Delete key to eliminate it. Or, right-click the icon and choose Remove from the shortcut menu that appears.

When you finish, just click the Send button as usual to send both the message and its attachment(s).

Formatting Your Messages

You can create fancy e-mail messages by composing your messages in HTML (Hypertext Markup Language) format. With this format, your messages can resemble full-fledged Web pages complete with headings, images, fancy fonts, hyperlinks, cool background colors, and more. For example, the first sample message that you're likely to get in Outlook Express, shown in Figure 8-8, uses a bunch of HTML formatting techniques that make the message look as fancy as some Web pages.

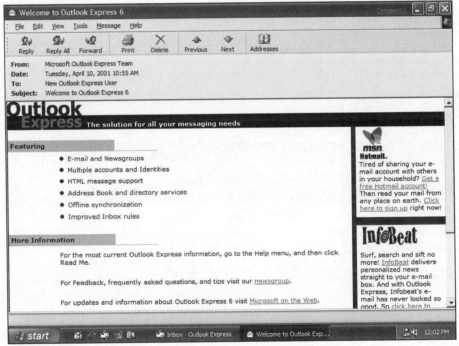

Figure 8-8: The Microsoft Outlook Express welcome message

When composing your e-mail message in the New Message window, you can choose between a Plain Text format or the fancier HTML format (also known as "Rich Text") by choosing Format from the New Message window's menu bar. You need to select the HTML option if you want to do any of the fancy formatting discussed in this section.

Caution   Not everyone is lucky enough to own an e-mail program that understands HTML. If the recipient's e-mail program can't deal with HTML formatting, your message usually appears as plain text with an HTML attachment (or sometimes as plain text with HTML statements in it). To view the formatted HTML message, the recipient can save the HTML attachment or text as an HTML file (with a .htm extension) and then open the saved file in any Web browser. For best results, use plain text format when sending messages to recipients whose e-mail programs do not handle HTML messages.

Using the Formatting toolbar

When you begin editing an HTML message, the Formatting toolbar appears just above the body of the message, as shown in Figure 8-9. You can use buttons on the toolbar to help you decorate your message in many ways. The basic steps for using the Formatting toolbar are simple:

1. Position the insertion point where you want to make a change or select a chunk of existing text to format.

> To select a chunk of text within your e-mail message, just drag the mouse pointer through the text. Optionally, you can double-click a single work to select just that word. To select an entire line or paragraph, triple-click it.

2. Click a button on the toolbar. (To determine the purpose of any Formatting toolbar button, point to it with your mouse. After a moment, a descriptive ToolTip will appear near the mouse pointer.)

3. If a drop-down menu appears below the button, click the option you want. If a dialog box opens, fill in the dialog box and choose OK.

4. If necessary, type new text. (Be careful! If you selected text in Step 1, your typing will replace the existing text.)

> If you do not see the Formatting toolbar, open the View ⇨ Toolbars menu in the New Message window and be sure the Formatting Bar option is checked. If it isn't, choose the option. If you still don't see the Formatting toolbar, choose Format ⇨ Rich Text (HTML) from the New Message window menu bar.

By the way, most of the options on the Formatting toolbar are available on the Insert and Format menus in the New Message window. You also can choose formatting options from the shortcut menu that appears when you right-click within selected text or at a particular spot in the message.

Changing the font, style, color, and size

You can use any of the first seven controls on the Formatting toolbar to change the appearance of text in the message. Here's how:

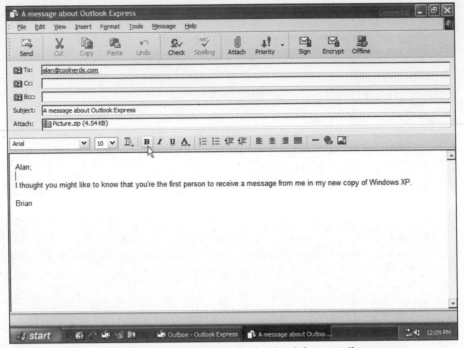

Figure 8-9: The Formatting toolbar above the body of the e-mail message

1. Position the insertion point where you want to type new text, or select a chunk of existing text.

2. Click the Font or Font Size drop-down arrow, or click the Paragraph Style, Bold, Italic, Underline, or Font Color button. If you chose Font, Font Size, Paragraph Style, or Font Color, click the option you want from the drop-down menu that appears. Repeat this step as needed.

3. Type new text (assuming you didn't select text in Step 1).

Figure 8-10 shows a sample message after I went crazy with the first seven controls on the Formatting toolbar. This figure resembles a ransom note, but it isn't.

The Bold, Italic, and Underline buttons are toggles. Click them once to turn on the effect; click them again to turn off the effect. You also can press shortcut keys to turn the effects on and off. Use Ctrl+B for bold, Ctrl+I for italic, and Ctrl+U for underline.

Instead of using shortcut keys or buttons on the Formatting toolbar, you can choose Format ➪ Font from the New Message window menu bar and then choose the font name, style, size, underlining, and color from one convenient Font dialog box (see Figure 8-11). After making your selections, click OK to save your changes.

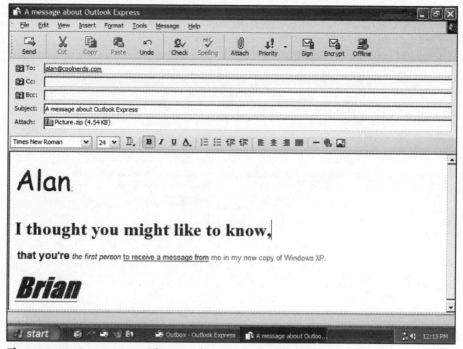

Figure 8-10: A message with several types of text formatting

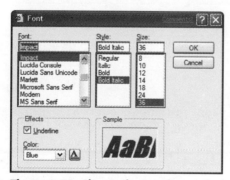

Figure 8-11: Choose font options using the Font dialog box.

Aligning text

Your text usually is left aligned, but you can center, right align, or justify text if you want (see Figure 8-12). To alter the text alignment, click in the paragraph or short line you want to change, or click where you're about to type a new paragraph or line. If you want to adjust several paragraphs or short lines at once, select them.

Now click the Align Left, Center, Align Right, or Justify button on the Formatting toolbar, or choose Format ⇨ Paragraph from the New Message window menu bar, and then choose Left, Center, Right, or Justify.

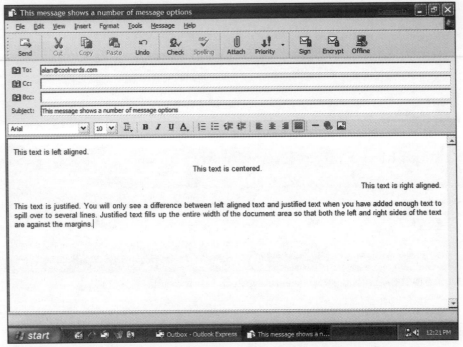

Figure 8-12: Some examples of left, center, right, and justified text alignment

Indenting and outdenting text

You can indent a paragraph by moving it in one tab stop (about five spaces) toward the right or you can outdent a paragraph by moving it out one tab stop toward the left, as shown in Figure 8-13. This is an excellent way to make certain paragraphs — such as quotations — stand out. The steps should be familiar by now:

1. Click the paragraph or short line you want to indent or outdent, or click where you're about to type a new paragraph or line. If you want to adjust several paragraphs or short lines at once, select them.

2. Click the Increase Indentation or Decrease Indentation button on the Formatting toolbar or choose Format ⇨ Increase Indent or Format ⇨ Decrease Indent from the New Message window menu bar.

That's all there is to it! As you'll see next, indenting and outdenting is also useful when you're typing lists.

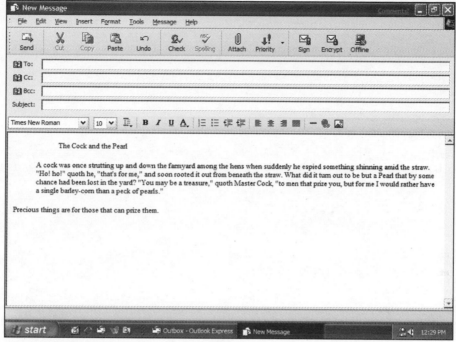

Figure 8-13: Indented and outdented text

Typing lists

I'm a great fan of bulleted and numbered lists (as you can tell from this book) because they make it easier to understand a series of choices or a logical sequence of steps. You can create lists like the ones shown in Figure 8-14 with a few keystrokes and mouse clicks. When you create a numbered list, new items are numbered automatically in their proper sequence. If you delete an item in the list, the numbering adjusts accordingly, as you would expect.

Typing a new list

Here's how to type a new list:

1. Click where you want the new list to start.

2. Do one of the following:

   • To create a numbered list, click the Formatting Numbers button on the Formatting toolbar or choose Format ➪ Style ➪ Numbered List from the New Message window menu bar. A number appears at the insertion point and the Formatting Numbers button will appear pushed in.

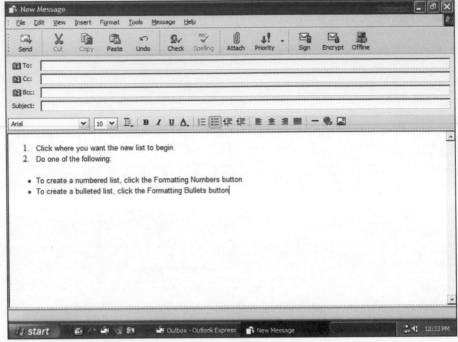

Figure 8-14: A numbered list with an indented bulleted list

- To create a bulleted list, click the Formatting Bullets button on the Formatting toolbar or choose Format ⇨ Style ⇨ Bulleted List from the New Message window menu bar. A bullet appears at the insertion point and the Formatting Bullets button will appear pushed in.

3. If you want to indent or outdent the current item, click the Increase Indentation or Decrease Indentation button on the Formatting toolbar (or choose the equivalent options on the New Message window's Format menu).

4. Type the next list item and press Enter. A new number or bullet will appear.

5. Repeat Steps 2 through 4 as needed.

When you finish typing the list, follow the steps given in the section "Removing numbers and bullets." (Alternatively, just hit the Enter key twice to turn off bullets or numbers.)

Tip The Formatting Bullets and Formatting Numbers buttons and the equivalent menu options are toggles. Choosing the button or option once turns on the numbered or bulleted list. Choosing it again turns off the list.

Creating a list from existing text

If your message already includes some paragraphs or short lines that would work better as a list, converting them is easy:

1. Select the paragraphs or lines you want to format into a list.

2. Click the Formatting Numbers or Formatting Bullets buttons and the Increase Indentation or Decrease Indentation buttons on the Formatting toolbar as needed (see Steps 2 and 3 of the procedure for typing a new list).

Creating a list within a list

You can even create a list within a list, like the bulleted list within the numbered list shown in Figure 8-14. As usual, you can make the change while you're typing a new list or by selecting text first. Follow these steps:

1. Position the insertion point where you want the indented list item to appear or select the existing paragraphs or lines you want to indent.

2. Click the Increase Indentation button on the Formatting toolbar or choose the equivalent menu options until you get the indentation level you want.

3. If you want to change the type of list, click the Formatting Numbers or Formatting Bullets button, or choose the equivalent menu options. A number or bullet appropriate to the indentation level appears.

4. If you did not select text in Step 1, type your list items, pressing Enter after each one.

Of course, you can return list items to their previous levels by outdenting. Simply repeat the previous four steps except, in Step 2, click the Decrease Indentation button on the Formatting toolbar as needed.

Removing numbers and bullets

You can remove the numbers or bullets from list items at any time. Simply select the items or position the insertion point anywhere in the item from which you want to remove the number or bullet. Then click the Formatting Numbers button (if it's a numbered item) or the Formatting Bullets button (if it's a bulleted item) on the Formatting toolbar until the number or bullet disappears. If necessary, increase or decrease the indentation level.

Tip You can remove numbers and bullets and return the text to its leftmost position by repeatedly clicking the Decrease Indentation button.

Inserting a picture

A great-looking picture of your pet, spouse, kid, or newest possession can spice up an e-mail message. You can insert many types of pictures, including scanned images and clip art, by following these steps:

1. Click in the message editing area where you want the image to appear.

2. Click the Insert Picture button on the Formatting toolbar, or choose Insert ⇨ Picture from the New Message window menu bar. You'll see the Picture dialog box shown in Figure 8-15.

3. In the Picture Source box, type the complete filename of the picture. Or, click the Browse button and then locate and double-click the picture's filename in the dialog box that appears (see Figure 8-16).

4. If you want to specify alternate text or various layout and spacing options, fill in the appropriate Alternate Text, Layout, and Spacing fields.

5. Click OK.

Your picture appears at the insertion point. Recipients who don't have HTML e-mail clients will see the image as a regular attachment, not as an inline image. Recipients whose e-mail clients have no graphics capability will see only the alternate text.

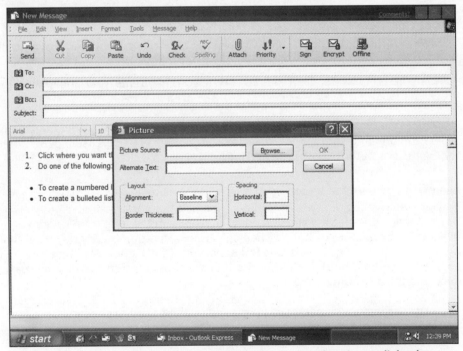

Figure 8-15: Add graphics to your e-mail messages using the Picture dialog box.

Figure 8-16: Select the picture you want from the list.

Note   Alternate text will appear in place of the image if the recipient's e-mail client has pictures turned off or cannot display them. Alternate text also appears while the image is loading.

Outlook Express can import images in GIF, JPEG (JPG), bitmap (BMP), Windows XPtafile (WMF), XBM, and ART formats. The default import formats are GIF and JPEG. You can choose a different format from the Files Of Type drop-down list shown at the bottom of Figure 8-16.

Inserting a hyperlink

By now, you've probably had experience browsing the World Wide Web and you know you can click hyperlinks on a Web page to jump to another place on the Internet or to perform some action, such as sending e-mail or downloading a file. Well, guess what? You can insert your own hyperlinks into any e-mail message (see Figure 8-17).

Outlook Express automatically creates hyperlinks from valid e-mail addresses and URLs as soon as you type them into a message and press the spacebar or Enter key. For example, after I type my e-mail address (alan@coolnerds.com) or the URL of my home page (http://www.coolnerds.com) and press the spacebar or the Enter key, Outlook Express automatically converts the text to an underlined blue hyperlink. The message recipient simply clicks the hyperlink to send me an e-mail message or to jump to my home page on the Web.

You also can create hyperlinks manually, using any text you want. For example, you may want your message to include a sentence, such as:

```
Click here to send me an e-mail message or click here to
download a heavenly recipe.
```

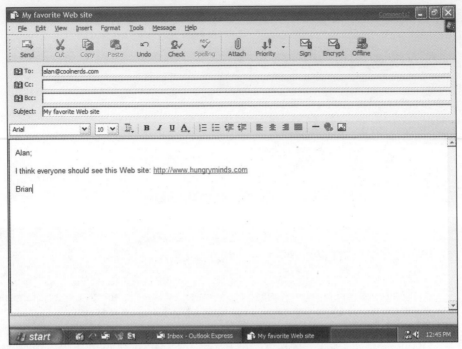

Figure 8-17: An e-mail message with an underlined hyperlink for http://www.hungryminds.com

In this example, the first appearance of the word "here" is a hyperlink that sends me an e-mail message; the second appearance of the word "here" is a hyperlink that sends my favorite recipe for cinnamon rolls to your computer (just kidding, I don't cook).

To create a hyperlink manually from any existing text, follow these steps:

1. Select the text you want to use as a hyperlink.

2. Click the Create Hyperlink button on the Formatting toolbar. You'll see the Hyperlink dialog box, shown in Figure 8-18.

3. Click the drop-down arrow in the Type box and select one of the types listed in Table 8-2. The type you select is filled in as the prefix in the URL box.

4. Click after the prefix in the URL box and type the rest of the URL.

5. Click OK.

The selected text becomes a hyperlink in your message.

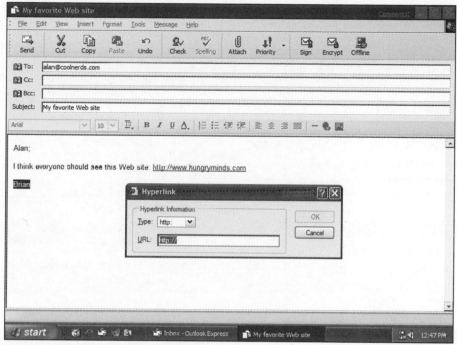

Figure 8-18: The Hyperlink dialog box

To change a hyperlink you created manually, repeat the preceding Steps 1 through 5. To change a manual hyperlink to plain text, select the hyperlink text, delete it, and then retype it.

Table 8-2	
Types of URLs You Can Use to Create Hyperlinks	
Sample Entry in Type the URL Box	*Description*
(other)	Any link that doesn't fit one of the options below
file:	Opens the file specified in the URL box on the recipient's computer (if it's there.) file://c:/windows/desktop/wrinkledpaper.bmp
ftp:	Downloads the file specified in the URL box ftp://ftp.microsoft.com
gopher:	Goes to the Gopher site specified in the URL box gopher://gopher.well.com

Continued

Table 8-2 (continued)	
Sample Entry in Type the URL Box	**Description**
http:	Goes to the Web page specified in the URL box http://www.hungryminds.com
https:	Goes to the secure Web page specified in the URL box https://www.securesite.com
mailto:	Sends a new message to the e-mail address specified in the URL box mailto:alan@coolnerds.com
news:	Goes to the newsgroup specified in the URL box news://news.newusers.questions
telnet:	Establishes a Telnet link to the computer specified in the URL box telnet:compuserve.com
wais	Establishes a link to a Wide Area Information Server (wais) wais://info.cern.ch

Choosing a background color or picture

Normally your e-mail message will have whatever background color is the default for the recipient's e-mail program or browser. You can, however, specify the background color or even use a picture as the background, as I did in Figure 8-19.

Specifying a colored background

To specify a colored background, choose Format ⇨ Background ⇨ Color from the New Message window menu bar and then choose a color from the menu that appears. You should try to pick a color that won't obliterate the message text (or reformat the text if necessary). For example, your recipient will have a hard time reading a message typed with black text on a purple background. The text might look rather cool, however, if you reformat it in boldface, a larger size, and the color white. (See the section "Changing the font, style, color, and size" earlier in this chapter.)

Specifying a picture background

To use a favorite picture or texture as a background, follow these steps:

1. Choose Format ⇨ Background ⇨ Picture from the New Message window menu bar. The Background Picture dialog box appears.

2. In the File box, type the path of a file on your own computer or click the drop-down arrow next to File and choose one of the picture files that comes with Outlook Express. Or, you can click the Browse button and then locate and double-click the picture file you want to use.

3. Choose OK.

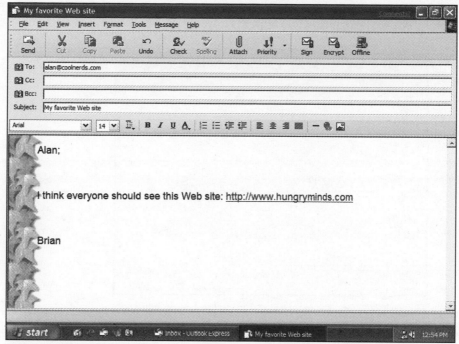

Figure 8-19: This message uses a picture of ivy, which comes with Outlook Express, as a background and big bold text for added readability.

The picture or texture you chose will be repeated as needed to fill up the background, as in Figure 8-19. Again, be careful to choose a picture that won't obscure the text in your message and type the message in an easy-to-read format.

Tip You may want to use indenting as I did in Figure 8-19 to improve the readability when you use a background image.

Note The pictures that come with Outlook Express are in the folder C:\Program Files\Common Files\Microsoft Shared\Stationery. You can copy your favorite GIF, JPEG (.JPG), or bitmap (.BMP) pictures to this folder. Then, they'll appear in the File drop-down list of the Background Picture dialog box and you can select them more quickly.

Inserting a text file or an HTML file

Let's suppose you already put together a plain text file containing your message (perhaps using Notepad) or you have an HTML Web page prepared. Now you want to e-mail the text or Web page to someone else. No sweat. Here's what you should do:

1. Click in your message where you want the text or HTML page to appear.

2. Choose Insert ➪ Text From File from the New Message window menu bar. The Insert Text File dialog box appears (see Figure 8-20).

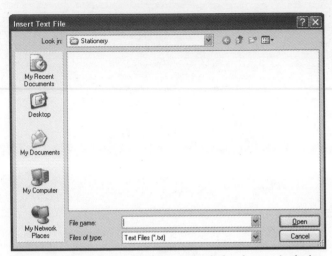

Figure 8-20: Use the Insert Text File dialog box to include a text or HTML file in your message.

3. Choose the type of file you want to insert from the Files of type drop-down list near the bottom of the dialog box. You can choose either Text Files (*.txt) to insert a plain text file or HTML Files (*.htm,*.html) to insert an HTML file.

4. Locate and double-click the file containing your text.

The plain text or HTML page appears in your message.

Tip
If you want to take a break while composing your message, choose File ➪ Save from the New Message window menu bar and then click OK if you see a dialog box informing you that the message has been saved in your Drafts folder. Then close the New Message window (File ➪ Close). When you're ready to finish composing the message, click the Drafts folder in the Outlook bar or the folder list and then double-click the message in the message list. Finish editing your message and send by clicking the Send button as usual.

Fixing "broken" HTML pictures and links

If the HTML file you inserted is at all fancy, it may have broken picture icons like the "view from my office" icon shown in Figure 8-21 and sometimes the hyperlinks won't work when the recipient clicks them.

What Is HTML?

HTML stands for Hypertext Markup Language, a language Web browsers and many e-mail programs interpret to display Web pages. You can create HTML pages from scratch, using Windows Notepad or other simple word processors, or you can use fancier word processors and specialized Web page design programs to create What You See Is What You Get (WYSI-WYG) Web pages. Microsoft Word and Corel WordPerfect are two word processors that can create Web pages. Microsoft FrontPage, and Netscape Compose, are examples of Web page design programs.

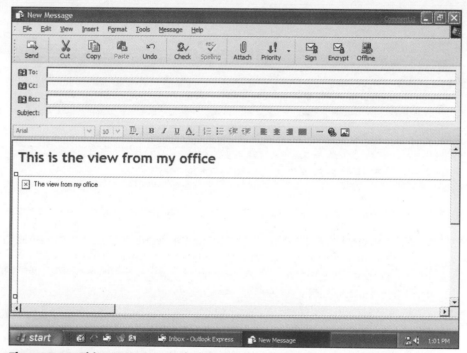

Figure 8-21: This HTML page includes a broken picture icon. I've selected the icon in this example.

Try the following methods to solve these problems:

✦ Broken picture icons are indicated by an x and an empty frame where the picture should appear. To fix a broken picture icon, click the icon and then click the Insert Picture button on the Formatting toolbar (or right-click the icon and choose Properties). Now complete the Picture Source box as explained earlier under "Inserting a picture." Figure 8-22 shows the page from Figure 8-21 after I fixed the broken picture icon.

Figure 8-22: The HTML page after I fixed the broken image icon

✦ Broken hyperlinks aren't obvious just by looking at them; however, they'll point to files or URLs unavailable to the recipient of your message. To fix a broken hyperlink (or to check a hyperlink for accuracy), select the hyperlink text, click the Insert Hyperlink button on the Formatting toolbar, and complete the Hyperlink dialog box, as explained earlier, in the section "Inserting a hyperlink."

 Note   Outlook Express will not let you save or send your messages until you fix all broken picture icons.

Sending a Web Page from the Internet

You can send a Web page directly from the Internet, if you like. To begin, open Microsoft Internet Explorer and visit the Web page you want to send. Then choose File ➪ Send ➪ Page By Email from the menu bar. Outlook Express will open and place the entire Web page — including all its pictures and hyperlinks — in a New Message window. When the page is finished loading into the New Message window, you can fill in the recipient's address, a subject, and any additional message text you want. Then send the message.

Spell checking your message

No one wants to seem careless or ignorant, especially when using e-mail to communicate with other people. One way to avoid bad impressions is to send messages free of embarrassing spelling errors. Outlook Express offers a built-in spelling checker that makes checking your spelling a breeze.

> **Note** To be honest, Outlook Express doesn't have its own spelling checker. Instead, it uses the spelling checker provided with the Microsoft Office programs (including Microsoft Word, Microsoft Excel, or Microsoft PowerPoint). If you do not have one of these programs installed, the spelling features are not available.

If the spelling checker doesn't start automatically when you click the Send button (or you want to spell check the message while you're composing it), choose Tools ➪ Spelling from the New Message window menu bar, or press F7. The spelling checker will start. If it doesn't find any errors, a dialog box informs you the spelling check is complete (click OK to clear it). If the spelling checker does find an error, you'll see a Spelling dialog box. The unrecognized word appears in the Not In Dictionary box just below the title bar.

Be aware, the spelling checker is not omniscient. Sometimes it fumes about a perfectly acceptable word. As I'll explain in a moment, you can add unrecognized (but properly spelled) words to the spelling checker's custom dictionary and you can change the spelling options so the spelling checker doesn't complain so much.

The buttons in the Spelling dialog box are as follows:

- ✦ **Ignore:** Click Ignore to ignore this error and move on to the next one.

- ✦ **Ignore All:** Click Ignore All to ignore this error throughout the entire message.

- ✦ **Change:** Click the word you want to use as a replacement in the Suggestions list (if it's not highlighted already) or edit the word in the Change To box. Then click the Change button to change the misspelled word to the word shown in the Change To box.

- ✦ **Change All:** Click the word you want to use as a replacement in the Suggestions list (if it isn't already highlighted) or edit the word in the Change To box. Then click Change All to change the same misspelled word throughout the entire message to the word shown in the Change To box.

- ✦ **Add:** Click this button to add the unrecognized word to the spelling checker's custom dictionary.

- ✦ **Suggest:** Type a word into the Change To box and then click Suggest to look up the word and display other possible spellings in the Suggestions list.

- ✦ **Options:** Click Options to open the Spelling Options dialog box, which enables you to customize the current spelling options. You can check or clear the check boxes, choose a language from the Language drop-down list, and even edit the custom dictionary, which contains words you've added via the Add button, plus any words you type in manually.

✦ **Undo Last:** Click Undo Last to undo your most recent change (if any) and skip back to the previous misspelled word.

✦ **Cancel (or Close):** Click Cancel or Close to stop the spelling check immediately.

A message appears when the spelling check is complete. Click OK to clear the message.

Tip　Your choices in the Spelling Options dialog box affect the current spelling check session and all future spelling check sessions. You'll learn another way to change the spelling checker options in "Customizing the default mail options," later in this chapter.

More About Sending and Receiving Messages

As mentioned earlier in this chapter, you can send your messages immediately — by clicking the Send button on the New Message window toolbar, for example. If you prefer to stack up your messages in your Outbox until you're ready to send the whole bunch, you can use the File ➪ Send Later option instead. Assuming you have some messages stacked in your Outbox, follow these simple steps to send them:

1. Open Outlook Express using whichever method you prefer (see "Starting Outlook Express").

2. If you want to see a list of messages waiting to be sent, click the Outbox icon in the Outlook bar or the folder list. A list of messages waiting to be sent appears in the message list, as in the example shown in Figure 8-24.

3. Do one of the following:

   • To send all the current messages and also to receive any messages waiting for you, click the Send/Recv button on the toolbar or press Ctrl+M. If you have more than one account, Outlook Express will send and receive e-mail for all your accounts automatically.

   • To send all the current messages and also receive any messages that are waiting for you, you also can choose Tools ➪ Send and Receive ➪ Send and Receive All. If you have multiple accounts, you'll see a list with options for choosing which account to use.

   • To send the pending messages without retrieving new ones, choose Tools ➪ Send and Receive ➪ Send All from the menu bar.

A dialog box will keep you posted on the progress and your computer will dial your service provider (if you use a modem to connect). When all the messages have been sent, the Outbox will be empty. Copies of the sent messages will be stored in the Sent Items box.

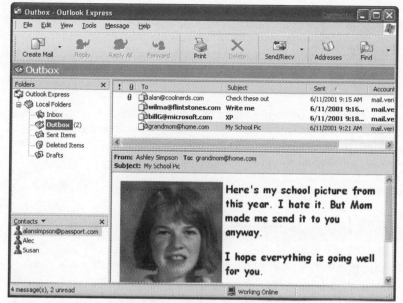

Figure 8-23: Messages waiting to be sent appear in Outlook Express's Outbox.

 Tip   You can change any message waiting in your Outbox. Simply open the Outbox, double-click the message you want to change in the message list, and change the message as needed. Then click the Send button on the toolbar (or press Alt+S).

If you close Outlook Express while unsent messages are still in your Outbox, you'll see a box telling you the following:

```
You have unsent messages in your Outbox. Do you want to send
them now?
```

This is a friendly reminder in case you composed a message and forgot to send it. You can choose Yes to send the messages immediately or choose No to leave them in the Outbox to send them later.

Reading Your Messages

Retrieving and viewing new Internet e-mail messages is easy. Just follow these steps:

1. Open Outlook Express using any of the techniques described in the section "Starting Outlook Express," earlier in this chapter.

2. Click the Send/Recv button (or press Ctrl+M).

Tip

If you want to check for new messages without sending any messages that are in the Outbox, use Tools ➪ Send and Receive ➪ Receive All.

You'll see some progress dialog boxes as Outlook Express sends any messages in your Outbox and then copies new messages from your e-mail server on the Internet to your PC.

To view the new messages, open the Inbox (a number appears next to the Inbox to indicate the number of unread messages it contains). New messages you haven't read yet are listed in boldface in the message list and are preceded by a closed envelope icon, as in the example shown in Figure 8-24. Messages containing attached files are preceded by a paperclip icon and those with a high or low priority are preceded by an exclamation point (!) or a down arrow, respectively.

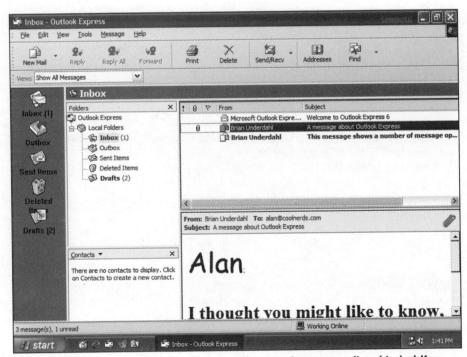

Figure 8-24: The Outlook Express Inbox with unread messages listed in boldface

Note

Don't panic if the boldface attribute suddenly disappears from the message line. This means you viewed the message for about five seconds (an interval you can adjust, as explained later in "Customizing the default mail options").

To read a specific message, click it. The preview pane at the bottom shows the contents of the e-mail message. If you prefer to open the message in a separate window, double-click it.

Tip

If you already have messages stored in one of the more popular e-mail programs, you can import them into Outlook Express. Importing old messages can be especially handy when you're switching from some other e-mail program to Outlook Express. See the section "Importing and Exporting Messages" for details.

When you finish reading the message, you can do any of the following:

✦ **Reply:** To send a reply to the author of the e-mail, click the Reply toolbar button or press Ctrl+R. Type your reply and click the Send toolbar button.

✦ **Reply All:** To reply to everyone who received the message (including those who received carbon copies), click the Reply All toolbar button or press Ctrl+Shift+R. Type your reply and click the Send button.

Caution

Before you choose Reply All, make sure you know who all the recipients will be. If you want to send a private message to just the sender, make sure you click the Reply button, and not Reply All.

✦ **Forward:** To forward the message to someone else, click the Forward (or Forward Message) toolbar button, or press Ctrl+F. Type the new recipient's name, type a message describing the forwarded information (optional), and then click the Send button.

✦ **Forward As Attachment:** To forward the message to someone else as an attachment to a message you've written, choose Message ⇨ Forward As Attachment from the menu bar. Type the new recipient's name, type a message describing the forwarded information (optional), and then click the Send toolbar button.

✦ **Delete:** To delete the message, click the Delete button or press Ctrl+D. Outlook Express moves the message to the Deleted Items folder.

✦ **Print:** To print the message, choose File ⇨ Print from the menu bar, or press Ctrl+P, or click the Print toolbar button if it's available.

✦ **Mark As Unread:** To mark the message line with boldface as a reminder to reread it later, choose Edit ⇨ Mark As Unread from the menu bar.

✦ **Mark As Read:** To remove the boldface and mark a message as read, choose Edit ⇨ Mark As Read, or press Ctrl+Q.

✦ **Mark All Read:** To mark all the messages as read, choose Edit ⇨ Mark All As Read.

✦ **View the Next Message:** To view the next message in the folder, click the Next button on the toolbar (if it's available) or press Ctrl+> (Ctrl plus the greater than symbol), or choose View ⇨ Next ⇨ Next Message from the menu bar. To read the next unread message, press Ctrl+U.

✦ **View the Previous Message:** To view the previous message in the folder, click the Previous button on the toolbar (if it's available), or press Ctrl+< (Ctrl plus the less than symbol), or choose View ⇨ Previous Message from the menu bar.

✦ **View the Message Properties**: To view details about the message, choose File ➪ Properties from the menu bar. Then click the General tab (to see general information) or the Details tab (to see the Internet headers for this message). To view the message headers and HTML source text, select the Details tab and then click the Message Source button. When you finish viewing the properties, click the Close (X) and OK buttons as needed.

Instead of using the toolbar buttons to reply to or forward the message, you can choose options from the Message menu. And if you're viewing the message in the message list (rather than in a separate window), you can right-click the message and decide its fate by choosing an option from the shortcut menu that appears. You'll find more about replying to messages, forwarding them, and deleting them in the later sections "Replying to a Message," "Forwarding a Message," and "Deleting Messages."

A Few Words About Junk Mail (Spam)

If people are sending you unwanted junk mail (also known as spam), never respond to the spammer directly. Instead, try to find out more about where the spam message came from by viewing its header information. To do this, open your Inbox, highlight the message, choose File ➪ Properties, select the Details tab, and look for an e-mail address next to the "From:" lines. You might see something like this:

```
From: "A. Spammer" <aspammer@spammerISP.com>
```

Unfortunately, the message header can be rather cryptic and it may be false if the spammer is masquerading as someone else. Nonetheless, this header information can help your Internet service provider (ISP) and the spammer's ISP to filter out the spam or to cancel the spammer's account.

Many ISPs have a specific policy about junk mail. You should check with your own ISP for details about how you can fight spam. Some ISPs ask you to notify their "abuse" or "postmaster" e-mail account when you receive spam. In this case, forward the spam message to your own ISP and to the spammer's ISP. At the top of the forwarded message, type something like this:

```
I received the attached spam e-mail, and I would appreciate
anything you can do to discourage this spammer from sending such
messages in the future. Many thanks!
```

When you finish typing this introductory text, send your message, and then delete the original spam from your Inbox.

Later in this chapter, you learn how to filter out unwanted messages from specific e-mail addresses. This tool can be handy for weeding out messages from repeat spammers. For more tips and information on dealing with junk e-mail, check out the antispamming Web site at http://www.dgl.com/docs/antispam.html.

Working with several messages at once

Working with several messages at once is often handy. For example, you might want to delete several messages, mark them as read (or unread), move them to another folder, open them in separate windows, and more. The first step is to click the folder containing the messages with which you want to work. Next, select (highlight) the messages, using any of the following techniques:

✦ To select one message, click it in the message list.

✦ To select all the messages, choose Edit ➪ Select All, or press Ctrl+A.

✦ To select several adjacent messages, click the first message you want to select and then hold down the Shift key while clicking the last message you want to select (this technique is called Shift+click).

✦ To select several nonadjacent messages, click the first message you want to select and then hold down the Ctrl key while clicking each additional message you want to select (this technique is called Ctrl+click). If you select a message by accident, Ctrl+click it.

Now you can work with all the selected messages at once. Here are some things you can do with them:

✦ Right-click any of the selected messages and choose an option from the shortcut menu that appears. Right-clicking is perhaps the easiest way to work with multiple messages.

✦ Choose File ➪ Open or nearly any option from the Edit menu.

✦ Click the Forward Message or Delete button on the toolbar.

✦ Drag any of the selected messages to another folder in the folder list (all the selected messages are moved to the new folder).

✦ Hold down the Ctrl key while dragging any of the selected messages to another folder in the folder list (all the selected messages are copied to the new folder).

You can create your own folders to organize your e-mail messages, and you can have the Inbox Assistant automatically move or copy incoming messages to specific folders. See "Creating your own folders" and "Using message rules," later in this chapter, for more information.

Finding and sorting messages

Eventually, you may end up with a huge number of messages in your Inbox and other folders within Outlook Express. Finding a particular message in that pile of mail could be like looking for the proverbial needle in the haystack. But thanks to the Find Message feature, it's easy to search for messages. Follow these steps to find the message(s) you want:

1. Starting from the main Outlook Express window, click the folder you want to search.

2. Choose Edit ➪ Find ➪ Message from the menu bar or press Ctrl+Shift+F. You'll see the Find Message dialog box.

3. To narrow the search, fill in as much information as you need about the messages you want to find. (It doesn't matter whether you type uppercase or lowercase letters.)

4. If you want to search a different message folder, click the Browse button. You also can choose whether to include subfolders of the selected folder by checking or unchecking the Include Subfolders box.

5. Click the Find Now button to begin the search.

Tip   In Step 3, you can specify partial words or names in the From, To, Subject, and Message fields. If you enter information into more than one field, Outlook treats each field as an "and" operation.

After you click Find Now, the Find Message dialog box expands to include an area for showing messages that match your search. If matches exist, they'll appear in the list, as shown in Figure 8-25. If no matches exist, the list will be empty and you see 0 message(s) in the status bar at the bottom of the dialog box.

The Find Message dialog box offers many cool ways to work with messages. For example, you can conduct another search by repeating Steps 3 through 5 of the previous find procedure. You also can do just about anything that works in the main Outlook Express window, including the following:

✦ Double-click a message to open it.

✦ Select one or more messages and then choose options from the File, Edit, View, or Compose menus in the Find Message dialog box.

✦ Select one or more messages, right-click your selection, and then choose an option from the shortcut menu.

✦ Select one or more messages and then delete them by pressing the Delete key. (For more information about deleting messages, see "Deleting Messages," later in this chapter.)

When you finish using the Find Message dialog box, you can close it by choosing File ➪ Close from the Find Message menu bar, by pressing Alt+F4, or by clicking the Close (X) button in the upper-right corner of the dialog box.

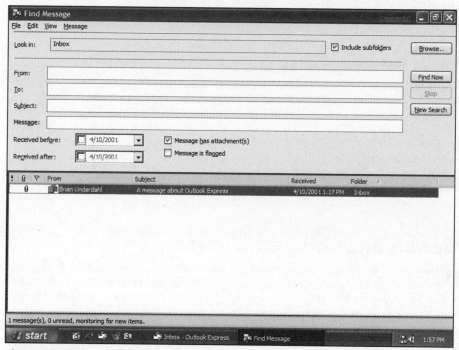

Figure 8-25: The Find Message dialog box after searching for messages that contain an attachment

Sorting the message list

Another quick way to find a message is to sort the message list. You can sort the list by any column in either ascending (A to Z) or descending (Z to A) order. To begin, click the icon for the folder you want to sort. Then, use any of the following methods to sort the message list:

✦ Click the column button at the top of the message list. For example, click the Subject column button to sort the messages by subject. If you click the column button again, the sort order is reversed. A small up-pointing triangle on the button indicates an ascending sort; a down-pointing triangle indicates a descending sort.

✦ Right-click the column button at the top of the message list and choose either Sort Ascending or Sort Descending.

✦ Choose View ➪ Sort By from the menu bar and then choose the column by which you want to sort. If you want to toggle the current sort order between ascending and descending order, choose View ➪ Sort By ➪ Sort Ascending. If the Sort Ascending option is checked, the list is sorted in ascending order. If it isn't checked, you get a descending sort.

You can add and remove columns in the message list, as explained later in "Customizing the Outlook Express window."

Finding text within a message

In addition to searching for a specific message, you can search for text within the message you're currently viewing in the message list or in a separate window. To do this, choose Edit ⇨ Find ⇨ Text in this message from the menu bar. Type the text you're looking for in the Find box and choose any options you want. You can decide whether to match the whole word only, whether to match the uppercase and lowercase letters you typed, and the search direction (up or down). Click the Find Next button to start the search. Find will highlight the next match it finds. You can continue clicking Find Next and highlighting matches until you find the match you want. When you finish searching, click Cancel.

Viewing and saving attachments

If a message includes an attachment, a paper-clip icon appears next to the message in the message list and also at the upper-right corner of the message in the preview pane. The icon for the actual file appears below the address header anytime you view it in a separate window. Figure 8-26 illustrates the same message opened in both the preview pane and in a separate window (left side of figure).

Viewing or saving the attachment is easy:

✦ If you highlighted the message in the preview pane, click the paperclip icon (attachment icon) at the upper-right corner of the message and then click the filename of the attachment you want to open.

✦ If you opened the message in a separate window, double-click the attachment icon. Or, for even more processing options including Open, Print, and Save As, right-click the attachment icon and choose an option from the shortcut menu.

What happens next depends on the type of information the attachment contains. If the attachment is an e-mail message, it will open in a separate window. If it's a compressed file (such as a .zip file), a program file, or a data file (such as a spreadsheet or word processing document), you'll usually see the Open Attachment Warning dialog box, shown in Figure 8-27. Now take either of the following actions:

✦ To open the attachment, click Open it, click OK, and then respond to any dialog boxes that appear.

✦ To save the attachment to disk, click "Save it to disk" and click OK. When the Save Attachment As dialog box appears, choose a folder from the Save In drop-down list, or the folder display beneath that in which to save the file. (Or choose Desktop from the Save In drop-down list to put the file right on your Windows desktop.) Don't forget to take a look at the file name near the bottom of the dialog box, so you'll recognize it later. Then click the Save button or press Enter.

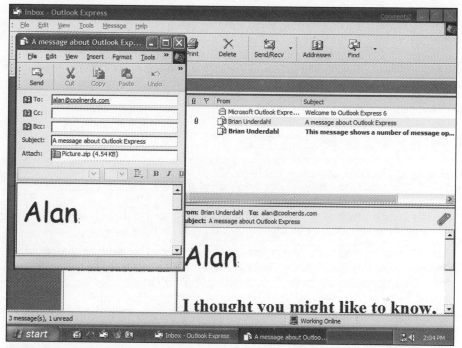

Figure 8-26: This message has an attachment, as shown in the preview pane and in a separate window.

 Caution   Be careful about opening a file if you haven't checked it for viruses. It's okay to save a file to disk and then check it for viruses, but after you open the file (by choosing "Open it" in the Open Attachment Warning dialog box or by double-clicking it in My Computer or Windows Explorer), you can expose your computer to any viruses the file contains. See Chapter 29, "Beefing Up Security," for tips on protecting yourself from e-mail viruses.

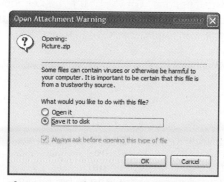

Figure 8-27: This dialog box enables you to open the attached file or to save it to disk.

If you save an attachment to disk, it's no different from a file you downloaded from the Web. Which, of course, means it's no different from any other file on your hard drive. As a rule, you can then just open that file by clicking (or double-clicking) its icon. If you run into any snags, see "Using Downloaded Files" in Chapter 6, and more general discussions of files and folders in Chapters 2 and 3. For more information on managing files and folders, refer to Chapters 12 and 13.

Replying to a Message

You can reply to any message you highlighted in the message list or that you're viewing in a separate window. First, do one of the following:

✦ To send a reply to the author of the e-mail, click the Reply toolbar button or press Ctrl+R (or choose Message ➪ Reply To Sender).

✦ To reply to everyone who received the message (including the people who received carbon copies), click the Reply All toolbar button or press Ctrl+Shift+R (or choose Message ➪ Reply To All).

A Reply window will open, as shown in Figure 8-28. Notice the To: box in the address area is already filled in with the recipient's e-mail name and the Subject line displays Re: (for reply) followed by the original subject name. The insertion point is positioned above the original message, which appears in the lower portion of the editing area. (If the message originally contained an attachment, the attachment is not included.)

Type your reply using any of the editing and formatting techniques discussed in the section "Composing a Message." Although you shouldn't need to, you also can change any items in the address and subject areas. When you finish typing your reply, send the message as usual (for example, click the Send button in the Reply window or press Alt+S).

Tip   You can choose whether to include the original message in the reply, as explained in the section "Customizing the default mail options." For the best reminder about what you're replying to, include the original message. You can always delete any extraneous text from the original message using standard editing techniques.

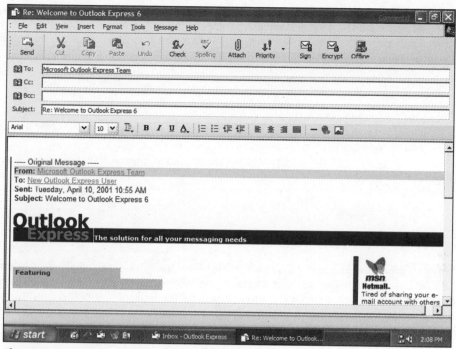

Figure 8-28: Preparing to reply to this message

Forwarding a Message

You can forward any message. Forwarding a message is similar to sending a reply, although these differences exist: Attachments are included in the forwarded message; the To: box in the address area is not filled in automatically; and the Subject: line is filled in with Fw: (for forward) followed by the original subject or it is blank.

To forward a message, follow these steps:

1. Highlight the message you want to forward in the message list or open it in a separate window.

2. Do one of the following:

   • To forward the message exactly as it originally appeared in your Inbox, click the Forward toolbar button or press Ctrl+F (or choose Message ➪ Forward). A Forward (Fw) window opens and shows the original message and its attachments, if any.

   • To forward the message as an attachment, choose Message ➪ Forward As Attachment. A New Message window opens with the original message appearing as an attachment icon.

3. Type the recipient's e-mail address in the To: box or use your Address Book to fill in the address (see "Using the Address Book," later in this chapter). If you want to forward the message to more than one recipient, type a semicolon between each recipient's e-mail address.

4. If you forwarded the message as an attachment, type a subject in the Subject: box.

5. Click the message editing area and type an introduction to the message you're forwarding. This introduction is optional, but it's helpful to tell recipients why you're forwarding the message.

6. Send the message as usual (for example, click the Send toolbar button or press Alt+S).

Deleting Messages

Deleting an unwanted message from any folder is easy. First, open the folder containing the message and open the message or select it in the message list. Then, click the Delete button on the toolbar or press Ctrl+D. If you selected messages in the message list, you can delete them in two other ways: Either press the Delete (Del) key on your keyboard or drag the selection to the Deleted Items folder.

Cross-Reference You can empty your Deleted Items folder automatically as soon as you exit Outlook Express, as explained in the section "Customizing the default mail options," later in this chapter

When you delete a message from any folder except the Deleted Items folder, you actually move it to the Deleted Items folder. So if you ever need to undelete a message, you can just move it to another folder. To do so, open the Deleted Items folder and select the message(s) you want to undelete in the message list. Then right-click the selected message(s), choose Move To from the shortcut menu, and double-click Inbox or whatever folder to which you want to move the message(s). Or, you can select messages in the Deleted Items folder and drag them to another folder in the folder list or the Outlook bar.

Caution When you delete a message from the Deleted Items folder, the message is removed from your hard disk and it cannot be undeleted.

Backing Up Your Messages

It's a good idea to back up your Outlook Express message folders to a floppy disk, Zip disk, or network drive. Backups can protect you against the loss of all your saved messages in the event of a hard disk crash and they provide some extra insurance just before or after you do a major cleanup in your message folders.

Compacting a Folder

Outlook Express compacts your message folders automatically to eliminate wasted space. You also can compact a folder manually at any time. First, open the folder you want to compact. Then choose File ⇨ Folder ⇨ Compact and wait a moment while the compactor cleans up the wasted space. (If you prefer to compact all the folders at once, choose File ⇨ Folder ⇨ Compact All Folders instead.)

Compacting is not the same as compressing. Outlook Express can directly use any folders it has compacted; you needn't decompress them in any way.

Each Outlook Express message folder is actually a file on your hard disk with a .dbx extension.

The general steps for backing up your messages are as follows:

1. Open the folder that contains your Outlook Express messages using Find, Windows Explorer, or My Computer. See the following section, "Finding your Outlook Express messages," for some tips on locating this folder.

2. Copy the message files to a backup folder on your computer, to a floppy disk or Zip disk, or to a network drive. Note, some message files may be too large to fit on a floppy disk.

Importing and Exporting Messages

If you recently switched from Eudora Pro, Eudora Light, Microsoft Exchange, Microsoft Internet Mail For Windows 3.1, Microsoft Outlook, Microsoft Windows Messaging, Netscape Communicator, or Netscape Mail, you may have a bunch of messages you want to import for use in Outlook Express. Conversely, you may want to export your Outlook Express messages for use in Microsoft Outlook or Microsoft Exchange, predecessors of Outlook Express. As the following sections explain, importing and exporting messages between Outlook Express and other e-mail programs is easy.

Note   The first time you start Outlook Express on your PC, you may be taken to the Outlook Express Import Wizard, which asks if you want to import messages from previously installed e-mail software.

Importing messages

To import messages from another e-mail program into Outlook Express, use the following steps:

1. Open Outlook Express and choose File ➪ Import ➪ Messages from the menu bar. An Outlook Express Import dialog box appears.

2. From the "Select an e-mail program to import from" list, choose the type of file to import. Your choices are Eudora Pro or Light (through V3.0), Microsoft Exchange, Microsoft Internet Mail (32-bit Version), Microsoft Internet Mail For Windows 3.1, Microsoft Outlook, Microsoft Outlook Express 4, Microsoft Outlook Express 5, Microsoft Windows Messaging, Netscape Communicator, and Netscape Mail (V2 or V3).

3. Click Next.

4. Respond to any prompts that appear. The prompts will depend on your choice in Step 2.

When importing is complete, the messages will appear in the appropriate Outlook Express folders (of course, all the original messages are still intact in your old e-mail program). To view the imported messages, simply click the Outlook Express folder in which you're interested.

Tip   If necessary, Outlook Express will create new folders to hold messages from the original e-mail program. For example, if the old e-mail program contained messages in a folder named "Good Stuff," a Good Stuff folder will appear in the Outlook Express folder list and Outlook bar, and it will contain messages from the Good Stuff folder in your old program.

Exporting messages

Use the following steps to export your Outlook Express messages to either Microsoft Outlook or Microsoft Exchange:

1. Open Outlook Express and choose File ➪ Export ➪ Messages from the menu bar.

2. When you see the message "This will Export messages from Outlook Express to Microsoft Outlook or Microsoft Exchange," click OK.

3. When the Choose Profile dialog box appears, choose a Microsoft Outlook or Microsoft Exchange profile from the Profile Name drop-down list and then click OK. (If you have no idea what profiles are, click the Help button in the Choose Profile dialog box.)

4. When prompted to select the folders to export, choose All Folders or choose Selected Folders, and then click, Shift+click, or Ctrl+click the folders you want to export.

5. Click OK to export the messages.

Using the Address Book

Outlook Express has a handy address book you can use to record, maintain, and find people's addresses, phone numbers, and, of course, e-mail addresses. You also can use the Address Book to fill in the e-mail addresses of your recipients automatically when you compose a new message or when you reply to or forward a message.

To get to the Address Book, use any of the following approaches:

✦ From the Windows XP desktop, click the Start button and choose All Programs ➪ Accessories ➪ Address Book.

✦ From any Outlook Express window, choose Tools ➪ Address Book from the menu bar or press Ctrl+Shift+B.

The Address Book window opens, perhaps empty if you've never used it before, as in Figure 8-29. Now you can add new contacts and new groups, change the properties of or delete any existing entry, search or print the Address Book, send mail to anyone in the Address Book, and more. When you finish using the Address Book window, click its Close (X) button in the upper-right corner or choose File ➪ Exit from its menu bar.

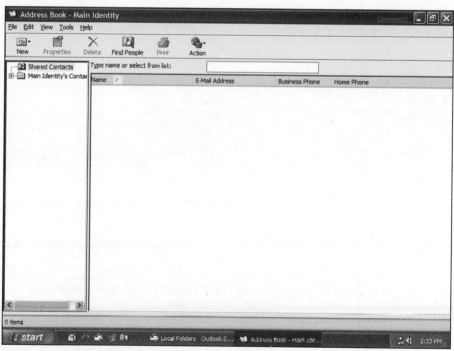

Figure 8-29: The Address Book prior to entering any names and addresses

Tip   As a shortcut while using Outlook Express, you can open the Address Book by clicking either the Addresses toolbar button on the toolbar. Or, if you're composing a message, you can click the book icon to the left of the To:, Cc: or Bcc: line in the message header. If you use the latter method, you're taken to the Select Recipients window shown later in Figure 8-35.

Adding names and addresses

Adding people's names and addresses to the Address Book is simple. First, open the Address Book. Then, click the New button on the toolbar and choose New Contact. Or, or choose File ➪ New Contact from the menu bar, or press Ctrl+N. The Properties dialog box, like the one shown in Figure 8-30, appears.

Tip   Anytime you're viewing an e-mail message in a separate window, you can quickly copy any underlined address in the From:, To:, Cc:, or Bcc: area to your Address Book. Simply right-click the address next to From: and choose Add To Address Book from the shortcut menu. You'll be taken to the Properties dialog box for this person as as explained in this section.

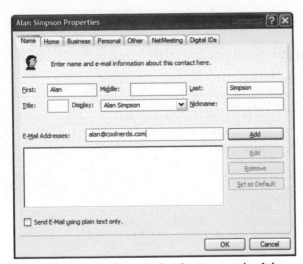

Figure 8-30: Sample entry for the Name tab of the Address Book

You can type in any person's name and (if applicable) e-mail address.

Note   When you enter the First, Middle, and Last name fields, Outlook Express automatically fills in the Display name field from your entries (you can edit the Display name field, of course). The Name column of your Address Book shows the Display name.

If the person has several e-mail addresses, you can type one at a time, clicking the Add button to record each one. The first address you enter is automatically assigned as the default e-mail address. You can change that, however, by clicking the e-mail address you'll send to most often and then clicking the Set as Default button. If you want to remove an e-mail address from the list, click it and then click the Remove button. To change an e-mail address, click it, click the Edit button, change the address, and press Enter.

Tip   If the contact has an e-mail program that cannot read HTML-formatted mail, select the Send E-Mail Using Plain Text Only box.

The Home, Business, Personal, Other, NetMeeting, and Digital IDs tabs enable you to record additional information about this person. For example, in Figure 8-31, I've typed some sample information into the Home tab.

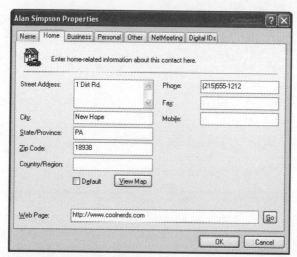

Figure 8-31: More sample information for one person in the Address Book

As explained in the section "Customizing the default mail options," which appears later in this chapter, you can have your Address Book updated automatically with the address of every e-mail message to which you respond. And if you already have an address book in Eudora Light, LDIF-LDAP Data Interchange Format, Microsoft Exchange, Microsoft Internet Mail for Windows 3.1, Netscape, Netscape Communicator, or a comma-separated text file, you can import it into your Address Book and save yourself a bunch of time as explained later in "Importing and exporting address books."

Creating groups and mailing lists

Suppose you have a group of friends who like to receive jokes by e-mail, or suppose you're organizing a family reunion, or maybe you're a project leader. When sending e-mail to all these folks, you certainly won't want to specify each person's e-mail address individually. Instead, you'll want to enter the name of a group — such as Joke list, or Reunion list, or Project team — and have Outlook Express automatically know to send your message to each address on the list. Creating a group of e-mail addresses is easy. As always, begin by opening the Address Book. Then follow these steps:

1. Choose File ➪ New Group from the menu bar or press Ctrl+G. A Properties dialog box appears. (Figure 8-32 shows a completed example.)

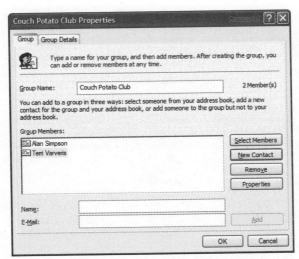

Figure 8-32: A completed group in the Group Properties dialog box

2. In the Group Name box, type the name for your group (for example, Project Team).

3. Do any of the following, as needed:

   • To select addresses already in your Address Book, click the Select Members button and then double-click the names of the people or groups you want to add to your group. When you finish, click OK.

   • To create a new Address Book entry on the fly and add it to the group, click the New Contact button, fill in the Properties dialog box (shown back in Figure 8-30), and click OK.

- To remove an entry from the group, click it and then click the Remove button. This does not remove the entry from your Address Book, just from the group itself.

- To update the details about any group member, click the member's entry and then click the Properties button (or double-click the member's entry). Edit the entry as needed and click OK.

4. If you want to add some notes about the group, click in the Notes box and type away.

5. When you finish creating the group, click OK in the Properties dialog box.

The group name will appear in the Address Book in boldface text, with a little group icon beside it. If you point to the group name with your mouse, a list of the group members will appear near the mouse pointer.

Tip You can point to any entry in the Address Book and Outlook Express will display the name and e-mail address in a pop-up box. Very cool! (If you don't see the pop-up box right away, try clicking an empty area in the list of names and e-mail addresses and then pointing to an entry.)

After you set up some groups, you can click any group in the list to see only the members of that group or click Address Book to view the entire Address Book.

Tip You can quickly send a message to group members while you're viewing the Groups List in the Address Book. To send a message to everyone in the group, click the name of the group and then choose Tools ➪ Action ➪ Send Mail. Or, to send to selected people in the group, click the name of the group, use the Shift+click or Ctrl+click technique to select the members in the right side of the window, and then choose Tools ➪ Action ➪ Send Mail. A New Message window will open with the group members listed automatically in the To: box of the message. This feature is cooler than an Eskimo's igloo!

Changing and deleting Address Book entries

Of course, you'll probably need to change the entries in your Address Book occasionally. It's easy. First, open the Address Book window and click the entry you want to change. Then, click the Properties button on the Address Book toolbar, or choose File ➪ Properties from the menu bar, or press Alt+Enter. As a shortcut, you can double-click the entry you want to change. Now change the entry using the same techniques you used to create it in the first place. When you finish, click OK to return to the Address Book window.

To delete an entry, highlight it in the Address Book. Or, if you want to delete multiple entries, select them by using the same Shift+click or Ctrl+click techniques discussed earlier in the section "Working with several messages at once." Then, click the Delete button on the Address Book toolbar, or choose File ➪ Delete from the menu bar, or press the Delete key. When prompted for confirmation, click Yes. Poof! The entries are gone.

Searching the Address Book

As your Address Book grows, you may have trouble finding a particular entry simply by scrolling up and down. But it's no problem at all because you can search for entries in several ways. The easiest method is to click the Type Name Or Select From List box and then type the first part of the name you're trying to find. As you type, Outlook Express highlights the closest matching entry. The more information you type, the narrower the search. In Figure 8-33, for example, I typed **ke** and Outlook Express immediately highlighted the name Keith.

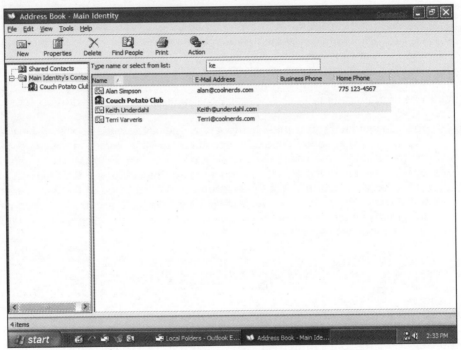

Figure 8-33: I'm searching for a person whose name begins with ke.

You also can find entries quickly by sorting your Address Book. The techniques are similar to those already discussed in the section "Sorting the message list." To sort by a particular column, click the column heading (click it again to reverse the sort order). You also can choose options from the View ➪ Sort By menu.

Doing fancy Find People searches

You can do an even fancier Find People search of your Address Book or various online directory services. To begin, click the Find People button on the Address Book toolbar, or choose Edit ➪ Find People from the menu bar, or press Ctrl+F. When the Find People dialog box appears, choose the name of the address book or directory you want to search in the Look in drop-down list, fill in the blanks with the text you want to look for on the People tab, and then click Find Now. (If you chose an online directory service, you may be prompted to connect to the Internet.) Figure 8-34 shows that I'm about to begin searching for Alan Simpson in the WhoWhere online directory.

 You'll learn more about online directory services in the section "Using online directory services," later in this chapter.

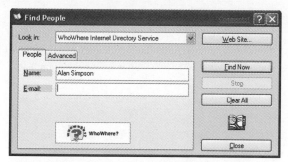

Figure 8-34: The Find People dialog box after choosing the WhoWhere directory, typing alan simpson in the Name box, and getting ready to click Find Now

You can work with any address shown at the bottom of the Find People dialog box. First, click the entry to highlight it. Then, do one of the following:

✦ To view or change the entry, click the Properties button or double-click the entry.

✦ To delete the entry, click the Delete button or press Delete and then choose Yes to confirm the deletion (available only if you're searching the Address Book).

✦ To add the entry to your Address Book, click the Add to Address Book button (available only if you're searching an online directory service).

If you want to do a new search, click the Clear All button; then, choose an address book or directory to search, fill in the boxes on the People tab, and click Find Now. If you want to visit the Web site for the currently selected online directory service, click the Web Site button. When you finish using the Find People dialog box, click Close and you'll return to the Address Book.

Choosing recipients from your Address Book

Several ways exist to choose recipients from your Address Book when you're composing a new message, replying to a message, or forwarding a message.

If you're starting from the Address Book, select the addresses you want to include in the To: box of a new message. You can use the click, Shift+click, and Ctrl+click selection methods discussed earlier. Now click the Action button on the toolbar and choose Send Mail or choose Tools ⇨ Action ⇨ Send Mail. A New Message window opens and the To: box includes the addresses you selected.

If you're starting from the New Message window, the Reply window, or the Forward window, click the little Rolodex card next to the To:, Cc:, or Bcc: box. You'll see a Select Recipients dialog box, like the one shown in Figure 8-35.

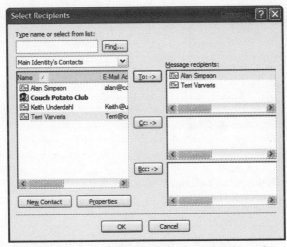

Figure 8-35: The Select Recipients dialog box after selecting two recipients and clicking the To: button

From here you can take any of the following actions as needed:

✦ To select the name(s) you want from the Name list, use the click, Shift+click, and Ctrl+click methods described earlier in the section "Working with several messages at once." Then, click the To:, Cc:, or Bcc: button depending on whether you want to add the names to the To:, Cc:, or Bcc: address boxes in your message.

✦ To highlight a name quickly in the Name list, click the "Type name or select from list" box and type the first part of the name (see "Searching the Address Book"). Now select the name you want (if it isn't highlighted already) and then click the To:, Cc:, or Bcc: button as appropriate.

✦ To do a Find People search, click the Find button and search as explained earlier in "Doing fancy Find People searches." After clicking Find Now, select the names you want and then click the To:, Cc:, or Bcc: button as appropriate.

When you finish using the Select Recipients dialog box, click OK. The e-mail recipient names you selected will appear in the address boxes of your message. (If you added a name by accident, simply click the name in the address box to select it and then press the Delete key.)

Now that you're an ace with your Address Book, why not try this great shortcut for specifying e-mail recipients? It works anytime you're using the New Message window, the Reply window, or the Forward window:

1. Click the To:, Cc:, or Bcc: box of the message as usual.

2. Type any part of a name or e-mail address that you know is in your Address Book. For example, type alan or simpson or coolnerds if you've entered my name and e-mail address in your Address Book. If you want to enter more than one recipient, type a semicolon, and then type the next name or e-mail address.

3. Repeat Steps 1 and 2 as needed.

4. If the correct recipient names aren't filled in automatically when you finish entering names, click the Check Names button on the toolbar or press Ctrl+K, or choose Tools ⇨ Check Names from the menu bar.

Outlook Express will do its best to match and fill in the names you chose. If it needs your help to decide which address to include, you'll see a Check Names dialog box, as shown in Figure 8-36. Click the address you want to use and then click OK (or click Show More Names, highlight the name you want, and then click OK).

Tip

If "Automatically complete e-mail addresses when composing" is checked on the Send tab of the Options dialog box — as it is by default — Outlook Express will fill in any match it finds in your Address Book as you type in the To:, Cc:, or Bcc: box of the message and you can skip Step 4. If more than one entry matches your typing, Outlook Express matches only the first entry it finds. For example, if your Address Book includes two Alans — Alan A. Abalone and Alan C. Simpson — Outlook Express matches Alan A. Abalone if you type alan. To match the entry for Alan C. Simpson in this example, enter simp or part of the e-mail address, such as cool. See the section "Personalizing Outlook Express," later in this chapter, for information on customizing the Send options.

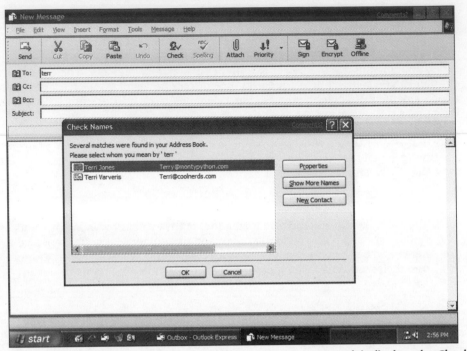

Figure 8-36: If Outlook Express can't match a name you entered, it displays the Check Names dialog box.

Printing your Address Book

Who was it that said you can't take it with you? If they were talking about the Address Book, they were wrong. You can easily print a paper copy of your Address Book to take on a trip or to drop into your little black book by following these steps:

1. Open the Address Book (click the Addresses button on the main Outlook Express toolbar).

2. If you only want to print certain addresses, select them with the usual click, Shift+click, Ctrl+click, or Find methods.

3. Click the Print button on the Address Book toolbar or choose File ➪ Print from the menu bar, or press Ctrl+P.

4. In the Print dialog box (see Figure 8-37), choose a printer, a print range, a print style, and the number of copies to print.

5. Click OK to start printing.

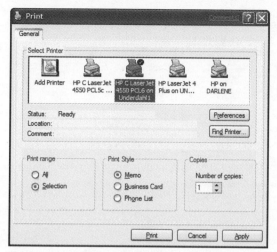

Figure 8-37: Use the Print dialog box to print a copy of your Address Book.

Using online directory services

The Internet is swarming with online directory services that enable you to look up e-mail addresses. Outlook Express can automatically access several of the most popular online directory services—Bigfoot, VeriSign, WhoWhere, and a local Active Directory is your company has such a service. To view or change the directory lists Outlook Express can search, choose Tools ➪ Accounts from the Address Book or main Outlook Express menu bar, and then click the Directory Service tab in the Internet Accounts dialog box (if it isn't selected already).

If you want to add a new directory service to the list, click the Add button (or click Add and then choose Directory Service). You'll be taken to the Internet Connection Wizard, which will prompt you for information including the Lightweight Directory Access Protocol (LDAP) server, whether the server requires you to log on, whether you want to check e-mail addresses using this directory service, and the name of the Internet directory service. Fill in each box and click Next or Finish to continue (you may need to contact the directory service if you're uncertain how to fill in the dialog boxes). When you finish adding the service, you'll see it in the list, as shown in Figure 8-38.

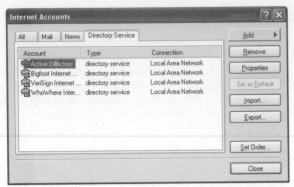

Figure 8-38: This is the Directory Service tab, which lists the online directory services.

Updating the directory service list is easy. First, click the name of the directory service you want to change. Then, click Remove to remove the service from the list, click Properties to view or change the settings you assigned in the Internet Connection Wizard, or click Set as Default to make this your default account. If you want to change the order used to check names when you send e-mail, click Set Order, move the directory services up or down in the list that appears, and click OK. When you finish using the Internet Accounts dialog box, click Close.

Tip   Although you can have Outlook Express check names against the online directory service when you're sending e-mail, everything will go faster if you search the online directory occasionally and add selected addresses to your local Address Book (as explained in the section "Doing fancy Find People searches").

Backing up your Address Book

Just as you'll want to back up your message folders, you'll also want to back up your Address Book. The Address Book is stored in a file named *username*.wab in the folder C:\Documents and Settings*username*\Application Data\ Microsoft\Address Book, where username is your e-mail name or network user name.

Even a large address book like mine will fit conveniently on a floppy disk, so compressing the Address Book files before backing them up isn't important. Simply use My Computer, Windows Explorer, or Find to open the C:\ Documents and Settings*username*\Application Data\Microsoft\Address Book folder. Then select the Address Book file and copy it to your backup disk.

Importing and exporting address books

If you used another e-mail program before switching to Outlook Express, you probably already have a bunch of addresses stored in an address book. Back in the bad old days, switching to a new e-mail program was a major pain; you had to reenter all your contact information from scratch. There was no way to import existing addresses into the new address book. Fortunately, those bad old days are over, at least where Outlook Express is concerned. You can import address books from several different e-mail programs into the Address Book. Likewise, you can export your Address Book to a file many other e-mail programs can import and use in their address books.

Importing an address book

To import an address book from another e-mail program into your Address Book, follow these steps:

1. Choose File ➪ Import ➪ OtherAddress Book from the Address Book or the main Outlook Express menu bar.

2. When the Address Book Import Tool dialog box appears, click the import format you want. Your choices are shown in Figure 8-39.

3. Click Import.

4. Respond to any dialog boxes that appear next. The prompts will depend upon your choice for the import format in Step 2.

5. When you see the message "Address book import has completed successfully," click OK and then click Close to exit the Address Book Import Tool dialog box.

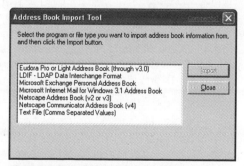

Figure 8-39: The Address Book Import Tool dialog box

Tip

When you import address books (or vCards), Outlook Express will check to see whether an address you're importing already exists in your Address Book. If it does, you'll be asked whether you want to replace the old entry with the new one. Choose Yes to replace the old entry or No to keep it.

The next time you open your Address Book, it will include any addresses you had before, plus all the addresses you imported.

Exporting your address book

Exporting your Address Book to a format another e-mail program can use is equally easy:

1. Choose File ➪ Export ➪ Address Book from the Address Book or the main Outlook Express menu bar.

2. When the Address Book Export Tool dialog box appears, click the export format you want. Your choices are Microsoft Exchange Personal Address Book and Text File (Comma Separated Values). Most e-mail programs can import comma-separated value text files if they can import any files at all. Click Export.

3. Respond to any additional dialog boxes that appear. The prompts will depend on your choice for the export format in Step 2.

4. When you see the message `Address book export has completed successfully`, click OK and then click Close to exit the Address Book Export Tool dialog box.

Importing and exporting vCards

VCards — or business cards in Outlook Express parlance — are a standardized electronic business card that can be exchanged between e-mail, address book, communications, personal planner, and other types of programs. vCards can even be exchanged between different types of devices and platforms, including desktop computers, laptops, personal digital assistants (PDAs), and telephony equipment. Thus, vCard files (which have a .vcf file extension) offer a flexible, universal format — something like Esperanto for the computerized address book world.

Outlook Express can import and export vCard files with ease. (Unfortunately, you can import or export just one vCard at a time, not an entire address book. Oh, well.)

Note

Importing a vCard file adds the file's information as an entry in your Address Book. Exporting a vCard creates a vCard file from an entry in your Address Book (you can send that vCard file to other digital devices and operating systems that accept them). You also can add vCards as signatures to outgoing messages, as explained in the section "Setting up an automatic signature," later in this chapter.

Importing from vCards

Follow these steps to import an address from a vCard file into your Address Book:

1. Open the Address Book.
2. Choose File ⇨ Import ⇨ Business Card (vCard) from the menu bar.
3. When prompted for a filename, locate and double-click the vCard file you want to import.

The selected address appears in a Properties dialog box like the one you use to create new e-mail addresses. Enter any additional information you want on the Personal, Home, Business, Other, NetMeeting, or Digital IDs tab, and then click OK. Voila! The new address appears in your Address Book.

Exporting to vCards

To export an address from your Address Book to a vCard file, follow these steps:

1. Open the Address Book.
2. Select the address you want to export. You can select only one address and groups aren't allowed.
3. Choose File ⇨ Export ⇨ Business Card (vCard) from the menu bar.
4. When prompted for a filename, type a filename for the address (for example, alan) and choose a drive and folder location, if you wish. You can omit the .vcf extension because Outlook Express will add it automatically.
5. Click Save.

The selected address is saved in vCard format to the location you specified in Step 4.

Personalizing Outlook Express

You can personalize both the appearance and behavior of Outlook Express to your liking. First I'll describe ways to customize the Outlook Express window. Then I'll explore ways to change the program's behavior, to create folders, and to filter incoming messages using the Inbox Assistant.

Customizing the Outlook Express window

Throughout this chapter, I've shown you examples of the Outlook Express window in which the Outlook bar, folder list, folder bar, tip of the day, toolbar, status bar, preview pane, and preview header are visible. The toolbar buttons include explanatory text, the message text appears in a medium-sized font, and the preview pane appears below the messages. You'll probably find the default setup easiest to use, but you certainly can change things, if you like.

Choosing what appears in the window

You can use options on the View menu of the main Outlook Express window to choose which features appear on-screen. The options are controlled by the Window Layout Properties dialog box, shown in Figure 8-40. To open this dialog box, choose View ⇨ Layout from the main Outlook Express menu bar.

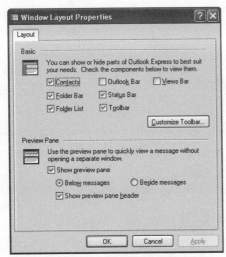

Figure 8-40: These are the options for the Window Layout Properties dialog box. Choose View ⇨ Layout to get here.

Arranging the preview pane

The preview pane enables you to preview your message by clicking it in the message list. You can hide the preview pane altogether or display it below messages or beside them. To begin, choose View ⇨ Layout from the main Outlook Express menu bar. Then, in the Window Layout Properties dialog box, do any of the following:

✦ To display the preview pane, check Show Preview Pane; to hide the preview pane, uncheck Show Preview Pane. When the preview pane is hidden, you must double-click a message in the message list to read it.

✦ To split the window so the preview pane appears next to the messages (see Figure 8-41), check Show Preview Pane and choose Beside Messages.

✦ To split the window so the preview pane appears below the messages (as shown throughout this chapter, except in Figure 8-41), check Show Preview Pane and choose Below Messages.

✦ To display or hide the preview pane header (the gray band above the message in the preview pane), check Show Preview Pane and check or uncheck Show Preview Pane Header.

✦ When you finish making changes, click OK.

Resizing the lists, panes, and columns

You can resize the lists, preview pane, or columns for easier viewing of the information they contain. Here's how:

1. Move the mouse pointer to the dividing line for the pane or the column you want to resize. The mouse pointer changes to a two-headed arrow.

2. Click and hold the left mouse button and drag the mouse in the direction of the arrows.

3. When the pane or the column is the size you want, release the mouse button.

That's it! If you don't like the results, simply repeat these three steps.

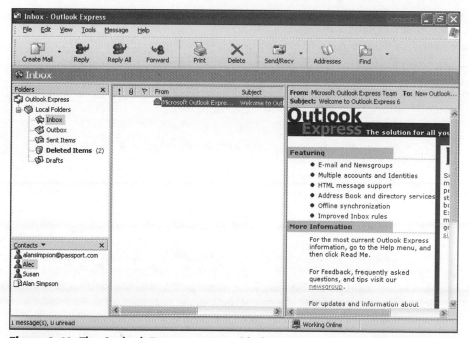

Figure 8-41: The Outlook Express screen with the preview pane displayed next to the messages

Configuring columns in the message list

In addition to resizing the columns, you can add or remove columns in the message list or reposition them by following these steps:

1. Choose View ➪ Columns from the main Outlook Express menu bar. You'll see the Columns dialog box, shown in Figure 8-42.

Figure 8-42: Use the Columns dialog box to configure columns.

2. Do any of the following:

   - To add a column to the message list, select the column you want to add.

   - To remove a column from the message list, deselect it.

   - To reposition a column in the message list, click its name and then click Move Up or Move Down as needed (this moves the column heading to the left or right, respectively, in the actual message list).

   - To return to the default columns for the message list, click the Reset button.

3. Click OK.

The new list of columns will appear in the Outlook Express message list. If necessary, you can resize the columns as explained in the previous section.

Tip

If you only want to reposition an existing column, you can skip the Columns dialog box altogether and use the drag-and-drop technique. That is, drag the column button left or right along the top of the message list until the column is where you want it, and then release the mouse button.

Customizing the toolbar

The main Outlook Express toolbar is customizable. You can add or remove its buttons, change its position, and choose whether to display its text labels. To begin, go to the main Outlook Express window and choose View ➪ Layout and click the Customize Toolbar button.

You'll see the Customize Toolbar dialog box shown in Figure 8-43. The techniques for customizing the toolbar buttons are similar to those for customizing the columns in the message list. You can double-click a button under Available Toolbar Buttons to add it to the toolbar or double-click a button under Current Toolbar Buttons to remove it. To reposition a button, click it under Toolbar Buttons and then click the Move Up or Move Down button as needed. Anytime you want to return to the default toolbar, click Reset. You can experiment with the alignment options and turn the text labels on and off by clicking the option you want. When you finish making changes, click Close.

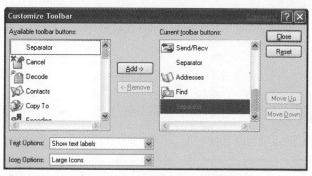

Figure 8-43: The Customize Toolbar dialog box

Tip   As a shortcut, you can drag the items from the Available Toolbar Buttons list in the Customize Toolbar dialog box to the Current Toolbar Buttons list and vice versa. You also can drag items in the Toolbar Buttons list up or down to reposition them.

Customizing the default mail options

Tons of options exist for customizing the way Outlook Express behaves, and most of them are available from the Options dialog box. To open this dialog box, choose Tools ➪ Options from the main Outlook Express menu. Next, click the tab you want to use, change the settings as needed, and then click OK to save your changes. In the following sections, we look at the General, Send, Read, and Connection tabs in the Options dialog box.

Tip

You can learn more about any option in the Options dialog box. Simply select the tab you want to use, click the question mark (?) button at the upper-right corner of the dialog box, and then click the option puzzling you. A description appears near the mouse pointer. To clear the description, press Esc.

General options

The General tab of the Options dialog box offers features that don't fall neatly into any other category (hence, the name General). As Figure 8-44 shows, all the options are toggles: When you check them, the feature is turned on; when you uncheck them, the feature is turned off. For example, you can choose whether to play a sound when new messages arrive, whether to check for new messages automatically (and how often to check), whether to empty deleted messages from the Deleted Items folder when you exit Outlook Express, and whether to put e-mail addresses of people you reply to in your Address Book automatically.

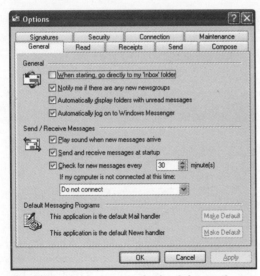

Figure 8-44: The General tab of the Options dialog box

Cross-Reference

The tabs in the Options dialog box contain some options that apply to e-mail and others that apply to newsgroups (the topic of Chapter 9).

Send options

Figure 8-45 shows the Send tab of the Options dialog box. As you can see, the Mail Sending Format area on this tab controls the format of messages you send. Check or clear the boxes as needed.

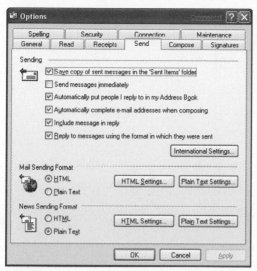

Figure 8-45: Use the Send tab of the Options dialog box to specify your sending options.

The default format for sending mail is HTML, but you can select either HTML or Plain Text in the Mail Sending Format area and then click the appropriate Settings button to change the settings as needed.

Tip   If you want to change the format of a message on which you're currently working, choose Format ➪ Rich Text (HTML) or Format ➪ Plain Text from the menu bar on the New Message, Reply, or Forward windows.

Read options

The options on the Read tab of the Options dialog box (see Figure 8-46) control what happens when Outlook Express delivers new messages from your service provider. You can choose whether to mark previewed messages as read and how long to wait before marking them. You also can choose the font used to display your messages.

Figure 8-46: Use the Read tab of the Options dialog box to specify incoming message options.

Connections options

The Connection tab of the Options dialog box, shown in Figure 8-47, makes life easier for people with modem connections to the Internet. From here, you can specify which connection to use. You also can choose whether you want Outlook Express to warn you to cancel a connection that isn't working (if you have more than one dial-up networking connection) and whether to hang up automatically when sending, receiving, or downloading messages.

Setting up an automatic signature

Outlook Express can automatically insert a signature at the bottom of your messages, which will save you time and trouble. To use the automatic signature options, choose Tools ➪ Options from the Outlook Express menu bar and select the Signatures tab, shown in Figure 8-48. Now, click the New button to enable the Edit signature box, shown in Figure 8-49. Choose the options you want, as described in the list that follows. When you finish, choose OK.

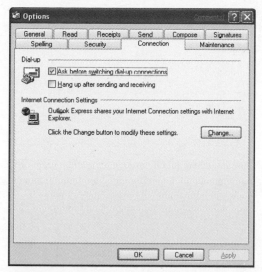

Figure 8-47: The Connection tab of the Options dialog box enables you to control your modem options.

Figure 8-48: The Signatures tab of the Options dialog box

Figure 8-49: The Signature tab box, after I filled in a Text signature

You can choose any of these Signature options:

✦ **Add signatures to all outgoing messages:** When checked, the signature text appears at the bottom of outgoing messages. When unchecked, the automatic signature does not appear and you must sign the messages yourself.

✦ **Don't add signatures to Replies and Forwards:** When checked, the signature text is not added to replies and forwards. When unchecked, it is added to replies and forwards.

✦ **Text:** When selected, the automatic signature uses text you typed in the box next to the Text option.

✦ **File:** When selected, the automatic signature uses text in the file specified next to the File option. (You can use the Browse button to help locate and insert the filename.) The signature file can be a text file (.txt) or an HTML file (.htm or .html).

Of course, you insert signatures and business cards automatically, as described here. You also can insert them manually anytime you like:

✦ If you set up a signature text or file, you can manually insert your signature in a message. Starting from the New Message, Reply, or Forward window, position the insertion point where the signature should appear in the editing area of your message. Then choose Insert ➪ Signature from the menu bar.

✦ If you set up a personal business card (vCard), you can insert it manually by choosing Insert ➪ My Business Card from the message window menu. The vCard icon will appear below the stamp icon in the message window. (To remove the vCard, choose Insert ➪ My Business Card again. The vCard icon will disappear.)

Tip   If you attach a vCard to your message or you receive a message with an attached vCard, the vCard appears in your message as a Rolodex card icon with a big V on it. You can then click or right-click the vCard icon and choose Open or Delete from the shortcut menu that appears.

Choosing custom stationery

People using snail mail (the slow stuff delivered by the post office) often pride themselves on the fancy stationery they use. With Outlook Express, your electronic mail messages can use stationery just as fancy. Or, if you'd rather not use fancy stationery, you can compose your messages in any font installed on your computer.

Tip   The stationery and font options only work for messages composed in rich text (HTML) format, rather than plain text format.

To use the automatic stationery options, choose Tools ➪ Options and select the Compose tab in the Options dialog box. Now, choose any of the options that follow, and when you finish using the Options dialog box, click OK:

✦ **Compose Font:** Click the Font Settings button in the Compose Font area to select the font used for outgoing messages. When the Font dialog box appears, choose the Font, Font Style, Size, Effects, and Color options you want and choose OK.

✦ **Stationery:** Choose either Mail or News.

✦ **Select:** After choosing Mail or News, click the Select button to specify the stationery file you want to use for outgoing messages. You see the Select Stationery dialog box, shown in Figure 8-50. Now do any of the following and then click OK to return to the Stationery dialog box:

    • To select an existing stationery design, click its name in the Stationery list. A thumbnail view of the stationery appears in the Preview box.

    • To select a design stored in a rich text (HTML) file on your computer, click the Look in list box and then locate and double-click the filename you want. HTML files have a .htm or .html extension.

    • To edit a stationery design, click the design you want to edit in the Stationery list and then click the Edit button. When you finish editing, choose File ➪ Exit.

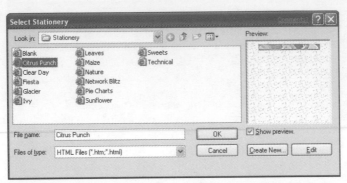

Figure 8-50: The Select Stationery dialog box appears when you click the Select button in the Options dialog box.

Tip   Before composing a new message, you can manually select a stationery file. Starting from the Outlook Express window, choose Message ➪ New Message Using and choose one of the stationery options listed. Or, choose Select Stationery and then locate and double-click the stationery file (.htm or .html) you want to use.

Leaving mail on the server

You already know how to customize your e-mail account settings by changing the settings in the mail account Properties dialog box, which opens when you choose Tools ➪ Accounts and double-click the name of the account you want to change. The Advanced tab in this dialog box offers a "Leave a copy of messages on server" option (see Figure 8-51). Most e-mail client programs have a similar option. As a general rule, if you use only one e-mail program, you'll want to leave this option deselected (unchecked) to keep mail from building up on your mail server.

If you use more than one program to check your e-mail, however, you should allow only one of those programs to remove the mail from the server. Otherwise, you may end up with some e-mail messages in one e-mail client program and some messages in another, which makes keeping track of messages difficult. If you choose to leave a copy of messages on the server, you also can choose when to delete the messages as Figure 8-51 shows.

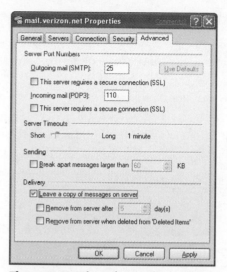

Figure 8-51: The Advanced tab of the mail account Properties dialog box enables you to choose whether to leave mail on your server and when to remove it.

Creating your own folders

Outlook Express automatically comes with the following folders for storing your e-mail messages:

✦ **Inbox:** Stores your incoming messages

✦ **Outbox:** Stores messages waiting to be sent

✦ **Sent Items:** Stores messages you already sent

✦ **Deleted Items:** Stores your deleted messages until you delete them manually or Outlook Express deletes them for you

✦ **Drafts:** Stores draft messages you've saved with the File ➪ Save command while composing them

Chances are, however, that you'll want to create some folders of your own to store copies of messages regarding specific projects or people. Folders offer a great way to organize your messages so you can find them easily.

Tip

When working with folders, be sure to display the folder list. If the folder list is not visible, choose View ➪ Layout, check Folder List, and click OK.

Creating folders is a breeze. Here are the steps to follow:

1. Starting from the main Outlook Express window, choose File ➪ Folder ➪ New from the menu. Or right-click any folder and choose New Folder from the shortcut menu. You'll see a Create Folder dialog box, as shown in Figure 8-52.

2. In the Folder Name box, type a name for the new folder.

3. Click the folder that should contain the new folder (that is, click the parent folder). If the parent folder is hidden within a higher-level folder, click the plus (+) sign next to the higher-level folders until you see the parent folder you want and then click the parent folder.

4. Click OK.

In Figure 8-52, I created a folder named News Project inside the Inbox folder. I typed the new folder name into the Folder Name box; then I clicked the Inbox folder and clicked OK.

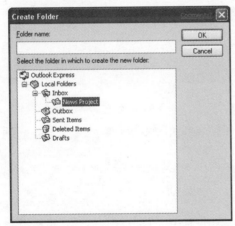

Figure 8-52: Creating a new folder named News Project below the Inbox folder

Using folders and subfolders

Any folders you create will appear in the folder list at the left side of the main Outlook Express window (top-level folders also will appear in the Outlook bar). Here's how to expand, collapse, and open a folder in the folder list:

✦ To expand a folder so its folders or subfolders are visible in the folders list, double-click the folder icon (for example, News Project, in Figure 8-53) or click the plus (+) sign next to the icon.

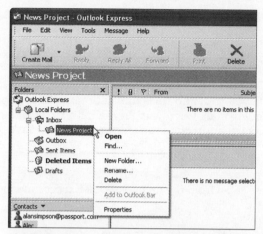

Figure 8-53: The News Project folder, which I right-clicked to display the shortcut menu

✦ To collapse a folder so its folders or subfolders are hidden, double-click the folder icon or click the minus (–) sign next to the icon.

✦ To open a folder so you can see its contents in the message list, click the folder icon (or right-click it and choose Open).

You can rename, delete, move, and copy any folder you create. Use the following techniques:

✦ To rename a folder, open the folder. Then right-click it and choose Rename, or choose File ⇨ Folder ⇨ Rename from the menu bar. Type a new folder name and click OK.

✦ To delete a folder and the messages it contains, open the folder. Then, press the Delete (Del) key on your keyboard or right-click the folder and choose Delete. You also can choose File ⇨ Folder ⇨ Delete from the menu bar. When prompted for confirmation, click Yes. (This action cannot be undone.)

✦ To move a folder and its contents to another folder, click the folder you want to move and drag it to the desired parent folder in the folder list.

Cross-Reference See "Working with several messages at once," earlier in this chapter, for information about moving and copying messages between folders.

Using message rules

Suppose someone has been sending you annoying e-mail messages and you want to delete that person's messages without reading them. Or, perhaps you want to move or copy certain messages automatically to specific folders. Or, maybe you want to send an automatic reply, such as

```
Gone fishin' and I won't be back until the twelfth of never.
```

to some or all of the messages you receive. All this and more is possible with a little help from message rules that enable you to set up rules and actions to take when Outlook Express delivers your incoming mail. Once you get the hang of using message rules (and it won't take long), you'll appreciate the amount of time it saves.

To add a new rule, follow these steps:

1. Choose Tools ⇨ Message Rules ⇨ Mail from the main Outlook Express menu bar.

2. Select conditions for your rule.

3. Select actions to take on messages that meet the specified conditions.

4. In the lower portion of the dialog box, click an underlined item and then edit it.

5. Click OK. You'll be returned to the Message Rules dialog box and your new rule will appear in the Description box, as shown in Figure 8-54.

You can repeat Steps 2–5 to set up as many rules as you need and you can adjust the rules, as I will explain in a moment. When you're happy with the list as it is, click OK. The next time you receive new messages, Outlook Express processes any messages that match the rules you set up.

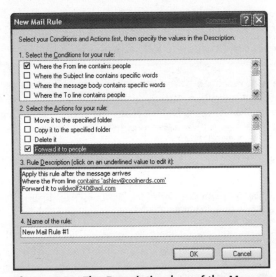

Figure 8-54: The Description box of the Message Rules after setting up some rules

Here are some points to remember about the message rules:

✦ Outlook Express processes only the rules checked in the rules list. It ignores rules that appear in the rules list, but aren't checked.

✦ If an incoming message matches more than one rule, Outlook Express will process it according to the first rule it matches and ignore the others. (Of course, if you've set up multiple actions in a single rule, Outlook Express will take all the actions you requested.)

You can adjust the rules in the Message Rules dialog box at any time:

✦ To turn off a rule temporarily, deselect (clear) the check box next to the rule. To turn the rule back on again, check the box once more. Turning off a rule and turning it back on is easier than removing the rule and re-creating it later.

✦ To remove a rule permanently, click it in the rules list and then click the Remove button.

✦ To change a rule, click it in the rules list and then click the Modify button (or double-click the rule's description). The Edit Mail Rule box will open and you can change any criteria or actions you want.

✦ To move a rule up or down in the Description list (and thus change the order in which the Inbox Assistant processes the rules), click the rule you want to move and then click the Move Up or Move Down button as needed.

Summary

Well, folks, that's about it for doing e-mail. As you've seen, Outlook Express is a powerful program that can simplify your electronic correspondence in dozens of ways. In the next chapter, we explore some more Internet goodies. But first, let's review the salient points covered in this chapter:

✦ Outlook Express comes with Windows XP and Internet Explorer and is installed automatically with those programs.

✦ To start Outlook Express from the Windows XP desktop, click the Start button and choose E-mail. Or, choose All Programs ➪ Outlook Express.

✦ To start Outlook Express from within Microsoft Internet Explorer, choose Tools ➪ Mail and News ➪ Read Mail.

✦ To configure Outlook Express to your own e-mail account(s), start Outlook Express and choose Tools ➪ Accounts. Click the Add button and choose Mail to add a new account.

✦ To compose a new mail message, click the Create Message button in its toolbar, or press Ctrl+N, or choose Message ⇨ New Message from the menu bar. You'll be taken to a New Message window where you can compose your message.

✦ To send a composed message, click the Send button in the New Message window, or choose File ⇨ Send Message from its menu bar. If you do not want to send the message immediately, choose File ⇨ Send Later instead (the message will be placed in the Outbox).

✦ To send all messages from the Outbox to their recipients, choose Tools ⇨ Send and Receive ⇨ Send and Receive All from Outlook Express's menu bar, or click the Send/Recv button on the toolbar.

✦ To check for new incoming mail, click the Send/Recv button on the Outlook Express toolbar. Be sure to select the Inbox folder in the folder list or Outlook bar.

✦ To read a message, click it. The message content appears in the preview pane of Outlook Express's window. If you prefer to open the message in a new window, double-click the message.

✦ You can reply to the message you're currently reading in two ways. If you want to reply to the author only, click the Reply button on the toolbar. Or, to reply to everyone who received this message, choose Reply to All on the toolbar.

✦ To delete the message you just read, click the Delete button on the toolbar.

✦ To create and use an address book, click the Windows XP Start button and choose All Programs ⇨ Accessories ⇨ Address Book. Or, if you're already in Outlook Express, click the Address Book button on the toolbar, or press Ctrl+Shift+B.

✦ To personalize the appearance of the Outlook Express window, choose View ⇨ Layout from Outlook Express's menu bar.

✦ To personalize the way Outlook Express operates, choose Tools ⇨ Options or Tools ⇨ Accounts.

✦   ✦   ✦

Participating in Usenet Newsgroups

Usenet is a popular service on the Internet that enables people who share a similar interest to post messages to one another. The "rooms" where people post their messages are called *newsgroups*. That name is a little strange, however, because few of the rooms have anything to do with what most of us consider "news." Instead, each newsgroup just focuses on a particular subject. People who know the subject, who are interested in the subject, or who are just looking for answers to a specific question about that subject make up the members of the newsgroup. When you seek a specific answer to a specific question, finding an appropriate newsgroup can take you straight to the people who can answer that question.

Newsgroup Buzzwords

Like all things computerish, newsgroups have their own concepts and terminology, as follows:

+ Each message in a newsgroup is officially called an article, although I'll stick with the term *message* in this book. An article or message might also be called a *post*.

+ A series of messages that originate from a single post is called a *thread*. For example, if I post a question and 9 people answer with messages of their own, those 10 messages constitute a thread.

+ Many newsgroups are *moderated* by people who screen messages for suitability to the newsgroup. Others are *unmoderated*, and messages pass through to the newsgroup unscreened (and uncensored).

✦ *Lurking* is hanging around a newsgroup to see what's being said without actually contributing anything. When you're new to a newsgroup, lurking for a while is a good idea, just to get an idea of what subject matter the group thinks is appropriate.

✦ *Flaming* is sending nasty messages to people in the group. If you post irrelevant messages to a group, you might get flamed! Anything that smacks of advertising in a newsgroup will surely result in flame mail directed at you!

✦ *Spamming* is sending blatant advertisements or sneaky ads disguised as newsgroup messages to a newsgroup. Highly unacceptable!

✦ *Netiquette* is observing proper newsgroup etiquette by not sending irrelevant comments and not spamming the group. A good *netizen* (network citizen) follows proper netiquette.

Newsgroups come and newsgroups go, and some aren't accessible on every newsgroup server. So don't be concerned if a newsgroup you read about in this book has disappeared by the time you sign on or if it is simply is unavailable.

Caution   Some newsgroups contain offensive material. Please do not let your kids wander newsgroups (or any other part of the Internet) unsupervised!

Each newsgroup discusses topics in a specific category. Newsgroup names reflect a hierarchy, starting with the least specific category and ending with the most specific one, as you read from left to right. A period (.) separates each subcategory from the next. For example, there's a newsgroup named `alt.humor.puns`. The *alt* stands for *alternative* and represents a wide range of newsgroups that deal in "alternative" subject matter. The remainder of the name is self-explanatory (unless you happen to feel that `humor.puns` is an oxymoron). Table 9-1 presents some examples of top-level categories.

Table 9-1
Some Newsgroup Main Categories, Descriptions, and Names

Main Category	Description	Sample Newsgroup Names
alt	Alternative topics	`alt.humor.puns,` `alt.pets.rabbits, alt.test`
bionet	Biology	`bionet.microbiology,` `bionet.mycology`
biz	Business	`biz.comp.hardware,` `biz.comp.software`
comp	Computers	`comp.human-factors, comp.jobs`
humanities	Arts and humanities	`humanities.classics,` `humanities.music`

Main Category	Description	Sample Newsgroup Names
misc	Miscellaneous	`misc.books.technical,` `misc.computers.forsale`
news	Usenet news network	`news.announce.newusers,` `news.answers`
rec	Recreation, arts, and hobbies	`rec.food.drink.coffee,` `rec.food.chocolate`
sci	Science	`sci.agriculture.beekeeping,` `sci.bio.food-science`
soc	Social topics	`soc.culture.punjab,` `soc.geneology.surnames`
talk	Debates, opinions	`talk.environment,` `talk.politics`

Setting Up Your Newsgroup Account

In this chapter, I assume you'll be using Outlook Express for all your newsgroup needs. Furthermore, I assume you've already set up Outlook Express for e-mail, as discussed in Chapter 8. As I discuss later in this chapter, however, there are plenty of newsgroups that you can access right through your Internet Explorer Web browser. So if you have any problems here, see the section titled "Doing Newsgroups with Internet Explorer," later in this chapter.

To set up Outlook Express as your newsreader, you need the name of the newsgroup server provided by your ISP. That should be included in the other account information they gave you, as discussed under "What You Need to Connect to the Internet" in Chapter 5. With that information handy, you're ready to get started:

1. If your computer doesn't have an "always on" connection to the Internet, go ahead and connect through your dial-up account now.

2. Start Outlook Express. Typically you can do this by clicking the Windows Start button and choosing E-Mail from the Start button. Otherwise, click the Start button and choose All Programs ⇨ Outlook Express.

Tip

If you want to add an e-mail option to your Start menu, right-click the Start button and choose Properties. Then click the Customize button. Choose E-mail under Show in Start Menu on the General tab. For more information, see "Reorganizing Your Start Menu" in Chapter 13.

3. Choose Tools ➪ Accounts from Outlook Express's menu bar. The Internet Accounts dialog box opens.

4. Click on the News tab.

5. If you see any accounts listed, somebody (or some program) has already configured Outlook Express for a news server. If that's the case, you can click the Close button to close the Internet Accounts dialog box. Then go straight to the section titled "Subscribing to Newsgroups."

6. Click the Add button and choose News. A wizard opens.

7. Answer each question posed by the wizard and then click the Next button. When you get to the page that asks for the name of your news server, make sure you enter it exactly as provided by your ISP. It will consist of three parts separated by dots, such as `news.myisp.net` or `nntp.someserver.net`.

After you've answered all the questions posed by the wizard you'll see the account name listed on the News tab of Internet accounts. You can then click the Close button in the Internet Accounts dialog box. When you do, you'll see a message asking whether you'd like to download newsgroups. Choose Yes. When the download is complete, you'll be taken to the Newsgroup Subscriptions dialog box, discussed next. You need not concern yourself with subscribing right now. You can close that dialog box if you want.

Subscribing to Newsgroups

After you've added a newsgroup server to your Internet accounts, Outlook Express will display its name in the list of folders at the left edge of the window. (If you don't see that list, choose View ➪ Layout from the Outlook Express menu bar. Then choose the Folder List icon and click the OK button.) In Figure 9-1, for example, the `news4.bellatlantic.net` item at the bottom of the Folders list is a newsgroup server. For future reference, keep in mind that whenever you want to interact with newsgroups, you'll just need to click the newsgroup server name in the Folders list. If you haven't subscribed to any newsgroups on that server, you'll be given the option to subscribe the first time you click the server name. You can view a list of available newsgroups and subscribe by right-clicking the newsgroup server name and choosing Newsgroups from the menu that appears.

Tip   Don't worry; you can instantly change Outlook Express back to your e-mail program by clicking Inbox under Local Folders in the leftmost pane.

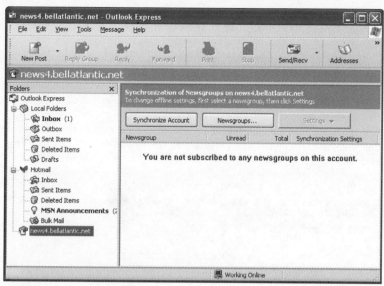

Figure 9-1: Clicking the name of your newsgroup server, or any newsgroup, instantly changes Outlook Express to a newsreader.

To interact with a newsgroup, you need to *subscribe* to it. This is nothing like a magazine subscription. It won't cost you anything, you won't be bombarded with renewal notices, and you can unsubscribe at any time. Subscribing to a newsgroup just places a quick link to the newsgroup beneath the news server name in the left column of Outlook Express and also downloads messages from the newsgroup to your computer so that you can start interacting.

To see what kinds of newsgroups are available on your news server, first make sure you've clicked your newsgroup server name in the Folders list. Then click the Newsgroups button in the pane on the right. The Newsgroups Subscriptions dialog box opens, displaying a list of all the newsgroups available to you. You can scroll through the list if you like. It is probably going to be quite lengthy. Optionally, you can type any word (or words) that describe the subject matter you're interested in. The list changes to include only newsgroups whose names contain that word (or words).

You can broaden your search by having Internet Explorer search both the newsgroup names and their descriptions. Just choose the Also Search Descriptions check box. If you've never downloaded the descriptions, you may have to wait a few minutes for the download to be completed.

Figure 9-2 shows an example where I've searched for the term *new user*. The list now contains only newsgroups that have that work in their name or description. To subscribe to a newsgroup, just click its name in the list, and then click the Subscribe button. Newsgroups to which you've described gain a little icon next to their name. In Figure 9-2, for instance, I've subscribed to the news.newusers.questions newsgroup. This is a good newsgroup for people who are newsgroup beginners.

Tip   Not all newsgroups have descriptions. To see any that are available, however, choose the Also Search Descriptions check box, as in Figure 9-2. If prompted to download descriptions, choose Yes.

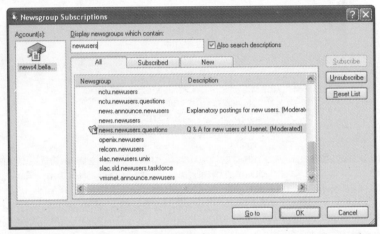

Figure 9-2: Here I've subscribed to the news.newusers.questions newsgroup.

You can subscribe to as many newsgroups as you want. When you've finished, just click the OK button near the bottom of the Newsgroup Subscriptions dialog box.

Viewing Newsgroup Messages

To see what's happening in a newsgroup, just click its name in the Folders list. Any new messages since your last visit (if any) will be downloaded to your computer and displayed in the pane on the right. (That may take a couple of minutes, depending on the speed of your connection). In Figure 9-3, for example, I've clicked the news.newusers.questions newsgroup in the Folders list.

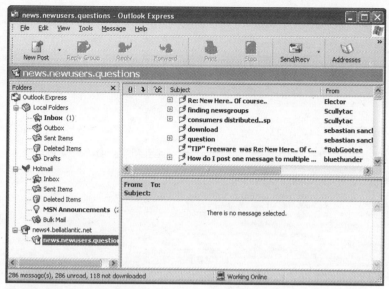

Figure 9-3: Seeing what's up in the `news.newusers.questions` newsgroup

The top pane shows message *headers*, where the header for each message is just its subject line, who sent the message, when the message was sent, and the size of the message. Notice that some message headers have a plus sign (+) next to them. Each such message is the beginning of a thread — perhaps a question that was asked by one of the newsgroup members. Clicking that plus sign reveals the rest of the messages in the thread — typically answers to the question posed by whomever sent the initial message. Messages that you've never read will be shown in **boldface**. Clicking a message header reveals the body of the message in the lower pane. Within a few seconds after you've clicked, the boldface in the message header will fade.

Tip

> To arrange message headers into chronological order, click the Sent column heading. Each time you click a particular heading, the sort order reverses. Hence, if the first click puts the headers in oldest-to-newest order, the next click will put them in newest-to-oldest order.

You can search through existing messages to see whether anybody has already brought up whatever's on your mind. If you're thinking of asking a question, for example, the answer might already be posted somewhere in the current messages. To find out, you can search through existing messages by clicking the Find button on the toolbar, or by choosing Edit ➪ Find ➪ Message from the menu bar. The Find Message dialog box opens, as shown in Figure 9-4.

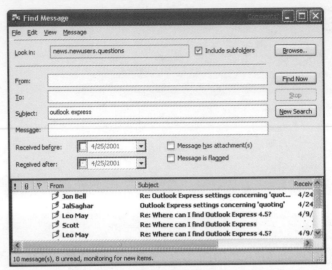

Figure 9-4: The Find Message dialog box

The dialog box offers many ways to search (although that's largely because it's the same dialog box you can use to search for e-mail messages). In a newsgroup, you will probably want to search through subject lines and messages. In Figure 9-4, for example, I've opted to search message subjects for the words *outlook express*. Click the Find Now button when you're ready to begin your search. The Find Message dialog box will expand to list messages (if any) that match your search criteria. For instance, you can see messages that have the words *outlook express* in their subject lines in the lower half of Figure 9-4. To read any found message, just double-click it in the lower pane. To close the Find Message dialog box, click its Close (X) button.

Posting a Newsgroup Message

If you have a question for the newsgroup, click the New Post button in the toolbar, or choose Message ➪ New Message from the menu bar. You'll come to the New Message dialog box shown in Figure 9-5. Be sure to type a *meaningful* subject into the subject line, because this is what appears as the message header. Most other newsgroup members will read the subject before deciding whether to open the message. Then type in your message, just as you would type an e-mail message. If you want to check the spelling before you send the message, choose Tools ➪ Spelling from the menu bar.

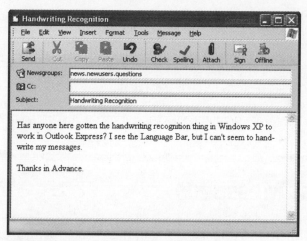

Figure 9-5: The New Message dialog box

When you've finished composing your message, just click the Send button. A dialog box will appear, telling you how the message will be handled. If Outlook Express isn't set up to send messages immediately, you'll see a dialog box telling you that the message will be placed in your Outbox and won't be sent until you click the Send and Receive (Send/Recv) button. You'll need to click the OK button and then click the Send and Receive button in Outlook Express to actually send the message. (Alternatively, you can click the little arrow on the button and choose Send All if you want to just send without receiving.)

If Outlook Express is set up to send messages immediately, you'll see a dialog box telling you that the message is being sent; remember, however, that it might not be visible right away. If the message doesn't appear soon, however, you might want to synchronize your PC with the news server, as discussed later in the section "Getting the Latest Messages."

Tip As when you're composing e-mail messages, the Language bar will appear when you are composing newsgroup messages. As discussed in Chapter 15, you can use speech or handwriting recognition to compose the message.

Replying to Newsgroup Messages

If you read a message and decide to post a reply, you can do so in a couple of ways:

✦ **Reply Group:** Your message is sent to the news server, and all newsgroup members can see it.

✦ **Reply:** Your message is sent to the poster's e-mail message, where only she will see your response.

To choose a reply option, click the Reply Group or Reply button on the toolbar. Alternatively, right-click the message to which you want to reply and choose Reply to Group or Reply to Sender. You'll be taken to the standard dialog box for composing messages. Just type in your message and click the Send button. Replies are handled in the same way as new posts are. After all, replies are messages as well. Therefore, when you click the Send button, you'll see a dialog box telling you how the message will be handled. If you don't see your reply for a while after sending it, you might want to synchronize your computer with the server, as discussed in the next section.

Getting the Latest Messages

When you post a message or a reply, you may not see your message right away in the newsgroups messages. There are several reasons for this — some of them on the server side where the messages are located. Those, you can do nothing about. You can ensure that you can download new messages at any time, however, just to make sure you have what's on the server. More often than not, your posts will be visible as soon as the new messages have been downloaded. To bring messages from the current newsgroup up-to-date, follow these steps:

1. In the Folders list, click the name of the newsgroup you want to bring up-to-date.

2. Choose Tools ➪ Synchronize Newsgroup from the Outlook Express menu bar.

3. In the Synchronize Newsgroup dialog box that appears, choose Get the Following Items. Then choose one of the following options:

   • **All Messages:** Gets all messages from the server. This can take a long time.

   • **New Messages Only:** Gets only those messages that aren't yet visible on your screen.

   • **Headers Only:** Downloads message headers only, which is quick. Remember, however, that clicking a message header does not reveal the body of the message. Instead, it only marks it for download. You need to repeat Steps 1 and 2 and then choose Get messages marked for download to see the bodies of the messages whose headers you click.

4. Click the OK button.

Keep in mind that if you want to view messages in chronological order, you need to click the Sent column heading to sort the message headers into ascending or descending order by date.

 Tip   To update messages for all your subscribed newsgroups, click the newsgroup server name in the Folders list and then click the Synchronize Account button.

You can adjust some additional settings to choose how all your messages — both e-mail messages and newsgroup messages — are handled. They're all available in the Options dialog box for Outlook Express, shown in Figure 9-6. To open that dialog box, choose Tools ➪ Options from the Outlook Express menu bar.

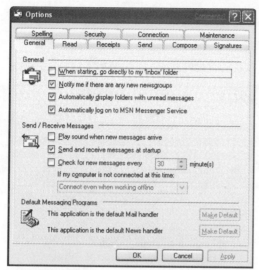

Figure 9-6: The Outlook Express Options dialog box

The Outlook Express Options dialog box enables you to set the following options:

✦ If you want messages to be updated automatically each time you start, choose the Send and receive messages at startup option on the General tab.

✦ If you want Outlook Express to update messages automatically, choose the Check for new messages every . . . option, and then specify how often you want Outlook Express to check. If you don't have an "always on" Internet connection, you also can choose whether you want the computer to dial in to your ISP when it's time to check for new messages.

✦ If you want your messages to be sent as soon as you click the Send button, choose the Send Messages Immediately option from the Send tab. If you don't choose this option, messages will be placed in your outbox until you click the Send and Receive button, or until you choose Tools ➪ Send and Receive from the menu bar.

Caution

The options discussed in this section apply to your e-mail messages as well. So if you don't want to change your current e-mail settings, don't make any changes to the settings described here.

Unsubscribing

If you find there are newsgroups that you're not using much and want to stop downloading their messages, just unsubscribe from the group. To do so, right-click the newsgroup's name in the Folders list and choose Unsubscribe. Alternatively, click the name of the newsgroup server and then click the Newsgroups button that appears. Click the Subscribed button, click the newsgroup name you want to leave, and then click the Unsubscribe button.

Newsgroups on the Web

Many newsgroups now make their homes on the Web. Sometimes they're called *message boards,* sometimes they're called *communities*. Regardless of what you call them, they all work on the same basic principal of posting messages to a server that all members of the group share. The main difference is that Web-based newsgroups don't require access to a news server, or even a newsreader such as Outlook Express. You can do everything you need to do right from your Web browser.

As an example, Figure 9-7 shows the list of "communities" available at `http://communities.microsoft.com`. To get there, just start Internet Explorer (not Outlook Express) to go to that URL. Because you'll be visiting a Web page, there's no telling exactly how it will look on the day you visit (although, in general, message boards work much the same as newsgroups). Your Web browser window will likely be divided into two or more panes. The top pane will show message headers. When you click a message header, the body of the message appears in the lower pane, just as in Outlook Express.

Along the top of the bottom pane, you'll see New Post, Post Reply, Subscription, and perhaps some other buttons, as in Figure 9-8. Use those buttons to post new messages, reply to existing messages, or subscribe/unsubscribe, just as you would in Outlook Express.

More On Outlook Express

This chapter and Chapter 8 cover a great many features of Outlook Express. Given the fact that this is a Windows book, however, and not an Internet or e-mail book, there's simply not enough space to cover every option in great detail. What you've learned here will certainly get you going with e-mail and newsgroups. In fact, you might never need to know anything more that what's presented in these chapters. If you do need more information, however, remember that Outlook Express has its own help system. Choose Help ➪ Contents and Index from the Outlook Express menu bar to access that help.

Figure 9-7: Home page of `http://communities.microsoft.com`

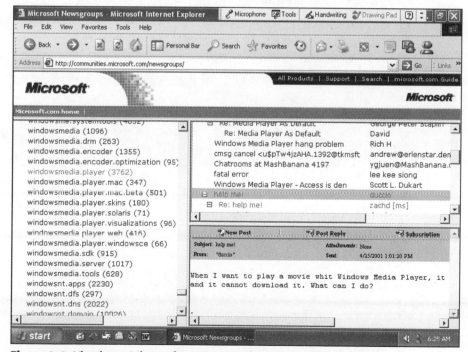

Figure 9-8: Viewing a Microsoft newsgroup through Internet Explorer

The Web offers some great ways to find newsgroup messages that deal with specific topics. If you have some burning question on your mind, you can often find the answer you're looking for just by searching through all the newsgroups through one of these services. Deja News at www.dejanews.com and America Online's Netfind at www.aol.com/netfind/newsgroups.html are great places to get started. Just use your Internet Explorer Web browser to visit either site. There you'll see instructions and options for searching through newsgroup messages. If you're lucky, you just might find that the question that's on your mind has already been answered in some newsgroup message(s).

Summary

In this chapter, you learned about Usenet newsgroups, yet another popular feature of the Internet. Here's a quick recap of the important points covered in this chapter:

✦ A newsgroup is a collection of messages sent to and from people who share an interest.

✦ You can use Outlook Express News to participate in Usenet newsgroups.

✦ To use Outlook Express as your newsreader, you must set up your account using the name of the news server as provided by your ISP.

✦ With Outlook Express as your newsreader, you can post messages and reply to messages using the same tools you use to create e-mail messages.

✦ Many communities and message boards on the Web provide newsgroup-like services, without the need for a news server or newsreader. Just use your Web browser instead.

✦   ✦   ✦

Windows Messenger, Games, and Such

You don't always have to be alone at a computer. Windows Messenger enables you to communicate with others who might be logged on as well. You also can use MSN Chat to meet up with others who share your interests in various chat rooms built around specific interests. And don't forget about the most important use of computers: games! You can join others online and compete in a wide range Internet games. This chapter introduces you to these features of Windows XP and steps you through the processes required to get started.

Setting Up a .NET Passport

To use some of the features described in this chapter and the next, you need to set up Microsoft .NET Passport. If you're thinking that sounds a little "fishy," it's really no big deal. All you're really doing is giving yourself a unique user name that identifies you on the MSN network, as well as other networks that support Microsoft Passports and Microsoft .NET Web services. It won't cost you anything and won't interfere with your existing ISP account or e-mail address. To set up a .NET passport, follow these steps:

1. Click the Start button and open Control Panel.

2. Open the User Accounts icon.

3. If your computer is set up for multiple user accounts, click your account name or picture.

4. Click Set up my account to use a .NET Passport.

5. Follow the instructions presented by the wizard.

The procedure is simple and self-explanatory. When you've finished, you'll be able to use the Windows Messenger program described in this chapter.

Starting Windows Messenger

An icon for Windows Messenger is usually visible in the Notifications area of the taskbar. If you see an *x* circled in red, that just means you're not signed in at the moment (or, you haven't set up your .NET Passport yet). To open Windows Messenger, you can do any of the following:

✦ Double-click the Windows Messenger icon in the Notifications area.

✦ Or, click that same icon and choose Open.

✦ Or, click the Start button and choose Windows Messenger.

Windows Messenger opens in a small window. If you're not signed in, you'll just see a prompt that says Click here to sign in. Just click that text to sign in. Once you're signed in, the window will look more like Figure 10-1. In that example, I've already set up some contacts, so your window won't look exactly like the example. But you can easily set up your own list of contacts, as described next.

Figure 10-1: The Windows Messenger window

Creating your contacts list

The next step is to create a contacts list — or "buddy list" as some services call it — of people with whom you want to interact online via the Messenger service. With the Windows Messenger window open on your screen, follow these steps to get started:

1. If the Windows Messenger indicates that you're not signed in, go ahead and click that blue underlined text to sign in.

2. Click the Add button in the Windows Messenger window. The Add a Contact Wizard starts.

3. Choose how you want to identify the contact. If you know the person's e-mail address or sign-in name, for example, choose the first option. If you don't know that, choose the second option. Then click the Next button.

4. Follow the instructions presented by the wizard to add a contact.

After you've set up at least one contact, you will see which of your contacts are currently online (and which are not) when you start Windows Messenger. For example, back in Figure 10-1 my contacts named Alec and Ashley are both online. The rest, listed below those names, are currently offline.

Starting a conversation

To communicate with one of your contacts, double-click the contact's name in the list. Alternatively, click the Send button and choose the contact's name from the menu that appears. In the Conversation window that appears, type a message in the lower text box. You can insert an *emoticon* (tiny picture) into your message by typing a series of characters. For example, typing :) displays a happy face. Table 10-1 lists the characters you type to insert emoticons. After typing your message, click the Send button to send it. The message moves the Conversation pane as in the example shown in Figure 10-2.

Tip　To see the actual emoticon pictures, choose Help ⇨ Help Topics from the Windows Messenger menu bar, and then choose Use Emoticons in Messages from the Web page that opens. Note that emoticons won't be visible until you press the Send button. If they still don't appear, choose Edit ⇨ Show Emoticons from the Conversation window's menu bar.

Figure 10-2: Preparing to send a message to Alec using the Conversation window

Table 10-1 Emoticons, and the Characters You'll Type to Display Them	
To Show	*Type*
Happy face	:-) or :)
Laughing	:-D or :D or :-d or :d or :-> or :>
Surprise	:-O or :o
Stick out tongue	:-P or :p
Wink	;-) or ;)
Sad	:-(or :(or :-< or :<
Puzzled	:-S or :S or :-s or :s
Angry	:-| or :|
Thumbs up	(Y) or (y)
Thumbs down	(N) or (n)
Love	(L) or (l)
Broken heart	(U) or (u)
Kiss	(K) or (k)
Gift	(G) or (g)

To Show	Type
Flower	(F) or (f)
Girl	(X) or (x)
Boy	(Z) or (z)
Camera	(P) or (p)
Beer	(B) or (b)
Martini	(D) or (d)
Phone	(T) or (t)
Cat	(@)
Coffee cup	(C) or (c)
Idea	(I) or (i)
Hot	(H) or (h)
Sleep	(S) or (s)
Star	(*)
Music	(8)
Envelope	(E) or (e)
Messenger icon	(M) or (m)
Vampire bat	:-[or :[

Click the Send button after you've finished typing your message. The recipient will see the message right away if he is in the Windows Messenger window. If that window isn't open, a notification will appear on his screen as in the example shown in Figure 10-3. Clicking the larger taskbar button to the left of the Notifications area will open the Conversation window. Now you can communicate with one another by typing in the lower window and clicking the Send button.

Tip   To choose a different font for your messages, click the Change Font option in the right pane, or choose Edit ⇨ Change from the Conversation window's menu bar.

Figure 10-3: What the recipient, Alec, might see when my message arrives

To get other contacts to join in the conversation, just click the Invite button and fill in the blanks as instructed. To end the session, just close the Windows Messenger dialog box. Alternatively, should you get a weirdo on the line whom you want to get rid of, just click the Block button to make her go away. Careful though — that person won't be able to reach you in the future, so don't block people you intend to communicate with later.

Tip   If the text in the conversation is too small to read, choose View ➪ Text Size from the Conversation window's menu bar, and try a larger text size.

Your "Do Not Disturb" option

If you don't want to receive messages, log off of the service. Then right-click the Windows Messenger icon in the Notifications area of the taskbar and choose Sign Out. Other people who have you listed as an online contact will then see you as being offline. The Windows Messenger icon in the Notifications area will display an *x* to indicate you're offline. When you want to sign back in, just right-click that icon and choose Sign In.

As an alternative to signing out, you can display a message that indicates you're away from the computer or busy. Right-click your Windows Messenger icon, choose My Status, and select an option from the submenu that appears (see Figure 10-4).

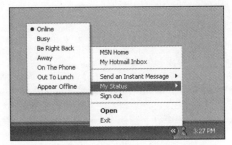

Figure 10-4: Choose any option to display your "status" in other peoples' contact lists.

Live voice and video

If your computer has a sound card and you have speakers and a microphone (or a headset) connected to your computer, you can switch to voice communications from the Conversation window. If you have a video camera (a "Web cam") connected, you can also view each other live. Just click the Start Camera and/or Talking button in the right pane. The first time you do this, a wizard will start to help you to make sure your equipment is configured correctly. Once you complete the wizard, your equipment should work just fine. Because the connection is going across the Internet rather than phone lines, you won't incur any long-distance charges.

Sending and receiving files

Once you're in a conversation with someone, you can send files to one another. To send a file, click the Send a File option in the right pane of the Conversation window. In the dialog box that appears, browse to the folder that contains the file you want to send. Then select the file by pointing to it (if you're using the single-click method to open icons), or by clicking it (if you're using "classic" style double-clicking), and then click the Open button in the dialog box.

The recipient will see a message indicating that you've sent the file. He will be given the option to accept or decline the file, along with all the standard "don't accept candy from strangers" type of warnings. When the recipient accepts the file, it is transferred. You (the sender) will see a message indicating when the transfer is complete. The recipient will see a message indicating that the file has been received, along with a link to the folder in which the file has been placed (typically the folder named My Received Files folder within that person's My Documents folder). Figure 10-5 shows an example where Alec has received a file named SurfPix.zip.

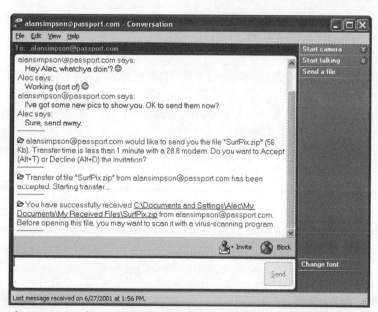

Figure 10-5: This contact has received a transferred file named SurfPix.zip.

Tip To send multiple files and speed transfers, consider using a compressed folder (a zipped file) as discussed under "Using Compressed Folders" in Chapter 12.

Saving "chats"

You can save an entire copy of your conversation ("chat") with someone, in case you ever need to refer to some information within that conversation later. To save a conversation:

1. Choose File ⇨ Save from the Conversation window's menu bar.

2. Optionally, navigate to the folder in which you want to place the conversation. Or, just use the suggested My Documents folder.

3. Enter a file name for the conversation, such as "Alec Conversation" and then click the Save button.

The conversation will be placed in a text (.txt) file. To review the conversation in the future, just navigate to the folder containing it using Windows Explorer. Then click (or double-click) the icon that represents the saved conversation.

More on Windows Messenger

As I write this chapter, Windows Messenger is still evolving. By the time you read this, the service might have many more features. To supplement what you've learned here, and to keep abreast of changes, use these resources:

✦ While you're in Windows Messenger, choose Help ⇨ Help Topics for help within that window.

✦ To see what version of the program you're currently using, choose Help ⇨ About Windows Messenger from its menu bar.

✦ For more general information about the service, use your Web browser to visit http://messenger.msn.com.

Chatting Online

MSN provides *chat rooms* in which people with common interests meet to chat. Chatting is a way to meet new people that share similar interests, get answers to burning questions, flirt, get into heated debates — whatever tickles your fancy. To get started with MSN Chat, you need to connect to the Internet in the usual manner. Then fire up Internet Explorer (or any other Web browser of your choosing), and visit the MSN Chat home page at http://chat.msn.com.

Right off the bat, you'll see some chat categories and rooms listed. Click any room that looks interesting, and you'll be taken to that chat room. You might need to download the current Chat component. If so, you'll see a message on the screen telling you so, and also how to do the download. You also might be asked to enter a nickname. You can type any nickname you like.

When you've finished downloading and answering any prompts, you'll be taken to your selected chat room. Figure 10-6 shows a sample chat room named Newbies, which, by the way, is a good place to get started.

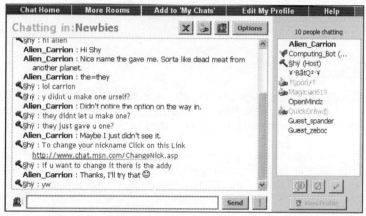

Figure 10-6: Entering a chat room

The large white pane on the left is where the conversations take place. The list of members to the right of that tells you how many people are in the chat room. A hammer icon represents the room's *host*—the person who runs the room. Some rooms have *bots* (sort of like robots) that scan incoming messages for inappropriate content (such as foul language) and prevent such messages from being displayed within the room. Everyone else in the list is currently a member of the room. The coffee cup icon indicates that a person is currently away from his keyboard.

Joining a conversation

Joining a conversation is easy. Just type whatever you want to say in the text box below the scrolling conversation. You can add any of the emoticons listed back in Table 10-1 just by typing the appropriate characters. The characters will be converted to the appropriate icon when you send the message. To send your typed message, click the Send button or press the Enter key. Your message appears on the screen preceded by your name, for all to see.

Whispering

You also can "whisper" to any one member so that only that person sees your message. To whisper, type your message normally. Then, in the members list, click the name of the person to whom you want to whisper. Optionally, you can whisper to several people by holding down the Ctrl key as you click member names. Then click the Whisper button below the list of member names. Only the selected member(s) will see your message.

If someone whispers to you, a button will blink in your Windows taskbar. Click that button to see the message in the Whisper box. You can continue to hold a private conversation with that person by typing your messages in the Whisper box. To return to the room at large, just close the Whisper box.

Taking action

You also can show "action," where your text appears in purple italicized text. Type your text, but don't include your name. For example, you might type "is thinking" or "is laughing hysterically." Then click the Action button rather than the Send button.

Tip   Chatters use some acronyms and abbreviations of their own. LOL means Laughing Out Loud. BRB means Be Right Back. NP means No Problem. K means OK. ROTFL means Rolling On The Floor Laughing, AWK means Away From Keyboard, and CYA means See Ya.

Ignoring pests

If anyone in the chat room gets on your nerves and you want to ignore that person, just click his name in the members list. Then click the Ignore button below the list. Optionally, you can just right-click the member's name in the list and choose Ignore. The symbol to the left of the member's name turns to an international "no" sign.

In some cases, when a member is sending a huge number of messages to you, Chat's auto-ignore feature will click in and start ignoring the person for you. Either way, after you've opted to ignore a member, that member's messages won't disturb you until you repeat the process to un-ignore him. That is, right-click that member's name and choose Ignore again.

Taking a break

As mentioned, a coffee cup icon indicates that the member is currently away from his keyboard or taking a break. If you want to take a break from your keyboard, just click the I'm Away button (which itself is labeled with a coffee cup icon) above the Conversation pane. Your name will then show the coffee cup icon in the members list.

Styling your chat

The Chat Options dialog box, shown in Figure 10-7, enables you to customize some features of Chat to your liking. To get to that dialog box, just click the Chat Room Options button above the Conversation pane. Change your nickname, the font and color used in your messages, or any of the other options to your liking. Then just click the OK button, as usual.

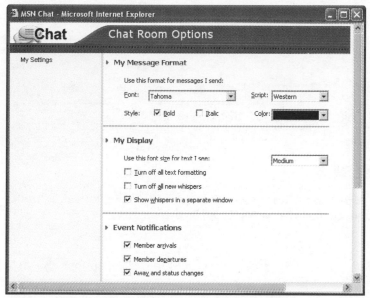

Figure 10-7: The Chat Options dialog box in MSN Chat

Creating Your Own Chat Room

To create your own chat room, navigate to the MSN Chat home page (http://chat.msn.com) and click the Create Your Own Chat Room option. You'll be taken to the options shown in Figure 10-8. As instructed, fill in the blanks, and then click the Go button. Note that when selecting a category, if you choose Unlisted, your chat room won't be listed under any of the categories in MSN's lists. Only people who know the exact name of your room will be able to join. This is a great way to use MSN Chat as you might use NetMeeting—to conduct a private meeting without outsiders joining in.

To invite people to your private chat room, tell them the exact name of your room, and have them browse to http://chat.msn.com. There they'll need to click the Join a Chat option in the left column of the page that opens. In the next page, have them type the exact name of your chat room and then click the Go button.

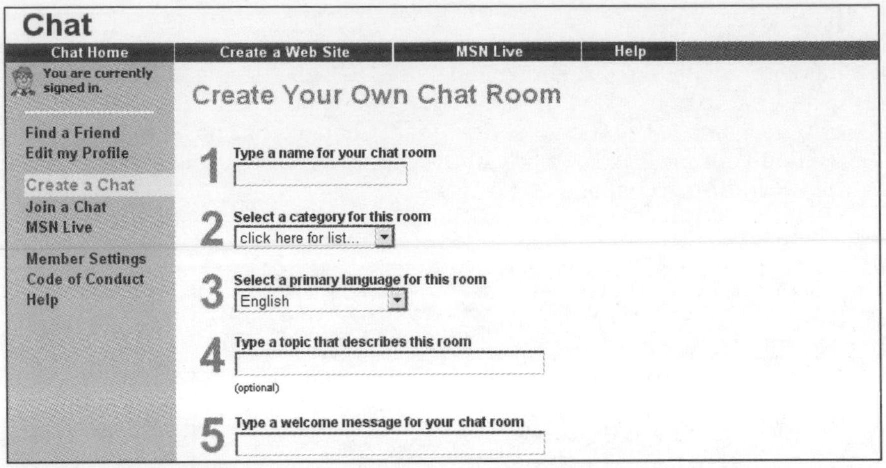

Figure 10-8: Web page for creating your own chat room

Fun and Games

The games that come with Windows XP are all available from the Games option on the Program menu. So to play a game, the steps are simple:

1. Click the Start button.

2. Choose All Programs ⇨ Accessories ⇨ Games to see the options shown in Figure 10-9.

3. Click the name of the game you want to play.

If the Games option isn't available on your Programs menu, or if you're missing any of the games shown in the figure, you can install them using the Windows Setup tab of Add/Remove programs. See Chapter 25 for details.

Some of the games, such as Solitaire, are meant to be played alone. When you open such a game, you'll often be taken to instructions on how to play the game. If the game you selected just displays the playing board, you can choose Help from that game's menu bar to learn how to play the game.

Other games are meant to be played online via the Internet. Those games, obviously, have the word *Internet* in their menu options. When you choose such a game, you'll likely be taken to a dialog box that introduces you to Zone.com — the MSN gaming zone. When you click the Play button, in that dialog box Windows will seek out other players for you. When it's time to play, the game board will open up, as in the example shown in Figure 10-10. You can use the Help option on the menu bar to learn more about the specific game you're playing.

Figure 10-9: Games that come with Windows XP

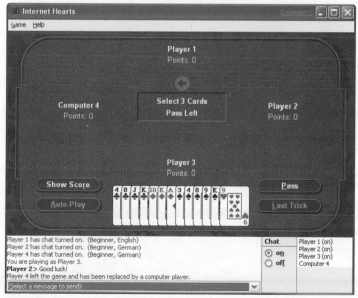

Figure 10-10: About to start a game of Internet Hearts

Chatting while gaming

Many Internet games give you the option to chat while playing. However, you're usually restricted to just a few phrases. For example, at the bottom of the Internet Hearts game board, you'll see the message Select a message to send in a drop-down list. To use chatting, first make sure the Chat option is turned on. Then select a message from the drop-down list. If any players speak some language other than the one you're using, those players will automatically see the message translated to their own language.

More fun at the Gaming Zone

The Internet games on the Windows XP Games menu are only a small selection of what's really available to play online. At the MSN Gaming Zone you'll find card games, adventures, sports, racing, and simulation games as well. In most cases, you can sign up for a game for free. Some games require subscriptions. However, you can usually use them for free on a trial basis. Note that you must be 13 or more years of age to play at the MSN Gaming Zone. To get to the Gaming Zone, open Internet Explorer, or any other Web browser, and go to http://zone.msn.com.

Summary

Here's a quick recap of the important points covered in this chapter:

✦ Setting up a .NET passport account will give you access to many of the features available through the Microsoft Network (MSN) and participating Web sites on the Internet.

✦ One such feature of a passport is Windows Messenger, which enables you to communicate in real-time with others on that network.

✦ The pages at http://chat.msn.com provides access to many popular chat rooms.

✦ To play games that came with Windows XP, click the Start button and choose All Programs ➪ Accessories ➪ Games.

✦ For more information on the larger world of online gaming, visit MSN's Gaming Zone at http://zone.msn.com.

✦   ✦   ✦

Online Conferencing with NetMeeting

Microsoft NetMeeting, which came with your copy of Windows XP, is one of the most powerful of all Microsoft Internet programs. Like Windows Messenger, NetMeeting enables you to communicate by chat, voice, and video, and also to transfer files via the Internet. But beyond that, you can use NetMeeting to conduct meetings, collaborate on projects, even take complete control of another computer from your own keyboard, mouse, and screen. It performs these feats of magic with the help of *Internet directory servers,* which you'll learn about in this chapter.

Gearing Up for NetMeeting

NetMeeting can work with many different directory servers on the Internet. In this chapter, I use the Microsoft Internet Directory server as an example. Before you get started with this chapter, you'll want to do two things (if you haven't already done them.) First, set up a .NET Passport, as described at the beginning of Chapter 10. Then set up a contacts list in Windows Messenger service, as described in Chapter 10. When you use NetMeeting with the Microsoft Internet Directory, the contact list you create for Windows Messenger will be the same as the list of people you can call through NetMeeting.

 Note Corporations can install a copy of NetMeeting server on their local area networks, for in-house conferencing. For more information on using NetMeeting in your business, see www.microsoft.com/windows/netmeeting.

If you plan to use voice and video with NetMeeting, be sure to install your microphone or headset, and/or or video camera (Web cam) as per the manufacturer's instructions. If you're mainly interested in using NetMeeting for collaboration or conferencing, you don't need those devices.

Starting NetMeeting

To start NetMeeting on your computer, click the Start button and choose All Programs ➪ Accessories ➪ Communications ➪ NetMeeting. The first time you start NetMeeting, you'll be taken to a wizard that helps you choose a directory server, identify yourself, and configure your audio gear. Like most wizards, it's self-explanatory. But don't worry if you're unable to complete each wizard page the first time through. You can always change whatever options you choose while in the wizard.

When you finish the wizard, the NetMeeting window opens on your desktop, looking something like Figure 11-1. Although its window is small, you'll be amazed at all the things you can do with this seemingly tiny program.

Figure 11-1: Microsoft NetMeeting

If you have a Web cam or other video recorder in place, but don't see a video image in the video frame (where the Windows NetMeeting logo appears in Figure 11-1), click the Start Video button just under that frame.

Placing a NetMeeting Call

Depending on how you responded to the wizard prompts the first time you ran NetMeeting, you may or may not be connected to a server as soon as NetMeeting starts. When you're logged on to a server, the tiny icon in the lower-right corner of NetMeeting's window has some color to it. If you're not logged on to a server, that icon is dim. If you need to log on, choose Call ⇨ Log On To *servername* from NetMeeting's menu bar. Then, the simplest way to place a call will be to go through the directory server, as follows:

1. Choose Call ⇨ Directory from NetMeeting's menu bar. The Find Someone dialog box opens. It lists online and offline contacts, as in Figure 11-2.

Figure 11-2: The Find Someone dialog box lists online and offline contacts.

2. Click the name of the person whom you want to call. You'll see a message stating that the person has been invited to join you in the call. The person you called will get notification of your incoming call in the dialog box shown in Figure 11-3.

Figure 11-3: The message that appears on the screen of the person you are calling

3. When the recipient accepts the call, NetMeeting displays the names of the people in the call, and the status bar shows `In a call`, as in Figure 11-4.

Figure 11-4: Alan Simpson and Alec Simpson in a NetMeeting call

Once you're in a call, use the three buttons below the video screen to fine-tune your audio and video settings. Pointing to a button, as always, displays the name of the button. You have the following choices:

✦ **Start/Stop Video:** If you have video capability, use this button to start or stop your video display.

✦ **Picture in Picture:** To show or hide your video output on your own screen, click this middle button. To view your own video in a separate window, choose View ➪ My Video (New Window) from NetMeeting's menu bar.

✦ **Participant List/Adjust Audio Volume:** You can switch between sliders for adjusting your microphone and speaker volume and a list of people currently participating in the call.

From here on out, the rest is easy. If both participants have sound capabilities, voice communications will start automatically and you can just start talking. If there's a problem, make sure the check boxes above the microphone and speaker sliders are selected, and their volumes are set comfortably. (If you see the participant list rather than the sliders, just click the Adjust Audio Volume button to view the sliders.) Use the leftmost of the first three buttons to start and stop video communications. The middle button enables you to see how your own image looks to the other person, if you have a Web cam attached.

You can invite others to join in your phone call as well. Just repeat the steps listed earlier to invite more people to join in. The names of all the people in the current call will be listed in the Name window. Be aware that you can communicate by voice or video with only one other person at a time. If several members are sending video images, for example, you can see only one person's video image. To choose which person's video you want to see, click her name in the list of people who are in the call. Likewise, to communicate by voice with one member, click that member's name in the list.

If you're planning to host a business conference online, you can set certain policies for the meeting, as described under "Hosting a Meeting" later in this chapter.

Ending a NetMeeting call

When you're ready to hang up, just click the Hang Up button. If you're viewing the participant list, you'll see it empty. The Not in a call indicator appears at the lower-left corner of NetMeeting's window when you're no longer in a call. And that, in a nutshell, is how you use the basic voice and video capabilities of NetMeeting. There are plenty of other tools and options to play around with though, as you'll learn in the sections that follow.

Audio/Video Tips

Before we get into more advanced features of NetMeeting, here are some useful tidbits that will help you get the most out of your voice and video calls. As mentioned, your computer needs a sound card, microphone (or headset), and speakers to use audio. Sound cards come in two basic "flavors," half-duplex and full-duplex. With half-duplex, the signal travels only one direction at a time. Therefore, only one person at a time can talk. Some of the early speakerphones used half-duplex. If you have experience with those, you know that the big downside to half-duplex is sound clipping. Each time one party starts talking, the first syllable or two tends to get cut off, which can really drive you crazy.

If your sound card is half-duplex, there's no way around the problem, except to replace your existing sound card with one that supports full-duplex. If your sound card has full-duplex (or if you're not sure whether it does or not) and you're getting sound clipping, confirm that the Enable full-duplex audio so I can speak while receiving audio option in NetMeeting is turned on. To do so, choose Tools ⇨ Options from NetMeeting's menu bar. Then click the Audio tab to get to the options shown in Figure 11-5. Check whether the Enable full-duplex audio so I can speak while receiving audio option is selected. If that option is disabled (dimmed), your sound card doesn't support full-duplex, and there's no way to turn full-duplex on.

The Audio tab in NetMeeting's Options dialog box is available only if your computer has audio capability.

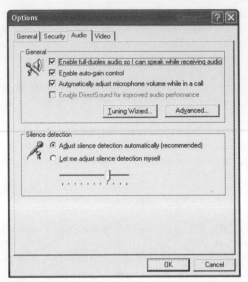

Figure 11-5: The Audio tab of NetMeeting's
Options dialog box

Other options on the Audio tab are summarized here. If an option is disabled in the dialog box, your sound card doesn't support that feature, and therefore it's not an option for you.

✦ **Enable auto-gain control:** Some sound cards offer an auto-gain feature that automatically adjusts the microphone volume as you speak. If your sound card offers this feature, selecting this option will make sure that NetMeeting uses that feature.

✦ **Automatically adjust microphone volume while in a call:** If your sound card does not support auto-gain, selecting this option will provide the equivalent of an auto-gain feature.

✦ **Enable DirectSound for improved audio performance:** If your sound system supports DirectSound, choosing this option improves performance by shortening the time between when audio is sent and received.

✦ **Tuning Wizard:** Runs the audio tuning wizard that appeared the first time you ran NetMeeting. The wizard can't be used while you're in a call.

✦ **Advanced:** Lets you choose a compression/decompression (codec) method for compressing sound. Choose this option only if you have some compelling reason to manually select a codec other than the default.

✦ **Silence detection:** Selecting automatic silence detection enables NetMeeting to filter out background noise automatically. If you prefer to adjust that yourself, choose the Let me adjust silence detection myself option, and then use the slider to increase or decrease silence detection.

While you're in a call, you can easily adjust audio settings without going to the Options dialog box. If you're currently viewing the participant list, click the Adjust Audio Volume button to view audio sliders. To turn off your microphone, clear the check box next to the microphone icon. To turn off your speakers, clear the check box next to the speaker icon. To adjust the volume of each, first make sure the item's check box is selected and then move the slider left or right to decrease or increase the volume.

NetMeeting video

Anybody who uses NetMeeting can receive video from another party. But you can send video only if you have a Web cam or other video device installed on your computer. Options for fine-tuning your video are on the Video tab of the Options dialog box shown in Figure 11-6. In NetMeeting, choose Tools ➪ Options from the menu bar, and then click the Video tab to get to those options. Note that if you don't have a video camera installed, most options will be disabled (dimmed).

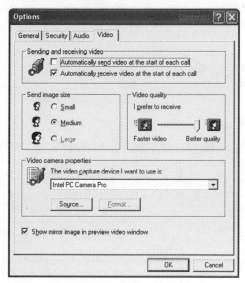

Figure 11-6: The Video tab in NetMeeting's Options dialog box

Your have the following options:

> ✦ **Automatically send video at the start of each call:** If selected, your video image is sent automatically as soon as the call starts. Otherwise, your video isn't sent until you click the Start Video button in NetMeeting, or choose Tools ➪ Video ➪ Send from the menu bar.

✦ **Automatically receive video at the start of each call:** If selected, a caller's video (if any) displays automatically. If not selected, a caller's video is hidden until you choose Tools ➪ Video ➪ Receive from NetMeeting's toolbar.

✦ **Send image size:** If selected, determines the size of the video image you're sending. Larger images require more bandwidth (connection speed) to transmit smoothly.

✦ **Video quality:** Bandwidth-hungry video can be smooth, or can have high picture quality, but not always both. The Video quality slider enables you to sacrifice picture quality for smoother motion if your bandwidth prevents you from having both qualities.

✦ **Video camera properties:** If you have multiple video devices attached to your computer, this option enables you to choose which device to use with NetMeeting. The Format and Tuning Wizard buttons work differently with different types of cameras.

✦ **Show mirror image in preview video window:** If selected, your image is reversed like a mirror, which we're accustomed to by experience with everyday mirrors. However, deselecting this option can actually speed video transmissions because NetMeeting doesn't have to "calculate" a mirror image from the actual image.

While you're in a call, you can do a lot more than just communicate with voice and video, as the following sections explain.

Chatting in NetMeeting

Chatting is a quick and easy way to communicate with others in a meeting. To chat, click the Chat button near the bottom of NetMeeting's window. Or choose Tools ➪ Chat from NetMeeting's menu bar. The Chat window opens, as in Figure 11-7, and its title bar indicates how many other people in your Current Call are using the same Chat window. Other peoples' messages will appear in the largest window automatically.

Figure 11-7: Using Chat in NetMeeting

To send a message, type whatever you want to say in the Message area. If you want to "whisper" (send a chat message to only one member of the meeting), choose that person's name from the Send To drop-down list before you send the message. When you're ready to transmit the message, press Enter or click the large button to the right of the message area.

You also can control how chats display on your screen using the Options menu in the Chat window. Choose View ⇨ Options from Chat's menu bar and make your selections from the dialog box that appears. To save a chat session, choose File ⇨ Save from Chat's menu bar. Choose a folder and file name for the chat and then click the Save button. The chat is saved as a text (.txt) file that you can open later using Notepad, WordPad, or any other word processing program. You also are given an opportunity to save the current chat session when you exit the Chat program (by closing the Chat window or choosing File ⇨ Exit from the Chat window's menu bar).

Using the Whiteboard

NetMeeting's Whiteboard is similar to Chat, but it enables you to communicate with pictures rather than text. All the members of the current call can draw simultaneously. And everyone sees whatever is placed in Whiteboard. Think of Whiteboard as the regular chalkboard or whiteboard often used in classrooms and meeting rooms. In this case, however, one person or several people can draw and write on the board at the same time. To start Whiteboard while in a NetMeeting call, just click the Whiteboard button near the bottom of NetMeeting's window. Alternatively, you can choose Tools ⇨ Whiteboard from its menu bar.

Whiteboard pops up on your screen, as well as on the screen of everyone else in the current call. With Whiteboard onscreen, you can draw using various tools, including Pen, Line, Unfilled Rectangle, Filled Rectangle, Unfilled Ellipse, and Filled Ellipse. To use a drawing tool, click the appropriate button on the toolbar and drag the tool across the large drawing area. If the drawing tools aren't visible, choose View ⇨ Tool Bar from Whiteboard's menus. You also can choose tools by right-clicking in the drawing area and making a selection from the shortcut menu that appears. Figure 11-8 shows the Whiteboard with some sample content.

Typing text in Whiteboard

You can type text using the Text toolbar button. After you click that button, you can choose a font and text color from options at the bottom of the Whiteboard window, or from the Tools menu in Whiteboard. Then click anywhere on Whiteboard and type your text.

Figure 11-8: The Whiteboard with some text, a drawing, and a pasted photo in it

Pasting pictures into Whiteboard

Any pictures you paste into Whiteboard are visible to everyone in the call who is viewing the Whiteboard. Use any of these techniques to paste an image into Whiteboard:

✦ If the image is on-screen in a program, select and copy whatever you want to send, using whatever works in that particular program. Typically, clicking the picture and pressing Ctrl+C is sufficient to copy the picture into the invisible Windows Clipboard. Then click in the Whiteboard and choose Edit ⇨ Paste.

✦ Optionally, you can click the Select Area button in Whiteboard, click OK if you see a message, drag a rectangle around anything on the screen that you want to paste, and then release the mouse button.

✦ Or, if you want to copy a specific window or dialog box into the Whiteboard, click the Select Window button. If a message appears, click its OK button. Then click the window that you want to copy into the Whiteboard.

After you've pasted an image (or anything else, for that matter) into the Whiteboard, you can easily move it. Click the Selector button in the toolbar, click the object you want to move, and then drag that object to some new position.

Erasing from Whiteboard

You can erase material from Whiteboard in a few ways:

✦ To erase the entire Whiteboard at once, choose Edit ⇨ Clear Page from the Whiteboard menu bar or press Ctrl+Del. Then choose Yes when asked for confirmation.

✦ To erase a drawn object or block of text, click the Eraser tool. Then click the object or chunk of text you want to erase. (To undo the deletion, choose Edit ➪ Undelete from the menus or press Ctrl+Z.)

✦ To delete individual letters rather than a whole block of text, choose Tools ➪ Text (or click the Text toolbar button), select the letters that you want to erase, and then press the Delete (Del) key.

Other Whiteboard features

The Zoom button in Whiteboard enables you to double the size of the image in Whiteboard. The Lock Contents button locks the Whiteboard's contents so that other meeting members cannot change it. The Remote Pointer button displays a pointing hand that you can drag with your mouse to call attention to parts of the screen.

You can store multiple pages in Whiteboard. To add a new page, click the Insert New Page button down near the lower-right corner of the Whiteboard window. Or, choose Edit ➪ Insert Page from the menus. A new, blank Whiteboard page appears on which you can draw, type, or paste pictures. To scroll through pages, use the First Page, Previous Page, Next Page, and Last Page buttons near the lower-right corner of the Whiteboard window. Or, type a page number into the Page text box (again, near the lower-right corner) and press Enter.

You can learn more about Whiteboard by choosing Help ➪ Help Topics from its menu bar. If you plan on using the Whiteboard often in your work (or play), you would do well to spend some time reading the Help pages, so that you'll know how to use everything that Whiteboard offers.

Sharing Applications

One of the most amazing features of NetMeeting is its capability to share applications. In fact, you can share applications even if everyone in the meeting does not have the same software you are sharing! Sharing is easy to do. The only bummer is that sharing can be a little slow. Nonetheless, if you want to try it, follow these steps:

1. Close any programs you do not want to share with others.

2. Start any program on your PC or open any document you want to share.

3. Click NetMeeting's Share button, or choose Tools ➪ Sharing. Then click the name of the application that you want to share and click the Share button.

4. Optionally, you can click the Allow Control button if you want others to be able to control the program. Or click the Prevent Control button to prevent others from being able to control the program.

A window that contains your shared programs and documents appears on everyone else's screen, as in the example shown in Figure 11-9 where Alec is sharing Microsoft Outlook with me. Whether others can *do* anything with that application depends on whether you've opted to enable control or prevent control. If you did enable control, selecting the Automatically accept requests for control option will enable other viewers to take control of the program immediately. If you don't select that option, other viewers will have to choose Control ⇨ Request Control from their menu bars to request control. You'll see a message indicating that someone has requested control, at which point you can either accept or reject the request.

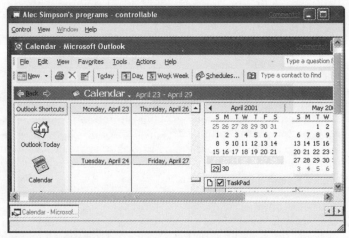

Figure 11-9: Microsoft Outlook's calendar function is shared using NetMeeting.

If you're the person who started sharing the application, you can stop sharing it just as easily by highlighting its name in the list of programs and choosing Unshare. Be careful what you share, especially when dealing with people you don't know well. If you open My Computer and share that, for instance, you essentially give the other person complete control over your computer! If you have any worries, keep your hand near the Esc key. If the other person starts doing something you don't like, a quick tap on the Esc key removes control from them.

Tip   Many programs in Microsoft Office have an Online Collaborate option on their Tools menu, which you can use to schedule and start online meetings right on the spot.

If several people are working on a shared document, remember that any and all changes made to the document are saved only if you save the changes (using File ⇨ Save in that application). Furthermore, the changes are saved only on your computer. If you want others in the meeting to have copies of the completed document, you must send them copies as discussed in the next section (or as e-mail attachments — whichever you prefer).

Transferring Files

To send files to someone in a NetMeeting call, click the Transfer Files button near the lower-right corner of NetMeeting's window. Or choose Tools ➪ File Transfer. Use the Add Files button to browse around your system and select the files you want to send. You can select as many files as you want to transfer. For example, Figure 11-10 shows that I've opted to send three files.

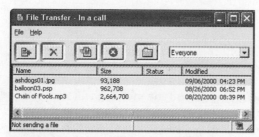

Figure 11-10: NetMeeting's File Transfer dialog box

You can use the "everyone" drop-down list to choose to whom you want to send the file(s) — everyone or a specific member. When you're ready to send, click the Send All button. The recipient(s) of the file(s) will see a dialog box like that shown in Figure 11-11 for each file you send. As the dialog box shows, the recipient has the option to Accept, Open, or Delete the file (as do you when someone transfers a file to you).

Figure 11-11: Receiving a file transferred by NetMeeting

By default, all files transferred by NetMeeting are stored in the \Program Files\NetMeeting\Received Files folder on the computer that received the file. You can get there via Windows Explorer. Or, in NetMeeting, click the Transfer Files button, and then click the View Received button in the File Transfer window's toolbar. If you prefer to store received files in some other folder, choose File ➪ Change Folder from the File Transfer window and specify a new location for the received files.

Hosting a Meeting

A NetMeeting meeting is really no different from any other type of call. However, you do need to make sure that everyone who is supposed to attend the meeting knows the time and place. The "place" should be a directory server, such as Microsoft Internet Directory, which everyone who is to attend the meeting will log on to before the meeting start time. You can save some time by making sure all participants have Passport or Hotmail accounts ahead of time. Then add all participants to your Instant Messenger list of contacts. That way, their names will be visible in the Find Someone dialog box as soon as you're ready to start your meeting.

As the host of the meeting, you get to choose the meeting time, the meeting name, password, security settings, and the list of people who can be invited to the meeting. You also can define which tools (for example, Chat and Whiteboard) can be used during the meeting. When it comes time to actually go online and conduct the meeting, here are the steps to follow:

1. Start NetMeeting and log on to the directory server you've chosen to act as the server.

2. Choose Call ➪ Host Meeting from NetMeeting's menu bar.

3. In the Host a Meeting dialog box, enter the name of the meeting (Figure 11-12).

4. Optionally, you can set these other meeting properties:

   • To require a password to enter the meeting, enter a Meeting Password.

   • To require security, select the Require Security option.

Note   Secure calls are data only, which means that you can't use voice and video during the meeting. You can learn more about different types of security available to you by looking up *secure* in NetMeeting's help index.

   • To make yourself grand wazoo of who can join the meeting, select the Only you can accept incoming calls and the Only you can place outgoing calls options for controlling incoming an outgoing calls.

   • Under Meeting Tools, choose the tools that meeting participants will be allowed to use.

5. Click OK.

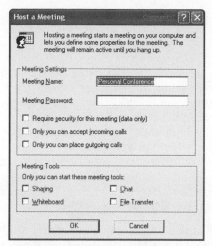

Figure 11-12: The Host a Meeting dialog box

As the host of the meeting, you can now log on to the appropriate server and start placing calls to meeting members. Probably the easiest way to do this is to choose Call ➪ Directory to view people (or buddies) on the server. Then just click the name of the person whom you want to call. As with any other NetMeeting call, the recipient will hear a ring and be given the option to accept or reject the call.

Being host also grants you the right to kick out anybody you want. Just right-click a name in the list of participants and choose Remove from Meeting.

Tip   If you have Microsoft Office, you also can conduct a meeting from most program's menu bars. Open the document you want to share, choose Tools ➪ Online Collaboration. Then choose Meet Now. If Microsoft Outlook is installed, you can choose Schedule Meeting to schedule the meeting for a later time.

When you're ready to end the meeting, just click your Hang Up button. For more information on setting up and conducting meetings, meeting security, and so forth, choose Help ➪ Help Topics from NetMeeting's menu bar. Then look up the word Host in the Index tab.

Controlling One PC from Another with RDS

Remote Desktop Sharing (RDS) is a NetMeeting-related capability that enables you to thoroughly control one computer from another computer using that computer's mouse, keyboard, and monitor. This is great for certain types of technical support. If you have a problem with your computer, for example, you can turn control of the computer over to an expert who can examine things from his current location. The expert might even be able to fix the problem on your screen as you watch.

Tip

If you're looking to give someone else control of your computer for technical support, you might find it easier to use the Remote Assistance feature. See the section titled "Remote Assistance" in Chapter 19.

If you have an "always on" connection to the Internet (such as cable or DSL) and your computer has its own IP address on the Internet, you also can access that computer *remotely* (that is, from any other computer on the Internet). For example, you can use RDS to share your computer's entire desktop and leave your computer on. Then, while you're out on the road, you could connect to the Internet and actually control that home or office computer from wherever you happen to be located at the moment.

Setting up RDS on the computer to be shared

To share control of a PC, you first need to be at that PC and do some configuring. You must have an account on the computer that has administrative privileges, and be logged on to that account. The account needs to have a password. You can use your existing account, or create a new account specifically for RDS. For this example, we'll go through the steps of creating a unique RDS account. Assuming you're already logged on with administrative privileges, here's how you would proceed:

Cross-Reference

Chapter 22 discusses user accounts and privileges in depth.

1. Click the Start button and choose Control Panel.

2. Open the User Accounts icon.

3. Choose Create A New Account.

4. Enter a name for the account, such as **RDS Users**, and click the Next button.

5. Choose Computer Administrator and then click the Create Account button.

6. Choose Change an Account.

7. Click the name of your new account (for instance, RDS Users).

8. Choose Create Password.

9. Enter a password (twice) and optionally a password hint (in case you forget).

Caution

As always, it's a good idea to write this password down and keep it in a safe place. If you plan on accessing this computer via the Internet, be sure to bring the password with you!

10. Click the Create Password button.

11. Close the User Accounts window and Control Panel by clicking their Close (X) buttons.

Determine the computer's name and IP address

Next you need to determine this computer's name and/or IP address. If you plan to manage this computer from within your local area network only, either the name or IP address will do. To access this computer via the Internet, you need the computer's IP address. To determine the computer's name, follow these steps:

1. Click the Start button, and then right-click My Computer and choose Properties.

2. Click the Computer Name tab. The computer's name appears next to Full Computer Name. Jot it down for future reference.

3. Click the Cancel button to close the dialog box without making any changes.

To determine the computer's IP address, follow these steps:

1. Start NetMeeting from the Start menu or any shortcut you created.

2. Choose Help ⇨ About Windows NetMeeting from NetMeeting's menu bar.

3. The computer's IP address appears near the bottom of the dialog box. Jot it down, and click the OK button.

Configuring RDS

The next step in allowing this computer to be operated remotely involves configuring NetMeeting to provide the capability. A simple wizard will help you do this:

1. If NetMeeting isn't already open on the desktop, go ahead and start NetMeeting normally.

2. Choose Tools ⇨ Remote Desktop Sharing from NetMeeting's menu bar.

3. Read the first couple of wizard screens and then click the Next button.

4. In the wizard screen that enables you to create a password-protected screen saver, choosing Yes will allow you to set up a screen saver that prevents others from using the computer while it's being used remotely. Click the Next button to display the Screen Saver tab of the Desktop Properties dialog box. To accept the suggested screen saver, just click the OK button to close the dialog box and return to the wizard.

5. Read the last wizard page, and then click its Finish button.

A new icon will be available in the Notification area of the desktop. That little icon will play an important role, as you'll learn next.

Before you leave, or turn over control . . .

Now that the computer is capable of being operated from afar, you can do some things to help make the whole process easier. For starters, if you created a separate account for remote use, such as our RDS Users account, log onto that account. If you want to be able to access some other account (such as your own account) from afar, log on to that account instead. Then consider changing the display resolution to 640 x 480, if possible. That will enable your entire desktop to fit inside a window on the calling computer, provided that computer is using some higher resolution. Also, if your computer has multiple monitors, you should disable all but the main monitor, because it's unlikely that the calling computer will be able to access the additional monitors. You can change the resolution and deactivate extra monitors via the Display Properties dialog box that appears when you right-click the desktop and choose Properties.

Next you need to set up the computer to "listen" for incoming calls that request control of the desktop. This step is vital, so it's imperative that you perform it before you leave the computer. Likewise, if you'll be turning over control of your computer to someone else, you must perform this step before that person calls in to take control of the computer. Here's how you tell the computer to "listen" for the incoming request:

1. Right-click the new NetMeeting icon in the Notification area, as in Figure 11-13.

2. Choose Activate Remote Desktop Sharing.

Figure 11-13: Select Activate Remote Desktop Sharing to allow this computer to be managed from afar.

Note   The new NetMeeting icon is available only in those user accounts in which you've already configured NetMeeting for RDS. If the Notification area icon isn't visible, but you're certain you're in an account where you've enabled RDS, restart the computer by clicking the Start button and choosing Turn Off Computer ⇨ Restart.

If you plan to leave the computer unattended while it's being used remotely, be sure that the computer is on and ready to accept the call when the time comes. If you're using power management options to power down your computer after a period of inactivity, disable those options before you leave the computer. Use the Power Options icon in Control Panel (Start ⇨ Control Panel) to set your System Standby option to Never. (It's okay to let the monitor and hard disk power down after a while.)

Some modern computers have a Wake On LAN capability built in to them. This enables the computer to go into a suspended state while not in use and then instantly "wake up" as soon as a request for resources comes through the network. If your computer has that capability, you'll probably need to set it up in the system BIOS. Typically the only way to get to the BIOS setup is to watch for a message that reads Press <*some key*> to Enter Setup right after you start the computer. You'll only have a few seconds to press the specified key. I can't give you much more advice than that though, because different computers have different BIOS chips and setup programs. You can check the written documentation that came with your system (or the system's motherboard) for more information on its BIOS capabilities and setup program.

The main thing to remember, however, is that if you want to access the computer from afar and nobody will be sitting there to accept your NetMeeting call, the computer has to be turned on and running when the call comes in. You can log off from the computer, however, by clicking the Start button and choosing Log Off ➪ Log Off.

Turning over control

If you'll just be turning over control of this computer to someone else, you're done. When that person dials in to the computer, you will probably just see him doing whatever it is he needs to do. The mouse pointer will just move about the screen as though Casper the Ghost were sitting at your computer working its keyboard and mouse. When that user hangs up, you get control back.

Now consider how it works from the other end, with you as the person who is elsewhere and calling in to control this computer.

Accessing an unattended desktop

Suppose you are away from the computer that's listening for RDS requests. You want to get into that computer and control it from your current location. To do so, you need to follow these steps:

1. On whatever computer you're using at the moment, start Microsoft NetMeeting.

2. Click the Place Call button.

3. In the To box, type the IP address of the remote computer. If you are calling from a computer that's part of the same local area network, you can enter the computer's name instead.

4. Select the Require security for this call option so that its check box is filled (this is important!), as in Figure 11-14.

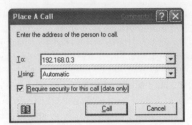

Figure 11-14: About to request control of a remote computer at IP address 192.168.0.3

5. Click the Call button in the dialog box.

6. In the next dialog box to appear, enter your user name (or the name of the account you created for RDS) and password, as in Figure 11-15. Note that the Domain option is required only when contacting networks that use the Windows NT/2000 domain system of security.

Figure 11-15: Entering the user (account name) and password required to access the remote computer

7. Click the OK button.

A window opens on your desktop, displaying whatever is currently visible on the remote computer's screen. From here on out, you can operate that computer normally within the window. If you choose View ➪ Full Screen from the window's menu bar, you will, in essence, replace your desktop with their desktop. You can use the Restore button that appears in the upper-right corner of the Full Screen view to reduce that remote desktop to a window, when convenient.

Transferring files during RDS

As you're working a computer from afar, you might think that you can copy files from that remote computer to the current computer just using standard drag-and-drop techniques. However, that's not how it works. Instead, what you need to do is run NetMeeting on the remote computer and click the Transfer Files button in that computer's copy of NetMeeting. Go through the standard method described earlier in this chapter to select and send the files that you want to copy. After you click the Send button, the files will, of course, be sent to the computer at which you're currently sitting. You can accept or reject them, just like you could if someone else had sent them to you. If you're not given an option to place them in a specific folder on the local computer, they'll probably end up in the `C:\Program Files\NetMeeting\ Received Files` folder, which is the default for storing transferred files.

Ending Remote Desktop Access

When you've finished using the remote computer, click the Hang Up button in NetMeeting's window. You can also close NetMeeting if you like.

More on NetMeeting

NetMeeting has so many capabilities that it would take a small book to cover all the possibilities. Because I have only one chapter to work with, I have limited my coverage to just the most important and widely used features of the product. For the rest of this chapter, I want to point out some of those capabilities and point you in the right direction for getting more out of NetMeeting.

Using Directory Services

You are not limited to using the Microsoft Internet Directory as your directory server. NetMeeting is compatible with a wide range of directory servers. The best source for finding compatible servers is probably the NetMeeting Zone at `www. netmeet.net`. You might want to read up on the latest information available from its home page. If you're just looking for other servers that work with NetMeeting, however, you can go straight to the page at `www.netmeet.net/bestservers.asp`.

Tip Directory server URLs typically follow the format `ils.domainname.com`, where ils is an acronym for Internet Locator Service (a service that finds people currently online). For example, the URL of the Microsoft Internet Directory is actually `ils.microsoft.com`. Of course, the URL of a directory server can be anything — the initial ils acronym is common, but by no means universal.

There are a couple of ways to log on to a server other than a Microsoft server. If you want to control whether your name will appear in that server, and whether you're logged on to a specific server when NetMeeting starts, your best bet is to add the directory server's URL to NetMeeting via the Options dialog box. Here are the exact steps:

1. From NetMeeting's menu bar choose Tools ⇨ Options.

2. Under Directory Settings, replace the contents of the Directory drop-down list with the URL of the directory server that you're interested in. For example, you could drag the mouse pointer through the Microsoft Internet Directory option to select it. Then type in some new directory URL, such as `ils.visitalk.com`.

3. If you don't want to be listed in that directory server's list of people online, select the Do Not List My Name option.

4. If you want to log on to a directory server automatically whenever NetMeeting starts, select the second option. Then choose the name of the directory that you want to log on to automatically from the Directory drop-down list.

5. Click OK.

Tip   You also can enter a new directory URL in the Select a directory drop-down list of the Find Someone dialog box, which opens after you choose Call ⇨ Directory from NetMeeting's menu bar.

Now whenever you're in NetMeeting and want to visit some server other than the one you're currently logged on to, just choose Call ⇨ Directory from NetMeeting's menu bar. Open the Select a Directory drop-down list and choose the directory that you want to log on to. To place a call to anyone in the list, just click her name and then click the Call button.

Gateways and gatekeepers

If you work for a large organization that uses gateways and/or gatekeepers to provide access to telephone and videoconferencing, you can log on to that server via NetMeeting. First you need to get the address, password, and any other relevant information about the server from your company's network administrator or system administrator. That person can best tell you how to use the server. Some of those servers will even let you dial directly to normal telephones via NetMeeting. Should you ever need to dial directly, you can use choose View ⇨ DialPad from NetMeeting's menu bar to get to the dialing pad.

Still more

As I said earlier, a single chapter in a book cannot really do justice to all that NetMeeting and all the various ILS servers on the Internet have to offer. Given that this is a book about Windows, however, rather than NetMeeting per se, a chapter is all I have to work with. You can find a lot more information online that will help you expand the basic skills and concepts that you learned here. Of course, NetMeeting's own Help menu offers plenty of information — just choose Help ➪ Help Topics from NetMeeting's menu bar. On the Web you can learn about the many different directory servers that support NetMeeting, keep up with new events as the technology evolves, and learn about some of the more esoteric features of NetMeeting from any of these Web sites:

- ✦ Microsoft's NetMeeting Page at `www.microsoft.com/windows/netmeeting`
- ✦ MSN Messenger page at `http://messenger.msn.com`
- ✦ MSN Hailstorm at `http://communities.msn.com/microsofthailstorm`
- ✦ CU-SeeMe World at `www.cuseemeworld.com`
- ✦ Conflab.com at `www.conflab.com`
- ✦ Helpmeeting at `www.helpmeeting.com`
- ✦ ILS Center at www.ilscenter.com

A search for the keywords "free long distance," "videoconference," "security certificate," or "NetMeeting" using any Web search engine is bound to turn up a lot more resources.

Summary

NetMeeting is one of the most powerful Internet tools in the Windows XP arsenal. As discussed in this chapter, it enables you to communicate online using voice, video, chat, and a whiteboard. You also can use NetMeeting to collaborate on projects, transfer files, and manage computers remotely. Here's a quick recap of the main techniques covered in this chapter:

- ✦ The easiest way to place a call in NetMeeting is to choose Call ➪ Directory from its menu bar to see who is online. Then click the name of the person you want to call.
- ✦ To "chat" (by typing messages) during a call, click the Chat button.
- ✦ NetMeeting's Whiteboard acts as a board on which you can place text and pictures. Click the Whiteboard button or choose Tools ➪ Whiteboard to open the board.

✦ To collaborate on a project in NetMeeting, open the document you want to share, and then click the Share Program button or choose Tools ➪ Sharing from NetMeeting's menu bar.

✦ To transfer files in NetMeeting, click the Transfer Files button.

✦ To finish a call, click the Hang Up button.

✦ To turn over control of your computer to a trusted expert, use Remote Desktop Sharing, available on NetMeeting's Tools menu.

✦ To control an unattended computer from afar, set the computer up to "listen" for RDS requests before leaving the computer. You can do so by right-clicking the NetMeeting Remote Desktop Sharing icon in the Notification area of the Windows taskbar.

✦   ✦   ✦

Have It Your Way

Windows XP is a very flexible program that you can customize to best suit your own needs and work style. Here you'll learn how to organize your programs and documents to make things easy to find in the future. You'll learn the important basic skills required for managing your work, including how to move, copy, delete, and rename files and folders. You'll learn how to customize your screen to your own tastes and comfort level. And finally, you'll learn how to use alternative input devices and methods including game controllers, speech recognition, and handwriting recognition.

General Housekeeping (Copying, Deleting, and So On)

As you gain experience in using your computer, creating documents, and so forth, you may find you occasionally need to manage your files. The term "manage" includes copying, moving, deleting, and renaming folders and files. It can also include compressing and uncompressing files that are stored in the popular Zip format. This chapter explains all the basic techniques you use to manage files and folders on your PC. As you'll see, you'll use the Windows Explorer (i.e., "Explorer") window discussed in Chapter 2 to perform all these tasks. So if you find yourself having trouble in this chapter, be sure to review Chapter 2 so you remember how to "get around" using that Explorer window.

Select, Then Do

Often, when moving, copying, or deleting files, you'll want to do so with more than one file at a time. It would be darn tedious if you had to, say, move or copy 100 files one at a time. So before we get into the specifics of these file management techniques, you'll want to learn how to *select* the files you intend to work with. Like just about everything else in Windows (and most Windows programs you'll use), the "Select, Then Do" rule applies. First you *select* the files you want to move, copy, or delete, and then you *do* the task, be it copying, moving, or deleting. There are many ways to select files. The general rule is to just use whichever technique is most convenient at the moment.

First, get to the files

To do anything with a file, or files, you first need to get to them via Explorer. As you may recall from Chapter 2, the Explorer window opens any time you click My Computer, My Documents, My Pictures, or any other location from the Start menu — as well as when you choose Search from the Start menu. For example, Figure 12-1 shows Explorer displaying the contents of my My Documents folder after choosing My Documents from the Start menu. In this example, I'm viewing the Folders pane, Explorer bar, and my files and folders in Icons view, with the Explorer window maximized to full-screen size.

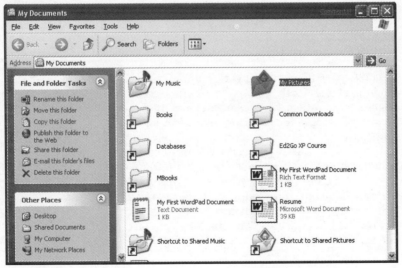

Figure 12-1: The contents of my My Documents folder in Explorer

Your My Documents will no doubt look different because there are so many different views to choose from, and because yours will no doubt contain different files and folders. But don't worry about that. We'll talk about the different views in moment. At this point your main concern is to navigate to the folder that contains the file(s) you want to move, copy, or delete. Just use the standard techniques described in Chapter 2 to do so. That is, open the folder that contains the file(s) by clicking (or double-clicking) its icon. Alternatively, choose the folder from the Other Places options in the Explorer bar. Or open the Folders list (by clicking the Folders button on the toolbar), and navigate in there.

Tip As mentioned in Chapter 2, the Explorer bar is visible only if Show Common Tasks in Folders is selected in Folder options. To show or hide the Explorer bar, choose Tools ➪ Folder Options from the Explorer menu bar.

Second, pick your view

After you have navigated to the folder that contains the files you want to manage, switch to whichever view you think will make it easiest to select the folders you plan to work with. As discussed in Chapter 2, your options are Thumbnails, Tiles, Icons, List, and Details. You can choose a view from the Views button in the Standard Buttons toolbar, or from the View menu, or by right-clicking within the files area and choosing View.

 Tip If you do not see the Standard Buttons toolbar, choose View ➪ Toolbars ➪ Standard Buttons from the menu.

Third, group things, if useful

If you plan to manage a group of files that have something in common, you can save some work by bunching those items in a list. To arrange the icons, choose View ➪ Arrange Icons By. Then, choose an option based on the following possibilities:

✦ **Name:** If the items you want to select have similar names (for example, they all start with the word *Chapter*), choose By Name to put the objects in alphabetic order by name.

✦ **Size:** If the items you want to select are the same size or you want to work with large items or small ones, choose By Size.

✦ **Type:** If the items you want to select are of a similar type (for instance, pictures), choose By Type.

✦ **Modified:** If the items you want to select were created or modified on or near a particular date, choose By Date. Files with similar dates will be grouped in the list.

 Tip If you select View ➪ Arrange Icons By ➪ Show in Groups, the icons will be arranged into groups of related items, based on your most recent selection from View ➪ Arrange Icons By (for instance, Name, Type, Size, and so on). To turn off grouping, choose View ➪ Arrange Icons By ➪ Show in Groups again.

You might find it easiest to select items if you use one of the views that displays small icons, such as the Icons, List, or Details view. However, feel free to choose any view you want.

Finally, select the items to move, copy, or delete

When you see the items you want to move, copy, or delete, you need to select the specific items. You can tell when an item is selected because it's colored differently than the unselected items. There are lots of ways to select items for moving, copying, or deleting. Any of the following methods will work. It's just a matter of choosing which method you like, or the method that you think will be most convenient for the task at hand.

Tip   All the following selection techniques apply to folders and files equally. When you select a folder, you automatically select all the files within that folder as well.

Selecting by dragging

A quick and easy way to select the items you want to manage is to just drag the mouse pointer through them. Move the mouse pointer to just outside the first item you want to select. Then hold down the mouse button and drag a frame (also called a *lasso*) around all the items you want to select. The items will be selected as you move the mouse pointer through them, and will remain selected after you release the mouse button. Figure 12-2 shows how I selected a bunch of files by dragging a frame around them.

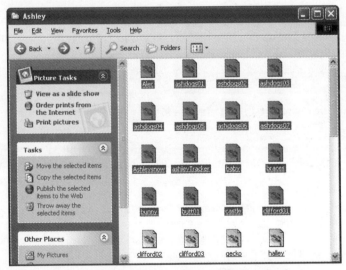

Figure 12-2: I selected all these files by dragging a frame around them.

Selecting non-adjacent files

In some cases, you'll want to select files that aren't adjacent to one another. In this case, you won't be able to just drag the mouse pointer through them. That's not a problem, however, because there are plenty of other ways to select a bunch of files. The exact technique you use depends on whether you're using the "single-click" or "double-click" method to open icons, as discussed in the sections that follow. Remember, you can choose between the single-click and double-click method at any time by choosing Tools ⇨ Folder Options from the Explorer menu bar and then making your choice under Click Items as Follows in the Folder Options dialog box that appears.

Selecting in Classic style

If you are using Classic-style clicking, you can select items using a combination of keyboard keys and the mouse. As you may recall, to Ctrl+click something means to hold down the Ctrl key while clicking. To Shift+click means to hold down the Shift key while clicking. And to Ctrl+Shift+click means to hold down the Ctrl and Shift keys while clicking. You might find it easiest to use the List or Details view when working in this manner. Anyway, here's how it all works:

✦ To select one item, click it. Any previously selected items are unselected instantly.

✦ To add another item to a selection, Ctrl+click it.

✦ To extend the selection to another item, Shift+click where you want to extend the selection.

✦ To create another extended selection without disturbing existing selections, Ctrl+click the first item in the range and then Ctrl+Shift+click the last item in the range.

✦ To deselect a selected item without disturbing the current selections, Ctrl+click the item you want to deselect.

Figure 12-3 shows an example in which I have selected several file names in List view, using Classic-style clicking. I started by clicking the topmost file name. The figure shows the keys I held down while clicking the mouse button to select other files in the list.

Selecting with Web-style navigation

If you are using Web-style clicking, you select items by pointing to them rather than clicking them. This approach can be tricky, especially if you're not all that adept at using a mouse yet. The main point to remember is that moving the mouse pointer over the item doesn't count as pointing. You need to actually rest the mouse pointer on the item for a moment. Other than that, the techniques are the same, except you point rather than click. Specifically, you can do the following:

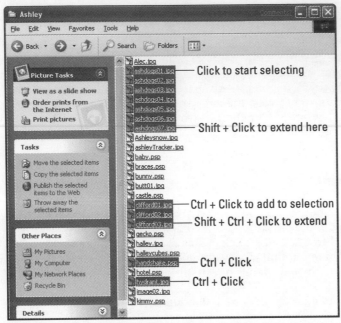

Figure 12-3: To select multiple items in Classic style, use the Ctrl and Shift keys while clicking.

✦ To select one item, point to it. The item will be selected, and any previously selected items will be unselected instantly.

✦ To add another item to a selection, Ctrl+point to it. To avoid mistakes, hold down the Ctrl key the whole time you move the mouse.

✦ To extend the selection to another item, Shift+point where you want to extend the selection. You can hold down the Shift key while you move the mouse pointer through the file names you want to select.

✦ To create another extended selection without disturbing existing selections, Ctrl+point to the first item in the range and then Ctrl+Shift+point to the last item in the range.

✦ To deselect a selected item without disturbing the current selections, Ctrl+point to the item you want to deselect.

Figure 12-4 shows an example in which I selected several file names in Web style. I started by pointing to the topmost file name. The figure shows the keys I held down while pointing the mouse to select other files in the list.

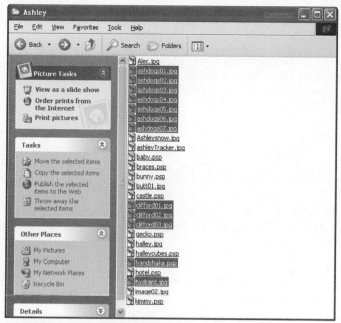

Figure 12-4: To select multiple items in Web style, use the Ctrl and Shift keys while pointing.

Shortcuts for selecting multiple files

Here are a couple of shortcuts for selecting files and folders in Explorer:

✦ To select all the items in the window, choose Edit ⇨ Select All or press Ctrl+A.

✦ To invert the current selection (deselect all the selected items and select all the deselected ones), choose Edit ⇨ Invert Selection.

Either method can be useful when you want to select most, but not all of, the items in the window. For example, you could select all the items in the window by pressing Ctrl+A. Then deselect the few you want to exclude by Ctrl+clicking them. Alternatively, you could start out by selecting the items you tend to exclude and then use Invert Selection to select all but those files you initially selected.

Finally, keep in mind that you can select a bunch of files just by dragging the mouse pointer through them. To exclude a few files from the selection, just Ctrl+click the files you want to eliminate from the selection.

Tip If there's at least one file selected in Explorer, and your hands happen to be on the keyboard, you can extend the selection by holding down the Shift key as you press the arrow keys on your keyboard.

Selecting across folders and drives

If the files you plan to manage aren't all in the same folder, you might need to work with one folder at a time. That is, go to the folder, select the files you want to manage and then move, copy, or delete them. Then, go to the next folder and repeat the process. However, if the files have something in common that you can search on, you can select files from multiple folders and move, copy, or delete them in one fell swoop.

Suppose, for example, that you have a digital camera that stores its pictures on your hard disk using .KDC as the extension. You routinely copy your digital photos to some other format, such as JPG, leaving you with two copies of each photo on your hard disk — one in the original KDC format, the other in the JPG format. You want to move the KDC files to a CD-ROM or some other medium to free up the disk space they're consuming. But those KDC files are sprinkled throughout many folders on your hard disk. You want to move them all in one fell swoop instead of painstakingly locating and moving them one folder at a time. Here's how you can do that:

1. If you're already in an Explorer window, click the Search button. Alternatively, click the Start button and choose Search.

2. In the Search Companion bar, specify the type of files you want to search for. In this example, you can choose Pictures, Music, or Video. Alternatively, you can choose All Files and Folders, because you'll eventually be narrowing things down to all files that have the .KDC extension.

3. Under Part or All of the Name, type ***.KDC**, which means "any file name followed by a .KDC extension." Note that upper/lowercase doesn't matter, because file names are not case-sensitive. The asterisk (*) stands for "any file name."

4. Under Look In, choose the area you want to search. In this example, choose Local Disk (C:), because you're looking for all the KDC files on your local hard disk.

5. Click the Search button and wait for the search to complete.

6. When the search is finished, you can choose Yes, Finished Searching in the Search Companion bar if you want to close that to make some room.

When the search is finished, the right pane will list all the KDC files on your hard disk, regardless of what folder each file is contained within, as in the example shown in Figure 12-5. There I've opted to display the search result in Details view, without the file name extensions hidden, so you can see that the files are indeed KDC files located in different folders.

At this point, you can select all the files in the right pane to move, copy, or delete using any of the techniques described earlier. And you can move, copy, or delete them using any of the techniques that follow.

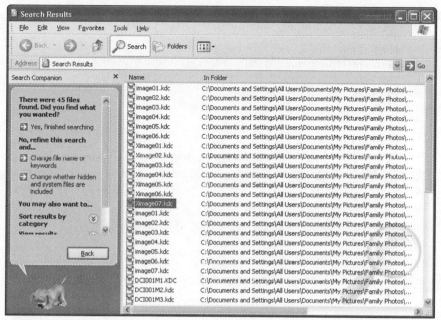

Figure 12-5: All the files on the hard disk that have .KDC as their file name extension are listed in the right pane.

Remember, Search gives you the ability to isolate all kinds of files. Searching for files with a .KDC extension was just an example. As discussed back in Chapter 2, you can search for "categories" of files, such as music or pictures. You can search only for document files, such as Word documents or Excel spreadsheets. You can search for files that were created during some time frame. The point is, you're not limited to working with one folder at a time. If the files you plan to move, copy, or delete aren't all in the same folder but do have something in common, you can use Search to make all their icons visible in the Explorer window. Then you can select the files to move, copy, or delete from the results of your search.

So much for selecting. . . . Now let's discuss the techniques for managing selected files.

Move, Copy, Delete, Rename

Before we discuss general techniques for copying, moving, and deleting files and folders, it's important that you understand those terms:

✦ To *copy* a file or folder means to make an exact duplicate of it, as you can with a photocopy machine. If you copy a file named MyLetter.doc from your My Documents folder to a floppy disk in drive A:, for example, you end up with two identical copies of MyLetter.doc—the original copy still in the My Documents folder, and a new copy on the floppy disk in A: drive.

✦ To *move* a file or folder means what the name implies—to change the item's location. If you move the file named MyLetter.doc from the My Documents folder to a folder named Letters within My Documents, for example, you still have only one copy of the MyLetter.doc file—the copy now in the subfolder named Letters.

✦ To *delete* a file or folder means to trash it permanently, so you end up with no copies of that file. Obviously, you need to use extreme caution when you delete things because you don't want to delete anything important. You'll occasionally want to delete things you no longer need to make more room for new stuff on your hard disk.

✦ To *rename* a file or folder means to change the name that appears under the icon. The file or folder is not moved, copied, or deleted.

Deleting Files and Folders

Deleting items is easy, but also risky because you might not be able to recover a file after you delete it. In *some* cases, deleted files are sent to the Recycle Bin, where you get a chance to change your mind before you permanently delete. However, in some situations, such as when you delete a file from a removable disk (such as a floppy), the Recycle Bin isn't used at all. Therefore extreme caution is always in order when selecting files to delete. Here are some important points to keep in mind to play it safe:

✦ Just because you don't recognize a file name doesn't mean you can delete it. Most of the files on your system belong to Windows and other programs on your system. Deleting such files could make the programs, or even your entire program, unusable.

✦ If you share a computer with other people, be careful you don't accidentally delete their stuff.

✦ Remember that if you delete a folder, you also delete all the files inside that folder! Use extreme caution here!

✦ If your computer is on a network, *never* delete an item on a shared folder from another computer. Doing so would *really* irritate the other person, and there may be no way to recover the deleted item!

✦ Only items you delete from your local hard disk (typically, drive C:) are sent to the Recycle Bin. Files on floppy disks, network drives, and other removable media are deleted permanently on the spot and they *cannot* be undeleted.

✦ Usually when you delete something, you'll see a message asking whether you're sure you want to do this. Pay attention to that message! If it says `Are you sure you want to delete file name?`, that means the file to be deleted will *not* be sent to the Recycle Bin if you choose Yes. Instead, the file will be permanently deleted on the spot. Choose wisely.

✦ When you delete a shortcut icon (which will display a curved arrow), you delete only that icon — not the program, folder, or file that the shortcut takes you to. When you delete a regular icon (one without the curved arrow), however, you delete the program, folder, or file that the icon represents.

Caution If you're trying to delete an installed program or some Windows component you rarely use, don't use any of the techniques discussed in this chapter. Instead, use Add or Remove Programs, as discussed in Chapter 16.

Now, with all these cautions out of the way, here's how you delete files and folders:

1. In Explorer, use any of the techniques discussed earlier to select the file(s) and/or folder(s) you want to delete.

Tip If you're looking to delete a single file or folder, you can just right-click that item and choose Delete from the menu that appears.

2. Do whichever of the following is most convenient (they all produce the same result):

   • Choose Delete The Selected Items under Tasks in the Explorer bar.

   • Or, press the Delete key.

   • Or, right-click any selected item and choose Delete from the menu that appears.

   • Or, drag the selected items to the Recycle Bin icon on your desktop, and drop them there.

3. You'll probably see a message asking whether you're sure you want to proceed. Assuming you are sure, go ahead and click the Yes button.

If you deleted from your local hard disk, the file or folder isn't actually removed from your hard disk. It's just moved to the Recycle Bin on that disk, and therefore still consumes just as much disk space as it did before you "deleted" it. To free up the disk space, you need to empty the Recycle Bin, as discussed under "Using the Recycle Bin" in the next section.

Note It may be possible to undo a deletion by pressing Ctrl+Z or choosing Edit ➪ Undo Delete from the Explorer menu bar. But you have to do it right away after you've deleted the items.

Using the Recycle Bin

The Recycle Bin acts as a temporary storage folder for files you delete. When you delete a file from your hard disk, it disappears from the current folder. A copy of it stays in the Recycle Bin, however, in case you change your mind later.

You can tell whether trash is in the Recycle Bin by looking at its icon on the desktop. If the Recycle Bin is empty, the trash can will be empty. If the Recycle Bin contains any trash, the trash can icon also will contain trash.

Recovering files from the Recycle Bin

To recover accidentally deleted files from the Recycle Bin, you need to restore them *before* you empty the Recycle Bin, because emptying the Recycle Bin permanently deletes all the files currently in the Recycle Bin. To recover the disk space those files are using, follow these steps:

1. Open the Recycle Bin icon on the desktop to view its contents (see Figure 12-6). The Recycle Bin looks like any other folder except, of course, for the words *Recycle Bin* in the title bar. You can choose options on the View menu to control the appearance of items in the folder.

Figure 12-6: The Recycle Bin open on the desktop

2. To save restored items, thereby saving them from permanent deletion, use whichever technique below is most convenient at the moment:

- To restore all the files in the Recycle Bin, click the Restore All Items option in the Explorer bar.

- To restore a single file or folder, right-click it and choose Restore from the shortcut menu.

- To restore multiple items, select the items you want to restore. Then right-click any selected item and choose Restore, or click the Restore Selected Items option on the Explorer bar.

The restored files and folders are placed back in their original locations and no longer appear within the Recycle Bin.

Permanently deleting files

Deleted files and folders in the Recycle Bin still occupy as much disk space as they did before you deleted them. In fact, the files are still on your hard disk—they're just hidden from all browsing tools except the Recycle Bin. To recover the disk space occupied by those recycled files, you must delete those files permanently. This procedure is called emptying the Recycle Bin.

Caution

Remember that after you empty the Recycle Bin, you cannot restore the files!

To empty the Recycle Bin, follow these steps:

1. Open the Recycle Bin icon on the desktop.

2. Make certain only the files you want to delete permanently are listed. (This is your last chance to change your mind and restore any files in the Recycle Bin before sending them permanently to software heaven. So be sure to restore any files that you don't want to permanently delete before going to Step 3.)

3. Click Empty the Recycle Bin under Recycle Bin Tasks in the Explorer bar. Or choose File ⇨ Empty Recycle Bin from the Recycle Bin menu bar.

4. Choose Yes when asked for confirmation.

The Recycle Bin is emptied and the space once occupied by those files is now free for other files.

Caution

Maybe it's just me, but I can't tell you how many times I've almost selected Empty Recycle Bin when I meant to restore all the items in the Recycle Bin to their original locations. Perhaps Microsoft should have title the option something like Burn Recycle Bin or Nuke Recycle Bin, just as an extra reminder that it really does blast the files out of existence!

Personalizing your Recycle Bin

You can customize the way the Recycle Bin works on your PC. To see your options, first close the Recycle Bin if it's open. Then right-click the Recycle Bin icon and choose Properties. You'll come to the Recycle Bin Properties dialog box, shown in Figure 12-7.

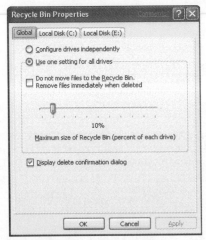

Figure 12-7: The Recycle Bin Properties dialog box

On the Global tab, you can choose the Use one setting for all drives option if you have only one local hard disk or if you have multiple hard disks, but you want each drive to use the same settings. Then you can do the following:

✦ To disable the Recycle Bin so that all files are permanently deleted immediately, check the check box labeled Do not move files to the Recycle Bin. Remove files immediately when deleted. (You'll be taking away your own safety net if you choose this option!)

✦ You can set a maximum size for the Recycle Bin as a percentage of the total drive space.

✦ You can hide the usual "Are you sure?" dialog box by clearing the check box next to Display delete confirmation dialog option.

If you have multiple hard disk drives and you want to configure each independently, choose the Configure drives independently option at the top of the Global tab. Then use the other tabs to set preferences for each drive independently.

Choose OK after making your selections.

Caution When you right-click the Recycle Bin, you'll probably notice an Empty Recycle Bin option. This option enables you to empty the Recycle Bin without opening it first. Unless you are absolutely certain you don't need any of the files in the Recycle Bin, this is dangerous to use!

So now that we've discussed all your options for getting rid of files, let's look at the many ways in which you can move files around and make copies of them for safe keeping, or to share with others.

Moving and Copying Folders and Files

There are lots of reasons for moving and copying files. For example, you might want to copy a file to a floppy disk to give to a friend. Or you might copy files to a CD-R or CD-RW disk as backups or to share with others. If your My Documents folder is getting so cluttered with files that it's hard to find the one you want, you might want to create some subfolders (as discussed in the next chapter) and move some files into the new folders. Or, perhaps you would like to make a copy of a file to edit in some program without changing the original file.

A couple of buzzwords that go along with moving and copying items:

✦ **Source:** The folder or disk *from* which you're copying items.

✦ **Destination (or target):** The folder or disk *to* which you're moving or copying items.

When the destination is a disk drive, make sure you insert a blank disk, or a disk with sufficient space on it, before you start the actual move or copy procedure. When browsing around for a disk drive in the sections that follow, remember they're listed under My Computer in the various navigation tools available to you.

Cross-Reference If you plan to copy files to a CD, see the section titled "Copying Files to a CD-R or CD-RW Disc" later in this chapter for specific instructions.

There are lots of ways to move and copy files. Choosing one method over another is just a matter of personal taste, or whichever method seems most convenient at the moment.

Moving and copying using tasks

The File and Folder Tasks area of the Explorer bar presents one way to move or copy files and folders. Here's how that works:

1. Select the items you want to move or copy, using any of the techniques described earlier in this chapter.

2. In the Explorer bar, choose Copy the Selected Items or Move the Selected Items depending on which you want to do (if only one file is selected, the singular "This File" will replace "Selected Items"). A small navigation window like the one in Figure 12-8 appears.

Figure 12-8: This small navigation window lets you choose a destination drive or directory for files you've selected to copy.

3. Navigate through the list of folder and files names to locate the destination you're moving or copying to. To expand an icon in the list and view its contents, click the plus sign (+) to the left of the item. To shrink an expanded item, click the minus sign (–) to its left.

Note   You can use the Make New Folder button to create a new folder in which to place the items. However, make sure you navigate to the appropriate parent folder first. To create a new folder within My Documents, for example, click My Documents before you click the Make New Folder button.

4. Click the name of the folder (or drive) to which you want to move or copy the items so that its name is selected in the list. In Figure 12-8, for example, I've selected a folder named Ashley within My Documents as the destination for the files to be copied.

5. Click the Copy or Move button.

All done. If you opted to move the items to the destination, their icons will disappear from the current Explorer window, because those files are no longer in the current folder.

Moving and copying using drag-and-drop

You also can use drag-and-drop to move and copy files. Some people prefer this method because they think it gives them a better feel for what's actually happening. Here's how it works:

1. Use any of the techniques described earlier in this chapter to select the items you want to move or copy.

2. Shrink the window down to make room on the desktop for a second window. The window you shrink only needs to be large enough to display at least one of your selected items.

3. Open another Explorer window (perhaps by choosing My Documents or some other destination from the Start menu).

4. Navigate to the destination drive or folder within this new window (or create a new folder in it, if you prefer). Then shrink that window down so that you can see both windows. In Figure 12-9, for example, I've selected files to copy in the folder named Alec. And I have opened a new, empty folder named Food Photos in two separate Explorer windows.

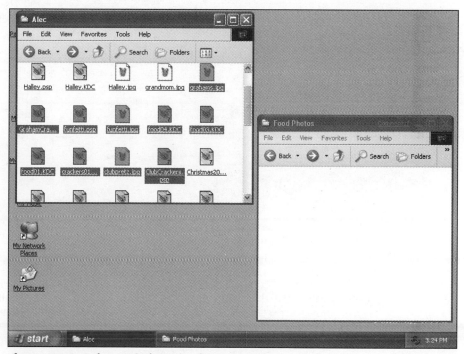

Figure 12-9: Explorer windows for the source (Alec) and destination (Food Photos) of the files I'm about to move.

5. Point to any selected item in the source window, hold down the secondary (right) mouse button, and then drag the "ghost image" into the destination folder.

6. Release the mouse button. Then choose Move Here or Copy Here from the menu that appears.

That's it! If you copied the items, both windows now contain icons for all those items. If you moved them, only the destination window for the item contains those icons, as in the example shown in Figure 12-10. You can, of course, tidy things up in either window by selecting a view and/or choosing View ⇨ Arrange Icons By from the window's menu bar.

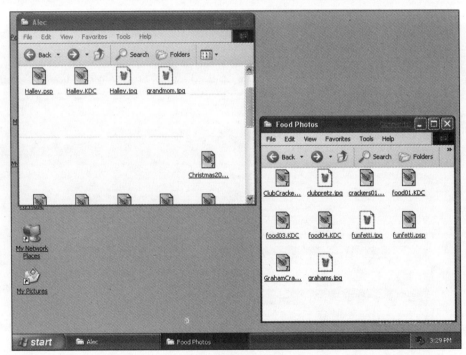

Figure 12-10: Results of moving selected items from the Alec folder to the Food Photos folder

Tip

If you get partway through a drag-and-drop operation and then change your mind, be aware that releasing the mouse button will place the selected files wherever the mouse pointer happens to be at that moment (which can get messy). However, if you press the Escape (Esc) button *before* you release the mouse button, the drag will be canceled before any files are moved or copied.

In the preceding steps, I recommended using the secondary (right) mouse button to drag the selected items. Personally, I prefer that method because I like being given the option to move or copy the items at that moment. However, you can drag the items using the primary (left) mouse button. If you do so, you won't be given any choices when you release the mouse button to drop the items. Instead, here's what will happen:

✦ If you drag to a different folder on the same disk, the selected items are moved to that location.

✦ If you drag to a different disk drive, the selected items are copied to that location.

If you drag the files with the left mouse button and you aren't sure what Windows XP intends to do with those items, look at the mouse pointer (without releasing the mouse button). The icon near the mouse pointer tells you what Windows intends to do, as follows:

✦ If you see a plus sign, Windows intends to copy the files (add them to the disk or folder).

✦ If you see a small arrow, Windows intends to create shortcut icons at the destination.

✦ If you see neither symbol, Windows intends to move the files to that location.

✦ If you see an international prohibited symbol, Windows intends to do nothing, because you're attempting an operation that's not allowed.

If Windows XP intends to do something you hadn't intended, you can force it to copy, move, or create a shortcut by pressing and holding down one of the following keys before you release the mouse button:

✦ **Ctrl:** Copies the selected item(s)

✦ **Shift:** Moves the selected item(s)

✦ **Shift+Ctrl:** Creates a shortcut to the selected files or folder

Remember, if you get mixed up in the middle of all of this, pressing the Escape key *before* you release the mouse button will cancel out the whole operation, leaving all the selected items safe and sound in their original location.

Using cut-and-paste to move and copy

Cut-and-paste (or copy-and-paste) offers yet another alternative for moving and copying files. Here's how this method works:

1. In an Explorer window, use any of the methods described earlier to select the items you want to move or copy.

2. Right-click any selected file's icon. In the menu that appears, choose Copy if you want to copy the items, or Cut if you want to move the items.

Caution

Once you copy or cut a file name, *do not* cut or copy any others until *after* you paste the current selection into the destination folder.

3. Navigate to the drive or folder to which you want to move or copy the items.

4. Choose Edit ⇨ Paste from that window's menu bar. Or, right-click some neutral area between icons inside the destination folder or drive and choose Paste from that menu.

All done.

Making a copy in the same folder

Sometimes it's helpful to have two copies of the same file in a single directory. For example, let's say you have a file named `January Newsletter.doc`. When February rolls around, you want to use January's newsletter as the starting point for your new newsletter. Instead of altering January's newsletter directly, you can keep that one and use a copy as the starting point for the new newsletter.

To do so, right-click the file you want to copy (`January Newsletter.doc` in this example) and choose Copy. Then right-click any neutral area near that icon and choose Paste. The new file will have the same name as the original, preceded by *Copy of*. To change the name of that new file, right-click it and choose Rename. Type in the new name (for instance, `February Newsletter.doc`) and press Enter. To open that new file for editing, just click (or double-click) it.

Tip

If the new icon is covered by others in the same window, just choose View ⇨ Arrange Icons By ⇨ Name to straighten things out. If you do so before renaming the new file, remember its name starts with the word *Copy*.

Undoing a move or copy

If you complete a move or copy operation and then change your mind, you can undo the action as long as you don't do any more moving or copying. (You can undo only one move/copy operation—the one you performed most recently.)

To undo a move or copy, you can just press the universal Undo key, Ctrl+Z. Alternatively, you can right-click within the source folder or destination folder (or desktop, if that was your source or destination) and choose Undo Move or Undo Copy. Or choose Edit ⇨ Undo from the source or destination window's menu bar. You might see a prompt asking whether it's okay to delete the files. Choosing Yes will delete only the copied file, which is okay because that's what's actually required to "undo" the copy.

Copying Files to a CD-R or CD-RW Disc

If your PC has a CD-R or CD-RW disk drive, you also can copy files to writeable discs using techniques very similar to those you've used earlier in the chapter. People often get confused about just what is and isn't possible with CDs, so let me first point out a couple of facts:

✦ You can't copy to a "regular" CD under any circumstances. You can copy only to CD-R and CD-RW discs (available at most computer and office-supply stores).

✦ If your system has only a regular CD-ROM drive, you can't copy to any kind of compact disc, not even a CD-R or CD-RW disc. You must have a CD-R or CD-RW disk *drive*, as well as the appropriate type of disc.

The difference between CD-R and CD-RW is as follows: With CD-R, you get to "burn once." That is, after you've copied some files to the disc, you're done. You can't go back and add still more files, and you can't delete things from the disc after you've completed the copy. CD-RW (Read/Write) discs are more like floppies and other more "normal" types of disks. That is, a single copy operation doesn't permanently "burn" the content onto the disc. You can still go back and add more files later, delete files, and so forth. However, to do that you need to be working with both a CD-RW drive and CD-RW disc. If either the drive or disc is CD-R, the "burn once" principle still applies.

In the past, you had to use special software to copy files to CD-R and CD-RW discs. That capability is built right in to Windows XP. So you can use the techniques described so far to create CDs. There are a couple of extra steps involved though. So here's what you want to do:

About Burning Audio CDs

When choosing files to copy to a CD, if you opt to copy music files, you'll be given options for creating (or "burning") a music CD (also known as an audio CD). An audio CD differs from a CD-ROM in that you can play it in *any* CD player, be it your car stereo, home stereo, or portable device, as well as your computer.

If you use the technique described here to create an audio CD, Windows Media Player will pop up in the middle of things, and you'll need to know how to use that program to finish the job.

I suggest that if you're interested in creating audio CDs, you learn how to do it with Windows Media Player, which is covered in Chapter 25. You'll probably find that the whole process is easier if you just use Media Player to do the whole job.

1. Insert a blank CD-R into your CD-R or CD-RW drive. Or insert a CD-RW disc into your CD-RW drive. Within a few seconds, an Explorer window will open displaying the contents of the disc (if any). You can shrink that window down to make room for a second Explorer window, which you can use to navigate to the folder from which you'll be copying files.

Tip If an Explorer window doesn't open automatically within a few seconds, open My Computer and click the CD-R or CD-RW drive's icon. To choose how Windows XP reacts when you insert a CD or DVD disc into its drive, see "Automating CDs and DVDs" later in this chapter.

2. Open My Documents (or My Computer, or anything else that opens into a Windows Explorer window), and navigate to the folder that contains the file(s) and/or folder(s) you want to copy.

3. Using any of the techniques described earlier in this chapter, select the files and/or folders that you want to move or copy to the CD.

4. Drag the selected item(s) into the Explorer window that represents the CD-R or CD-RW disc. The file icons will appear in the *staging area* under the heading Files Ready to Be Written to the CD, as in Figure 12-11. The down arrow on each icon in the staging area indicates that the file has not yet been written to the CD.

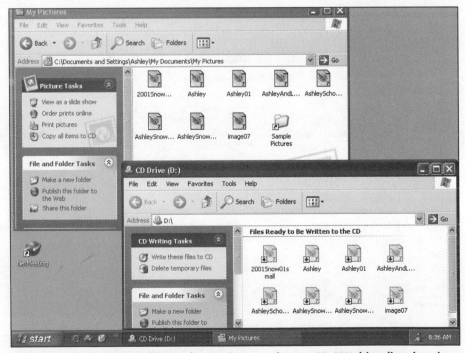

Figure 12-11: Temporary files in the staging area for my CD-RW drive, listed under Files Ready to Be Written to the CD

5. If necessary, you can repeat Steps 2 through 4 to add as many files as will fit on the CD.

Tip

If you change your mind about any files to be written to the CD, you can click the Delete Temporary Files option under CD Writing Tasks to remove them all. Or, right-click any file and choose Delete to remove it from the list.

6. When you're ready to create the CD, click the Write These Files to CD under CD Writing Tasks in the Explorer bar. The CD Burning Wizard shown in Figure 12-12 starts.

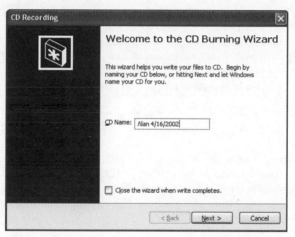

Figure 12-12: First page of the CD Burning Wizard

7. If this is the first time you've written to the CD-RW, you can change the name of the CD. (This is the name that appears under the CD's icon in the Explorer window.) By default, the wizard suggests your user name followed by the date. Click the Next button.

Note

At this point, if you selected music files for the staging area, the wizard will let you choose between creating an audio CD, or copying normally. I suggest you copy normally here, if that was your intent. If you want to create an audio CD, you would be better off canceling the operation, and then using Media Player, described in Chapter 25, to create the audio CD.

8. You'll see a progress indicator keeping you informed of how much time is required to complete the process. When the process is finished, the wizard will reappear. Click the Finish button to close the wizard.

The CD will probably be ejected from the drive, leaving the Explorer window's contents empty. To verify that the copy was performed successfully, just insert that CD into the CD-ROM drive of any computer.

Troubleshooting CD recording

If you have any problems recording to a CD-R or CD-RW drive, make sure writing is enabled. If you encounter multiple errors while trying to record to CDs, you might need to select a slower recording speed. You can get to the appropriate options by opening My Computer, right-clicking the drive's icon, and choosing Properties. Click the Recording tab and make your selections from the options provided.

Deleting files from CD-RW discs

CD-RW discs provide a little more flexibility than CD-R discs, in that you can delete files that are already on the disc. However, you have to delete them all in one fell swoop—you cannot delete them individually. To get started, insert the CD-RW disc into your CD-RW drive. If you're prompted for an action, choose Open Folder to View Files. If nothing happens within a few seconds, open My Computer and then open the drive's icon. When you get to the Explorer window for the drive, files that are currently on the disc will be listed under Files Currently on the CD.

 Caution   This operation will permanently erase all the files on the CD-RW. There is no Recycle Bin or Undo. So think before you act!

If you need to keep copies of any of the files that are currently on the disc, make sure you copy them to your My Documents folder, desktop, or any other folder on your hard disk. When you're ready to permanently delete *all* the files that are currently on the disc, choose Erase This CD-RW under CD Writing Tasks in the Explorer bar. A wizard will open and delete all the files from the disc. The Explorer window for the disc will then be empty.

When things don't fit

When moving and copying files—especially to external media such as floppy, CD, and Zip disks, keep in mind that there's a limit to how much stuff you can actually place on a disk. For example, a floppy disk holds only about 1.2MB of data. A CD-R or CD-RW usually holds somewhere between 650 and 750MB (or say half a gigabyte, or about as much as 600 floppies). Other media, such as Zip disks, come in a variety of capacities.

 Note   A kilobyte (K) is about 1,000 bytes, a megabyte (MB) is about 1,000 kilobytes, and a gigabyte is about 1,000 megabytes.

If you attempt to move or copy too much stuff to a disk, you'll see some kind of message indicating that the destination is full. You might have to insert another disk to continue the move/copy, or you might have to cancel the operation altogether, depending on the problem at hand and the error message that appears. Although none of this is disastrous, it can be avoided by checking to see how much space is available on the destination disk and how much stuff you've selected to copy to that disk before you begin the move or copy operation.

To see how much space is available on a removable disk, insert the disk into its drive. Then use My Computer in the Start menu to get to the icons for your drives. Right-click the drive that contains the disk you want to check, and choose Properties from the pop-up menu. The Properties dialog box will show the capacity of the disk, as well as how much used space and free space is available. In Figure 12-13, for example, I'm checking the capacity of a floppy disk in drive A:. There's only about 263K left on that disk.

While you're selecting files to copy to the disk, use the Details area of the Explorer bar to see how much you've selected. In Figure 12-14, for example, I've selected five files on my hard disk to be copied. The Details pane tells me that the total size of those selected files is 241K. Which is about all that will fit into the available space on the sample floppy mentioned earlier!

If you want to squeeze as much stuff as possible onto a removable disk, consider compressing the files before selecting them to be copied. You can do that in the traditional way, by using a third-party compression program. Alternatively, you can first move or copy the files to a compressed folder, as described a little later in this chapter.

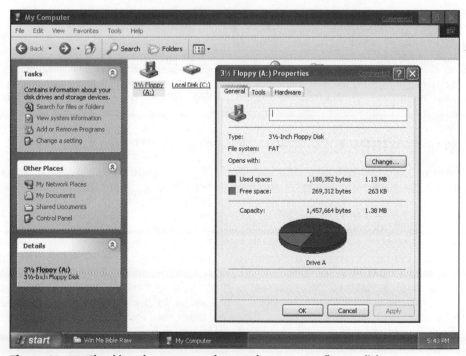

Figure 12-13: Checking the amount of unused space on a floppy disk

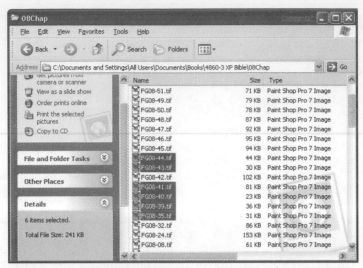

Figure 12-14: The Details section of the Explorer pane shows the total size of all the selected files.

Renaming a File or Folder

You can easily change the name of a file or folder. However, a word of caution regarding file name extensions is appropriate here. Many file names have a *file name extension,* which is a dot (period) followed by one or more letters, such as .exe, .doc, or .jpg. The extension tells Windows what kind of information the file contains. Normally, file name extensions are hidden so that you don't see them; you need not concern yourself about accidentally changing them.

If you're about to rename a file and notice that it has a file name extension, don't change the extension. If you try to, Windows will present a warning that reads:

```
If you change a file name extension, the file may become
unusable. Are you sure you want to change it?
```

Click the No button to keep the existing file name. Then go ahead and rename the file again, but leave the extension unchanged. You can do so after right-clicking the file's icon and choosing Rename. Just click to the left of the file name extension and then drag the mouse pointer all the way to the left, or press Ctrl+Home to extend the selection all the way to the left. The new name you type will replace only the selected portion of the name—not the extension.

Cross-Reference For information on hiding and displaying file name extensions, see the section titled "Viewing and Hiding File Info" in Chapter 2. For an in-depth discussion about how Windows uses file name extensions, see Chapter 33.

Tip

The Web site at `http://filext.com` maintains a comprehensive list of all file name extensions, with a brief description of the type of file each extension represents.

I guess I just told you how to rename a file. But here are the exact step-by-step instructions anyway:

1. Right-click the icon of the file or folder you want to rename. (There's no point in selecting files first, because you can only rename one file or folder at a time.)

2. Choose Rename from the shortcut menu and then edit the current name or type a new one.

3. Press Enter or click anywhere just outside the icon to save your change.

Note

Files on read-only media, such as a CD-ROM, cannot be renamed or deleted.

If you change your mind immediately after renaming a file, press Ctrl+X or right-click next to the file name and choose Undo Rename from the shortcut menu.

Using Compressed Folders (Zip Files)

As you know, every file you store on your computer's disk drives takes up a certain amount of disk space, represented as the file's size. It's possible to *compress* a file to reduce its size so that it takes up less space. Doing so not only conserves space on your hard disk, it also is handy for squeezing more data onto a removable disk, such as a floppy. You also can compress multiple files into a single *compressed folder* or *Zip file,* which makes it easier to attach the files to an e-mail message. The resulting compressed file will also be smaller than all the original uncompressed files, making transfer across the Internet go more quickly. In fact, many files that you download from the Internet will be compressed. The senders compress the files to reduce your download time.

Note that I said you can compress files into a compressed folder or Zip file. In reality, the two are one in the same. On a Windows XP computer that has no other compression program installed, Zip files display with an icon that looks like a manila file folder with a zipper on it. Because a Zip file can actually contain one or more compressed files, the term *folder* is used, as is the folder icon, because folders (not files) in Windows can always contain multiple files.

Caution

If you install *any* third-party Zip program on your Windows XP computer, compressed files will, essentially, cease to exist on that computer. Your Zip files will be treated in the traditional manner. Compressed folders work only on Windows XP machines that have no third-party compression programs installed!

If you have a third-party Zip program and want to compress some files, you need to use whatever techniques that program requires to compress files. Assuming you're using the built-in Windows XP compression, the next section describes a quick and easy way to copy some files/folders to a compressed folder.

Quick and easy compressed folders

If you just want to compress some files into a compressed folder (that is, a Zip file) to e-mail them to someone, here's the quick and easy way to do so:

1. Open My Computer or any other Explorer window and navigate to the folder that contains the files you want to compress.

2. Select the files/folders to compress.

3. Right-click any selected item and choose Send To ➪ Compressed (zipped) Folder.

A new folder with a zipper icon will appear at the bottom of the current Explorer window. Initially, its name will be the same as whichever file you right-clicked in Step 3. You can change that name by right-clicking the compressed folder's icon and choosing Rename.

Tip   If you want to e-mail that compressed folder to someone right now, right-click its icon and choose Send To ➪ Mail Recipient. More on e-mailing compressed folders in a moment.

Note that these steps *copy* the selected files to the compressed folder. You haven't gained any disk space using that method. In fact, you've lost some disk space because now you have both the original copies and the compressed copies of the files on your hard disk. If you're looking to *move* a bunch of files to a compressed folder, and/or the files to compress are spread across several folders on your hard disk, you can use the method described next rather than the quick and easy method just described.

When the quick and easy method of compressing files and folders doesn't achieve the results you're looking for, you can use a two-step method to move or copy files to a compressed folder. The first step is to create a new, empty compressed folder, as follows:

1. Using the standard Explorer window, navigate to the folder that will contain the new compressed folder. (For instance, My Documents will do nicely.)

2. Choose File ➪ New ➪ Compressed (zipped) Folder from the Explorer menu bar. Or, right-click within the files area and choose New ➪ Compressed (zipped) Folder from the shortcut menu. A folder named New Compressed (zipped) Folder appears. (It will show the file name extension .zip if you're not hiding file name extensions.)

3. If you want to change the name of the folder, type in the new name now. (If the .zip extension is visible, don't change that!) Alternatively, you can change its name at any time by right-clicking and choosing Rename.

In Figure 12-15, I have created a couple of compressed folders within My Documents. Their zippered icons are visible in the lower part of the Explorer window. Remember that compressed *folders* aren't really folders at all — they're actually Zip files. Notice that in Thumbnails view, which is what Figure 12-15 is using, the compressed folder icons aren't as big as the icons for the regular folders. In fact, the compressed folder icons are the same size as the regular file icons. Furthermore, when you arrange the icons by name, the compressed "folders" are alphabetized with the rest of the files in the folder, *not* with the regular folders. But of course, that's not important to using the compressed folders.

Figure 12-15: Compressed folders have a zipper on their icon, like the two near the bottom of this Explorer window.

Moving/copying files to a compressed folder

After you've created a compressed folder, you can easily move or copy any files or folders into it. For starters, you can open the compressed folder by clicking (or double-clicking) its icon. Size its window to make room for other Explorer windows. Then open My Computer, My Documents, or any other Explorer window, and navigate to the folder that contains the files/folders you want to compress. Select the files/folders you want to compress, using any of the techniques described earlier in this chapter. Then copy or move those files to the compressed folder by right-dragging and then dropping them into the compressed folder.

Tip   It's not really necessary to open the compressed folder to move/copy items into it. You can drop selected items onto the folder's icon instead.

Remember that if you *move* the files into the compressed folder, they will no longer be available from their original location. You'll have to open the compressed folder to get at those files and folders. Do this only if your hard disk is getting full and you want to use compression as a way to gain back some disk (or if you intend to move the compressed folder to some external medium such as a floppy disk).

E-mailing your compressed files

If you compressed your files to make it quicker and easier to e-mail them to some-one, there are a couple of ways you can attach the compressed files to someone. The quickest way is to right-click the compressed folder and choose Send To ➪ Mail Recipient. Your e-mail client program (for instance, Outlook Express) will open a window that enables you to compose your e-mail message, as in Figure 12-16. The compressed file (that is, the Zip file) is already attached, and the Subject is filled in with the name of the file you're sending. You just need to fill in the recipient's e-mail address in the To portion and add any text to the body and then click the Send button.

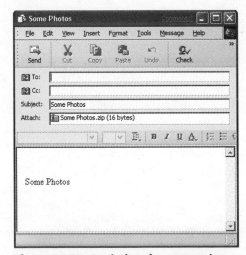

Figure 12-16: A window for composing an e-mail message, with the Some Photos compressed folder already attached

Optionally, you can compose your e-mail in the traditional manner and attach the compressed folder just as you would attach any normal file to an e-mail message, as discussed in Chapter 8.

When the recipient gets your message, the file will be like any other attachment. The recipient can use her e-mail program to save the attachment to her own hard disk. If she doesn't have Windows XP (or some other version of Windows that supports compressed folders), the file will be saved as a regular Zip file, with the normal icon for their system, in whatever folder she places the icon. If she has a version of Windows that supports compressed folders and no third-party compression program installed, the saved attachment will appear as a compressed folder in her system.

Uncompressing files

There are several ways to deal with files that are within a compressed folder. Probably the simplest way to do so is to *extract* normal, uncompressed copies of the files out of the folder and into some normal folder on your computer, such as My Documents. To do so, follow these steps:

1. Right-click the compressed folder's icon and choose Extract All. An Extraction Wizard will open.

2. Click Next on the first page of the wizard. On the second wizard page, use the Browse button to navigate to the folder in which you want to place the normal, uncompressed copies of the files. Then click OK.

3. Click the Next button to extract. If you want to open the folder in which you placed the extracted files, choose the Show Extracted Files option on the last wizard page.

4. Click the Finish button.

After the files have been extracted, it's not necessary to keep the original compressed folder. You can right-click its icon and choose Delete if you want to get rid of it.

As an alternative to extracting all the files from a compressed folder in one fell swoop, you can extract them individually. This comes in handy if you want to put different files in the compressed folder into several different folders on your hard disk. For example, if the compressed folder contains pictures and text documents, you might want to put the pictures in your My Pictures folder and the text documents in your My Documents folder. To extract files individually, follow these steps:

1. Open the compressed folder by clicking (or double-clicking) its icon. Its contents appear in a "normal looking" Explorer window.

2. Shrink that open Explorer window down a bit to make room for another Explorer window.

3. Open My Documents, My Computer, or any other Explorer window, and navigate to the folder into which you want to place normal, uncompressed files. Shrink that window down a bit too so that you can see both open Explorer windows.

4. In the compressed folder's Explorer window, select the files/folders you want to uncompress to the other Explorer window.

5. Right-drag the selected items from the compressed folder to the normal folder and choose Copy Here or Move here, depending on which you want to do.

You can repeat Steps 3–5 to move or copy different files from the compressed folder to different folders on your hard drive.

Caution

Some programs cannot be run while they are contained in a compressed folder. If you find that a particular program won't run in a compressed folder, just move the program and its associated files to a regular un-compressed folder. Then open the program file from within that normal, uncompressed folder.

Note

If you have formatted your hard drive using NTFS — the *NT File System* — you also have the option of using NTFS file compression on your entire hard drive. NTFS file compression is not related to compressed folders or Zip files and so does not have any effect on files you send or receive. See "NTFS File Compression" in Chapter 31 for more information.

Other compression types

Windows XP compressed folders use Zip compression mainly because that's the most popular method for transferring compressed files from one Windows computer to the next. However, Zip isn't the only compression method out there. Macintosh users often use a program named StuffIt to compress files. These compressed files often have the .sit file name extension. UNIX and Linux users sometimes compress files to Tape Archive (.tar) or gzip (.g or .gz) format. Still others will create self-extracting files (.exe) that automatically decompress as soon as you open their icons.

If you attempt to open a compressed file that Windows cannot decompress, you'll either be taken to an Open With window or a dialog box that enables you to search the Web for programs that might be able to open the file. If the Open With list opens, there's no harm in trying one of the listed programs. You might have to try several to find one that works. It's also quite possible that none of the listed programs will work!

If instead of the Open With list, you're taken to the option that enables you to browse the Web for appropriate programs, you can choose that option to see what suggestions are listed. Before you download any programs to open the file, remember that if the program you download also handles Zip files, you may lose the ability to use the built-in Windows XP compressed folders capability. Your best bet might be to reply to the person who sent you the compressed file and ask whether he can send a Zip file instead.

If you really need the flexibility to work with a wide variety of compression formats, your best bet might be to do some research on Windows XP–compatible programs. First, go to a download site such as http://download.cnet.com. Then search for the file name extension of the type of file you're interested in (for instance, .sit, .tar, or whatever). Try to find any information about Windows XP compatibility on products that the search finds. Also, jot down the name and manufacturer of possible products.

Next, check the software compatibility list for Windows XP by clicking the Start button, choosing Help and Support, and clicking the Find compatible hardware and software for Windows XP link. Use the Product Search, Manufacturer Search, or Software Lists option to try to find as much information as possible. (In Software Lists, use the Utilities category.) If you can find a compatible product that *doesn't* support Zip files, you stand a better chance of being able to hold onto the compressed folders feature of Windows XP, as opposed to having to rely on a third-party program to handle all your Zip files.

Freeing Read-Only Files

Occasionally, you may come across a file flagged as read-only (sometimes abbreviated R/O), meaning you can view the file, but you can't make any changes to it. In a few cases, the file might have been intentionally made read-only so that you can't tamper with it. Files copied from CD-ROMs and downloaded from the Internet might be flagged as read-only for no good reason, other than the fact that they used to reside on a read-only CD-ROM disc. To clear the read-only status, thereby converting it back to a normal read-write (R/W) file, follow these steps:

1. Close the file (if it's open) so that you can get to its icon.

2. If you aren't already there, navigate to the folder that contains the read-only file(s).

3. Right-click the file you want to convert to read-write (or right-click any one of the selected files) and choose Properties.

4. In the dialog box that appears, click the General tab if it isn't already on top (see Figure 12-17).

5. Clear the check mark from the Read-only check box and then click the OK button.

Note   Files on read-only media, such as CD-ROMs, cannot be converted to read-write.

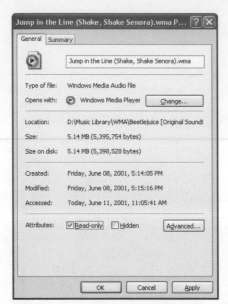

Figure 12-17: Use a file's Properties
dialog box to change its read-only status.

The file (or selected files) will behave as normal read-write files from this point. To
make a file read-only, repeat the steps, but check—rather than clear—that Read-
only check box.

Automating CDs and DVDs

Many CD-ROM and DVD discs contain a file named `autorun.inf`, which tells
Windows what to do when the disc is inserted into its drive. For example, when you
purchase a program on CD, inserting the CD will often start the program required to
install that program onto your computer. If the disc doesn't contain an autorun file,
Windows might present a prompt asking what you want to do with the disc, as in
Figure 12-18. Or it may just open the CD in a folder or some program.

Tip   To explore the contents of a CD or DVD, open My Computer, right-click the drive's
icon and choose Explore.

Figure 12-18: A sample Windows XP prompt asking how you want to handle an inserted CD or DVD

You can choose an action from the list provided, and you can also opt to always take the same action whenever a similar disc is inserted into the drive. But of course, as in all things Windows, you're never committed to a specific action. You can select a new default action for any type of disc at any time. Here's how:

1. Open My Computer and then right-click the icon for the CD or DVD drive.

2. Choose Properties, and then click the AutoPlay tab to get to the options shown in Figure 12-19.

3. From the drop-down list, choose a content type. For example, if you want to select an action for discs that contain a DVD movie, choose DVD Movie from the drop-down list. Then. . . .

   • If you want Windows to perform some action automatically, select the first option button, Select an Action to Perform, and then click the action you want Windows to perform (for instance, Play Using Windows Media Player).

   • Or, if you want Windows to display the prompt asking you which action you want to perform, select the second option button, Prompt Me Each Time.

4. Click the OK button.

That's all there is to it. If ever you want to go back to the original settings that Windows XP used when first installed, repeat Steps 1 and 2 and choose Restore Defaults.

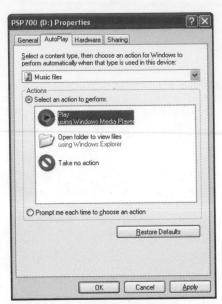

Figure 12-19: The AutoPlay tab of a
CD or DVD drive's Properties dialog box

Changing the Name of Your C: Drive

Your hard disk, named C:, also has a *volume label,* which is an additional, slightly
more descriptive name. On most computers, this label is Local Disk. If you have
multiple hard drives, such as C: and D:, they might both be labeled Local Disk. If
you connect a bunch of computers together in a local area network and go browsing around through all the computers, you're going to end up seeing a whole lot of
drives named Local Disk, which can become pretty confusing.

You can change the volume label of any hard disk, if you're so inclined. To do so,
open My Computer from your Start menu or navigate to My Computer within any
Explorer window. Then right-click the icon for a hard drive and choose Properties.
Type a new name in the box titled Label. (This name can be no more than 11 characters long.) Click OK when finished. The name you entered replaces Local Disk (or
whatever the original name was) in My Computer as well as in all other navigation
windows.

You can use the same technique to name or rename a floppy disk in a floppy drive,
but you can't rename read-only disk drives (including CD-ROMs). The label that
appears with these drive names will always change to reflect the current contents
of the drive.

Using DOS Commands to Manage Files

If you're familiar with DOS commands, you may be relieved to know you still can use the CD, COPY, ERASE, DEL, MOVE, XCOPY, and REN commands to navigate and to move, copy, and delete files and folders. (If you're unfamiliar with DOS commands, don't worry. You don't need to use them.)

To use the DOS commands, first click the Start button, point to All Programs, Accessories, and choose Command Prompt. The command prompt displays (typically C:\Documents and Settings*yourusername*>), and you can enter DOS commands. For brief help with a command, enter the command followed by a space and /? — for example, del /?. (Remember, always press Enter after typing any DOS command.)

Tip   To see a list of the DOS commands you can use, type **help** at the command prompt.

To close the DOS window, enter the exit command at the command prompt.

A number of books are available if you want to learn more about DOS. Check out *DOS For Dummies,* by Dan Gookin, published by Hungry Minds, for an introduction to DOS.

Summary

Here's a quick recap of the most important points covered in this chapter:

✦ To select an object to move, copy, or delete, click the object (Classic style) or point to it with your mouse (Web style).

✦ To select several objects, you can drag a frame around them. Alternatively, use Ctrl+click, Shift+click, and Shift+Ctrl+click with Classic-style clicking or Ctrl+point, Shift+point, and Shift+Ctrl+point with Web-style clicking.

✦ To move or copy selected objects, hold down the right mouse button and drag to the destination. Then release the mouse button and choose Copy Here or Move Here from the shortcut menu that appears.

✦ As an alternative to using drag-and-drop, you can right-click any selected file and choose Copy if you want to copy or Cut if you want to move. Then open the destination folder, right-click some neutral area within that folder and choose Paste.

✦ If you have a CD-R or CD-RW drive, you can save files to writeable disks using the standard file manipulation techniques. Just remember that you need to write the files to the disc after they have been copied to the staging area.

✦ To rename an object, right-click the object and choose Rename from the shortcut menu.

✦ You can use the compressed folders feature to work with Zip files using the standard Windows XP methods for moving or copying files between folders.

✦ To delete selected objects, press the Delete key. Or, right-click a selected object and choose Delete from the shortcut menu.

✦ Remember, objects you delete from your local hard disk(s) (only) are sent to the Recycle Bin. They continue to use disk space until you empty the bin.

✦ To undelete deleted items, open the Recycle Bin, select the items you want to restore, and then choose File ➪ Restore from Recycle Bin's menu bar.

✦ To delete objects permanently and recover their disk space, choose File ➪ Empty Recycle Bin from the Recycle Bin's menu bar.

✦ To convert a read-only file to read-write, right-click the file's icon and choose Properties. Then clear the Read-only check box on the General tab of the dialog box that appears. Choose OK.

✦   ✦   ✦

Organizing Your Virtual Office

It seems we're all busier today than we would like to be, these days. And just about everyone is looking for ways to work smarter, not harder. A big part of achieving that goal centers around organization — the ability to find the things you need when you need them. Obviously I can't help you organize your entire life. (My own life could stand quite a bit of reorganization!) But I can help you get things organized on your computer so that at least that tiny part of your life is more efficient.

There are a couple of ways to get organized on your computer so that you can work smarter, and not harder. One has to do with how you organize the materials you work with. The sections dealing with folders in this chapter show you how to do that. The other has to do with how you set up your desktop, Start menu, and taskbar, which is also covered in this chapter.

About Folders

As you know, the word *document* refers to anything on a computer that's not a program. For example, pictures, video, and music are all examples of documents. Most programs that you use enable you to create documents as well, such as spreadsheets, databases, letters, and so forth. Images — from digital cameras, scanners, clip art collections — are also documents.

Each document is stored as a file on your hard disk. All the files that make up your programs, and Windows itself, are also stored on your hard disk. So at any given time your hard disk probably contains thousands of files.

To prevent you from having to look at all these files all the time, the files are divided into separate folders. You've already seen examples of folders in preceding chapters, such as the My Documents folder, which is the ideal place to store any documents you create, download, or copy onto your hard disk from floppies, CD-ROMs, and so forth.

Windows XP itself is stored in a folder named WINDOWS. Most programs you install (as well as the programs that come with Windows) are stored in a folder named Program Folders. Both the WINDOWS and Program Files folders contain still more folders. As a general rule, you never want to mess around with those folders. Doing so can really create havoc on your system, making it unusable. So it's best to allow Windows and the programs you install to create and manage those folders on their own.

The My Documents folder, which is created automatically by Windows, is the folder into which you'll want to place your own documents. Chances are, your My Documents folder already contains a couple of subfolders as well, named My Pictures and My Music. As their names imply, these are good for storing pictures and music files.

As your collection of documents grows, your My Documents, My Pictures, My Music, and any other folders might start growing to a point where they become unwieldy. For example, if you do a lot of work with pictures, your My Pictures folder might end up containing hundreds, or thousands of files. Technically, that's okay, because there is no limit to how many files a folder can contain. From an organizational standpoint, however, it's bound to be a pain, because every time you go looking for a specific picture in that lengthy list of files, you're going to have to sift through all those file names. It's better to find a way to organize those files into separate, smaller folders, where each folder contains relatively few files. That way, you can locate the file you're looking for just by going to the appropriate folder first, and then looking through the smaller set of filenames within that folder.

The joy of folder terminology

As with all things computer, certain concepts and buzzwords (big yawn here) go along with the whole business of folders. For starters, files (and folders) are stored on *disks*. The thing that spins the disk around, reads information from, and writes information to, the disk is called the *disk drive*, or *drive* for short. Removable disks are the ones that you can actually see and take out of their drives, such as floppy disks and CD-ROMs. The files that are "always in" your computer are stored on the non-removable *fixed disk* (also called the *hard disk*) inside your computer. Although you never actually see that disk, it too spins around inside its drive.

Disk drives, as you can see when you open My Computer from the Start menu, are given simple, one-letter names followed by a colon. In virtually all systems, the floppy disk drive is named A:, and the hard disk is named C:. Your CD-ROM or DVD drive may be named D: or E:, as in the example shown in Figure 13-1. Your computer might have additional drives.

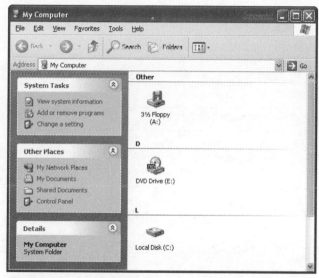

Figure 13-1: A sample My Computer view of a PC with a hard disk (C:), floppy drive (A:), and DVD drive (E:)

Every disk, be it your hard disk or a removable disks, contains one or more folders. The one folder that every disk contains is called the root folder or root directory, and its name is just a backslash character (\). The *root* folder gets its name from the fact that all the folders on any disk are organized in a hierarchical *inverted tree* format. At the base of this upside down tree is the root folder, from which all other folders "branch out."

Note   The terms *folder* and *directory* mean exactly the same thing — a place on a disk where files (and perhaps additional folders) are stored. The older term *directory* isn't used much any more though.

Figure 13-2 shows an example of a folder hierarchy with the root folder at the top. Although the hierarchical view of a folder structure doesn't really show it, all folders (except the root) are contained within other folders. Any folder that appears below another folder in the hierarchy is actually contained within the folder above it. Hence, *all* the folders within the hierarchy shown in Figure 13-2 are actually contained within the root folder. The folders named My Music and My Pictures at the lower left of the hierarchy are actually contained within the My Documents folder. My Documents, in turn, is contained within the Documents and Settings\ yourusername (where *yourusername* is the name you log on with).

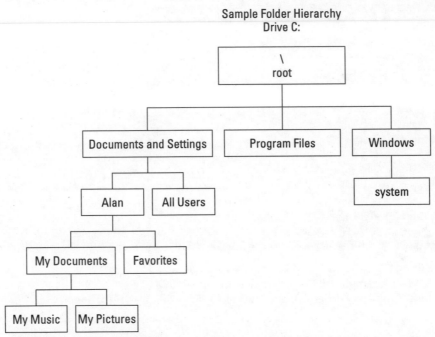

Figure 13-2: A sample folder hierarchy. The root folder, named \, is always the uppermost folder in the hierarchy, and contains all other folders within the hierarchy.

Parents and children

The relationships among folders are often described in the same manner as relationships in a family tree are described. A folder that contains another folder is called the *parent* to that folder. For example, the My Documents folder is the parent to the My Music and My Pictures folders. Likewise, My Music and My Pictures are *children* of the My Documents folder. Because My Music and My Pictures share the same parent, they can be called *siblings*.

Carrying the family tree analogy further, one *could* say that the folder named Alan is the grandparent to the My Music and My Pictures folders. However, you'll never hear those terms. In fact, more often than not, you'll probably only hear the term *parent* used within the context of folder hierarchies. And that term is always used to refer to the folder that's immediately above a given folder in the hierarchy. You also might hear the parent referred to as the *containing folder* or *container* because it does, indeed, contain the folders that are its children. Thus, in the hierarchy, the folder named Alan is the *parent*, and the *container*, and the *containing folder* to the My Documents folder beneath it.

As if that's not enough terminology to turn a fairly simple concept into a confusing mess, there's actually more.

Folders and subfolders

A folder that's contained within another folder is often called a *subfolder*. However, a folder is a folder is a folder, and there's no difference between a folder and a sub-folder. Each is just a place on the disk where files are stored. All the folders in the hierarchy are actually subfolders of the root folder, because they're all contained within the root folder. But you won't often hear people referring to the My Documents *sub*folder.

About the only time you'll hear that term is when one is referring specifically to a folder that's contained within the current folder. When viewing the contents of the My Documents folder, for example, referring to the My Pictures subfolder is just a shortcut way of referring to the My Pictures folder that is specifically contained within *this* My Documents folder. But the important point to keep in mind is that the terms *folder* and *subfolder* refer to exactly the same thing—a folder.

Paths

Last in our exciting tour of folder terminology is the term *path*, which refers to the complete "road map" that a computer needs to follow to get to a specific file. Suppose, for example, that the My Pictures folder shown back in Figure 13-2 contains a file named Passport.jpg. The path that explains the *exact* location of that file on the computer would be expressed as follows:

```
C:\Documents and Settings\Alan\My Documents\My
Pictures\Passport.jpg
```

The C: part refers to hard disk drive, which contains the entire folder hierarchy. Backslashes are used to separate the various parts of the name. Therefore, the path here specifies the Passport.jpg file in the My Pictures folder, which is contained within the My Documents folder, which is contained within the Alan folder, which is contained within the Documents and Settings folder, which is contained within the root folder of hard disk drive C: (whew). Later in this chapter, under "Viewing the Path," I show how you can view the complete path to most files and folders in Explorer.

Note Whereas UNIX and the Internet use forward slashes (/) to separate names within a path, Windows always uses backslashes (\).

After all those terms and concepts, you may be thinking folders are something that's to be avoided like the plague. However, actually creating and using folders is a lot easier than talking about them. And there are good reasons for creating folders, which brings us to. . . .

Why create folders?

You create folders on your hard disk for the same reason you create folders for your paper filing cabinet — to organize your material to make it easier to find in the future. A good rule of thumb to follow is to put all your own documents within the folder named My Documents. None of your Windows or program files will ever use that folder, so it's a "safe" area in which to place all your own files, rearrange them into new folders, and so forth.

When you open your My Documents folder (which you can do by clicking the Start button and choosing My Documents), you'll probably see that it already contains at least a couple subfolders, such as My Pictures and My Music. As their names imply, these folders are good places to store pictures and music files.

As time goes by and your collection of documents (including picture and music files) grows, any one of those folders might end up containing hundreds, if not thousands, of files. There's nothing wrong with that technically, because there's really no limit to the number of files a folder can hold. However, when the list of files within a folder becomes so lengthy that it takes you a long time to locate any specific file, you're just not using your PC, or your time, very efficiently. Better to start creating folders within those folders, to group your files into some meaningful order, so you can more easily zero in on specific documents you're looking for.

For example, Figure 13-3 shows the contents of the My Documents folder on one of my computers. Notice that instead of having a ton of files listed there, I have my documents broken down into subfolders. The Books folder, for instance, holds all the files for any books I'm working on. I occasionally do work as an expert witness in court cases, and all the documents for those jobs I place in the Expert Witness folder, and so forth.

As you know from the start of this chapter, any folder can contain still more folders. For example, Figure 13-4 shows the contents of my My Music folder, where I have grouped songs by artist. Figure 13-5 shows the contents of my My Pictures folder, where I have organized pictures into several folders as well. In that example, I'm using the Thumbnails view (View ➪ Thumbnails from the menu bar), which enables me to see small thumbnail images of pictures within folders, as well as the larger views of the pictures that I haven't put into subfolders.

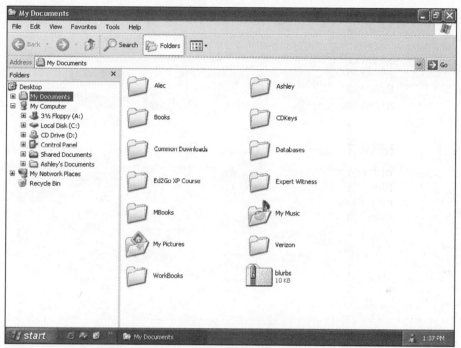

Figure 13-3: A sample My Documents folder, categorized into several subfolders

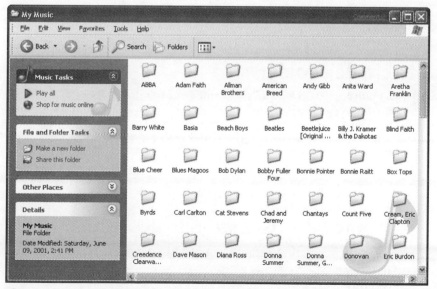

Figure 13-4: A sample My Music folder, with files arranged into subfolders by artist

Figure 13-5: A sample My Pictures folder in Thumbnails view, showing some folders as well as individual picture files

Of course, all of these examples are *just* examples. You're free to organize your files into whatever organizational scheme works best for you.

How to create a folder

Creating folders is easy. And as with most things in Windows, there are several ways to do it. All the methods produce the same result — a new, empty folder. Deciding which method to use is just a matter of what seems most convenient at the moment. In Explorer, the general procedure is as follows:

1. In Explorer, navigate to the folder in which you want to place a new folder (for instance, My Documents, My Pictures, My Music, or whatever).

2. Do either of the following:

   - Choose File ➪ New ➪ Folder from the Explorer menu bar.

   - Or, right-click at about where you want to place the new folder and choose New ➪ Folder.

3. A new folder named `New Folder` appears, with its name already selected for editing, as in Figure 13-6.

Figure 13-6: A new folder created, with its name selected and ready for you to type a new name.

4. Type in any name you like, then press Enter or click anywhere outside the new folder.

5. If you want to tidy things up and put the folder into alphabetic order by name with your other folders, choose View ➪ Arrange Icons By ➪ Name.

That's all there is to it. If you like, you can now move any existing documents into the new folder, using any of the techniques described back in Chapter 12. Should you decide to rename the folder later, just right-click it, choose Rename, and enter a new name.

Creating a folder while saving a document

If you're an experienced computer user, and are already creating and saving documents on your own, you'll be happy to know that most programs enable you to create new folders "on-the-fly" the first time you save a new document (or when you choose File ➪ Save As from the program's menu bar to save a new copy of the document with a different name). When the Save As dialog box appears, first use the Save In drop-down list or any other tools available in the Save As dialog box to navigate to the parent folder. If you're going to create this new folder within your My Documents folder, for example, navigate to the My Documents folder.

Then, in the toolbar of the Save As dialog box, look for the Create New Folder button, which usually appears as a manila file folder with an asterisk. In Figure 13-7 the mouse pointer is resting on that button and a ToolTip appears just under the mouse pointer. Click that button, type in a name for the new folder, and click OK. In most programs that new folder opens automatically at this point. So now you can just enter a file name for the document and click the Save button.

Folder tips and tricks

Before we wrap up this rather lengthy discussion of folders, here are a few more sections offering some tips and tricks for working with and navigating through folders.

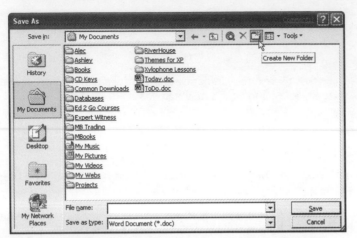

Figure 13-7: Most programs provide a Create New Folder button in their Save As dialog box, so you can create a new folder while saving a document.

Customizing folder icons

You can jazz up any folder so that it displays a special icon when viewed in Thumbnails view. Your icon image can be a picture in bitmap, JPEG, or GIF format. If you change your mind about using the image, you can remove it easily.

Customizing any folder icon is a snap, thanks to a wizard that steps you through the procedure:

1. Using Explorer, get to where you can see the icon for the My Pictures, Shared Pictures, or any other folder that contains pictures, and switch to Thumbnails view (View ➪ Thumbnails). Then select the folder you want to customize.

2. Right-click the folder, choose Properties, and click the Customize tab. Figure 13-8 shows the Customize tab of the Properties dialog box that appears.

3. Do one of the following:

   - To use an existing picture in bitmap, JPEG, or GIF format, click the Choose Picture option.

   - To remove the custom icon, click Restore Default.

4. If you are adding a picture, choose the picture you want to use and click Open.

5. Click OK to apply your changes.

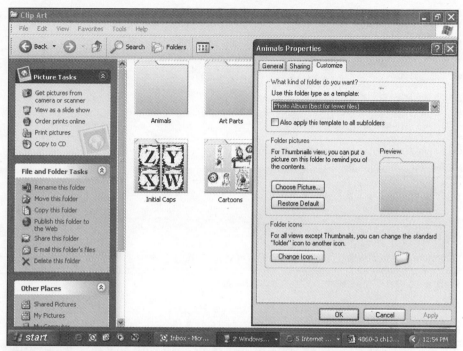

Figure 13-8: Use this dialog box to customize the current folder or to remove customization.

Caution If you select View ➪ Customize this Folder from the menu in step 2, you'll be customizing the parent folder rather than one of the folders contained in the parent folder.

Tip You can use the template options on the Customize tab of the Properties dialog box to choose special viewing templates for specific types of folder content. For example, you might want to choose Photo Album to display fairly large thumbnails for a folder you use to hold digital photos.

Your folder will have the custom icon anytime you open the folder that contains it — as long as the parent folder is set to display Thumbnails view, that is. Figure 13-9 shows an example in which I selected a graphic image for the icons for two of the folders in the ClipArt folder.

Note Any time the view is changed from Thumbnails to any other of the view options, the custom icons disappear. They return if the view is switched back to Thumbnails view.

The Customize tab also gives you the option to select a different "standard" icon if you don't want to add an image to the folder's icon.

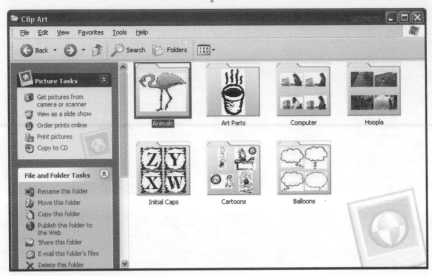

Figure 13-9: Folders with custom icon images

Finding a lost folder

If you lose track of a folder, you can always locate it with Search. Click the Start button and then click Search. Choose All Files and Folders, and then enter all or part of the name of the name of the folder you're looking for. Under Look In, select the C: drive and select (check) the Include subfolders option (under More advanced options). Then click the Search button.

Note   You can broaden the search beyond the local hard disk by choosing My Computer in the Look In list.

Viewing the path

Normally, Explorer shows only the name of the folder you're currently viewing in its title bar. You can opt to display the full path of the current folder in the optional Address bar, in the title bar, or both. Here's how:

1. In Explorer, choose Tools ➪ Folder Options (or in Control Panel, open the Folder Options icon).

2. Click the View tab.

3. If you want to see the full path in the Explorer Address bar, choose Display the full path in the address bar option, as in Figure 13-10.

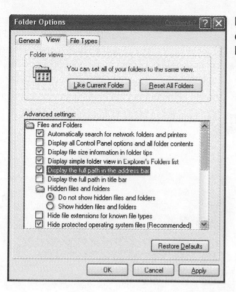

Figure 13-10: In this dialog box, I have opted to display the full path to a file or folder in Explorer's Address bar.

4. If you want to see the full path in the title bar, choose Display the full path in the title bar option.

5. Click the OK button.

Where's the My Documents Folder?

If you're accustomed to earlier versions of Windows, you might be surprised to discover that your My Documents folder is no longer in the root folder of the C: drive, where it used to be. As the Address bar and Folders list in Figure 13-11 show, it's actually now under `C:\Documents and Settings\yourusername`. This little change is so transparent, and so well hidden, you might not even discover it for quite a while after upgrading to XP.

The reason for the change has to do with the improved support for multiple users in Windows XP. That topic is discussed in depth in Chapter 22. But for now, suffice it to say that the Folders list at the left of Figure 13-11 illustrates, each user will have her own folder within the Documents and Settings folder. That folder, in turn, contains `Cookies`, `Desktop` `settings`, `Favorites`, a `My Documents` folder, and more, for each user. Exactly which of those folders actually comes into play while Windows is running is determined by the user's name.

Depending on the options you selected, you'll see the full path to a folder whenever you're viewing an actual folder on a disk in Explorer. For example, in Figure 13-11, I'm viewing the `My Pictures folder`. The title bar shows only that folder name. But the Address bar shows the complete path to that folder, `C:\Documents and Settings\Alan\My Documents\My Pictures`.

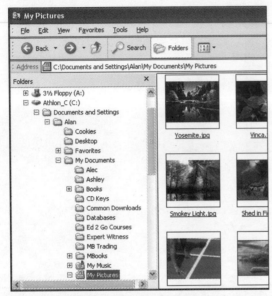

Figure 13-11: The title bar shows only the name of the current folder, but the Address bar shows the complete path.

The title bar always displays. But the Address bar is optional. You can turn it on and off by choosing View ➪ Toolbars ➪ Address bar. Be aware that not all items you view in Explorer will have a path to display. For example, "special" items such as Desktop, My Computer, Recycle Bin, and even My Documents, do not display a path, despite the fact that technically, many of these items really are just folders on the hard disk, as we'll discuss next.

Tip   If for whatever reason you ever need to type out the complete path to a folder, you can use standard cut-and-paste as a shortcut. Drag the mouse pointer through the path name in the Address bar, and then press Ctrl+C. Move the cursor to where you want to paste the path, and press Ctrl+V.

Windows XP special folders

You may have noticed some of the things that appear on (or are accessible from) the Windows desktop seem to have some regular folder hidden behind them. For example, the Start menu is really a specialized view of a standard folder named `\Documents and Settings\yourusername\Start Menu` (where *yourusername* is the user name you are logged on to). I don't recommend you play around with the contents of these special folders directly. Let Windows handle that. If you're an experienced user, or are just curious about things that go on behind the scenes, however, you might be interested to know that quite a few desktop items are only special views of regular folders on your hard disk, as listed in Table 13-1.

Table 13-1
Desktop Items That Display Special Folders and Their Paths

Item	Folder
Auto-Start Programs	`\Documents and Settings\yourusername \Start Menu\Programs\ StartUp`
Desktop	`\Documents and Settings\yourusername \Desktop`
Favorites	`\Documents and Settings\yourusername \Favorites`
All Programs menu	`\Documents and Settings\yourusername \Start Menu\Programs`
Send To menu	`\Documents and Settings\yourusername \SendTo`
Start menu	`\Documents and Settings\yourusername \Start Menu`

I suppose our foray into folders here may have gone beyond the basics of what you really *need* to know to better organize the contents of your My Documents folder. If all you really remember from this is the fact that you can easily create folders to better organize the files within your My Documents folder, then you're doing just fine.

Beyond organizing your documents is the ability to organize your desktop to better suit your own needs. So we'll get into that now, starting with (what else?), the Start menu.

Reorganizing Your Start Menu

The Start button, as you know, is the starting point for many activities you'll perform on your computer. And as such, the better you organize your Start menu, the easier it will be to get things started. Windows does a pretty good job of organizing your Start menu as you work. It keeps track of recently used documents and programs, and also provides access to the most widely used Windows features. However, there are ways to further customize the Start menu to your own liking, as you'll learn here.

Controlling the list of programs

The left side of the Start menu displays quick access to recently used programs. You might have noticed that items above the thin gray line within that menu never change. We say those options are "pinned" to the menu. Items below the thin gray line change quite frequently, to reflect programs you've used recently. You might want to change things around a bit there. For example, you might want to put some different programs above the thin gray line so that they're always available on the menu. Or, you might want to remove a program that you used recently, but don't intend to use again for a while. These things are easy to do. If you right-click on any program name in that menu, you'll see options similar to those shown in Figure 13-12, where I've right-clicked on Windows Movie Maker in the lower half of the menu.

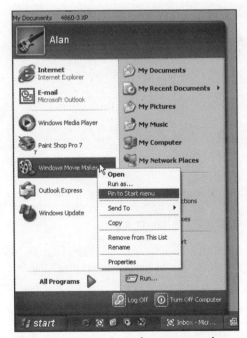

Figure 13-12: Options that appear when you right-click a program name in the Start menu

You'll want to focus on these main options:

✦ **Pin to start menu:** Pins the item to the upper portion of the menu, so it never gets "bumped" by recently used programs.

✦ **Unpin from Start menu:** If the item is already pinned to the menu, this option "unpins" it.

✦ **Remove from this list:** Takes the item off the menu.

✦ **Rename:** Lets you change the name that the option displays.

So Many Techniques, So Little Time

As you'll quickly discover, Windows XP offers many ways to accomplish the same tasks—from organizing your Start menu to opening icons—and you may wonder why. Well, I guess the short answer is "different strokes for different folks." Some people like to do things one way, whereas others prefer to use a different method. The long answer is that the more ways you know to accomplish a task, the easier it is to pick the best tool for the job at hand.

Consider how handy it is to know several routes between work and home. If you know only one route, you might be stymied if a storm, a water-main break, or a traffic jam blocks your normal route. If you know several routes, however, you can find alternative ways to home or work when your usual route is blocked.

The same holds true for Windows XP. If you know one way to do something and it works—fine, use it! But sometimes knowing another method can save you time and keystrokes or mouse clicks, depending on what you're currently doing. So, for example, if you already have Explorer open and you have a burning desire to rearrange your Start menu, have at it with Windows Explorer. If Windows Explorer isn't open, however, you might prefer right-clicking the Start button or the taskbar to begin your Start-menu housekeeping chores because these methods tend to be easier than Explorer.

Of course, you don't have to learn every method under the sun. Just use the method you like best. When you're ready to learn a new technique or a shortcut, you can always return to this book for tips.

As you know, when you click All Programs at the bottom of the program list, you see a larger menu providing access to all your programs. If you want to pin one of those programs to your Start menu, just drag it from the All Programs menu and drop it into the list of programs on your Start menu.

Putting shortcuts in the start menu

You're not limited to adding programs to the Start menu. You can also add shortcuts to favorite folders and documents to that menu, again using a simple drag-and-drop procedure. In Explorer, browse to the icon for any folder or document you want to be able to access from the Start menu. Then drag that icon to the Start button and drop it there. The next time you click the Start button, you'll see the new option up near the top of the Start menu.

Using large or small start menu icons

If your Start menu is getting too large, you can use smaller icons to make more space. Follow these steps:

1. Right-click an empty part of the taskbar and then choose Properties.

2. Click the Start Menu tab.

3. Click the Customize button.

4. To use smaller icons, select the Small icons option. To use larger icons, select the Large icons option.

5. Click the OK button to close the Customize Start Menu dialog box.

6. Click the OK button to close the Taskbar and Start Menu Properties dialog box.

When you click the Start button, you'll see that your Start menu is using whichever size icons you chose in Step 4.

Adding and deleting start menu items

The right half of the Start menu provides access to features that all Windows users have, not programs that are unique to your system. You can also control the options that are available on that menu:

1. Right-click the Start button and choose Properties.

2. Click the Start Menu tab.

3. Choose Start menu, and then click the Customize button.

4. Click the Advanced tab to get to the options shown in Figure 13-13.

Figure 13-13: The Advanced tab of the Customize Start Menu dialog box

5. Use the scroll bar under Start Menu Items to choose which options you want to display, and which you don't. Some items will give you the following choices:

- **Display as a link:** Clicking the option will open the associated dialog box or folder.

- **Display as a menu:** Clicking the option will display the contents of the associated dialog box or folder in a submenu.

- **Don't display this item:** The item won't appear on the menu at all.

6. If you want to have quick access to documents you have recently created, choose the List My Most Recently Opened Documents check box near the bottom of the dialog box.

7. If you want to control how many of your frequently used programs appear in the lower half of the programs side of the Start menu, click the General tab and choose a number from the Number of Programs on Start Menu option.

8. To add or delete the Internet option from the left side of the menu, or choose which Web browser opens when you click that option, make your selection from the Internet check box and drop-down list on the General tab.

9. To add or delete the E-mail menu option, and/or choose which program opens for e-mail, make your selection from the E-mail option on the General tab.

10. Click the OK button to close the Customize Start Menu dialog box.

11. Click the OK button to close the Taskbar and Start Menu Properties dialog box.

Start menu appearance and behavior

The Advanced tab of the Customize Start Menu dialog box also offers the following options for controlling the appearance and behavior of your Start menu:

✦ **Open submenus when I pause on them with my mouse:** When selected, you can display a submenu simply by pointing to the option that leads to the submenu. If you clear this check box, you need to actually click the item to open the submenu.

✦ **Highlight newly installed programs:** When selected, newly installed programs on the All Programs menu will be highlighted.

Tip

If you prefer the Start menu appearance from previous versions of Windows, select the Classic Start menu option on the Start Menu tab of the Taskbar and Start Menu Properties dialog box.

Rearranging menu items

You can easily rearrange "pinned" items at the top of the Start menu, as well as items that appear inside the All Programs and Favorites submenus. Here's how:

1. Click the Start button and then point to (do not click) the item you want to move.

2. If you want to rearrange items in the Favorites or All Programs menus, open the appropriate menu.

> **Note** The Favorites option on the Start menu is available only if you have selected Favorites Menu from the Start Menu Items list discussed earlier in this chapter under "Adding and Deleting Start Menu Items."

3. Hold down the left mouse button while dragging the item to its new destination. The destination can be the top of the Start menu or any spot within the All Programs or Favorites folders and subfolders.

4. When the black horizontal bar is positioned where you want the menu item to appear, release the mouse button.

Deleting menu items

To remove an item from the Start menu, click the Start button and then point to (don't click) the option you want to delete. Right-click the item you want to delete, choose Delete (or Remove from This List, depending on which option appears in the context menu that is displayed). If you choose Delete, you will be asked for confirmation before the item is deleted.

Organizing your all programs menu

As mentioned, the All Programs menu provides access to all the programs on your system. You also can add new menus — groups of items — to the Start menu. If you have lots of installed programs, and that menu is too lengthy, you can group some of those programs into submenus, thereby reducing the length of the menu.

Suppose, for example, that you have installed one of the Microsoft Office suites. When you click the Start button and open All Programs, each program within the suite is listed individually as in Figure 13-14. To reduce the size of your All Programs menu, you want to put all those icons into a subfolder named Microsoft Office. Here's how you can do that:

1. Right-click the Start button and choose Open (or Open All Users) to get to your Start Menu folder.

2. Open the Programs folder.

3. Right-click within the Programs folder and choose New ➪ Folder.

4. Type in a new name for the folder to whatever you want the submenu option to appear as on the All Programs menu. For this example, I name that folder Microsoft Office.

5. Drag any shortcut icons that you want to put into the submenu right onto the new folder icon, and drop them there. The icon will seem to disappear, but it has actually just been moved into the new folder.

After you have finished, you can close the Explorer window.

Now you can click the Start button, open All Programs, and point to your new submenu option to see what you've accomplished. In Figure 13-15, I have moved individual Microsoft Office programs from All Programs into the new Microsoft Office submenu.

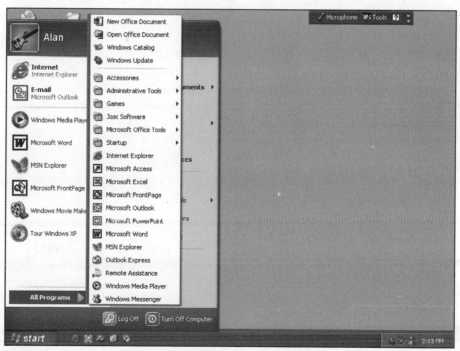

Figure 13-14: Microsoft Office programs listed individually on the All Programs menu

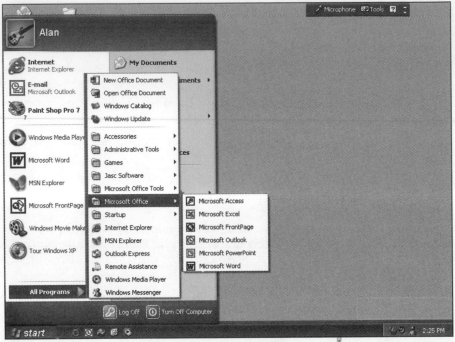

Figure 13-15: The contents of my new Microsoft Office submenu

If an item on your All Programs menu is buried within a submenu, and you would prefer that it be accessible right from the All Programs menu, just click the Start button, open All Programs, and work your way to the item of interest. But don't click the item. Instead, use the secondary (right) mouse button to drag the item into the All Programs menu, and then drop it where you want to place it. When you release the mouse button, choose Copy Here (if you also want to keep a copy of the item in the original submenu). Alternatively, choose Move Here if you want to move the item from its subfolder.

Clearing the My Recent Documents Menu

The My Recent Documents submenu on the Start menu keeps track of recently saved document files. So if you need to reopen that document in the near future, you can click the Start button, point to My Recent Documents, and then click the name of the document you want to open.

Tip   If your Start menu doesn't have a My Recent Documents option, you can add it from the Start Menu Items list discussed earlier under "Adding and Deleting Start Menu Items."

If your My Recent Documents menu is cluttered with files you don't open anymore, follow these simple steps to clear the My Recent Documents menu and start with a clean slate:

1. Right-click the taskbar and then choose Properties.
2. Click the Start Menu tab.
3. Click the Customize button.
4. Click the Advanced tab.
5. Click the Clear List button.
6. Click OK.
7. Click OK again.

That's all there is to that! If ever you want to delete a single file from the My Recent Documents menu, open the menu, right-click the item you want to delete, and choose Delete.

Note The My Recent Documents menu doesn't keep track of every document you open and close. Instead, it only keeps track of the last 15 documents created or edited with programs that enable such tracking. Most Windows programs do support the My Recent Documents menu.

Using and Organizing the Favorites Menu

Most people use the Favorites menu to store links to favorite Web sites on the World Wide Web. As discussed back in Chapter 6, you can easily add whatever Web page you're viewing at the moment to your list of favorites by choosing Favorites ⇨ Add to Favorites from the Internet Explorer menu bar.

Tip If the Favorites menu does not appear on your Start menu, select the Favorites menu option on the Advanced tab of the Customize Start Menu dialog box described under "Adding and Deleting Start Menu Items" earlier in this chapter.

You also can use the Favorites menu to store links to favorite things on your own PC. In fact, the Favorites menu available in Windows Explorer is identical to the Favorites menu in Internet Explorer. (For that matter, just in case you hadn't noticed, pretty much everything about Internet Explorer and Windows Explorer is identical!) Suppose, for example, that I want to put a quick link to my Windows XP Bible folder into the Favorites menu. All I have to do is get to this folder via Explorer and choose Favorites ⇨ Add to Favorites, as in Figure 13-16.

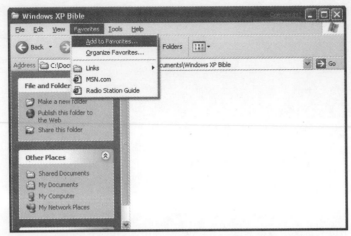

Figure 13-16: About to add the Windows XP Bible folder to my Favorites menu

You'll come to the dialog box shown in Figure 13-17. You can click the OK button to finish the job.

Figure 13-17: The Add Favorite dialog box enables you to add items to your Favorites menu.

From this point on, you can click the Start button and point to Favorites to get to that shortcut icon. For example, you can see the Windows XP Bible folder icon at the bottom of the Favorites menu shown in Figure 13-18.

The Favorites menu offers the handy Organize Favorites dialog box, shown in Figure 13-19, which makes it especially easy to organize the contents of this menu. To get to the Organize Favorites dialog box, choose Favorites ⇨ Organize Favorites from any menu bar that offers those options. (If you're at the desktop, you can open the Start menu, right-click Favorites, choose Open, and choose Favorites ⇨ Organize Favorites from its menu.)

Figure 13-18: Shortcut to Windows XP Bible folder added to my Favorites menu

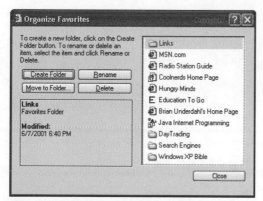

Figure 13-19: Use the Organize Favorites dialog box to manage your collection of favorites.

Once you're in the dialog box, the rest is simple. Just click whatever icon you want to move, rename, or delete, and then click the appropriate button beneath the icons. Follow the instructions onscreen and you're done. Click the Close button when you finish organizing. To see the results of your efforts, click the Start button, point to Favorites, and look at the contents of the Favorites menu.

Personalizing the Taskbar

The taskbar is another important tool on your desktop. The following list provides a quick review of the taskbar's purpose:

✦ Every open window has a button on the taskbar. To bring any window to the forefront onscreen, click its taskbar button.

✦ To close or resize any open window (even one buried in a stack), right-click its taskbar button and choose the appropriate option from the menu that appears.

✦ To tidy up (arrange) all the open windows, right-click an empty part of the taskbar (not a button in the taskbar) and then choose Cascade Windows or one of the Tile Windows options. You also can minimize all the windows from that menu.

✦ A little clock usually appears in the taskbar, showing the current time. Point to the clock to see the current date; double-click the clock to change the current date and time. (At the end of this chapter, I explain how to display or hide the clock.)

✦ Some hardware devices (such as sound cards and printers) display an icon in the taskbar while they are running. Typically, you can click, right-click, or double-click that icon to get more information about — or even to control — the device.

Handy little gadget, that taskbar. The following sections explain some ways you can personalize it.

Sizing and positioning the taskbar

You can put the taskbar along any edge of the screen. Whichever edge you prefer is just a matter of personal taste. To move the taskbar, point to an empty area of the taskbar and then drag the taskbar to some other edge of the screen.

Note   You cannot make any changes to the taskbar if the Lock the Taskbar option is selected on the right-click Taskbar menu.

To size the taskbar, rest the mouse pointer right on the top of the taskbar so that the mouse pointer turns into a two-headed arrow. Then drag the edge of the taskbar toward the center of the screen to enlarge it or toward the closest edge of the screen to narrow it. In Figure 13-20, for example, I dragged the taskbar to the right edge of the screen and then widened it by dragging its innermost edge toward the center of the screen.

Note

If you make the taskbar too skinny, the Start button disappears and the taskbar changes to a thin blue line. Don't panic. Just move your mouse pointer to the thin blue line. When the pointer becomes a two-headed arrow, drag the edge of the taskbar toward the middle of the screen. The taskbar widens and the Start button reappears.

Hiding the taskbar

If you don't want the taskbar eating up valuable space on your screen, you can have it go into hiding, automatically, whenever you're not using it. Follow these steps:

1. Right-click an empty part of the taskbar, and then choose Properties.

2. To control whether the taskbar appears on top of other windows, select or clear Keep the Taskbar on top of other windows. If you select this option, open windows never cover the taskbar. If you clear this option, open windows may cover the taskbar.

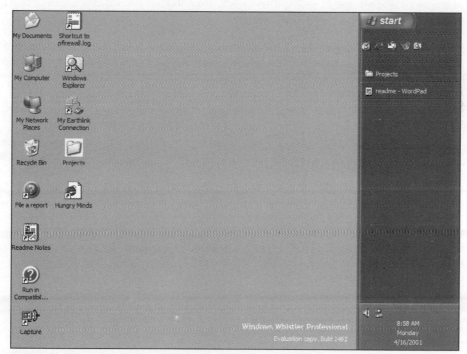

Figure 13-20: Taskbar along right edge of screen — and widened

3. To control whether the taskbar hides automatically, select or clear Auto-hide the Taskbar. If you select Auto-hide the Taskbar, the taskbar shrinks to a thin line along the edge of the screen when it isn't in use. If you clear this option, the taskbar never shrinks to a thin line.

4. Click OK.

I suggest you leave the Keep the Taskbar on top of other windows option selected. No good reason exists to allow other windows to cover the taskbar. If the taskbar gets in your way, however, select the Auto-hide the Taskbar option so that it's tucked away, but within easy reach. To redisplay the shrunken taskbar, point to the thin line.

Controlling the notification area

The right side of the taskbar contains an area known as the Notification area. (In previous versions of Windows, this was called the System Tray.) The Taskbar tab of the Taskbar and Start Menu Properties dialog box contains options you can use to control the icons that display in the Notification area.

The little clock that appears at the right edge of the Notification area is entirely optional. To turn it on or off, open the Taskbar and Start Menu Properties dialog box. On the Taskbar tab, clear the check box next to Show the Clock if you want to hide the time. Otherwise, select this check box (so that it contains a check mark) to make the time visible in the taskbar.

To hide icons you haven't used in some time, select the Hide inactive icons check box. You can also click the Customize button to select the display options for each individual Notification area icon.

After you have finished making your selections, close the dialog boxes to apply your changes.

Using desktop toolbars

In Chapter 4, you learned about the Quick Launch toolbar, yet another good repository for shortcuts to your favorite programs. Windows XP also has three other special toolbars:

✦ **Address:** Displays an Address box in which you can type Internet addresses or the names of disk drives, folders, and files on your computer. After you press Enter, Internet Explorer takes you to the place you chose. See Chapters 7 and 8 for more information.

✦ **Links:** Displays shortcut buttons for visiting handy places on the Internet. Click a button to visit that place. Again, see Chapters 7 and 8 for more information on the Internet.

✦ **Desktop:** Displays a button for each item on your desktop, just as the taskbar does. This toolbar can float (be placed anywhere on-screen).

Note On some systems, a Language bar containing options such as Microphone, Handwriting, and such might also be visible. See "Using Speech Recognition" in Chapter 15 for information on that one.

To turn any of these toolbars on or off, follow these steps:

1. Right-click some neutral area of the taskbar and point to Toolbars (see Figure 13-21).

2. To display — or hide — a toolbar, click its name (checked toolbars are already on display).

Figure 13-21: Optional toolbars are readily accessible from the toolbar's right-click menu.

Positioning and sizing toolbars

You can position and size desktop toolbars in several ways, all of them easy. When the desktop toolbars appear on the taskbar (their normal location), use these methods to position and size them:

✦ To resize a desktop toolbar, point to the vertical dots near the left or right edge of the toolbar and then drag left or right, or double-click to expand or contract.

✦ To move a toolbar out of the taskbar and onto the desktop, point to the vertical dots at the left edge of the toolbar you want to move. Then drag this toolbar out to the desktop and release the mouse button.

Figure 13-22 shows an example in which I opened all four toolbars — Address, Desktop, Links, and Quick Launch — and then dragged them all out to the Windows desktop.

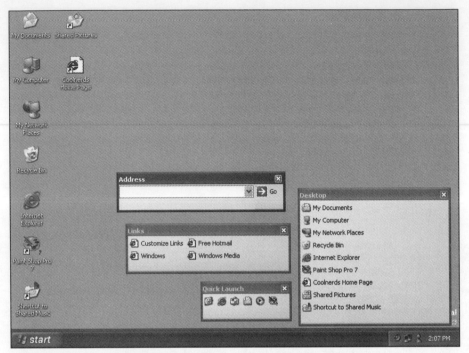

Figure 13-22: The four desktop toolbars appear as floating windows.

When the toolbars appear as floating windows, you can resize and position them in these ways:

✦ To move a floating toolbar, drag the toolbar's title bar to some new spot. You can drag the toolbar back onto the taskbar so that it again becomes part of the taskbar, or to any edge of the screen to anchor it there.

✦ To resize a floating toolbar, drag any corner or edge of the toolbar's window.

Other ways to customize desktop toolbars

You can choose from a host of handy options for customizing a desktop toolbar or any button on it. Just right-click any empty spot on a desktop toolbar or any desktop toolbar button and choose the option you want.

For example, when you right-click an empty spot on a toolbar, you can choose whether to display buttons as large or small icons, to show or hide text descriptions below the buttons, and to close the toolbar.

Creating new desktop toolbars

You can create a toolbar that automatically includes buttons for items within any folder on your computer or for an address on the Internet. Your custom toolbar will stick around until you close it.

To create a custom toolbar, follow these steps:

1. Right-click an empty part of the taskbar and choose Toolbars ➪ New Toolbar.

2. When the New Toolbar dialog box appears (see Figure 13-23), click a folder in the list or type a full Internet address (see Chapter 6).

3. Click the OK button.

Figure 13-23: The New Toolbar dialog box enables you to create toolbar access to any folder.

Your toolbar will appear on the taskbar. To get a better view, you can drag it by its little vertical bar up onto the desktop, as in the example shown in Figure 13-24. But remember one important point: When you close the toolbar, it's gone for good — so you don't want to go to a lot of trouble making it pretty. If you need more permanent toolbar access to favorite items, I suggest you use the Quick Launch toolbar rather than a new toolbar.

The taskbar clock

In case you ever wonder what the date is, you can rest the mouse pointer on the time. The current date (according to your computer's clock) appears in a ToolTip, as in Figure 13-25.

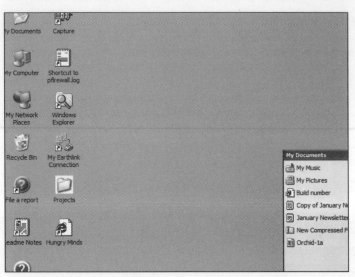

Figure 13-24: A new toolbar created from my My Documents folder

Figure 13-25: Point to the taskbar's clock to view the current date.

If your taskbar clock is showing the wrong date and/or time, here's how you can set it straight:

1. Double-click the clock indicator. Or choose Start ⇨ Control Panel and open the Date and Time icon to reveal the dialog box shown in Figure 13-26.

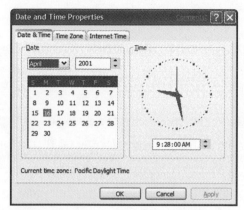

Figure 13-26: The Date/Time dialog box enables you to set the current date and time.

2. Choose the correct date and set the correct time.

3. To set your time zone, click the Time Zone tab and then choose your time zone from the list.

4. To automatically synchronize your system clock to a time server on the Internet, click the Internet Time tab and choose the Automatically synchronize with an Internet time server option. You also can choose the server to use from the drop-down list.

5. Click the OK button to save your settings and close the dialog box.

Note

The Date and Time Properties dialog box sets the date and time for your entire computer system, not just for the taskbar clock. If your files keep getting stamped with wrong dates or your personal calendars keep opening with the wrong dates, changing the date in the Date and Time Properties dialog box will take care of those problems, too!

Summary

Windows XP has lots of great stuff for organizing and personalizing your folders and desktop. Here are the main points to remember:

✦ To create a folder, open the drive or folder in which you want to place the folder. Then right-click some neutral area between existing icons and choose New ➪ Folder.

✦ To customize the appearance of a single folder, choose View ➪ Customize This Folder from that folder's menu bar.

✦ To add a new icon to the top of the Start menu, drag a copy of the icon to the Start button.

✦ To rearrange items in the Start menu, drag items to new locations.

✦ To clear the My Recent Documents menu, right-click the taskbar, choose Properties, click the Start Menu tab, click Customize, click the Advanced tab, and click the Clear List button.

✦ To hide/display desktop toolbars, right-click the taskbar and point to Toolbars.

✦ To size the taskbar, drag its inner edge (the edge nearest the center of the screen).

✦ To move the taskbar, drag the entire taskbar to any edge of the screen.

✦ To change your computer's date/time, double-click the clock indicator at the right side of the taskbar. Or, click the Start button and choose Control Panel, and then open the Date and Time icon.

✦   ✦   ✦

Personalizing the Screen

In Chapter 13, you found out ways in which you can organize your My Documents folder, Start menu, and other
desktop items to work smarter, not harder. As you learn in
this chapter, you can also personalize your screen to suit your
tastes and needs in lots of ways. Elements such as screen
background color, the size of text and objects on-screen, the
appearance of dates, times, and numbers, and the arrangement of the menu bar and toolbars in Explorer-type windows
are all discussed. Fun stuff!

Customizing the Screen

Personalizing the display properties — that is, your screen,
background, and so on — is easy in Windows XP. But first,
always, always, always adjust the brightness, contrast, and
sizing controls (if any) on your monitor to get the best possible picture before you mess with the display properties. Then,
if you do change the display properties in Windows XP, adjust
those controls again after you finish to get the best possible
picture from your new settings.

Follow these steps to change the display properties:

1. Right-click on the desktop and choose Properties. Or,
   click the Start button and choose Control Panel and then
   open the Display icon. Either way, you see the Display
   Properties dialog box, shown in Figure 14-1.

2. Click any tab near the top of the dialog box and then
   choose any options within that tab. The sample window
   in the middle of the dialog box gives you a preview of
   the way your current selection will look on-screen.

Figure 14-1: Use the Display Properties
dialog box to personalize your screen.

3. To apply your selection to the screen without leaving the dialog box, click the
Apply button.

4. After you finish, click OK to save all your selections or click Cancel to save
only the settings you have already applied (if any).

The following sections describe in detail the various options in the Display
Properties dialog box. You also can get instant help in the Display Properties dialog
box by clicking the question mark (?) button and then clicking the option with
which you need help. Alternatively, click the option you need help with and then
press the Help key (F1).

Choosing a theme

A *theme* is a collection of many different screen customization settings, saved as a
single file with a name. The Themes tab of the Display Properties dialog box, shown
back in Figure 14-1, enables you to choose from a variety of predefined themes.
When you select a theme from the drop-down list, the preview window under
Sample gives you an idea of how that theme will look. As in all dialog boxes, the
theme you select isn't applied to your actual desktop until you click the Apply or
OK button.

You also can create your own themes. As you make selections from the Desktop,
Appearance, and other tabs in the Display Properties dialog box, Windows saves

those settings with whatever theme is currently selected. Clicking the Save As button on the Themes tab enables you to save the current settings to a new theme. Any theme you save will be added to the Theme drop-down list. You can turn that theme on or off just by making a selection from that list. In the sections that follow, we'll look at the other tabs of the Display Properties dialog box, which enable you to customize the screen. Keep in mind that after you've customized the screen to your liking, you can always return to the Themes tab and save all those settings as a new theme.

Screen resolution and color quality

The size of items on your screen and the quality of pictures on your screen are determined mainly by the Screen Resolution and Color Quality options on the Settings tab of the Display Properties dialog box, shown in Figure 14-2. The Screen resolution slider determines how many pixels are visible on your screen (where each pixel is a tiny dot of light, too small to see). Basically, the higher you set the screen resolution, the more stuff will fit on your screen.

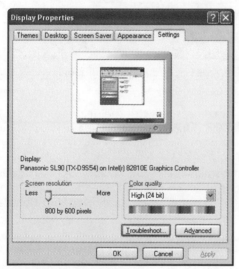

Figure 14-2: The Settings tab of the Display Properties dialog box

For example, Figure 14-3 shows three windows on the desktop — one for Calculator, one for Paint, and one for a Windows Media Player — at the low resolution of 800 x 600 pixels. I need to overlap the windows on this screen because of the small desktop area I'm using. (Most screens in this book are shown at 800x600 resolution.)

Figure 14-3: Three windows with the desktop area at 800 x 600 resolution

Figure 14-4 shows the same three windows on-screen with the desktop area set to 1024 x 768 pixels. I now have room to spread things out more because each item on the screen is smaller.

Note   If you're unable to adjust the screen resolution and color quality, the appropriate driver for your graphics adapter card may not be installed. See the sections titled "Troubleshooting Adapter and Monitor Problems" and "Maximizing Your Options" later in this chapter for help.

Graphics card manufacturers often recommend choosing a desktop area based on the physical size of your screen. It's up to you, however, to decide what's comfortable for your eyes. Also, because changing the desktop area on the fly is so easy, you can choose whatever desktop area is most convenient for the work you're currently doing.

Tip   You usually can magnify or shrink the document within a Windows program without fussing with the Desktop Area setting. Choose View ➪ Zoom in the current program or search the program's help system for the word *zoom*.

Figure 14-4: The same three windows at 1024x768 resolution

The Color Quality option determines how many colors are visible on your screen. Basically, the higher the color quality, the better things will look—especially photographs and video, which require many colors. The only downside to a high color quality is that it eats up computing resources, which can slow things down. If you have a reasonably fast computer, however, setting the color quality to the highest setting available will give you the best display.

Troubleshooting adapter and monitor problems

If you have problems with your screen display, the Video Display Troubleshooter may be your best bet for getting them resolved. To run the troubleshooter, just click the Troubleshoot button on the Settings tab of the Display Properties dialog box. If the troubleshooter doesn't help solve your problem and you're stuck at a very low screen resolution and color quality, you may need to manually install drivers for your graphics adapter card and/or monitor, as discussed next.

Maximizing your options

In the sections that follow, we'll be looking at some of the more advanced options of the Display Properties dialog box. Remember that the range of options from which you can choose varies from one computer to the next because many of these options directly affect settings on your computer's make and model of graphics adapter and monitor. It makes these adjustments via the hardware's *drivers*. A driver is a small program that tells the operating system (for instance, Windows) how to interact with the hardware device.

Usually, when you (or your computer manufacturer) install Windows, Windows automatically detects your graphics adapter and monitor and installs the appropriate drivers. However, Windows doesn't come with a driver for every graphics card and monitor on the market. When Windows doesn't recognize your hardware, it installs a simplified "generic" driver, which usually provides for a very limited range of options. To expand your available options and take full advantage of your hardware, you might need to install the driver manually. The driver will usually be on a disk that came with your computer, monitor, or graphics card.

You can determine whether Windows has installed drivers for your hardware through the Advanced display settings. To get to those settings, follow these steps:

1. Click the Settings tab in the Display Properties dialog box.
2. Click the Advanced button.

A Properties dialog box that contains tabs for your display adapter and monitor will open. In the next sections, you learn how to determine whether Window has installed the appropriate drivers for your hardware. If it hasn't, you can install the appropriate drivers yourself, as discussed under "Updating Video Drivers" later in this chapter.

Checking your graphics adapter

To reveal information about your computer's graphics adapter, click the Adapter tab in the Advanced Display Properties dialog box (see Figure 14-5). If Windows was unable to detect your graphics adapter, you might see a generic name, such as `Plug and Play Graphics Adapter` listed there instead. You also may discover that you're limited to 16 colors. If that's the case, you should update the driver manually, as discussed in a moment.

Checking your monitor settings

To reveal information about your monitor, click the Monitor tab in the Advanced Display Properties dialog box. As with your display adapter, a generic name listed under Monitor Type indicates that Windows didn't recognize your monitor and hence has installed a generic driver. If necessary, you can install a specific driver, as discussed next.

Figure 14-5: Sample Adapter tab of the
Advanced Display Properties dialog box

Updating video drivers

If you need to update the drivers for your adapter and/or monitor, you have a couple of options for installing the appropriate driver:

✦ If the instructions that came with your computer suggest running a specific
   program to install the drivers, follow those instructions and skip the rest of
   the material in this section.

Caution

If Windows XP has installed a driver for your hardware, it's best to keep that driver
instead of reverting to the driver on the disk. The driver on the disk might be older
and not compatible with Windows XP.

✦ If you have no such instructions (or they didn't work), you can use the Update
   Driver Wizard to search for and install a driver.

To use the Update Driver Wizard, follow these steps:

1. If you have a driver disk for your adapter card or monitor, place it in the
   appropriate drive of your computer.

2. In the Advanced Display Properties dialog box, click the Adapter tab or the
   Monitor tab, depending on which type of driver you'll be installing.

3. Click the Driver tab in the dialog box that opens.

4. Click the Update Driver button to start the Hardware Update Wizard.

5. Choose the Install the software automatically (Recommended) option and then click the Next button.

6. Follow the instructions provided by the wizard.

If Windows XP cannot find a better driver, you may have to search other resources to find an appropriate driver. You can contact the computer manufacturer (or the monitor/graphics card manufacturer) to find out whether a Windows XP driver is available. Many manufacturers now have Web sites from where you can download drivers on the spot.

Optionally, you can check the Windows Update Web site for updated drivers. Click the Start button, choose Help and Support, and click on the Windows Update link. In the left pane, click Pick Updates to Install. Within a few seconds, an expanded list of different types of updates will display. Click Driver Updates to search for a driver for your hardware.

Choosing a desktop appearance

The Appearance tab of the Display Properties dialog box, shown in Figure 14-6, lets you control many aspects of how Windows looks on your screen. To get to the options, right-click the desktop and choose Properties. Then click the Appearance tab. You can use the drop-down lists to choose from a variety of predefined appearance settings. As usual, the preview area will show you how your selection will look. Remember, though, that your selection doesn't actually take effect until you click the Apply or OK button.

Figure 14-6: The Appearance tab of the Display Properties dialog box

If you need very precise control over the size of icons, windows, and text on your screen, you can click the Advanced button on the Appearance tab. You'll be taken to the Advanced Appearance options. You can choose specific items for which you can adjust the size and color, such as ToolTips or menus. After you've selected an item, you can choose fonts, sizes, colors, and so forth, as appropriate, for the item you've selected from the drop-down list.

When you've finished fine-tuning the size and appearance of individual items, you can save them as a theme. Click OK to close the Advanced Appearance dialog box. Then click the Themes tab in the Display Properties dialog box. There, click the Save As button and enter a file name for your new theme. In the future, you can choose between any of the original themes (appearances) that come with Windows XP or the custom appearance settings you've created. Just open the Display Properties dialog box as usual. Then, on the Themes tab, select an option from the Theme drop-down list.

Appearance special effects

Click the Effects button on the Appearance tab to open dialog box where you can set special effects, such as fading for ToolTips and menus as well as smoothing of screen fonts to get rid of jagged-looking text. Before you make any selections, however, be aware of two things:

✦ If your computer is sluggish, these special effects might slow it down. Clearing any special effects might speed things up.

✦ Not all display cards can portray all effects, so don't be surprised if some items are disabled.

Feel free to experiment with any settings. You need to close all open dialog boxes by clicking their OK buttons to see the effects of any selections you make. As always, if you decide to disable any selected effects, you can just return to the Effects dialog box and clear the check box next to any effect you activated.

Choosing a background

The Desktop tab of the Display Properties dialog box enables you to put a picture (wallpaper) on the desktop and to select a background color. If your monitor is slow, you can use this option to remove the background and speed things up. Either way, follow these steps:

1. Open the Display Properties dialog box, as discussed earlier, and click the Desktop tab (see Figure 14-7).

2. To use a picture or pattern for your desktop background, choose an option from the Background list. Or, click the Browse button and locate and double-click the picture or HTML file you want to use.

3. If you chose a picture or pattern, you can choose an option from the Position drop-down list to determine how you want that item displayed. The Center option centers the image in the middle of the desktop; Tile makes a repeated pattern from the image (useful for small patterns). Stretch stretches the image to cover your desktop.

4. To choose a background color, click the down arrow at the right of the Color box to expand the color palette. Then select a color (or click Other to specify a custom color).

5. Click OK to save your selection.

Figure 14-7: The Desktop tab of the Display Properties dialog box

Managing desktop icons

Chapter 4 introduced you to a variety of techniques for placing shortcuts to favorite programs right on your desktop. The Customize Desktop button on the Desktop tab of the Display Properties dialog box offers some tools for working with the built-in icons, such as My Computer and Recycle Bin, as well as the Desktop Cleanup Wizard. When you click the Customize Desktop button, the Desktop Items dialog box displays, as shown in Figure 14-8.

From the top of the dialog box, you can choose which icons you want to display by selecting or clearing their check boxes. Optionally, you can customize the appearance of an icon by clicking its image near the middle of the dialog box and then clicking the Change Icon button. In the Change Icon dialog box that opens, click any icon to select it and then click the OK button. Should you ever want to revert back to the original icons, you can click the Restore Default button.

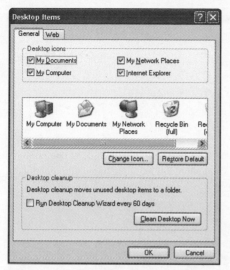

Figure 14-8: The Desktop Items dialog box

Cleaning up the desktop

If you have a tendency to clutter up your desktop with lots of icons, you can use the Desktop Cleanup Wizard to review how long it has been since you last used certain desktop icons and also choose which icons you want to delete. You can run the wizard manually by clicking the Clean Desktop Now button in the Desktop Icons dialog box. Optionally, you can have Windows run the wizard automatically every 60 days.

For more information on customizing icons, see "Changing Icons" in Chapter 30. For information on adding Web pages or Web components to your desktop, see "Using the Active Desktop" in Chapter 7.

Choosing a screen saver

A screen saver is a moving pattern that appears on your screen after some amount of idle time. By idle time, I mean a period in which no mouse or keyboard activity has occurred. The purpose of a screen saver is to prevent burn-in, a condition caused by keeping an unchanging image on-screen too long. Burn-in causes the screen on some older monitors to become blurry and lose some clarity. Many people use screen savers even on more modern monitors, just for the fun of it.

Windows XP offers you many built-in screen savers. To select one of them, follow these steps:

1. If you aren't in the Display Properties dialog box, right-click the desktop and choose Properties.

2. Click the Screen Saver tab (see Figure 14-9).

3. Choose a screen saver from the Screen Saver drop-down list.

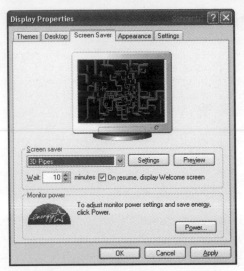

Figure 14-9: The Screen Saver tab of the Display Properties dialog box

4. Then do any of the following:

- To customize the screen saver you selected, click the Settings button and then choose among the options that appear. Click OK when you finish.

- To preview the currently selected screen saver and settings, click the Preview button. (To turn off the preview, move the mouse pointer a little.)

- To specify how long the PC must be inactive before the screen saver kicks in, specify the number of minutes in the Wait box.

- To have the screen saver return to the logon screen when deactivated, choose the "On resume, display Welcome screen" option.

5. Click the OK button after making your selections.

You won't see any immediate result, because the screen saver won't kick in until the computer has been idle for the number of minutes you specified while making your selections.

When the screen saver kicks in, your Windows XP desktop disappears, and a moving pattern or blank screen appears. To return to your Windows XP desktop, move the mouse pointer a little or press any key. If you opted to have the screen saver display the Welcome screen, you'll be taken to the logon options. Click your username or picture to get back to your desktop. If your user account is password-protected, you'll need to enter your password again to continue.

Accessibility for Physical Impairments

Up until now, the settings I've shown you in this chapter have been pretty much focused on just making your PC a bit more fun to use. There's certainly nothing wrong with having a little fun, but if you have physical challenges that make using a computer difficult, you probably have more important things in mind—such as being able to use your system productively.

Windows XP comes with a tool—the Accessibility Wizard—that can help make using a PC a whole lot easier for someone with vision, hearing, or mobility problems. There's no reason why almost anyone can't have the benefit of using a modern Windows XP-based PC.

Tip If several people share this computer, be sure to log on as the person to whom the accessibility features will apply. Optionally, you can create a separate account for accessibility features, as described in Chapter 20.

To use the Accessibility Wizard, follow these steps:

1. Click the Start button and choose All Programs ➪ Accessories ➪ Accessibility ➪ Accessibility Wizard.

2. On the first page of the wizard, click the Next button to get to the Text Size options shown in Figure 14-10.

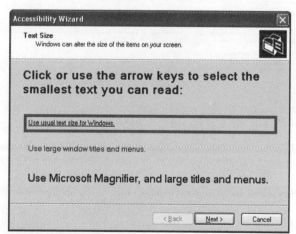

Figure 14-10: Use the Accessibility Wizard to help configure a PC so that it is easier to use.

3. Choose the text size that works best for you and then click the Next button.

4. On the Display Settings screen shown in Figure 14-11, choose the display options appropriate for your needs:

- **Change the font size:** Increases the size of the type in menus, titles bars, and other screen elements controlled by Windows XP.

- **Switch to a lower screen resolution:** Reduces the screen resolution so that everything on the screen appears somewhat larger. This option is not available if your screen is already set to the smallest allowable resolution.

- **Use Microsoft Magnifier:** Dedicates a portion of the screen to a window that greatly magnifies the area around the mouse pointer.

- **Disable personalized menus:** Prevents Windows XP from hiding menu items that haven't been used in some time. This makes the menus less confusing because items remain in the same location on the menus.

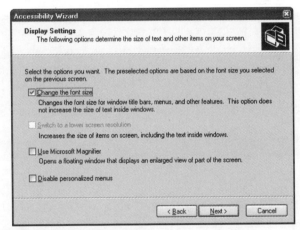

Figure 14-11: The Display Settings page of the Accessibility Wizard

5. Click the Next button to get to the Set Wizard Options page and then select any statements that apply to you, as summarized here:

- **I am blind or have difficulty seeing things on screen:** Instructs the Accessibility Wizard to choose settings that help people with vision problems.

- **I am deaf or have difficulty hearing sounds from the computer:** Instructs the Accessibility Wizard to choose settings — such as flashing a title bar — when Windows XP would normally use an audible prompt to get the user's attention.

- **I have difficulty using the keyboard or mouse:** Instructs the Accessibility Wizard to set options, such as StickyKeys, that make it easier to use a computer with a pointing stick or one hand.

- **I want to set administrative options:** Instructs the Accessibility Wizard to open the Accessibility Utility Manager in which you can set default startup options for accessibility options.

6. After you have made your selections, click Next to continue.

At this point, the Accessibility Wizard might ask more questions, depending on your selections so far. Follow the on-screen prompts to continue setting up the accessibility options you need. When you get to the last wizard page and click the Start button, your settings will be applied. You can activate and deactivate specific utilities by clicking the Start button and choosing All Programs ➪ Accessories ➪ Accessibility. Options on the submenu that appears are summarized in the sections that follow.

The Magnifier

To use the Magnifier, click the Start button and choose All Programs ➪ Accessories ➪ Accessibility Options ➪ Magnifier. The Magnifier Settings dialog box opens, and the desktop splits into two panes, as shown in Figure 14-12. The upper pane magnifies the area surrounding the mouse pointer, keyboard focus, and text editing. You can choose additional options from the Magnifier Settings dialog box. To leave the magnifier on but hide the dialog box, click the Minimize button in the Magnifier Settings dialog box. Closing the Magnifier Settings dialog box will also turn off the Magnifier.

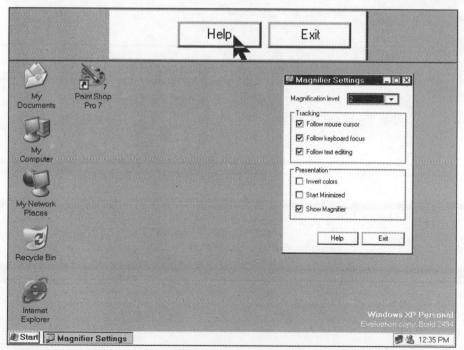

Figure 14-12: The Magnifier turned on, and the Magnifier Settings dialog box

The Narrator

To open Microsoft Narrator, click the Start button and choose All Programs ⇨ Accessories ⇨ Accessibility Options ⇨ Narrator. This program uses text-to-speech to read on-screen text aloud, including dialog box options, menu commands, and typed text. The Narrator dialog box also opens, enabling you to choose options for how the Narrator works. The Help button in the dialog box provides more information on using the program. The Voice button in that same dialog box enables you to choose a voice for the Narrator.

The On-Screen Keyboard

The On-Screen Keyboard makes it possible to type by using the mouse (see Figure 14-13). To activate the keyboard, click the Start button and choose All Programs ⇨ Accessories ⇨ Accessibility Options ⇨ On-Screen Keyboard. To type using the On-Screen Keyboard, click the keys you want to type. To adjust settings for the keyboard, choose options from its menu bar.

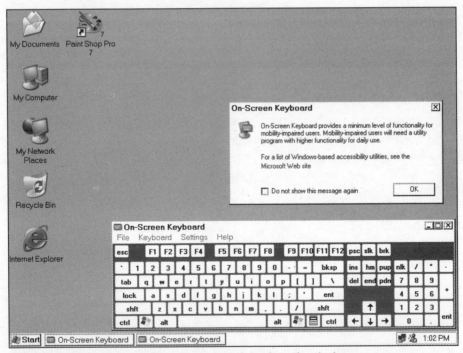

Figure 14-13: The Microsoft On-Screen Keyboard on the desktop

Automating accessibility programs

The accessibility Utility Manager, shown in Figure 14-14, enables you to automate the Magnifier, Narrator, and On-Screen Keyboard. You can start the Utility Manager by pressing the Windows key+U either at the desktop, or at the Welcome screen. Optionally, you can click the Start button and choose All Programs ➪ Accessories ➪ Accessibility Options ➪ Utility Manager.

Note The Windows key is the one that shows the flying window icon. It's placed between the Ctrl and Alt keys on most keyboards.

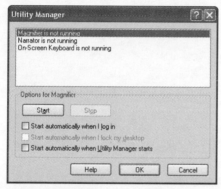

Figure 14-14: The accessibility options Utility Manager

To use the dialog box, click one of the program names — Magnifier, Narrator, or On-Screen Keyboard — in the top half of the dialog box. Then, use options in the lower half of the dialog box to start or stop that program to have the program start automatically when you log on or to have the program start when the Utility Manager program starts. If your computer is a member of a domain, you also can have the program start automatically when you lock the computer.

Note To lock or unlock the desktop in a domain environment, press the Windows key+L. In a non-domain environment, pressing those keys will take you to the Welcome screen.

Tweaking Accessibility Wizard options

The Accessibility Wizard provides the easiest way to choose and adjust accessibility options. However, you also can choose and adjust those settings via the Accessibility Options dialog box shown in Figure 14-15.

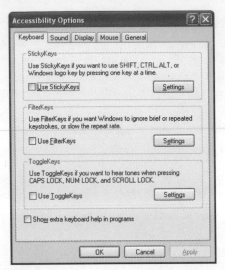

Figure 14-15: The Accessibility Options
dialog box

To get to Accessibility Options dialog box, follow these steps:

1. Click the Start button and open Control Panel.

2. If Control Panel opens in the Category view, click the Accessibility Options link.

3. Open the Accessibility Options icon.

In the sections that follow, we'll look at various options for using and fine-tuning the accessibility options available from this dialog box.

StickyKeys

If you have difficulty typing combination keystrokes, such as Ctrl+Esc, Shift+F1, or Alt+Z, try using the StickyKeys feature. With StickyKeys enabled, you can make the modifier keys (Ctrl, Alt, and Shift keys) stick after you press them, so you needn't hold down any of those keys to press a combination keystroke. Instead, you press and release the Ctrl, Shift, or Alt key (or any combination thereof) and then press and release the nonmodifier key, which will be any key on the keyboard except Ctrl, Alt, or Shift. Pressing and releasing the nonmodifier key automatically releases the modifier key(s).

You also can tap the modifier key twice to keep that key locked down. To unlock the modifier key, press the modifier key a third time. As you lock and release StickyKeys, a small indicator near the lower-right corner of the Windows desktop provides some visual feedback as to which keys are currently locked down.

FilterKeys

If you are double-pressing keys by holding them down too long or typing extra characters because your finger brushes nearby keys, use the FilterKeys option to change the sensitivity of the keyboard.

ToggleKeys

The Caps Lock, Num Lock, and Scroll Lock keys on the keyboard all act as toggles, meaning you can press the key to turn the feature on and off. Most keyboards have small indicator lights that light up when one of those keys is in the "on" position. If you're visually impaired, it might not be so easy to see those indicators. The ToggleKeys option provides an auditory cue that informs you of the status of the key. When one of those keys is turned on, a high-pitched sound plays. Turning off one of those keys plays a low-pitched tone.

SoundSentry and ShowSounds

If your hearing is impaired, you might want to try SoundSentry or ShowSounds. (These options appear on the Sound tab of the Accessibility Options dialog box.) Windows uses small beeps and other sounds to provide extra feedback. You also can have SoundSentry put up visual cues along with the sounds so that you can see when the sound is being played. ShowSounds allows programs that use speech or other audible cues to provide text on the screen, much like close-captioned TV.

MouseKeys

MouseKeys (on the Mouse tab) enables you to use the keyboard to move the mouse, click things, and so forth. When MouseKeys is activated, you can control the mouse as follows (be sure to use only the keys on the numeric keypad):

✦ **Move the pointer:** Press (or hold down) the numeric keys surrounding the number 5. The 7, 9, 1, and 3 keys move the pointer diagonally. The 8, 4, 6, and 2 keys move the pointer in the direction of the arrow shown in the key.

✦ **Click:** Press the 5 key in the middle of the keypad.

✦ **Double-click:** Press the plus sign (+) key or press the 5 key twice, fast.

✦ **Drag (left mouse button):** Point to the object, press the insert (0) key to begin dragging, use the numeric keys surrounding the 5 to move the mouse pointer; then press Delete (.) to complete the operation.

✦ **Right-click:** Position the mouse pointer and press the minus sign (-) key. Then press the 5 key to click or the plus sign (+) key to double-click.

✦ **Right-drag (right mouse button):** Point to the object you want to drag, press the minus sign (-) key, and then press the insert (0) key to lock down that button. Use the numeric keys surrounding the number 5 to drag. Then press the Delete (.) key to complete the drag.

✦ **Return to standard clicking:** Press the slash (/) key. This is useful if the 5 key is right-clicking when you want it to click. (If a shortcut menu is open, press Alt or Esc before pressing the slash key.)

✦ **Click both mouse buttons:** Press and release the asterisk (*) key.

✦ **Jump the mouse pointer in large increments across the screen:** Hold down the Ctrl key as you move the mouse pointer with the numeric keys surrounding the number 5.

✦ **Slow the movement of the mouse pointer (as when you need to position it precisely):** Hold down the Shift key as you move the mouse pointer with the numeric keys surrounding the number 5.

Even if you're not physically impaired, you might find MouseKeys a handy option, especially if you need to position the mouse precisely in your work. Precise positioning is easier to do with the numeric keypad than with the mouse. It's also handy if you're suffering from mouse shoulder (a pain in your shoulder) or repetitive stress syndrome pains.

Tip   When the MouseKeys feature is active, you can mix mouse actions with numeric keypad actions in any way that's convenient.

Accessibility time-out and status indicator

If disabled and non-disabled users share a PC, you might want to activate the Automatic Reset and Notification features:

✦ The Automatic Reset feature turns off the accessibility features (except the SerialKey device) and returns to the regular settings after the PC has been idle for a specified period.

✦ The Notification feature warns all users when the accessibility features are active and can provide audio feedback when a feature is turned on or off. The indicator also tells MouseKeys and StickyKeys users when a key or mouse button is locked down.

To activate either of these options, click the General tab of the Accessibility Options dialog box. Then select the Automatic Reset and Notification options you want to use and set the idle time (if any) for turning off the accessibility options.

SerialKeys alternative input devices

Windows XP also provides built-in support for alternative input devices, including eye-gaze systems and head pointers. Typically, you can plug any such SerialKey device into an available serial port. You needn't disconnect the mouse first. To give an alternative input device its own serial port, install the device according to the manufacturer's instructions. Then, in the General tab of the Accessibility Options dialog box, select the Use Serial Keys option and click the Settings button to specify the serial port and baud rate for the alternative input device.

Using shortcuts to activate/deactivate accessibility options

If you activate the shortcut key for each accessibility option you enable, you can use the keys listed in Table 14-1 to turn those options on and off.

Table 14-1
Emergency Hot Keys for Turning Accessibility Options On and Off

Accessibility Option	Hot Key
FilterKeys	Hold down right Shift key for 8 seconds.
High-Contrast mode	Left Alt+Left Shift and then Print Screen.
MouseKeys	Left Alt+Left Shift and then Num Lock.
StickyKeys	Press Shift 5 times.
ToggleKeys	Hold down Num Lock for 5 seconds.

Date, Time, Currency, and Number Formats

The world has many standards for displaying dates, times, numbers, and currency values. The United States uses a period as a decimal point, whereas Great Britain uses a comma. The Regional Settings dialog box in Windows XP enables you to specify the formats you want to use on your PC. Most Windows programs use whatever date, time, currency, and number format you specify in the Regional and Language Options dialog box. You needn't pick the same settings for every program on your system. To choose regional formats, follow these steps:

1. Click the Start button and open Control Panel.

2. If Control Panel opens in Category view, click the Date, Time, Language, and Regional Options link.

3. Open the Regional and Language Options icon. The Regional and Language Options dialog box displays, as shown in Figure 14-16.

On the Regional Options tab, you can select a country from the drop-down list to choose your international formats. The Samples below your selection will provide examples of how numbers, currency values, and so forth will appear on-screen. Optionally, you can click the Customize button to set the number, currency, time, and date formats independently.

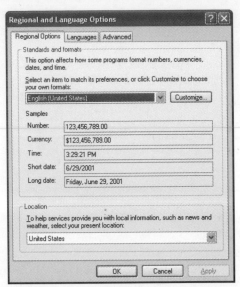

Figure 14-16: Use the Regional Settings Properties dialog box to customize numeric, currency, time, and date formats for your region.

Summary

In this chapter, you've seen umpteen different ways to control the exact appearance of your Windows XP desktop. Let's review the most important options discussed in this chapter:

✦ To personalize your screen settings, right-click the desktop and choose Properties. The Display Properties dialog box appears.

✦ To change the background, click the Desktop tab in the Display Properties dialog box.

✦ To change the screen saver, click the Screen Saver tab in the Display Properties dialog box.

✦ To change the screen appearance (colors, sizes, and buttons), click the Appearance tab in the Display Properties dialog box.

✦ To change the color palette, resolution (desktop area), and display type, click the Settings tab.

✦ The Desktop Items dialog box enables you to change the appearance of your My Computer, My Documents, My Network Places, and Recycle Bin icons.

✦ To configure your system for use by someone with vision, hearing, or mobility problems, click the Start button and then choose All Programs ➪ Accessories ➪ Accessibility ➪ Accessibility Wizard.

✦ To change the date, time, and format of numbers and currencies, go to the Control Panel (choose Start ➪ Control Panel). Then open the Regional and Language Options icon.

✦   ✦   ✦

Speech, Handwriting, Joysticks, and More

Anything that you use to interact with your computer is generally referred to as an *input device*. Most people use a mouse and keyboard as their main input devices. So naturally, we all want those things to work smoothly and easily. But mice and keyboards aren't the only devices out there. You also can use joysticks and other game controllers. Some programs even enable you to use your voice and a microphone to interact with your computer. Still others support writing and drawing tablets, which allow you to interact with the computer in a pen-and-paper-like fashion. In this chapter, you'll learn how to tweak all these devices so that they'll best suit your own needs.

Personalizing the Mouse

There are many ways to personalize your mouse to make it work better for you. If you find it difficult to see the mouse pointer to zero-in on items on your screen, or if you just want to change the appearance of your mouse pointers, you can use the Mouse Properties dialog box to customize the behavior of your mouse.

Cross-Reference The Accessibility Wizard discussed in Chapter 15 offers more ways of customizing the mouse, specifically geared toward people with visual and motor impairments.

To customize your mouse pointers, follow these steps:

1. Open the Control Panel by clicking the Start button and choosing Control Panel. (If you don't see a Control Panel option, see the sidebar titled "Can't Find Control Panel?")

2. If Control Panel opens in Category view, click the Switch to Classic View option in the Explorer bar.

3. Open the Mouse icon to get to the Mouse Properties dialog box, shown in Figure 15-1.

4. Choose options, as described in the following sections, to tailor your mouse to your liking and then click the OK button.

Figure 15-1: Use the Mouse Properties dialog box to fine-tune the behavior of your mouse.

Can't Find the Control Panel?

If you don't see a Control Panel option on your Start menu, right-click the Start button and choose Properties. Choose Start Menu and then click the Customize button. On the Advanced tab, select Display as Link under the Control Panel option under Show the items on the Start menu. Then close both open dialog boxes by clicking their OK buttons.

If you're using the classic-style Start menu, click the Start button and choose Settings ⇨ Control Panel.

Mice for lefties

If you're left-handed and you want the main mouse button to be below your left index finger, select the Switch primary and secondary buttons option near the top of the Buttons tab in the Mouse Properties dialog box. After you make this change, you must "think in reverse" when you're told to use the left or right mouse button. Table 15-1 shows how the standard terminology becomes backward for lefties.

Taking control of double-clicking

If you find double-clicking is a problem, you can speed or slow the double-click speed. If you can't seem to double-click fast enough, for example, slow down the double-click speed. Or, if you often double-click when you mean to make two separate clicks, speed up the double-click rate.

Table 15-1	
Lefties Need to Use Different Buttons for Common Mouse Activities	
Standard Terminology	*Lefties Use This Mouse Button*
Click	Right mouse button
Double-click	Right mouse button
Drag	Right mouse button
Right-click	Left mouse button
Right-drag	Left mouse button

Tip Some mice come with their own programs that enable you to tweak the mouse even more than the Mouse Properties dialog box enables you to. This is especially true if your mouse has any unique features such as a third button, a wheel, or a touchpad. If you have some kind of written documentation for your mouse, you should look at it and see what else is possible.

The Double-Click Speed option on the Buttons tab enables you to determine how fast two clicks must be for interpretation as a double-click. To find the double-click speed that works best for you, try the following steps:

1. Drag the slider below Double-Click Speed to the Fast end of the scale.

2. Double-click the sample folder icon, using your normal double-click speed.

3. If the folder doesn't open, drag the slider bar slightly toward Slow.

4. Repeat Steps 2 and 3 until you find a comfortable double-click speed.

Using ClickLock

If you find that selecting or dragging items with your mouse is difficult, you might want to give the ClickLock feature a try. When this option is activated, you can highlight or drag objects without continuously holding down the mouse button.

To select this option, add a check to the Turn on ClickLock check box. Then click the Settings button and use the slider to adjust the length of time you need to hold down the mouse button to turn on ClickLock. You can experiment with the delay slider to see when you have a comfortable setting.

When ClickLock has been activated, you click a second time to release the lock. It might take some time to get used to using this option.

Controlling the mouse motion

If you find zeroing-in on things with the mouse pointer difficult, slow down the mouse-motion speed. Alternatively, if you must move the mouse too far to get from point A to point B onscreen, speed up the mouse-pointer speed. On laptop LCD screens (and some others), the mouse pointer might fade, or even disappear, when you move the mouse. To solve this irritating problem, turn on the pointer trails.

Tip   When you use a projector to give a demonstration onscreen, turn on the pointer trails to make following the mouse across the screen easier for your audience.

To control the mouse speed and trails, click the Pointer Options tab in the Mouse Properties dialog box (see Figure 15-2). To adjust the speed of the pointer, drag the slider in the Motion slider bar toward the Slow or Fast end of the bar. To test your current setting, click the Apply button and then try moving the mouse around. To see your full range of options, apply the slowest speed and test the mouse. Then apply the faster speed and try the mouse again.

Turning on the Enhance Pointer Precision option will make it easier to zero-in on specific items on the screen, even when you have your pointer speed set high. It accomplishes this by automatically adjusting the speed and precision of the pointer when you're moving the mouse in tiny increments and when you decelerate the mouse after moving a large distance.

The Snap To option, if selected, automatically moves the mouse pointer to the default button in a dialog box as soon as the dialog box opens. The default button in most dialog boxes is the OK button and always has a colored border or some other visual effect that makes it stand out from other buttons in the box.

To turn on pointer trails, select the Display pointer trails check box. The trails turn on immediately and will be visible as soon as you move the mouse. To control the length of the trails, drag the slider to the Short or Long end of the slider bar.

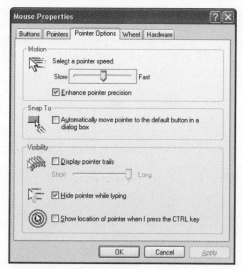

Figure 15-2: Options for controlling mouse speed and pointer trails

If you find that the mouse pointer is distracting while you are typing, select the Hide pointer while typing box. This will hide the mouse pointer when you are typing, but it will reappear when you stop typing or move the mouse.

Finally, if you often find that you just lose track of the mouse pointer location, select the Show location of pointer when I press the CTRL key box. When this option is selected, Windows XP displays a set of circles that draw your attention to the mouse pointer whenever you press the Ctrl key.

 Tip   If you have serious problems with your mouse, click the Hardware tab in the Mouse Properties dialog box and then click the Troubleshoot button.

Choosing mouse pointers

Are you bored with the same old pointer? Do you have problems seeing the mouse pointer? If so, you might want to try some of the alternative pointers, quite a few of which come with Windows XP. The choices available to you are on the Pointers tab in the Mouse Properties dialog box (see Figure 15-3). In this example, I've already chosen a scheme called Windows Animated.

To begin, open the Scheme drop-down list and then experiment with the different options offered. When you find a scheme you want, you can customize it further, if you like. Click any mouse pointer in the list and then click the Browse button to try another pointer. If you select a different pointer and then change your mind, click the Use Default button to return to the default pointer.

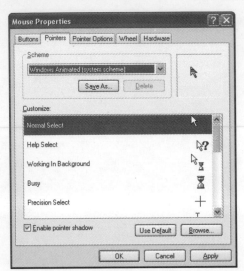

Figure 15-3: The Pointers tab in the Mouse Properties dialog box

To give your desktop a 3D appearance, select the Enable pointer shadow check box. This will make it seem as though your mouse pointer is floating a short distance above the desktop.

After mixing your own mouse pointer scheme, you can click the Save As button and give your new scheme a name. You can delete the scheme currently shown in the drop-down list by clicking the Delete button.

If you have Internet access, you can download some cool collections of animated cursors. To find some possible resources, use your Web browser to go to any of the large search engines, such as www.yahoo.com and search for Windows+mouse+pointers or Windows+XP+mouse+pointers. If you visit some of the sites listed, you're likely to find quite a few sets you can download for free.

Tip   Files that contain cursors have the .cur extension. Animated cursors use the .ani extension. Use Start ➪ Search to search your entire hard disk for *.cur or *.ani files to explore all the cursors available on your hard disk.

Customizing the mouse wheel

If your mouse has a wheel, you can control how far things scroll each time you rotate the wheel one notch. Click the Wheel tab and make your selection from the options that appear.

Personalizing the Keyboard

The keyboard is another important input device. And, as you might expect, Windows XP offers several options for fine-tuning its behavior. For example, you can control *typematic* settings, such as the length of time you have to hold down a key before it starts repeating, as well as how quickly the keystroke repeats. To adjust keyboard settings, follow these steps:

1. Open the Control Panel (click Start ⇨ Control Panel).

2. In Classic view, open the Keyboard icon to get to the Keyboard Properties dialog box shown in Figure 15-4.

3. Make your selections, as discussed in the following sections and then click the OK button to close the dialog box and save your settings.

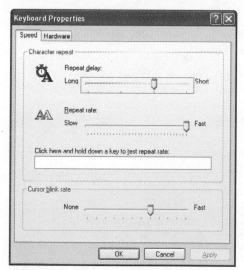

Figure 15-4: The Keyboard Properties dialog box

Cross-Reference   Additional keyboard options for people with motor and visual impairments are available through the Accessibility Wizard, covered in Chapter 14.

Controlling the keyboard's responsiveness

Most keyboards are typematic, which means that if you hold down a key long enough, it starts repeating automatically. If you're a slow typist, you might accidentally type the same letter two or more times. To correct the problem, adjust the Repeat Delay slider to a longer delay. A longer delay requires that you hold down the key longer before auto-repeat typing starts.

You also can use the Repeat Rate slider bar to determine how fast the key repeats as you hold it down. You can test either selection just by typing in the text box below the sliders after making a change to either slider.

Cross-Reference If you have serious problems with your keyboard, click the Hardware tab and then click the Troubleshoot button.

Controlling the Cursor blink speed

The Cursor blink rate section of the Keyboard Properties dialog box enables you to determine how fast the blinking cursor (also called the *insertion point*) blinks. Drag the slider to the None or Fast end of the Cursor blink rate bar and watch the sample blinking cursor. The idea is to find a speed that's in sync with your own cosmic biorhythms or, perhaps, the pace of life in your locale. In San Diego, for example, people like slow-blinking cursors; in New York City, they like their cursors blinking at full-on, high-anxiety speed (hurry! hurry!).

Multiple-language keyboarding

For people who work in multiple languages, Windows XP offers some handy options for adjusting your keyboard to work in a specific language, including the following:

✦ Easy switching from the keyboard layout used in one language to the keyboard layout for another language

✦ Automatic font substitution when switching among different languages (fonts are discussed in Chapter 19)

✦ Correct sorting and comparison rules for different locales and cultures

The options for controlling language-related keyboard options are in the Text Services dialog box shown in Figure 15-5. To get to those options, follow these steps:

1. Click the Start button and choose Control Panel.

2. If you're in Category view, switch to Classic view.

3. Open the Regional and Language Options icon.

4. Click the Languages tab in the dialog box that opens.

5. Click the Details button.

The following sections examine techniques for installing multiple-language support and using multiple-language keyboard layouts.

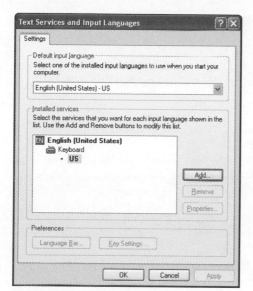

Figure 15-5: The Text Services and Input Languages dialog box

Setting keyboard languages and layouts

The first step is to choose specific languages and keyboard layouts appropriate to your work. Follow these steps:

1. Windows XP may need to install specific languages during this procedure, so close all open programs (although not the current dialog boxes) and save your work; then gather your original Windows XP CD-ROM.

2. On the Text Services and Input Languages dialog box, click the Add button and choose a language from the drop-down list (see Figure 15-6).

3. Choose a keyboard layout for the currently selected language and choose OK.

4. Repeat Steps 2 and 3 to add as many languages as you want.

5. If you want to use a shortcut key for switching languages, click the Key Settings button. Then choose the options you prefer.

6. If you want to switch languages by clicking an icon on the taskbar, click the Language Bar button and choose your preferred options.

7. Click OK when you finish making your selections.

As usual, if any additional instructions appear onscreen, be certain to read and follow them.

Figure 15-6: Many languages are offered in the Add Input language dialog box.

Switching among languages and layouts

After you select one or more foreign languages and layouts, switching among them is easy. If you selected Enable indicator on taskbar while you chose layouts, you see a two-letter abbreviation at the right end of the taskbar indicating which language is currently in use — for example, EN if you're working in English.

To switch to another language and keyboard layout, do either of the following:

✦ Click the language indicator in the taskbar and then click the language you want to use (see Figure 15-7).

✦ Press the shortcut keys you indicated (for example, Left Alt+Shift). Each time you press the shortcut key, you will cycle to the next available language. (You won't get any feedback about which language you chose unless you enabled the indicator on the taskbar.)

Figure 15-7: Clicking the EN indicator to switch to another language

Now you can fire up your word processing program and type with the currently selected language and keyboard layout. In fact, you can switch to another language and layout on the spot. Anything new you type will use the language, layout, and (if applicable) font for that language. In a true multilingually aware program, you can even select existing text and change it to whatever language and font you're currently using.

Removing languages

If ever you decide to eliminate a foreign language keyboard layout, return to the Text Services dialog box. Click any language option you want to eliminate and click the Remove button. Then click the OK button to save your changes and close the dialog box.

Adding and Calibrating a Game Controller

Some computer games play better using a joystick, steering wheel, or video game-style control pad or another game controller. Game controllers are, of course, entirely optional. So if you don't feel you need one, don't bother to read this section. Also, be aware that game controllers work only with certain kinds of games, not with the Windows XP desktop. For example, many drive games support steering wheels and foot pedals. Games that involve flying might support joysticks. Some shoot-em-up games support video game-style gamepads. The only way to know for sure which input devices a particular game supports is by reading about the game in which you're interested.

Many different kinds of game controllers exist, as a quick visit to your local Comput-O-Rama superstore will prove. I should point out, however, that Windows XP has built-in support for many different types of controllers. You'll almost certainly find that whatever type you buy is supported.

Adding a game controller

Because so many different kinds of game controllers exist, I can't guarantee the simple installation instructions will work for every product on the market. But they're worth a try. (If these instructions don't work, you'll probably need to follow the installation instructions that came with your game controller.) Anyway, here are the steps you must follow to install a game controller:

> If your game controller plugs into a USB port, there's no need to shut down the computer. Just plug in the controller and watch the Notification area for automatic detection of the device. Then skip to Step 4.

1. Close all open programs and documents and save any work in progress (to play it safe). Shut down the computer.

2. Plug the game controller into the appropriate plug on the back of your PC.

3. Restart the computer. If Windows detects the game controller at startup, follow the instructions that appear on-screen.

4. Open the Control Panel and then open the Gaming Controllers icon.

5. Select your game controller from the list and click the OK button. Alternatively, if your game controller isn't listed, click the Add button and follow the instructions on-screen.

6. If Windows successfully locates your controller, the Status column will read OK, as in Figure 15-8, where I successfully added a joystick.

Figure 15-8: A Sidewinder joystick is successfully attached.

Calibrating and testing the controller

Once the controller is installed and you're given the OK status, you'll want to calibrate the controller. Doing this tells Windows about the buttons on your device, the range of motion it has, and so forth. Calibration is pretty easy; just follow these steps:

1. Click the name of the controller you want to calibrate and then click the Properties button. The Game Controller Properties dialog box appears.

2. Click the Settings tab and then click the Calibrate button (see Figure 15-9).

3. Follow the instructions on-screen to calibrate your controller.

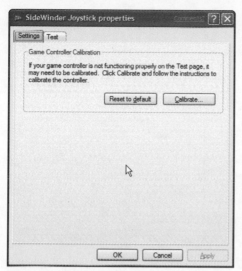

Figure 15-9: Use the Calibrate button to tune your game controller to your PC.

4. When you finish the calibration, click the Test tab in the Game Controller Properties dialog box and try out your controller. The test page will provide options relevant to your controller, as in the example shown in Figure 15-10.

5. If necessary, repeat the calibration and test until the game controller appears to work properly. Then click OK to close the Game Controller Properties dialog box and click OK again to close the Game Controllers dialog box.

The game controller won't work on the desktop. When you fire up a game that supports this kind of controller, however, the controller should work fine. If not, check the documentation or Help screens that came with the game to see whether you need to select any special options to activate the game controller.

If you experience severe problems with your game controller, you might have a hardware conflict or some other problem. Click the Troubleshoot button in the Game Controllers dialog box for help in solving the problem.

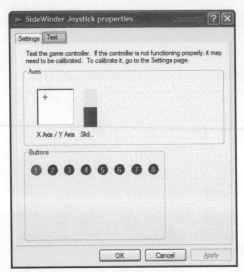

Figure 15-10: The test page for a Sidewinder joystick

Talk, Don't Type

Movies about the future always have totally hands-free computers, to which the actors can just bark orders to get whatever they want. I think it's safe to say we're still pretty far from totally hands-free computing. But computer speech recognition has come a long way over the past few years. There now exists speech-recognition engines that can deal with normal, continuous speech (unlike earlier technologies that required you speak one word at a time, with a substantial pause in between).

Windows XP is the first version of Windows to actually provide support for speech recognition. It's pretty limited support at the moment. Windows XP doesn't come with speech recognition built in. And the Windows XP interface itself doesn't respond to speech. If you have the right hardware and software, however, you can install it all into Windows XP. You can then "train" your speech recognition to recognize your voice and use it in any and all programs on your computer that are capable of accepting voice input.

Speech recognition requirements

To use speech recognition, your computer needs the following hardware and software:

✦ A high-quality close-talk (headset) microphone with gain adjustment. Gain adjustment automatically adjusts the input sound level for your computer. Microsoft recommends using a headset with a USB connector, as opposed to one that plugs into your sound card.

Note
I used a Telex USB headset microphone while writing this chapter. I just plugged it into the USB port, and then waited for the Notification area of the taskbar to tell me the new hardware was installed and ready for use.

✦ A 400 megahertz (MHz) or faster computer with 128 megabytes (MB) of memory.

Tip
If you're not sure of your computer's speed or how much RAM it has, open the System icon in Control Panel. Look under the Computer heading on the General tab for the info you need.

✦ Microsoft Internet Explorer 5.0 or later.

✦ An installed speech recognition engine.

As mentioned, Windows XP doesn't come with a speech-recognition engine of its own. However, many newer computers come with a speech-recognition engine built right in. Microsoft Office XP also comes with a speech-recognition engine. So you might already have an engine installed on your system. To find out, open the Speech icon in Control Panel (Classic view). If you see a tab labeled Speech Recognition, as in Figure 15-11, you're ready to roll.

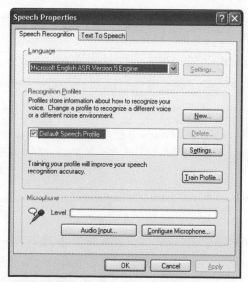

Figure 15-11: The Speech Recognition tab in the Speech Properties dialog box

If the engine is not installed, but you have Microsoft Office XP (a.k.a. Microsoft Word 2002), you can install the speech recognition from Word. Here's how:

1. Start Microsoft Word.

2. Choose Tools ⇨ Speech from its menu bar.

The engine will be installed and available in all programs that support speech recognition. Once the engine is installed, you need to configure your microphone and go through a little training procedure before you can start using it. You can do so in Windows by creating your own *speech profile*. If you installed the speech-recognition engine from Microsoft Word 2002, you can exit that program first.

Creating a speech profile

The best way to set up your speech-recognition system is to create your own speech profile in Windows XP. Doing so will take you through a wizard that simplifies the process. And if you share a computer with other users, your speech profile will automatically be selected and ready to go each time you log on to the computer.

The process of creating a speech profile takes about 10 or 15 minutes. Try to set aside a time when you won't be disturbed, and try to make the room as quiet as possible. When you're ready to roll, follow these steps:

1. Open Control Panel.

2. In Classic view, open the Speech icon and click the Speech Recognition tab.

3. Click the New button to create a new profile.

4. When the wizard starts, just follow the instructions it presents on the screen.

The wizard helps you adjust your microphone settings and takes you through a speech-training procedure. When training is finished you have the option of doing more training or clicking the Finish button to end training. You'll be returned to the Speech Properties dialog box, where you'll see your name added to the list of training profiles. You can click the OK button to close that dialog box and save your settings.

Using speech recognition

Here, in a nutshell, is how speech recognition works. When you start a program that supports speech recognition, (such as Internet Explorer, Outlook Express, or any program from the latest version of Microsoft Office) the *Language bar* opens automatically. (Actually, the cursor needs to be positioned to a control that's capable of accepting speech input. So if the Language bar doesn't appear immediately, it should appear when you click an appropriate control, such as a text box within a Web page.)

To use speech recognition, don your microphone and click the Microphone option on the bar. The language bar expands to show options relevant to the program you're using. If you're in Microsoft Word, for example, the bar expands to look like Figure 15-12.

Note   The first time you use Speech Recognition in a Microsoft Office program, you'll be taken through a second training session. Then, you'll be taken through a Speech Recognition tutorial.

Figure 15-12: The Language bar, as it appears in Microsoft Word

The Dictation option in the toolbar enables you to type by speaking. The Voice Command option enables you to choose menu options by saying their names. You can choose either option by clicking it or by speaking the option you want. (For instance, say the word "dictation" or the words "voice command.") When Voice Command is selected, you can just say the names of menu items to select them. For instance, in Word, saying "edit" opens the Edit menu in Word. Saying the Word "expand" expands the menu to show all of its options. To select an option from the menu, speak the option. For example, saying "select all" would choose the Select All option from the Edit menu.

The Dictation option types the words you speak. If you switch to dictation in Microsoft Word and start speaking, for example, your spoken words will be typed into the document. You can "speak" punctuation marks and special key names as you go. If you say, "My name is Alan comma what is yours question mark new paragraph," you end up with something resembling

    My name is Alan, what is yours?

The words "new paragraph" in Word have the same effect as pressing the Enter key, so the cursor moves down in Word.

Things work differently in different programs. When you're composing an e-mail message in Outlook Express (Version 6.0), clicking the Microphone option in the Language bar displays only a Dictating box because that program doesn't support voice commands. You still need to type the recipient's e-mail address and the subject of the message — those boxes don't accept dictation. After you have positioned the cursor in the main body of the message, however, you can start dictating. If you speak the words "I am dictating this message period how about that question mark next line next line," for example, you end up with something like . . .

    I am dictating this message. How about that?

. . . with the cursor moved down two lines.

Tip   If ever you need to determine which version of a specific program you're using, choose Help ➪ About from that program's menu bar.

Versions 5.5 and later of Microsoft Internet Explorer also provide some limited dictation capabilities. You can't select menu options or fill in Internet Explorer's Address bar using dictation. However, when the cursor is in some field within a Web page — such as a Search text box or a text box on a form — you can dictate your text into the text box.

To turn off the microphone and end dictation at any time, just click the Microphone button in the Language bar again.

Like I said, we're still a long way from the hands-free computing of science fiction. You'll still need to use your mouse and keyboard quite often, even while donning your trusty headset. But it's a start. If you can't type worth beans, speech dictation can be very helpful indeed.

Fine-tuning speech recognition

The more you train speech recognition, the better it will work. Once you've gotten started with speech recognition, you can click the Tools button on the Language bar and choose Training to go through some more training procedures. It works the other way around too. As you use speech recognition, it will train you. You'll gradually develop a consistent speaking style that leads to better accuracy in your dictation.

Tip   To learn more about using speech recognition within a specific program, open that program's help and search for the word. You also might want to visit http://office.microsoft.com and search for the words *recognition* and *speech*.

Using Handwriting Recognition

Handwriting recognition enables you to enter text by writing rather than by typing. As with speech recognition, handwriting recognition isn't a feature of Windows XP per se. However, you can install and remove handwriting-recognition engines through Windows, as discussed later in this chapter. Also, like speech recognition, it takes some time and practice to get things working the way you might like. Don't throw out your keyboard just yet.

There are a couple of ways to use handwriting recognition. For one, you can write by holding down the primary mouse button as you move the mouse to write the characters you want. That approach isn't easy, but it is possible. More realistically, you'll probably want to use some kind of handwriting input tool, such as a pen stylus and tablet. You also can use more advanced 3D drawing and CAD tablets. In case you have never seen such devices, Figure 5-13 shows a couple of examples from Wacom Technology Corp. On the left is the Wacom Graphire tablet. On the right, Wacom's fancier PL 500 LCD tablet.

Figure 15-13: Wacom Inc's Graphire (left) and PL 500 LCD (right) tablets

Tip   For more information on Wacom tablets, visit their Web site at www.wacom.com. To locate products that are compatible with Windows XP, check out the hardware compatibility list at Microsoft's Web site (www.microsoft.com/hcl).

Should you decide to take the tablet approach, make sure you find a Windows XP-compatible product. And, install it as per the manufacturer's instructions. You'll also want to read the documentation that came with the tablet because it might offer features and capabilities that go beyond those described in this chapter.

Some programs, such as Microsoft Word 2002 (which comes with the Microsoft Office XP suite) support handwriting recognition right out of the box. After you've installed such a program, the Language bar will open automatically when you start the appropriate program, and will reveal a Handwriting option. If you have installed Word 2002, but don't see a Handwriting option on the Language bar when you start Word, you might need to install handwriting recognition separately. Here's how:

1. In Control Panel, open the Add or Remove Programs icon.

2. Click your Microsoft Office XP program and then click the Change button that appears.

3. Choose Add or Remove Features and then click the Next button.

4. Expand the Office Shared Features and Alternative User Input options as in Figure 15-14. If handwriting recognition *isn't* installed, it will be marked with an X as in the figure.

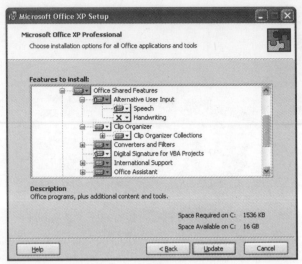

Figure 15-14: In this example, handwriting recognition is not installed yet.

5. Click Handwriting and then choose Run from My Computer.

6. Click in the Update button and follow the instructions on the screen.

When the installation is complete, click the OK button in the Office Setup dialog box that appears. You can then close the Add or Remove Programs window. The next time you start Word, the Handwriting option should appear automatically on the Language bar. When you click the Handwriting option in the Language bar, you'll see the options shown in Figure 15-15. In the sections that follow, I briefly describe how each tool works.

Figure 15-15: The Handwriting options allow you to choose where to write.

Using the Writing Pad

The Writing Pad displays its own window for accepting handwriting input. To use it in Word, you first need to position the cursor to the place in the document where you want to insert text. Then, using the buttons at the right side of the Writing Pad, you can choose whether you want your handwritten text to appear handwritten — exactly as you wrote it — or as typed text. To have the text appear in handwritten form, click the Ink Bottle button. To convert handwritten text to typed text, click the T button just to the right of the Ink Bottle button. Then using your mouse or tablet stylus, write your text along the blue line in the Writing Pad. In Figure 15-16, for example, I wrote the word *Howdy*, which Word then recognized and converted to typed text in the document.

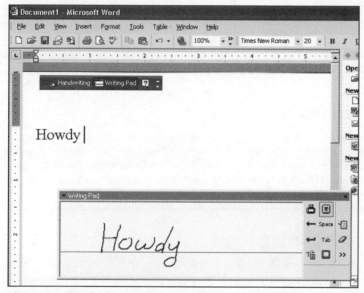

Figure 15-16: The handwritten word "Howdy" converted to typed text in a Word 2002 document

When writing in the pad, your handwritten text is inserted into the document as you go along. More specifically, the text is inserted when

✦ You reach the end of the line in the Writing Pad.

✦ You complete a word.

✦ You stop writing for a couple of seconds.

✦ You click the Recognize Now button in the Writing Pad.

Tip   To see the name of a button in the Writing Pad, point to it for a moment.

You can insert spaces and tabs, and press Backspace or Enter, by clicking on those buttons in the Writing Pad. If you're using a tablet and stylus, it's sufficient to tap on the buttons on your tablet. If you click the Expand (>>) option, the pad widens to display buttons for navigating up, down, left, and right. You also can control whether handwritten text is recognized automatically, how quickly it's recognized, and colors by clicking the small down-pointing arrow to the left of Writing Pad's title and choosing Options.

Using Write Anywhere

As the name implies, the Write Anywhere handwriting-recognition option enables you to write anywhere within a document that supports that feature. Switching to Write Anywhere removes the writing box and underline, leaving just the Ink Bottle, Text, Backspace, and other buttons visible on the screen. To write in this mode, you need to move the cursor to about where you want the text to appear in the document. Then write your text, again using your mouse or tablet stylus. As in Writing Pad, you can choose options by clicking the down-pointing arrow to the left of the Write Anywhere title.

Using Drawing Pad

The Drawing Pad option enables you to draw using either your tablet stylus or mouse. Unlike the preceding two options, Drawing Pad never attempts to convert your entry to text. Instead, you can doodle and draw, clicking the Remove Last Stroke button as needed to undo your most recent pen stroke. To insert the picture into the document, click the Insert Drawing button.

Help with handwriting tools

As mentioned, handwriting recognition isn't really a feature of Windows XP per se. Instead, it's a feature of certain programs. Whether you use it, and how you use it, depends largely on the program you're using at the moment. If you want to learn more about the three handwriting tools described here, you can click the down-pointing triangle in the upper-left corner of the pad and choose Help. Optionally, search the program you're using for specifics. In Figure 15-17, for example, I chose Help ⇨ Microsoft Word Help from Word's menu bar. Then I clicked the Index tab and searched for the word *handwriting*. As you can see, there are quite a few topics on the subject.

Installing and removing recognition engines

As I write this chapter, handwriting recognition is available for Simplified Chinese, Traditional Chinese, English, Japanese, and Korean. These languages are available with the Microsoft Office XP Multilingual User Interface Pack, which also includes Input Method Editors (IMEs) to convert typed text to complex Asian characters. To check for additional languages, go to the Microsoft Office download center at http://office.microsoft.com/Downloads. Choose the Add-ins and Extras option and click Update List. If you need to install handwriting recognition for additional languages, follow these steps:

1. Open Control Panel and then open the Regional and Language Options icon.

2. Click the Languages tab and then click the Details button.

3. Click the Add button and then choose a language from the Input Language drop-down list.

4. If there's a handwriting-recognition engine available for the language you have selected, the Handwriting Recognition check box will be available. Select that check box. If appropriate, select an engine from the drop-down list.

5. Click the OK button and follow the on-screen instructions.

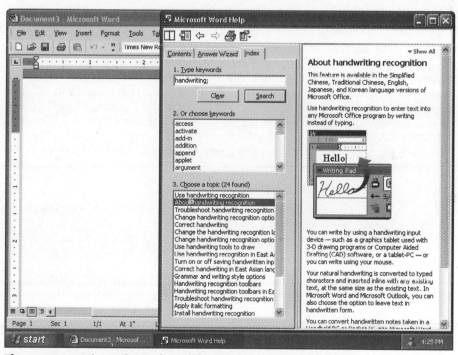

Figure 15-17: Microsoft Word 2002 handwriting-recognition help

Managing the Language Bar and Text Services

The Language bar can be a bit confusing because it seems to appear and disappear as you switch from one program to the next. The fact that Windows XP provides a means of installing recognition engines, but neither provides nor supports those engines itself, makes things all the more confusing. It helps to understand that the role of the Language bar is to provide access to *text services*. Text services are any of the following:

✦ **Keyboard layouts:** Language-specific keyboards, as discussed earlier in this chapter

✦ **Input Method Editors (IMEs):** Special programs that enable you to type East Asian characters with your keyboard

✦ **Speech recognition:** Converts speech to text, as described earlier in this chapter

✦ **Handwriting recognition:** Converts handwritten words to typed text

Normally, the Language bar appears automatically whenever a program that supports a text service is running in the active window. The Language bar will display options for activating/deactivating text services relevant to that particular program. If the Language bar never appears, it might be turned off entirely. (This would happen if you right-clicked the bar and chose Close the Language bar.) You can follow these steps to bring the Language bar back into action:

1. Click the Start button and open Control Panel. If it opens in Category view, switch to Classic view.

2. Open the Regional and Language Options icon.

3. On the Languages tab, click the Details button to get to the Text Services and Input Languages dialog box.

4. Click the Language Bar button under Preferences.

The Language Bar Settings dialog box, shown near the lower-right corner of Figure 15-18, presents options for displaying the Language bar as follows:

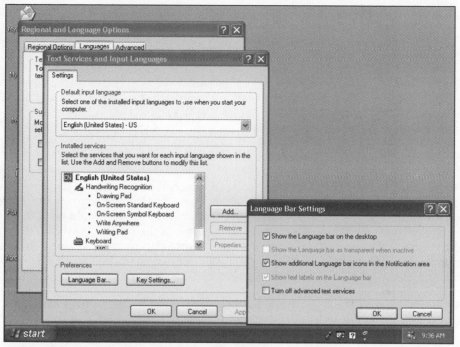

Figure 15-18: The Language Bar Settings dialog box near the lower-right corner of the screen

✦ **Show the Language bar on the desktop:** If this check box is cleared, the Language bar will never be visible. Make sure this check box is selected.

✦ **Show the Language bar as transparent when inactive:** Selecting this option gives the Language bar a translucent appearance when it's not active, allowing you some view of text behind the bar. Pointing to the bar makes it opaque again.

✦ **Show additional Language bar icons in the Notification area:** If selected, this option displays buttons from the Language bar in the Notification area whenever the Language bar is minimized. Otherwise, only a tiny Restore/Options button or language indicator (for instance, EN for English) will be visible when the Language bar is minimized.

✦ **Show text labels on the Language bar:** If selected, the Language bar shows the names of buttons, rather than just icons.

✦ **Turn off advanced text services:** This option turns off all installed text services, including speech and handwriting recognition. Because those options use computer resources, turning them off when not in use can help speed up a sluggish computer.

If you have any installed text services that you never use, you can save computer resources by removing those services. On the Settings tab of the Text and Input Services dialog box (also visible in Figure 15-18), click the service you want to remove under Installed Services. Then click the Remove button. If you work with multiple languages, you also can use the Key Settings button in that same dialog box to create custom shortcut keys for switching between languages.

When the Language bar is visible on-screen, you can move it about the screen by dragging the dots at the left edge of the bar. To minimize the Language bar, click the tiny Minimize button near its upper-right corner. Alternatively, right-click the Language bar and choose Minimize. The buttons on the bar are moved to the right edge of the taskbar. You can then click the Restore button at the upper-right corner of those taskbar buttons to restore the Language bar. Or, right-click that area of the taskbar and choose Restore the Language bar.

While the Language bar is visible, you can right-click it to get to the following options:

✦ **Minimize:** Reduces the bar to a taskbar item

✦ **Transparency:** Turns the transparency effect on and off

✦ **Text labels:** Shows/hides text labels on the bar

✦ **Vertical:** Switches the bar to a vertical orientation

✦ **Additional icons in the taskbar:** Shows/hides individual Language bar buttons when the bar is minimized

✦ **Settings:** Opens the Text Services and Input Languages dialog box, which includes the Language Bar button for setting options

✦ **Close the Language bar:** Removes the Language bar from the screen altogether. To bring it back, you need to return to the Language Bar Settings dialog box via Control Panel (Steps 1–4 at the start of this section) and choose the Show the Language bar on the desktop option.

The Tools button on the Language barz and the Options button (the tiny down-pointing arrow at the lower-right corner of the Language bar), each present options relevant to the text service and program you're using at the moment. Remember, different programs support text services in different ways. So your best bet on using text services within a specific program is the Help menu for that specific program. For general help with the Language bar, click the Help button in the bar and then click the Language Bar Help option that appears.

Summary

Keep in mind that all the dialog boxes for personalizing your input devices are in Control Panel, which you can open by clicking the Start button and choosing Control Panel. If categories rather than icons appear onscreen, choose Switch to Classic View. Then. . . .

✦ To personalize your mouse or mouse pointers, open the Mouse icon.

✦ To personalize your keyboard, open the Keyboard icon.

✦ To add or recalibrate a game controller, open the Gaming Options icon.

✦ To change accessibility options, use the Accessibility Options icon.

✦ To install or fine-tune speech recognition, use the Speech icon.

✦ To add or remove handwriting-recognition services, use the Text Services dialog box.

✦   ✦   ✦

Growth, Maintenance, and General Tweaking

In this part you'll learn how to get the most from Windows XP and your computer. You'll learn how to expand your system with new hardware and new programs. You'll learn how to protect your investment, and how to recover from "disasters," both large and small. Keep your computer secure, up-to-date, and running at its fullest potential with the skills you'll learn here. You'll also discover new techniques for creating and managing multiple user accounts. Those of you running Windows XP on notebook computers will learn how to get the most from Windows XP while you're on the road.

Installing and Removing Programs

Virtually every Windows program, whether it is delivered to you on floppy disks, on a CD-ROM, or over the Internet, comes with its own installation program. That program, which you need run only once, will install all the files necessary to make the program work on your computer. In most cases, the installation program also creates one more icon on your All Programs menu, enabling you to start the installed program from the Windows Start button.

Installing New Programs

For those of you who are new to PC biz, some pointers on when you do, and don't, need to use the techniques in this chapter are in order:

✦ If you are trying to install a driver for a new piece of hardware, see Chapter 27.

✦ If you are trying to copy files, such as other people's documents or clip art, use the general copying techniques discussed in Chapter 12.

✦ Documents, such as pictures or music you've downloaded from the Internet, don't need to be installed. Those you can open just by clicking their icons. Only programs need to be installed using the techniques described in this chapter.

✦ If you're trying to install fonts that you've purchased or downloaded, see the section titled "Installing Fonts" near the end of this chapter.

With that in mind, let's look at the techniques you'll use to install various types of programs.

Installing from a CD-ROM

The vast majority of programs you purchase these days will be stored on CD-ROM. The installation procedure generally goes something like this:

1. Before you start, save all work in progress and then close all open programs on the Windows desktop.

2. Insert the program's CD into your CD-ROM drive.

3. Wait at least 30 seconds to see whether the CD autostarts.

4. If the CD starts automatically, installation instructions will probably be on-screen. Follow those instructions to complete the installation.

When the installation is complete, you can start the installed program by clicking the Start button, choosing All Programs, and then locating the new option for starting the program on the All Programs menu. If you can't find an icon for starting the newly installed program, try rebooting first. That is, remove the CD from your CD-ROM drive, click the Start button, and choose Turn Off Computer ⇨ Restart. Then check the All Programs menu once again for the new program's icon.

If you insert the CD into the CD-ROM drive and nothing appears on-screen after a minute or so, the CD may not be capable of autostarting. In that case, you can follow these steps instead (with the CD still in the CD-ROM drive):

1. Click the Start button and choose My Computer.

2. Click the icon for your CD-ROM (or DVD) drive.

3. Wait a few seconds to see whether the CD autostarts. If it does, follow any instructions that appear on-screen and skip the remaining steps.

4. Look for a file named setup, setup.exe, or install, and then click (or double-click) its icon. Follow the instructions that appear on-screen and skip the remaining steps here.

5. If you've gotten this far, you'll need more information to start the installation procedure. Look for a file named README on the CD. Click (or double-click) that icon for more instructions.

If all else fails, you might try the installation procedure used for installing programs from floppy disks, as discussed next.

Installing from Floppy Disks

Some programs may be delivered to you on floppy disks. To install such a program, follow these steps:

1. Put the program's Setup disk (usually disk #1) in the floppy disk drive.

2. Remove any CD from the CD-ROM drive.

3. Click the Start button and choose Control Panel.

 Note If Control Panel isn't an option on your Start menu, right-click the Start button and choose Properties. Click the Customize button and then click the Advanced tab. Under Start Menu Items, choose the Display as Link option under Control Panel. Close both open dialog boxes by clicking their OK buttons. You should then see Control Panel as an option on the Start menu after you click the Start button.

4. If you're in Category view, choose Add or Remove Programs. If you're in Classic view, double-click the Add or Remove Programs icon. Either way you'll end up in the Add or Remove Programs dialog box shown in Figure 16-1.

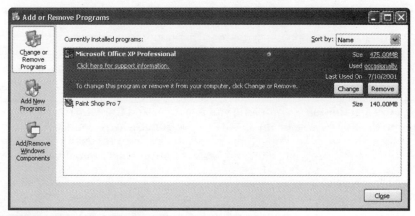

Figure 16-1: The Add or Remove Programs dialog box

5. Click Add New Programs In the left column to get to the options shown in Figure 16-2.

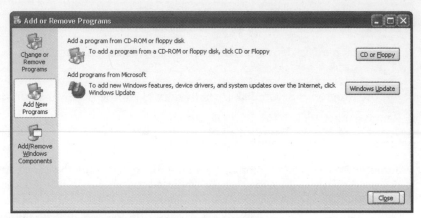

Figure 16-2: Options for adding a new program

6. Click the CD or Floppy button.

7. Because you've already placed the program's disk in the floppy disk drive, click the Next button in the first page of the wizard that opens.

8. The wizard searches the floppy for setup.exe or a similarly named file. If it finds such a file, the wizard displays its name. Just click the Finish button and follow any additional instructions that appear on-screen.

Note   If the wizard cannot find a setup program, refer to the section "Programs That Have No Setup" later in this chapter.

When the installation is complete, you may be asked to restart your computer. Remove the floppy disk or the CD-ROM disk from the drive and put the disks in a safe place for use as backups. If the screen tells you to restart the computer before trying to run the program, click the Restart button on-screen, if any. If no Restart

Check the README.TXT File

Many programs come with a file named README.TXT on the first floppy disk or the CD-ROM. Often this file contains information relevant to installing the program. If you want to read this file before installing, first use My Computer, Windows Explorer, or Find to locate that README.TXT file on the installation floppy disk or CD. Then open that icon. (If Windows asks which program to use, choose Notepad.)

If you want to print the README.TXT file, choose File ➪ Print from Notepad's menu bar. When you finish with README.TXT, close Notepad by clicking its Close (X) button. If you're asked about saving changes to README.TXT, choose No (because you haven't made any intentional changes to that file).

button appears, go to the desktop, click the Start button, choose Turn Off Computer ⇨ Restart. After the computer starts up, click the Start button and choose All Programs. An icon for starting the newly installed program should be visible on the menu now, most likely somewhere near the bottom of that menu.

Installing Downloaded Programs

There are thousands of programs available on the Internet that you can download, install, and then use right on the spot. Some of them are *freeware,* meaning that the program is entirely free of cost. Some are *shareware,* meaning that you can download and use the program free of charge (although you'll be expected to register and purchase the program, if you like it, at some point in time). You can also download *evaluation versions* of some programs. These often have a time limit on them, or they may be missing some features that the full program offers. After you've had a chance to evaluate the version you have, the manufacturer hopes you'll want to buy the full-blown, unlimited version of the program. Still other programs require that you pay up front, even before you download the program.

You can find downloadable programs at many Web sites, which you can visit using Microsoft Internet Explorer. One of the largest repositories of downloadable programs is TUCOWS at `www.tucows.com`. MSN's Computing Central, at `http://computingcentral.msn.com` also offers lots of downloadable programs. Typically, when you choose a program to download, you'll see some instructions for using the program. You may want to print out any information that appears on the Web page by choosing File ⇨ Print from the Internet Explorer menu bar. Then click whatever button or link enables you to start the download procedure.

You may see a dialog box like the one in Figure 16-3. If you do, choose the Save This Program to Disk option and then click the OK button.

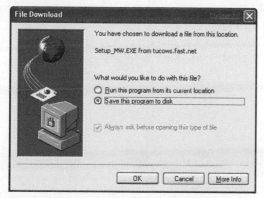

Figure 16-3: Options for downloading a program from the Internet

The Save As dialog box appears next. To make it easy to find the file's icon later, choose Desktop from the Save In drop-down list near the top of the Save As dialog box. (You actually can put the file in any folder you want; just don't forget where you put it!) Next, note the name of the file being downloaded in the File Name box. In Figure 16-4, for example, I have opted to download the file Setup_MW.EXE to my Windows desktop. Click the Save button to begin the download.

When the download is finished, the Download Complete dialog box displays. You can close that by clicking its Close button. If you downloaded the file to some folder other than your desktop, you can click the Open Folder button (if available) to open the folder in which you placed the downloaded file. Otherwise, you can click the Close button to close that dialog box.

It's always a good idea to close all open programs prior to installing a new program. So if Internet Explorer (or any other program) is still open on the desktop, be sure to close it. Then, if you downloaded a program to your desktop, just click (or double-click) the file's icon to start the installation. If you downloaded the file to some other folder, such as My Documents, you need to navigate to that folder first, using Windows Explorer. Then click (or double-click) the icon for the downloaded file.

The installation procedure begins. I can't help you much with that because it varies from one program to the next. If you just follow the instructions presented on the screen, however, you should have no problems.

When the installation is complete, you should be able to locate the icon for starting the installed program in All Programs. (Click the Start button and choose All Programs, as usual.) If you can't find such an icon, you might need to reboot your computer. Click the Start button and choose Turn Off Computer ⇨ Restart.

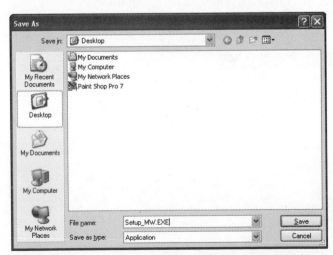

Figure 16-4: About to save Setup_MW.EXE to my Windows Desktop

Once the program is installed and running, it's not entirely necessary to keep the file that you originally downloaded (although you may want to hold onto it as a backup). So rather than deleting the file to remove it from your desktop, you can just move it to some other folder, if you want.

Tip   I keep copies of the original download files in a folder named Common Download within my Shared Documents folder. That way, I can get to the program to install from any user account and from any computer on my local area network.

Installing Missing Windows Components

When you (or whoever) installed Windows XP on your PC, the installation procedure made some decisions about which components to install and which not to install. You're not stuck with those decisions, however. If you can't find a program that supposedly comes with Windows XP, you can follow these instructions to install that program:

1. If you purchased and installed Windows XP yourself or if your computer came with a Windows XP CD, get that CD within reach, as you may need it.

2. At the Windows desktop, click the Start button and choose Control Panel.

3. Open the Add or Remove Programs icon.

4. Click Add/Remove Windows Components in the left pane of the dialog box to open the Windows Components Wizard, shown in Figure 16-5.

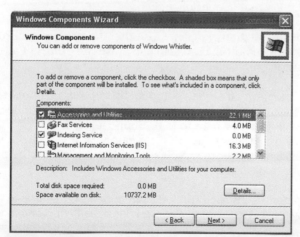

Figure 16-5: First page of the Windows Components Wizard

5. If you don't see the component you want to install, it might be within a category of components. Click any option and then click the Details button (if it's enabled) to view components within that category.

Tip   Some listed components are actually categories of components. Some are not. The only way to determine whether an item in the list is a category is to click the item (not its check box). If the item is a category, the Details button will be enabled. If the item is a single component, the Details button will be disabled (dimmed).

6. Any component that isn't already installed will be indicated with an empty check box. To install a component, click its empty check box.

Caution   Clearing the check box next to an installed component will remove that component from your computer. Be careful that you don't inadvertently remove components that you want to keep. If you accidentally clear some check boxes and aren't sure which one you've cleared, click the Cancel button in the dialog box (or press the Escape key) to cancel the whole procedure.

7. You can repeat Steps 5 and 6 to select as many components as you want. If you're in a categories dialog box, such as the Accessories And Utilities dialog box, click its Close button until you get back to the Windows Components Wizard.

8. Click the Next button.

9. If any components require that you insert your original Windows XP CD, you'll see an instruction to that effect.

10. Follow the instructions that appear on-screen.

After you've finished the installation, you can close the Add or Remove Programs dialog box by clicking its Close button. You also can close the Control Panel by clicking its Close (X) button.

The icon(s) for starting the newly installed component(s) program should available from within the All Programs menu. The category from which you installed the component might give you a clue as to where to look. Suppose, for instance, that you installed a game from the Accessories And Utilities category. If you click the Start button and choose All Programs ⇨ Games, you should be able to find the program's startup icon on the menu that opens.

Note   The procedure for removing installed Windows components is identical to the procedure for installing them. However, to remove an installed component, you just clear its check box in Step 6.

Removing Installed Programs

You might want to remove an installed program for any number of reasons. Maybe you decide that you don't like a program and you want to free the disk space it's using. Or, perhaps you bought a competing program from a different vendor and now you need to make some room on the disk to install this program.

As a general rule, when you upgrade to a new version of an existing program, you should not uninstall the earlier version first. The upgrade program will expect, perhaps even require, the earlier version to be installed. If you're in doubt, check the program's upgrade instructions.

Finally, be aware that uninstalling a program will likely remove the program's folder from your hard disk. If you created any documents with that program and saved them within that program's folder (as opposed to your My Documents folder), those documents will be erased. If you think that there my be some documents you need within the program's folder, be sure to move them to My Documents or some other independent folder prior to removing the installed program. Most programs are installed within their own subfolder under the Program Files folder on your hard disk.

To remove an installed program, first close all open programs and save any documents you're working on. Then follow these steps:

1. Click the Windows Start button and choose Control Panel.

2. Open the Add or Remove Programs icon.

3. Click the name of the program you want to remove. Its line will expand to display information about the program, including its size, how frequently you use it, and the date you last used the program, as shown in Figure 16-6.

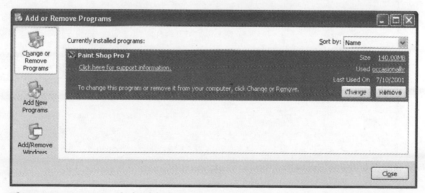

Figure 16-6: Currently highlighting Paint Shop Pro 7 in my list of installed programs

4. Click the Change/Remove button.

5. If given the option to select an uninstall method, choose Automatic.

6. Follow any remaining instructions that appear on-screen and click the Finish button to complete the removal. If prompted to restart your computer, go ahead and do so.

Installing Fonts

Like programs, fonts that you purchase or download need to be installed before you can use them. The procedure for installing fonts differs from the procedure for installing programs. If you've purchased a set of fonts on disk, you would do well to follow the manufacturer's instructions to install the fonts, because they might provide a custom program. If you've downloaded fonts from the Internet or don't have instructions for installing fonts from a disk, use the procedure described here. You can use this procedure to install OpenType, TrueType, Type 1, and raster fonts:

1. If the fonts to be installed are on a floppy disk or CD-ROM, insert the disk into the appropriate drive on your computer.

2. Click the Start button and choose Control Panel.

3. In Classic view, open the Fonts icon. An icon for each font currently installed appears, as in the example shown in Figure 16-7.

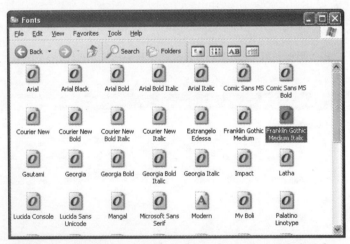

Figure 16-7: The Fonts window shows fonts that are already installed.

Tip To see what a font looks like, click (or double-click) its icon in the Fonts folder.

4. From the Font window's menu bar, choose File ➪ Install New Font.

5. If the fonts are not on drive C:, use the Drives drop-down list to select the drive in which you placed the fonts disk.

6. Under Folders, navigate to the folder that contains the fonts you want to install. Fonts within that folder will be listed in the dialog box.

7. Select the font you want to install. To install multiple fonts, use Ctrl+click, Shift+click, or the Select All button. In Figure 16-8, for example, I have selected four fonts to install.

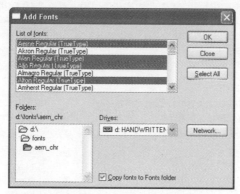

Figure 16-8: Fonts to be installed are selected in the Add Fonts dialog box.

8. Click the OK button.

The new fonts will be added to the Fonts folder. They also should be visible in any program that supports fonts after choosing Format ➪ Font from that program's menu bar.

Tip As an alternative to using the File ➪ Install New Font menu option, you can just drag font files into the Fonts window.

PCL fonts

Some Hewlett-Packard and compatible printers ship with fonts of their own, in the form of PCL (Printer Control Language) and PDL (Page Description Language) fonts. These are often referred to as *external fonts* or *PCL soft fonts*. Check the documentation that came with your printer for exact installation techniques on such fonts. However, the general procedure goes like this:

1. Insert the disk that contains the fonts into the appropriate drive on your computer.

2. Click the Start button and open Control Panel.

3. In Classic view, open the Printer and Faxes icon.

4. Right-click the printer's icon and choose Properties.

5. On the Device Settings tab, click External Fonts, and then click Properties.

6. In the New Soft Font Directory text box, type the path to the drive and directory in which the soft fonts are located.

7. Click Open, and then, under New Soft Fonts, click each font that you want to install. Then click the Add button.

You can add as many fonts as you want in Step 7. Should you decide to remove installed soft fonts at some time in the future, repeat Steps 1–5. Under Installed Soft Fonts, click the font you want to remove and then click on Delete.

Cartridge fonts

Some older printers offer fonts on cartridges. To use a font, you plug the cartridge into a slot on the printer. To make those fonts visible from within Windows and your programs, however, you need to install the cartridge by following these steps:

1. Insert the font cartridge(s) into the printer.

2. Click the Start button and open Control Panel.

3. In Classic view, open the Printers and Faxes icon.

4. Right-click the icon of the printer for which you're installing cartridge fonts and choose Properties.

5. Click the Device Settings tab.

6. Under Installed Font Cartridges, click the slot number of an installed cartridge.

The fonts on the cartridge should be visible in all your programs that support the use of fonts.

Summary

Installing and removing programs is generally pretty easy in Windows XP. Here's a quick recap of the various ways you can install and uninstall programs:

✦ To install a program that was delivered to you on a CD, place the CD in your CD-ROM drive and wait a few seconds for installation instructions to appear on-screen.

✦ If the CD doesn't display installation instructions automatically, use the same procedure you would use to install a program from a floppy disk.

✦ To install a program from a floppy disk, click the Start button, choose Control Panel, and open the Add or Remove Programs icon. Then click the Add New Programs option in the left pane of the dialog box that opens.

✦ To install a program you downloaded from the Internet, just click (or double-click) its icon, and follow the instructions that appear on-screen.

✦ To install missing Windows components, or remove installed components, open the Add or Remove Programs icon in Control Panel. Then click the Add/Remove Windows Components option in the left pane.

✦ To remove an installed program, click the name of the program you want to remove in the Add or Remove Programs dialog box. Then click the program you want to remove, and click the Change/Remove button that appears.

✦ To install OpenType, TrueType, Type 1, and raster fonts, open the Fonts icon in Control Panel, and choose File ⇨ Install New Font from its menu bar.

✦   ✦   ✦

Installing and Removing Hardware

There are tons of cool gadgets that you can plug into your PC to add more power, more functionality, and more fun. Officially these gadgets are called *hardware devices* or just *devices* for short. There are two main categories of such devices. *External devices* are ones that plug into the computer through some sort of cable. You don't need to take the computer apart to install external devices. Then there are *internal devices,* which plug into the computer's motherboard, inside the computer. All devices require *device drivers* (often called *drivers* for short) to work. The driver is a small program that tells your operating system, Windows XP in this case, how to use the device. As you'll learn in this chapter, managing hardware on a computer is all about managing both the hardware and the drivers that make that hardware work.

Meet Your Hardware

To manage hardware on your computer, you first need to become familiar with the System Properties and Device Manager dialog boxes. To open either one, follow these steps:

1. Click the Windows Start button and choose Control Panel.

 If Control Panel isn't available on your Start menu, see "Reorganizing Your Start Menu" in Chapter 13 for information on adding that option. If you're using the Classic Start menu, you'll find Control Panel under the Settings option.

2. If Control Panel opens in Categories view, choose the Performance and Maintenance category. Open the System icon to reveal the System Properties dialog box shown in Figure 17-1.

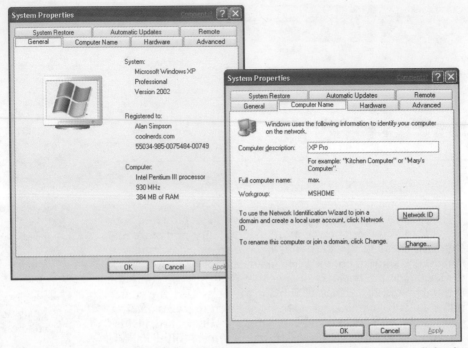

Figure 17-1: The General and Computer Name tabs of the System Properties dialog box

The General tab of the System Properties dialog box, shown on the left side of Figure 17-1, shows some basic information about your computer system, including the manufacturer, the type and speed of the processor, the amount of random access memory (RAM) installed, and so forth. The Computer Name tab, shown on the right side of Figure 17-1, shows the computer's name, description, and work-group (if any). You can change the computer's description or name from here, as well as its network identification.

Cross-Reference   Part VI in this book discusses local area networks, workgroups, and other network-related topics.

The Hardware tab provides access to various hardware-related options on your computer, including Device Manager. Clicking the Device Manager button on that tab opens the Device Manager program shown in Figure 17-2. Device Manager gives you a clear view of all the hardware currently installed on your computer, organized into categories. To expand a category and see specific hardware items within that category, click the plus sign (+) to the left of the category name.

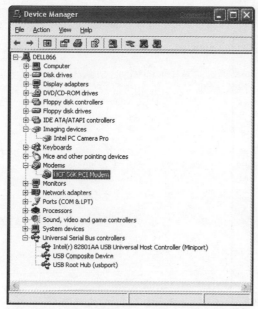

Figure 17-2: The Device Manager window shows installed hardware, organized into categories.

Device Manager uses tiny icons to identify hardware that's not working at the moment, as follows:

✦ **Disabled device:** A device that's capable of working, but is currently disabled, is marked with a red X, like the HCF 56K PCI Modem shown in Figure 17-2.

✦ **Unknown device:** A hardware device that Windows XP doesn't recognize, and therefore can't use, is identified by a question mark (?), as in the example shown in Figure 17-3.

✦ **Problem device:** If an installed device is recognized, but not working properly, it will display an exclamation point icon, like the ATI WDM Rage Theater Video option shown in Figure 17-3.

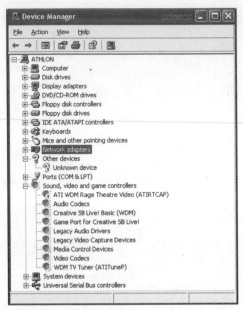

Figure 17-3: This computer contains one unknown hardware device, and one problematic device.

Quick and easy troubleshooting

You can learn more about any installed device by right-clicking its name and choosing Properties. A Properties dialog box for that specific device will open. The exact contents of the dialog box will vary from one device to the next. But often, you can fix a troubled device from options within that Properties dialog box. For instance, Figure 17-4 shows the Properties dialog boxes for an unknown device and a problem device. Clicking the Reinstall Driver or Troubleshoot button in one of those dialog boxes will start a wizard or take you to a help screen for solving the problem.

If you're new to the whole business of working with hardware, the help and troubleshooting options for dealing with unknown or problematic devices might be a little over your head. By the time you finish this chapter, however, you'll have enough understanding to use those options productively.

Enabling and disabling devices

To disable a device, right-click its name and choose Disable. To enable a disabled device, just right-click the device and choose Enable. This perhaps brings up the question, why would one want to do this? Well, I have an example. I intentionally disabled the HCF PCI 56K Modem shown back in Figure 17-2 after I set up my local area network. I didn't need the modem anymore because all the computers on my network connect through a single modem and Internet account on another computer.

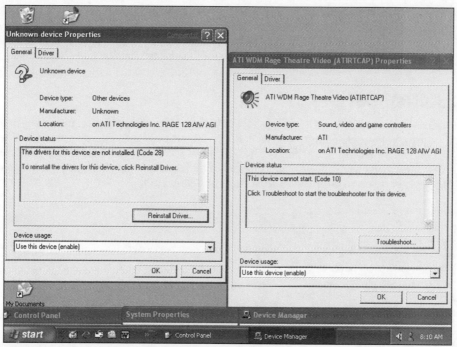

Figure 17-4: Properties dialog boxes for an unknown device and a problematic device

Note Not all devices can be disabled. For example, you cannot disable your computer's hard disk. If you could, your computer would stop working right on the spot.

I could open up the computer and actually remove the modem. But, then again, if some network problem makes it impossible to get to the Internet through my network, I can use that installed modem as a backup. I would just have to reactivate the modem by right-clicking its name and choosing Enable. Of course, I would also have to connect the modem to a phone line, use Internet Options in Control Panel to make sure requests to access the Internet go through the modem instead of through the LAN, and set up my Internet account information on that computer. But at least I wouldn't have to reinstall the modem and its drivers.

Hardware Terminology

When you start delving into computer hardware, you'll be faced with a whole new terminology, not to mention the ubiquitous acronyms such as AGP, PCI, USB, and so forth. So before we get into the specific steps for actually installing and removing hardware devices, let's get some terms and concepts straight. My goal here isn't to turn you into a total hardware guru—there's just not enough room in this Windows XP book to cover such a broad area in depth. If this chapter piques your interest and you want to learn more, there are entire books and courses—usually under the general category of "Upgrading and Repairing PCs" or "A+ Certification"—that go into hardware in depth. What you learn here, however, will enable you to install, troubleshoot, and remove the most common hardware devices on the market.

External devices

External hardware devices are physical objects, such as modems, mice, keyboards, monitors, scanners, cameras, and so forth, which plug into the system unit. Figure 17-5 shows an example of the *ports* (also called *jacks*) on the back of a system unit into which you can plug external devices. The jacks shown there are fairly typical, although your computer might look different from this.

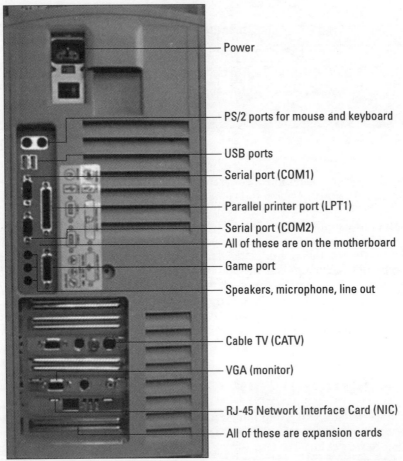

Figure 17-5: External hardware devices plug into ports (also called jacks) on the back of the system unit.

Before you purchase an external device to add to your computer, you want to be sure that you have a plug available for the device. If you buy a modem that hooks into a serial port, for example, you must have a serial port available into which to plug this device. If you want to buy speakers or a camera that hooks into the USB port, your computer must have an available USB port. Let's discuss some of the different types of plugs you might encounter and what kinds of devices might plug into them:

✦ **Power:** The power port is used for one thing only, to plug the PC into the wall socket for power. No devices are ever hooked into the power port.

✦ **Parallel printer port:** Also known as the LPT1 port, the parallel printer port is generally used to connect a parallel printer. You also can plug some portable devices, such as Zip drives, into the parallel port. On the back of the computer, the parallel port generally contains 25 little sockets and the parallel cable has 25 pins on its plug. The plug itself is often referred to as a DB25.

✦ **Serial port:** The serial port is used primarily for communications devices, such as modems. Some mice and other devices can also plug into that port. The plug on a serial port is usually a DB9. (It has nine pins on the male plug and nine sockets on the female plug.) Occasionally, a PC will have a 25-pin serial port that looks like a parallel port. The serial port on the back of the PC usually is male (has pins), however, and the plug itself is female.

✦ **USB ports:** Available only in computers made after 1997, the universal serial bus (USB) port offers the ultimate in Plug-and-Play convenience. Typically, you can plug the device into the port and start using it. Common hardware devices that use the USB port include cameras, scanners, and speakers.

✦ **SCSI (not shown):** SCSI (pronounced scuzzy) stands for Small Computer System Interface. Unlike other components, SCSI devices can be daisy chained, meaning you can plug several devices into a single plug. The first device connects to the plug, the second device connects to the first device, the third device plugs into the second device, and so forth. Conventional SCSI supports up to seven devices on a single plug. Ultra Wide SCSI supports up to 15 devices.

✦ **Speakers, microphone, line out:** If your computer has sound capability, you probably have a plug for a microphone, a plug for speakers, and perhaps Line In and Line Out plugs for connecting stereos and other audio equipment. There may also be a separate port for digital sound, into which you would plug digital speakers.

✦ **Game port:** The game port plug is used to connect joysticks and other input devices. On most PCs, this plug is near the plugs for the speakers and the microphone. The port resembles the serial and parallel ports, but contains 15 sockets, making it larger than the serial port, but smaller than the parallel port.

✦ **VGA or SVGA:** Similar in size to a serial port, but with three rows of pins or sockets, rather than two, for a total of 15 sockets. The port on the computer is generally female; the plug itself is male. A monitor is the only device that plugs into a VGA or SVGA port.

✦ **RJ-45:** This resembles a slightly oversized telephone jack. It's used mainly for networking cables (as discussed in Part VI). The RJ-45 may also be used to connect a *broadband modem* — such as those used with cable and DSL Internet services.

✦ **PS/2:** PS/2 ports are used for mice and keyboards. Older computers may not have these ports. Instead, the keyboard plugs into a special keyboard port on the back of the PC and the mouse may plug into one of the serial ports.

✦ **CATV:** If your computer has TV capabilities, you'll probably find a standard cable TV plug (CATV) somewhere on its back. You hook your cable TV cable into that port.

Internal devices (cards)

Internal hardware devices include things such as your disk drives, processor, and RAM, all of which plug into specific slots on the motherboard. Unless you're a very experienced hardware person, however, you're probably not going to want to mess with those items. Finding devices that exactly match the capabilities of your motherboard can be daunting, even if you know the exact make and model of your motherboard.

Aside from those specific devices, another whole class of internal devices come in the form of circuit boards, also known simply as *cards*. Figure 17-6 shows an example of what such a card looks like. The cards plug into *expansion slots* on the motherboard inside the computer. From the outside, all you see is the jack that the card exposes. For example, note the CATV, VGA, and RJ-45 ports on the back of the system unit shown in Figure 17-5. Those are all internal cards that are plugged into the computer's motherboard. We know this because they're all housed within expansion slots. The rest of the ports all represent *onboard devices*. Which is to say, the circuits to which those other ports connect are actually part of the motherboard itself, as opposed to being part of an internal card that has been added to the motherboard.

Figure 17-6: A sample card that plugs into an expansion slot. Only the port facing you is visible from outside the computer.

Not all motherboards are alike. For example, some motherboards have *onboard sound,* which means you don't need an internal card to add sound capabilities. The computer in Figure 17-5 has onboard sound capabilities, as witnessed by the fact that the jacks for sound are on the motherboard, as opposed to being on a card that's plugged into an expansion slot. Some motherboards have onboard video, which means that you can plug your monitor into the motherboard without the need for a separate video card. The motherboard in the system unit shown in Figure 17-5 does not have onboard video. The monitor on that computer plugs into a VGA port, which is on an internal card in one of the expansion slots.

Just as there are different sizes and shapes of plugs outside the computer, there are different sizes and shapes of expansion card plugs on the motherboard inside the computer. Figure 17-7 shows an example of a computer with its outside case removed and its motherboard partially exposed. Figure 17-8 shows a sample motherboard "in the raw" — before it has been put inside a computer.

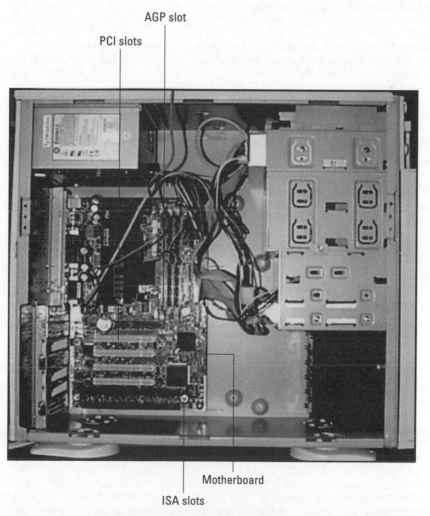

Figure 17-7: Motherboard inside a PC's system unit

Figure 17-8: A motherboard in the raw

Caution Never remove your computer's case while the computer is turned on, or even plugged in. Always shut down the computer, and unplug the power cord, before attempting to remove the cover!

Different motherboards offer different types of slots into which you can plug internal devices. Most, however, offer some combination of the following:

✦ **PCI slots:** The Peripheral Components Interface (PCI) slot is a general-purpose slot found in most modern computers. PCI slots support *Plug and Play*, a technology that simplifies adding internal cards to your computer. Most computers have at least two PCI slots, although this varies with the size of the motherboard and the size of the system unit in general. PCI slots are usually white or light tan in color.

✦ **AGP slot:** The Advanced Graphics Port (AGP) is strictly for AGP video cards. Most motherboards have only one such slot. The AGP slot is about the same size as a PCI slot. As a rule, however, it's colored brown or dark gray and is not aligned with the PCI slots.

✦ **AMR slot:** Some newer motherboards offer an Audio/Modem Riser (AMR) slot, into which you can plug an AMR sound card, modem, or sound/modem combined card. The sample motherboard shown in Figure 17-8 has an AMR slot.

✦ **DIMM, SIMM, and RDRAM slots:** Every motherboard has at least one slot for holding RAM (random access memory) chips. Random access memory stores whatever it is you're working on at the moment in your PC. Which is to say, anything that's open on your desktop is currently in RAM. Most modern motherboards offer DIMM (dual inline memory module) or the faster (and much more expensive) RDRAM (RAMBUS dynamic random access memory) slots.

✦ **ISA and EISA slots:** Industry Standard Architecture (ISA) and Extended Industry Standard Architecture (EISA) slots have been around since the earliest PCs. These are something of "dinosaurs" these days, and most modern motherboards only offer one such slot, if any. These ports don't support Plug and Play, which makes installing ISA and EISA cards quite complex. The modern motherboard in Figure 17-8 does not have any ISA or EISA slots.

If you're thinking that adding an external device is a lot easier and safer than adding an internal device, you're absolutely correct. In fact, the easiest type of device to install is any device that plugs into a USB port at the back of the system unit. So we'll start with a discussion of those devices.

Before You Install or Remove Anything

Be aware that installing new hardware will change some sensitive and critical files on your PC. Most of the time, hardware installation goes pretty smoothly, and you won't have any problems. If, by chance, a new hardware device causes your computer to act erratically, however, you might want to "back up" to where you were before adding the new hardware. The best way to do this is to set up a *system restore point* just before you install new hardware. That way, if things go wrong after the hardware is restored, you can remove the hardware and easily restore the computer to its previous state. See "Using System Restore" in Chapter 18 for more information on using System Restore.

Installing/Removing USB and IEEE 1394 Devices

USB (universal serial bus) is the most modern and convenient way to add external devices to your computer. As a general rule, you just plug the device into the USB port while the computer is running, and that's all there is to it! However, general rules don't always apply. So before you do this, here's a caution.

Caution Always read the installation instructions that came with your USB or IEEE 1394 device before you attempt to install it. It may require drivers that aren't built in to Windows XP. The device might not work until those drivers are installed.

What holds true for USB devices also holds true for IEEE 1394 (also known as FireWire) devices. The only differences are as follows:

1. Most newer computers have USB ports built in, very few have IEEE 1394 ports.
2. IEEE 1394 is faster than USB.

FireWire is a bit more expensive than USB due to its extremely high speed. It's great for transferring digital video to your PC. Because relatively few people need to do that sort of thing, however, you rarely find a computer with a FireWire port built right in. If you want to add FireWire capability to a computer that doesn't have it, you need to purchase and install an IEEE 1394 card, which will add the appropriate port to your computer. Because FireWire is relatively rare, however, I'll just refer to USB in the paragraphs that follow in this section. If you happen to have an IEEE

1394 port on your computer, just remember that what applies to USB devices applies to IEEE 1394 devices as well. You just have to plug them into an IEEE 1394 port rather than a USB port.

Before you purchase a USB device, you need to make sure your computer has USB ports. If the USB ports already have devices plugged into them, you have a couple of options. For one, understand that USB devices are hot swappable, which means you can plug them in and unplug them with the computer turned on. Therefore, if one of your current devices is something you use only occasionally, you can unplug it when you're not using it, and plug in some other device. Of course, this isn't terribly convenient (particularly if the devices currently using your USB ports are things you need to use all the time, such as your mouse and keyboard).

An alternative is to get a *USB hub* into which you can plug more devices. You can find these devices at most computer stores, or order online from a retailer such as tigerdirect.com, cyberguys.com, or cdw.com. (Search for the phrase *USB hub* at any of those Web sites.) Specifically, you're looking for a hub that plugs into one USB port and offers two or more USB ports of its own, so that you can plug multiple devices into a single USB slot.

Caution   Actually, a search for *USB hub* will probably return lots of products at any of these sites. Here I'm talking specifically about the type of hub that enables you to plug two or more USB devices into a single USB port on your computer.

The only drawback to using a USB hub is that there is a limit to how much "stuff" can travel through the USB port at one time (specifically, about 12 megabits — twelve million bits — per second). That's a lot of data and screamin' fast — don't get me wrong. If you pile your mouse, keyboard, printer, modem, speakers, microphone, and kitchen sink all onto one USB port, however, things may start to slow down. So if you buy a new mouse, keyboard, printer, or whatever, you might want to stick with the traditional PS/2 and parallel printer ports for those devices, to conserve USB resources.

Anyway, the "usual" technique for installing a USB device is as follows:

1. Close all open programs and windows on your Windows desktop.

2. Plug the device into the USB port.

3. Watch the Notification area of the taskbar for the message shown in Figure 17-9.

Figure 17-9: A USB device has been detected, its drivers have been installed, and it's now ready for use.

That's it; you're ready to use the device. Once again, however, be sure to follow any instructions that came with the device for proper use and installation.

Note   A USB or IEEE 1394 device is visible in Device Manager only when it's plugged into the appropriate port on the computer. If you plug a USB headset into your USB port, for example, you'll see that device listed under Sound, Video, and Game Controllers in Device Manager.

Removing a USB or IEEE 1394 device is generally a simple matter of unplugging it from the port. One exception, however, is a disk drive, which may require that you click some icon in the Notification area before removing the drive. If in doubt, check the documentation that came with the device. Alternatively point to any icons in the Notification area for possible options.

As a general rule, you don't need to go through the rigmarole discussed in the following section to remove a USB or IEEE 1394 device. If you absolutely must remove the drivers for such a device, be sure to read the manufacturer's instructions on how to do that. It can be tricky. Fortunately, it's rarely necessary; when you unplug the device, the drivers temporarily "disappear" and then magically reappear when you plug the device back in next time.

Installing/Removing non-USB External Devices

External devices that plug into any port other than USB (or IEEE 1394) usually require a bit more work than USB devices. Specifically, you often need to install the *device drivers* for the device. A driver is a program that allows the device to interact with your computer's operating system—Windows XP in this book. As always, your best bet is to refer to the device manufacturer's instructions for specific step-by-step instructions. I can tell you what to expect, however, and how it all works in general.

Cross-Reference   The procedure for installing a device attached to some other computer in a local area network differs from the procedure discussed in this chapter. See Chapter 27 for information on installing network devices.

Caution   If you're going to be replacing one device with another—say you just bought a new printer to replace the existing printer—remove the existing printer's drivers before you install the new printer.

The first step will usually be to close all open windows on your desktop, saving any work in progress, of course. Then shut down the computer all the way by clicking the Start button and choosing Turn Off Computer ⇨ Turn Off. If you see a message telling you it is now safe to turn off your computer, you'll need to turn it off, usually by holding in the main on/off switch for a few seconds. If you don't see a message indicating that it's now safe to turn off your computer and the screen goes completely blank, Windows has already turned the computer off "all the way." Not all computers have that capability though.

Next you need to plug the external device into the appropriate port on your system unit, plug the device into the wall socket (if the device requires its own power source), and then turn your computer back on. What happens next depends on whether Windows XP recognizes the new device and whether Windows XP has drivers for that device built in.

If Windows XP recognizes the device and has drivers for the device already built in, the procedure will be much like the procedure for installing a USB device. The Notification area of the taskbar will inform you that the device has been found, Windows will install the drivers, and you'll see a message indicating the device is installed and ready to use. If that happens, you're done. If the device came with any additional software of its own, however, you'll want to install that as well, following the manufacturer's instructions.

If Windows XP recognizes the device, but has no immediate access to drivers for the device, you'll see instructions for adding it, telling you to either insert your original Windows XP CD-ROM or the manufacturer's disk. Beyond that, however, I cannot tell you much more other than to follow the instructions on your screen, as well as the device manufacturer's instructions. Just too many possible scenarios might follow at this point for me to generalize.

Cross-Reference If you're adding a game controller, tablet, or some kind of speech-recognition device, see Chapter 15 for tips and techniques on installing and configuring those devices. For cameras and scanners, see Chapter 23.

If Windows doesn't recognize the device at all during startup, first make sure the device is plugged in and turned on. If you discover that the device wasn't turned on and plugged in, shut down Windows again by clicking the Start button and choosing Turn Off Computer ➪ Turn Off. If necessary, shut down the computer using the power switch. Then turn on the external device, check all connections, and turn on the computer again. If Windows doesn't recognize the device this time, then the device you're trying to install isn't Plug-and-Play compatible. Your best bet in that case is to follow the device manufacturer's instructions for installing the device. If that's not an option, the Add Hardware Wizard might be able to help. Click the Start button and choose Control Panel. If you're in Category view, switch to Classic view. Open the Add Hardware icon and follow the instructions presented on the screen. The wizard will tell whether the device is already installed and also will help you troubleshoot the installation procedure or device.

If you're not sure whether the device was installed correctly or if you need to troubleshoot the device, see the section titled "Troubleshooting Hardware Devices" later in this chapter.

When you remove a non-USB external device from your system, Windows doesn't automatically remove the drivers for that device. In many cases, this is a good thing, because you may plan on plugging the device back in again in the future. If you have a digital camera that plugs into a serial port on your computer, for example, you don't want to have to remove, and then reinstall, the device drivers for that camera every time you attach or detach the camera.

On the other hand, if you're permanently removing a device, as is the case when you're going to replace it with some other device, it's probably to your advantage to remove the device drivers. The drivers will serve no purpose after the device is gone — and could, conceivably, interfere with the drivers for the new device. To remove the devices drivers for an installed external device, follow these steps:

1. Leave the device turned on and plugged into the computer, as usual.

2. Click the Start button and open the Control Panel.

3. If you're in Category view, switch to Classic view.

4. Open the System icon.

5. Click the Hardware tab.

6. Click the Device Manager button. A list of categories of devices appears.

7. Click whichever category seems to best describe the type of device you want to remove to display installed devices within that category.

Note   Some devices might be stored under some unintuitive categories. For example, my HP printer is installed under Dot4 and Dot4Print.

8. Right-click the device you plan to remove and choose Uninstall. In Figure 17-10, for example, I'm about to remove a modem.

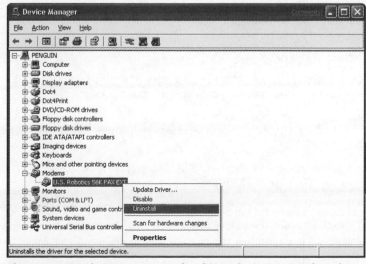

Figure 17-10: About to remove the drivers for an external modem I'm planning on replacing

The drivers will be removed. Make sure you physically unplug the device before you restart the computer in the future. Otherwise, if the device is still plugged in the next time you restart, Windows will probably detect the device and just reinstall its drivers!

Installing/Removing Internal Cards

Installing internal cards is a bit more complex than installing external devices, mainly because you need to open the system case and probably dig around through a bunch of cables to get the card into its slot. Furthermore, it's really important that you read the card manufacturer's instructions before you try to install the card. Here I explain how the procedure goes, in general. Be aware, however, that no two cards are exactly alike. So the manufacturer's instructions are always your best bet.

 If you're replacing an existing card in your computer, be sure to remove the old card's drivers before you install the new card. Leaving the old drivers installed could cause the device to misbehave.

Suppose, for example, that you have a card in hand and are ready to install it. The general procedure goes like this:

1. Close all open windows on your desktop.

2. Click the Start button and choose Turn Off Computer ➪ Turn Off.

3. If you see the message that it's now safe to turn off your computer, press and hold down the computer's main on/off switch for a few seconds until the computer powers down.

4. Remove the power plug from the back of the system unit. This might sound like overkill, but it's not. Failure to remove the power cord can result in irreparable damage to your computer!

5. Remove the computer's case.

6. Touch something metal (other than the computer) to ground yourself. Even a tiny static electricity spark on the motherboard can ruin it!.

7. Place the card in the appropriate type of slot — AGP, PCI, or whatever. Make sure you get it down in there real snug, and screw it down like all the other cards in your system.

8. Put the case back on the computer, plug the computer back in, and turn the computer back on. Then pray. (Kidding.)

What happens next depends on the card you installed. I have seen Windows XP detect and install a card without providing any sort of on-screen feedback. I had to go into Device Manager to see whether the card was actually installed. More likely, however, you'll see some kind of feedback indicating that the card has been installed, as in Figure 17-11. You might also see additional instructions for using the card. If so, follow those instructions.

Figure 17-11: Windows has detected a newly installed Ethernet card.

Finally, if the card came with any special software of its own, install that as well. Once again, you need to rely on the manufacturer's instructions for that information.

If you want to replace an existing board with a new board, first remove the existing board's drivers and then remove the board itself. The procedure for removing an internal card is identical to the procedure for removing an external device, as discussed earlier in this chapter. That is, in the Device Manager dialog box, right-click the name of the card you want to remove and choose Uninstall. However, Windows might display a message asking whether you want to restart your computer after it has finished removing the device's driver. You definitely want to answer No in response to that question; because if you restart the computer with the card still in its slot, Windows will just reinstall the card! Then close the Device Manager dialog box, Systems Properties dialog box, and Control Panel.

Caution

If you restart the computer prior to removing the card from its slot, Windows will just reinstall the card's drivers when it restarts. You'll never get rid of the card at that rate!

A Note on AGP Cards

AGP cards can be difficult to "get snug." You need to push hard enough to get the card well seated, although not so hard as to break anything! If you try to start your computer with an improperly seated AGP card, the computer will probably beep a few times at startup, and the screen will remain blank. If that happens, shut down and unplug everything and give that AGP card a little more push to get it seated properly.

Some AGP cards come with a retainer that helps the card stay in place. Be sure to read the instructions that came with your AGP card to see whether you need the retainer. And if so, look there for instructions on installing and using the retainer.

Finally, shut down the computer by clicking the Start button and choosing Turn Off Computer ⇨ Turn Off. As always, if you see a message indicating that it's now safe to turn off your computer, hold down the computer's power button for a few seconds to finish shutting down.

To remove the card, make sure you unplug the power cord from the system unit. You don't want *any* power coming into the computer at this point. Then remove the computer case and ground yourself by touching something metal. Then remove the card from its slot.

If you're planning to replace the card you removed, you can go ahead and insert the new card now.

Troubleshooting Hardware Devices

In the event that you have any problems with an installed hardware device, you can do several things to troubleshoot the device. As mentioned earlier in this chapter, you can right-click the device's entry in Device Manager, choose Properties, and click the Troubleshooting button in the device's Properties dialog box — assuming there is a Troubleshooting button available in that dialog box. Although this is a good first step, you also can take some other approaches.

My Mouse Died

If your mouse is the device causing you problems, you need to use the keyboard to get to the troubleshooters. Just press the F1 key at the desktop to get started. Alternatively, you can press the Windows key on your keyboard, or Ctrl+Esc, to open the menu. Then use the arrow keys to move to the Control Panel option and press Enter to select that option. If you end up in the Category view of Control Panel, press Tab or Shift+Tab until the Switch to Classic View option is highlighted. Then press Enter to select that option. In Classic view, use the arrow keys to move the highlighter to the Mouse icon, and press Enter to open that icon.

When the Mouse Properties dialog box opens, press Ctrlt+Shift+Tab to get to the Hardware tab. To select the Troubleshoot button on that tab, press Alt+T. Within the troubleshooter, you need to use a combination of the Tab, Shift+Tab, and arrow keys to move from item to item. To select an option button in the troubleshooter, press the Spacebar while the option you want is selected. Press Tab as necessary to highlight the Next button (or any other button), and press Enter to select the currently highlighted button. For more information on getting around in dialog boxes without a mouse, refer to "Using Dialog Boxes" in Chapter 2.

Using hardware troubleshooters

If a new hardware device won't work or if something that worked before has stopped working properly, a device conflict exists. The quickest and easiest way to resolve a device conflict is to use a troubleshooter. Follow these steps:

1. Click the Start button and choose Help and Support.

2. Choose Fixing a Problem.

3. Select whichever option in the left pane best describes the type of problem you're trying to fix.

4. Then select a troubleshooter or other option from the right pane.

5. Follow the on-screen instructions.

In Figure 17-12, I have selected the Hardware and System Device Problems option in the left pane to reveal the options in the right pane. As you can see, there are troubleshooters for a variety of hardware devices, as well as options for performing specific hardware-related tasks.

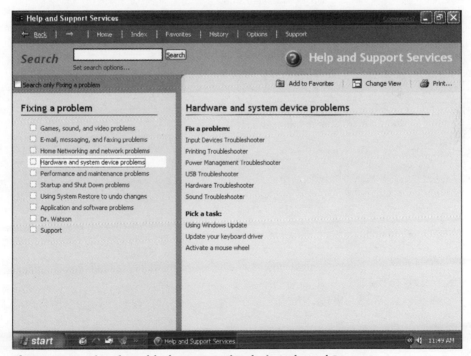

Figure 17-12: List of troubleshooters and tasks in Help and Support

If your chosen troubleshooter doesn't find any problems, something else is wrong. Check the manual that came with your new device for specific troubleshooting tips or try some of the troubleshooting methods described in the following sections.

Managing device drivers

Any problem you have with a device might actually be caused by the device driver. Before you go looking for a new driver, however, you might want to check the date and version of your existing driver. Here's how:

1. In Device Manager, right-click the device you're interested in and choose Properties.

2. Click the Driver tab in the device's Properties dialog box that opens.

The Driver tab will tell you who provided the driver, the date and version of the driver, and its signer. It also will present you with some options for working with the driver, as in Figure 17-13. The Driver Details button provides even more information, including the location and file name of the driver on your hard disk.

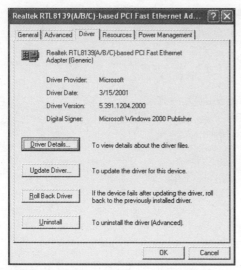

Figure 17-13: The Driver tab in the Properties dialog box for an installed device

After you know the version and date of your existing driver, there are a couple of ways that you can look around to see whether there is a newer, better version of the driver around:

✦ Run Windows Update. (Click the Start button and choose Help and Support ⇨ Keep Your Computer Up-to-Date with Windows Update.)

 Cross-Reference For more information on Windows Update, see Chapter 19.

✦ Contact the device manufacturer and inquire about recent drivers.

If you find an updated driver in Windows Update, you can probably download and install it in one fell swoop. Be sure to read any instructions that accompany the driver on the Windows Update Web page.

If you end up downloading a driver to a file on your hard disk, or it's delivered to you on a CD-ROM or floppy disk, you need to update your current driver using that file. To do so, click the Update Driver button on the Driver tab shown back in Figure 17-13. Then follow the instructions presented by the Hardware Update Wizard that opens on your computer.

If you discover that the newer driver only makes matters worse, you can click the Roll Back Driver button to return to the previously installed drivers. If things *really* get out of hand, see Chapter 18.

Who Is the Digital Signer?

Digital signatures are used to identify who released the driver to the public. The idea is to prevent people from sending out faulty drivers that mess up the device by making them accountable. If someone sends out a bad driver on purpose, he either has to sign it (which makes the driver traceable back to him!) or he needs to send it out unsigned.

If you attempt to install an unsigned driver, a warning displays, giving you a chance to reconsider. If you feel confident that the driver is from a reliable source, you can proceed with installing the new driver. Otherwise, you can bail out. If you're a system administrator, you can prevent unsigned drivers from being installed by choosing Clock from the Driver Signing dialog box. To get to that dialog box, click the Hardware tab, click System Properties, and then click the Driver Signing button.

Summary

Hardware installation with Windows XP is usually a fairly simple, straightforward procedure. If you're not familiar with all the terminology, however, it can seem like a daunting task. Hopefully, what you've learned in this chapter will be enough to help you install just about any hardware device you want. Here's a quick recap of the most important points:

✦ All hardware devices connect to your computer either externally (using plugs on the outside of the PC) or internally (using slots inside the PC).

✦ No matter what kind of hardware device you're installing, always follow the manufacturer's installation instructions first. This chapter can't possibly cover all the thousands of hardware devices available for modern PCs.

✦ Installing a USB or IEEE 1394 device is a simple matter of plugging the device into the appropriate port on your computer. There's no need to shut down the system first.

✦ Other external devices require that you shut down the computer, connect the device, turn the device on, and then restart the computer. In most cases, Windows detects and installs the device during its startup procedure.

✦ Virtually all devices require a *driver*, which is a program that tells your operating system how to use the device.

✦ You can manage and troubleshoot devices and their drivers via Device Manager, which is accessible from the Hardware tab of the System Properties dialog box.

✦   ✦   ✦

Disaster Prevention and Recovery

Plan for the best; prepare for the worst. Windows XP enables you to do just that. This chapter introduces you to various features of Windows XP that can help you prevent a crisis. But it doesn't stop there. This chapter shows you how to recover from disasters with the aid of built-in capabilities in Windows XP.

Using System Restore

System Restore is a great tool for recovering from the type of "disaster" that occurs when some change makes the entire system perform poorly. System Restore automatically copies all your important system files to a folder on your hard disk. If installing some program, adding a new hardware device, changing the Registry, or making some other significant change causes the system to run poorly, you can use System Restore to bring things back to where they were before you made the change.

System Restore settings

When activated, System Restore automatically creates a *restore point* (also called a *system checkpoint*) when it detects that you're about to make some change that could compromise the system. The restore point is, essentially, an exact copy of all your important System files at a specific point in time. Because System Restore stores the copies on your hard disk, you need to set aside some space for that capability.

 Note   System Restore affects only Windows System files, not your documents.

To activate System Restore as well as to set aside some disk space for its files, you use the System Restore tab of the System Properties dialog box, shown in Figure 18-1.

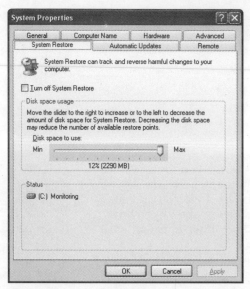

Figure 18-1: The System Restore tab of the System Properties dialog box

To get to the System Properties dialog box, follow these steps:

1. Click the Start button and open Control Panel.

2. In Classic view, open the System icon.

3. Click the System Restore tab.

The "Turn off System Restore" check box should be left blank; otherwise, you won't be able to use this feature. You can adjust the slider under "Disk space to use" to determine how much disk space you're willing to devote to this feature. Reducing the amount of disk space set aside for System Restore will allow more disk space for your programs and documents. On the other hand, the more disk space you allow for System Restore, the more restore points you can create.

If you have multiple hard drives, you can turn System Restore on or off and adjust disk space usage on the drives independently. You'll see each drive listed in the dialog box as well as a Settings button. Just click any drive and then click the Settings button to get to the options. In most cases, the system files that System Restore backs up will all be on your C: drive. So unless you've done an unusual installation where you've placed some of those files on a separate hard disk, there's really no need to activate System Restore on additional drives.

Creating restore points

Even though System Restore creates restore points automatically, you may want to create your own manually from time to time. Suppose, for example, that you're about to install some new program or hardware device or you're thinking about trying out an unsigned driver for some device, or doing anything else that affects the computer at a system level. If you create a restore point and the change doesn't work out, you can easily bring the computer back to this restore point, thereby erasing all changes made to the system since that point in time. To create a restore point, follow these steps:

1. Click the Start button and choose All Programs ➪ Accessories ➪ System Tools ➪ System Restore.

2. Choose Create a Restore Point and then click the Next button.

3. Type in a brief description of your restore point (for instance, Pre Program X Installation) and then click the Create button.

The date and time of the restore point, as well as your description, appear on-screen. Click the Close button.

Returning to a restore point

Whether you've manually created your own restore point or not, you can always restore the system to an earlier time by following these steps. First, if installing a program caused the problem, uninstall that program, if possible, using Add/Remove Programs in Control Panel. If installing hardware or a driver created the problem, you would do well to uninstall the hardware and remove it from the system. Otherwise, it might just get reinstalled the next time you start Windows. If a hardware device driver is causing a problem, you might want to "roll back" to the earlier driver as well. Then follow these steps to fully restore your system:

Cross-Reference See Chapter 16 and Chapter 17 if you need any help removing software or hardware.

1. Start System Restore. (Click the Start button and choose All Programs ➪ Accessories ➪ System Tools ➪ System Restore.)

2. Choose Restore My Computer to an Earlier Time and then click the Next button.

3. In the calendar, any date in boldface has a restore point associated with it. Click the date to which you want to restore.

4. In the list of available restore points, click the appropriate restore point, as in Figure 18-2.

5. Click the Next button.

6. Follow the instructions on-screen.

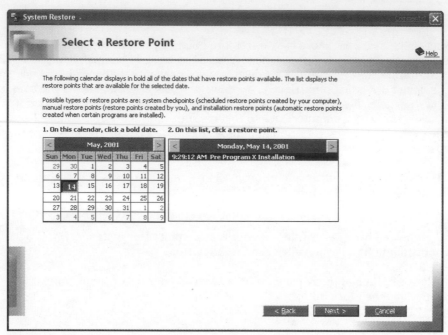

Figure 18-2: Choose a restore date and point from the options shown here.

After the computer restarts, you'll see a message on the screen telling you whether the restoration was successful. In the unlikely event that the restoration doesn't help, you can run System Restore again and then either undo the last restoration or return the system to an even earlier date.

Recovering When Windows Hangs

Occasionally, your computer might freeze up, or *hang,* leaving you with a mouse and keyboard that seem to do nothing. The problem is usually caused by two running programs that conflict with one another. Although not a major disaster, this can cause you to lose any unsaved work in a document. (Hence, the reminder to save your work often!) Although you might not be able to recover any unsaved work, you can get the system functioning again by following these steps:

1. Press Ctrl+Alt+Del. (Hold down all three keys on the keyboard and then release all three.) The Windows Task Manager, shown in Figure 18-3, will open in the desktop.

Tip   You also can start Task Manager by right-clicking an unused space on the taskbar and choosing Task Manager. While Task Manager is the active window, press the F1 key to bring up its help system.

Figure 18-3: The Windows XP Task Manager

2. Click any program listed as Not Responding (as opposed to Running) and then
   click the End Task button.

When you get to a point where all programs shown are listed as Running, you can
close Task Manager by clicking its Close (X) button. I recommend that if you have
any unsaved work remaining on the screen at this time, you go in and save that
work right away.

If ending tasks that aren't responding isn't enough to get your system working properly, you can log off, shut down, or restart your computer from Task Manager. Just
choose Shut Down from its menu bar, and make your selection from the menu.

System Startup Problems

If Windows XP can't start up normally, first be sure to remove all disks from your
floppy and CD-ROM drives and then try restarting again. If Windows can't boot up
from the hard drive, it will typically start in *Safe mode*. (You also can start in Safe
mode manually by pressing the F8 key as the computer is starting.) This mode
loads the absolute minimum number of drivers required to get your system going
so that you can troubleshoot the startup problem. It also launches the Safe Mode
Troubleshooter, shown in Figure 18-4.

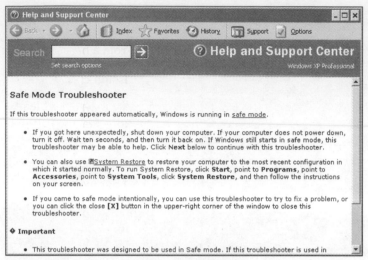

Figure 18-4: The Safe Mode Troubleshooter

One potential quick fix might be to just close the troubleshooter and then run System Restore, as described earlier in this chapter. If running System Restore doesn't get your system running normally and if the computer continues to start up in Safe mode, you'll want to step through the troubleshooter to solve the problem. Read all the information and instructions presented on each page of the troubleshooter. Describe your problem when given choices and click the Next button. If your system can be salvaged, the troubleshooter should help you get your system back to normal.

Then again, if the problem is that your hard disk has crashed and is no longer operable, well, then you really do have a bit of a disaster on your hands. When that happens, the only solution is to get a new hard drive. That drive, of course, will be entirely empty, and everything on your original hard drive might be lost for good. The only way to prepare yourself for this worst of all possible disasters is to make backup copies of your hard disk.

Disaster Recovery Services

It's not impossible to recover data from a crashed hard disk. But the process requires a *clean room* and highly specialized skills. In other words, it's darn expensive. Furthermore, there's no way of knowing in advance just how much data, if any, can be recovered from the drive. So you might have to shell out a good deal of money to recover little, or nothing, of any real value. Still, sometimes that's a chance you'll just have to take.

Data recovery services, as they're called, are few and far between and not always easy to find. Your best bet is to use your favorite search engine on the Web to search for the phrase *data recovery*. If you can't find one locally, you'll need to remove the hard drive from your system and ship it to the service center.

Making Backups

The only way to truly prevent the loss of important data from a hard disk crash is to make backups of your data to some other medium. Large corporations use sophisticated and expensive systems to back up their "mission-critical" data, often on a moment-by-moment basis. Such systems, however, are usually too expensive and complex for the average home and small business. This hard reality leaves most folks with the somewhat odious task of making backups manually from time to time.

The key factor that makes backups so odious is that it takes a whole lot of time and storage to back up an entire hard disk. Making backups to floppy disks is usually out of the question, because it would take thousands of floppies just to back up a single hard disk. A magnetic tape drive is a more realistic backup device. However, people often stop using them because they're slow and often difficult to manage. Zip disks and CD-RW drives are good, but you might need quite a few disks to back up a drive.

What's really needed is an approach that makes backing up your hard drive a less odious task. First you must realize that, on any given day, the contents of your hard drive will change very little. Sure, you might create and change several documents during the day. But those changes have no effect on 99 percent of the files stored on your hard disk. So backing up your entire hard disk on a daily basis is obviously overkill. In the sections that follow, we'll look at a couple of alternatives for backing up only those files that have actually changed since your last backup.

Tip An external Zip drive that plugs into a USB port is handy for making backups from multiple computers, because it's easy to move from one computer to the next.

Quick and easy document backups

When a hard disk crashes, the biggest loss is usually your own documents. Assuming you've kept your original Windows XP CD-ROM as well as the CD-ROMs for any programs you've purchased and any that came with your computer system, you can always reinstall all those programs from the original discs. You will, of course, lose any personal settings you created in those programs. As a rule, however, it's not too tough to repeat the steps necessary to create your settings should you ever have to reinstall the programs from scratch.

Caution Whenever you purchase a new program, be sure to store the original CD-ROM, as well as any CD key or serial number, in a safe place. You just never know when you might need to reinstall that program in the future.

If you keep all your documents in your My Documents folder (as well as subfolders within My Documents), it's easy to see which files have been created or changed during any given day, week, or month. Just use the Search bar in Explorer to locate files within My Documents that were created or modified within some range of dates.

Backing up those recently modified files then is just a matter of copying them to some other medium (assuming that medium has sufficient space for the files). If you have a CD-R or CD-RW drive, for example, you can select all the files listed in the results of the search, right-click, and choose Send To ⇨ Writable CD. You can then repeat the procedure to back up any documents in your Shared Documents folder as well.

Tip   Both Microsoft Outlook and Outlook Express offer options for exporting your Contacts and Messages, and other folders to files. If you export those items to your My Documents folder from time to time, you can back them up along with other files in that folder. The Personal File Folder format (.pst) is especially handy for this type of backup, because it's easy to import the files later.

Although this approach doesn't back up things such as your collection of favorites, dial-up networking accounts, or personal program settings, it does make a backup copy of your recent work, which is certainly better than nothing! To back up those other items, you can use the Files and Settings Transfer Wizard. This program is designed to help you transfer personal items from one Windows XP computer to another. However, there's no rule that says you can't use it to create backups!

The Files and Settings Transfer Wizard

The Files and Settings Transfer Wizard is a handy tool for copying documents, display settings, desktop shortcuts, dial-up connections, and other personal items from one Windows XP computer to another. If you create such a disk, however, you can just as easily use it to restore those items to your new hard disk in the event of a disk crash. You still need to install Windows XP and all your programs onto that new hard disk, of course, but at least you wouldn't have to re-create all the items the wizard has copied for you.

When you use the wizard, it prompts you for a disk drive on which to store the items. You can use your floppy drive. Of course, it might take quite a few floppies to store the files, depending on how much stuff you plan to back up. If you have some other type of drive with removable storage, such as a Zip drive, you can use that instead. Put a blank disk in the drive before you start the wizard.

If you have a CD-R or CD-RW drive, you can use that to store your files and settings as well. However, the wizard doesn't seem to handle such drives too well, nor can it split the files across multiple disks. Therefore, you'll need to do some fancy footwork to get it all to work. For starters, you'll want to create a couple of folders, perhaps one named FSTWSettings, to store your settings. Then create a second folder, perhaps named FSTWFiles, to store your files. When you run the wizard, store your settings in one folder. Then you need to run the wizard a second time and store your files in another folder. If any of the folders are especially large, you might even need to split their contents into several folders. When the wizard completes its task, you can use the Send To ⇨ Writable CD options described in Chapter 12 to copy each of the folders that the wizard creates to a separate disk.

To use the wizard, just follow these steps:

1. Click the Start button and choose All Programs ➪ Accessories ➪ System Tools ➪ Files and Settings Transfer Wizard.

2. Click the Next button on the first wizard page. Then choose Old Computer from the second wizard page and click its Next button.

3. From the third wizard page, choose the drive or folder to which you want to copy the files.

4. On the fourth wizard page, you have the option of transferring settings only, files only, or both, as shown in Figure 18-5. You also can choose Customize to make more specific selections.

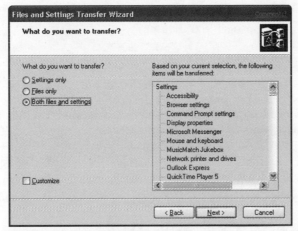

Figure 18-5: Choose which items you want to "transfer" from this wizard page.

 Note   The term *files* in this context refers to document files only. The wizard doesn't transfer programs or Windows System files.

5. If you did choose Customize in Step 4, you'll see a list of items that will be transferred, as in Figure 18-6. You can add and remove settings, folders, files, and file types using the buttons to the right of the list.

From here on it's just a matter of following the instructions on the screen. When the process is done, the selected disk drive (or folder) contains a subfolder named USMT2.UNC. If you're using a CD-R or CD-RW, you need to burn that folder (not its contents) to the disk. That is, you right-click the folder's icon and choose Sent To ➪ Writable CD.

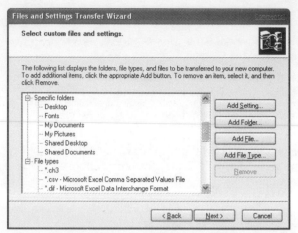

Figure 18-6: This wizard page appears if you choose Customize in the preceding page.

To transfer your settings or files to a new computer (or an old computer with a new hard disk), you want to create your user account. Insert the disk to which you copied the USMT2.UNC folder into the appropriate drive on that computer. On the first wizard page, you can choose the option that reads I have already collected my files and settings from my old computer and then click the Next button. On the second wizard page, choose the drive into which you placed the disk, click the Next button and follow the instructions on-screen.

Introducing Microsoft Backup

The safest way to back up your hard disk is to use hardware and software designed for that purpose. Many backup devices come with their own programs that you can use. Windows XP Professional edition comes with Microsoft Backup, (also know as the Backup utility), which works with a variety of storage devices. Before you use Backup, you need to understand some of the concepts and terminology involved. First on the list is the *archive attribute*.

If you right-click any file, choose Properties, and then click the Advanced button on the General tab, you'll notice a check box labeled File is ready for archiving. Although you *can* select or deselect this check box yourself, there's really no need to, because Backup takes care of that attribute for you. Whenever you run Backup to back up files, it automatically clears that check box — which is to say, it "turns off" the file's archive attribute. Later, if you change the file, Windows automatically turns the archive attribute back on, indicating that the file has changed since it was last backed up. Likewise, any new files you create automatically have their archive attributes turned on, because they've never been backed up. In this way, Windows and backup programs have a means to discriminate between files that have, and have not, changed since the last backup.

Understanding backup types

Microsoft Backup supports a variety of backup types (also known as *backup strategies*). The variety of types give you some leeway in deciding how you want to back up files given available resources, including the type of device you're backing up to, how critical the data being backed up is, and so forth. Regardless of which strategy you choose, you always have the option of backing up an entire disk or just selected files and folder. You can perform the following types of backups:

✦ **Normal backup:** Backs up the disk or selected files and folders, regardless of the current archive attribute settings. It also clears the archive attribute of every file that has been backed up to support future incremental or differential backups.

✦ **Incremental Backup:** Backs up only selected files whose archive attribute is turned on and then clears the archive attributes of each backed up file. The strategy is incremental in that the first incremental backup copies only files that have changed since the most recent normal backup. The second incremental backup copies only files that have changed since the first incremental backup, and so forth. Each incremental backup must be stored on a separate medium, or in a separate file.

✦ **Differential backup:** Copies only selected files that have changed since the most recent normal or incremental backup. However, it does not clear the archive attribute of backed-up files. Therefore, you could perform two differential backups to two separate media with the same results — both backups would contain all the files that have changed since the last normal or incremental backup.

✦ **Daily backup:** Copies all the files that have changed on that day, but does not change their archive attributes. Hence, you could run a quick daily backup on any given day without compromising the integrity of your incremental backups.

✦ **Copy backup:** Copies selected files without changing their archive attributes. As with a daily backup, this enables you to use the Backup program to copy some files without compromising the integrity of your incremental backups.

The trade-offs between the various strategies are safety versus the cost in terms of time and backup media. The normal backup provides the greatest safety, because it backs up all the selected files and folders. It doesn't take archive attributes into account, however, so it backs up files that haven't changed since the last backup. If you don't overwrite a previous backup file when using this approach, you'll end up with a lot of huge backup files, which in turn means a lot of tapes or disks.

Different companies use different combinations of strategies. Finding the strategy that works best for you might require some experimentation. A good approach might be to perform a normal backup on some given day (say once a week, once a month, or even, just once!). Then perform differential backups on other days. The differential backup takes longer than an incremental backup, because it copies *all* files that have changed since the last normal backup. And the number of files being copied with each backup increases. If you reuse the same disk or tape for each differential backup, however, at least you know where all the most recent backups are located. Also, you don't end up spending a fortune on tapes and disks. In an emergency, you can restore your entire hard disk by first restoring from the most recent normal backup and then restoring from the differential backup.

Starting Microsoft Backup

Microsoft Backup, which comes with Windows XP Professional edition, can be used in two different ways. The easiest is the Backup Wizard, which takes you step-by-step through the backup procedure. The other, called Advanced mode, isn't quite so friendly. In the Advanced mode, you want switch to a wizard by choosing an option from the Tools menu. In the wizard, you can click the Advanced button to switch to Advanced mode. The very first time you run Backup, it will start with the wizard.

Microsoft Backup provides three main capabilities:

✦ **Backup:** Creates backup copies of files on the hard disk.

✦ **Restore:** Restores backed up files to the hard disk.

✦ **Create an Automated System Recovery disk:** Creates a complete backup of the computer's entire hard drive, as well as a floppy disk from which you can automatically restore from that backup.

To start Microsoft Backup, click the Start button and choose All Programs ➪ Accessories ➪ System Tools ➪ Backup. The first time you start it, the Backup Utility Wizard opens. The second page of that wizard, shown in Figure 18-7, provides options for performing any of the three main capabilities that the program offers. If you're ever in the Advanced mode, shown in Figure 18-8, and want to get to the wizard, choose Tools ➪ Switch to Wizard Mode from the Backup Utility menu bar.

Managing Removable Storage Libraries

Windows XP includes a tool for managing removable storage media, such as optical disks and tapes, as well as the libraries that robotic changers and jukeboxes offer. Dubbed just *Removable Storage,* this program enables you to electronically label individual disks and tapes, to catalog and track media, to perform drive-cleaning operations, and to control drives, slots, and doors that the devices offer. Removable Storage works in conjunction with Backup to simplify the management of large collections of backup media.

You'll find Removable Storage in the Computer Management console. Open the Control Panel, and in Classic view, open the Administrative Tools icon. Choose Computer Management, and then click Removable Storage, under Storage, in the console tree (left pane). For more information on using Removable Storage, press F1 or choose Help ➪ Help Topics from the Computer Management menu bar. In the Help contents, click the Removable Storage book.

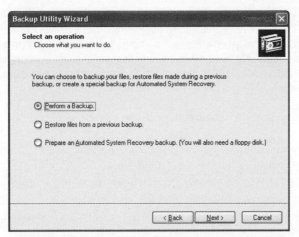

Figure 18-7: This wizard page provides access to the three main capabilities of the Microsoft Backup utility.

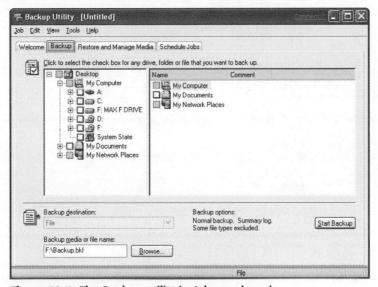

Figure 18-8: The Backup utility in Advanced mode

Be aware that Backup does not just copy files to the backup medium. Instead, it combines all the files and folders into one huge file that has a .bkf extension. The only way to get to specific files within that larger file is through the Restore capability that Backup offers.

Backing up with Backup

To back up files using the wizard, first prepare your backup medium. If you're using a new, blank tape, for example, you might need to *format* the tape by following the manufacturer's instructions or by using the Removable Storage utility described in the sidebar earlier in this chapter. Then follow these steps:

1. Choose Perform a Backup from the wizard page shown back in Figure 18-7.

2. On the next wizard page, choose one of the following options:

    - **Back up everything:** Literally backs up everything on the computer.

    - **Back up selected files:** Allows you to choose specific drives or folders to back up.

    - **Only back up the System State data:** Backs up the Registry, COM+ Class Registration files, boot files, Certificate Services database, Active Directory, SYSVOL directory, Cluster service information, IIS Metadirectory, and protected System files (for advanced users).

3. If you opted to back up selected items only, you'll be taken to the wizard page shown in Figure 18-9, where you can select specific drives and/or folders to back up. Make your selections and click the Next button.

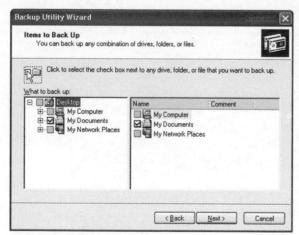

Figure 18-9: This wizard page enables you to choose specific drives and/or folders to back up.

4. On the next wizard page, choose the type of medium you're backing up to. Or, if you're backing up to a folder, use the Browse button to select the folder and type in a file name for the resulting backup file. Be sure to add the .bkf extension to whatever file name you enter, as in the example shown in Figure 18-10. Click the Next button.

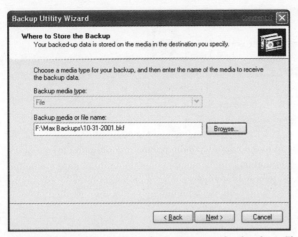

Figure 18-10: Choosing where to store the backup file

5. At this point, a Completing the Backup Wizard page appears summarizing the options you selected. If you want to perform anything other than a "normal" backup or if you're using Remote Storage to manage media libraries, click the Advanced button. You'll be taken to a wizard page that enables you to choose a type of backup and presented with an option to back up files that have migrated to Remote Storage.

What happens next depends largely on the selections you have made along the way. Just follow the instructions on each wizard page until you get to the last page. Clicking the Finish button at that point will back up the files, creating the final .bkf file. On the final wizard page, you can click the Report button to view a descriptive report of the backup in Notepad. Choose File ⇨ Print from Notepad's menu bar to create a printed record of the report.

Restoring backed up files

If disaster strikes, and you lose all or part of the contents of your hard drive, you can use the Restore side of Microsoft Backup to recover backed-up files. Assuming you've already installed Windows XP on some new replacement drive, here are the steps: You can run Microsoft Backup and choose Restore Files from a Previous Backup from the options shown back in Figure 18-7. You'll be taken to the page shown in Figure 18-11, where you can select the media from which you want to restore files. As instructed on the screen, you can double-click any item in the right column to isolate its contents and then choose specific items to restore. Or to just restore all the files from a medium, select that item's check box in the right-hand column. Click the Next button and the wizard will walk you through the steps required to restore the files.

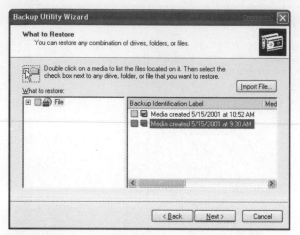

Figure 18-11: Choose items to restore from this wizard page.

More on Backup

In this chapter, I have touched on only the most basic capabilities of using Microsoft Backup to back up and restore files. The program actually offers a wide range of backup options suitable for all types of work environments. To learn more about Backup, go to its Advanced mode and choose Help ➪ Help Topics from the menu bar. There you can use the Contents tab to learn about other capabilities or use the Index or Search tab to look up information about specific topics.

Summary

In this chapter we've looked at tools and techniques for recovering from "disasters" ranging from minor inconveniences to total hard disk crashes. Here's a quick recap of the important points covered in this chapter:

✦ When a system change causes your computer to misbehave, you can use System Restore to return important system files to a previous state.

✦ Creating a restore point in system restore just before installing new hardware or software will make it easier to recover from any problems caused by the new installation.

✦ When Windows freezes up (hangs), press Ctrl+Alt+Del to bring up Task Manager, which you can use to end any tasks that are not responding.

✦ When a problem prevents your computer from booting normally off the hard disk, Windows will start in Safe mode, where you can use a troubleshooter to solve the problem.

✦ You can also get to Safe mode by pressing the F8 key as the system is starting.

✦ You can easily back up new and recently changed documents by using the Search Explorer bar to isolate files modified within some range of dates. Then copy all the matching files to some other medium.

✦ The Files and Settings Transfer Wizard, designed to help you transfer your files and settings to a new computer, is also a convenient way to back up those items.

✦ Microsoft Backup provides an extensive set of tools and options for creating, managing, and restoring from backup media.

✦   ✦   ✦

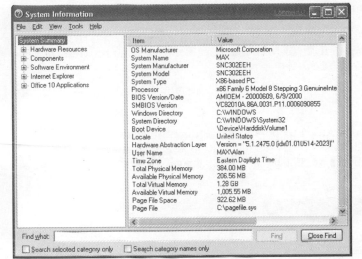

Figure 19-3: The System Information applet

You can search System Information for specific information using the Find What text box. Getting back to the IRQ example, for instance, you could type **IRQ** into the Find What box and click the Find button to quickly locate relevant information. If Find returns too much information, you can limit the search to a specific category, or to just category names, using the check boxes near the bottom of the window. Clicking the Find Next button will repeat the search, limiting the results to your selection(s). The System Information applet includes its own Help, accessible from the menu bar, which you can use to get more information on using the applet.

Now that you know where you can look to get information about your computer, let's look at some ways you can maintain, optimize, and troubleshoot your computer.

Performing Routine Maintenance

An overcrowded, highly fragmented hard disk can slow down even the speediest of computers. Furthermore, we all tend to gather up some "junk" on our hard disks, such as temporary files, which can waste space. Windows XP provides a couple of handy tools for cleaning up your hard disk and helping it run at top speed.

Tip   Help and Support provides a quick shortcut to many tools for maintaining your computer, maximizing performance, and troubleshooting. Click the Start button, choose Help and Support, and then click the Performance and Maintenance option.

Updates, Maintenance, and Monitoring

A sluggish computer can be a real bore, especially if you paid good money and were expecting more. Sometimes, a computer that once ran fast will start to run more slowly, leaving you wondering just what's going on. Without some knowledge of your system and the skills necessary to improve its performance, it's not easy to identify and clear the performance bottlenecks that are dragging you down. This chapter covers tools and techniques for getting the most from your computer, ranging from routine maintenance to advanced "tweaking."

Getting Information about Your System

Before we get into the "how to" aspects of this chapter, I want to introduce you to some places where you can go to get information about your system. The most basic and commonly required information about your system is in the System Properties dialog box shown in Figure 19-1.

Tip   If you have a My Computer icon on your desktop, you can right-click it and choose Properties to get to the System Properties dialog box.

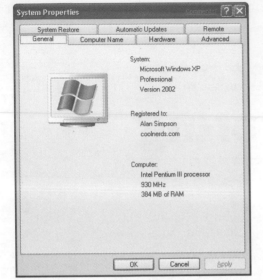

Figure 19-1: The System Properties dialog box

To access the System Properties dialog box, follow these steps:

1. Click the Start button and open Control Panel.

2. If Control Panel opens in Category view, click Performance and Maintenance.

3. Open the System icon.

The General tab displays the most basic information, including the type of microprocessor installed in this computer, its speed, and the amount of random access memory (RAM) installed. Other tabs provide additional information, as well as options for making changes to some options, as you'll learn throughout this chapter.

Know your hard drive

Modern programs, multimedia files, and the like all consume a lot of space on your hard disk. So it's good to check to see how much space is available on the disk from time to time. Furthermore, Windows XP supports a variety of *file systems,* including FAT, FAT32, and NTFS. The file system used by your hard disk will impact some of the Windows XP features that are available to you.

Cross-Reference Chapter 31 discusses NTFS in detail and provides instructions for converting a FAT partition to NTFS.

To get a quick glimpse of the file system and available space on a disk, follow these steps:

1. Open My Computer, either from the Start menu, or from the desktop (if available).

2. Right-click the drive in which you are interested (C: represents your hard disk) and choose Properties.

The disk's Properties dialog box opens as in the example shown in Figure 19-2. In that example, the disk uses the NTFS file system. It has a capacity of 27.3 gigabytes. Currently 4.92 gigabytes are in use, leaving 22.4 gigabytes free.

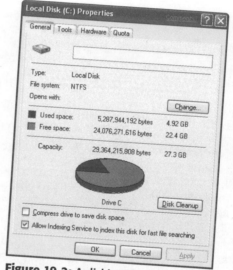

Figure 19-2: A disk's Properties dialog box

Extensive system information

Extensive information about your system is available through the System Information applet that comes with Windows XP. The vast majority of that information is meaningful only to highly trained technicians. If you're ever getting technical support over the phone and an expert asks you some obscure question about IRQ or some such thing, you can use System Information to locate the appropriate information.

To open the applet, click the Start button and choose All Programs ➪ Accessories ➪ System Tools ➪ System Information. The left pane lists categories of information that you can expand and contract using the + and – boxes. The right pane shows the contents of the currently selected category. For example, Figure 19-3 shows the contents of the System Summary category on one of my computers.

Using Disk Cleanup

When disk space is tight or when you just want to make sure you're not bogging down your computer with a bunch of unnecessary files, you can use Disk Cleanup to clean things up. Here's how:

1. Close all open windows and programs on your desktop. (Don't forget to save any unsaved work first!)

2. Click the Start menu and choose All Programs ⇨ Accessories ⇨ System Tools ⇨ Disk Cleanup.

3. From the Select Drive dialog box that appears, choose the drive you want to clean up. Typically this will be drive C:, where most of your files are probably stored. Then click the OK button.

4. In the Disk Cleanup dialog box that appears next, select the items you want to eliminate (see Figure 19-4). If you're not sure what an item describes, click it and read the description below the list.

Caution   If you delete files from the Recycle Bin, you won't be able to recover them later. You might want to check the bin before selecting that option in Disk Cleanup.

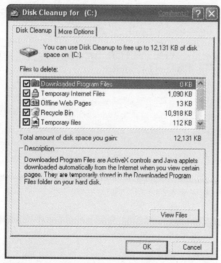

Figure 19-4: Choosing files to delete in Disk Cleanup

5. If disk space is really tight, you can click the More Options button and choose Windows Components, Installed Programs, and System Restore points to remove. However, be forewarned that the items you select will be deleted, and there's no way to "undo" the deletion!

6. Click the OK button after making your selections. You'll be given one last chance to change your mind. If you're sure you want to delete the selected items, click the Yes button.

Disk Cleanup briefly displays a progress report as it removes the selected files from your disk. To see how much free space is now available on the disk, you can view its properties as in the example shown back in Figure 19-2.

Checking for disk errors

Occasionally, a hard disk can develop *bad sectors,* which can't be written to or read from accurately. A disk might also develop *logical errors,* where some data that doesn't appear to be associated with any actual file is consuming disk space. You can maximize the performance of a hard disk by having Windows fix any logical errors and attempt to recover any bad sectors. The procedure might take a few minutes, during which time you won't be able to use the computer. You also might need to restart the computer, so be sure to save any unsaved work. Then follow these steps to check your disk:

1. Close all open windows and programs.

2. Open My Computer.

3. Right-click the icon for the drive you want to check and choose Properties.

4. Click on the Tools tab and then click the Check Now button.

5. Choose whether you want to fix logical errors (the first option), attempt to recover bad sectors, or both, as in Figure 19-5.

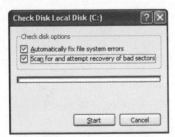

Figure 19-5: About to check a hard disk for errors

6. Click the Start button.

If Windows is unable to perform the task, a message appears that tells you so and gives you the option to perform the task at next startup. If you choose Yes, click the Start button and choose Turn Off Computer ➪ Restart. Windows will check and repair the disk prior to bringing you back to the desktop.

Using Disk Defragmenter

As time goes by and you add and delete files, your hard disk can become *fragmented*. That's because when you delete a file, Windows just frees up the space that the file was using, leaving sort of a "hole" where the file used to be. When you create a new file, Windows fills the available holes. If the new file is larger than a given hole, it might actually fill several holes. The holes might be spread around different portions of the disk, causing the drive head that reads the file to jump around in order to read the entire file. The result is slower performance. If your hard disk is noisy enough, you can actually hear the drive head jumping around the disk.

To get things working smoothly again, you can *defragment* the disk. Doing so puts all the files into nice, contiguous sections of the disk that the drive head can read smoothly without jumping all over the place.

Before you defragment a disk, you would do well to clean off any files you don't need. Doing so will reduce the amount of time it takes to perform the task and also make for more efficient use of the disk. The process is likely to take anywhere from several minutes to several hours. During that time, you shouldn't use the computer, because changing the contents of the drive will only confuse things for Defragmenter, often causing it to start over! So plan to start Defrag just before you'll be away from the machine. When you're ready to defragment, follow these steps:

1. Close all open windows and programs on your desktop. (Don't forget to save any unsaved work!)

2. Click the Start button and choose All Programs ⇨ Accessories ⇨ System Tools ⇨ Disk Defragmenter.

To analyze the current status of the disk, click the Analyze button. The Analysis display in the window will give you a color coded, graphical view of fragmented, contiguous (unfragmented), and unmovable files, as well as the available free space, as in the example shown in Figure 19-6. A dialog box also appears, telling you whether you really need to defragment the disk and giving you the option of viewing a report that further describes the analysis.

To defragment, click the Defragment button and then wait. When the process is done, the Defragmentation display will show the results of the task. If all went well, you shouldn't see any red bars in that display. Some items that were originally sprinkled across the unused white space may be shifted to the left, making them more contiguous with other files that are already stored in that portion of the disk.

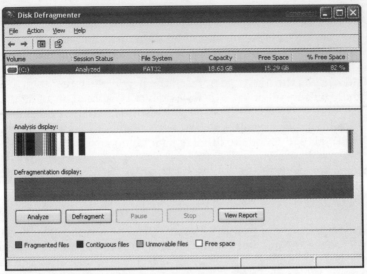

Figure 19-6: Disk Defragmenter, after analyzing a disk

Cleaning up your desktop

There's always a temptation to add a lot of shortcut icons to the desktop, because it's so readily available. As time goes by, however, your desktop can get pretty cluttered up. The Desktop Cleanup Wizard can help you find the least-used icons and delete them from your desktop. To get to the wizard, follow these steps:

1. Right-click the Desktop and choose Properties.

2. Click the Desktop tab.

3. Click the Customize Desktop button. The Desktop Items dialog box opens. Click the General tab to get to the options shown in Figure 19-7.

4. If you want to get rid of any of the "permanent" desktop icons, such as My Computer, clear their check marks.

5. If you want Windows to automatically run the Desktop Cleanup Wizard to clean off your unused icons periodically, choose the Run Desktop Cleanup Wizard every 60 days option.

6. To run the Desktop Cleanup Wizard, click the Clean Desktop Now button.

The wizard will list all your desktop icons along with the date each was last used. To remove an icon, just select its check box. Click the Next button and follow the instructions on the screen.

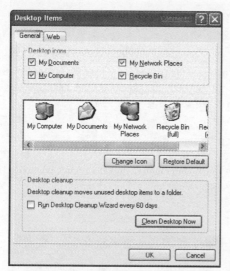

Figure 19-7: The Desktop Items dialog box helps you manage your desktop icons.

Keeping Windows Up-to-Date

If you have access to the Internet, you can use Windows Update to check for, and to download, any Windows XP files that have been changed or improved since your original purchase of Windows XP. The procedure is simple:

1. If you have a dial-up connection to the Internet, connect to your ISP normally.

2. Click the Start button and choose Help and Support.

3. Click Keep your computer up-to-date with Windows Update.

You'll be connected to the Windows Update Web site. I can't say for certain exactly what you'll see there because it's all online and subject to change at any time. Most likely you will see a Scan for updates option, as in Figure 19-8, which you can click to locate and select the latest updates.

Cross-Reference You can keep your computer up to date automatically, without visiting Windows Update or waiting for files to download. For details, see Chapter 7.

Windows Update and Security

There are some sophisticated programmers out there, often referred to as *crackers*, who like to break into people's computers, either to steal information or just to be malicious. One way they accomplish this is by finding "security holes" in programs on computer systems. These are not particularly easy to find, and nobody is even aware of a security hole until some cracker finds it.

When such a hole is discovered in a Microsoft program, Microsoft quickly creates a *patch* that covers the hole. These patches, called security updates, are always posted on the Windows Update Web site. So by updating your computer online, you not only keep up-to-date on changes and new features, you also make your computer more secure.

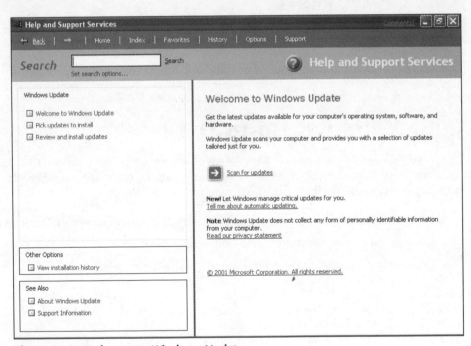

Figure 19-8: Welcome to Windows Update.

Monitoring System Performance

If your computer is feeling sluggish, you can use Task Manager to take a peek at exactly what's going on. There are a couple of different ways you can start Task Manager:

✦ Right-click the empty area of the taskbar that's just to the left of the Notification area and choose Task Manager.

✦ Or, press Ctrl+Alt+Del.

When Task Manager opens, it initially displays the Applications tab, which lists each application program currently open in the system. As mentioned in Chapter 18, you can stop an errant program by clicking it and then clicking the End Task button.

The Processes tab, shown in Figure 19-9, gives you a much more detailed view of all running *processes*. A process is essentially anything that requires attention from the CPU (central processing unit). Every running program is a process, as is every running *service*. A service, in turn, is usually some small, specific "low-level" feature that's running in the background. For example, spoolsv.exe (Spool service) accepts print jobs that are being spooled to a printer.

The User Name column indicates who initiated the process. Processes with SYSTEM, LOCAL SERVICE, NETWORK SERVICE, and other user names are ones that were started automatically as opposed to by a specific person. The percentage of CPU resources that a process is using at any time is displayed in the CPU column. At any given time, most processes are idle, which means that they're ready for action if called upon, but not currently using any processor time.

Tip   You can get detailed information about and gain very fine control over services via the Services icon in Administrative Tools. However, you don't want to mess with services unless you really know what you're doing. A detailed description of all services is beyond the scope of this book.

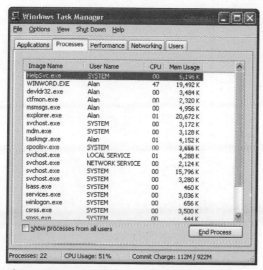

Figure 19-9: The Processes tab in Windows Task Manager

The amount of memory (RAM) that a process is using is shown in the Mem Usage column. If you leave Task Manager open for a while as you start, use, and stop programs, you'll start to get a sense of which programs hog up the most resources (in terms of CPU time and memory). You can get more performance out of your computer by remembering to close those programs while they're not in use.

You *can* end a process in Task Manager by right-clicking and choosing End Process. Some processes are critical to the system functioning properly, however, so you really don't want to do this. You're better off sticking to ending *just* the programs you started. To play it safe, exit the program normally, such as by right-clicking its taskbar button and choosing Close.

The Performance tab, shown in Figure 19-10, gives you a graphical view of CPU and memory usage. If you leave this tab open while using your computer, you'll probably be surprised to see how much CPU resources are required by a seemingly trivial event, such as dragging some icon or window around on the screen. You can also see a tiny graphical representation of current CPU usage in the Notification area of the taskbar while Task Manager is open.

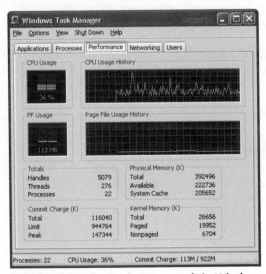

Figure 19-10: The Performance tab in Windows Task Manager

If the CPU usage history tends to stay near the top of the chart, you're working your computer's processor to the max. More than likely, you're also causing the system to be sluggish. Closing some open programs might help you gain back some of those resources and keep the system moving at a brisker pace (or at least, provide a good excuse for buying a newer, faster computer).

Real Memory versus Virtual Memory

The total amount of memory available on your system is the sum of real memory (a.k.a. RAM or *physical memory*) plus *virtual memory*. Virtual memory is a portion of the hard disk that's set aside to look like RAM to the system. Unfortunately, virtual memory is *much* slower than real memory, and excessive use of it can really bog down system performance. As a rule, Windows moves processes that aren't getting much action into virtual memory, to leave as much real memory as possible to the processes that are seeing a lot of action. So at least it's efficient.

On the other hand, if you run memory-intensive programs that fill up RAM, those too will start spilling over into virtual memory. When that happens, things will really start to slow down. If your hard disk is noisy enough, you might even hear the drive head clicking away madly, even when you're not opening or closing any files. When that starts happening often and your computer seems to be running like molasses in Antarctica, you can be confident that just adding more RAM to your system will improve its performance significantly.

Likewise, if the Page File Usage history is trailing along near the top of the chart, you're taxing available memory, causing everything to run slower. In that case, just adding more RAM to your system without even going to a faster processor is likely to give you a noticeable improvement in performance!

Are We Optimized Yet?

Keeping your hard disk in tip-top shape and being aware of how you're using available resources on your computer are key to getting the best performance from it. But you also can gain some efficiency through the Performance Options dialog box shown in Figure 19-11. To get there, follow these steps:

1. Right-click the My Computer icon on your desktop and choose Properties. Or open Control Panel and then open the System icon in Classic view.

2. Click the Advanced tab.

3. Click the Settings button under Performance.

The Visual Effects tab lets you enable and disable various visual effects that appear on the screen. These effects can be real resource hogs. And if you're more interested in speed than in "pretty," you can probably squeeze some more performance out of your overall system.

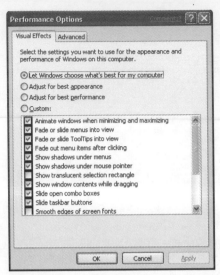

Figure 19-11: The Performance Options dialog box

Note   If your system isn't capable of displaying a visual effect, its option will be disabled.

The four main options available on the tab are self-explanatory. You can let Windows choose the settings, adjust for best appearance, adjust for best performance, or choose Custom and use the check boxes to select and clear various visual effects.

On the Advanced tab of Performance Options, shown in Figure 19-12, you can either give Programs or Background services priority in accessing the resources of your CPU. Choosing Programs will help your programs run their fastest. Choosing Background Services will give priority to those processes that you didn't start yourself. Under Memory Usage, you can optimize for Programs (the programs you run), or the *System cache,* which is memory used by those Windows processes you didn't start yourself.

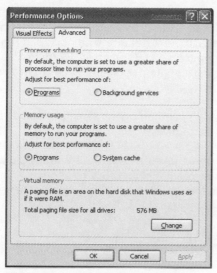

Figure 19-12: The Advanced tab of
Performance Options settings

The Change button under Virtual memory takes you to the options shown in Figure
19-13. These let you fine-tune virtual memory, described in the sidebar earlier in this
chapter. If you find that your system often runs out of memory and can't start some
programs or if the Memory Usage history in the performance monitor is always
creeping along the top of the chart, you can increase the size of your virtual memory. You would get better performance by adding more physical RAM. However, in a
pinch — such as when you need more memory right now — this will help.

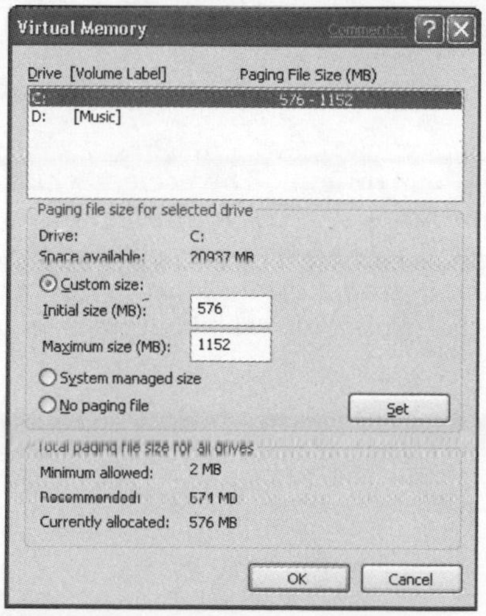

Figure 19-13: The Virtual Memory
dialog box

If you have multiple hard disks, you can choose which one you want to use for virtual memory. If you have two hard disks, C: and D:, and you rarely use D:, moving virtual memory to that disk might help increase performance. The reason is that drive C:'s drive head is usually pretty busy opening programs and documents, saving files, and so forth. Using a separate drive prevents the paging file from having to compete for attention with all those other activities.

 Note   If the extra hard drive is really just a separate partition on the same physical drive, it won't help to move virtual memory to that "drive."

You also can choose to set a custom size for virtual memory, or let Windows manage its size. By default, Windows sets the size of virtual memory to about 1.5 times the size of physical memory. The No paging file option turns off the virtual memory capability altogether, leaving you with only physical RAM.

Note   The term *paging file* refers to the area of your hard disk that's used for virtual memory. When using virtual memory, Windows actually swaps information between physical RAM and this invisible paging file.

If you change the current selection, you need to click the Set button to activate the change. If you decrease the size of virtual memory, you won't really see any effect until you restart the computer.

Troubleshooting

When things don't work right, the Windows XP troubleshooters are a good first step to solving the problem. To get to the troubleshooters, follow these steps:

1. Click the Start button.
2. Choose Help and Support.
3. Click Fixing a Problem.

Select an option in the left column to see additional options. Then select whichever option best describes your problem. Eventually you will come to the troubleshooter, like the example shown in Figure 19-14. Choose whichever option best describes your problem and then click the Next button. The troubleshooter takes you step-by-step through the procedure of diagnosing and resolving the problem.

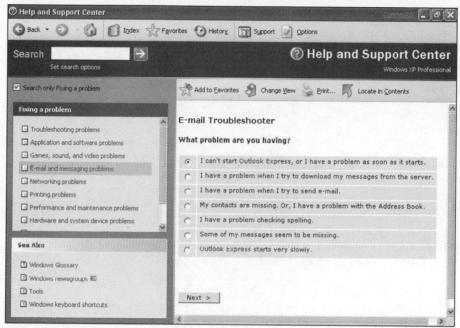

Figure 19-14: Using a troubleshooter in Help and Support

Other support

When all else fails, it might be time to call on the pros — or at least, someone more knowledgeable about the topic than yourself. The Windows newsgroups are a good resource for "free" support (although Microsoft offers a wide range of support options beyond newsgroups). To check out what's available for getting support, follow these steps:

1. Click the Start button.

2. Choose Help and Support.

3. Click Support on the toolbar.

On the Help and Support Center page, shown in Figure 19-15, you can learn more about different support options available to you by clicking any option in the left column.

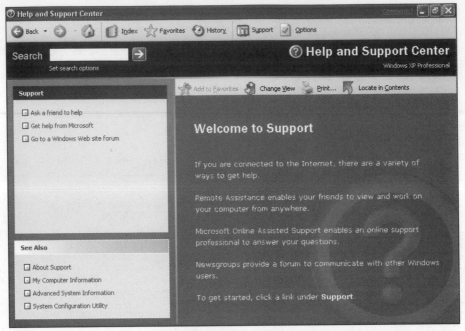

Figure 19-15: Support overview and options in Help and Support

Remote Assistance

Remote Assistance is a feature of Windows XP that enables you to get live assistance right on your desktop through a network connection (including an Internet connection). To use it, you must first make sure the feature is enabled on your computer, by following these steps:

1. Get to the System Properties dialog box, either by right-clicking the My Computer icon on your desktop and choosing Properties, or by opening the System icon in Control Panel.

2. Click the Remote tab.

3. Make sure the Allow Remote Assistance invitations to be sent from this computer option is selected, as in Figure 19-16.

4. Optionally, you can click the Advanced button to place limitations on the assistant (the person who will be helping you). You have the following options:

   • **Allow this computer to be controlled remotely:** Selecting this option allows the assistant to make changes to your computer settings.

   • **Set the maximum amount of time invitations can remain open:** Sets a time limit on how long a request for assistance remains active.

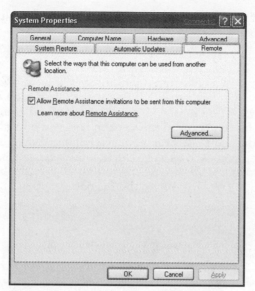

Figure 19-16: The Remote tab in System Properties

5. Click the OK button(s) to close the dialog box(es).

Cross-Reference Windows XP Professional also offers a Remote Desktop option, discussed in Chapter 34. That feature is similar to Remote Desktop Sharing, available to all Windows XP users, and covered in Chapter 11. Unlike Remote Assistance, the Remote Desktop options enable you to control an unattended computer from afar. No invitations are required.

The next step, of course, is to find the expert who is willing to give you assistance. This could be someone within your own company who is on your same network. By the time you read this, however, there will most likely be consultants and other computer firms offering some type of remote assistance. The only requirement, on the assistant side, is that they too be running some version of Windows XP (well that, and sufficient knowledge to solve the problem.) You need that person's e-mail address. To ensure that *only* the person you request can gain access to your computer, you can send the potential assistant a password. The assistant will be prompted to enter that password before gaining access to your computer.

With those items squared away, here's how to send a request for remote assistance:

1. Click the Start button and choose Help and Support.
2. Click the Support button on the toolbar.
3. Click Ask a friend to help in the left column.
4. Choose Invite someone to help you in the right column.

5. You'll come to options for contacting the assistant, such as through e-mail or Instant Messenger. Make your selection and click Continue.

6. Follow the instructions on the screen.

When the recipient of the message accepts your invitation, you'll be informed through a dialog box. If you have already agreed on a password, you can type it into this dialog box. The assistant will be prompted to enter the password at her end as soon as you do. Click the Start button to begin the session. You can now close the Help and Support Center window and close or minimize anything else on your desktop that's not relevant. However, you need to leave the Remote Assistance window open (see Figure 19-17). If that window gets in the way, either you or the expert assistant can minimize it. But don't close it during the session.

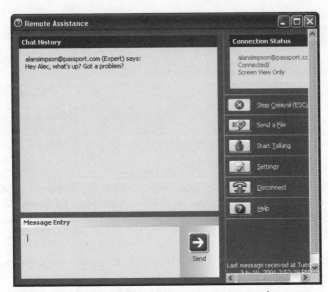

Figure 19-17: A Remote Assistance session underway

You can type a message to send to the expert assistant in the Message Entry box and then click the Send button to display the message on the recipient's screen. Optionally, if both of you have speakers and a microphone, you can click Start Talking to initiate a voice conversation.

As the recipient

As the recipient of assistance (the person who sent the invitation), you'll mainly just see the Remote Assistance box. Initially, the assistant will be able to view, but not use, your computer. When the assistant attempts to take control of your computer, you'll see a dialog box. You can click the Yes button. From then on, you are just along for the ride (although you can still send and receive Chat messages or communicate by voice while the expert assistant has control of your computer).

Note To take back control of your computer at any time, click Stop Control in the Remote Assistance window. Or, press the Escape (Esc) or Alt+C keys.

As the assistant

If you're the person providing assistance, a large window opens on your screen, showing the other person's desktop, as in Figure 19-18. To request control of the other person's computer, click the Take Control button. Anything you do inside that window takes place on the other person's computer. In other words, your mouse and keyboard operate their computer, and you can do anything you would do on your own computer. Outside that window, you can use your own computer normally. If you need to send a file to the other person's computer, click the Send a File button. (That person also can send you a file, if need be.)

If you need to turn control back over to the other person, click the Release Control button. Anything that person does will be visible on your own screen.

To end a Remote Assistance session, either person can click the Disconnect button. The connection terminates immediately.

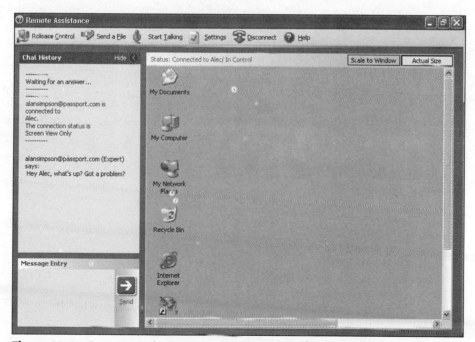

Figure 19-18: Remote Assistance, as seen from the assistant's side

Summary

In this chapter you have learned how to gather information about your computer, monitor its performance, perform routing maintenance, keep it up-to-date, and tweak settings that will help it deliver its best. Here's a quick recap of the important points covered in this chapter:

✦ The System Properties dialog box displays general information about your computer, such as its processor speed and available RAM.

✦ A disk drive's Properties dialog box shows you how much space is available on the drive.

✦ More extensive information about your system is available through the System Information applet.

✦ The Disk Cleanup Wizard can help you get rid of junk on your hard drive that's just wasting space and maybe even hurting your system's performance.

✦ Disk Defragmenter can keep a hard disk running at top speed by rearranging files into smooth, contiguous blocks on the disk.

✦ To keep Windows up-to-date and provide the maximum security, use Windows Update to download current security updates.

✦ Task Manager offers several tools for monitoring your system's performance, which can also help you identify performance bottlenecks.

✦ The Performance Settings dialog box provides options that can further improve your system's performance.

✦ The troubleshooters, available through Help and Support, provide the best means of solving common computer problems.

✦ Remote Assistance enables you to turn control of your computer over to an expert who can (hopefully) help you solve more complex problems.

✦   ✦   ✦

Managing Multiple Users

Windows NT and Windows 2000, both designed for the corporate environment, have enabled users to create and manage multiple user accounts for quite some time. Windows XP is the first version to offer this capability in both its Professional and Home editions. The beauty of having multiple user accounts, even in a home environment, is that each user can have his own settings, desktop icons, favorites, and other personal items, without trampling on the preferences of other people who share the same computer.

Understanding User Accounts

When you create two or more user accounts on a computer, starting Windows initially displays the Welcome screen shown in Figure 20-1. You'll see a picture and name for each user account you've created. To log on, a user just needs to click his account name or picture. If his account is password-protected, he must enter a password as well.

Every computer has at least one user dubbed the Administrator, who has "omnipotent" powers over that computer, including the ability to add and remove hardware and software, create user accounts, and so forth. Windows XP also provides for a Limited account, where the user has far fewer privileges. Table 20-1 summarizes the differences between the Administrator and Limited accounts.

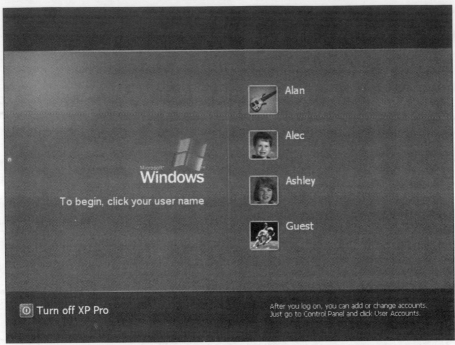

Figure 20-1: The Welcome screen for a computer with four user accounts

Table 20-1		
User Accounts and Their Privileges		
	Administrator	*Limited*
Install hardware and software	X	
Make systemwide changes	X	
Access and read all non-private files	X	
Create and delete user accounts	X	
Change other people's accounts	X	
Change own account name or type	X	
Change own account picture	X	X
Create, change, or remove own password	X	X

Creating and managing user accounts is easy. Just follow these steps:

1. Click the Start button and open Control Panel.
2. Open the User Accounts icon.

Cross-Reference If Control Panel isn't available on your Start menu, see "Adding and Deleting Start Menu Items" in Chapter 13 for information on adding it.

A window titled User Accounts opens, as in the example shown in Figure 20-2. From this one window you can add, change, and delete accounts. The window differs a little from most programs and dialog boxes, in that you navigate by clicking options within the window and then click the Back button to return to the preceding window.

Creating a new account

To create a new user account, click the Create a New Account option in User Accounts. Enter a name for the account (most likely the name of the person who will be using the account). Then click the Next button. Pick the account type on the next page and click the Create Account option. That's it! You're returned to the User Accounts window where you'll see the new account with an automatically assigned picture. Initially, the account won't have a password. But you can easily change that.

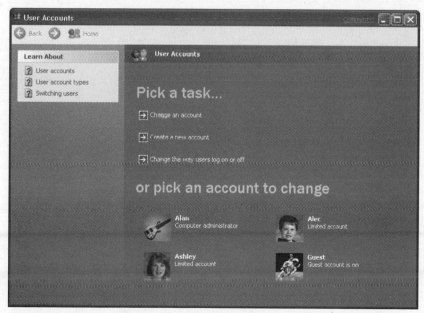

Figure 20-2: The User Accounts window lets you manage user accounts.

Custom User Account Pictures

When you opt to change a user account, you are given the option to change the account picture. Choosing that option displays several stock pictures that you can use, as well as an option to Browse for More Pictures. Clicking that option displays an Open dialog box, where you can choose any picture stored it BMP, GIF, JPG, or PNG format as your picture. As in any Open dialog box, you also can navigate to other folders. Use the View Menu button in the Open dialog box's toolbar to view thumbnails of images in the current folder.

The picture you choose will be sized to fit within the space allotted on the Welcome screen and at the top of the Start menu. For best results, consider using Paint or some more sophisticated graphics program to crop and size an image to 48 x 48 pixels before you select it as a user account picture. If the picture is a photograph, save it as a JPEG (.jpg) file for the best color quality.

Changing an account

To change an existing use account, click the Change an Account option in User Accounts. Click the account you want to change to see the options shown in Figure 20-3. The options are self-explanatory — you can change the account name, picture, or type, create a password (if none exists), or delete the account.

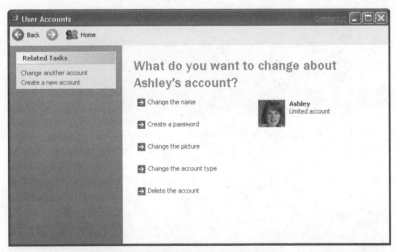

Figure 20-3: Options for changing a user's account

Deleting an account

To delete an account, choose Delete the Account. You'll be given the option to either keep, or delete, the user's files. If this user is just moving to some other computer, you can choose Keep Files. Doing so will create an icon with the user's name on the Windows desktop. The folder will contain that user's My Documents folder and desktop settings. You can then copy that folder to a disk, another computer on a LAN, or write it to a CD if you have a CD-R or CD-RW drive. If you choose Delete Files, all that user's files are deleted, and there won't be any way to recover them. So think carefully before you choose!

The Guest Account

In addition to accounts for specific users, you can activate a Guest account. This account allows anyone to log on as a "guest," with the same basic privileges as a Limited user account. Which is to say, the guest can run programs and such, but cannot make changes to the system.

To turn the Guest account on or off, click the Guest account picture in the User Accounts window. You'll be taken to a page that enables you to turn the account on or off.

Changing User Logon and Logoff

As computer administrator, you also have the option to determine how users log on and off. Choosing this option presents the choices shown in Figure 20-4. Clearing the first option, Use the Welcome screen, prevents the Welcome screen from appearing. Instead a simple logon box will display, without showing all user names. This might be preferred in a high-security setting where you don't want users to know each other's logon names.

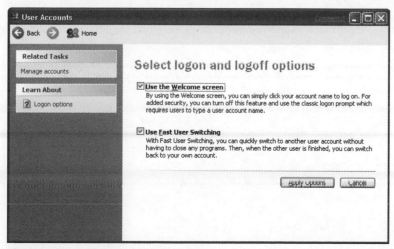

Figure 20-4: Logon and logoff options

If you allow for fast switching among user accounts, any user can temporarily log off from her account without closing open programs and documents. This is handy when another user needs access to the computer for a few minutes. With fast switching, any user can click the Start button and choose Log Off to view the options shown in Figure 20-5. Choosing Switch User will bring up the Welcome screen, where the other user can log on. When that person is finished with her task, she can then log off, which brings back the Welcome screen. The first user then just clicks on her account name or picture to get right back to where she left off.

Figure 20-5: With fast switching, a user can choose Switch User to leave his programs and documents on the desktop while another user logs on.

Account Security and Privacy

As mentioned, Windows XP provides each user account with his own My Documents folder, and additional folders for storing desktop settings, favorites, and other preferences. However, it offers very little in the way of privacy. An administrator can easily open any other user's `My Documents` folder just by opening My Computer. Each user's My Documents folder is clearly identified as *Username*'s Documents (for instance, `Alan's Documents`, `Alec's Documents`, and so forth). The folders list also provides easy access to each user's Documents and Settings, as in Figure 20-6.

Note   A user's My Documents and other folders aren't created until the user actually logs on for the first time.

On a hard disk formatted with the FAT32 file system, Limited user accounts have just as much free reign as Administrator accounts. That is, a user with a Limited account can open My Computer and easily access all other users' `My Documents` and other folders. If the hard disk is formatted using the NTFS file system, however, Limited accounts access only their own folders.

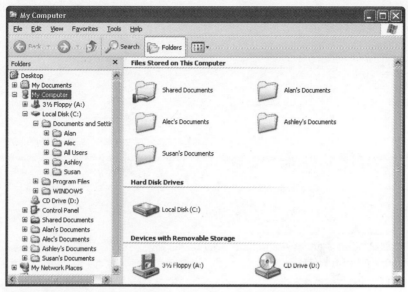

Figure 20-6: An administrator can easily access all other users' My Documents and other folders.

Cross-Reference To learn more about FAT32 and NTFS, see Chapter 31.

For example, Figure 20-7 shows the results of Limited user Susan opening My Computer. Only her My Documents folder (Susan's Documents) is displayed (along with Shared Documents, to which all users have access). The folders list does show folders for other users under Documents and Settings. If the Limited user attempts to open one of those folders, however, she gets an Access is denied message, because Limited users (on an NTFS file system) are not allowed to access other users' stuff.

Suffice it to say, the default settings for privacy and security are pretty casual with user accounts. This may be fine for many home and small business settings. If you're looking to keep other users out of your My Documents and other folders, you do have some options:

✦ Both Home and Professional edition users can password-protect accounts and make their My Documents folder private. See Chapter 29 for more information.

✦ Professional edition system administrators can use the industrial-strength security features found in Windows NT and Windows 2000. See Chapter 32 for more information.

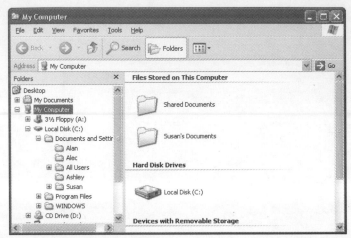

Figure 20-7: A Limited user cannot access other users' My Documents and other folders.

Regardless of how you set up security and privacy, the Shared Documents folder is, by default, the one folder on the system that all users have access to. Likewise, the Shared Pictures and Shared Music folders within Shared Documents, as well as any additional folders you create within Shared Documents, are accessible to all users.

Sharing Documents

Anything that the users want to share among themselves should be placed in the Shared Documents folder, or one of its subfolders. As you might recall, there are several quick ways to get to the Shared Documents folder:

✦ Open My Computer and then open the Shared Documents icon.

✦ Open My Documents and then click Shared Documents under Other Places.

✦ In the folders list of any Explorer window, expand My Computer and then open Shared Documents.

✦ The Address drop-down list (if visible) in the Explorer window includes a direct link to Shared Documents.

As discussed in Chapter 4, you also can create your own shortcuts to Shared Documents.

When you save a document for the first time, the Save As dialog box that appears when you save a document or downloaded file that's to be saved to disk will provide easy access to either folder. Typically, the Save As dialog box opens to your My Documents folder. You can simplify navigation to My Documents folders by adding shortcuts to those folders to your My Documents folders. In Figure 20-8, for example, all the shortcut icons actually point to folders that are within the Shared Documents folder. Therefore, I can navigate to one of those folders just by clicking the appropriate icon, instead of navigating via the Save In drop-down list.

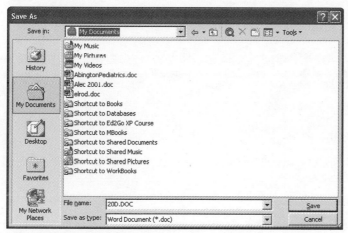

Figure 20-8: Shortcuts within My Documents also work in a program's Save As dialog box.

See "My Documents Shortcuts to Shared Documents" in Chapter 4 if you need help creating shortcuts from My Documents to Shared Documents.

Any user, whether he has an Administrator or Limited account, can move and copy files to and from the Shared Documents folder and its subfolders using any of the techniques described in Chapter 12.

Where User Account Information Is Stored

Windows XP automatically places each user's settings, favorites, and so forth within folders that represent that user's account. So, as a rule, there's no need to actually go into those folders and mess with things. In case you're curious, however, here's how it works. The Documents and Settings folder on the hard disk (drive C:) contains a folder for each user. The name of the folder is the same as the user's name. In Figure 20-9, for example, I opened My Computer and expanded the Local Disk C:, Documents and Settings, and Alan folders. Normally when you do this, only a few folders appear beneath the user's account name, because the others are hidden. To reveal the hidden folders, choose Tools ➪ Folder Options from the Explorer menu bar. Click the View tab and choose Show Hidden Files and Folders under Advanced settings.

Figure 20-9: The subfolders for the user account Alan appear in the folders list.

 Caution As a rule, hidden folders contain files you don't really want to mess with. Generally, therefore, it's best to keep them hidden. If you need to take them out of hiding for some reason, remember to rehide them after you've finished whatever it is you needed to do.

The names of the subfolders pretty well sum up what they contain. For example, Favorites keeps track of the individual user's Internet favorites. Desktop contains custom desktop shortcuts that the user has created, and so forth. The user's My Documents folder is contained within the user's subfolder as well.

The All Users folder contains a similar set of subfolders, as well as the Shared Documents folder. As the folder name implies, documents and settings in the All Users subfolders apply to all users of the computer, as well as to any new accounts you create.

Summary

Managing user accounts in Windows XP is easy, thanks to the simple User Accounts window that's accessible through Control Panel. Each user is given a personal My Documents folder, as well as other folders for storing favorites, desktop settings, and other personal preferences. Here's a quick recap of the important points covered in this chapter:

✦ Windows XP provides for two types of user accounts, Administrator accounts and Limited accounts.

✦ Administrator accounts have free reign over the entire system, can install programs, and can view the contents of other users' files.

✦ Limited accounts can run programs and save documents, but cannot install programs, make changes that affect the entire system, or view other users' files (on an NTFS file system).

✦ Administrators can create, change, and delete user accounts through the User Accounts icon in Control Panel.

✦ Limited users can change only their own account information through the User Accounts icon in Control Panel.

✦ All users have access to documents in the Shared Documents folder, as well as all of its subfolders.

✦   ✦   ✦

Road Warrior Tools and Techniques

Notebook computers pose some unique challenges for Windows XP users — especially if you need to work with copies of files stored on a computer or network back at the office. In this chapter, you'll learn techniques for getting the most out of your computer while on the road.

Conserving Power

Power conservation is everyone's concern. Many of the techniques described here are applicable to regular-sized PCs as well as notebooks. If you have ever had your notebook's battery die in the middle of something important, however, you can appreciate the importance of getting the most from that battery.

Windows XP provides power options designed to help all computer users conserve power. To get to the power options, follow these steps:

1. Click the Start button and open Control Panel.

2. If Control Panel opens in Category view, choose Performance and Maintenance ⇨ Power Options. In Classic view, open the Power Options icon.

The Power Schemes tab of the Power Options Properties dialog box, shown in Figure 21-1, provides some options for selecting and creating power schemes. You can choose from any of several predefined power schemes using the drop-down list. You also can change a power scheme or create an entirely new one.

Figure 21-1: The Power Schemes tab of
the Power Options Properties dialog box

Note   Options available in the Power Options Properties dialog box may vary from one
computer to the next, because different computers have different power options
built in to them.

To change an existing scheme, choose your options from the drop-down lists under
Settings. Here's what each option does:

✦ **Turn off monitor:** Turns off the monitor to conserve the power required to
keep the monitor lit. Moving the mouse or pressing any key turns the monitor
back on.

✦ **Turn off hard disks:** "Spins down" the disk, to conserve energy. As soon as
you open or save a file, the disk automatically starts spinning again. The only
thing you will notice is a slight delay as the disk gets back up to speed.

✦ **System standby:** Puts the computer in Standby mode, where it consumes minimal power. The computer quickly returns to its previous state as soon as you
move the mouse pointer or press a key.

✦ **System hibernates:** Like Standby, puts the computer into hibernation, where
it consumes minimal power. Moving the mouse or pressing the key brings the
system back to where you left off, although not quite as quickly as the
Standby mode.

If you change any settings, and want to save them as a new power scheme, click the
Save As button and enter a file name. The new scheme will then be available from
the drop-down list at any time in the future.

On the Advanced tab of the Power Options Properties dialog box, you can
choose whether you want the power icon to always be visible on the taskbar (see

Figure 21-2). It's a good idea to select this option if you will be using batteries to run your computer, because it can help warn you when the batteries run low.

Figure 21-2: The Advanced tab of the Power Options Properties dialog box

Standby versus Hibernate

As you may know, everything that's "in your computer" is stored on the hard disk. Whatever you happen to be working on at the moment is stored in random access memory (RAM). That's because RAM is much faster than a disk. So storing your current work there makes things move along more quickly. The problem with RAM is that it's *volatile* — meaning that when the computer is turned off or loses power, everything in RAM is instantly and permanently erased!

When your system goes into Standby mode, it uses just enough power to keep the current contents of RAM intact. So, when you bring the computer back up, everything on your screen is exactly as you left it. If the computer is turned off or loses power during Standby, however, RAM gets wiped out. If you left any unsaved work on the desktop, that will be gone.

Hibernate works a little differently. Before your computer goes into hibernation, it "takes a snapshot" of RAM's contents and stores that on the hard disk. The hard disk isn't volatile, so even if the computer loses power during hibernation, there is no loss. When you bring the computer out of hibernation, it just copies the snapshot from the disk back into RAM, returning the computer to exactly where you left off.

Of course, the smart thing to do is to save your work often. In most programs, it's a simple matter of clicking the Save button on the toolbar, or pressing Ctrl+S, or choosing File ⇨ Save from the menu bar.

If you select the second option, Prompt for password, then whenever the computer goes into Standby or Hibernate mode, you will need to enter a password to get back to the desktop. If you choose this option, make sure you think up a good password and write it down somewhere (just in case you forget it). Otherwise, you may lock yourself out of your own computer!

Under Power Options, you can choose how the main power button on your computer behaves. If your computer has a Sleep button, you can control its behavior as well. You have the following options:

✦ **Do nothing:** Disables the button.

✦ **Ask me what to do:** Pressing the button will display some options on the screen for you to choose from.

✦ **Sleep:** Pressing the button will put the computer into "Sleep" mode.

✦ **Hibernate:** Pressing the button will put the computer into hibernation.

✦ **Shut down:** Pressing the button will completely shut down the computer so that it consumes no power at all.

The Sleep mode is similar to Standby mode in that the computer consumes minimal power. If your computer has a Wake On LAN capability, the Sleep mode might be your best bet. With Wake On LAN enabled, the computer "wakes up" whenever a request for resources comes to the computer through a LAN or dial-up connection. Getting Wake On LAN to work can be tricky, however, because it's actually a function of your network interface card and computer's BIOS (Basic Input/Output System). As such, you may need to refer to the manufacturer's instructions for the specifics of using that capability on your own system.

Using hibernation

If your computer has the capability to hibernate, chances are that feature is enabled automatically. If it doesn't seem to be available or if you want to disable hibernation, however, use the Hibernate tab, shown in Figure 21-3, of the Power Options Properties dialog box to make your selection.

Uninterruptible power supplies

An uninterruptible power supply (UPS) is a hardware device that maintains a steady power output. If you live in an area where the power is subject to outages or brownouts, a UPS is a must to keep your computer(s) from shutting down or rebooting every time there's a problem with the power. In the event of a complete power outage, the UPS can keep power going to your computer long enough for you to save any work in progress and shut down normally. The UPS tab in the Power Options Properties dialog box lets you check the condition of your UPS.

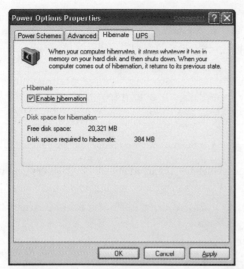

Figure 21-3: The Hibernate tab of the Power
Options Properties dialog box

Managing Multiple Dial-Up Connections

Using dial-up connections while on the road—whether they be to access the
Internet, your computer back home, or your office network—can be a real pain.
The main reason is that exactly how you dial the number of the source you're trying to reach will vary from one location to the next. When you're dialing from outside your own area code, for example, you must dial 1 before dialing the area code
and number. When you're in a hotel room, you may need to dial 8 to get an outside
line or 9 before dialing long distance. The Windows XP Dialing Properties dialog box
greatly simplifies matters by enabling you to change dial-out settings on-the-fly. You
also can create and save different "dial from" locations, in case your travels require
you to return to the same place often.

Define where you're dialing from

The first step is to tell Windows about the location you're dialing *from*. Here's how:

1. Click the Start button and open Control Panel.

2. If Control Panel opens in Category view, switch to the Classic view.

3. Open the Phone and Modem Options icon.

4. On the Dialing Rules tab, click the New button. The New Location dialog box
   opens.

5. On the General tab, fill in the blanks to define how and where you're dialing *from*. The Location Name can be any name you like. Make sure you also fill in the area code you're dialing from, as well as any other dialing rules, as in the example shown in Figure 21-4.

6. On the Area Code Rules tab, click the New button and define dialing rules for the location you're dialing *to*. In Figure 21-5, for example, I have set up the rules to dial a 1 plus the area code when dialing to the 516 area code from my current location.

7. Click OK when you're done.

8. If you use a calling card, click the Calling Card tab and specify the type of card you're using, the account number, and PIN.

9. Click the OK button. Then click the OK button in the Phone and Modem Options dialog box to save your settings.

Figure 21-4: Sample General tab of the New Location dialog box location

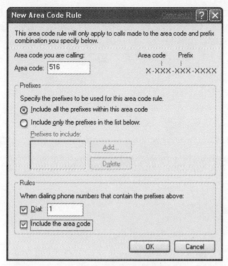

Figure 21-5: The Area Code Rule tab of the New Location dialog box

Disable auto-dialing

To ensure that the Connect dialog box prompts you for the location you're dialing from, follow these steps:

1. In Control Panel, open the Network Connections icon.

2. Right-click the icon for dialing into your ISP and choose Properties.

3. Click the Options tab.

4. Select the Prompt for phone number check box if it isn't already selected. If, for whatever reason, you also need to use a different user name and/or password for this connection, choose Prompt for name and password, certificate, etc. as well.

5. Click the OK button.

Now you're ready to connect.

Making the connection

Now you're ready to make the connection. Assuming you're still in the Network Connections window, just click (or double-click) the icon for dialing to your ISP. You can also open the shortcut icon on your desktop or open Network Connections from the Start menu or Control Panel and then open the icon for dialing your ISP.

The Connect dialog box will open with options that enable you to choose the location you're dialing from, as in Figure 21-6. Select your current location and click the Dial button. Should you have any problems, you can use the Dialing Rules button right there in the Connect dialog box to adjust your settings.

Figure 21-6: Choose your current location from the Dialing from drop-down list.

Avoiding long-distance charges on the road

Keep in mind that if you dial your usual local access number while on the road, you're likely to run up some long-distance charges while you're connected. The only way to avoid that is to see whether your ISP offers a local access number for the area from which you are dialing. Many large ISPs have local access numbers throughout the country. Typically, you can get to the list of numbers by going to the ISP's home page on the World Wide Web and searching for *local access numbers*. Or, you can call them by voice and tell them the area code and dialing prefix for your current location to see what's available.

If you do get a new local access number for your current location, you can just replace the phone number that appears next to Dial in the Connect dialog box with the number you want to dial. When you click the Dial button, Windows will ask whether you want to make this change permanent. Choose No if you want to keep your original local access number in tact.

The Help button in the Connect dialog box takes you to help topics for all types of network connections. In the Contents tab, the Dial-Up Connections, Configure Dial-Up Options, and Troubleshooting books provide information that's relevant to dial-up connections.

Creating Direct Cable and Infrared Connections

If you have a notebook or handheld computer and need to transfer files to and from your PC, you have several solutions available to you. One of the most commonly used is the *docking station,* also called a *port replicator.* Most manufacturers of notebook computers sell docking stations as accessory items. If your notebook has a USB port, you can also purchase third-party "generic" docking stations that provide *hot docking,* the ability to connect the notebook to a PC without turning either computer off.

Many modern portable computers also come with infrared devices, which enable you to transfer files between computers. After you install the appropriate hardware and software, as per the manufacturer's instructions, you can transfer files between the two computers. If the software for your infrared connection doesn't work with Windows XP, you can use the procedure discussed in this section to set up the connection. Assuming you have set up the infrared hardware, the Connection Wizard described later will enable you to choose that hardware as the connection device.

As an alternative to those approaches, many inexpensive third-party products enable you to connect two computers to share an Internet connection or transfer files from one computer to the next. Parallel Technologies, at www.lpt.com, offers many such solutions.

Finally, there's the Windows XP Direct Cable Connection (DCC) option. It's important to understand, however, that this type of connection isn't like any of those described earlier. Direct Cable Connection enables you to connect your portable computer to a PC that already has *shared resources* on it and to access those shared resources. For a computer to have shared resources, it needs to be a member of a local area network (LAN). In other words, whereas the preceding solutions enable you to connect two stand-alone computers together, Direct Cable Connection enables you to connect a portable computer to a LAN, via any single computer in that LAN. What makes this approach unique is that the portable computer doesn't need an Ethernet card. Instead, you can connect to the LAN through a cable or infrared device.

Before I continue, let me tell you about a couple of disadvantages to direct cable connections. They are slow as molasses in Antarctica. If you need to transfer files often, you would do well to set up a local area network to connect the computer, as discussed in Part VI of this book. In addition, although the Direct Cable Connection feature does work, a lot of people seem to have problems getting it to work with particular hardware configurations. The Windows support newsgroups are filled with lots of questions, and few answers, about getting this type of connection to work. If you're willing to forge ahead and give it a try, however, the first thing you need is some kind of connection device. You can use any of the following:

✦ A DirectParallel cable for connecting to printer ports. (To use this type of connection, the stand-alone computer must be running Windows XP or Windows 2000.)

✦ A wireless infrared connection device.

✦ A null modem cable specifically wired for computer-to-computer connections. Also requires that the serial ports are able to act as null modem devices.

Tip   Parallel Technologies, at `www.1pt.com`, sells a variety of cables specifically designed for connecting two computers. They are also a great resource for exploring different ways you might connect your computers.

In addition to the connection device, you need to configure both computers for direct cable connection. One computer will act as the *host*. This is the computer connected to the LAN and having shared resources that can be accessed by other computers. The other computer is the *guest*—the stand-alone portable computer that doesn't have a direct connection to the network.

Setting up the host computer

First, keep in mind that the guest computer will have access only to shared resources on the host. So you need to share any folders or devices you need access to from the guest. Typically, the Shared Documents folder on the host will already be shared. If you want to share anything else, do as described in Chapter 27.

Then, create an incoming connection icon in that computer's Network Connections dialog box to enable the direct cable connection. Here's how:

1. On the host computer, click the Start button and choose All Programs ➪ Accessories ➪ Communications ➪ Network Connections.

2. Under Network Tasks, click Create a New Connection.

3. Click the Next button and choose Set Up an Advanced Connection and then click Next.

4. Choose Accept Incoming Connections and then click Next.

5. Under Connection Devices, choose the hardware or cable type you'll be using to make the connection and click Next.

6. When asked about VPN connection, you can choose the Do not allow option, because this isn't really relevant to direct cable connections. Click the Next button.

7. In the User Permissions page, select the users who will be allowed to access this computer through a direct cable connection. If need be, you can click Add to create a new user account and password. Click Next.

8. Under Networking Software, you can accept the default selections by clicking the Next button.

9. Click the Finish button.

The connection will be named Incoming Connections and will be visible in your Network Connections window, as in Figure 21-7.

Figure 21-7: On the host computer, the icon for a direct cable connection appears as an Incoming Connections icon.

 Tip
 To add a Network Connections option to your Start menu, right-click the Start button and choose Properties. Click the Customize button and then click the Advanced tab. Choose the Display As or Link To option under Network Connection in the list of Start menu items.

To ensure that you will be able to log on to the host computer, you can relax the security settings a bit. This is particularly important if you're connecting via a small portable device that won't allow you to log on. Here's how:

1. Right-click the Incoming Connections icon you just created and choose Properties.

2. Click the Users tab.

3. Choose the last check box: Always allow directly connected devices.

4. Click the OK button to save your change and close the dialog box.

Now you're ready to set up the guest computer.

Setting up the guest computer

Now you need to go to the other (guest) computer, and set up an icon for making the connection:

1. On the guest computer, click the Start button and choose All Programs ➪ Accessories ➪ Communications ➪ Network Connections.

2. Under Network Tasks, choose Create a New Connection. Click the Next button.

3. Choose Set Up an Advanced Connection and then click Next.

4. Choose Connect Directly to Another Computer and then click Next.

5. Choose Guest and click Next.

6. Type in the name of the computer to which you'll be connecting and then click Next.

Tip   If you're not sure of the host computer's name, go to that computer, open Control Panel, and open the System icon. On the Computer Name tab, you will see the name next to Full computer name.

7. On the Select a Device page, choose the hardware or cable type you'll be using for the connection and then click Next.

8. On the last wizard page, you can opt to create a desktop icon for the connection. Click the Finish button.

A Connect dialog box displays. If the two computers are already connected via cable, you can make the connection by clicking, entering the user name and password you entered on the host, and clicking the Connect button. If you're not quite ready for that, you can just click the Cancel button and connect later.

Making the direct connection

To use the direct connection, connect the computers with the cable, or position the infrared hardware accordingly. Then, on the guest computer, open the icon that represents the direct connection. It will have the same name as the computer to which you're connecting. If you didn't opt to create a desktop shortcut for the connection, open Network Connections to get to the icon. When prompted, enter the user name and password that you specified while setting up the host computer and click the

Connect button. After verifying your username and password, you'll be connected. The icon for the connection will show Connected (in Tiles view). If you open the Network Connections window on the host computer, you'll see an icon for the connection there as well.

After the computers have been connected, you should be able to access the shared resources of the LAN. If all the computers in the network share an Internet connection, for example, you should be able to open Internet Explorer on the guest computer and start browsing the Web.

Theoretically, you should be able to open My Network Places and access shared folders on the network as well. However, with slow direct cable connections, this approach doesn't always work. Often, you must search for other computers on the LAN by following these steps:

1. On the guest computer, click the Start button and choose Search.

2. In the Search Companion, choose Computers or People.

3. Choose the option labeled A computer on the network.

4. Under Computer Name, type the name of the computer you're looking for and click the Search button.

When entering the name of the computer to search for, do not use the leading slashes specified by the Universal Naming Convention. Just type the name, as in **Max**.

After the computer has been found, you can click (or double-click) its name in the right column to view its share resources. In Figure 21-8, for example, I searched for a computer named Max on my LAN. Once it was found, I opened its icon and can now see the two shared folders on that computer, named SharedDocs and MaxBackup. I could then copy files to or from those folders using any of the standard procedures discussed in Chapter 12. To print a document via the printer on Max, I can drag the icon for the document file that I want to print onto the Printer icon.

Closing a direct cable connection

Before you disconnect the two computers, you should close the connection on the guest computer. In Network Connections, right-click the icon for the connection and choose Disconnect. On the guest computer, the icon in Network Connections shows Disconnected. On the host, the icon for the connection disappears, and the Incoming Connections icon shows No clients attached.

Figure 21-8: Icons for shared resources on a network computer named Max

Speeding up serial connections

If you connect the two computers through a serial cable, you can maximize the speed of the connection by cranking up the speed of the serial port to the max on both computers. (If the serial port speed on the two computers doesn't match, the slower speed is used.) To set your serial card's connection speed, follow these steps:

1. Click the Start button and open Control Panel in Classic view.

2. Open the System icon.

3. Click the Hardware tab and then click the Device Manager button.

4. Expand the Ports (COM & LPT) category.

5. Right-click the COM port that you want to speed up (for instance, COM1) and choose Properties.

6. On the Port Settings tab, choose the fastest speed available from the Bits per second drop-down list.

7. Click the OK button.

   Remember to repeat the process on both computers to get the maximum transfer rate.

The Virtual Briefcase

Many people use their portable PC as a kind of virtual briefcase. Perhaps you generally do your work on a desktop PC. To take your work on the road, you copy the appropriate files from the desktop PC to your laptop for editing on the road. When you get back to the office, you copy the updated files from the portable PC back to the desktop PC. The one problem is things can get confusing. Fortunately, the Windows XP Briefcase helps reduce the confusion and simplifies the entire process.

Tip   The Briefcase works best when you have no physical connection between the two computers, or if both computers use the Home edition of Windows XP. If the portable computer connects to a network through an Ethernet card or some other network connection, and the host computer has Windows XP Professional or Server edition installed, the Synchronization tool, discussed under "Working Offline" later in this chapter, may be more convenient.

There are three basic steps to using Briefcase, as follows:

1. Before you go on the road, create a briefcase. Pack it with files you want to take on the road. Take the briefcase with you on the road.

2. On the road, open the briefcase and open any files you want to work on from within the briefcase.

3. When you get back to the office, unpack the briefcase. Windows automatically updates any files on the stationary PC to match any changes you made on the road.

Caution   Briefcase relies on your computer's internal calendar and clock to determine which version of a document is the most current version, so make sure your clocks are in sync. Double-click the current time in the taskbar to set the current date and time.

To get started, you need to create and pack a briefcase. How you do that depends on whether you're using a removable disk, or if the two computers can be connected through a direct cable connection.

Packing a briefcase with unconnected computers

If you don't have any way to connect the two computers with a cable, use a removable disk to store the briefcase. You can use floppies if both computers have a floppy drive. However, the downside to this is that floppies hold so little information (1.2 MB), meaning that you cannot pack much of anything into your briefcase. If possible, you're better off using some kind of portable USB drive that you can easily connect to either computer and take with you on the road. In the following example, I will be using an external Zip drive that connects to my computers through a USB port.

First, create the briefcase on the stationary computer. You can create the briefcase within any folder you want, such as My Documents or Shared Documents. Just open the folder, right-click some neutral area between icons and choose New ⇨ Briefcase. An icon named New Briefcase appears.

Next, in a separate Explorer window, navigate to the folder that contains the document files you want to take with you. Select the icon(s) for the documents you want to take and then drag them onto the Briefcase icon and drop them there. Optionally, you can open the briefcase by clicking or double-clicking its icon. Then you can drag the icons into the open briefcase, which displays the current contents of the briefcase. You can navigate around and drag files from any folder into the briefcase. Figure 21-9 shows an example where I have dragged some icons into an open briefcase in the top window.

Figure 21-9: The upper window is an open briefcase with some document files in it.

After you have finished packing the briefcase, close it (if you opened it) by clicking the Up button on the toolbar to switch to the parent folder. The Briefcase icon should be visible in the open window. Next, insert a disk into the removable disk drive, open My Computer, and open the drive's icon. Then drag the Briefcase icon into the open window for the removable disk. In Figure 21-10, for example, I dragged the briefcase to a disk in my removable Zip drive, E:.

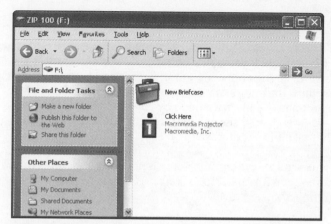

Figure 21-10: The New Briefcase icon is now on the Zip disk in drive E:.

Now you just need to remember to take the disk with you (and the drive as well, if your portable computer doesn't have a drive for that type of disk).

Packing a briefcase with connected computers

If the stationary and portable computers are connected via a direct cable connection, you can create the briefcase right on the hard disk of the portable computer. Just open any folder on the portable computer's hard drive, right-click any neutral area within that folder, and choose New ➪ Briefcase. You can open the briefcase by clicking or double-clicking its icon.

When the computers are connected, use your portable computer to navigate to the folder(s) on the stationary computer that contain the files you want to take along. Drag the icons for those document files into the briefcase that's on your portable computer. You can then close all open windows and disconnect the computers.

On the road

When you're on the road and want to make changes to any files that are in the briefcase, open the briefcase icon. Needless to say, if the briefcase is on a removable disk, you must insert that disk first. Once the briefcase is open, you can open any document within it by clicking or double-clicking the document's icon. When you save your work, the changes are saved within the briefcase. The date and time is recorded within the briefcase as well.

When you get back

When you get back from your trip, you can synchronize the files in the briefcase with the files on the stationary computer. If you connect the computers through a direct cable connection, you must make the connection first. If you used a removable disk, you need to insert the disk into the stationary computer and open its icon in My Computer once again. Then open the Briefcase icon by clicking or double-clicking as usual. Once the briefcase is open, you'll see a task labeled Update All Items in the Explorer bar. Just click that task to synchronize the files, and you're done.

If, for whatever reason, you want to synchronize only a portion of the files in the briefcase, you can select the icon for that/those file(s). Then click Update This Item under Briefcase Tasks in the Explorer bar.

Making orphans

If you ever want to separate files that are stored in a briefcase from their counterparts outside the briefcase, open the briefcase as usual. Then choose Briefcase ➪ Split from Original from the Briefcase menu bar. The status of the file within the briefcase will change to Orphan, meaning that the file no longer has a counterpart outside the briefcase. You can no longer synchronize that file with files outside the briefcase. To move the orphan file out of the briefcase, you can right-click its icon within the briefcase and choose Cut. Then, use Explorer to navigate to the folder in which you want to place the file, right-click within that folder, and choose Paste.

Working Offline

Windows XP Professional offers Synchronization Manager, a tool that helps you work with shared resources on a LAN even while you're not connected to the LAN. If you have a notebook computer running the Professional edition and you often use it on the road, you can use Synchronization Manager to synchronize the files on your notebook with the files on the LAN each time you reconnect to the LAN.

A few buzzwords go with the synchronization process. A computer that's occasionally disconnected from the network is called a *stand-alone* computer, whether it's a full PC or a notebook. The specific shared files that the stand-alone computer can access are called *offline files*. The process of working with those offline files is called *working offline*. After you make changes to the offline files, and then reconnect to the network, the process of bringing the original files up-to-date with the changes you made offline is called *synchronization*.

A *shared resource* or *share* on a LAN is some file or folder that other computers in the LAN can access. Offline files need to be shares, or stored within a shared folder. The Shared Documents folder on a Windows XP computer is shared across the LAN automatically. So that folder, or any subfolder within it, is a good candidate for working offline.

See Chapter 27 for more information on sharing folders.

To work with offline files, you need to first go through three steps to enable that capability on your stand-alone computer.

Step 1: Enable working offline

Working offline requires that the Faster User Switching feature of user accounts be disabled. To check that feature, click the Start button, open Control Panel, and open the User Accounts icon. Choose Change the way users log on or off and clear the Use Fast User Switching check box, if it's selected. Click the Apply button. You can then close the User Accounts window and Control Panel.

Next you need to enable synchronization on the stand-alone computer and choose some related options. Suppose, for instance, that your stand-alone computer is named Athlon. To enable working offline on that computer, follow these steps:

1. Open My Computer. (Click the Start button and choose My Computer if you don't have a desktop shortcut.)

2. Choose Tools ➪ Folder Options from My Computer's menu bar.

3. On the Offline Files tab, make sure Enable offline files is selected, as in Figure 21-11.

4. Choose any other options as convenient. If you need more information about an option, click the question mark button (?) in the upper-right corner of the Folder Options dialog box and then click the option you're interested in.

The Create an Offline Files shortcut on the desktop is a handy option, because it makes it easy to get to those files when you're working offline.

5. Click the OK button.

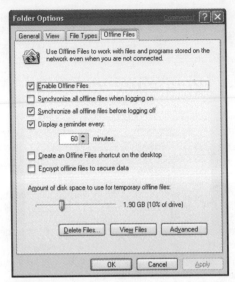

Figure 21-11: The Offline Files tab in the Folder Options dialog box

Step 2: Map network drives

The next step requires mapping a network drive to any shared resource on the LAN that contains files you want to be able to work with while you're offline.

Note   The term *network drive* stems from the fact that the icon to the shared folder appears in My Computer with a drive letter assigned to it and can be accessed *as though* it were a drive. The item that the icon represents need not be a drive — it can be a folder.

For the sake of example, suppose that you want to access one or more files in the Shared Documents folder of the computer named Max. Your stand-alone computer (Athlon in this example) needs to be connected to the LAN for this step. While sitting at Athlon, here's how you would map a network drive to the Shared Documents folder on Max:

1. Open My Computer and choose Tools ➪ Map Network Drive.

2. Choose an available drive letter.

3. Click the Browse button and navigate to the folder you want to make available offline. Click the folder's name and then click the OK button.

4. To ensure that you're automatically reconnected to the shared resource whenever you go online, make sure Reconnect at logon is selected.

In the Map Network Drive dialog box, the folder that the network drive icon will represent is shown in UNC format, \\COMPUTERNAME\sharename. For example, the shared documents folder on the computer named Max appears as \\Max\Documents. Click the Finish button. An icon for the shared resource appears under Network Drives in My Computer. For example, the icon named Documents on 'Max' (Z:) in Figure 21-12 represents the Shared Documents folder from the computer named Max.

Figure 21-12: A network drive, Z:, mapped to the Shared Documents folder on a computer named Max

If you want to, you can repeat the steps to create network drives for other shared resources on the LAN.

Step 3: Make the folder available offline

For each network drive you create, you then need to follow these steps to make the shared resource available for working offline:

1. In My Computer, select the network drive icon(s) that you want to be able to access offline. Optionally, if you just want to make certain items within the shared folder accessible offline, you can open the network drive icon and select those specific files and/or folders.

2. Choose File ➪ Make Available Offline from the menu bar. The Offline Files Wizard opens.

3. The wizard explains how synchronization works and also gives you the option of synchronizing files automatically when you log on/log off. Just follow along, make your selections, and click the Finish button when you're done.

Tip   Automating synchronization when you log on and off is the best way to guarantee that your stand-alone computer is always in sync with the shared resource on the LAN.

The wizard copies the files from the shared resource to the Offline Files folder of your local computer. You're done! Now let's look at how you can work with those files offline.

Using offline files

When you're not connected to the LAN and want to work with offline files, just open the Offline Files icon on your desktop. Alternatively, if you don't have a desktop shortcut, open My Computer, choose Tools ➪ Folder Options, click the Offline Files tab, and then click the View Files button. The contents of the folder will be visible in a standard Explorer icon. To work with a file, just click (or double-click) it as you would any other document's icon.

Getting back in sync

When your get your computer reconnected to the network and log on, the files between your computer and the network will automatically be synchronized, if you opted to allow for automatic synchronization. Otherwise, you synchronize manually. To do so, open the Offline Files shortcut icon on the desktop, or open My Computer. Choose Tools ➪ Synchronize from the menu bar. Select the item(s) you want to synchronize, as in Figure 21-13, and click the Synchronize button.

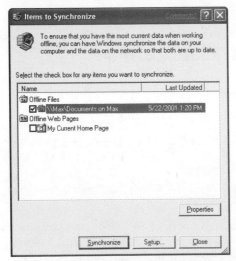

Figure 21-13: Manually selecting items to be synchronized

Deleting offline files

If you want to eliminate any of your offline files so that they're no longer synchronized, open My Computer or your Offline Files folder and choose Tools ➪ Folder Options. On the Offline Files tab (see Figure 21-14), click the Delete Files button. As instructed in the confirmation dialog box, select the items that you want to delete. Then choose whether you just want to delete the "temporary" copies on your own computer or delete both those and the original, unedited copies as well. Then click the OK button.

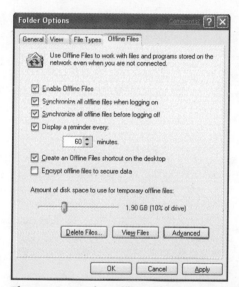

Figure 21-14: The Offline Files tab provides many options for controlling synchronization.

Changing synchronization options

If you want to change any settings that you originally chose in the Offline Files Wizard or when enabling offline files, just open your Offline Files folder, or My Computer. Choose Tools ➪ Folder Options form the menu bar, and click the Offline Files tab, as usual. Make your new selections and then click OK.

Summary

In this chapter, we've looked at techniques for getting the most from a notebook computer — or any other stand-alone computer, for that matter. Here's a quick recap of the important points covered in this chapter:

✦ The Power Options icon in Control Panel enables you to manage power resources and conserve battery power.

✦ When you're on the road and need to make a dial-up connection, you can simply create and choose a new location that you're dialing *from,* as opposed to creating an entirely new network connection.

✦ Direct Cable Connection enables you to connect a stand-alone computer to a LAN without using an Ethernet card.

✦ Briefcase is a handy tool for keeping files from two computers in sync with one another.

✦ Windows XP Professional offers Synchronization, a tool to simplify working with shared files on a network while you're offline.

✦   ✦   ✦

Work and Play

Whether you use your computer for work, play, or both, this part will teach how to handle all different kinds of documents. First you'll learn the basic skills for working with text and numbers. Then you'll learn all about working with pictures, including photos from a digital camera or scanner. You'll also learn all the new techniques for working with music, including how to create your own custom audio CDs. If you have a video camera, you can use Windows Movie Maker to produce your own custom movies complete with sound track, narration, and special effects.

Numbers, Text, and Pictures

This chapter is all about some basic skills and concepts for working with numbers, text, and pictures in Windows XP. Here you'll also learn about some of the handy Windows XP *applets* that help you work with those different types of data. You'll also learn some important basic skills for moving and copying stuff between different types of documents and different programs. We'll start with the simplest applet of all, the Calculator, which, as its name implies, helps you work with numbers.

Using the Calculator

To help you work with numbers, Windows XP offers the Calculator applet. Qualifying as the easiest-to-use program on the planet, Calculator works much like your standard pocket calculator. To start the Calculator, click the Start button and choose All Programs ➪ Accessories ➪ Calculator. The calculator pops up on-screen, as in Figure 22-1.

Figure 22-1: The Calculator applet

When the calculator is visible on the screen, you can click its buttons with your mouse, exactly as you would press the buttons on a regular calculator. To calculate 24 times 19, for example, just click the following buttons in the order shown:

24×19=

Note   Computers generally use an asterisk (*) to represent multiplication — not an *x* or a dot. So when you type a formula into Calculator, such as 2 times 3, you would actually type 2*3. Division is handled by the / character. For example 10/5 (ten divided by five) equals 2. Addition uses the plus (+) character; subtraction uses a hyphen (-).

To calculate 15% of $34, you type (using the keyboard) the following:

0.15*34=

Or, you click (using the mouse and Calculator) the following buttons:

0.15×34=

The result equals 5.1 (or $5.10).

If your math needs go beyond basic arithmetic, you can switch to the scientific calculator shown in Figure 22-2. To get there, choose View ➪ Scientific from Calculator's menu bar.

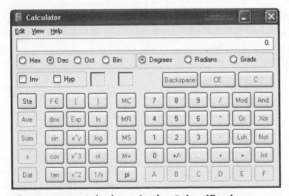

Figure 22-2: Calculator in the Scientific view

I'm not going to go into all the advanced math that the scientific calculator offers — largely because, I don't know what half that stuff is about. Suffice it to say that if your work requires the more advanced math capabilities of a scientific calculator, you have one on your screen. If you need any help with Calculator, just choose Help ➪ Help Topics from its menu bar.

Special Note for HTML Authors

If you're a Web author who's into HTML and scripting languages, you might be happy to find that the scientific calculator can convert from hexadecimal to decimal and vice versa. This is handy when you need to convert an RGB triplet, such as FFFFFF, to a decimal number for use with a Java applet, ActiveX control, or script. To convert #FFFFFF to decimal, for instance, click the Hex option button, type **FFFFFF** and then choose the Dec number system. The result is 16777215, which is, indeed, the correct decimal equivalent of the hex number.

To convert from decimal to hex, click the Dec radio button, type in the decimal number, and click the Hex option button. When typing hex numbers into HTML tags, remember to use the leading pound sign (#). For example, to use FFFFFF as a page's background color, the correct tag is `<BODY BGCOLOR="#FFFFFF">`.

Using Notepad

Windows XP offers a few handy applets for working with text. Notepad, the simpler of the two, is especially designed for working with plain ASCII text. This means you can't do anything fancy with fonts, boldface, graphic images, or anything like that. All you can do is type text. But this is good because certain kinds of files must be plain text. For example, you can edit the HTML and JavaScript source code of Web pages using Notepad. In the unlikely event that you need to edit some important system text file, such as a batch file (`.bat`), initialization file (`.ini`), or log file (`.log`), Notepad is your best bet because it won't put any weird invisible formatting characters that might otherwise cause the file (and possibly your entire computer) from functioning correctly.

To start Notepad, click the Start button and choose All Programs ➪ Accessories ➪ Notepad. When Notepad first opens, it shows a blank page. If you want to use Notepad to edit a specific file, you can right-click that file's icon and choose Open With ➪ Notepad. Notepad opens with the text file already displayed and ready for editing. For example, Figure 22-3 shows the source code (HTML and JavaScript) for a Web page.

Caution   If you open a non-text file with Notepad, you'll see a bunch of weird looking characters. *Do not* save that file! Choose File ➪ Exit and then choose No if asked about saving any changes to the document.

When you're in Notepad, you can type text in much the same way you type on paper. When you finish typing a line of text, press Enter to move to the next line.

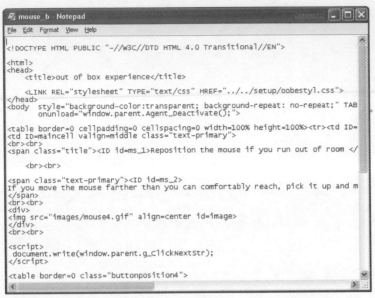

Figure 22-3: Notepad showing the source code of a Web page
(`.htm` file)

To edit (change) text, use the standard techniques discussed under "Changing Text" in Chapter 2. In addition, you can do the following:

✦ Press Enter as necessary to insert blank lines.

✦ To delete a blank line, move the blinking cursor to the blank line you want to delete and then press the Delete (Del) key.

✦ To type the current date and time into the document, choose Edit ➪ Time/Date.

✦ To locate a particular word or phrase in the document, choose Edit ➪ Find from Notepad's menu bar, type whatever it is you're looking for, and then click the Find Next button.

✦ To print the current document, choose File ➪ Print from Notepad's menu bar. Or, you can choose File ➪ Page Setup to choose a specific printer, paper size, and other print options.

To save your work, choose File ➪ Save from Notepad's menu bar and then enter a file name. Notepad automatically adds a `.txt` extension to whatever name you provide. As always, you can get additional help by choosing Help ➪ Help Topics from Notepad's menu bar. And, as always, you can close Notepad when you're done by clicking its Close (X) button, or by choosing File ➪ Exit from its menu bar.

Using WordPad

WordPad is another handy applet for working with text. Unlike Notepad, however, which creates plain, simple text files, WordPad can help you create true word processing documents with fonts, boldface, and other print features. To start WordPad, click the Start button and choose All Programs ➪ Accessories ➪ WordPad. A fresh, new page for typing and editing displays.

Note　　WordPad is actually a trimmed-down and simplified version of Microsoft Word, a program you can purchase separately.

Typing in WordPad is much the same as typing on paper. One important difference exists, however: When typing a paragraph, you do not want to press Enter at the end of each line. Instead, keep typing right past the right margin. The text automatically word wraps (break between two words). Press Enter only at the end of the paragraph. You can press Enter twice if you want to insert a blank line.

While typing in WordPad, you'll notice a blinking vertical line near where you're typing. That's called the *insertion point* or *cursor* and shows where the next text you type will appear. You can move the cursor around through any existing text using the arrow keys on your keyboard. You also can make the cursor jump to a specific character in your text by clicking that character with your mouse.

Fonts and formatting in WordPad

Fonts are styles of print that you can use to give your document some character. Like virtually all programs you'll ever use, WordPad works on the "select, then do" principle for applying fonts. To change the font of a chunk of text you've typed, for example, first select that text by dragging the mouse pointer across it. Then you can choose a font from the Fonts drop-down list in the toolbar and a size from the font Size drop-down list. Optionally, you can choose Format ➪ Font from WordPad's menu bar and choose your font and size from the Fonts dialog box that opens.

You also can apply boldface, italics, underlining, and a font color to the selected text using other buttons on the toolbar, or the Fonts dialog box. The toolbar also provides buttons for aligning text to the left or right margin and centering text. You can even select two or more lines of typed text and make them into a bulleted list by clicking the Bullets button in the toolbar. Figure 22-4 shows a sample document where I have used some of these formatting features in WordPad.

Tip　　If you're not sure what a button in WordPad's toolbar is for, point to the button and then read its description in the status bar at the bottom of WordPad's window.

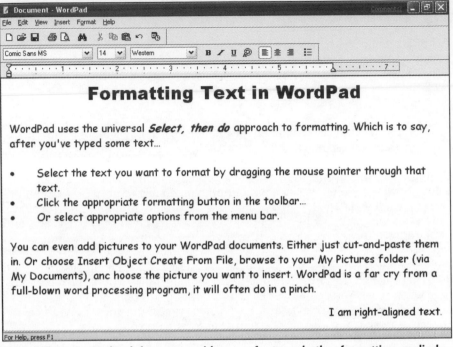

Figure 22-4: A WordPad document with some fonts and other formatting applied to the text

Editing in WordPad

To make changes to text in WordPad, click anywhere that you want to type new text and just start typing. To delete text, first select the text you want to delete by dragging the mouse pointer through it. Then press the Delete (Del) key. You also can use the Delete and Backspace keys to delete text to the right or left (respectively) of the cursor.

If you make a change to your document that you decide you don't like, choose Edit ➪ Undo from WordPad's menu bar to undo the change. To move text in a WordPad document, select the text you want to move. Then drag that selected text to wherever you want to place it.

Printing and saving in WordPad

To print the document you're editing in WordPad, choose File ➪ Print from WordPad's menu bar. Or, click the Print button on the toolbar. To save your document, click the Save button on the toolbar or choose File ➪ Save from WordPad's menu bar.

I show you more examples of working with WordPad in the following sections. Meanwhile, if you ever need help while you're working in WordPad, look into its Help. Press F1 or choose Help ➪ Help Topics from WordPad's menu bar.

Using Character Map

Character Map is a handy applet for typing special characters not found on the keyboard — such as (c) for copyright and (r) for registered trademark and _ for summation. Character Map works with any application that supports special characters, including WordPad. To use Character Map while you're typing a document, follow these steps:

1. Click the Start button and choose All Programs ➪ Accessories ➪ System Tools ➪ Character Map.

2. Use the Font drop-down list to choose a font. (Different fonts offer different characters to choose from.) In Figure 22-5, for example, I chose the Wingdings fonts, which offers all kinds of symbols.

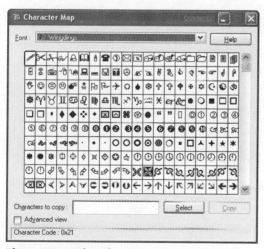

Figure 22-5: The Character Map applet with the Wingdings font selected

3. To get a close-up look at a character, point to the character you want to inspect and then hold down the primary mouse button.

4. To select a character, click it and then click the Select button. The Characters to copy text box will show the character to be copied. You can repeat this step to select as many characters as you want.

5. To paste the character(s) into your document, first click any visible portion of the document's program window or the program's taskbar button to make it the active widow. Then, in the document, right-click where you want to place the character(s) and choose Paste.

If you want to change the size of the pasted characters, select them by dragging the mouse pointer through them. Then choose a new size from the Font Size drop-down list in WordPad's toolbar. Or, choose Format ⇨ Font and select a new size from the Fonts dialog box that opens.

Using Image Preview

Image Preview is an applet that pops up on its own when you open a graphics image (or fax) that isn't associated with any other graphics program. You also can open any picture in Image Preview by right-clicking the picture's icon and choosing Preview. To open several images at once, select the image's icons in any Explorer window. Then right-click any selected icon and choose Preview. One picture will appear within Image Preview, as in the example shown in Figure 22-6.

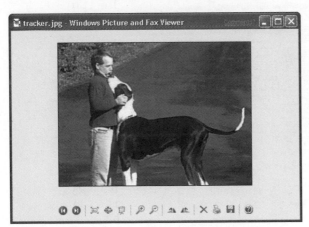

Figure 22-6: The Image Preview applet displaying a photograph

Buttons in the toolbar across the top of the window provide some rudimentary options for working with the image. To get an idea of what a specific button does, just point to the button for a moment. Here's what the buttons offer:

✦ **Previous Image/ Next Image:** If several pictures are open, enables you to view the next or previous image.

✦ **Best Fit:** Displays the picture at the largest size possible within the window.

✦ **Actual Size:** Shows the picture at its actual size.

✦ **Start Slide Show:** Starts a full-screen slide show of all the pictures in the current folder. Clicking the Close (X) button near the upper-right corner of the screen returns you to the viewer.

✦ **Zoom In:** Clicking this button turns the mouse pointer into a little magnifying glass. Click any part of the picture to zoom in on that spot.

✦ **Zoom Out:** Does the opposite of Zoom In.

✦ **Rotate Clockwise:** Rotates the picture clockwise 90 degrees.

✦ **Rotate Counterclockwise:** Rotates the picture counterclockwise 90 degrees.

✦ **Delete:** Deletes the image file from your disk.

Caution

The Delete button does *not* just remove the picture from the Image Preview window—it actually deletes the file from your hard disk!

✦ **Print:** Prints the picture.

✦ **Copy to:** Enables you to save a copy of the image to your hard disk with any file name you want.

✦ **Edit:** Closes the viewer and opens the picture in an editing program, such as Paint.

✦ **Help:** Brings up the Help for Image Preview, where you can learn more about the program.

As with any window, you can close Image Preview by clicking the Close (X) button in its upper-right corner.

Editing Pictures with Paint

Whereas Image Preview just lets you look at images, Paint enables you to change them. As WordPad is to full-blown word processing programs, Paint is to full-blown graphics programs — it's a scaled-down version with just a handful of features. To start Paint, click the Start button and choose All Programs ⇨ Accessories ⇨ Paint. Initially, you are taken to a blank canvas within the program.

You can actually draw in Paint. First choose a line color by clicking the color you want down in the little color palette near the bottom of the window. You also can choose a fill color, which comes into play when drawing filled shapes, by right-clicking any of the colors in the palette. Then pick a drawing tool from the left side of the window. If you're interested in learning how to draw with Paint, choose Help ⇨ Help Topics from its menu bar and then click any book that appears in the contents pane at the left of the Help window.

Getting Pictures into Paint

For those of us who can't draw worth beans, Paint can serve as a tool for working with existing pictures and photographs. Suppose, for example, that you're browsing through some pictures in your My Pictures folder and you see a picture you want to edit or crop or whatever. To open the picture in Paint, you can right-click its icon (or thumbnail) and then choose Open With ⇨ Paint from the shortcut menu that pops up. Or, you can start Paint from the Start menu (Start ⇨ All Programs ⇨ Accessories ⇨ Paint.) Then choose File ⇨ Open from its menu bar to open any picture file.

You can often use Paint to edit pictures that aren't even on your hard disk. Suppose, for example, that you're browsing the Web with Internet Explorer and come across a picture or photo that you want to have a copy of. All you need to do is start up Paint from the Start button. Then, in Internet Explorer right-click the picture you're interested in and choose Copy. Then go back to Paint and choose Edit ⇨ Paste from its menu bar.

 Note   Of course, I'm not condoning swiping copyrighted pictures off of Web sites. I assume you'll use the utmost caution to make sure you don't break any copyright laws when you cut-and-paste into Paint.

If all else fails, you can take a snapshot of the screen and then paste that into Paint, as discussed under "Printing the Screen," later in this chapter. Then crop out anything you don't want in your final picture.

Nothing much seems to happen, but the snapshot of the screen is in the Windows Clipboard at this point. To paste it into Paint, choose Edit ⇨ Paste from Paint's menu bar.

Rotating pictures in Paint

If you hold the camera sideways when taking a picture with a digital camera, the image you see on your screen will also be sideways, such as the example shown in Figure 22-7.

To rotate the image upright, follow these steps:

1. Choose Image ⇨ Flip/Rotate from Paint's menu bar.

2. In the Flip and Rotate dialog box that appears, choose Rotate by Angle.

3. Choose 90° and then click the OK button.

The image rotates accordingly, as in Figure 22-8. If your image turns upside down, choose Image ⇨ Flip/Rotate ⇨ Flip Vertical.

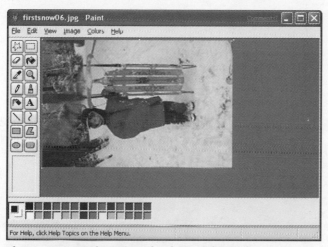

Figure 22-7: A photo in Paint, before flipping it

Figure 22-8: A photo in Paint after rotating it 90 degrees

Cropping pictures in Paint

Another common problem with photographs is when the picture is taken from too far away, leaving a whole lot of extra background that's perhaps not all that relevant to the real subject of the photo. In this case, the solution is to crop the picture by just cutting out any unwanted background. To crop a picture in Paint, follow these steps:

1. Click the Rectangular Selection tool on the toolbar at the left side of Paint's window. (It is the upper-right button.)

2. Point to any corner where you want to begin the cropping and then drag a frame around that portion of the image you want to keep, as in the example shown in Figure 22-9.

Figure 22-9: Here I've dragged a selection rectangle around a portion of a photo.

3. Choose Edit ⇨ Copy from Paint's menu bar. A copy of the selected portion of the picture is placed in the Windows Clipboard.

4. Open another instance of Paint by clicking the Windows Start button and choosing All Programs ⇨ Accessories ⇨ Paint. The new instance of Paint opens with a blank canvas. The rest of the steps must take place in this new Paint window.

5. Choose Image ⇨ Attributes from the menu bar. Set the Width and Height each to 1, to minimize the size of the canvas. Click the OK button.

6. Choose Edit ⇨ Paste from the menu bar. The cropped image appears as in Figure 22-10.

Now you can choose File ⇨ Save to save the new, cropped copy of the image with a new file name.

Figure 22-10: The cropped image in Paint

If you plan to edit a lot of pictures, do not rely too much on Paint as your editor. As mentioned, it's a far cry from a true graphics editing program. If you happen to have Microsoft Office XP, you will be much better off using the Photo Editor program that comes with that program suite. I point out some other options in the next chapter, as the discussion delves deeper into working with pictures.

Cut-and-Paste between Documents

You might have noticed most of the sample applets support a particular type of document or information. For instance, Calculator is used to do math with numbers. WordPad and Notepad both focus on written text. And Paint is dedicated to working with pictures. Which brings up the question, "What if I want to create a written document with a picture in it?" Good question!

The way you move elements (text, graphics, and so on) from one document or program into another is called cut-and-paste, or copy-and-paste. To do this, follow these steps:

1. Select whatever you want to move or copy, using the following as your guideline:

   • To select text, drag the mouse pointer through the text you want to select.

- To select a single picture, click it once.

- To select the number currently showing in Calculator, choose Edit ➪ Copy from Calculator's menu bar.

- To select an entire document or picture, choose Edit ➪ Select All from the program's menu bar.

2. When the item is selected, choose Edit ➪ Copy from the program's menu bar or press Ctrl+C. A copy of the selection goes into the Windows Clipboard.

Note   You cannot copy a picture from Image Preview into the Windows Clipboard. You have to open the image in Paint or some other graphics program instead. You cannot really paste text into a picture either. However, you can paste a picture or a number into text.

3. In the document in which you want to place the picture or number, click at about where you want to insert the copy. Then press Ctrl+V or choose Edit ➪ Copy from that program's menu bar, or right-click the spot where you want to paste and choose Paste from the pop-up menu.

Let me show you an example. Figure 22-11 shows two separate documents in two separate programs — a graphic image in Paint and some text typed in WordPad.

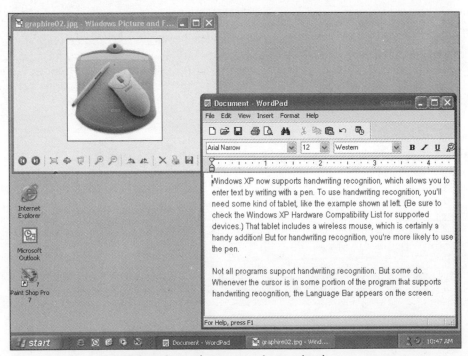

Figure 22-11: A picture in Paint and some text in WordPad

Suppose you want to put a copy of the picture inside the written document in WordPad. It's not too difficult. Just follow these steps:

1. In Paint, choose Edit ➪ Select All to select the picture. Then choose Edit ➪ Copy to copy it to the Windows Clipboard.

2. In WordPad, click at about where you want to place the picture. In my example, I clicked near the upper-left corner of the document.

3. Press Ctrl+V or choose Edit ➪ Paste from WordPad's menu bar.

4. The picture is pasted and also has sizing handles. You can drag any corner or edge to size the picture.

Figure 22-12 shows the results. It's not ideal. Figure 22-13 shows a Microsoft Word document with lots of pictures thrown in. As you can probably guess, Word gives you much better control over the exact size and placement of the pictures within a document. The important point is, however, the basic cut-and-paste techniques described here will work in virtually every Windows program you ever use. So do keep them in mind!

Figure 22-12: The picture has been pasted in the WordPad document.

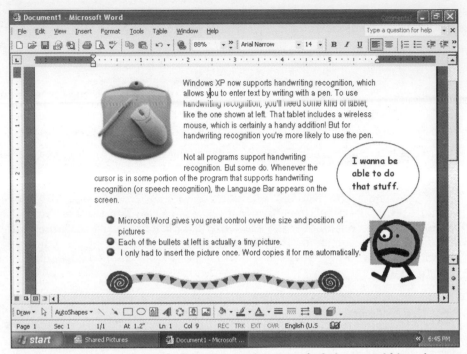

Figure 22-13: Microsoft Word offers very precise control of pictures within a document.

I should also point out that as an alternative to the Clipboard, you can use *scraps*, discussed in Chapter 28, to move and copy material from one document to another.

Printing the Screen

In the olden days of DOS, you would print whatever was on your screen by pressing the Print Screen (Prnt Scrn) key on your keyboard. In Windows, this works a little differently. First you capture the screen to the Windows Clipboard. Then you can paste it into Paint or any other graphics program and print it from there.

You can capture the screen in two ways:

✦ Press the Print Screen key if you want to capture the entire screen.

✦ Hold down the Alt key and press Print Screen if you want to capture only the current window (whichever window on the screen has the colored title bar).

Nothing appears to happen, but the Windows Clipboard receives a copy of the screen or window. You can verify this by opening the Clipboard Viewer, if you like. To print or save this image, you need to open Paint or some other graphics program and then choose Edit ⇨ Paste from that program's menu bar. A copy of the image will be loaded into the graphics program.

At this point, the screen capture is like any other graphics image. You can edit it by using the graphics program. You can save it by choosing File ⇨ Save or print it by choosing File ⇨ Print from the graphics program's menu bar.

Summary

In this chapter, you learned about some of the applets that come with Windows XP, as well as some general ways to move and copy stuff from one document to another. Here's a quick recap of the important points covered in this chapter:

✦ The Windows applets provide some simple tools for working with numbers, text, and pictures.

✦ The Calculator applet works like a standard pocket calculator.

✦ The Notepad applet is good for working with plain, unformatted text.

✦ The WordPad applet is a miniature word processing program capable of displaying fancy text, fonts, pictures, and special characters.

✦ The Character Map applet enables you to insert special characters — characters not normally found on the keyboard — into a document.

✦ The Paint applet enables you to draw pictures and to perform some rudimentary editing on photographs and other graphics images.

✦ To put something into the Windows Clipboard, select the thing to move/copy and then choose Edit ⇨ Copy or Edit ⇨ Cut from this program's menu bar.

✦ To copy something from the Clipboard into another document, click at about where you want to place the object. Then choose Edit ⇨ Paste from that program's menu bar, or right-click and choose Paste.

✦ Keyboard alternatives for cut-and-paste are as follows: Ctrl+C copies the selection to the Clipboard, Ctrl+X moves the selection to the Clipboard, and Ctrl+V pastes the Clipboard contents at the current cursor position.

✦ Use the Print Screen and Alt+Print Screen keys to puts screenshots in the Windows Clipboard. Then paste the snapshot into any graphics program by choosing Edit ⇨ Paste.

✦   ✦   ✦

Cameras, Scanners, and Faxes

Windows XP has made working with pictures easier (and more fun) than ever. You can get pictures onto your computer from a wide variety of sources, including cameras, scanners, faxes, screen shots, and clip art. All pictures, regardless of their source, are referred to as *digital images* in tech talk. Regardless of where a digital image originated, the tools and techniques for working with them are pretty much the same. Chapter 22 has already discussed some of the basics of working with pictures. This chapter goes much deeper into the subject to give you total mastery of working with the many different types of digital images you're likely to come across.

Pictures Are Documents

Every picture (digital image) on your computer is a document stored in a file. There are lots of different programs available for working with digital images. You met two of them that come with Windows XP in Chapter 22: Image Preview and Paint. If you happen to own Microsoft Office XP, you might also have Microsoft Photo Editor installed on your computer, which provides some basic editing capabilities for working with pictures. Many third-party graphics programs provide even greater picture-editing capabilities. For example, Jasc's Paint Shop Pro (www.jasc.com) is a very high-powered yet easy to use program that gives you total control over virtually all types of images (as well as animations). Adobe's PhotoShop (www.adobe.com) is another high-powered program for working with pictures.

Like any document file, digital images can be stored in any folder on any disk. To give you a little help in keeping your pictures organized and some extra tools for working with images,

Windows comes with the following two folders already created on your hard disk for storing your pictures.

✦ **My Pictures:** Stores pictures you want to keep private. Other people who use this computer (as well as other people who have access to this computer) can't see your `My Pictures` folder. Your `My Pictures` folder is inside your `My Documents` folder

✦ **Shared Pictures:** Stores pictures that all users of this computer (as well as other people who have access to this computer through a network) can see the `Shared Pictures` folder is inside the `Shared Documents` folder.

Windows provides several handy shortcuts for opening both folders. To get to My Pictures, for example, you can just click the Start button and choose My Pictures. Or, if My Pictures isn't on your Start menu, open My Documents, and then open the My Pictures icon in Explorer's window. When you are in the My Pictures folder, you can jump to the Shared Pictures folder by choosing Shared Pictures from Other Places in the Explorer bar.

You can easily move or copy pictures between the two folders by opening them both, and dragging the picture icons from one folder to the other. When you are in the My Pictures folder, for example, clicking Shared Pictures takes you to that folder. Then, choosing My Pictures from the Start menu again opens that folder in a separate Explorer window. From there you can just size and position the two Explorer windows as in the example shown in Figure 23-1.

Figure 23-1: The My Pictures and Shared Pictures folders both open on the desktop

Here are some quick tips to give yourself easy access to both folders:

✦ If My Pictures isn't an option on your Start menu, you can add it by right-clicking the Start button and choosing Properties. Click the Customize button. Under Start Menu Items on the Advanced tab, choose Display as Link under My Pictures.

Cross-Reference

For more information on customizing your Start menu, see "Reorganizing Your Start Menu" in Chapter 13. See Chapter 4 for more information on creating desktop shortcuts.

✦ To create a desktop shortcut to your My Pictures folder, open My Documents. Then right-drag the My Pictures icon out to the desktop, release the right mouse button, and choose Create Shortcuts Here. You can use the same technique to create a Quick Launch toolbar shortcut to the folder.

✦ To create a desktop shortcut to your Shared Pictures folder, open Shared Documents. Then right-drag the Shared Pictures icon out to the desktop, release the right mouse button, and choose Create Shortcuts Here. You can use the same technique to create a Quick Launch toolbar shortcut to the folder.

Explorer views of pictures

As you learned back in Chapter 3, Explorer offers several ways to view the contents of a folder. You can choose a view from the View menu in the Explorer menu bar or the Views button on the toolbar. Two of the available views are especially well suited to folders that contain a lot of pictures:

✦ **Thumbnails:** Displays each picture as a small "thumbnail" image. Subfolders appear as manila file folders with small images of pictures within the subfolder. Both My Pictures and Shared Folders back in Figure 23-1 are currently in Thumbnails view.

✦ **Filmstrip:** Images within the folder appear as thumbnails along the bottom of the Explorer window. The currently selected image is enlarged above the thumbnails, as in Figure 23-2. Buttons beneath the large image enable you to scroll through images, zoom in, zoom out, and rotate the current image.

Note

Files that don't contain pictures, or contain pictures in formats that Windows XP doesn't recognize, display as icons in Thumbnails and Filmstrip views.

A third option is to view the pictures as a slide show. This option isn't available from the View menu or Views button. Instead, you choose View as Slide Show from the Picture Tasks lists in the Explorer bar. As the name implies, each picture from the folder appears on the screen, full size, for a few seconds, as shown in Figure 23-3. (This makes for a great screensaver!) A toolbar in the upper-right corner provides buttons for starting, pausing, and stopping the slide show, as well as for scrolling to the next or preceding picture. The toolbar will actually disappear within a few seconds. As soon as you move the mouse, however, it will reappear. Clicking the Close (X) button on the toolbar ends the slide show and takes you back to where you left off.

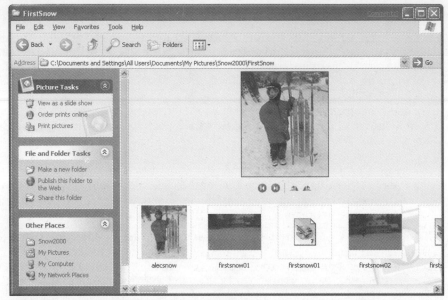

Figure 23-2: The Filmstrip view of a folder that contains pictures

Figure 23-3: One picture from a slide show

Customizing picture folders

In Thumbnails view, subfolders that contain pictures usually display four tiny images from pictures within the subfolder. As you add, move, and delete pictures, those tiny images might get out of sync with the current contents of the folder. To bring the tiny pictures up-to-date with the folder's current contents, right-click the folder's icon and choose Refresh Thumbnail.

Built-in folders such as My Pictures already have certain default settings that determine how the contents of the folder will be displayed. For folders that you create yourself, you can choose how the folder's contents are displayed. First select the icon(s) for the folder(s) you want to change using any of the selection methods described under "Select, Then Do" in Chapter 12. Then choose View ➪ Customize This Folder from the Explorer menu bar. (Optionally, you can right-click the icon, choose Properties, and then click the Customize tab.) The folder's Properties dialog box opens. On the Customize tab, you'll see the options shown in Figure 23-4.

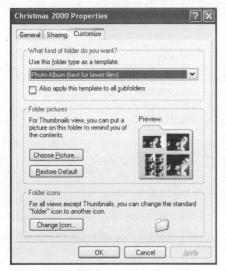

Figure 23-4: The Customize tab for a folder

The drop-down list near the top of the dialog box provides the following two options that are especially relevant to folders that contain a lot of pictures:

✦ **Pictures (best for many files):** Sets the default view for the folder when it's first opened to Thumbnails.

✦ **Photo Album (best for fewer files):** Sets the default view for the folder when it's first opened to Filmstrip.

You can opt to apply your choice to all subfolders within the folder you're currently customizing.

Under Folder Pictures, you have two options:

✦ **Choose Picture:** Enables you to replace the four tiny pictures with a single larger picture from the file.

✦ **Restore Default:** Returns you to the four tiny pictures look.

The last option, Folder Icons, enables you to change the icon for the folder. However, it has no effect on the Thumbnails view of the folder.

Picture Tasks

The Picture Tasks options at the top of the Explorer bar enable you to perform some basic tasks with the selected pictures in the folder. I already described the View as Slide Show task earlier in the chapter.

 Even though thumbnails look different from regular icons, they're still icons. And you can select them using any of the techniques described under "Select, Then Do" in Chapter 12.

Here's a quick summary of the other available options:

✦ **Get Pictures from Camera or Scanner:** Available only if you have a camera, Web cam, or scanner attached to your computer, this option starts a wizard that enables you to get pictures from any of those devices. See "Getting the Picture" later in this chapter for more.

✦ **Order Prints Online:** Starts up a wizard that enables you to order prints, in a variety of formats, from a service provider on the Internet.

✦ **Print Pictures:** Starts a wizard that enables you to print the selected pictures in any of a variety of sizes ranging from full page to tiny stickers.

✦ **Set as Desktop Background:** This task is available only when a single picture within the folder is selected and the picture is in BMP, GIF, JPG, JPEG, DIB, or PNG format. Choosing this option sets your desktop background image to the selected picture.

 If you choose the third option, but then change your mind, you can right-click the desktop, choose Properties, and then select another picture, or no picture, from the Desktop tab in the Display Properties dialog box that opens.

Opening Pictures

Clicking (or double-clicking) a picture's icon opens that picture in the default program for viewing that type of picture. The default program might be Image Preview, or it might be Microsoft Photo Editor if Microsoft Office 2000 is installed. It really doesn't matter which is the default, however, because if you have multiple graphics programs installed, you can choose which program you want to open the picture by following these simple steps:

1. Right-click the icon for the picture you want to open.

Tip

With some graphics programs, you can select several images to open before right-clicking and choosing Open With. The program will then open all the selected images.

2. Choose Open With from the pop-up menu to reveal the submenu shown in Figure 23-5.

3. Select the program you want to use to work with the picture. Or, select the Choose Program option for a larger list of programs from which to choose.

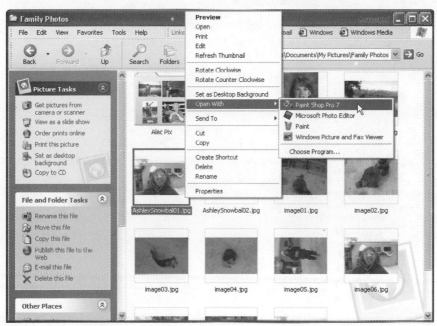

Figure 23-5: The Open With submenu on one of my computers

If you ever want to change the default program used for opening a picture when you open its icon, see Chapter 30.

Maximizing Picture Quality

As you know, the Print This Picture or Print Pictures task from an Explorer window enables you to print any selected pictures from a folder, without going through any special program. You should be aware, however, that many printers give you a choice of print qualities to select from for your printed pictures, ranging from "draft" (fast, but low quality) to "high" (slow, but good quality.) When you print from some program by choosing File ⇨ Print, the Print dialog box opens. If you see a Properties button in that Print dialog box, you can adjust features that are unique to your make and model of printer. When I print a picture from Paint Shop Pro and click the Properties button in its Print dialog box, for example, I come to the options shown in Figure 23-6. As the title bar of the dialog box implies, these are features that are unique to my HP OfficeJet R80 printer.

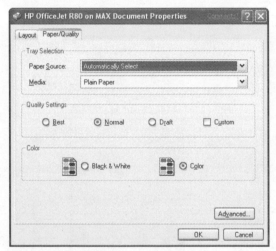

Figure 23-6: The Properties dialog box for my HP printer lets me choose a print quality, among other options.

The default settings, Plain Paper and Normal quality, give me decent picture output. If I choose HP Premium Photo Paper from the Media drop-down list (and put that type of paper in the printer), and choose Best under Quality Settings, however, I get *much* better results!

Tip   Even the modest Paint program that comes with Windows XP enables me to choose a paper and print quality on my HP OfficeJet printer. In its Print dialog box, however, I have to click the Preferences button rather than the Properties button.

The color depth of your desktop has a big impact on the size and quality of images as they appear on your screen. Basically, the higher the color depth, the better photos and such will look. You can set the color depth of your screen by right-clicking the desktop and choosing Properties. On the Settings tab, the higher you set the Color Quality option, the better your photos will look.

Chapter 14 describes Display Properties settings in depth.

Now for Some Technical Stuff

Windows XP has made working with digital images easier than ever. You can accomplish a lot without knowing much about all the technical behind-the-scenes stuff that goes into making pictures work. If you ever plan to get serious about working with digital images, however, it will definitely help to know some of the technicalities involved. There's a lot more going on than at first meets the eye. For starters, there is not just one "type" of file used for all types of pictures. To the contrary, there are a whole lot of them.

Digital image file types

Perhaps the most perplexing thing about digital images is the wide range of file formats used to store these images. Table 23-1 lists types of image files and the file name extensions typically used to name images stored in each format.

Table 23-1 Some of the File Formats Used for Storing Digital Images	
Format	**Filename Extension**
Amiga	.iff
Autodesk Drawing Interchange	.dxf
CompuServe Graphics Interchange	.gif
Computer Graphics Metafile	.cgm
Corel Clipart	.cmx
CorelDraw Drawing	.cdr
Deluxe Paint	.lbm
Dr. Halo	.cut
Encapsulated PostScript	.eps, .ai, .ps
FlashPix	.fpx
GEM Paint	.img
HP Graphics Language	.hgl
Joint Photographic Experts Group	.jpg, .jif, .jpeg
Kodak Digital Camera	.kdc

Continued

Table 23-1 *(continued)*

Format	Filename Extension
Kodak Photo CD	.pcd
Lotus PIC	.pic
Macintosh PICT	.pct
MacPaint	.mac
Micrografx Draw	.drw
Microsoft Paint	.msp
Paint Shop Pro	.psp
PC Paint	.pic
Photoshop	.psd
Portable Bitmap	.pbm
Portable Greymap	.pgm
Portable Network Graphics	.png
Portable Pixelmap	.ppm
Raw File Format	.raw
SciTex Continuous Tone	.sct, .ct
Sun RasterImage	.ras
Tagged Image File Format	.tif, .tiff
Truevision Targa	.tga
Ventura/GEM Drawing	.gem
Windows Clipboard	.clp
Windows Enhanced Metafile	.emf
Windows Metafile	.wmf
Windows or CompuServe RLE	.rle
Windows or OS/2 Bitmap	.pmp
Windows or OS/2 Device Independent Bitmap	.dib
WordPerfect Bitmap or Vector	.wpg
Zsoft Multipage Paintbrush	.dcx
Zsoft Paintbrush	.pcx

Normally, Windows XP hides file name extensions from you, so you might not know what format a particular image is stored in. If your My Pictures folder already contains a bunch of pictures and you view that folder in Thumbnails view, for example, you'll see thumbnails of the images along with their file names. If you switch to the Tiles view (by choosing View ➪ Tiles from the Explorer menu bar), each image's type is shown along with the name. In Figure 23-7, for example, each icon represents a picture. However, even though each is a picture, their icons and descriptions vary quite a bit. Some are KDC files, some are Paint Shop Pro 7 images, as well as some TIF and WMF images.

Figure 23-7: Icons for some digital images in Tiles view

You might notice that the file names in Figure 23-7 are also displaying the usually hidden file name extensions, such as .kdc, .psp, .wmf, and .tif. To view file name extensions, choose Tools ➪ Folder Options from the Explorer menu bar. On the View tab, clear the Hide file extensions for known file types check box.

Bitmap versus vector images

Despite the many different file formats and extensions, digital image formats can be broken down into two main categories: *bitmap* images and *vector* images. Bitmap images are made up of tiny colored dots, which you can see if you look at an image with a magnifying glass. The bitmap file essentially just stores information about the color of each dot. The vast majority of image files, including those from cameras and scanners, are bitmap images.

Vector images store information about the size, curvature, and length of lines in the drawing, as well as color information. Vector images are relatively rare, and created only with illustration programs used by professional artists. In other words some—but not all—line drawings and other hand-drawn art images are stored in vector file format. Although a handful of programs can read and write only one type of image or the other, plenty of programs can read and write both types.

Image quality and file size

When computer people talk about image quality, they're not talking about whether an image is "good" (the subject is smiling) or "bad" (the subject has one eye closed and is drooling). They're talking about the *resolution* (the nubmer of dots per inch) and *color depth* (the number of unique colors) contained within the image. Simply stated, the higher the resolution and color depth, the higher the "quality" of the image. The reason it matters is that the higher the quality of the image, the larger the file required to store the image. And the larger the file, the more disk space it eats up and the longer it takes to transmit across a wire, as on a network like the Internet.

An image's resolution is measured in dots per inch (dpi). The term *dot* here is synonymous with *pixel* — one tiny little dot on a computer screen or printed page. If you look at a computer monitor or printed page with a strong enough magnifying glass, you can see that all images are actually made up of tiny dots. The advantage of using a high resolution (lots of dots per inch) is that you get a sharper, crisper image and the dots sort of "disappear." (You probably never thought of your computer screen as an array of lighted dots — but it is!)

Color depth refers to the number of unique colors in the image. As an example of an image with a low color depth, think again of a comic strip in a newspaper. Because there is no shading in such images, the cartoonist can get away with using only a few unique colors. In some cases, only 16 unique colors is sufficient. In others, 256 colors are required.

Since each dot's color needs to be stored as part of the graphic image's file, the more possible colors there are in the image, the more *bits* of information it takes to define each color. A *bit* is the smallest unit of information a computer can work with. The bit can have only two possible values, either "on" (or 1) or "off" (or 0). Therefore, if you use one bit to store information about colors, you get only two choices of colors, 0 or 1. Those two values translate to black and white. So if the entire image requires a million dots to render, but there are only two possible colors per dot, the image could be expressed with exactly 1 million bits — one bit per dot.

Suppose, however, that the image needs at least 16 unique colors. In that case, you need four bits of data to define each dot's color. Why four? Because if you look at all the combination of four bits where each bit can be either 1 or 0 — 0000, 0001, 0011, 0010, 1111 — you end up with 16 possible combinations of 1s and 0s. Therefore, if the picture contains a million bits and requires four bits to express the color of each dot, the picture requires four million bits (or 500,000 bytes — 4 million bits / 8-bits) of disk space to store — which makes the file four times as large as the image in pure black and white.

If the picture requires 256 unique colors, you need eight bits of information to store each unique color value. Hence a picture with a million dots would then require 8 million bits of information—eight times the amount of disk space required by the black-and-white picture containing a million bits. The real world contains many millions of colors. Hence, a photograph of the real world will also contain many millions of colors. To be able to express the color of each dot in a photograph containing millions of colors, you might need 24 bits, or 32 bits of information to express each color. So a graphic image file that contains a million dots will require 24 million, or 32 million bits of disk space (3 million or 4 million bytes, respectively).

For graphics professionals, size often equates to cost. The bigger the file, the more disk space it eats up, and the longer it takes to print, transmit across a network, and so forth. Disk space and time cost money. So when you're dealing with thousands of images, you're naturally inclined to try to use the smallest file size possible—but not at the expense of totally ruining the image. As a somewhat extreme example of how color depth will affect the quality and file size of an image, Figure 23-8 shows an example of a photograph at 1-, 4-, and 24-bit resolutions. The 1-bit photo's file is a tiny 2.5K in size, although it's severely lacking in detail. The 24-bit (16-million color) image looks best, but is considerably larger, file-size-wise, at 65.8K color. As you can see, no setting helps the "quality" of that goofy-looking smile!

Note   The 1-bit black-and-white resolution really is just black and white, with no shades of gray in between. What we call "black and white" in TV and photographs is really called *grayscale*. The images in this book are grayscale.

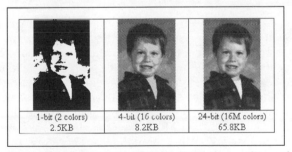

| 1-bit (2 colors) | 4-bit (16 colors) | 24-bit (16M colors) |
| 2.5KB | 8.2KB | 65.8KB |

Figure 23-8: How color depth affects the quality and file size of a photograph

GIF and JPEG

Two of the most widely used image formats today are GIF (CompuServe Graphics Interchange Format) and JPEG (Joint Photographic Experts Group). Their popularity stems from the fact that they were the first image types supported on the Internet. The GIF format provides for a nice, small file size, which is ideal for transmitting pictures across the Internet. GIF also enables the creator to define one color as "transparent," allowing the image to have a transparent background in the example shown in Figure 23-9. The only problem with GIF is that it's limited to an 8-bit pixel depth (256 colors), which doesn't cut it for photographs. The JPEG format, on the other hand, allows for millions of colors and is therefore used for publishing photographs on the Web.

Paths to My Pictures and Shared Pictures

It's pretty easy to get to `My Pictures` and `Shared Pictures` in Windows XP, as well as in XP-aware programs. When you start using XP-unaware programs, however, their Open and Save dialog boxes might not have quick and easy options for jumping to those folders. In fact, you might not even be able to find a folder named `Shared Pictures`. That's because `My Pictures` and `Shared Pictures` are really "shortcuts" to the actual folders.

The "true" path to My Pictures is `C:\Documents and Settings\`*your user name*`\My Documents\My Pictures`, where *your user name* is the name you logged on with. The path to Shared Pictures is `C:\Documents and Settings\All Users\Shared Documents\Shared Pictures`.

Whether you'll ever really need to navigate through those folder sequences, I can't say. But in case you ever do, at least you know where to look now!

Installing Cameras and Scanners

As you probably know, a digital camera is like any other camera—except that there is no film. Instead, the photos you take are stored electronically inside the camera. To view the photos, you need to *download* them to your PC, where each photo is stored as a file. A scanner is sort of like a camera, although it doesn't have a lens. Instead, you lay down some piece of paper that you want to *digitize* (copy to a digital image), and scan the image. The two processes might not seem very similar. In both cases, however, you're taking a picture of something, and sending that picture to a file on the computer's disk. From a Windows XP perspective, both tasks are just a matter of downloading digital images and putting them in files. Therefore, the techniques for downloading digital images from a camera and for acquiring digital images from scanners are very similar in Windows XP. In fact, scanners and cameras are generally lumped together under the generic term *imaging devices*.

The procedures for installing the two different types of devices are similar as well. Your best bet for installing any hardware device is always to refer to the manufacturer's instructions first. If the device was created before Windows XP was released, however, you might not see instructions specifically for installing in Windows XP. As such, you can try the generic techniques described here to see whether Windows XP has its own drivers for the device. If it does, you might be better off using the newer Windows XP drivers than the drivers that shipped with your imaging device.

Cross-Reference As discussed in Chapter 17, a driver is a small program that tells your operating system (Windows XP) how to use a piece of hardware.

The easiest way to check for Windows XP drivers is to try to install the device without using the manufacturer's drivers. How you get started depends on a couple of factors:

✦ If the device plugs into a USB or IEEE 1394 (FireWire) port, there's no need to shut down the computer. Instead, connect the cable to the device, turn on the device, and then plug the device into the appropriate port on the computer.

✦ If the device connects through some other port, you should shut down Windows and then connect the cable to the device and to the computer as well. Then restart the computer.

Keep an eye on the Notification area of the taskbar. If Windows recognizes the new device, it will install the appropriate drivers and display a message telling you when the device is ready for use. Be aware that the drivers are installed only once—not every time you plug in the device. Therefore, if you unplug your camera and then plug it back in later, you might not see any notification on-screen. But that's okay, the camera should still work just fine.

If Windows XP doesn't recognize the new device, that doesn't necessarily mean it doesn't have drivers for the device. The Scanner and Camera Installation Wizard might be able to help you find an appropriate driver. With the device still plugged into the computer and the device still turned on, follow these steps to give the wizard a whirl:

1. Click the Windows Start button and open Control Panel.

2. If Control Panel opens in Category view, switch to Classic view.

3. Open the Scanners and Cameras icon.

4. Under Imaging Tasks, choose Add an imaging device.

5. Follow the instructions presented by the wizard.

If, during the course of going through the wizard, you find the make and model of your camera, great! By the time you complete the wizard, your camera will be installed and ready to use. If your camera isn't listed in the wizard's lists of manufacturers and models, but you have a driver's disk for your camera, you can insert the disk into a disk drive and click the Have Disk button in that same wizard page to browse to the setup information (.inf) file for your camera.

If all else fails (you know what I'm gonna say next), follow the instructions. The device manufacturer's instructions, that is.

Getting the picture

If Windows XP doesn't recognize your imaging device, use the manufacturer's software to download (or acquire) images from your camera or scanner. If the installed device is one that Windows XP does recognize, you will see an option titled Get pictures from camera or scanner listed under Picture Tasks in the Explorer bar while you're viewing the contents of your My Pictures or Shared Pictures folder (or a subfolder from within either of those). Clicking that option starts the Scanner and Camera Wizard, which takes you step-by-step through the process of downloading images from your device. After you've finished, the image(s) appear in whichever folder you specified. Figure 23-9 shows an example where I acquired a photograph from a scanner and am currently viewing it in Filmstrip view.

Tip   If you have a Web cam attached to your computer, the Scanner and Camera Wizard can help you make a "snapshot" from whatever the Web cam is seeing!

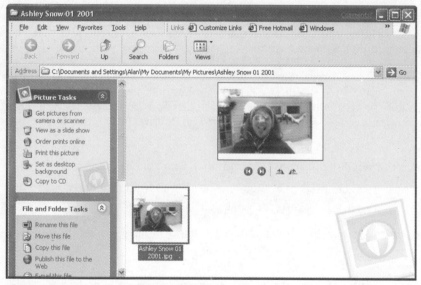

Figure 23-9: A scanned image in Filmstrip view

Organizing pictures

You can store a lot of information about a picture within the picture's file. That information won't appear in the picture, of course. However, it will be available in the picture's Properties dialog box and in the Details view within the Explorer window. To see what's available, just right-click any picture's icon and choose Properties. Then click the Summary tab. There you can choose between a Simple view or an Advanced view of the picture's summary information. Figure 23-10 shows both views.

Editing Faxes and Scanned Documents

Regardless of the type of information you scan, the resulting file is stored as a digital image. Even if you scan a sheet of paper that has nothing but written text on it, you end up with a graphic image file. The same is true of files faxed directly to your computer. The resulting file is a graphic image that can be edited only with a graphics program, and not a word processing program.

To convert a graphic image of a text file to a document that you can edit with a word processing program or text editor, you need to purchase an Optical Character Recognition (OCR) program. There are many on the market to choose from, as a visit to your local brick-and-mortar or online software store will reveal. The main trick is to know which format the scanned text documents or faxes are stored in. You can get that information from the documentation that came with the scanner or fax card, although you also can just look at the file name extension of any files that were created by the scanner or fax card. Then it's just a matter of finding an OCR program that can read that type of file and convert it to a text document.

Of course, if you can get the people who sent you the fax to just e-mail you a copy of the document instead, you'll save yourself a world of headaches!

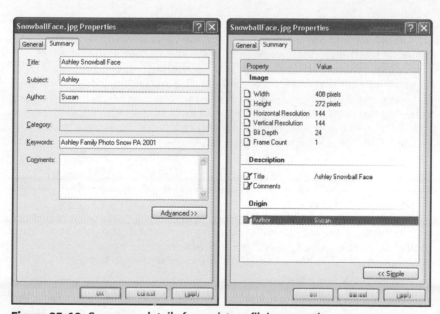

Figure 23-10: Summary details for a picture file's properties

Later, when viewing the contents of the picture's folder in Explorer, you can switch to Details view by choosing View ⇨ Details or choosing Details from the Views button on the Explorer toolbar. Then, choose View ⇨ Choose Details from the Explorer menu bar to determine which details you want to see about all the pictures in the folder. You also can arrange the files by any detail by clicking the heading at the top of any column.

Cross-Reference   See "Choosing Details to View" in Chapter 2 for more information on Details view.

Pictures on the Internet

If you have a .NET Passport, you can upload your pictures to the Web. Alternatively, if you have some kind of online storage, such as that provided by Xdrive, you can upload your pictures to that "extra drive." For these types of accounts, you don't need any special Web authoring skills or even a real Web site, per se. You just select the pictures you want to publish and upload them to the Web storage space.

Tip   If you haven't created a .NET Passport but would like to, click the Start button, open Control Panel, and open the User Accounts icon. Then click your account name and picture and choose Set up my account to use a .NET Passport.

In My Pictures, Shared Folders, or any other folder that contains the pictures you want to publish, select the pictures you want to upload to the Web. (Remember, even though thumbnails don't look like regular icons, you can still use all the standard selection techniques described under "Select, Then Do" in Chapter 12.) Then choose Publish the selected items to the Web under File and Folder Tasks in the Explorer bar. The Web Publishing Wizard opens. The steps you take through the wizard depend on where you're publishing your pictures, whether you already have a .NET Passport, and so forth. But the wizard is self-explanatory, and you shouldn't have any problems following along.

Caution   If you create a new Passport or Hotmail account, be sure to write down the e-mail address and password you provide. If you forget either one, you won't be able to access the site in the future!

If the Web Publishing Wizard has finished and you have clicked the Finish button, you will find an icon named My Pictures within your My Network Places folder. Clicking that icon displays the pictures on your site within an Explorer window. The URL for the site will be as follows:

    http://www.msnusers.com/**your e-mail address**/files/*folder name*

If your Passport e-mail address is howdy@passport.com and you placed your pictures in the folder named My Pictures on the Web, for example, the URL for viewing the pictures will be as follows:

```
http://www.msnusers.com/howdy@passport.com/files/My Pictures on
the Web
```

Any blank spaces in the URL will automatically be converted to %20, but don't worry about that. That's just the symbol for a blank space, which is required on the Internet. When you get to the site, you'll see your picture file names and icons listed, as in Figure 23-11. To view a picture, click its file name or icon. You can use options in the left column to Delete, Copy, Move, Rename, and Add files, or to change various file settings.

If you want to put some photos online for other people on the Internet to view, you can create your own MSN Community and photo album. Using Internet Explorer, go to www.msn.com. When you get there, click the Passport sign in icon if you haven't already logged on with your .NET Passport. Then, in the rightmost column under Communities, click My Web Sites. If you want to create an online photo album that other people on the Internet can view, choose Create a Community and follow the instructions presented by the Web pages that follow. When you have finished, you can choose Photo Albums from the left column to create albums and add photos to them.

Be aware that this whole business of publishing to MSN Web sites is really an "MSN thing," and not a Windows XP thing. As such, it could change at any time. If you have any problems, be sure to check out the latest news and options at www.msn.com.

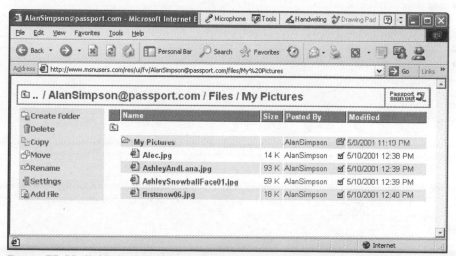

Figure 23-11: Published photos available through a Web site at MSN

E-Mailing Pictures

You also can e-mail any selected picture(s) to one or more e-mail recipients by following these simple steps:

1. Right-click the picture you want to send or select the pictures to send and right-click any one of them.

2. Choose Send To ⇨ Mail Recipient.

3. You'll see an option to resize the pictures for faster transfer or keep the original sizes. If you're sending many photos, you might want to make them smaller. Click OK after making your selection.

4. Fill in the e-mail recipient name(s), and type any message you want, as in the example shown in Figure 23-12.

Figure 23-12: About to send an e-mail with an attached picture

 Tip   To send the picture to multiple recipients, just separate their e-mail addresses with semicolons (;) in the To: or Cc: box.

5. Click the Send button.

Don't forget that if you have set up your e-mail program to place sent items in your Outbox, you need to open your e-mail program and use the Send and Receive button to send the e-mail message.

Summary

Like I said at the outset, Windows XP has made working with pictures easier and more fun than ever. Here's a quick recap of the main points covered in this chapter:

✦ All pictures are digital images and are stored in files just like any other document.

✦ The My Pictures folder that Windows XP creates automatically within My Documents is ideal for storing pictures you want to keep private.

✦ Use the Shared Pictures folder to store pictures that you want to share with other users of this computer, as well as other users on a local area network (LAN).

✦ The Thumbnails and Filmstrip views in Windows Explorer are ideal for viewing the contents of folders that contain pictures.

✦ Both My Pictures and Shared Pictures offer Picture Tasks in the Explorer bar, which are handy for working with pictures.

✦ The quality of a digital image, in technical terms, has to do with the picture's resolution (dots per inch) and color depth (also called pixel depth).

✦ The higher the quality of the image, the larger the file needed to store the image.

✦ Cameras, Web cams, and scanners are all considered *imaging devices*, and the Explorer bar in the My Pictures folder offers tools for acquiring images from those devices.

✦ You can add detailed information about a picture to its file properties by right-clicking the picture, choosing Properties, and clicking the Summary tab.

✦ You can copy pictures to external drives on MSN or some other service by selecting the picture(s) to upload and choosing Publish . . . to the Web from the Explorer bar.

✦ If you're interested in publishing your pictures online in a nice photo album format, your best bet might be to set up a Photo Album Web site through an MSN community.

✦ To e-mail a picture, right-click the picture, choose Send To ➪ Mail Recipient, and enter the recipient address(es), as with any other normal e-mail message.

✦   ✦   ✦

Sounds, Music, Video, and DVD

Windows Media Player, which comes with Windows XP, has become something of a universal multimedia player for music, video, and DVD. There are plenty of third-party players for these different types of multimedia files. As far as I know, they should all continue to work fine in Windows XP. To keep this chapter from being any longer than it already is, however, I focus on Windows Media Player 8.0 (often referred to as WMP8.0). But first, let's focus on the one problem that seems to perplex many a computer, getting that darn sound to work!

Get Your Sound Working

Nearly every PC built these days comes with sound capability built right in. A computer that doesn't have sound capability just needs a *sound card* added to it. There are dozens of sound cards to choose from, as a visit to your local computer store (or online computer store) will verify. You'll need speakers to go with that sound card, of course. If you want to listen to audio CDs, you need a CD-ROM drive as well. Assuming that you do have at least a sound card and speakers in your PC, let's look at how you can control the sound.

Assuming you do have speakers and a sound card already, make sure the speakers are connected to the appropriate port on the sound card. If you're using powered speakers, make sure the speakers are plugged in, turned on, and the volume is cranked up enough so that you can hear any sound coming from the speakers. Personally, I prefer to keep my speakers cranked all the way up and then control the volume from the Windows XP taskbar. If you use this method, however, make sure you turn down the taskbar volume a bit before you crank up your speakers too loud. You wouldn't want to blast yourself with too much sound.

When you are certain that your speakers can make some audible sound, the next step is to learn to select audio devices and adjust volume using Windows XP.

Tip   The Sound Troubleshooter is a good tool for fixing problems with sound. To get to it, click the Start button and choose Help and Support. Then choose Fixing a Problem and select the Games, Sound and Video Problems option.

Get some music playing

If you want to have some sound playing while you fiddle with the various controls you're about to learn about, just stick any audio CD into your computer's CD-ROM drive. Typically, Windows Media Player opens and just starts playing the CD. Note that Media Player has its own volume control, however, as discussed a little later in this chapter.

Alternatively, you can play some MIDI files. If you don't know the location of any off-hand, use Search to search your entire hard drive for All Files Types that match `*.mid`. When Search returns a list of files that match your search criteria, just click (or double-click) any file's icon to start playing it.

Cross-Reference   If you need a reminder on using Search, see "Searching for Lost Files" in Chapter 2.

To test other types of sound files, use Search to search your hard disk for "pictures, music, or video," and choose Music and Sound. You needn't specify a name. When you click the Search button, a list of sound and music files displays. You can play any one by clicking (or double-clicking) its icon.

Windows XP volume controls

Your sound card has its own volume controls that are independent of the volume controls on the speakers — much like the volume control on a stereo. However, there's probably no visible volume knob on your computer. You control the sound card's volume from your screen. Here's how:

1. Click the Start button and choose Control Panel. If Control Panel opens in Category view, choose Sounds, Speech, and Audio Devices option.

2. Open the Sounds and Audio Devices icon. Initially, you'll be taken to the Volume tab shown in Figure 24-1.

Caution   With headphones, too much volume can actually damage your ears. Be sure to hold the headphones away from your ears while you adjust volume so that you don't hurt yourself!

Figure 24-1: The Volume tab of the Sounds and Audio Devices dialog box

3. If you want a volume control on your taskbar, choose the Place volume icon in the taskbar check box, as in the figure.

4. Click the Apply button.

5. A tiny speaker icon appears in the taskbar. From now on, you can adjust your sound volume by clicking that icon and dragging the slider, as shown in Figure 24-2.

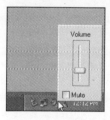

Figure 24-2: The volume control slider on the Windows taskbar

The Volume tab, under Device Volume, also offers you these other options:

✦ **Volume slider:** General sound card volume, linked to the slider that's accessible from the taskbar (moving one moves the other).

✦ **Mute:** If selected, no sound will come from the sound card.

✦ **Advanced:** Takes you to the "mixer" for setting the volume of individual types of sound, as discussed later in this chapter.

Under Speaker Settings, you have the following options:

✦ **Speaker volume:** Enables you to set the right and left speaker volume for all speakers attached to this computer.

✦ **Advanced:** Enables you to maximize speaker performance by choosing a speaker setup that best resembles your own and to adjust other settings relevant to your particular sound card and speakers.

Choosing preferred playback devices

You might have multiple devices capable of playing and recording sound. For example, the computer I'm sitting at right now has a sound card and speakers. It also has an audio headset with a speaker and a microphone. Most of the time, I prefer to use my large external speakers for playing sound. For recording voice (or talking on the Internet), however, I prefer the microphone on the headset. Choosing your preferred devices in Windows XP is pretty easy. In the Sounds and Audio Devices Properties dialog box shown back in Figure 24-1, just follow these steps:

1. Click the Audio tab to reveal the options shown in Figure 24-3.

2. Using the available drop-down lists, choose your preferred device for sound playback, recording, and MIDI music.

3. Optionally, you can adjust the volume of each device individually using the Volume button. You'll be taken to the mixer described later in this chapter.

4. Optionally, you can use the Advanced button (if enabled) to adjust other settings that are relevant to your audio devices.

Figure 24-3: The Audio tab of the Sounds and Audio Devices Properties dialog box

The Use only default devices option will limit your sound recording and playback to the devices you have selected. You probably don't want to select that option until you have all your devices working properly. If it turns out that two or more devices are playing or recording sound, you can choose that option to limit sounds to your chosen default devices.

If you use voice communications, such as speech recognition, narration, and so forth, you can select devices for voice sound. Click the Voice tab to reveal the options shown in Figure 24-4 and choose your devices. Choosing the Test Hardware button will fire up a wizard that will let you test and adjust your voice hardware. If you have a headset or any other microphone, choose this option to get all that squared away now.

Figure 24-4: The Voice tab of the Sounds and Audio Devices Properties dialog box

At this point, you click the OK button in the Sounds and Audio Devices Properties dialog box and save your settings. You can, of course, change your preferred devices at any time. If you have a headset for voice as well as a microphone and you prefer to use the microphone, for example, you can just go into the Sounds and Multimedia Properties dialog box and choose the microphone as your preferred device for voice capture. If you're not sure which device to use for each of the different types of sound, just use the default settings that were in the dialog box when you first opened it.

Using the mixer

Yet another program, called the *mixer,* enables you to adjust the *relative* volume and sensitivity of different types of sounds your sound hardware can play and record. There are a couple of ways to open the mixer:

✦ Double-click the little speaker icon in the indicators section of the taskbar.

✦ Or, click the Start button and choose All Programs ➪ Accessories ➪ Entertainment ➪ Volume Control.

✦ Or, click the Volume button on any device in the Sounds and Audio Devices Properties dialog box.

The mixer will open displaying a separate volume control slider for each type of playable sound, as in the example shown in Figure 24-5. Initially, the mixer shows volume controls for various playback devices, as well as types of sounds.

Note   The controls available through the mixer come from the capabilities of your sound card. Your mixer might look different and not offer the same options as the examples presented here.

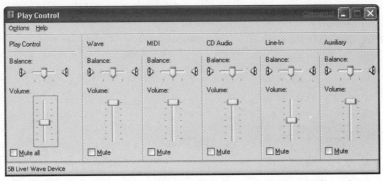

Figure 24-5: The Play Control side of the volume control (the mixer)

The first column in the sample mixer shown, labeled Play Control, is (yet again) another general volume control for the sound card. If you open the little speaker icon in the taskbar and move its volume control slider up and down, you'll see that the Play Control slider in the mixer moves right along with it. The remaining sliders affect the volume of specific types of sound (for instance, Wave and MIDI files), as well as other devices on your system, as follows:

✦ **CD Audio:** Controls the volume of music being played in your computer's CD-ROM drive.

✦ **Line-In:** Adjusts the volume of any device attached to your sound card's Line-In device.

✦ **Auxiliary:** Adjusts the volume of devices attached to the Aux In port on the sound card *inside* the computer.

The Line-In device adjusts the playback volume of any device that's connected to the Line-In port of your sound card. This would typically be some kind of music player or video camera that you connect directly to that port. If you use any such devices and *do* want to hear the sound coming from that device through your computer speakers, make sure the Line-In device is not muted, and its volume control slider is cranked up a bit.

Your sound card may also have an Aux In port on it, inside the computer. If you didn't install the sound card yourself, you might not know whether anything is connected to that port. If you have, say, both a DVD and CD-ROM drive, an IEEE 1394 port, or some kind of port for connecting a video camera to your computer, however, there's a good chance that the device is connected to the Aux In port of your sound card. If you want to hear that device played through your computer speakers, make sure that the Auxiliary volume control is not muted and that its volume control is cranked up a bit.

Adjusting recording volume

The mixer also has a separate set of controls for setting the volume of any devices you use to record sound. To get to those controls, follow these steps:

1. Choose Options ⇨ Properties from the mixer's menu bar.
2. Choose the Recording option.
3. Click the OK button.

Now the mixer shows volume sliders for various types of devices from which you can record sound. Note that the Mute check boxes have been replaced with Select check boxes, as shown in Figure 24-6. If you want to record from a specific device, you must choose its Select check box and crank its volume slider up a bit. You can record from only one device at a time. So if you're able to record from many devices, you need to return to these options and choose the device you want to record from at the moment.

Once again, be aware that the Line-In and Auxiliary items can be important here. If you have trouble recording from some devices, it's quite possible that the device is connected to the Aux In port inside the computer or the Line In port on the sound card. If ever you have trouble recording from some device, such as a video camera, chances are its recording volume slider is either not selected or is turned down too low.

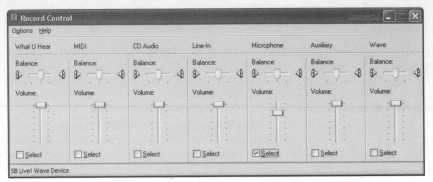

Figure 24-6: The Record Control side of the volume control (the mixer)

Adding devices to the mixer

If you have a sound device on your computer that's not included in the mixer, you can add that device. Choose Options ⇨ Properties and then choose either Playback or Recording, depending on whether you want to add a playback or recording volume control. Then choose which items you want to display volume controls for from the list of items in the dialog box.

Bass, treble, and balance

Back on the Play side of the mixer, you can adjust the balance of any device by moving the Balance slider to the left or right. To adjust bass and treble, click the Advanced button under Play Control. If you don't see that button, choose Options ⇨ Advanced Controls from the mixer's menu bar. The options that appear will vary from one sound card to the next. However, the Bass and Treble controls shown in Figure 24-7 are fairly common (I think).

Figure 24-7: Bass and Treble settings

Using Windows Media Player

Windows Media Player is a general-purpose program for playing all kinds of multi-media files, including audio and video files. When you open a file that Media Player is capable of playing, the program usually starts automatically. You can also start it yourself at any time by clicking the Start button and choosing All Programs ⇨ Accessories ⇨ Entertainment ⇨ Windows Media Player. If you have an Internet connection, Media Player might automatically connect you to WindowsMedia.com and display its home page.

Media Player also can be displayed in a variety of "skins," so it's tough to say exactly how it will look when it first opens on your screen. The default appearance is shown in Figure 24-8.

Tip   If the title bar and menu bar aren't visible in Media Player, click the Show menu bar button near the upper-left corner of the Media Player window to display them.

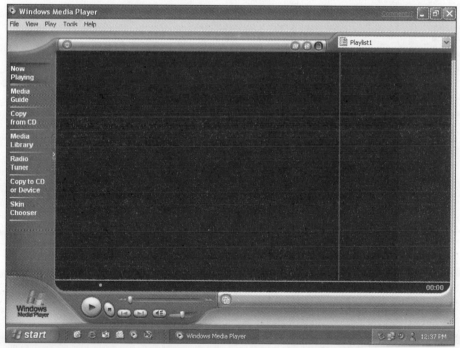

Figure 24-8: Windows Media Player

Although Media Player might not look like a powerhouse program at first glance, here are some of the things you can do with it:

✦ Play audio CDs and copy tracks (songs) to your hard disk

✦ Burn your own custom audio CDs

✦ Watch videos and DVDs

✦ Find and play streaming media from the Web

✦ Create and organize libraries of favorite music and video files

✦ Create and listen to custom *playlists* (collections of songs)

✦ Download music to a portable listening device

✦ Listen to radio stations from all over the world

The most important controls for playing multimedia files are those along the bottom of Media Player. As always, you can point to any control to see its name in a ToolTip. If you've ever worked a VCR, tape player, or CD player, these main controls should be familiar to you. Media Player's controls include the following:

✦ **Play/Pause:** Plays or pauses the current multimedia file

✦ **Stop:** Stops playback

✦ **Seek:** Shows progress as a file is being played, and also enables you to skip ahead by dragging the box or clicking somewhere along the slider

✦ **Mute:** Shuts off the volume without stopping playback

✦ **Volume:** Adjusts the sound volume of the playback

✦ **Previous track:** Jumps to previous track in the current playlist

✦ **Rewind:** Jumps to beginning of file currently being played

✦ **Fast forward:** Moves forward at higher speed through current file

✦ **Next track:** Jumps to beginning of next track in the playlist

✦ **Switch to compact mode:** Displays a smaller Media Player window

The Windows Media Player is capable of playing many different types of multimedia files, as listed in Table 24-1.

Table 24-1
Multimedia File Formats Windows Media Player Can Play

Format	Common File Name Extensions
AIFF audio	.aif, .aifc, .aiff
AU audio	.au, .snd
CD audio track	.cda
DVD video	(none)
Indeo Video Format	.ivf
MIDI audio	.mid, .midi, .rmi
MP3 music	.mp3, .m3u
MPEG (Motion Picture Experts Group)	.mpeg, .mpg, .m1v, .mp2, .mp3, .mpa, .mpe, .mpv2, .mp2v, .m3u, .pls
Video file	.avi
Wave audio	.wav
Windows Media audio file	.wma, .wax
Windows Media audio/video file	.wmv, .wmx
Windows Media file	.asf, .asx, .wm, .wmx, .wmp

Opening any of the files in the table automatically launches Media Player and starts playing the file. If you happen to have some other player that you prefer for a specific type of multimedia, you can choose Tools ➪ Options from Media Player's menu bar, and then click the File Types tab. Clear the check box next to any type of multimedia file that you don't want Media Player to play.

Different ways to view media player

There are many different ways to view Media Player, including Full mode and Skin mode. To switch to Skin mode, choose View ➪ Skin Mode from Media Player's menu bar. Or, click the Switch to Skin Mode button centered near the bottom of the window. The window shrinks, and you'll also see an anchor window near the lower-right corner of your screen, an in Figure 24-9. Buttons along the edge of the compacted window slide out the playlist and equalizer controls. To return to Full mode, click the button in the anchor window and choose Switch to Full Mode.

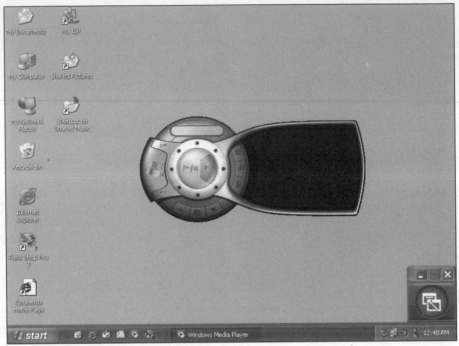

Figure 24-9: Media Player in Skin mode

Tip   If you minimize Media Player's window, it will shrink to the taskbar button but continue playing. If you close Media Player, it will stop playing.

You can dramatically alter the appearance of Media Player by choosing *skins*. The easiest way to play around with different skins is to go to Full mode and then click the Skin Chooser button in the left column of the player. As you click different skins, you'll get a preview, as in the example shown in Figure 24-10. Click the Apply Skin button above the list to apply the currently selected skin.

Keeping Media Player Up-to-Date

Windows Media Player is so tied into the Internet that it's likely to evolve more quickly than other components of Windows XP. To see what version of Media Player you're using at the moment, choose Help ⇨ About Windows Media Player from its menu bar. To check for updates, just choose Help ⇨ Check for Player Updates from Media Player's menu bar. As discussed under "Media Player Properties," you also can have Media Player check for updates automatically from time to time.

Figure 24-10: Use the Skin Chooser to give Media Player a whole new look.

New skins become available on the Internet all the time. To see whether there are any you would like to have, click the More Skins button. When you get to the Web site, click any skin you want to download.

Not all skins have the full range of options, menu bars, and so forth that Media Player offers. So you might need to switch back to the default Full mode from time to time to get at some features. Look for a Return to Full Mode button on your applied skin when you need to get back to all of Media Player's capabilities.

Media Player properties

You can customize some aspects of how Media Player behaves on your computer by choosing Tools ➪ Options and then clicking the Player tab. There you can choose how often you want Media Player to check for updates to itself on the Internet. You also have other options:

✦ **Download codecs automatically:** If selected, Media Player automatically downloads any codec you need to play a specific multimedia file, if that codec isn't already installed on your computer.

Note

A *codec* (compressor/decompressor) is a tiny program used to compress and decompress multimedia files. Windows XP comes with the most common codecs already installed.

✦ **Allow Internet site to uniquely identify your player:** Selecting this option allows servers on the Internet to adjust streaming media to your Internet connection.

Streaming media is multimedia content played as it is being downloaded. Allowing Internet sites to uniquely identify your player does not send any personal information about you to the Internet site.

✦ **Acquire licenses automatically:** If selected, the license for any protected content you purchase and download from the Internet will be downloaded automatically. If you clear this option, you'll be prompted before the license is sent.

✦ **Start player in Media Guide:** If you don't want Media Player to connect to the Internet each time you start it, clear this check box.

✦ **Display on top when in skin mode:** Keeps the compact Media Player on top of all other open windows on your desktop.

✦ **Display anchor window when in Skin mode:** If you deselect this option, you'll no longer see the anchor window on the desktop when you switch Media Player to Full mode.

✦ **Allow screen saver during playback:** Clearing this option will prevent your screensaver from kicking in while you're viewing a video or DVD through Media Player.

✦ **Add items to Media Library when played:** If selected, items are automatically added to the Media Library (discussed in a moment) as they are played.

✦ **Include items from removable media:** Available only if the preceding item is selected. Selecting this option adds items that have not been copied to your hard disk to the Media Library.

Be forewarned that if you choose that last item, your Media Library will display content that's not on your hard disk. This can be frustrating because the content can't actually be played without the disk in the drive!

Media library

Media Player's media library categorizes all the multimedia content on your hard disk(s) that it's capable of playing. To view your current media library, go into Full mode in Media Player and click the Media Library button in the left column. Be aware that the Media Library isn't automatically updated on its own as you add new songs or other multimedia content to your hard disk. For Media Library to accurately reflect all the multimedia files on your hard disk, follow these steps:

1. Choose Tools ➪ Search for Media Files from Media Player's menu bar.

2. In the Search for Media Files dialog box that opens, choose All Drives from the Search on drop-down list. Or, if you prefer, you can limit the search to a specific drive and folder. Optionally, you can click the Advanced tab to reject small sound effects files and video files.

3. Click the Search button.

4. When the search is complete, click the Close button.

The left column now presents a categorized list of all available media files categorized into a variety of categories (a.k.a. *playlists*). As with a folders list, you can expand and contract categories by clicking the plus (+) or minus (–) sign next to the category name. The categories under Audio include the following:

✦ **All Audio:** Lists all the audio files on you hard disk — even those that aren't categorized

✦ **Album:** Lists available albums

✦ **Artists:** Lists all available artists

✦ **Genre:** Lists available genres

> **Note** Songs that you didn't copy from a recognized CD might not be available in the Album, Artist, or Genre lists. The All Audio option is the only one that's guaranteed to show all available audio files.

You can play any category or any item within a category by double-clicking its icon or by right-clicking and choosing Play. Optionally, you can choose a playlist (category) from the drop-down list near the upper-right corner of Media Player's window. Note that when you make a selection from the drop-down list, the right pane shows the contents of that category, which is not necessarily the same as the category selected in the left pane.

Figure 24-11 shows a sample Media Library displaying the contents of the All Audio category. The larger pane on the right lists all the available songs on my hard disks. To ensure that your right pane is showing all your audio files, choose All Audio from the drop-down list near the upper-right corner.

In Case You're Wondering

You might have noticed that some of the file names in Figure 24-11 refer to drive D:. That's a second hard drive on that particular computer, not a CD ROM drive. I use that drive mainly for music files, which can hog up quite a bit of disk space. As indicated at the bottom of the pane on the right, the 868 songs are in my All Audio category 3.42 GB of disk space. Probably half those songs are WMA files copied at the highest quality. However, some are also small MP3 files.

Figure 24-11: The contents of the All Audio category in Media Library

Because All Audio lists all the audio files on your hard disk (not just songs you copied from audio CDs), you might come across some "mystery" files. The columns in the right pane can help you straighten things out. There may be more columns that can fit within Media Player. Use the horizontal scroll bar at the bottom of the list to scroll to other columns. As with most column displays in Windows, you can do the following:

✦ Click any column heading to sort (alphabetize) the list by that column. Each time you click the sort order switches from ascending to descending order.

✦ Size columns by dragging the thin line that separates the column headings.

✦ Move columns by dragging their column headings to the left or right.

In Figure 24-11, for example, my audio files are listed in ascending alphabetic order by name. I dragged the Filename column into view, because that helps me see where each file is located and provides some clues regarding "mystery" files or repeat titles. In a moment, I'll explain how you can add category information to your uncategorized music files to get them to fit better within the available categories.

If you come across any files in your Media Library that you want to get rid of, just right-click the file and choose Delete from Library. Doing so does not remove the file from your hard disk, just from the Media Library. To see other information about a particular file, right-click it and choose Properties. If your library is large and you want to search for a specific file, click the Search button near the top of the Media Library list. The songs found during the search will appear in Search Results under the My Playlists category.

Organizing Media Library

The information that Media Library uses to categorize multimedia content comes from certain various properties stored within each multimedia file. Normally you don't see that information. Furthermore, not all files have the appropriate information within their properties. Such files end up being listed with "unknown" artist, album, and genre information, and vague titles, such as "Track 1." This is especially true of songs copied from CDs that aren't recognized by Media Player, as well as many items that are downloaded from the Internet. Such items are accessible only from the all-encompassing All Audio category, and "unknown" categories within Artist, Album, and Genre categories.

This can be a real bummer if you have a ton of multimedia content that you've organized into nice neat folders and subfolders. Intuitively, it might seem as though Media Player should be able to determine the artist, album, genre, and title of a song based on the folder and file names you have defined. As mentioned, however, Media Library doesn't use file or folder information to categorize multimedia content. It uses file properties that are usually invisible. There are a couple of ways to fix the problem though.

While viewing songs in Media Player with the Media Library tab selected, you can change a song's title, artist, album, genre, and other information. To change the title, right-click the existing title and choose Edit. Type in the new title and press Enter.

You can change the Artist, Album, Genre, and other fields for several songs in one fell swoop. If you previously put the songs into folder by artist, album, genre or whatever, clicking the Filename column heading will arrange the songs into groups by folder name. You can then select several songs by dragging the mouse pointer through some blank area near the Filename column or any other column. That can be a little tricky though. Alternatively, you can click the first song you want to change and then hold down the Shift key and click the last song to extend the selection to that song. Or, click the first song you want to change and then Ctrl+click the songs you want to add to the selection. Then you can right-click the item you want to change (for instance, Artist), and choose Edit Selected Items. Type in the new value (for example, the artist's name) and press Enter.

As an alternative to doing all of this in Media Player, you can do it in an Explorer window. If you do so before you choose Tools ➪ Search for Media Files from Media Player's menu bar, the songs will be properly categorized when you do read them into the Media Library. To change songs title, artist, genre, and other information in

Explorer, open the folder that contains the music you want to change. Choose View ⇨ Details to view detailed information about each file. Then choose View ⇨ Choose Details and make sure the title, artist, album, and genre details are selected. Then drag all those columns into view so that you can get a clear picture of current settings, as in Figure 24-12.

To change the detail properties of a single song, right-click that song and choose Properties. If all the songs share the same artist, album, and/or genre name, you can select all of them, right-click, and choose Properties. In the Properties dialog box, open the Summary tab. There you can choose between Simple and Advanced views. In the Advanced view, you can click and fill in the Artist, Album Title, Title, and Genre field, as in the example shown in Figure 24-13. (There I'm filling in information for a group of selected songs—so it wouldn't make sense to change the title.)

Click OK, and the files will get the new values. Later, when you choose Tools ⇨ Search for Media Files from Media Player's menu bar, it will use the information to categorize the songs as it adds them to its Media Library.

Tip

When typing in song titles, you can copy-and-paste from the song's file name instead of retyping the title from scratch. Right-click the existing file name and choose Rename and then press Ctrl+C. The file name will be copied to the Windows Clipboard. Click some neutral area outside the file name to close without renaming. Then right-click again and choose Properties. On the summary tab, click in the Title field and press Ctrl+V to paste.

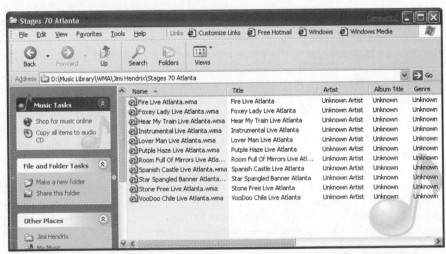

Figure 24-12: Songs with Title, Artist, Album, and Genre detail fields listed

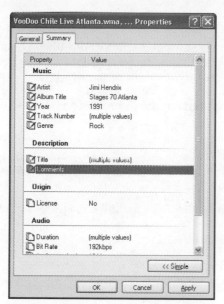

Figure 24-13: New artist, album, and genre information for selected songs

As you move, copy, and rename things in Explorer or in Media Player, Windows does an admirable job of keeping the Media Library in sync with what's currently on the hard disk. Do keep in mind, however, that when you add new content to the hard disk, that content is not necessarily added to your Media Library automatically. You need to choose Tools ➪ Search for Media Files in Media Player to ensure that Media Library truly reflects all the multimedia files currently available on your hard disk.

Likewise, if you delete multimedia content from your hard disk through Explorer, the deletion will not be reflected in Media Library. The song (or whatever) will still be listed in Media Library. When you try to play the song, you'll get an error message. To delete the song from Media Library, right-click the song and choose Delete from Library.

Media Player has its own "Recycle Bin" of sorts — The Deleted Items folder at the bottom of the category list. If you *accidentally* delete a song from Media Library, you can get it back by opening the Deleted Items folder, right-clicking the item you want to restore and choosing Restore. Doing so, however, just puts the item back into the library — it doesn't restore the file if you deleted it from the hard disk. To get rid of items that truly don't represent files on your hard disk, right-click the Deleted Items folder and choose Empty Deleted Items.

Media Library properties

You can control access to your Media Library through its Properties dialog box. In Media Player, choose Tools ⇨ Options and then click the Media Library tab to get to the options shown in Figure 24-14. The access rights of other applications refers to any other multimedia players that might share your Media Library. The access rights of Internet sites refers to other computers on the Internet. You can assign the following rights:

✦ **No access:** Your Media Library is invisible to them.

✦ **Read-only access:** They can view and play items in the Media Library, but not change the library.

✦ **Full access:** They can view, play, add to, delete from, and change the contents of your Media Library.

Figure 24-14: Media library properties

 Protected content can be played only on the computer that it was originally copied to, regardless of the options you choose in the Media Library tab. More on this topic under "Copying Audio CDs," later in this chapter.

License management

Online communities such as Napster (www.napster.com), which enable people to swap music files, have given the recording industry some major headaches. After all, how can they sell music when it's so easy to get it for free? One way of dealing with the problem has been to include licensing information in all purchased music.

The license is actually stored within the song and copied along with the song to the computer on which the purchased music was placed. When you play the song on that computer, Media Player looks for the license information and then plays the song. If you try to play the song on some other computer that doesn't have the license, however, the song won't play. This holds true whether you e-mail the song to the other computer, the other computer downloads the song from your computer, or even if the computer is just a member of your local area network.

Be aware of one potential problem with music that you've purchased and downloaded online. If the song is accidentally erased, or a bad disk crash wipes out the songs and licenses, you are plain out of luck. Even the simple act of upgrading your computer to a new operating system can mess up your licenses! Just backing up the songs to some other medium won't help. To play it safe, you need to back up the songs and the licenses. To back up your licenses to a floppy disk, follow these steps:

1. Insert a blank, formatted floppy disk into your floppy drive.

2. Choose Tools ➪ License Management from Media Player's menu bar.

3. Use the Browse button to choose your floppy disk drive.

4. Click Backup Now.

 Note   To learn more about licensed files and copyright issues, choose Help ➪ Help Topics from Media Player's menu bar. Under Contents, choose Understanding Digital Media Concepts ➪ Understanding Licensed Files.

If you ever need to restore the licenses from the floppy disk, repeat the steps using the floppy disk to which you copied your licenses in Step 1, rather than a blank disk. When you get to Step 4, choose Restore Now.

Playing Audio CDs

If your computer has a CD-ROM drive, you can use it to play standard audio CDs — the same CDs you play in your home or car stereo. The process is simple:

1. Put the audio CD into the CD-ROM drive, label side up, just as in a stereo.

2. Wait for Media Player to open. (If it doesn't open within a minute, open My Computer on your desktop and then click or double-click the icon for your CD-ROM drive.)

3. If the music doesn't start playing automatically, click the Play button in Media Player.

Use the volume control slider near the bottom of Media Player to adjust the volume of the CD. If the CD you're listening to contains song titles, you'll see those titles in the right pane. If the CD does not contain song titles, but you have an Internet connection, Media Player will attempt to look up the CD on the Internet and display the title of each track on the CD in the Playlist at the right side of Media Player, as in Figure 24-15. If song titles aren't available on the CD or the Internet, songs on the CD will just be listed as Track 1, Track 2, and so forth.

Note   I guess when CD audios were first invented, they didn't think to put the track titles right on the CD. Perhaps they hadn't thought of people using their computers to listen to them! Some newer audio CDs do put titles right on the CD though.

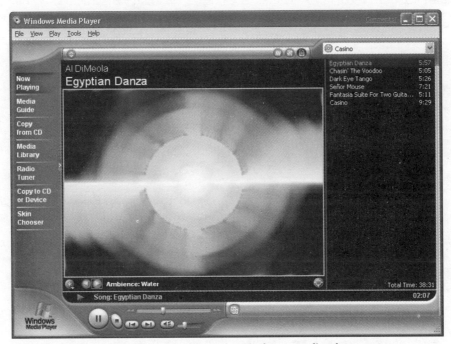

Figure 24-15: Listening to an audio CD in Windows Media Player

When the Now Playing tab is selected at the left side of Media Player, you'll also see a visualization of the music being played. You can try out different visualizations using the buttons just beneath the current visualization. To expand or shrink the size of the visualization, click the Hide Playlist in Now Playing button near the upper-right corner of Media Player. You also can show or hide equalizer settings by clicking the Show Equalizer and Settings in Now Playing button that's also near the upper-right corner of Media Player's window. When the equalizer opens, you'll see a Select View button near its lower-left corner, which gives you some different ways to view the equalizer. You also can choose View ⇨ Now Playing Tools from the menu bar to play around with different settings.

Tip   New visualizations also become available online from time to time. To see what's new, choose Tools ⇨ Download Visualizations. You'll be taken to a Web page where you can pick and choose the visualizations you want to download.

By default, all the songs on the CD are played in the order in which they appear. If nothing is playing, clicking the Play button starts the playback. If you want to listen to a specific song, just double-click its name or track number in the right column. If you would like Media Player to play every song on the CD, but in random order, click the Turn Shuffle On button up near the top of the Media Player's window.

Some audio CDs have their own players that pop up after you insert the CD in your drive. If you prefer to use Media Player to that player, cancel that player. Then open Media Player and click the CD Audio tab to view the disk's contents. Click the Play button to play the CD.

Copying Audio CDs

You can copy music from any audio CD to your hard disk. Later you can listen to the CD, or any song from the CD, or any selection of songs from any CDs, on your computer without inserting the original audio CD into your CD-ROM drive. If your computer has a CD-R or CD-RW drive, you also can create your own custom CDs from any songs you've copied to your hard disk. Windows XP comes with two folders already created for storing music:

✦ **My Music:** If you want to keep your music private, so that no other users of this computer have access to your songs, put the songs in My Music. You find this folder inside your My Documents folder.

✦ **Shared Music:** If you want anyone who uses this computer to be able to play the songs, copy the songs to the Shared Music folder, which you find inside the Shared Documents folder.

Choosing a folder

To choose where you want to put copied songs, follow these steps:

1. Choose Tools ➪ Options from Media Player's menu bar.

2. Click the Copy Music tab.

3. Click the Change button under Copy music to this location.

4. To copy to your My Music folder, choose My Music under My Documents in the Browse for Folder list. Otherwise, choose Shared Music under My Computer and Shared Documents, as in Figure 24-16.

Tip

Media Player automatically creates one or more subfolders for the copied music. So there's no need to create your own subfolder within My Music or Shared Music.

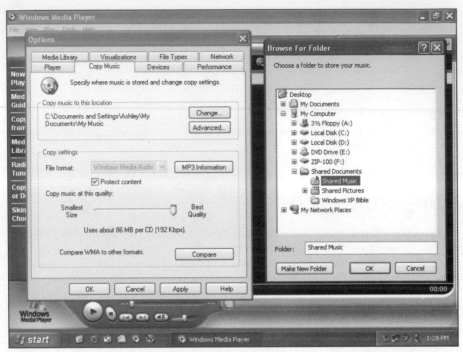

Figure 24-16: Choosing a location for copied music

Choosing a format and quality

As shipped, Media Player enables you to copy music in Microsoft's Windows Media Audio (.wma) format only. With that format, you can opt to protect the content (so that it can be played only on the computer to which the music was copied). You can also choose a quality. The higher the quality you choose, the larger the resulting file, but the better the sound.

Tip   If you're on a LAN, other computers on the LAN will also have access to music in the Shared Music folder. However, they will only be able to play unprotected songs.

Clicking the MP3 Information button will take you to a Web page that describes Microsoft's current stance on the ever-controversial MP3 format for recording music. As you may know, MP3 was the most popular format used on the Napster site, where users traded music files without paying fees. That site has since been shut down by the courts. As I write this chapter, it's not clear whether Media Player will support copying files to the MP3 format. Click that button to visit the Web site and see what's up.

Copying CD tracks

After you've made your selections as to where to put the copied songs, the format and (optionally) copying is simple. First, put the CD you want to copy into your CD-ROM drive. Media Player will attempt to display the song titles, although this might take a few seconds. Click the Copy from CD button in the taskbar at the left edge of the Media Player window. You'll see a list of check boxes next to track titles (or track numbers if Media Player wasn't able to get the song titles), as in Figure 24-17. Select the check box for songs you want to copy and clear the check boxes for songs you don't want to copy.

Figure 24-17: The CD Audio tab of Media Player

> **Tip** There are usually more columns of information in the CD Audio display than are initially visible. To see other columns, use the scroll bar below the list. You can adjust column widths by dragging the thin line that separates the column headings.

When you've selected the songs to copy, click the Copy Music button. If you didn't opt to protect copied content, you'll see a dialog box explaining music protection, along with a disclaimer should you decide to select the Do not protect content check box. Make your decision and click the OK button. The Copy Status column keeps you informed of the progress. It might take a few minutes, but you can do other things during that time. (Well, anything that doesn't require that you remove the audio CD from your CD-ROM drive!) When the Copy Status column indicates that all songs are Copied to Library, you're done. Then you can remove the CD from your CD-ROM drive.

But Those Titles Are Wrong!

Sometimes Media Player doesn't get the song titles right. This is especially true of CDs that come in two-volume sets and compilation CDs. If you end up with the wrong song titles, click the Get Names button. You'll be taken online, where you can try to track down the appropriate song titles. You definitely want to do this *before* you copy the CD. Otherwise, the songs will be copied to all the wrong folders with all the wrong song titles!

To see the results, open the folder to which you copied the songs. The songs will be in a folder that has the artist's name. So if you copied songs from a compilation CD, the songs might be spread across several folders. If the CD you copied was recognized by the Internet, you'll see a little picture of the CD cover on the folder when you're in Thumbnails view. If you've copied several CDs from the same artist, the songs will be in separate subfolders within the artist's folder, as in Figure 24-18.

Figure 24-18: The contents of one artist's folder within my Shared Music folder

After the files are copied to your hard disk, you can rename files and folders, move things around, and so forth. Each song is just a file, so you can use any of the standard techniques for selecting, copying, moving, renaming, and deleting files, as discussed in Chapter 12.

Playing copied music

To play a song that's been copied to your hard disk, just click (or double-click) its file name or icon. Optionally, you can use the Play option under Music Tasks to play multiple songs while you're in the My Music or Shared Music folder:

✦ To play all the songs in the folder, don't select anything. Just click the Play All music task.

✦ To play all the songs within a folder, select the folder. Then click Play Selection.

✦ To play several songs within a folder, open the folder, select the songs you want to play, and click Play Selection.

Regardless of which method you use, Media Player opens and starts playing the music. Your Media Library within Media Player is updated to reflect the additions. If, for whatever reason, it isn't, you can choose Tools ➪ Search for Media Files from Media Player's menu bar to bring Media Library up-to-date.

Music on the Internet

Audio CDs are certainly a good source of music. But these days the Internet is also home to tons of recorded music. However, unlike radios and CDs, which deliver music smoothly and evenly to your ears, the Internet has no capability to send data at a smooth, even rate. In fact, delivery of data over the Internet is often pretty choppy and unpredictable. You usually don't notice this when you're viewing Web pages or downloading files. If you try to listen to a song or view a video as it's being downloaded from the Internet, however, the choppiness will be quite apparent — especially if you're using a modem and dial-up account as opposed to a broadband connection, such as cable or DSL.

Music and video, which are intended to be listened to and viewed smoothly, are called *streaming media*. Windows Media Player uses *buffering* to minimize the choppiness that's likely to occur with streaming media. With buffering, you don't have to wait for the entire file to be downloaded before you can start listening to it. Instead, a good chunk of the file is first downloaded and stored in a *buffer* — a place in the computer's memory for temporarily storing data. When the buffer is filled (or partially filled), playback begins even though the file hasn't been fully downloaded. As long as your Internet connection can fill the buffer faster than your computer plays the streaming media, you'll get smooth continuous playback without the interruptions normally caused by the manner in which the Internet transfers data from one computer to another.

Intelligent streaming is a form of streaming that goes to even greater lengths to ensure that you get the best quality playback possible. Intelligent streaming depends on media being encoded at multiple *bit rates*. The program receiving the data being sent analyzes the network to get a sense of how much bandwidth (speed) is currently available. Then the program chooses whichever *bit rate* is best suited to current network conditions. The higher the bit rate, the better the sound quality. The range for downloaded media goes from about 28 Kbps (28,000 bits per second) to 100 Kbps (100,000 bits per second), with the largest number being the highest quality. Sometimes the highest quality transmission is shown as T1, which is a high-speed connection to the Internet. If you have a broadband connection, such as DSL or cable, you may be able to listen to streaming media at that highest quality level.

Remember that none of this really has anything to do with downloading music — it applies only to listening to music as it's being sent to your computer. When you download music to a file on your hard disk, there's no need for the transmission to be a smooth one, because you won't be listening to the music until after the file has been downloaded to your computer. More on downloading in a moment.

Internet music file formats

One other important feature of music that's stored on the Internet is that not all songs are available in the same format. Unlike audio CDs, which always store songs in CDA format, songs on the Internet are available in several flavors. Windows Media Player can play songs stored in the popular MP3 (.mp3) format, as well as all the other formats listed earlier in Table 20-1. However, it can't play songs stored in RealAudio (.ram) or Liquid Audio (.lqt) format. For those formats you need to download the appropriate players from www.realaudio.com and www.liquidaudio.com, respectively.

In many cases, you also are given a choice of file quality to download. If you plan to just listen to the song as it's being streamed to your computer, pick a quality that matches the speed of your Internet connection (although Media Player can also select the appropriate speed automatically). If you are copying the file to your hard disk, however, you are better off downloading the highest-quality copy you can get.

As a rule, it's easy to tell which file is the highest quality. The higher the bps (or Kbps), the higher the quality of the recording. Higher quality also means a larger file and longer download time. But again, if you're copying it to your hard disk you really don't care how "smooth" the delivery is; it's worth it to go for the highest quality. You also might come across some sites that list T1 as a quality rating. Consider that to be the highest quality available.

Downloading to the Media Library

Finally, if you want Windows Media Player to add downloaded music that you've purchased to its own Media Library, choose Tools ➪ Options from Media Player's menu bar. Then click the Media Library tab and select the Automatically add purchased music to my library option. When you do so, Media Player attempts to organize downloaded music in the same manner that it organizes music copied from audio CDs. If you don't choose this option or if you end up in a site that forces you to choose the folder where you want to store the file, don't worry about it. You can always add the song to your Media Library later by choosing Tools ➪ Search for Media Files from Media Player's menu bar.

Now that you have a basic understanding of all these issues, you're ready to go online and start looking for music that you like.

Finding music online

Your search for music online can begin from Windows Media Player itself. Just click the Media Guide tab on the left side of window, and the larger window will show you the home page for WindowsMedia.com on the Web. You also can get there by choosing Shop for Music Online from the Explorer bar while viewing your My Music or Shared Music folder in Explorer. WindowsMedia.com will offer links to other sites that offer music online.

As you cruise around these sites, you'll find samples to listen to, as well as files to download. Just listening is almost always free. However, you might not be able to listen to the entire track—only a portion of it; downloading may require a license and possibly a payment. Specific download instructions will have to come from the Web site you're downloading from, but the procedure is similar to that used in most downloads. After you choose Save File to Disk from the dialog box that appears, navigate to your My Music or Shared Music folder, if that's where you want to place the downloaded file.

 Tip
    If you're looking for music from a specific artist or group, consider going to a general search engine such as www.yahoo.com and looking up the artist's or group's name. You might find their home page, which may, in turn, point you to some places for downloading their music.

Playing downloaded music

After you've downloaded a song from the Internet, you can play it just as you would any other song on your computer. Navigate to the song's file icon through Windows Explorer and then click (or double-click) the file's icon. The file will play in Media Player if it's MP3 or WMA. Otherwise, it will play in the program best suited to that format.

Creating Custom Playlists

A *playlist* is a selection of songs from your Media Library that you can play in a series or in random order. For example, you might create a playlist titled Dinner Music containing soft songs that you can listen to while dining. You could create another playlist titled Dance Music for wild, late-night parties. You can create as few or as many playlists as you like. Any song from any category can belong to any number of playlists, giving you total flexibility.

To create a playlist in Media Player, first make sure the Media Library button is selected at the left side of the window. Then click the New Playlist button and enter any name of your choosing. Click OK. The new playlist appears beneath My Playlists in the left pane.

To add songs to your playlist, stay in the Media Library tab and open whichever category best suits your needs: All Audio, Album, Artist, or Genre. To add a song to a playlist, click the song and then click the Add to Playlist button. Choose the playlist to which you want to add the song. You can select multiple songs by dragging the mouse pointer down through the empty space to the right of the song titles. Or, click the first song you want to select and then hold down the Ctrl key as you click additional songs you want to select. Then click the Add to Playlist button to add all the selected songs to a playlist.

> **Tip**   You also can add songs to a playlist by right-clicking the song name and choosing Add to Playlist.

Figure 24-19 shows a sample playlist I created from my Media Library. Clicking the playlist name displays its contents in the right pane. (You also can select a playlist from the drop-down list in the upper-right corner.) To play a playlist, click the first song in the list and then click the Play button. Optionally, you can click the Shuffle button to the left of the drop-down list prior to clicking the Play button to play the songs in random order.

To rearrange songs in a playlist, click the song you want to move and drag it up or down. Or click the song and use the Up and Down buttons above the playlist to move the song. To delete a song from the playlist, click the song and then click the Delete (X) button. Then choose Delete from Playlist. Note that doing so will not delete the song from your Media Library, nor from your hard disk.

If you have a CD-R or CD-RW drive, you can also "burn" all the songs from a playlist to an audio CD, as discussed next.

Figure 24-19: A sample custom playlist under My Playlists in the left pane

Creating Custom Audio CDs

As you know, an audio CD is one that can be played in virtually any CD player, be it your car stereo, a portable player, or the CD-ROM drive of a computer. If your computer has a CD-R or CD-RW drive, you can "burn" a custom playlist to an audio CD. You'll need a blank CD-R or CD-RW disk, available at most computer, music, and office-supply stores. The capacity of these disks is often expressed in "minutes," indicating how many minutes of music you can put on the disk.

Caution | Songs copied to CD-R disks can be played in any CD player, but songs copied to CD-RW disks can be played only in computer CD-RW drives. You can copy to CD-R disks in either CD-R or CD-RW drives.

Before you get started, be aware that if your sound hardware (CD drive, sound card, speakers) supports digital recording and playback, you can use error correction to remove pops and other sounds caused by scratches on the CD. In Media Player, choose Tools ➪ Options and click the Devices tab. Then click the device you're using and click the Properties button to see your available options. Clicking the Help button in the drive's Properties dialog box will provide additional information. After you close the dialog box, you're ready to create your audio CD.

Note   Whether a protected song can be copied to an audio CD is determined by its license, which in turn is created by the owner of the copyright.

The first step is to create a playlist of the songs you want to copy to the CD, as discussed in the preceding section. Then just follow these steps:

1. Put the blank CD-R or CD-RW disk in the drive.

2. In Media Player, click the Media Library tab and then click the name of the playlist that you want to copy to the audio CD.

3. Click the Copy to CD or Device button in the taskbar at left or choose File ➪ Copy ➪ Copy to Audio CD from Media Player's menu bar. Media Player will split into two panes with Music to Copy in the left pane, and any music that's already on the disk in the right pane. (A CD-R disk needs to be completely blank, a CD-RW disk just needs to have sufficient space for the songs to be copied.)

4. If the songs in the left pane don't match your playlist, select the playlist you want to copy from the drop-down list at the top of the column. Typically, custom playlists are listed at the top of the list that drops down.

5. If there are more songs in the left pane than can fit on the CD, some will be marked Will Not Fit. If necessary, you can deselect any songs by clearing their check marks to make room for songs that might not otherwise fit. You also can rearrange the songs in the left column by dragging them up and down.

 Tip   If you want to add more songs to the playlist, click the Media Library tab and select your songs normally. Then click the Portable Device tab to get back to your two-pane view. Then choose your playlist name from the drop-down list under Music to Copy.

6. When all the songs that are checked are shown as Ready to Copy, as in Figure 24-20, click the Copy Music button near the upper-right corner of Media Player's window.

7. Wait.

Windows Media Player will make two passes through the playlist. On the first pass, it creates a copy of each song in the CDA format required on audio CDs. On the second pass, it copies each of those copied songs. When it has finished copying all the songs, the Status column of all the songs in the playlist will be marked as Complete. You can then remove the disk from its drive.

 Tip   If the you're concerned about the right column not showing copied files, choose View ➪ Refresh from Media Player's menu bar while the CD is still in its drive.

Keep in the mind that the CD you created is just like any other audio CD you purchased from a store. Which is to say, each track (song) is stored in CDA format, and titled Track 1, Track 2, and so forth.

Figure 24-20: Ready to burn an audio CD from a Media Player playlist

Copying Music to Portable Devices

Portable players (also called *MP3 players* and *digital audio players*) are small audio devices that can store and play music without a disk or tape. To use such devices, you download music from your computer's hard disk to the device. All players come with their own software for downloading, and you can certainly continue to use that software in Windows XP. However, Windows XP has added support for downloading music to some portable players directly from Media Player.

Tip For the most recent list of hardware that's compatible with Windows XP, click the Start button and choose Help And Support ⇨ Find compatible hardware and software for Windows XP. Or visit www.microsoft.com/hcl on the Web.

You can copy virtually any unprotected music to a portable device. Whether licensed music can be played is determined by the owner of the copyright. In some cases, you might need a hardware serial number, provided with the portable device, to copy protected content. In other cases, the protected content might not play at all on a portable device.

Caution As always, step one to using any hardware device is to read the manufacturer's instructions. If you have any problems with the techniques described here, just use the software that came with your portable player.

Setting a device's sound quality

If you're using a portable device that Windows XP recognizes, you can set a recording quality prior to copying. As usual, the higher the quality you select, the larger the resulting files, and therefore, the fewer songs you can fit onto the medium. To set a quality for your portable device in Media Player, follow these steps:

1. Make sure your device is turned on and plugged into the computer as per the manufacturer's instructions.

2. In Media Player, choose Tools ➪ Options.

3. Click the Devices tab and wait a few seconds for Windows to scan your connected devices.

4. When you see the device you want to copy to, click it and then click the Properties button. The device's Properties dialog box opens, as in the example shown in Figure 24-21 (although yours may look different).

Figure 24-21: Sound quality settings for a portable digital music player

5. Make your selections from the options provided and then click the OK button.

Copying the songs

Next, if you haven't already done so, create a playlist of the songs you want to copy to the portable device. Click the Copy to CD or Device tab in the taskbar along the left edge of the Media Player window. As when copying to a CD, the player will split into two columns. The left column, titled Music to Copy, lists songs from the playlist to be copied. Use the check boxes to select the songs you want to copy. The right column will display the name of the device and any songs that are already on the portable device, as in Figure 24-22. If the wrong device is selected in that column, just choose the device name from the drop-down list at the top of that column.

If there are already songs in the portable device, they list in the right column titled Music on Device. You can delete songs from that column by right-clicking and choosing Delete from Playlist. That will make more room for songs listed in the left column.

Note   If the left column doesn't look right, make sure your playlist is selected in the drop-down list under Music to Copy.

Figure 24-22: Ready to copy songs to a portable device

When you're ready to copy, click the Copy Music button near the top of Media Player's window. It will take a few minutes as Media Player inspects, converts, and then copies each song to the device. When all the selected songs in the left column show Complete in their status column, you're done. You can close Media Player, and use the portable device as per the manufacturer's instructions.

Internet Radio

Many radio stations now broadcast over the Internet, which means that you can listen to the station no matter where you are in relation to its broadcast origin. Just open Windows Media Player in the normal manner and click Radio Tuner in the left column. Media Player splits into two panes. On the left, the PRESETS pane lists featured radio stations, which serve only as examples. Hundreds of radio stations are actually available on the Internet. The right pane, titled STATION FINDER, enables you to explore available radio stations. Using the Find By drop-down list, you can choose how you want to search for available radio stations, by Format, Language, Location, and so forth. Once you make a selection, a second drop-down list appears. Making a selection from that drop-down list displays stations that match your criteria. For example, Figure 24-23 shows the results of searching for radio stations with a 60s format. (The Search button in the upper-right corner enables you to search by several criteria.)

Figure 24-23: The Radio Tuner tab in Media Player

To listen to a radio station, double-click it. You might have to wait a couple of seconds before you hear the station. (The station's Web page will open in Internet Explorer as well.)

To create your own custom collection of favorite radio stations, choose My Presets from the drop-down list under PRESETS. To add a station to your Preset list, click the station in the right pane, and then click the <<< button. To remove a station from your Presets list, click the >>> button. The stations you select as presets will also be added to the Media Library, under Radio Tuner Presets. To stop listening to a station, click the Stop button. Simple!

DVD and Video

Media Player also acts as a video and DVD player. If you have already updated Your Media Library, any existing videos on your hard disk will be listed under Video, categorized under All Clips, and by Author, as in the left pane of Figure 24-24. If you have a DVD drive, you can watch the DVD currently in the drive by choosing your DVD drive and the DVD title from the "playlists" drop-down list near the upper-right corner of the window, as is also shown in that figure.

Figure 24-24: Available video files in the left pane, DVD drive available in the drop-down list

While a video is playing, you can use the Play, Pause, Volume, Rewind, Fast Forward, and other controls near the bottom of Media Player's window just as you would on a VCR or DVD player. You'll also notice a tiny Full Screen button, which you can click to show the video full screen, as it would appear on a TV. (Or choose View ➪ Full Screen from Media Player's menu bar.) In the full-screen view, you can right-click to reveal some basic controls, as well as an Exit Full Screen option to return to Media Player. Any features unique to the DVD you're watching at the moment will also be available on that right-click menu.

On some videos, switching to full-screen view will display a menu strip along the top of the screen and some semi-transparent Media Player controls along the bottom of the screen. Both will gradually fade away. But just moving the mouse pointer will bring them back into view. Of course, you can always right-click in full-screen view to see other options.

If you have a DVD drive installed, the Options dialog box for Media Player (which you get to by choosing Tools ➪ Options) will include a DVD tab, as shown in Figure 24-25. From there you can set Parental Controls. For example, setting the rating to PG-13 prevents the kids from watching DVDs with any more mature rating. Many DVDs are multilingual. The DVD tab also enables you to select a language for subtitles, audio, and menu displays presented by the current DVD.

Figure 24-25: The DVD tab of Media Player's Options dialog box

Recording Sound with Sound Player

If you want to record voice or other sound that doesn't come prepackaged from an audio CD or from the Internet, you can use Sound Player. It's really only useful for recording small sound clips, perhaps up to a minute or so in length. If you ever need to create such sounds, however, the Sound Recorder applet will help you do the job.

Tip   For lengthier recordings, such as when copying LPs or longer voice narrations, the audio capabilities of Windows Movie Maker, described in Chapter 25, is the preferred tool.

To record your own voice with Sound Recorder, you first need to have a microphone or headset plugged into your sound card or computer. To test that device, open the Sounds and Audio Devices Properties dialog box, described earlier in this chapter. On the Voice tab, select your microphone under Voice Recording and click the Test Hardware button to try it out.

> **Tip** Files created with Sound Recorder are stored in Wave (`.wav`) format, which is the most common format used for voice and small sound effects.

To start Sound Recorder, click the Start button and choose All Programs ➪ Accessories ➪ Entertainment ➪ Sound Recorder. Before you start recording, you can set a sound quality by choosing Edit ➪ Audio Properties from Sound Recorder's menu bar. Under Sound Recording, choose your recording device and then click the Advanced button to choose a Sample Rate Conversion Quality setting. As usual, the higher the quality you select, the larger the file used to store the recording. You also can click the Volume button to display a little volume slider for making further adjustments (see Figure 24-26).

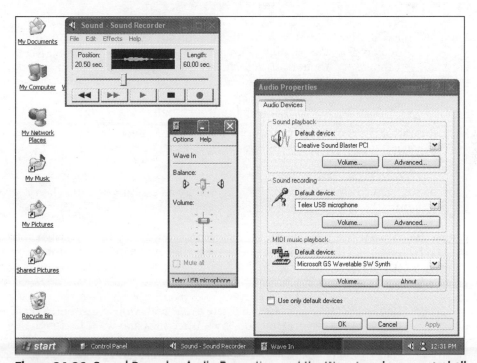

Figure 24-26: Sound Recorder, Audio Properties, and the Wave In volume control all on the screen

When you're ready to record, choose File ➪ New from Sound Recorder's menu bar, just to make sure you're starting with an empty Wave file. Then click the Record button (red dot) and start talking (or making whatever sound you want to record). When you've finished recording, click the square Stop button.

To hear the recording, click the Rewind button and then click the Play button. To save the recording, choose File ➪ Save. You can add echo to the file, play it in reverse, and increase or decrease its speed or volume by making selections from the Effects menu. The effects are additive. For example, choosing Add Echo once adds some echo, choosing that again adds more echo. Don't forget to save the file again after making your selections.

In the future, opening the Wave file from an Explorer window is likely to open Media Player to play the file. To get the file back into Sound Recorder in the future, run Sound Recorder and choose File ➪ Open from its menu bar.

Assigning Sound Effects to Events

You can assign sounds, stored in Wave files, to various events that occur in Windows. You can play one sound when Windows starts, for example, another when an error message appears on-screen, and so on. To assign system sounds, follow these steps:

1. Click the Start button and choose Control Panel.

2. If Control Panel opens in Category view, choose Sounds, Speech, and Audio Devices. Open the Sounds and Audio Devices icon.

3. Click the Sounds tab.

4. If you want to check out and possibly modify an existing sound scheme, select one from the Sound Scheme drop-down list.

Under Program Events, you'll see a list of "events" to which you can assign sound effects. For example, the Asterisk event occurs whenever a message containing an asterisk icon pops up on the screen. The Close Program event occurs whenever you close an open program's window.

To assign a sound effect to an event, click the event and choose a sound from the drop-down list. Or, if you've created your own Wave files and want to assign one of those to the event, click the Browse button, navigate to the folder that contains your Wave file and then click the file's icon. To hear the sound you've selected, click the Play Sound button just to left of the Browse button.

Tip   The Internet is home to thousands of tiny sound effects files stored in Wave format, most of which you can download for free. To explore, go to any search engine and search for some phrase, such as "free wave files."

To save your sound scheme, click the Save As button and give it a file name. Click the OK button. In the future, you can use this new sound scheme, or any other, by returning to the Sounds tab and selecting it from the Sound Scheme drop-down list.

Summary

Whew — Windows XP and Media Player 8 have made some great strides in turning the PC into a device for playing audio, video, and DVD. The main points covered in this chapter include the following:

✦ If you have any problems with sound, the Sounds and Audio Devices dialog box, the Volume Control (mixer), and Sound Troubleshooter can all help you to get things working.

✦ In addition to the volume knobs on your speakers, you can use the volume control slider on the taskbar and the Volume Control (mixer) applet to control volume from your mouse.

✦ Windows Media Player 8 can play most multimedia files and will open automatically when you open any file compatible with that program.

✦ To play an audio CD, just put the CD in your computer's CD-ROM or DVD drive.

✦ To copy an audio CD to your hard disk, use the Copy from CD tab in Media Player.

✦ You can use Media Player to create custom audio CDs and to copy music to some portable digital audio players.

✦ You also can use Media Player to listen to the radio, to watch DVDs, and to watch videos.

✦ Sound Recorder is a small applet that enables you to record voice and small sound effects to Wave files.

✦ The Sounds tab in the Sounds and Audio Devices Properties enables you to create your own custom sound schemes.

✦   ✦   ✦

Fun with Windows Movie Maker

If you have a video camera, you can use Windows Movie
Maker to create your own custom movies, created from
any video clips you have. You can even add your own soundtrack or narration, and put in some cool transition effects
between scenes. The movies you create with Movie Maker can
be viewed by anyone who has a copy of Windows Media
Player (Version 7 or later). This means you can e-mail the
movies you make to anyone who has an e-mail account. If you
have your own Web site, you can publish your movies there
as well for people to download.

Windows Movie Maker Hardware Requirements

All modern video cameras enable you to record both sound
and video. The files required to store that kind of information
tend to be large, and it takes considerable hardware horse-
power to play videos smoothly on a PC. So although any computer capable of running XP will run Movie Maker, a faster PC
with lots of RAM will provide the best performance. The PC
will also need a video card capable of capturing video, or an
IEEE 1394 port if that's what your camera connects to.

Note   You can find a list of Windows XP-compatible IEEE 1394 and digital capture devices in the hardware compatibility list available through Windows Help and Support as well as at www.microsoft.com/hcl.

Of course, you also need a cable to connect your video camera, or whatever, to your computer. I say "or whatever" because Movie Maker is actually capable of recording from many different types of devices, including TVs, VCRs, CD players, radios, LPs, Web cams, even other computers. The only requirement is that the device you are recording from must have the same kind of "out" jacks. For example, many music devices have a Line Out jack. If your sound card has a Line In jack, you just need a cable to connect the Line Out jack from the player to the Line In jack on the sound card.

TVs, VCRs, and many analog video cameras often have an A/V Out jack, SVideo jack, or separate Video Out and Audio Out jacks. If your graphics card (or video capture card) has corresponding "In" jacks, you'll just need a cable to connect the jacks on the two devices. You can even send video only to the graphics card, and audio to the sound card. You can find cables to connect virtually any combination of jacks at most electronics stores.

Getting to Know Windows Movie Maker

Starting Windows Movie Maker is easy. In fact, it's automatic with digital video cameras that connect through an IEEE 1394 (FireWire) port. If you plug the cable into the camera, turn on the camera in VCR (not Camera) mode, and then plug it into the computer, Movie Maker will start up automatically. For other types of devices, you can start Movie Maker like any other program.

1. Click the Start button.
2. Choose All Programs ➪ Accessories ➪ Windows Movie Maker.

When Windows Movie Maker starts, it will look like Figure 25-1. The names of the various components discussed in this chapter are pointed out in the figure.

Buzzwords

As with most things in life, creating movies has its own set of jargon and buzzwords. So before we get any deeper into Movie Maker, let's take a moment to define some terms so that you'll know what I'm talking about as you progress through this chapter:

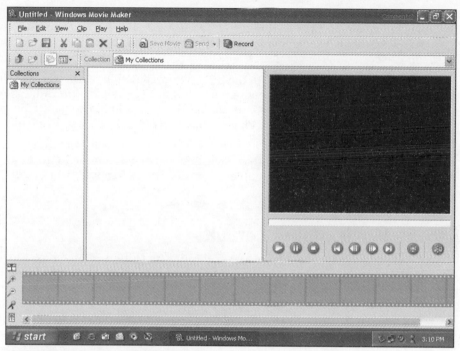

Figure 25-1: Windows Movie Maker

✦ **Capture:** Means the same thing as *to record*. More specifically, it means to convert incoming video and/or audio to digital data that can be stored in a file on a computer disk.

✦ **Capture card:** A graphics card that has capture capabilities built right in (such as the ATI All In Wonder card), or an add-on card specifically designed for recording (capturing) output from a playback device. For example, an IEEE 1394 FireWire card can capture digital video and therefore act as a capture card (also called a *capture device*).

✦ **Clip:** A small segment of audio or video content, much like a single scene in a regular movie. Most movies are made from a series of short clips.

✦ **Collection:** A folder in Movie Maker for organizing the clips from which your movie will be produced.

✦ **Content:** In the media biz, this general term refers to audio, video, text, and images that make up your production or movie. Also called *source content* or *source material*.

✦ **Frame:** A video is composed of many still images played in rapid succession. Each one of those still images is a *frame*.

✦ **Movie File:** The Windows Movie File (.wmv) file that results from combining clips into a movie and saving that movie as a file.

✦ **Playback device:** Any device capable of playing audio or video, such as a VCR, a video camera in VCR mode, a CD player, or a Web cam. The "out" port(s) of the playback device need to be connected to the "in" ports of the capture card on your computer.

✦ **Player:** Unlike *playback device*, the term *player* generally refers to some kind of software that can display content on a computer. For example, Microsoft Media Player is the *player* for movies that you create in Movie Maker. So anyone who has Microsoft Media Player can view (but not necessarily change) the movies you create.

✦ **Project:** A collection of clips that have already been assembled into a movie, although not necessarily a completed movie. This is a movie "work in progress."

Setting Movie Maker defaults

You can set some *defaults* for Movie Maker through its Options dialog box. The defaults are just settings that are automatically selected when Movie Maker starts, and you can certainly change them at any time. To set the defaults, you need to close the Record dialog box, if it's open. Then choose View ⇨ Options from Movie Maker's menu bar to get to the Options dialog box, shown in Figure 25-2.

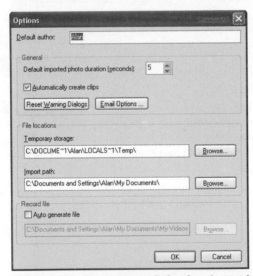

Figure 25-2: The Options dialog box in Movie Maker for setting general defaults

Within the Options dialog boxes, you can choose from among the following options:

✦ **Default author:** This is the name of the person who will be given the title Director in the movies you create. You can put your own name here.

✦ **Default imported photo duration:** Some video cameras can shoot photos that remain fixed on-screen while the video is playing. If your camera has this capability, use this option to set the default duration for displaying these still photos.

✦ **Automatically create clips:** When recording video, Movie Maker can automatically divide a lengthy segment into smaller, more manageable clips. It creates a new clip whenever the scene in one video frame completely differs from the scene in the previous video frame. I recommend you select this option so that you don't end up with one long video clip that you need to "cut up" later manually.

✦ **E-mail options:** You can send clips as e-mail attachments directly from Movie Maker by choosing File ➪ Send Movie To. Use the Email Options button to specify which e-mail program you want Movie Maker to use when mailing clips.

✦ **Temporary storage:** Select a drive and directory where you want Movie Maker to store temporary files as you record video.

✦ **Import path:** If you already have video you'll be importing into Movie Maker, set this option to the drive and directory where most of those clips are stored. Later, when you choose File ➪ Import, Movie Maker will initially look for clips in the folder you specify.

✦ **Auto generate file:** Selecting this option tells Movie Maker to automatically generate a movie file when a preset recording limit has been reached. This is handy when copying very lengthy video when you might want to leave the computer unattended. If you choose that option, you also can select where you want to place the movie file. The files that are created automatically will have generic names such as `Tape1.wma`, `Tap2.wma`, and so forth.

Click the OK button after you've finished making your selections.

Connecting hardware

As previously mentioned, there are no hard-and-fast rules for connecting your video hardware to your computer. For a digital video camera that connects through a FireWire port, however, the procedure will go like this:

1. Leave the computer turned on.

2. Turn on the camera in VCR (not camera) mode.

3. Put the tape you plan to record from into the camera.

4. Plug the FireWire cable into the camera.

5. Plug the FireWire cable into the computer.

With this approach, Windows Movie Maker starts automatically and displays a dialog box like the one shown in Figure 25-3. You can choose where you want to start recording from, or choose the third option if you're not ready to start recording just yet. You'll be taken to the Record window with your camera already selected as the video and audio recording device, as in the example shown in Figure 25-3.

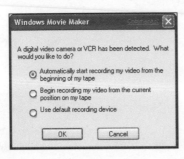

Figure 25-3: Plugging a digital video camera into a FireWire port automatically brings up this dialog box.

Caution

Incorrect connections can damage electronic devices beyond repair. Your best bet is to refer to the instructions provided by the device manufacturers.

For other devices, connect the device to your video or audio card according to the card manufacturer's instructions. You then need to start Movie Maker from the Start menu if you haven't already done so.

Selecting the device from which you're recording

If Windows XP can't detect the playback device from which you're recording, you need to do so yourself. This step can be tricky because the correct choice isn't always obvious. Furthermore, for audio, you need to make sure that the device is selected on the Recording side of the Volume Control applet (mixer) discussed in Chapter 24. If you are recording from an audio device attached to the Line In jack on your sound card, for example, the Line In jack on the recording side of Volume Control must be selected. To be able to hear the sound coming in through the Line In jack, the Line In Volume control on the Playback side of the Volume Control must not be muted, and its volume slider must be turned up a little.

You then need to select the device from which you plan to record in Movie Maker's Record dialog box. Click the Record button in Move Maker's toolbar or choose File ⇨ Record from its menu bar to open that dialog box. Once you're in the Record dialog box, use the Record drop-down list to choose Video and Audio, Audio Only, or Video Only to specify what you want to record. Then, if necessary, click the Change Device option to specify from where you'll be recording.

Choosing recording options

Before you actually start recording, you can make some additional selections from the Record dialog box, as follows:

✦ **Record time limit:** If selected, recording stops automatically after the duration you set in the drop-down list to the right of the check box.

✦ **Create clips:** If selected, automatically separates recorded material into smaller more easily managed "clips." This option is especially helpful when recording video.

✦ **Disable preview while capturing:** If selected, turns off the large Preview monitor in the dialog box that otherwise shows the video content you're capturing.

✦ **Setting:** Enables you to choose a quality for the material being recorded. As usual, the higher the quality, the larger the resulting files.

Unless your hard disk space is very limited, I recommend recording at the highest quality. You can always create smaller, lower quality movies from the high-quality clips at a later time. That's easier than going back and recapturing content to get a higher quality later.

Capturing Content

Recording content from a digital video camera is pretty easy, because you can use the Digital Video Camera Controls at the bottom of the dialog box to work your video camera from your computer screen. To play the tape so that you can see what's going to be recorded, for example, click the Play button. To rewind the tape, click the Rewind button. While the tape is paused, you can even use the Previous Frame and Next Frame buttons to move frame-by-frame through the tape to select exactly from where you want to start recording. Finally, if you want the captured content to be placed in its own collection under My Collections, click the My Collections icon at the top of the collections list to select that as the parent collection for your new collection.

To start recording, just click the Record button that's right under the Preview frame. The content being recorded will appear in the Preview frame, a blinking Recording message will appear, and the Record button will change to a Stop button, as in Figure 25-4.

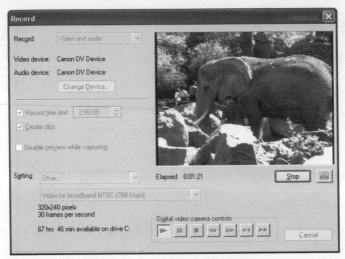

Figure 25-4: Video being captured appears in the Preview box.

For other content, get the device that will be the playback device ready to play the content you want to record. Then click the Record button in Movie Maker's Record dialog box and start playing the content to be recorded. If the content contains video, the video in the Preview box appears.

When you're ready to stop recording, click the Stop button. The Save Windows Media File dialog box opens, as shown in Figure 25-5. Give the content a file name and click the Save button. It might take a few seconds for the content to be saved. When that's finished, the content displays in a collection that has the same name as whatever you named the file, divided into clips, as in the example shown in Figure 25-6.

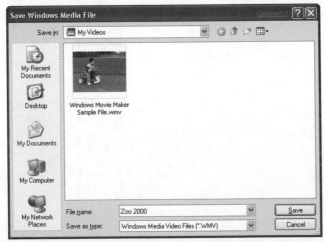

Figure 25-5: The Save Windows Media File dialog box

Tip As with physical material, you can easily trim media content that's too long. But you can't "stretch" content that's too short. There's no need to be *exact* when recording content. It is important to err in favor of recording too much, rather than too little, content.

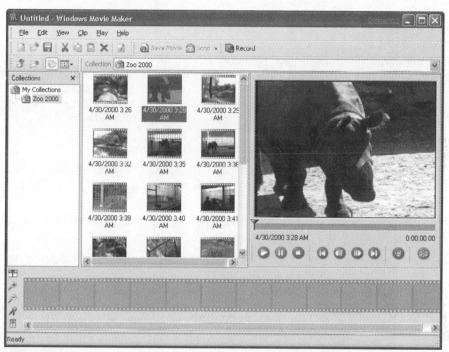

Figure 25-6: Captured content divided into clips in my Zoo 2000 collection

Making Stills from Video

You can take a snapshot of any frame in your video, in essence creating a digital photograph, just like a photo you take with a regular camera. You do this in the Record dialog box. But don't click the Record button to capture video. Instead, you just need to play the tape until the frame you want to shoot appears in the Preview box. This is a little easier with a digital video camera because you only need to get close to the frame. Then you can use the Previous Frame and Next Frames buttons in the Digital Video Camera Controls within the Record dialog box to zero-in on the exact frame.

Anyway, regardless of how you do it, once the frame that you want to photograph appears in the Preview window, just click the Take Photo button, which is just to the right of the Record button in the Record dialog box. When you do, the Save Photo dialog box opens. You can navigate to the folder where you want to save the picture (for instance, My Pictures or Shared Pictures), and then type in a file name. Click the Save button. The file is saved with a .jpeg extension in the current collection.

Capturing content is just one way to get it into Movie Maker. If you already have multimedia content on your hard disk, such as songs copied from audio CDs, pictures from cameras, downloaded (non-copyrighted) material, or whatever, you can just *import* that content into a collection.

Importing Existing Content

You can import existing content from your hard disk into a Movie Maker as well. To add the content to an existing collection, click the name of the collection into which you want to import the content. To place the content in a new collection, click My Collections and then click the New Collection button on the Collections toolbar. Type in a name for the collection and press Enter. Then follow these steps:

1. Choose File ⇨ Import from Movie Maker's menu bar.

2. In the Select the File to Import dialog box that appears, use the Look In drop-down list to navigate to the drive and directory that contains the file(s) you want to import.

3. Optionally, if you want to limit the display to a particular type of file, choose an option from the Files of Type drop-down list.

4. If you want to import several files from the current folder, select their names by using any of the standard selection methods, such as dragging the mouse pointer or using Ctrl+click. Otherwise, just point to (or click) the file to import.

5. If you want Movie Maker to automatically create clips from the imported content, choose the Create Clips for Video Files check box near the bottom of the dialog box.

6. Click the Open button to import the selected files.

A brief delay occurs as Movie Maker converts the data to the appropriate format for Movie Maker. Movie Maker also divides the file into clips if you have opted to have it do so. When the job is done, the imported file displays as one or more clips within the collection. Depending on the content you imported, the clips might just have generic names such as `Clip 1`, `Clip 2`, and so forth. Or, it uses the file name to name each clip. In Figure 25-7, for example, I have imported some songs I copied from an audio CD into a collection named Audio Only.

When you have content to work with in one or more collections, the hard part is over, and the fun begins.

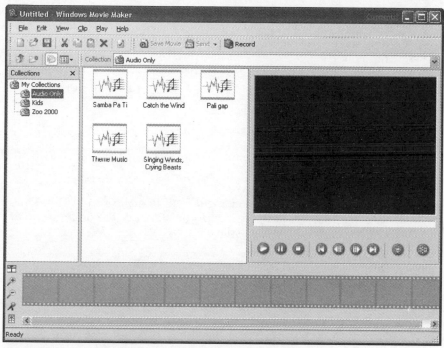

Figure 25-7: Imported songs in my Audio Only collection

Working with Clips

The movies you create with Movie Maker can contain any combination of clips from any combination of collections. Before you put a clip into a movie, you might want to preview it, and possibly trim some material off the beginning or end. To preview a clip, just click its icon in the Collections area. If it's a video clip, the first frame appears in the Preview area. You can then use the tools beneath the Preview area to play the clip. To see the name of a tool, just point to it. You can choose from the following tools:

✦ **Seek bar:** Drag the pointer on the seek bar to the left and right to move frame-by-frame through the video.

✦ **Play:** Plays the video, or resumes play if the video is paused.

✦ **Pause:** Pauses playback at the current frame.

✦ **Stop:** Stops playback and removes the clip from the monitor.

✦ **Back:** Moves back one frame if the video is paused.

✦ **Previous Frame:** Moves forward one frame if the video is paused or not playing yet.

✦ **Next Frame:** Jumps back to the first frame in the video.

✦ **Forward:** Jumps ahead to the last frame in the video.

✦ **Full Screen:** Hides Movie Maker and displays the video full-screen. Click anywhere on the screen to return to Movie Maker.

✦ **Split Clip:** Tells Movie Maker to split the clip into two clips at the current frame.

More on splitting clips in a moment.

Editing clips

Before you do anything with a clip, you might want to make a copy of it. That way, in the unlikely event that you mess up a clip, you still have the original clip at your disposal. To copy a clip, follow these steps:

1. In the Collections area, right-click the clip you want to copy.

2. Choose Copy.

3. Choose Edit ⇨ Paste from the menu bar (or press Ctrl+V).

The copy is placed at the bottom of the collection with the same name as the original, followed by the number 1.

To rename a clip, right-click its icon in the Collections area and choose Rename. Type in the new name and press Enter.

Splitting one clip into two

Suppose you have a clip that's quite lengthy, and you want to insert one or more scenes (or still pictures) into the clip in your movie. No problem. Just split the one clip into two or more clips that you can work with independently. Here's how:

1. With the clip in the Preview window, play the clip to about where you want to split it. Then click the Pause button.

2. If necessary, use the Previous Frame and Next Frame buttons to zero-in on the exact frame at which you want to make the split.

3. Click the Split Clip button or choose Clip ⇨ Split from the menu bar.

Now two clips appear in the Collections area where there was once only one. Everything up to the split point has the original clip name. Everything beyond the clip point has the original name followed by a number, such as (1).

Combining clips

You also can combine clips. Be aware, however, that it's not necessary to do this to create a movie. As you'll learn, a movie is a series of clips, and the more clips you have to work with, the more flexibility you have in arranging the clips. Nonetheless, Movie Maker doesn't always do a perfect job of dividing a video into clips. And there might be instances when you just want to combine two or more clips into one, perhaps because you have no intent of separating the clips within the movie. Whatever your motivation, here's how you can combine multiple clips into one:

1. In the Collections area, click the first clip.

2. Hold down the Ctrl key and click the clip that you want to append to the first one.

3. Choose Clip ⇨ Combine from Movie Maker's menu bar.

The icon for the second clip disappears; the original clip now contains the content of both clips. You can click the clip, and then click the Play button, to verify.

Managing clips

You can work with clips in the Collections area in much the same way you work with files in the Explorer window. You also can work with collections in much the same way you work with folders. To move or copy a clip to another collection, for example, right-drag the clip to the collection to which you want to move or add it. Then release the mouse button and choose Move or Copy.

You can view clips as thumbnails, a list of icons, or a detailed list by choosing the appropriate option from the View menu, or the Views button in the Collections toolbar.

Clips, like files, also have properties. To keep better records about each of your clips, you can also add an author, date, rating, and description to the clip's properties. Just right-click the clip's name and choose Properties to get to its Properties dialog box.

Clips don't have file names, however, because they're not files. Instead, they're more like "pointers" to the file from which they originated. This is a good thing, because it protects the original underlying content. After capturing content earlier in this chapter, for example, I saved that content to a file named Zoo 2000 in the My Videos folder. Regardless of what I do to the clips in the Zoo 2000 *collection,* the file remains unchanged. So, if I somehow made a mess of my clips and wanted to get back to the originals, I could just create a new collection, and then use File ⇨ Import to import the Zoo 2000 file from My Videos into that new collection.

Saving your project

After you've started editing your clips, you have begun a *project.* To play it safe, and to make sure you can resume from where you left off later, choose File ⇨ Save Project. Give the project a file name, such as My First Movie and click the Save button. By default, the project will be saved as a Windows Movie Maker Project (.mswmm) file.

To return to your project at any time in the future, you can open Movie Maker, choose File ➪ Open Project, and select the name of the project from the Open dialog box. Alternatively, you can just click (or double-click) the project's icon in Windows Explorer.

Producing a Movie

A movie is a collection of clips played in a specific order. This is as true in Movie Maker as it is in real movies. In a real movie or TV show, scenes aren't shot in the order you see them at the theater. Instead, they shoot all the scenes based on location, set, costumes, who's in the scene, and so forth. Then, all those scenes are assembled into a story that (one hopes) makes sense.

In Movie Maker, you assemble your movie in the workspace down near the bottom of the Movie Maker window. There are two ways to view the contents of the workspace:

✦ **Storyboard:** Shows the contents of the workspace as a series of clips without regard to the duration of each clip (top of Figure 25-8).

✦ **Timeline:** Shows the contents of the workspace as a flow of content along a timeline in which the size of each clip is proportional to the amount of time it takes up in the movie (bottom of Figure 25-8).

Figure 25-8: Storyboard (top) and timeline (bottom) of a movie

You can switch views at any time by clicking the Storyboard or Timeline button at the left of the strip. Or, right-click the workspace and choose any option, or choose View ➪ Storyboard or View ➪ Timeline from Movie Maker's menu bar.

Adding clips to the workspace

Initially you might find it easiest to build your movie in the Storyboard view. To add a video clip or picture to the movie, do whichever of the following is most convenient for you at the moment:

✦ Right-click the clip that you want to add to the movie and choose Add to Storyboard or Add to Timeline.

✦ Click the clip you want to add to the movie and choose Clip ⇨ Add to Storyboard/Timeline.

✦ Drag the clip to where you want it to appear in the Storyboard/Timeline and drop it there.

✦ Or select several clips using Ctrl+click, Shift+click, or Edit ⇨ Select All (Ctrl+A). Then drag any selected clip to the workspace.

That's all there is to it. If you make a mistake, you can delete a clip from the story-board or timeline just by right-clicking it and choosing Delete. Doing so *only* removes the clip from the workspace and doesn't remove the clip from its collection. Of course, you can add clips from any collection—they don't all have to come from the same collection.

To change the order of clips in the storyboard, just drag any clip to a new location in the workspace and drop it there.

Previewing your movie

You can preview how your finished movie is going to look at any time. Just keep in mind that there's a difference between playing a movie and playing a clip. To view the entire movie, click the first frame in the storyboard or timeline. (If you don't, the movie starts playing from the current scene or position in the timeline.) Then choose Play ⇨ Play Entire Storyboard/Timeline from Movie Maker's menu bar. The entire movie plays in the Preview window. The Play, Pause, Stop, and other buttons beneath the Preview window control the action of the entire movie, not just a specific clip.

Adding transition effects

You can add *cross-fade transitions* between clips in your movie, where one scene fades out while the other fades in. This eliminates the abrupt changes between scenes within your movie. To add a transition, follow these steps:

1. Go to the Timeline view in the workspace (View ⇨ Timeline).

2. Optionally, click the Zoom In and Zoom Out buttons to the left of the timeline to expand or contract the size of the scenes in the timeline.

3. Decide which two clips you want to place a transition effect between and then click the clip the right side of the two. It becomes surrounded by a blue frame, and its portion of the timeline is highlighted.

4. Drag the selected scene to the left so that it partially overlaps the scene that precedes it. The larger the overlap, the longer the transition between the frames.

To watch the effect, choose Play ➭ Play/Pause. To move to where the transition effect takes place, drag the vertical bar and arrow that's moving through the time-line to the left of the transition effect. If you decide the effect is too long or too short, just repeat Steps 1–4 to reposition the scene on the right side of the effect.

Trimming scenes

If you decide that a scene is running to long, you can trim frames off the front and/or back to shorten the scene. To do so, you set starting and ending *trim points* within the scene. Only content between the two scenes plays when you view the movie. Here's how to set the trim points:

1. Set the workspace to the Storyboard view. (Choose View ➭ Storyboard from the menu bar or click the Storyboard button.)

2. In the storyboard, click the frame that represents the scene you want to trim.

3. Click the Play button to start playing the current clip.

4. If you want to trim some material off the beginning of the clip, click the Pause button when you get to about where you want to set the trim point. You can use the Seek bar, Previous Frame, and Next Frame button to zero-in on a frame.

5. Choose Clip ➭ Set Start Trim Point from the menu bar to set the starting trim point. Content to the left of the trim point will be excluded from the movie.

7. To trim some content off the end of the scene, use the same buttons to zero-in on the last frame you want the movie to show.

8. Choose Clip ➭ Set End Trim Point to set the trim point. Content that follows that trim point will not be included in the final movie.

Clicking the Play button below the Preview window will now play the trimmed scene. If you change your mind or want to set different trim pointers, choose Clip ➭ Clear Trim Points from the menu bar. Note that trimming the scene in the movie has no effect on the original clip. If you want to see the clip again without the trim points, play the original clip from the Collections area rather than the movie. (Or just clear the trim points.)

Adding still photos to your movie

You can add still images, including photographs, to a movie as well. The source of the image doesn't matter. It can be a scanned image, screen shot, or any other type of digital image discussed back in Chapter 23. All that matters is that it be in BMP, DIB, JPG, JPEG, JPE, JFIF, or GIF format. If you haven't already done so, import the image(s) into Movie Maker, as discussed under "Importing Existing Content" earlier in this chapter. Of course, any still images that you created using the Take Photo button in the Record dialog box will already be in a collection.

Tip You can create slide shows without video clips by adding a series of still photos to a storyboard. You can then spice that up by adding an audio track and/or narration as described a little later in this chapter.

To add a photo to your movie, follow these steps:

1. Open the collection that contains the photo.

2. In the Collections area, right-click the image's icon and choose Add to Storyboard.

The picture will be added to the storyboard, and will look like any other clip. To reposition it within the movie, just drag it to the left or right as appropriate. By default, the image will appear for however long you set the default duration for photos in the Options dialog box. You can shorten its duration by setting a trim point. You also can set transition effects as you would with a regular video clip.

Adding audio to your movie

You can insert audio clips into your movie in much the same way you insert video clips and still photos. If you haven't already done so, import the audio files into a collection, where they'll display as clips — as in the example provided under "Importing Existing Content" earlier in this chapter. Then to add the audio clip to your movie, follow these steps:

1. Switch to the Timeline view in the workspace.

2. Drag the audio clip's icon into the timeline at about where you want it to start playing.

The audio track appears below the timeline as a bar that contains the clip's name, as in the example shown in Figure 25-9, where I've added the sound clip titled Samba Pa Ti. As necessary, you can drag the blue bar to the left or right to control exactly when the audio clip will start to play.

To try it out, choose Play ➪ Play Entire Storyboard/Timeline. You can drag the timeline bar to the start of the music. If your movie already had audio, you'll hear the original audio as well as the new clip. To adjust the relative volumes, click the Set Audio Levels button down near the timeline, or choose Edit ➪ Audio Levels from the menu bar. Use the slider in the Audio Levels dialog box, also shown in Figure 25-9, to give either the Video track or the Audio track the higher volume. For example, dragging the slider to the left lowers the volume of the audio clip.

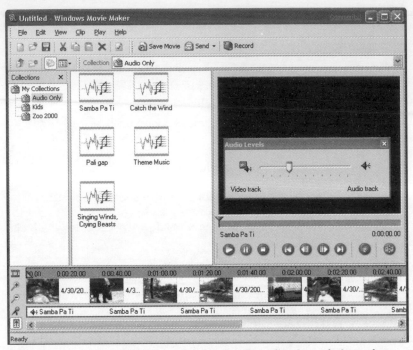

Figure 25-9: Audio track below the timeline for adjusting relative volumes

If the audio clip is longer than the movie, the clip will actually play after the video has stopped. So you'll probably want to limit the length of any audio track to the length of the movie. You can get an accurate measure of the movie's length by going to the Timeline view and dragging the vertical bar that crosses the timeline to the end of the movie. The timer beneath the monitor will show the duration of the movie up to where the vertical line is resting. For example, 0:3:25:03 indicates that the movie is about 3 minutes and 25 seconds long.

To create a shortened copy of your sound clip, click its name in the Collections area and then click the Play button under the monitor. As the sound plays, the duration appears beneath the monitor. You can drag the Seek bar to quickly move toward the desired time duration and then click the Pause button when you reach that spot. Choosing Clip ➪ Split from the menu at that point splits the audio clip into two clips. The first (original) clip will then be the length of the movie. Right-click the existing clip beneath the timeline and choose Delete to delete it. Then drag the new shortened clip to the timeline in its place.

Narrating a movie

You can also narrate a movie as it's playing. You need a microphone or headset plugged into your sound card to do this. Assuming you have already taken care of all that (as discussed back in Chapter 24), narrating the movie will be pretty easy. Just follow these steps:

1. Click the collection to which you want to add the recorded narration, or create a new collection.

2. Switch the workspace to the Timeline view. (Choose View ⇨ Timeline from Movie Maker's menu bar.)

3. Choose File ⇨ Record Narration from the menu bar. The Record Narration Track dialog box opens, as shown in Figure 25-10.

Figure 25-10: The Record Narration Track dialog box

4. If necessary, click the Change button to choose the device you'll be narrating from (for instance, Telex USB microphone in my example). Then click OK.

5. To prevent any audio from the movie's existing soundtrack from playing while you're narrating, choose the Mute video soundtrack option.

6. Speak into the microphone and watch for a reaction on the Record level indicator. If necessary, drag the slider up or down to increase or decrease the microphone sensitivity. You want the loudest noises (only) to just reach the top of the bar.

7. When you're ready to start narrating, click the Record button.

8. As the movie plays in the monitor, speak into the microphone and narrate the movie.

9. When you get to the end of the movie, or whenever you want to stop narration, click the Stop button in the Record Narration Track dialog box.

10. When prompted, choose a folder to save the narration in and enter a file name with the .wav extension. Then click the Save button.

The narration appears as a clip in the current collection and also is added to the movie automatically beneath the timeline. If there's already an audio track there, the narration track is inserted to the left of it. The narration is an added audio track, the same as any other audio clips.

To test, click the Start button and choose Play ⇨ Play Entire Storyboard/Timeline as usual. If necessary you can drag the Time bar in the timeline to the start of the narration. To adjust the volume of the narration in relation to any audio coming from the video, click the Set Audio Levels button.

To hear the narration while watching the movie, just play the movie as you normally would. (Choose Play ⇨ Play Entire Play/Pause from the menu bar.) If you're not happy with the narration and want to try again, delete the current narration by right-clicking that bluish line and choose Delete from the menu that appears.

As with video clips and photos, audio clips can also be overlapped. To make two audio tracks overlap one another, first drag them both to the workspace. Initially, the audio clips will not overlap. But you can drag the clip on the right to the left so that it covers the first audio track, either entirely or partially. Wherever the two tracks overlap, the audio plays simultaneously.

Keep in mind that if any video clips already contain audio, that audio also plays. Things can get pretty complicated this way. So if you're thinking about adding a soundtrack to your movie, and the video clips already have audio of their own, you might want to limit yourself to just adding background music or narration to the movie, but not both.

Creating the Final Product

The true final product from a movie is a Windows Movie File (`.wmv`) that can be played by anyone who has Windows Media Player on his computer. As with most things multimedia, you can control the size of the resulting file by controlling the quality of the movie. You might want to save copies of the movie at different quality settings, just to see the results. To do so, follow these steps:

1. Choose File ⇨ Save Movie, or click the Save Movie button on the toolbar. The Save Movie dialog box shown in Figure 25-11 appears.

2. Choose a quality from the Setting drop-down list. When you do, the information below the drop-down list changes to show you the specs of your selection, including frame size, frames per second, and download time at various modem speeds.

Tip   E-mail isn't the only way to share movies with others. If the movie is large, you can always burn it to a CD-R or CD-RW disc and mail it to people. That way, you don't have to be so concerned about its size.

3. Optionally, add a Title, Author, Date, Rating, and Description in the dialog box.

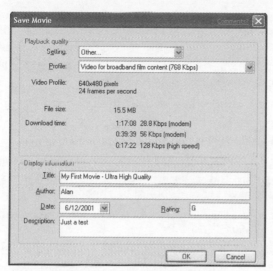

Figure 25-11: The Save Movie dialog box

4. Click the OK button. A Save As dialog box appears.

5. Choose a folder from the Save In drop-down list and then enter a file name for the movie.

6. Click the Save button.

You'll be given the option to watch the movie on the spot. Click Yes if you want to view the movie now.

To try out your movie at different qualities, repeat all these steps, but choose a different quality for each save in Step 2 and enter a unique file name for each in Step 5 (for example, `My First Movie Low Quality`, `My First Movie Ultra High Quality`, and so forth).

As with any file, you (or anyone else who has Windows Media Player) can watch the movie by clicking its file name in any Explorer window.

Summary

This chapter has covered all the basic skills and techniques you need to create your own movies using the new Windows Movie Maker. It all boils down to gathering a collection of video clips, still images, and/or audio clips, and then organizing them along a timeline into a cohesive movie. The main points to remember from this chapter include the following:

✦ Microsoft Movie Player can import clips in a variety of multimedia formats and organize them into a single movie that's stored as a single file with a `.wmv` extension.

✦ You can create clips by *capturing* content from analog and digital video cameras, VCRs, microphones, Web cams, and other devices.

✦ You also can create clips by importing content already stored on your hard disk.

✦ A *collection* is similar to a folder and acts as a container for organizing video, still images, and audio clip files.

✦ To create a movie, drag clips to the workspace at the bottom of the screen. You can display the clips in either Storyboard or Timeline view.

✦ The order of clips along the storyboard/timeline indicates the order in which they will display in the movie.

✦ The Play pull-down menu in Movie Maker offers commands for watching the movie as a whole.

✦ A movie "work in progress" is referred to as a *project* and can be saved via File ⇨ Save Project from Movie Maker's menu bar.

✦ The end result of a project is a single movie stored as a `.wmv` file, which can be viewed by anyone who has Microsoft Media Player.

✦   ✦   ✦

Local Area Networks

Gone are the days when you had to be an electrical engineer to get your computers to talk to each other in a network. In this part you'll learn how to purchase hardware for connecting your computers, and how to use the Network Setup Wizard to get your computers working in harmony. You'll learn how all the computers can share a single Internet account and printer. You'll discover how to share files, folders, and drives, so users at different computers can collaborate on projects. You'll also learn how to create shortcuts to all your favorites shared resources on the network. Finally, you'll learn techniques for beefing up security to protect your network from Internet hackers.

Create Your Own LAN

If you find yourself using floppy, or other, removable disks to copy files from one computer to another, you need a LAN. If you have several computers, but only one has Internet access, you need a LAN. If you find that you have the same document stored on several computers and can't keep track of which computer has the latest copy, you need a LAN. If only one of your computers has a CD-R or CD-RW drive and you want to burn a CD from some other computer, you need a LAN. There was a time when the cost and complexity of creating a LAN was too much for the average home or small business. As you'll learn in this chapter, however, those days are long gone.

Why Create a LAN?

In a nutshell, a *local area network*, or LAN, is just two or more computers connected to one another with cables. (However, even the cables are optional!) With the help of the networking software built in to Windows XP, the connected computers can *share resources*. The resources that the computers share can be just about anything — a printer, Internet access, disk space — whatever. The practical time- and money-saving advantages of owning a LAN are many, including the following:

- ✦ If only one PC in the LAN has a printer, a CD-ROM, CD-R, CD-RW, or Zip drive, every PC in the LAN can use that hardware.

- ✦ If only one PC has Internet access, every PC in the LAN can access the Internet through that one Internet connection and Internet account.

- ✦ You never need to use floppies or any other type of disk to copy files from one computer to another. You can move and copy files from one computer to another on the LAN using everyday drag-and-drop techniques.

✦ If you have a large collection of pictures or music files, you need store them on only one computer in the LAN. You can view, edit, and play those files from any computer on the LAN.

Cross-Reference As discussed in Chapter 24, some restrictions apply to playing music on multiple computers on a LAN.

✦ If several people work with the same data—such as a customer list, inventory list, or orders—all this information can reside on one PC. Each user in the LAN will have access to this always-current data.

As you can see, there are many advantages to setting up a LAN. I suppose the big concern for most people is how complicated it is. The truth is, networking *can* be a pretty complex subject. Many large corporations have specialized *network administrators* whose main job is to build and maintain the network. That job takes a lot of technical knowledge. However, here in this book, the goal isn't to make you a network administrator or networking guru. Instead, I just want to show you the quick and easy way to set up a perfectly good, fully functional LAN. By the time you finish this chapter, you'll know just that.

Planning the LAN

Before setting up a LAN, you first must plan your equipment purchase. For a relatively small LAN (say, no more that eight computers), you essentially have three choices:

✦ Traditional Ethernet

✦ Phone-line network

✦ Wireless network

The sections that follow discuss the pros and cons of each .

Traditional Ethernet LANs

Traditional Ethernet LANs require that each computer in the LAN have an Ethernet hardware device attached to it. Each computer then connects to a central *Ethernet hub* using Ethernet cable, as in Figure 26-1. Historically, the Ethernet device for each computer has been a *network interface card* (NIC). Which is to say, an expansion card that you have to install by taking the computer apart—a task that many find intimidating. Fortunately, external Ethernet adapters are available these days, which you can connect to your computer through a USB or IEEE 1394 port.

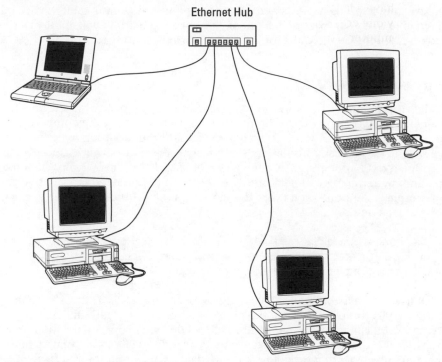

Figure 26-1: A traditional Ethernet LAN requires that all computers connect to a hub.

You also need an Ethernet hub and must decide where you're going to place the hub. You need to plug the hub into the wall, so it needs to be near an outlet. Finally, you need sufficient cable to connect each computer to that hub. Specifically, you want TPE category 5 cable with RJ-45 connectors at each end.

Caution   You need a hub even if you're connecting only two computers together in the LAN. A wire running from one computer to the next without a hub won't work!

If you decide to go with this approach, be aware that you can choose among three different speeds for Ethernet connections: 10 Mbps (million bits per second.), 100 Mbps, and 1000 Mbps (gigabit). Even the slower 10 Mbps speed is pretty fast — almost 200 times faster than a 56K modem! If you decide to splurge on one of the faster options, however, you'll want to make sure all your hardware is rated for that speed. Otherwise, everything will run at whichever component has the slowest speed.

The big drawback to using traditional Ethernet is, of course, having to run those cables. In your home, they are not a pretty sight. In an office environment, where you might not be so concerned about some extra cables, you still have to worry about creating tripping hazards and such. One solution to running all those cables yourself is to use your existing telephone line wires instead, because they're already hidden inside the walls for you. Which brings us to the. . . .

Phone-line Networks

With the rise in popularity of networking within the home has come the advent of home networking kits that use existing phone lines to connect the computers. For each computer in the network, you still need an Ethernet adapter. As with traditional networks, you can purchase either internal cards, or newer external adapters that connect to the computer through a USB or IEEE 1394 (FireWire) port. You don't need a hub with this type of network. The only "cable" you need is a relatively small, simple "telephone"-style wire that connects the Ethernet adapter to the nearest phone jack on the wall.

Tip   If a phone is already plugged into the wall jack that you want to use for your network, you can get a simple "splitter" that will enable you to plug both the phone and network adapter into the jack.

You can use your existing "voice" phone lines for the network. The voice signals and network signals traveling through the phone lines are, essentially, invisible to one another. So you can use your phone normally while using your LAN without one interfering with the other. If you also use that same phone line for a dial-up Internet connection, however, things could get pretty dicey. You would do well to get a second phone number and use that one for your Internet connection. Use your existing phone number for the network and your normal voice communications.

Tip   Having the Internet dial-up connection on its own phone line also means that people who call while you're on the Internet won't get a busy signal!

The only slight drawback to a phone-line network is that it's not quite as speedy as a "dedicated" Ethernet LAN. Currently, I think the maximum speed you can get from a phone-line network is about 1 Mbps. That's still about 17 times faster than a 56K modem, however, and not likely to cause you any heartache on a home or small business LAN. And it's a heck of a lot faster than copying files to floppy disks and *walking* them from one computer to the next!

Wireless network

The wireless approach to networking has one obvious big advantage: You don't need Ethernet cables or phone lines. With this approach, each computer in the network still gets its own Ethernet adapter. As always, this might be an internal card that you have to install yourself. Or it can be an external device you just plug into an existing USB or IEEE 1394 port. In either case, the adapter is essentially an antenna that sends signals to a special wireless Ethernet hub.

Despite the obvious convenience of going wireless, you need to be aware of some potential disadvantages. One is that there's a limit to how far the signals will travel. You need to estimate your distance requirements before you go shopping and make sure you get a wireless networking kit that can reach far enough to meet your needs.

Then again, there's a chance that the radio signals used by your networking hub will extend well beyond your home or apartment. If so, some outsider could actually tap into your network using his own equipment. Unless you happen to have evil computer geniuses as neighbors or are dealing in top-secret materials that some wealthy, powerful organization or government might want to tap into, this is probably not much of a threat.

Finally, you do need to be aware that virtually all electronic devices generate radio signals. And sometimes those signals "collide" and cause problems. For example, it's possible that the radio signals emanating from a radio, TV, microwave oven, or cordless telephone handset might interfere with your network (or vice versa). The solution to that potential problem is to purchase wireless networking hardware that enables you to choose from a selection of frequencies ("channels") to use for the network. That way, if you discover some interference among your electrical devices, you can just switch the network to another channel to stop the interference.

Setting Up Your Hardware

After you have decided on and purchased your networking hardware, you need to set it all up. I can't really help you much there. You need to rely on the manufacturer's instructions for that. Fortunately the manufacturers of home networking kits are well aware of the fact that they're not selling these products to corporate network administrators. So the instructions should be reasonably straightforward and jargon-free. I can give you some advice, however, based on my own experience with setting up LANs using Windows XP.

If you need to shut down the computers to install your hardware, as when you're installing internal cards, go ahead and shut them *all* down until the networking hardware is all installed and in place. If you're installing a traditional Ethernet LAN, make sure to connect all the computers to the hub before turning on any of the computers.

If you don't need to shut down first, as when you're just plugging your Ethernet adapter into a USB hub, you might see a little message on the screen asking whether you want to start the Network Setup Wizard as soon as you plug in each adapter. I advise *not* starting up the wizard until you've plugged in *all* the adapters. When all the networking hardware is in place, *then* you can go to the next step of actually setting up your LAN. If two or more computers in the LAN will be sharing a single Internet connection, however, there are some concepts and terms you'll want to become familiar with first.

Sharing an Internet Connection

Although the Network Setup Wizard will allow the computers in your LAN to share a single Internet connection and account, you need to be aware of some limitations. Simply stated, not all ISPs are particularly fond of Internet Connection Sharing (ICS)—for the obvious reason that they would prefer that you purchase a separate account for each computer, because that would mean more income for them. Currently, however, the only ISP that will *not* work with Windows ICS is America Online.

As far as I know, all other types of Internet connections do work with ICS. Just because it works, however, doesn't mean you automatically have license to use it. If, by chance, your ISP finds out you're using your account from more than one computer and they complain that you're violating your agreement, don't blame me. When I say you *can* do it, I mean it's technically possible. I'm not granting you permission to violate your agreement with your ISP.

Note Technically, America Online isn't really an Internet service provider (ISP). Instead, it's a separate network that provides Internet access as sort of a "value-added" feature to its own network.

A couple of concepts and buzzwords go along with the whole ICS thing. First of all, the Network Setup Wizard, which you'll use to set up your network, assumes that one computer in the LAN will act as the *ICS server* (also called the *ICS host*)—that is, the computer that has the physical connection to the Internet via a modem. All the other computers in the LAN, which don't have their own modems, are called ICS *clients*.

New Feature When you use the Network Setup Wizard to set up your LAN, you have the option to set up a *firewall* on the ICS host. A firewall is a program designed to keep intruders out of your local area network. It also keeps track of any attempts to access your LAN from the outside world (via the Internet) so that you can see whether any such attempts have actually been made.

Cross-Reference Chapter 29 discusses how you use the installed firewall.

The downside to a firewall is that it can sometimes interfere with normal, innocent communications between computers on the Internet. However, you can disable the firewall at any time if it becomes a nuisance. When you have finished the task that the firewall was interfering with, you can easily turn the firewall back on. So you can go ahead and install the firewall when the Network Setup Wizard presents the opportunity. So with those buzzwords and concepts out of the way, it's time for the last step in the procedure, which is. . . .

Setting Up Your LAN

When you have all your LAN hardware in place, you're ready to actually set up your network. The job is pretty easy, thanks to the Network Setup Wizard. Here's how you use it:

1. With all the LAN hardware in place, start up all the computers in the LAN, and turn on all peripherals (such as any printers) as well.

2. If one Windows XP computer in the LAN will be providing Internet access to all (or some) of the computers in the LAN, go to that computer first and connect to the Internet. Remember, that computer is referred to as the *ICS host* or *ICS server*.

> **Caution**
>
> If the ICS host is running some version of Windows other than XP, ignore Step 2. Instead, go to the ICS host computer and make sure it is connected to the Internet. That is, if that computer uses a dial-up connection, go ahead and log on to your ISP normally. Then go to any Windows XP computer in the LAN and go to Step 3.

3. Click the Start button, and choose All Programs ⇨ Accessories ⇨ Communications ⇨ Network Setup Wizard. The Network Setup Wizard starts.

4. Follow the instructions on each wizard page, followed by a click of the Next button. Windows can usually detect your Internet connection. If it isn't sure, you'll get to some options like those in Figure 26-2. Make sure you read the options carefully and choose the right one; otherwise, the Internet Connection Sharing won't work properly!

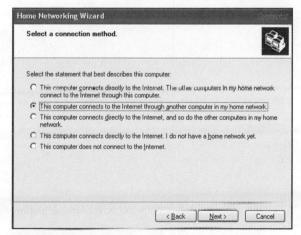

Figure 26-2: Read and respond to this Network Setup Wizard page carefully!

5. Just keep following the instructions presented by each wizard page, followed by a press of the Next key, and then click the Finish button on the last wizard page.

Repeat Steps 3–5 on each computer in the LAN. If one of the computers in the LAN is providing a shared Internet connection, stay logged on to your ISP. After you have run the Network Setup Wizard on each computer in the LAN, you're ready to test the network.

A Quick LAN Test

If one of the computers in your LAN has a printer connected, you can check to see whether it's accessible from other computers in the LAN now. Go to each computer and try to print something. It doesn't matter what you print — just open some document and choose File ➪ Print from the program's menu bar. If the printer appears under Select Printer, the printer is available from that computer. To print to that printer, just click its name and click the Print button.

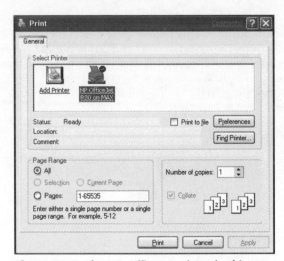

Figure 26-3: The HP OfficeJet printer in this dialog box is actually connected to another computer in my LAN.

If the printer is not available yet, you can always share it and access it later, as discussed in Chapter 27.

To check your Internet connection, try opening Internet Explorer (or any other Internet-related program) on each computer. If you can access the Web or any other Internet service from the computer, you know your ICS is working on each computer, and there's nothing more you need to do. If ICS is not working on a particular computer, run the Network Setup Wizard on that computer and make sure you choose the This computer connects to the Internet through another computer in my home network option when you get the Connection Methods page in the wizard.

To view and access other shared resources, use My Network Places.

Introducing My Network Places

After you have set up your LAN, your initial access to other computers in the LAN is available through My Network Places. You have two ways to get there:

✦ Open My Computer or My Documents (or just about any other Explorer window) and choose My Network Places from the list of Other Places.

✦ Or, click the Start button and choose My Network Places.

Tip

If My Network Places is not available on your Start menu, right-click the Start button and choose Properties. Click the Customize button next to the Start Menu option. On the Advanced tab, choose My Network Places from the list of items to display on the menu. You also can add a My Network Places icon to your desktop. Right-click the desktop, choose Properties, click the Desktop tab, click the Customize Desktop button, and then choose My Network Places under Desktop Icons.

Initially, My Network Places will open looking something like the example shown in Figure 26-4. Each of the folder icons in the window represents the Shared Documents folder of a Windows XP computer in the same *workgroup*. (I discuss that term in a moment.) If you don't see folders for all the computers in your LAN, don't worry about it just yet. As you'll learn in Chapter 27, it's easy to share folders.

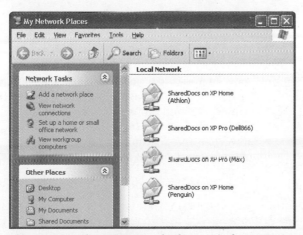

Figure 26-4: The My Network Places window on one of the computers in my LAN

Clicking (or double-clicking) a folder icon reveals the contents of that folder (if any) in a standard Explorer window. You can move and copy files from one computer to the next just by dragging icons into, and out of, that Explorer window—exactly the same techniques you use to move and copy files among folders on a single computer.

Cross-Reference   See Chapter 12 for information about moving and copying files.

A workgroup is just all the computers in the LAN that share the same workgroup name. The Network Setup Wizard initially places all the computers in a workgroup named Mshome. The View Workgroup Computers option under Network Tasks in the Explorer bar lists all the computers in your workgroup, as in the example shown in Figure 26-5.

Figure 26-5: Viewing all the computers in the Mshome workgroup

Computers Outside the Workgroup

As mentioned, the Network Setup Wizard suggests placing all your computers in a single workgroup named Mshome. However, it's not always possible to do that. For example, your ISP might require that the workgroup name of the computer that connects to the Internet be something else, such as the ISP's business name. In a large business, there might be several workgroups within the network. To view other computers in the network, follow these steps:

1. Choose View Workgroup Computers under Network Tasks in the Explorer bar of My Network Places.

2. Under Other Places, choose Microsoft Windows Network. You'll see an icon for each workgroup to which you're connected.

3. Under Other Places, choose Entire Network.

Depending on what's available on your network, you'll see icons for different types of networks. For example, Figure 26-6 shows icons for the three different types of networks, as follows:

✦ **Microsoft Terminal Services:** Relevant only to networks that use software from the open group. Not really relevant to the type of network being created here.

✦ **Microsoft Windows Network:** This icon represents the network you created using the Network Setup Wizard.

✦ **Web Client Network:** Provides access to Web servers on the LAN (if any). Not directly relevant to the network being described here.

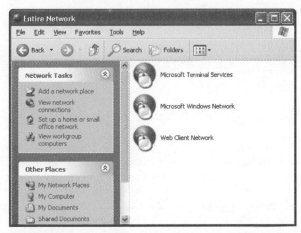

Figure 26-6: The Entire Network view provides access to all types of available networks.

As you'll learn in Chapter 27, you can share resources from virtually any computer in your network. Then you can add "shortcuts" to those places to your My Network Places window. You also can change a computer's workgroup membership, as discussed under "Computer Name, Description, and Workgroup" later in this chapter.

Introducing Network Connections

Another network-related "place" on your computer is the one named Network Connections. There are a couple of ways to get to this place.

✦ Choose View Network Connections under Network Tasks on the My Network Places Explorer bar.

✦ Or, click the Start button and choose All Programs ➪ Accessories ➪ Communications ➪ Network Connections.

An Explorer window named Network Connections opens and presents icons representing different types of network connections installed on your computer, as in the example shown in Figure 26-7.

Figure 26-7: The Network Connections place

The Local Area Connection icon provides access to a dialog box that provides information and options regarding this specific computer's connection to the LAN, as well as to the Internet. Opening that icon initially reveals just the status and activity of the connection, as on the left side of Figure 26-8. The Support tab, also shown in Figure 26-8, provides more advanced information about the connection, such as the current computer's IP address and so forth, as shown on the right side of the figure. For the most part, you really need not concern yourself with all that technical stuff right now. The whole purpose of the Network Setup Wizard is to handle all that for you automatically, behind the scenes.

Finally, clicking the Properties button on the General tab takes you to the Local Area Connection Properties dialog box shown in Figure 26-9. There are many options and settings available through this dialog box. Once again, however, at this stage of the game, you shouldn't have to concern yourself with all of that because the wizard should have taken care of everything for you. I might point out, however, that if you want this computer to be visible on your LAN, you must select the Client for Microsoft Networks check box. And if you want to be able to access resources (including files and folders) from this computer via the network, you must select the File and Printer Sharing for Microsoft Networks check box.

Figure 26-8: Some technical details about the current computer's connection to my network

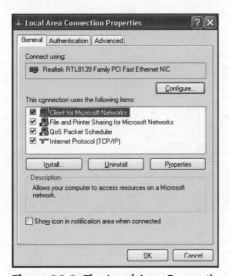

Figure 26-9: The Local Area Connection Properties dialog box for one computer in my LAN

The main things to keep in mind at this point are that most (if not all) accessing of resources on your LAN will take place through My Network Places. Unless you happen to be a trained network administrator or are currently getting support from one over the telephone, you probably won't need to use the Local Area Connection Properties dialog box very often. The whole idea behind the Network Setup Wizard (and to some extent, Windows XP itself) is to enable you to set up and use your network without first studying all the technical intricacies that go into making networks work!

Computer Name, Description, and Workgroup

On a more practical and less technical vein, people who set up their first network often discover that the names, descriptions, or workgroups they initially assign to computers in the LAN are perhaps less than ideal. Perhaps they wish they had put all the computers into the same workgroup for easier access through My Network Places. Or maybe the name or description they assigned to a computer isn't really enough to identify the computer when browsing around through all the computers in the LAN. Not to worry—you can change any computer's name, description, or workgroup membership at any time. Here's how:

1. Go to the computer whose name, description, or workgroup membership you want to change.

2. Click the Start button and choose Control Panel. If it opens in Category view, switch to the Classic view.

3. Open the System icon and then click the Computer Name tab to reveal the options shown in Figure 26-10.

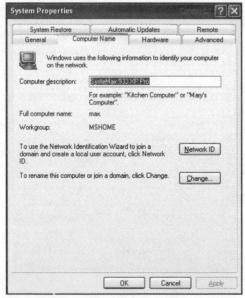

Figure 26-10: The Computer Name tab of the System Properties dialog box

4. To change the computer's description, just type in a new description in the text box provided.

5. To change the computer's name or workgroup membership, click the Change button to reveal the options shown in Figure 26-11. A Computer Name Changes dialog box appears. In this dialog box, you can change the computer's name and/or workgroup name.

Figure 26-11: Use this dialog box to change a computer's name or workgroup membership.

6. Close both open dialog boxes. If prompted to restart your computer, go ahead and do so.

Note Only the Professional Edition offers the option to make the computer a member of a domain. A *domain* is a group of computers that can be managed centrally from a Windows Server edition domain controller.

When you go to another computer in the LAN and open My Network Places, you might not see the results of your changes. But you needn't concern yourself with that just now. As you'll learn in Chapter 27, the icons in My Network Places are just "shortcuts" to resources available on your LAN. And you can easily add, change, and delete shortcuts at any time.

Troubleshooting Your LAN

If at any time you have problems with your LAN, your first step in solving the problem should be to run the Home Networking Troubleshooter. Before you do, however, keep in mind that you really haven't learned yet how to share resources and to access shared resources on the LAN, so there's really no "problem" with that. At this stage of the game, you only want to use the troubleshooter if you cannot seem to access your LAN at all, or if your Internet connection isn't working on all of your computers. To run the troubleshooter, follow these steps:

1. Close all open programs and documents.

2. Click the Start button and choose Help and Support.

3. Choose Fixing a Problem from the opening Help page.

4. Choose Network Problems from the left column of the next page.

5. Click Home and Small Office Networking Troubleshooter in the right column of the next page to get to the first page of the troubleshooter, shown in Figure 26-12.

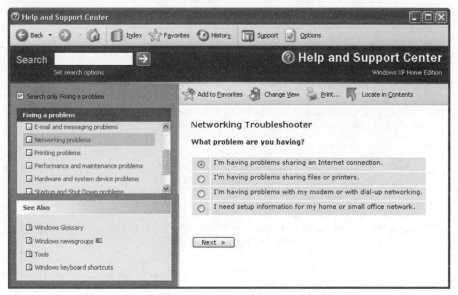

Figure 26-12: First page of the Home Networking Troubleshooter

6. Choose whichever option best describes your problem, click the Next button, and follow the instructions provided by the troubleshooter.

In the next chapter, you'll learn how to *really* put your LAN to work. Do keep in mind that if you run into any problems there, you can always run the Home Networking Troubleshooter to solve those problems.

Summary

In this chapter, you have learned how to set up a local area network using the Windows XP Network Setup Wizard. This list recaps the important points:

✦ A local area network (LAN) allows computers to share resources, such as folders, drives, printers, and an Internet connection.

✦ To create a LAN, you first need to purchase and install LAN hardware.

✦ After you have installed all the LAN hardware, you can use the Network Setup Wizard to connect together all the computers in the LAN.

✦ Your main tool for accessing shared folders on your LAN is My Network Places, available from the Start menu as well as from Other Places in most Explorer windows.

✦ To troubleshoot your LAN, use the Home Networking Troubleshooter available in Help and Support.

✦   ✦   ✦

Sharing Resources on a LAN

The whole purpose of setting up a LAN is to share resources. I suppose we could define "resource" in context as "anything that's useful." The Home Networking Wizard might have already set up some resources for sharing on your network, including your Internet connection, printer(s), and the Shared Documents folder from every Windows XP computer in the LAN. In this chapter, you'll learn to pick and choose the resources you want to share, and not to share.

Sharing Documents

Any documents that you have placed in the Shared Documents folder of any computer in the LAN will automatically be available to any computer in the LAN. The same holds true for the Shared Music and Shared Pictures subfolder within the Shared Documents folder. Suppose, for example, that I put a bunch of pictures in the Shared Documents folder on the computer named Max. To view those pictures while I'm sitting at some other computer in the LAN, I just need to open My Network Places on that computer. Within My Network Places I then just need to open the Documents on Max folder, and then the Shared Pictures icon within that folder. The entire contents of the Shared Pictures folder on Max are now as accessible to me as they would be if they were on whatever computer I happen to be sitting at.

Keep in mind that you're in a standard Explorer window while viewing the contents of the Shared Documents folder from some other computer. As such, you have all the same options available to you that you do when working with files stored on the computer's local hard disk. For example, you can change your view of the icons using options from the View menu or the Views button in the Explorer toolbar. You can move, copy, delete, and rename any file using any of the standard techniques discussed in Chapter 12.

There is one exception to otherwise "normal behavior" of the Shared Documents folder. You cannot play "protected" music that was copied to the Shared Music file on any computer other than the one to which you originally copied the music. Even though the song itself is still on the original drive, when you open the song from some other computer in the LAN, Media Player checks the local computer for a copy of the license. Because the license isn't on the local computer, Media Player will refuse to play the song. Of course, you can play any *unprotected* songs across the network. Which gives you something to think about next time you're using Media Player to copy songs from a CD to your hard disk. (I shall leave it at that.)

Cross-Reference   Copying songs from audio CDs, and the licensing issues that go along with that, are covered in Chapter 24.

Aside from protected music, it's all really pretty simple. On a stand-alone computer not connected to a LAN, files in the Shared Documents folder (and its subfolders) are accessible to all users of that computer. When you then connect that computer to a LAN, those same files are *also* accessible to all other users on that LAN. In other words, on a LAN the Shared Documents folder plays the dual role of sharing files both among users of a single computer as well as users on other computers in the LAN. So, if there are any files in your My Documents folder that you want to share with others, you can just move (or copy) them into the Shared Documents folder.

Although the Shared Documents folder is shared *by default* (automatically), it's certainly not the only folder that *can* be shared. The fact of the matter is you can share *any* folder on your hard drive across the network, as discussed next.

Sharing a Folder

You can share any folder on your PC with others in the network. When you share a folder, you automatically share all the documents and subfolders within that folder. Sharing a folder is easy. Just follow these steps:

1. On the computer containing the folder that you want to share, open My Documents or My Computer and navigate to the icon for the folder that you want to share.

Tip   Remember, the Shared Documents folder and all its subfolders are automatically shared across the network. When you open My Computer, you'll see the hand beneath the Shared Documents folder icon.

2. Right-click the folder's icon and choose Sharing and Security.

3. Select the Share this folder on the network check box, as in Figure 27-1.

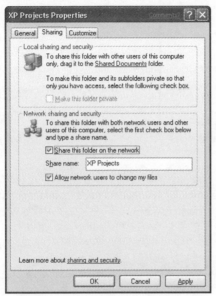

Figure 27-1: The Sharing tab of a folder's Properties dialog box

4. Give the folder a share name of your own choosing. Note that My Network Places will later display the description and name of the computer that this folder is on, so you need not include any of that information in the name you provide.

5. If you want others to be able to change and delete files that are in this folder, choose the Allow other users to change my files check box. If you don't select that option, other network users can view the files, but not change them.

Note   If you don't allow other users to change files in the current folder, those users will have "read-only" access to the folder. This means that they can view the contents of the folder, but cannot add files to the folder, delete files from the folder, or make any changes to documents stored in the folder.

6. Click the OK button to close the dialog box.

In the example presented in Figure 27-1, I opened the My Documents folder on a computer named Max, and within that folder I shared a folder named XP Projects. After closing the dialog box, the shared folder has a hand beneath its icon, as in Figure 27-2, to indicate that the folder is now shared.

Figure 27-2: Shared folders display a hand icon
like the XP Projects icon shown here.

If I were now to go to some other Windows XP computer in the network and open
My Network Places, I would see an icon for that shared folder, as in Figure 27-3.
Opening that icon would, of course, display the contents of that folder.

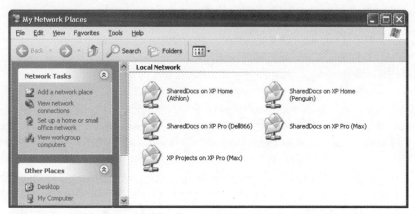

Figure 27-3: The shared folder from my Max computer as viewed from My
Network Places on another computer in the LAN (bottom left)

If you change your mind and decide to "unshare" the folder in the future, just repeat
the preceding steps. But this time, deselect the Share this folder on the network
check box.

Saving to a shared folder

Suppose that you're working on some document on one computer and decide you
want to save it on a shared folder on some other computer. Or you download a file

from the Internet and want to save that file to a shared folder on some other computer. Whether you choose File ⇨ Save from a program's menu bar or opt to save a downloaded file to disk, you'll be taken to the Save As dialog box shown in Figure 27-4.

Note   Not all programs have identical Save As dialog boxes. But most will offer some means of getting to shared folders on a LAN.

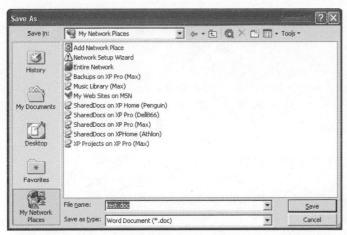

Figure 27-4: The Save As dialog box with My Network Places selected from the Save in drop-down list

From the Save in drop-down list near the top of the dialog box, choose My Network Places. Doing so will present the same set of icons you see when you open My Network Places, as in the figure. From there, just open (or navigate to) the shared folder on which you want to store the file. Give the file a name in the File name text box, just as you would when saving a file to your local hard disk. Then click the Save button.

Opening documents from shared folders

The same process works for opening documents stored on other computers in the LAN. Suppose, for example, that I want to edit a document named Course Outline.doc that's stored in the XP Projects folder on my Max computer. At the moment, however, I happen to be sitting at some other computer. I have two options here. I can start from the Windows Desktop, open My Network Places, open the icon for the XP Projects folder on Max, and then open the Course Outline document. Assuming this computer has a program that can open DOC files, such as WordPad or Microsoft Word, the document opens right up.

The other choice is to start the program first and choose File ⇨ Open from its menu bar. In the Open dialog box that appears, I would choose My Network Places from the Look In dialog box, which would show an icon for the XP Projects folder on Max. Opening that icon, in turn, would reveal the contents of that folder. Then, I would just need to click (or double-click) the icon for the Course Outline document to open it on this computer.

When you save the document, it will be saved in its original location. However, you can choose File ⇨ Save As from the program's menu bar instead. Then, in the Save As dialog box that opens, choose some other location and/or filename for this newly edited version of the document. If you do, the original file that you opened will remain unchanged. Only the new copy you save will reflect any changes you made to the document.

Tip   If you open a document from a shared folder that's read-only, you cannot edit that document directly. If you choose File ⇨ Save As and save it on your local computer, however, you can change the copy that's now on your local computer.

Moving and copying between computers

You can easily move and copy files between shared folders on the LAN. Before you *copy* files to another shared folder, however, be aware that you might be setting yourself up for some potential confusion. Suppose, for example, that the My Documents folder on a computer named Max contains a file named Chapter 1. You then copy that file to the My Documents folder on a computer named Dell866. At that moment, the two copies are identical. If later you edit one of those documents, the copies will no longer be identical. It doesn't take long before you're totally confused about which copy on which computer is the most recent copy. Therefore, your best bet might be to *move* files from one computer to another, so you always have just the one copy.

Tip   On the other hand, *copying* files to another computer on the LAN is a quick and easy way to make backups. Just remember to never edit the backups—only the originals!

The rest is simple. Select the files you want to move or copy. Then, using the secondary (right) mouse button, drag any selected file to the other window. Release the mouse button and choose either Copy Here or Move Here, depending on which you want to do.

Figure 27-5: The My Documents folder on the computer named Max, and the XP Projects folder on the computer named Max, are both open.

Bringing My Network Places Up-to-Date

Your My Network Places window will usually display an icon for any shared resource you create on some other computer on the LAN. If it doesn't do so right away, you can give it a little kick by choosing View ➪ Refresh from its menu bar. If that fails, you can follow these steps to create the shortcut yourself:

1. In My Network Places, choose Add a Network Place under Network Tasks in the Explorer bar. The Add Network Place Wizard opens. Click the Next button.

2. Click Choose Another Network Location and then click the Next button.

3. Click the Browse button. The Browse for Folder dialog box opens.

4. If the item you're looking for doesn't appear in the initial list, you can click the plus sign (+) on any category to expand it. Other workgroups and computers in your LAN will be in the Entire Network category.

5. Navigate to the shared resource you're trying to locate. In Figure 27-6, for example, I have navigated to a shared folder named Verizon on the Penguin computer in my Mshome workgroup.

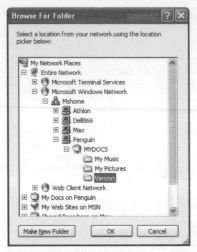

Figure 27-6: Here I have navigated to a shared folder on the computer named Penguin.

6. Click the item to which you want to create the shortcut and then click the OK button. The path to the item you selected appears in the text box.

7. Click the Next button and (optionally) enter a more descriptive name for the shortcut.

8. Click the Next button. Then click the Finish button in the last wizard page.

The contents of the shared folder might appear in an Explorer window. If that's not handy at the moment, you can just close the window by clicking its Close (X) button. In My Network Places, you'll see your new shortcut as an icon with whatever name you provided in Step 7.

Getting rid of dead shortcuts

One thing that My Network Places is not so good at is getting rid of icons for items no longer being shared. If I were to "unshare" XP Projects on Max, for example, its folder would remain in My Network Places on all the computers in the LAN! Trying to open that icon would just display an error message indicating that the folder isn't accessible.

Fortunately, the icons in My Network Places are just shortcuts to network resources. Therefore, you can delete those icons without affecting the file (or other resource) that the icon represents. You delete icons in My Network Places just as you delete any other icons — by right-clicking the icon and choosing Delete.

Renaming My Network Places icons

You can rename any icon in your My Network Places window, to whatever you want. Likewise, you can rename an icon in My Network Places by right-clicking and choosing Rename. Because you're only renaming the "shortcut" in My Network Places, the underlying resource that the icon represents won't be affected. Suppose, for example, that you don't want to see the computer descriptions in the network icons, just the computer names. No problem. Just right-click any icon, choose Rename, and type in the new name. In Figure 27-7, I renamed the icons in My Network Places on one of my computers to show only the computer name.

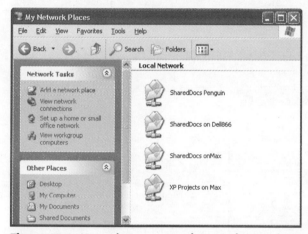

Figure 27-7: Here I have renamed some shortcut icons to shared resources in My Network Places.

Tip   To create a desktop or Quick Launch toolbar shortcut to a resource on the LAN, just right-drag the resources icon from My Network Places to wherever you want to place the icon. Then release the right mouse button and choose Create Shortcuts Here.

Sharing Drives

You can share entire drives in a LAN, which presents a lot of advantages. If one of the computers in your LAN is a notebook that doesn't have its own CD-ROM or floppy drive, for example, it can just use the shared CD-ROM or floppy drive from some other computer in the LAN. If you have a Zip drive on one of your computers, you might want to share it with other computers in the network.

As you might recall, the drives on any computer are accessible from the My Computer view in Explorer. You can open that by clicking the Start button and choosing My Computer, or by choosing My Computer from Other Places in the Explorer bar. To share any drive listed in My Computer, follow these steps:

1. In My Computer, right-click the icon for the drive you want to share, and choose Sharing and Security.

2. Initially, you'll see a warning about sharing the root of a drive. However, the warning pertains more to sharing your hard disk than a removable drive. So you can click the link to continue.

3. In the Sharing tab of the dialog box that opens, choose Share This Folder (even though the thing you're sharing is actually a drive as opposed to a folder).

4. Type in a share name, as in the example shown in Figure 27-8.

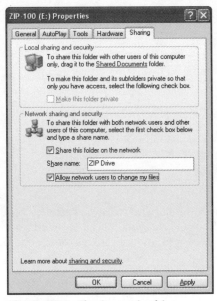

Figure 27-8: Sharing a Zip drive

5. Click the OK button.

The icon for the drive gains a little "hand" image, just as shared folders do. Then the My Network Places Explorer window on all the computers in the LAN will gain an icon for accessing the drive, as in the example shown in Figure 27-9. Opening the icon will display the contents of the drive (if any).

Using a Shared CD Drive

If you share a CD-ROM drive, there are a couple of catches to accessing it from a remote computer on the LAN. When you insert a CD that starts automatically into the CD-ROM drive, for example, the program starts on the local computer only. If you want to install a program from that CD on a remote computer, you need to open the drive's icon within My Network Places to get to the disk's contents. Optionally, you can right-click the icon and choose Explore to view the contents of the CD.

To burn files to a CD-R or CD-RW drive from a remote computer, you need to be sitting at the computer that's local to the drive. So, at the remote computer, you first need to put all the files that you want to burn to the CD in some shared folder. Then, at the computer that's local to the CD-R or CD-RW drive, open My Network Places and the icon for the shared folder. Then you can copy files from that shared folder onto the CD-R or CD-RW drive.

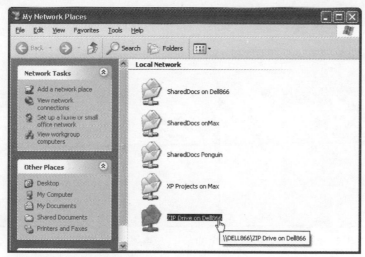

Figure 27-9: Shared Zip drive as viewed from another computer in the network

Sharing a Printer

A printer that's connected to any computer on the LAN can be shared or unshared. The default, in most cases, is to share the printer. To see whether an installed printer is already shared on the LAN, check the Print dialog box on some computer other than the computer that the computer to which the printer is physically attached, as discussed under "A Quick LAN Test" in Chapter 26.

To specifically share (or unshare) a printer, follow these steps:

1. Go to the computer to which the printer is physically connected. (Make sure the printer is properly installed and working from that computer.)

2. Click the Start button and choose Control Panel. In Classic view, open the Printers and Faxes icon. You should see an icon for the installed printer. (If the printer is currently being shared, that icon will have the "sharing hand" on it.)

3. Right-click the printer's icon and choose Sharing to get to the Sharing tab of the printer's Properties dialog box, as in Figure 27-10.

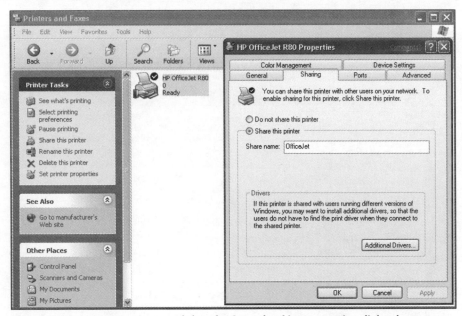

Figure 27-10: A printer icon and the Sharing tab of its Properties dialog box

4. Choose whether to share (or not share) the printer. If you opt to share the printer, you can give it a share name.

5. Click the OK button. You also can close any remaining open windows.

Using a Shared Printer

To access the printer from a remote computer, go ahead and print normally. For example, choose File ➪ Print from the menu bar of whatever program you're using at the moment. From the Print dialog box, choose the name of the printer you want to print to (if available). If your Print dialog box has a drop-down list of printer names, for instance, open the drop-down list and choose your preferred printer. Then click the Print or OK button, as usual.

If the shared printer is not available from a remote computer, you need to add the printer to your list of available printers. This is easy to do. Just follow these steps:

1. At the computer that needs access to the shared printer, click the Start button and open Control Panel.

2. In Classic view, open the Printers and Faxes icon.

3. Click the Add Printer icon.

4. In the Add Printer Wizard that opens, click the Next button and choose the Printer Connection option, as in Figure 27-11.

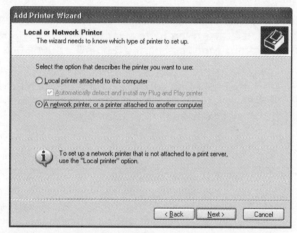

Figure 27-11: Choose Printer Connection to add a shared printer to a computer's list of available printers.

5. Click the Next button, and follow the instructions provided by the wizard.

The wizard will help you browse the network for available shared printers and will provide instructions for installing the printer you selected. When you have finished the wizard, the printer will be available in all programs' Print dialog boxes.

Summary

Setting up and using a network has never been so easy. By default, the Shared Documents folder (as well as the Shared Music and Shared Pictures subfolders) are shared across computers in the network. Therefore, sharing a file is as easy as moving or copying it to one of those folders. Printers are shared by default as well.

As you've learned in this chapter, you also have the option of sharing (or unsharing) any folder, printer, or drive. Here's a quick recap of the important points covered in this chapter:

✦ To share or unshare a folder, right-click the folder's icon in Explorer and choose Sharing and Security. Make your selections from the Sharing tab of the dialog box that opens.

✦ The `My Network Places` folder on each Windows XP computer in the LAN automatically displays shared folders across the network.

✦ Because the `My Network Places` folder actually contains shortcuts to shared resources on the LAN, you can freely rename and delete those icons without disrupting the shared devices.

✦ To add a new share to `My Network Places`, choose Add a Network Place from the list of available Network Tasks in the Explorer bar.

✦ To share a drive, open My Computer, select the drive you want to share, hold down the Ctrl key, right-click the drive's icon, and choose Sharing and Security. Make your selections from the Sharing tab of the dialog box that opens.

✦ To share or unshare a printer, open Control Panel and then open the Printers and Faxes icon. Right-click the icon for the printer you want to share or unshare and choose the Sharing option.

✦   ✦   ✦

Cool LAN Tricks

It's always best to know the tricks of the trade. That applies to making the most of your LAN. This chapter shows you various tricks to optimize your LAN experiences.

Cut-and-Paste across Computers

As you probably know, you can cut-and-paste (or copy-and-paste) text and such across any two open documents in the same computer. But what if you want to copy something from one document to a document on another computer? Well, you can't exactly do it with the Windows Clipboard. But you can with *scraps*. These scraps need to be placed in a shared folder to which the other computer can have access. The Shared Documents folder, or some new subfolder within it, will do just fine.

> **Note** Unfortunately, not all programs support scraps. When working with documents that do, however, they make for an easy way to share "chunks" of documents rather than entire files.

Suppose, for example, that the user named Alec, on the computer named Dell 866, is working on some document along with other people on the same network. For whatever reason, he wants to copy some material he's working in such a way that other people on the LAN can paste the material into their documents. First, Alec creates a new subfolder named Alec's Scraps within the Shared Documents folder on his computer. He opens that folder and leaves it open on the desktop.

Next, he selects whatever it is he wants to copy—a chunk of text, a picture, or whatever—and then chooses Edit ⇨ Copy. The selected item is in the Windows Clipboard. To make that item available to other LAN members, he just needs to right-click anywhere within his Alec's Scraps folder and choose Paste. Each time he pastes into the folder, any new file with the word *scrap* in its file name is created in the folder. In Tiles view, the document's type appears as Scrap Object. In Figure 28-1, for example, Alec has pasted two scraps from a Microsoft Word document into his Alec's Scraps folder.

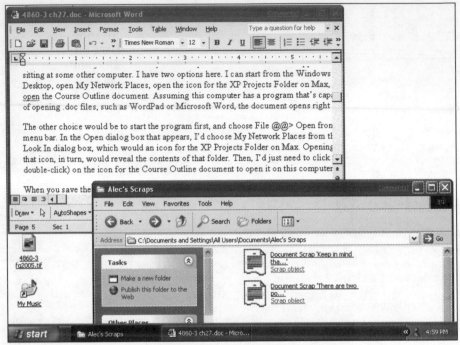

Figure 28-1: Three scraps pasted into the Alec's Scraps folder

Suppose now that user Ashley, who is on a different computer in the LAN, wants to paste those scraps into some documents she's working on. She just needs to open My Network Places and navigate to the shared Alec's Scraps folder. To copy a scrap into her own computer's Windows Clipboard, she just right-clicks the scraps icon and chooses Copy. At this point, it's just as though she had copied the material from her own computer. To insert the scrap into a document, she just right-clicks wherever she wants to place the scrap, and it lands in her document. Simple!

Protecting Shared Documents

This section heading might seem like an oxymoron. I mean, if you want to protect a document and keep it private, why would you share it in the first place? Answer: Perhaps you occasionally work at other computers in the LAN and want to access some of your documents at other computers. You just don't want anyone else to have access to the document from a shared computer. The simplest way to do this is to password-protect the document as you save it to a shared folder.

The exact technique for password-protecting a shared document varies from one program to the next. I cannot even say for certain that all programs will support it. Using Microsoft Excel as an example, however, let's say you're about to save a work-sheet that you want to access from other computers in the LAN, but keep other people out of it. Choose File ⇨ Save As and then choose Shared Documents from the Save in drop-down list to make the file's icon available from all computers in the LAN. Prior to clicking that Save button, however, click Tools in the Save As dialog box and choose General Options. This brings up the dialog box shown in Figure 28-2.

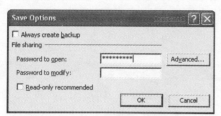

Figure 28-2: Save Options for a Microsoft Excel 2002 worksheet

To prevent others from opening the file, enter a password for Password to open. Needless to say, you don't want to forget this password or you won't be able to open the document yourself — ever! Use the same password for every document. If you start making them up on a document-by-document basis — trust me on this — you'll wish you hadn't. (The voice of experience here.) Click OK and then click Save to save the document.

Other users can see the document's icon. When they attempt to open the document, however, they'll be prompted for the password. If they don't enter the correct password, the file won't open.

If you want others to be able to see, but not change, the document, leave the Password to open option blank and enter a Password to modify instead. Upon opening the file, other users are prompted for the password to make modifications. If they can't enter the appropriate password, they can open the document only in read-only mode. This, in turn, prevents them from changing the document.

Creating Network Drives

A *network drive* is any shared drive, or even just a folder within some drive, that "looks like" a disk drive to Windows XP. In fact, the network drive will appear in My Computer as a drive. This makes it very easy to get to the shared resource because you don't have to dig around in My Network Places to get at it. The drive is also accessible within older programs that don't provide easy access to My Network

Places. The first step is to share the folder or drive, as described in Chapter 27. Then, on some other computer in the LAN, follow these steps:

1. Open My Computer.

2. Choose Tools ➪ Map Network Drive.

3. Select a drive letter for the shared resource from the Drive drop-down list.

4. Click the Browse button to browse shared resources on the network. In the example shown in Figure 28-3, for example, I've browsed to a Zip drive I previously shared on the computer named Dell866 in one of by computers. Click the item and then click the OK button.

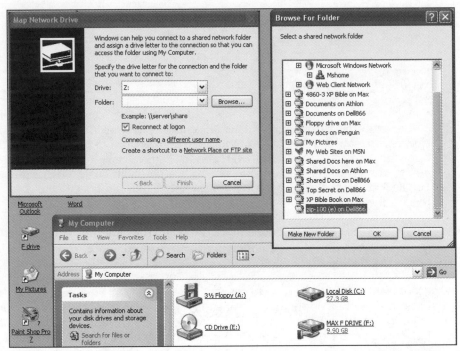

Figure 28-3: Mapping a network drive in My Computer on one machine to a shared Zip drive on another machine

5. To make sure the shared device is available each time you log on to this computer, choose the Reconnect at logon option.

Caution If you don't select Reconnect at logon, the mapped network drive will be available only until you log off. To reconnect in future sessions, you'll need to repeat all the steps here.

6. Click the Finish button.

7. If you want the drive to be available to other people who use this computer, repeat Steps 2–5. Before clicking the Finish button in Step 6, choose a different user name and enter the user's name and password.

From now on the shared folder or drive will be readily available whenever you open your My Computer icon. To move or copy files to/from the shared resource, open its icon in My Computer. The contents of the resource will display in a standard Windows Explorer window, where you can move and copy files normally. From a program's Save As dialog box, the shared resource will be available under My Computer in the Save in drop-down list.

Sharing Fonts

A large collection of fonts can consume a fair amount of disk space. In a LAN, it's not really necessary to install all your fonts on each and every computer. Instead, you can install fonts that you want to change across computers into a shared folder on one PC in the LAN. Then you can make them accessible to other computers in the LAN without actually copying the font files to each PC.

The first step is to place the font files to be shared in some shared folder. In the example shown in Figure 28-4, I created a folder named Shared Fonts within the `Shared Documents` folder on one of my computers, named Max. Each is a TrueType font, as indicated by the `.ttf` file name extension. I just copied all those TTF files from a font collection on CD-ROM that I purchased.

Figure 28-4: A bunch of TrueType font files in a folder named Shared Fonts within Shared Documents on my computer named Max

Copying font files from a CD-ROM or other disk (or downloading them) isn't the same as installing the fonts. To be accessible to your programs that use fonts, the fonts still need to be installed. But they don't need to be copied from their current folder. Installing the fonts on the computer that you copied the fonts to will be slightly different from installing them on other computers. On the computer that houses the `Shared Fonts` folder, here's how you install the fonts:

1. Click the Start button and choose Control Panel.

2. In Classic view, open the `Fonts` folder.

3. Choose File ⇨ Install New Font from the `Fonts` folder's menu bar.

4. In the folders list, browse to the folder that contains the fonts. In My example, that would require going through C:, `Documents and Settings`, `All Users`, `Documents`, and then double-clicking the `Shared Fonts` folder. The names of the fonts in the folder should appear under List of fonts.

5. Clear the Copy fonts to `Fonts` folder check box, as in Figure 28-5, because you don't really need two copies of all the font files on your hard disk.

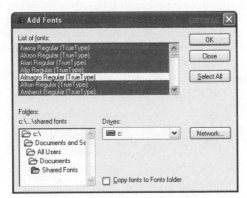

Figure 28-5: About to install some fonts from my Shared Fonts folder, without actually copying the font files

6. Select the fonts to install from the list of fonts. You can click the Select All button to select all the fonts. Optionally, you can use the Ctrl+click and Shift+click methods to select individual fonts or groups of fonts.

7. Click the OK button.

The fonts will be installed and the dialog box will close. Within the Fonts dialog box, icons for the installed fonts will all show the little curved "shortcut arrow," because each installed font is just a "pointer" to the actual font file in another folder. To verify that the fonts have been installed, open any program in which you use fonts. The newly installed fonts should be available in that program's Fonts dialog box as well as any Font drop-down lists that are available in that program.

The procedure is almost the same on other computers on the LAN. However, you will first want to map a network drive to the folder that contains the shared fonts. In Figure 28-6, for example, I went to another computer on the LAN, opened My Computer, and am in the processes of mapping a drive letter to the Shared Fonts folder on the computer named Max. When done, the Shared Fonts folder appears as a Network Drive in My Computer.

At this point, the procedure for installing the fonts on this computer is pretty much the same as installing them on the original computer. Open the Fonts folder in Control Panel and choose File ⇨ Install New Font. From the Drives drop-down list, however, you want to select the network drive that points to the Shared Fonts folder. In Figure 28-7, for example, I selected drive y:, which is the letter I used when creating the network drive. Once again, clear the Copy fonts to Fonts folder check box if you don't want to copy the actual font files. Select the fonts to install from the list of fonts and click OK.

You'll see a warning that the fonts might not be available in future sessions — which is certainly true — such as when the computer that contains the fonts is shut down! (That problem is easily avoided by selecting the Copy fonts to Fonts folder option. Which is fine, if you don't mind having the font files consuming disk space on this computer.) After you've finished installing the fonts, you can once again verify their availability by checking the list of available fonts in any program that supports fonts.

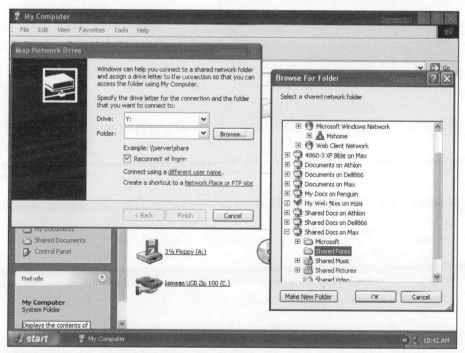

Figure 28-6: Mapping a drive letter to the Shared Fonts folder on the computer named Max from a different computer in the LAN

Sending Instant Messages

Earlier versions of Windows included a little utility named Win Popup that made it easy for people on the LAN to send instant messages to one another. I haven't seen any sign of that in XP. But all is not lost. If each LAN member sets up a Hotmail or Passport account, he can add the other members to his contacts list in Instant Messenger, as discussed in Chapter 10. Then they can send messages to one another through Instant Messenger.

Virtual Private Networks

Many businesses now allow users to connect to their internal network through virtual private networking (VPN) technology. It's called "virtual" private networking because you can use a public network (that is, the Internet) as sort of a bridge between the internal private network and the remote (client) computer that's connecting. If your company supports VPN, you need to know the VPN host name or IP address to make the connection. Typically the company's network administrator can give you that information. Once you have that information, making the connection is easy. Just follow these steps:

1. Open My Network Places on the client computer and choose View Network Connections under Network Tasks.

2. Click Create a New Connection under Network Tasks. On the first page of the wizard that opens, click the Next button.

3. On the Network Connection Type page, choose Connect to the network at my workplace and then click Next.

4. Choose Virtual Private Network connection and click Next.

5. Type in a name to be used as the icon's label and then click the Next button.

6. If you're using a dial-up modem, you'll see an option asking whether you want to dial automatically when making this connection. Choose either option and then click the Next button.

7. Enter the host name or IP address provided by the network administrator and click Next.

8. On the last wizard page, choose whether you want to add a shortcut icon for this connection to your desktop. Then click the Finish button.

A new icon will appear in the Network Connections dialog box. Opening that icon will take you through the steps required to log on to the private network.

Other Connections

Computer networking is an enormous topic, and not one that can be fully covered in a few chapters within a general Windows book. Hopefully, what you have learned up to this point will help you start creating and using your own LAN in a home or small business environment. Other types of connections that you can make with Windows XP are summarized here. For more information on any given topic, check out the Help menu in the Network Connections window, or search Windows Help and Support for the words shown in boldface:

✦ **Incoming connections:** Enables you to set up your computer as a remote access server so that external computers can connect through modems, virtual private networking, or directly through a cable or infrared device.

✦ **UNIX:** You can connect to UNIX and Linux networks, typically by mapping a network drive to the shared resource.

✦ **NetWare:** Windows XP includes the NWLink IPX/SPX/NetBIOS Compatible Transport Protocol, which you can use to connect to shared resources on a Novell NetWare network.

Summary

This chapter provided some tips and techniques for getting the most out of your local area network. Here's a quick recap of the important points covered in this chapter:

✦ To cut-and-paste (or copy-and-paste) across computers on a LAN, just paste the Clipboard's contents into a shared folder by right-clicking within the folder and choosing Paste.

✦ To protecting shared documents on a LAN, password-protect the document from the program's Save As dialog box.

✦ To create a My Computer shortcut to a shared drive or folder, choose Tools ➪ Map Network Drive from My Computer's menu bar.

✦ To share fonts across a network, place your font files in a shared folder. Then install them from that folder on computers throughout the LAN.

✦ You can use MSN Instant Messenger to send instant messages to other members of the LAN, provided each has a Hotmail or Passport account.

✦ To connect to a virtual private network (VPN), choose Make New Connection in the Network Connections window. Then choose Connect to the network at my workplace option when the wizard asks for your connection type.

✦   ✦   ✦

Beefing Up Security

This chapter covers some tools and techniques for
improving security and privacy on your computer. Your
computer need not be a member of a network, nor even connected to the Internet, to use some of these techniques. You
can use some of the techniques described here to beef up
security and privacy on any Windows XP computer that supports multiple-user accounts and/or connects to the Internet.

User Account Security

If you set up multiple-user accounts on your computer, as discussed in Chapter 20, you may be alarmed to discover that
your "private" My Documents folder isn't really very private
at all. Suppose, for example, that your user name is Susan,
and you're the administrator. You have created some Limited
accounts for other users. One of these other users logs on to
the computer, opens the My Computer icon, and, lo and
behold, there's a clearly identified link to your My Documents
folder right there in plain view, as shown in Figure 29-1. To
your dismay, you discover that all these other users can open
your My Documents folder and do as they please. What gives?
Two things:

- ◆ Windows XP doesn't bother to make anything private on
  a user account that isn't password-protected.

- ◆ On a hard disk that's formatted with the FAT32 file system, nothing *can* be made private. So user account passwords don't really matter much beyond the initial logon.

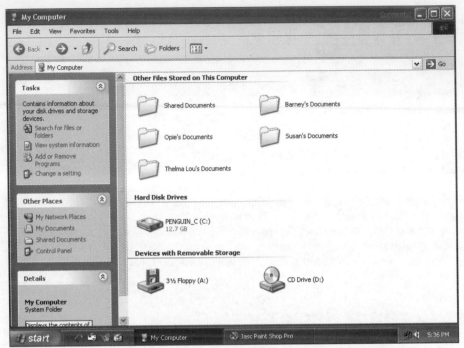

Figure 29-1: Other users' My Documents folders are clearly identified in My Computer in Home edition using the FAT32 file system.

If you're looking to gain some privacy, the first thing you need to do is check to see whether your hard disk is formatted using FAT32. If it is, you need to convert it to NTFS. Exactly how you go about doing that is explained in the sections titled "What's My File System?" and "Converting a File System to NTFS" in Chapter 31.

The second step to protecting your privacy is to password protect your user account if you haven't already done so.

Password-protecting accounts

Any user can password-protect his account. It's important to do so if you want any privacy at all on the local computer. If you don't password-protect your account, anybody can sit down at the computer, log on as you, and have free reign over everything in your account. Creating passwords is easy. Just follow these steps:

1. Click the Start button and open Control Panel.

2. Open the User Accounts icon.

3. Choose Change an Account.

4. If you're an administrator, click the account name you want to password-protect.

5. Choose Create a Password.

Caution

If you're an administrator and you forget your password, you will *permanently* lock yourself out of your account. To play it safe, create a password reset disk right after you password-protect your account, as described a little later in this chapter.

Caution

Never take passwords lightly! Remember that passwords are always case-sensitive. The password PASSWORD is highly overused, and the first one every hacker tries when attempting to break into an account.

6. Type your password (twice) and type a hint to remind yourself of the password in case you forget; then click the Create Password button.

7. When asked whether you would like to make your personal documents private, as in Figure 29-2, choose Yes, Make Private. (This option won't appear if the hard disk is using the FAT32 file system, or if you're password-protecting a Limited account in the Professional edition.)

Note

In Windows XP Professional edition, password-protected user account documents are private by default, so the option to make the account private doesn't appear. In the Professional edition, user accounts can be managed through Local Users and Groups, as discussed in Chapter 32.

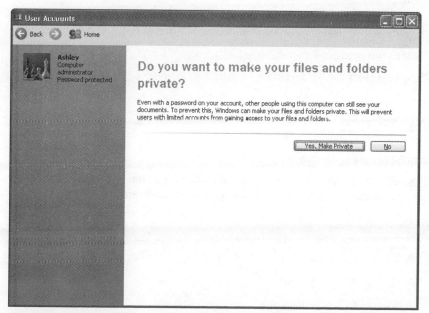

Figure 29-2: Choosing Yes, Make Private hides your My Documents folder from other users.

After password-protecting your account, you are prompted to enter your password each time you log on. If you have a Limited account yourself, other users with Limited accounts will no longer be able to view and open your My Documents folder through My Computer. (However, anyone with an administrator account can still get to your stuff.) If you just password-protected your own Administrator account, you've just blocked out everyone, even other people with Administrator accounts. Remember these key points:

✦ There essentially is no privacy on a hard disk that's using the FAT32 file system.

✦ On an NTFS hard disk, user accounts need to be password-protected to gain any privacy.

✦ Limited accounts have limited privacy in that they can't "hide" from administrative accounts.

Changing your privacy settings

Should you ever need to enable or disable privacy after password-protecting your user account, you can do so by following these steps:

1. Open My Computer and then open the icon for your local hard disk (drive C:).

2. Click Folders in the toolbar and expand the My Computer category.

3. Expand the icon for your hard drive (for instance, Local Disk C:).

4. Click Documents and Settings to reveal user folders.

5. Right-click the folder icon for your own account and choose Properties.

6. Click the Sharing tab (see Figure 29-3).

7. Clear or select the Make this folder private option and then click the OK button.

Note   Limited accounts are always private to other limited accounts, so there is no option to turn privacy on and off.

Cross-Reference   Chapter 32 describes the more advanced techniques that computer administrators can use to manage user accounts and groups in the Professional edition.

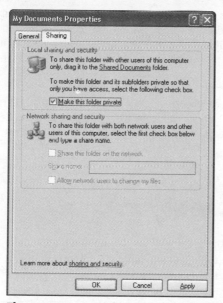

Figure 29-3: An account's privacy is set
on the Sharing tab of its Properties dialog
box within the Documents and Settings folder.

Recovering lost passwords

If you're an administrator and a user forgets his password, you can easily get that
user back online by creating a new password for him. Go into User Accounts, click
the user's account name or picture, and choose Change the Password. Create the
new password and hint; then click Change Password. Optionally, you can delete the
user's password so that the account is no longer password protected.

If you're the only person on this computer who has an Administrator account and
you forget your own password, the only way to get back into your account is
through the password reset disk (assuming you already created one!), as described
in the next section.

Creating a password reset disk

As an administrator, you should create a password reset disk for yourself, just in
case you forget your password at some time in the future. You'll need a blank floppy
disk. To create the disk, follow these steps:

1. In your own account, open Control Panel and open User Accounts.

2. Click your account name/picture.

3. Choose Prevent a Forgotten Password under Related Tasks in the Explorer bar.

The Forgotten Password Wizard will take you step-by-step through the procedure. When you're done, you need to store the disk in a safe place where you can find it in an emergency. Furthermore, be aware that anybody can use this disk to log on to your account without a password. So this is one disk you definitely don't want to leave laying around.

To use the password reset disk in the future, go ahead and log on normally. When prompted for your password, click the -> button to try to log on without a password. In the message box that pops up, click the link that enables you to log on with your password reset disk. Another wizard will appear, helping you to create a new password and log on.

Protecting yourself from yourself

Just because you have granted yourself an administrator account doesn't mean you have to use it all the time. You can create a second, more limited account for yourself and use it in your day-to-day work that doesn't require administrative privileges. Doing so prevents you from inadvertently making sweeping changes to your system. Furthermore, being logged in as an administrator risks allowing Trojan horses (seemingly innocent programs designed to wreak havoc) to damage your system, perhaps before you realize what's happening.

If a Web site downloads a Trojan horse to your computer that then starts executing itself, for example, it can gain the privileges of the account you are logged into, which, if you currently have administrative privileges, can give it free reign over the system. If you were logged on with a Limited account at the time, the Trojan horse might not be able to do its dirty work in your Limited account.

If you're working in your Limited account and need administrative privileges, you don't need to close everything to switch to your administrative account. Just click the Start button and choose Log Off ➪ Switch User.

 Tip   In the Professional edition of Windows XP, you can create an account for yourself within the Power Users group, to minimize your restrictions and still keep your computer relatively safe.

As an alternative to switching user accounts, you can use Run As to start a program as an administrator. In the Start menu or in Control Panel, hold down the Shift-key and click the icon for the program you want to run. Choose Run As from the menu bar. Select The Following User, and enter your administrative account user name and password.

Beefing Up Internet Security

It's no secret that the Internet isn't exactly the safest place for your computer to hang out. People (who apparently have nothing better to do with their time) use the Internet to spread viruses, break into private computers and networks, and generally make nuisances of themselves. This section introduces techniques to protect your computer, or even your entire network, from invasion from the ever-public Internet.

Using Internet Connection Firewall (ICF)

Windows XP comes with an Internet Connection Firewall (ICF) that you can use to protect a single computer that's connected to the Internet, or a whole network of computers that share an Internet connection. The firewall detects attempted *hacks* (attempts to access your system from the Internet) and blocks them. You also can enable firewall *logging,* which enables you to review any attempted hacks into your system.

If you use the Home Networking Wizard to set up a local area network and share a single Internet connection, the firewall is automatically set up on the ICS (Internet Connection Sharing) *host.* The host is the computer to which the modem is physically connected. On a single computer that doesn't share its Internet connection, the firewall is disabled by default. You can enable it by following these steps:

1. At the computer to which the modem is connected, open Network Connections. (Click the Start button and choose All Programs ⇨ Accessories ⇨ Communications ⇨ Network Connections.)

 Tip   Network Connections is also available under Other Places in My Network Places. You also can use the method described under "Adding and Deleting Start Menu Items" to add a Network Connections item to your Start menu.

System Administrator Cautions

Don't use the Internet Connection Firewall if your network already has a firewall or proxy server. Don't use it in an existing network that uses Windows 2000 or XP domain controllers, DHCP servers, DNS servers, gateways, or static IP addresses.

If your network uses a remote exchange server to handle e-mail, a firewall will prevent the server from automatically sending e-mail message notifications to Microsoft Outlook 2000 users. That's because the remote procedure call (RCP) that sends the notification has been initiated outside the firewall. Outlook 2000 users can still send and receive e-mail messages normally. However, they need to manually check for new messages from their own computers, so the process begins within the firewall.

2. Right-click the icon that defines your Internet connection and choose Properties.

3. Click the Advanced tab.

On the Advanced tab of the dialog box, you can enable or disable the firewall with a simple check box option (see Figure 29-4). That's all there is to it. The firewall does its job behind the scenes, so no further intervention on your part is required. On a network that shares an Internet connection, other computers in the network are automatically protected because all network traffic takes place through the firewall.

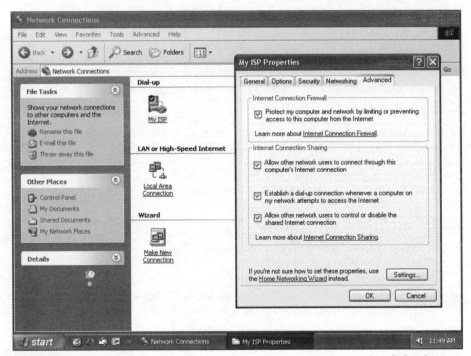

Figure 29-4: The Advanced tab of an Internet connection's Properties dialog box

Caution   Do not enable the firewall in Network Connections icons on any local area connections, virtual private networking (VPN) connections, or any other non-Internet connections.

Using ICF logging

You can keep track of the firewall's activities by allowing ICF logging. To activate (or deactivate) logging, follow these steps:

1. Open Network Connections on the computer on which you enabled the firewall.

2. Right-click the Internet connection's icon and choose Properties.

3. Click the Advanced tab and then click the Settings button.

4. Click the Security Logging tab to get to the options shown in Figure 29-5.

Figure 29-5: Options for tracking the firewall's activities to a log file

5. Choose Log Dropped Packets to keep track of attempted hacks.

6. Optionally, you can change the location, name, and maximum size of the log.

7. Click the OK buttons in the open dialog boxes to save your choices.

If you're currently connected to the Internet, you will see a message indicating that the log file will be started the next time you connect. To view the log, browse to the folder and click the log file's icon. It's a text file, so will automatically open in Notepad. Any unsuccessful attempts to hack into your system will be listed.

Should you ever decide to stop logging, just repeat the preceding steps and clear the check box.

Advanced firewall options

The Advanced Settings tab shown back in Figure 29-5 offers quite a few other options not covered here. This is largely because they're more relevant to server editions of Windows XP than to the Personal and Home editions covered in this book. As a recap, here's what they offer:

✦ **Services:** Enables an administrator to select Internet services to which outsiders can gain access through the firewall.

✦ **Programs:** Enables you to create custom firewall settings for programs that need to be able to accept outside requests that were not initiated from within the firewall.

✦ **ICMP (Internet Control Message Protocol):** Enables fine-tuning of what the firewall accepts and rejects and the messages that are sent to outside requests.

Tip   The Learn More About Internet Connection Firewall link in the modem's Properties dialog box provides additional information about the advanced settings.

Beefing up Internet Explorer security

On Internet Explorer, you can beef up security from by placing restrictions on Web sites. In Internet Explorer, choose Tools ⇨ Internet Options and then click the Security tab to get to the options shown in Figure 29-6. Note that there are four predefined Web content zones shown. Each zone can be assigned a security level, as discussed in a moment.

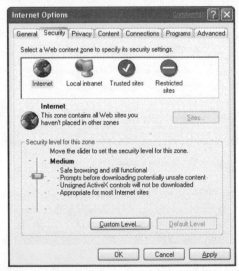

Figure 29-6: Microsoft Internet Explorer 6 security options

The default security level for each zone is summarized in the following list. The higher the security, the greater the restrictions that are placed on the zone:

✦ **Internet:** All new Internet Web sites that you have never visited before are placed in this zone. Default security level is Medium.

✦ **Local intranet:** Includes Web sites available from your company's own intranet, as opposed to sites on the public Internet. Default security level is Medium Low.

✦ **Trusted sites:** Initially empty, you can place Web sites that you trust into this category to maximize their access to your computer. Default security level is Low.

✦ **Restricted sites:** Initially empty, you can place Web sites that you would visit, but don't entirely trust, into this category. Default security level is High.

To view or change a zone's security level, first click its icon. The lower half of the dialog box shows the current security level for the zone. You can adjust the current level by moving the slider up and down. Optionally, you can click the Default Level button to accept the default settings for the zone, or click the Custom Level button to set very specific limitations for all Web sites within the zone.

Because the Internet zone applies to all new Web sites that you visit, you cannot add sites to that zone. However, you can add sites that you visit frequently to the other zones. Click the icon for the zone to which you want to add a Web site and then click the Sites button. Then type the URL of the site you want to restrict into the Add text box and click the Add button. Each site that you add will be listed, as in Figure 29-7. Future visits to those sites will enforce their new security zone setting.

Figure 29-7: Some Web sites added to the Restricted zone

Protecting Yourself from E-Mail Viruses

E-mail message attachments are one of the most common means of spreading viruses from one computer to the next. Just opening the attachment will install the virus onto your computer, where it will wreak its havoc (or play its prank). Most likely, it will then start to call upon your e-mail program to start sending copies of itself to people in your list of contacts. Needless to say, this doesn't exactly please people in your contacts lists.

Microsoft Outlook Express 6, which comes with Windows XP, has beefed up security against e-mail viruses somewhat. To get to its security options, follow these steps:

1. Open Outlook Express and click your Inbox.

2. Choose Tools ⇨ Options from Outlook Express's menu bar.

3. Click the Security tab to see the options shown in Figure 29-8.

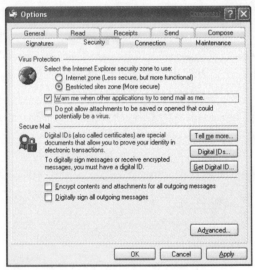

Figure 29-8: Security options for Outlook Express 6

The Virus Protection options are pretty self-explanatory. The Restricted sites zone refers to the settings that you define in Internet Explorer's security settings, as described in the preceding section. The Warn me option displays a message when some other program on your computer (which could be a virus) attempts to use Outlook Express to send out an e-mail message. The Do not allow option places major restrictions on you, because it prevents you from opening many different types of attachments.

Digital IDs

Digital IDs are a means of authenticating e-mail messages as being "the real thing," and not a forged document from an imposter. You also can use digital IDs to encrypt messages so that they cannot be intercepted and read by prying eyes. Digital IDs are not really a feature of Windows, however. They're provided by online services such as VeriSign. To learn more about them and to get your own digital ID, click the Tell Me More button on the Security tab shown back in Figure 29-8.

Note that none of these options can actually detect a virus. They just warn you when something that *could* be a virus (or contain a virus) is at hand. To really detect, prevent, and remove viruses, you need some kind of third-party virus-protection software. To ensure you're getting something that's compatible with Windows XP, check the Compatible Hardware and Software link in Help and Support.

Summary

This chapter has looked at ways to beef up security on small networks, and even stand-alone computers. Here's a quick recap of the important points covered in this chapter:

✦ The first step to preventing users from having easy access to each other's My Documents folder is to use the NTFS file system in your hard disk.

✦ The second step to keeping users' My Documents folders secure and private is to password-protect the user accounts.

✦ The Internet Connection Firewall can be used to protect a single computer or entire network from hackers on the Internet.

✦ Internet Explorer 6 enables you to set security zones for unvisited Web sites, sites on a local intranet, and sites you visit regularly.

✦ Outlook Express 6 offers some limited protection against viruses in the form of warnings that alert you to content that could contain a virus.

✦   ✦   ✦

Advanced Stuff

In this part you'll learn about some of the more advanced technical features of Windows XP. We'll take a look behind the scenes at how Windows XP associates documents with programs, and how you can customize those associations. We'll look at the modern NTFS file system, the advantages it offers, and how you can convert to that system if you so desire. We'll look deep inside the Windows Registry, which provides more advanced "tweaking" options than the Control Panel icons. We'll also look at some of the more advanced features of Windows XP Professional Edition, geared toward corporate users and administrators.

File Icons, Associations, and Properties

This chapter shows you some ways to refine how you work with documents and programs. In particular, I focus on how you can decide exactly which program opens when you click or double-click a document folder's icon. I also discuss some ways to control the appearance of icons on your screen. And, finally, I discuss some of the advanced settings for files and folders.

Registering Documents with Programs

As I mention in earlier chapters, opening a document directly from Windows usually opens the program associated with (or registered to) that type of file. The file's type is determined by its file name extension. For example, opening a file with the .htm extension automatically opens that document in Microsoft Internet Explorer or whatever Web browser is currently your default browser.

As mentioned in Chapter 4, you can give yourself more flexibility by adding favorite programs to your Send To menu. This way, instead of only opening a document by clicking (or double-clicking) its icon, you can right-click the icon, choose Send To and then select the program with which to open the document. If you create your own Web pages (HTML documents with the .htm extension), for example, you might want to add Microsoft Internet Explorer, Notepad, WordPad, FrontPage Express, and any other Web-authoring aids to your Send To menu. This way, you can right-click any HTML file and send it to whatever program best suits your needs.

Note Remember, however, that if you share your PC with other users, each user's Send To menu will be based on whatever modifications that user has made, because Windows XP remembers each user's personalized settings.

Occasionally, however, you will want to ensure that clicking (or double-clicking) a document file sends the document to a specific program. For example, the graphic images you see throughout this book are TIF files. (TIF is one of many graphic image file types.) When I click (or double-click) a program with the .tif extension, the graphic image opens in the Kodak Imaging program on my PC. But I would like the image to open in Adobe Photoshop, which is my preferred graphics imaging program. Making this change is pretty easy.

First, you might want to search your hard disk to make sure you have files with the appropriate file name extension to work with by following these steps:

1. Click the Start button and choose Search.

2. In the Part or all of the file name text box, type the file name extension you want to change without any periods. For example, I would type ***.tif**.

3. Click the Search button and wait for a list of files to appear, as shown in Figure 30-1.

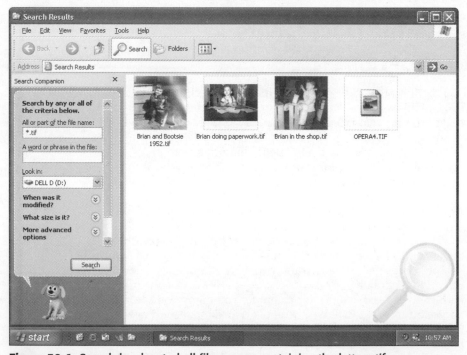

Figure 30-1: Search has located all file names containing the letters *tif*.

When you're satisfied that there are indeed some files to work with, you can go ahead and set up a new association by following these steps:

1. Open Explorer and choose Tools ⇨ Folder Options.

 Tip
Don't try to change any file associations in the Search window. You must open Explorer to see the File Types tab.

2. Click the File Types tab.

3. Scroll to and click the file type you want to change. In Figure 30-2, for example, I clicked TIF Image.

Figure 30-2: I'm about to change current associations for TIF Images.

4. Click the Change button. The Open With dialog box appears (see Figure 30-3).

Figure 30-3: The Open With dialog box

5. Click the name of the program that you want to open that file type.

6. Click OK to save your settings and close the dialog box.

This should do the trick. You can close the Folder Options dialog box by clicking its OK button. To verify that the association was successful, find a file name with the extension you reassociated (.tif, in my example). Click or double-click this file's icon; it should open in the program you specified (Adobe Photoshop, in my example). From now on, all files with this extension will open in the specified program.

Creating a New Association

If a file name extension has never before been associated with a program, it's easy to create an association. Just click (or double-click) the type of file that has no association. Suppose, for example, that I click a file named myLetter.let in My Computer, and the .let extension has never been associated with any program before. The Windows Cannot Open File dialog box appears. Click the Select the Program from a List button to display the Open With dialog box, enabling you to choose which program you want to use to open this file.

Tip If you don't want to select the correct program manually, you can click the Use the Web service to find the appropriate program button in the Windows Cannot Open File dialog box. Your PC will then attempt to look up the file extension on the Internet.

Now suppose that you want to use WordPad to open files with the .let extension. In the Open With dialog box, you can type in a plain-English description of the .let extension, choose an opening program from the list of available programs and make sure that the Always use this program to open these files check box is selected. In Figure 30-4, for example, I defined the .let extension as My Letters, chose WordPad as the associated program, and selected the check box so that all LET files open in WordPad when clicked (or double-clicked).

Figure 30-4: Files with the .let filename extension will now open in WordPad.

After making my selections, clicking the OK button finishes up the job. From now on, opening any file with the .let extension will send that file to WordPad.

Changing Icons

Windows XP automatically puts an icon on every file on your system. But you're not stuck with those icons. In most cases, you can change to some other icon. The first step is to get to the Change Icon button for the file type you want to re-iconize (for lack of a better term). How you do this depends on the type of file you want to change. Try whichever of the following methods seems most appropriate to the situation at hand. (If one approach doesn't work, you can always try another.)

✦ To change icons for permanent desktop items such as My Computer and the Recycle Bin, right-click some neutral area of the desktop, choose Properties, and click the Desktop tab. Finally, click the Customize Desktop button to get to the options shown in Figure 30-5.

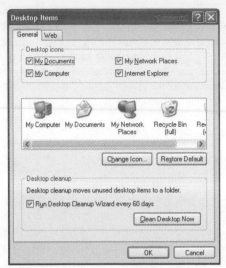

Figure 30-5: The Change Icon
button for permanent desktop icons

✦ To change the icon for a shortcut, right-click the shortcut icon and choose
Properties to get to the dialog box shown in Figure 30-6.

Figure 30-6: The Change Icon button
also appears on the Shortcut tab of
the Properties sheet.

✦ To change the icon representing a type of document, click the Start button, choose Control Panel, and open the Folder Options icon. Click the File Types tab, scroll to and click the type of file for which you want to choose a new icon, and then click the Advanced button. The Change Icon button appears at the top of the Edit File Type dialog box, as in Figure 30-7.

Figure 30-7: The Change Icon button is also available in the Edit File Type dialog box.

Regardless of how you get to a Change Icon button, when you click it, you'll come to a dialog box that looks something like the example shown in Figure 30-8. To select one of the icons shown, click it and then click the OK button. No biggie there.

Figure 30-8: The Change Icon dialog box

What may not be too apparent from this dialog box is that you aren't limited to the icons appearing in the Change Icon dialog box. You can apply any icon file (a file with the .ico extension). The tricky part is finding additional icons. Some icons are stored right on the hard disk with an .ico extension. Others are stored inside files with the .exe or .dll extension. I don't know for certain what icon files are available on your computer, but you should have the two that come with Windows XP:

✦ C:\WINDOWS\SYSTEM32\shell32.dll

✦ C:\WINDOWS\ SYSTEM32\Moricons.dll

Note   In Windows XP, the name of the Windows folder is stored in a system variable called %SystemRoot%. When you browse for icons, you may see this name in place of Windows in the path name.

To view the icons in either the shell32.dll file or the Moricons.dll file, browse to the appropriate folder and open the file. Or, type the path into the Look for icons in this file text box. In Figure 30-9, for example, I'm viewing the collection of icons in the shell32.dll file. As you can see in the figure, this file offers a lot of icons. You can use the scroll bar at the bottom of the icons to scroll to the right and view even more icons. To choose one of those icons, click it and then click the OK button.

Figure 30-9: Icons from the shell32.dll file visible in the Change Icon dialog box

If you download or purchase additional icons, you can install from those files as well. The exact procedure depends on the product you purchased. You need to refer to this product's documentation for details. Suppose, however, that you have installed the RISS Icon Pack from the www.tucows.com Web site or some other location.

To access those icons, use the Browse button to get to the folder where those icons are stored (C:\Rissicon, in this example). You'll see a bunch of files with the .dll extension. Click one of those files and then click the Open button. Icons in this file are then visible. To choose one, click it and then click the OK button. After making your selection, close whatever dialog boxes remain open using their OK or Close (X) buttons.

If you have Internet access and you want to surf for icons, search for icons using a relevant search term, such as *Windows+icons*.

You also can create your own icons if you have a program capable of saving images in the ICO format. Some popular products in this category include IconEdit Pro and IconForge icon editor. You can go to your favorite search engine and search for something similar to *icon+edit* to see what you find.

Other File Properties

As previously mentioned, the best way to find out what you can do with some object on your screen is to right-click that object and look at the menu that appears. If a Properties option is in this menu, selecting it will give you some options for changing characteristics of the object.

Suppose, for example, that I am browsing around my computer and I right-click a file name and choose Properties. Most (although not all) files will display something similar to the example shown in Figure 30-10. (If the dialog box contains multiple tabs, the General tab will show information similar to that in the example.)

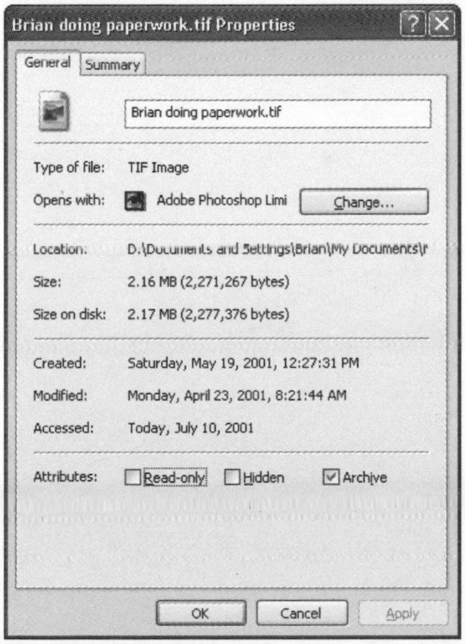

Figure 30-10: General options for a TIF image file

Much of the information on the General tab tells you about the file, its type, location, size, and the file name. You also can see the date and time the file was created, last modified, and last opened (accessed).

The Attributes at the bottom of the list enable you to tweak the behavior of the file a little more. Those options are as follows:

✦ **Read-Only:** If selected, you can open the file and view it, but you cannot change the contents of the file. (If you share a computer with others, selecting this option can keep other people from changing the file's contents.)

✦ **Archive:** If selected, this check box means the file has changed since the last backup. Hence, this copy of the file will be backed up the next time you do a backup of the disk.

✦ **Hidden:** If selected, the file will have no file name or icon visible on-screen, unless you go into Folder Options and opt to Show hidden files and folders on the View tab, as in Figure 30-11. (You'll need to do this yourself to find the file in the future!)

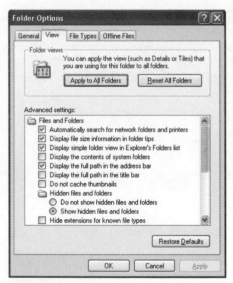

Figure 30-11: The Hidden Files and Folders options in the View tab of Folder Options

After you finish making your selections, click the OK button to save your changes and close the dialog box.

Advanced Settings in Folder Options

The View tab of the Folder Options dialog box offers some advanced settings to give you more control over the appearance and behavior of folders and icons.

Here's how to use access the View tab:

1. Click the Start button, choose Control Panel, and open the Folder Options icon.

2. Click the View tab to get to the options shown in Figure 30-12.

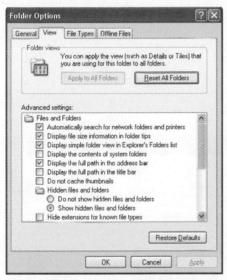

Figure 30-12: Advanced folder options

In the following sections, I summarize what the various options offer. For future reference, however, be aware that for more information on any option, you can click the question mark (?) button near the upper-right corner of the dialog box and then click the option with which you need help.

The Reset All Folders button

The Reset All Folders button, when clicked, returns all folders to the view defined when you first installed Windows XP. This view generally shows an icon and other information for every folder. Figure 30-13 shows an example, using the My Computer folder. In this example, the icon for drive C: is currently selected (highlighted). The Details pane shows that drive C: has a capacity of 37.2 gigabytes.

Figure 30-13: How My Computer looks after resetting all folders

Files and folders options

The options listed under Advanced Settings are all toggles in the sense they can either be turned on (checked), or turned off (not checked). Clicking a check box checks or unchecks that box. Here's what each of those options does:

✦ **Automatically search for network folders and printers:** If selected, this makes option it easier for you to use shared network resources because Windows XP will look for them whenever you start your system.

✦ **Display all Control Panel options and all folder contents:** If selected, this option ensures that you will be able to quickly find all the items in the Control Panel, rather than just the simpler ones.

✦ **Display file size information in folder tips:** When selected, this option shows the size of files in a folder even if Web content is not enabled for the folder.

✦ **Display simple folder view in Explorer's Folders list:** When selected, this option automatically displays the contents of a folder when you select it in the Folders list without requiring you to double-click to open the folder.

✦ **Display the full path in the address bar:** When selected, the address bar of each folder in My Computer displays the complete path to the folder you're viewing.

✦ **Display the full path in title bar:** When selected, the title bar of each folder in My Computer shows the complete path to the folder you're viewing in DOS format (for example, `C:\Windows\System`). When clear, only the name of the current folder appears in the title bar (for example, `System`). This option is similar to the Display the full path in address bar option, and you need only to choose one or the other of these options.

✦ **Hidden files and folders:** The two options under Hidden files and folders enable you to choose which types of files are visible and which are invisible. Hidden files are ones that have been declared hidden in the file's properties, as discussed under "Other File Properties" earlier in this chapter.

✦ **Hide file extensions for known file types:** When selected, the file name extension of any registered document type is hidden when viewed in My Computer. When cleared, file name extensions appear for all files.

✦ **Hide protected operating system files (Recommended):** System files are files that are critical to Windows XP, so hiding those files prevents you from accidentally deleting them.

✦ **Launch folder windows in a separate process:** This option opens a new window when you open a different folder instead of using an existing open window. Use this option to make it easier to drag and drop items between folders.

✦ **Remember each folder's view settings:** When selected, this option ensures that any changes you made to a folder while it is open are saved with that folder. The next time you open the folder, it will look the same as it did last time you closed it. Clearing this option prevents folder options from being saved.

✦ **Restore previous folder windows at logon:** This option ensures that the same folders will be opened when you log back on after logging off your computer.

✦ **Show Control Panel in My Computer:** This option displays the Control Panel icon in the My Computer folder.

✦ **Show encrypted or compressed NTFS files in color:** This option makes it easier for you to identify encrypted or compressed NTFS files by showing their file names in color in Explorer. This option is useful only if your hard drive is formatted with the NTFS file system.

✦ **Show pop-up description for folder and desktop items:** When selected, this option enables the large ToolTips that some folders and icons offer to appear when you rest the mouse pointer over the item. Clearing this option prevents those ToolTips from showing.

✦ **Use Search Companion for searching:** This option enables Windows XP to use the Search Companion Explorer bar to help you find items on your computer, your network, or the Internet.

Restore Defaults button

The Restore Defaults button under the Advanced Settings returns all the check boxes under Advanced Settings to the settings that were in place when you first installed Windows XP on your PC. In other words, clicking this button undoes any custom settings that you have made since Windows XP was first installed.

The Apply to All Folders button

The Apply to All Folders button is available for selection only when you access the Folder Options through My Computer or some other folder. (Open My Computer and choose Tools ⇨ Folder Options from its menu bar and then click the View tab.)

 Tip   If you click this button, all folders will receive whatever settings you just applied to the current folder.

If you get to the advanced options through the Start button, all folders will automatically inherit whatever settings you choose. Because the button would serve no purpose in this case, it is grayed out and unavailable.

Some additional visual settings

Windows XP has a few additional options that are accessible through the Display Properties dialog box. To get there, right-click the desktop, choose Properties, click the Appearance tab, and click the Effects button.

✦ **Use the following transition effect for menus and tooltips:** When selected, this option enables you to choose the way menus and ToolTips appear on-screen.

✦ **Use the following method to smooth edges of screen fonts:** When selected, enables you to choose an option that gets rid of the jagged look some icons produce on screen. The only downside to this option is that it slows screen performance a little, but probably not enough to be noticeable on most PCs.

✦ **Use large icons:** This option replaces the standard-size desktop icons with ones that are much larger. This may be useful if you have trouble viewing the screen.

✦ **Show shadows under menus:** This option gives the menus a three dimensional appearance.

✦ **Show window contents while dragging:** If selected, any time you drag a window across the desktop, the contents of the window will remain visible as you drag. If not selected, dragging a window across the screen shows only a ghost outline of the window being dragged. This option can slow performance although not to a noticeable degree on most PCs.

✦ **Hide underlined letters for keyboard navigation until I press the Alt key:** Removes the underlines from menu hotkeys unless you press the Alt key. This can make the menus a little easier to read if you primarily navigate using the mouse.

Summary

In this chapter, I discussed some of the more advanced personalization features of Windows XP. Here's a quick recap of the important points covered in this chapter.

✦ Most of the advanced settings for tweaking files and folders are in the File Types and View tabs of the Folder Options dialog box.

✦ To get to the Folder Options dialog box and make selections that will affect all folders and files, click the Start button, choose Control Panel, and open the Folder Options icon.

✦ One way to change which program opens when you click (or double-click) a document icon is to delete the icon's current association in the File Types tab. Then reopen the document to get to the Open With dialog box and choose the associated program from the list that appears.

✦ You also can change associations between document types and programs by working in the File Types tab directly.

✦ To change the icons used for My Computer and other permanent desktop icons, right-click the desktop, choose Properties, click the Desktop tab, click Customize Desktop, choose an icon to change, and then click the Change Icon button.

✦ To change the icon for a shortcut, right-click the shortcut, choose Properties, and then click the Change Icon button.

✦ To change the icon for a file type (for example, all TIF files), click the Start button, choose Control Panel, and open the Folder Options icon. On the File Types tab, click the file type that you want to change, click the Edit button, and then click the Change Icon button.

✦ When the Change Icon dialog box appears, you can use the Browse button to locate and select icons that aren't initially visible within this dialog box.

✦ You can change a file's advanced properties by right-clicking the file and choosing Properties. The exact options that appear depend on the type of file with which you're working.

✦ To adjust more advanced settings of all folders and files, click the Start button, choose Control Panel, open the Folder Options icon, and make your selections from options on the View tab.

✦   ✦   ✦

Partitions, Volumes, and NTFS

Every operating system uses a *file system* to organize the contents of a hard disk. The file system greatly influences the capabilities of the drive. Windows XP provides support for the FAT (also called FAT16) file system used by DOS, the FAT32 file system, as well as the NTFS file system. In this chapter, you'll learn about these different types of file systems, as well as how to use unique features of NTFS.

Drives, Partitions, and Volumes

Your computer's hard disk drive is a *device* that's installed inside the system unit. Basically it's a rectangular box that's small enough to fit comfortably in the palm of your hand. The box contains one or more disks that spin around and one drive head per disk that moves across the spinning disk to read and write data. The drive is permanently sealed to keep out contaminants. If you were open the box, you would ruin the drive (unless you happened to be in a clean room and knew exactly what you were doing).

The actual hard disk(s) inside the hard drive can be *partitioned* to look like two or more disks to the computer. Typically, computer manufacturers create one big partition on the hard disk, using all of its available storage space. That partition, in turn, becomes your local drive C:. In truth, however, a hard disk can split into two or more partitions. Each partition will look like a separate disk to the computer.

You can install a different operating system on each partition. For example, one partition could be home to Windows, the other home to Linux. When you start that computer, a *dual-boot* option appears, where you can choose which operating system you want to use. Optionally, all the partitions can be used for a single operating system. Each partition will just appear as a separate drive icon within My Computer.

Before a partition can be used, it needs to be *formatted*, during which time the partition is set up to support a particular file system, such as NTFS or FAT32. After the partition has been formatted, it's then called a *volume*. In My Computer, each volume appears as a separate local hard disk drive with its own drive letter name. For example, Figure 31-1 shows the contents of My Computer on my Max computer. In common parlance, we would say that there are six drives available to Max, A:, C:, D:, E:, F:, and Z:. In truth, however, drives C: and F: are just two different volumes on one physical hard disk drive.

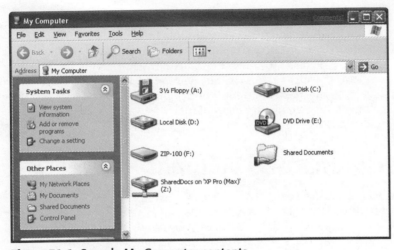

Figure 31-1: Sample My Computer contents

Any hard disk volume can be formatted using the FAT, FAT32, or NTFS file system. Because each type of file system offers different capabilities, it's good to know what file system a particular volume is using.

What's My File System?

Unless you, personally, installed Windows XP on a fresh, unformatted hard disk, you probably don't know which file system your hard disk is formatted with. But it's easy to find out. Just follow these steps:

1. Open My Computer.

2. Right-click the icon for your C: drive (or any other "hard drive," if you have more than one).

3. Choose Properties.

The General tab of the drive's Properties dialog box shows the file system being using on that drive. For example, Figure 31-2 shows the Properties for the aforementioned C: and F: drives. As you can see, drive C: is using the NTFS file system; drive F: is using the FAT32 file system. The dialog box for drive C: has a couple of extra options to choose from beneath the pie chart. That's because of differences between the two file systems.

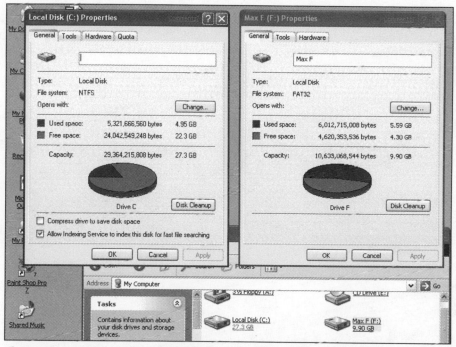

Figure 31-2: The Properties dialog boxes for drives C: and F: on my Max computer

Repartitioning a Disk

After a disk has been partitioned and used, repartitioning the disk is no small feat. Some third-party programs, such as Partition Magic (www.powerquest.com), enable you to change existing partitions without destroying data. However, repartitioning is always risky to existing data, so you should always make a backup of your hard disk before you even *think* about repartitioning. There is no "undelete" or "undo" when it comes to repartitioning a hard disk!

You also can repartition a hard disk by performing a clean install of Windows XP, as described in Appendix A. However, that approach will definitely destroy all the data on the hard disk. If you're just looking to convert a FAT or FAT32 volume to NTFS, no partitioning is required. As you'll learn later in this chapter, you can do that using the convert command.

NTFS versus FAT32

The FAT (file allocation table) file system was originally created for DOS and was the reason for the old 8.3 file name limitation at that time. (For those of you who missed all that, the 8.3 refers to the fact that a file name could be up to 8 characters in length, followed by a 3-letter file name extension.) FAT32 came along later and, among other enhancements, extended the file name limitation to 256 characters.

NTFS (New Technology File System) was created for the Windows NT product line, which was eventually renamed to Windows 2000. NTFS, like NT itself, was designed for the corporate environment, placing a strong emphasis on networking and network security. Table 31-1 compares the capabilities and features of the three file systems.

Table 31-1
Comparison of NTFS, FAT32, and FAT File Systems

	NTFS	*FAT32*	*FAT*
Maximum Volume Size	2 TB*	32 GB	4 GB
Maximum File Size	Unlimited**	2 GB	4 GB
Drive Compression	Yes	No	No
Indexing Service	Yes	No	No
Encryption	Yes	No	No
Mounted Drives	Yes	No	No
Disk Quotas	Yes	No	No
NT Domains	Yes	No	No
Active Directory	Yes	No	No

*TB stands for terabyte, one trillion bytes, or roughly 1,000 gigabytes.

**The maximum file size is equal to the size of the volume.

Because the file systems have evolved over time, not all operating systems are compatible with all file systems. If you install multiple operating systems on a single computer, you might end up with "invisible" file systems. If you boot up a computer in Windows 95, for example, any NTFS volumes on that computer would be invisible. On the other hand, most modern distributions of Linux can read NTFS partitions. So if you boot up in that operating system, the contents of the NTFS partition would be visible. Table 31-2 summarizes the compatibilities among different Microsoft operating system versions and file systems.

Table 31-2
File Systems and Operating System Compatibilities

	NTFS	FAT32	FAT
Windows XP	X	X	X
Windows 2000	X	X	X
Windows NT 4*	X*	X	X
Windows NT	X		
Windows 98		X	X
Windows 95 (OSR2)		X	X
OS/2			X
MS-DOS			X

* Windows NT 4.0 used NTFS 4. Windows 2000 and XP use the newer NTFS 5. Windows NT 4.0 with Service Pack 4 can access some, but not all, files on NTFS 5 volumes.

Converting a File System to NTFS

You can convert a FAT or FAT32 volume to NTFS using the Convert program that comes with Windows XP. Once you do, however, there's no way back. Which is to say, there is no "unconvert," nor is there any program to convert NTFS volumes to other file systems. So be sure you want to do this first.

Caution   Even though Convert can change a FAT or FAT32 volume without destroying data, you should back up the volume before you convert. You just never know when things might go wrong.

When you are sure you want to convert, follow these steps:

1. Close all open windows on your desktop.
2. Click the Start button and choose All Programs ➪ Accessories ➪ Command Prompt.
3. Type the command below, replacing *driveletter* with the drive letter of the volume you want to convert (for instance, **c:** or **d:**):

   ```
   convert driveletter: /fs:ntfs
   ```

4. Press the Enter key and then follow any instructions that appear on screen.
5. When you want to close the command-prompt window, type **exit** and press Enter.

If some open program or other activity prevents the program from converting the volume immediately, you'll be given the option to have it run the next time you start your computer.

NTFS File Compression

NTFS offers the ability to automatically compress and decompress files as you save and open them. As the name implies, compressed files use less disk space. Unlike the compressed folders discussed in Chapter 12, NTFS compression is completely transparent. Which is to say, you don't have to do anything to compress or decompress the files. When you save a file to a compressed drive or folder, the file is automatically compressed. When you reopen the file, it's automatically decompressed. To compress an NTFS folder or volume, follow these steps:

1. Right-click the folder's icon in Explorer or the drive's icon in My Computer and choose Properties.

2. If you right-clicked a drive icon in Step 1, choose Compress drive to save disk space. Then click OK and skip the remaining steps.

3. On the General tab, click the Advanced button to reveal the dialog box shown in Figure 31-3.

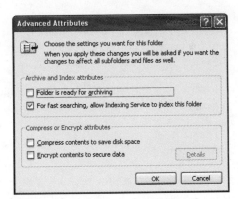

Figure 31-3: Advanced attributes for folders stored in an NTFS volume

4. Click the OK button.

That's all there is to it. Any files already in the folder or volume, as well as any files you save, move, or copy to it, are compressed automatically. Should you change your mind, repeat the steps and clear the Compress check box.

Windows XP Professional also supports encryption, as discussed in Chapter 33.

NTFS Indexing Service

NTFS also supports the *Indexing Service*, which is a tool that allows the Search Assistant to locate files more quickly. By default, the service is turned on, and the index is updated automatically as you create, move, copy, and delete files. If, for whatever reason, you want to verify or turn off the indexing service, follow these steps:

1. In Windows Explorer, right-click the icon for the folder or file in question and choose Properties.

2. On the General tab, click the Advanced button to get to the options shown in Figure 31-3.

3. Select or clear the check box labeled `For fast searching, allow Indexing Service to index this file` check box and then click the OK button.

If you changed the attribute for a folder, you'll be asked whether you want to apply the setting to all files and subfolders within the folder.

Summary

In this chapter, you learned about volumes, file systems, and NTFS. As you'll learn in the next chapter, NTFS in conjunction with Windows XP Professional provides for extensive security on corporate networks. Before we get into all that though, let's review the basic concepts discussed in this chapter:

✦ A single hard disk drive can be divided into partitions, where each partition appears as a separate disk to the computer.

✦ A partition can be formatted using a variety of file systems, including FAT, FAT32, and NTFS.

✦ Once formatted, a hard disk partition is referred to as a volume, even though it appears as a drive in My Computer.

✦ NTFS volumes offer some advantages over FAT partitions, including automatic compression and indexing.

✦ You can convert a FAT partition to NTFS. But Windows XP offers no tools for converting NTFS partitions to FAT.

✦ ✦ ✦

Advanced Security Administration

In a corporate environment, it's often important to control access to resources more tightly than in a home or small business environment. To that extent, Windows XP Professional provides the more advanced level of security found in Windows NT and Windows 2000. At the very core of the advanced security features of Professional are the concepts of *user accounts* and *groups*. The person in charge of managing user accounts and groups is generally referred to as the *system administrator*. That person controls access to resources on the computer by granting and denying *permissions* to users and groups.

User Accounts and Groups

To create and manage local user accounts and groups (those specific to a given computer), the system administrator can use the Computer Management tool, which is accessible through the Administrative Tools in Control Panel. Expanding the Local Users and Groups category in the *console tree* (left panel) reveals two subcategories: one named Users, the other named Groups, as in Figure 32-1.

Note   Managing domain users and groups is a feature of Windows XP Server editions, and hence isn't covered in this book.

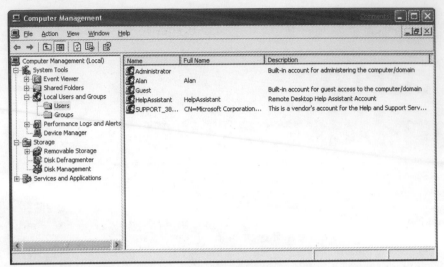

Figure 32-1: Local Users and Groups is available in Computer Management in Windows XP Professional.

Windows XP Professional automatically creates some user accounts, including the following:

✦ **Administrator:** Provides "omnipotent" access to the system, and is the account used by the system administrator.

✦ **Guest:** Provides limited access to people who log on as Guest.

✦ **HelpAssistant:** Provides access to any user who accesses this computer as an assistant.

Other accounts can be created within Computer Management, or through the User Accounts program described back in Chapter 20, or even automatically through certain features that are installed and used on the system.

Any user can be a member of one or more security *groups*. The administrator can create groups, or can use any of the predefined groups shown in Figure 32-2. The description next to each group name provides a basic summary of the privileges automatically assigned to all members of that group.

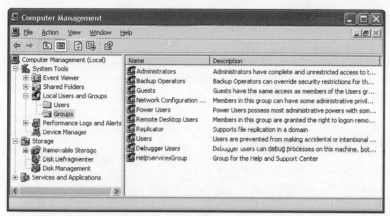

Figure 32-2: Security groups that are built into Windows XP Professional

Working with user accounts

To create a new user account via Computer Management, click Users under Local Users and Groups, and then choose Action ➪ New User. The New User dialog box opens, as shown in Figure 32-3. Then fill in the blanks and select options as summarized here:

✦ **User name:** This is the name the user logs on with. It must be unique (no two users can share the same user name), must be no more than 20 characters in length, and cannot contain any of the following characters / \ " [ ] < > : ; , | = + * ?

✦ **Full name:** The person's complete name.

✦ **Description:** Any descriptive text that you care to add about this user account.

✦ **Password:** The password the user will type to log on to the system, up to a maximum of 256 characters. Passwords are case-sensitive, meaning the user must type the password using the exact upper/lowercase letters you type here.

✦ **Confirm password:** To verify that you typed the password as intended, type it again here.

✦ **User must change password at next logon:** If selected, requires that the user to make up her own password the first (or next) time she logs on. Deselecting this option will enable the options that follow.

✦ **User cannot change password:** If selected, prevents the user from changing her own password.

✦ **Password never expires:** If selected, overrides the Maximum Password Age option defined in the Users group (as described later).

✦ **Account is disabled:** Creates the account and retains the account information. But the user cannot log on until the account is enabled. This option is sometimes used when modifying an existing account, to temporarily disable a user's logon privileges.

Figure 32-3: The New User dialog box

Tip   As in many dialog boxes, you can click the question mark button (?) in New User, and then click any option for more information.

Click the Create button when done. The information is saved and the dialog box remains open, in case you want to create more user accounts. Click the Close button to close the dialog box.

To modify an existing account in Computer Management, right-click the account and choose Properties. To change only the account name, right-click and choose Rename. To delete an account, right-click and choose Delete.

Assigning group membership

As mentioned, any user can belong to any number of security groups. By default, every user is added to the Users group. To change a user's group membership, right-click the user's name and choose Properties. Or double-click the user's name. Then click the Member Of tab in the dialog box that opens. The groups to which the user currently belongs are listed. To add this user to an existing group, click the Add button. The Select Groups dialog box opens. You need to type in the group names, separated by semicolons. To verify correct typing, click the Check Names button. The name of the computer followed by a backslash will be added to each group name, as in Figure 32-4.

Tip   As discussed in a moment, you can do this the other way around. That is, you can open a group, and then enter the names of users who belong to that group.

The Object Types, Locations, and Advanced options are available for working with objects other than groups. In a domain, for example, you can use groups defined on some other computer in the domain. Clicking OK returns you to the Member Of tab, which will now include any groups you selected.

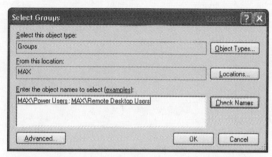

Figure 32-4: The Select Groups dialog box after typing a couple of group names and clicking Check Names

To remove a user from a group, click the group name, and then click the Remove button.

Profiles

The Profile tab in the Properties dialog box, shown in Figure 32-5, enables you to change some features of the user's profile. When you're creating an account for the local computer, leaving these options empty is essentially the same as creating the account through the User Accounts program in Control Panel. Which is to say, the first time the user logs on, Windows will create a subfolder with the user's name in Documents and Settings, give the user his own My Documents folders, and so forth.

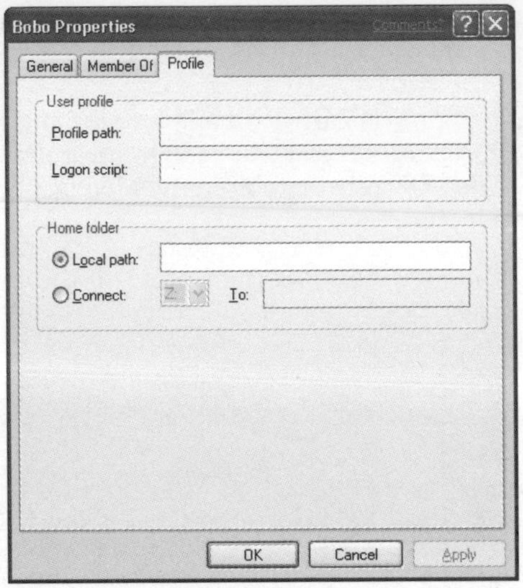

Bobo Properties

General | Member Of | Profile

User profile

Profile path: _____

Logon script: _____

Home folder

⊙ Local path: _____

○ Connect: Z ▾ To: _____

[OK] [Cancel] [Apply]

Figure 32-5: The Profile tab

A network administrator, on the other hand, can use the Profile tab to create a *roaming user profile*. This type of profile is stored on the local computer as well as on a server. That way, when the user logs on to some other computer in the network, she retains her desktop options and other settings at that computer. To create a roaming profile, enter the location of the roaming profiles folder as the profile path. Use the universal naming convention (UNC)—for example, \\server01\profiles.

 Note   On the server, the folder that contains user profiles must be shared with Full Access granted to all users.

If you have created a logon script for the user, enter the path to the script. The script itself can be any executable with the .bat, .cmd, or .exe extension. You can use the environment variable %username% to refer to the account user name. For example, entering **\\server01\profiles\%username%** will point to a file with the same name as the current user in the profiles folder of the computer named server01.

Under the Home folder, the Local Path option enables you to define a default folder for documents on the local computer. If left empty, this will be the user's local My Documents folder. If you prefer to use a folder on a network server as the user's home folder, select Connect. Then select an available drive letter to assign to the path and enter the path to the folder in UNC format.

Working with groups

Working with groups is similar to working with users. To create a new group, for example, click Groups in the left column of Computer Management and then choose Action ➪ New Group. In the New Group dialog box that appears, enter the group name, description, and optionally, click the Add button to add users to the group.

To rename, change, or delete an existing group, right-click the group name and choose the appropriate option. You cannot delete the Administrators or Guests groups.

Tip   Even though you cannot delete the Guests group, you can disable the Guest user account. Click Users in the left column in Computer Management, double-click the Guest account, and choose Account Is Disabled.

The predefined groups are all oriented toward different types of computer users. In a corporate environment, you might want to create groups based on departments and job types. For example, you might create a group named Accounting Admins. Later, you could give users in that group the permission to create, read, modify, and delete files relevant to the accounting department. Then create another group, perhaps named Accounting Staff. Later, you could give members of that group permission to open and read certain files, but not to modify them.

Still later, if a member of the Accounting Staff group gets promoted, extending her privileges would be a simple matter of making her a member of the Accounting Admins group. At this stage of the game, you're just creating group names and descriptions — you'll grant permissions later. So feel free to think up and create as many groups as you think might be useful in your organization. Of course, you needn't get it perfect the first time. You can add, change, and delete groups at any time.

You can close the Computer Management window when you are finished working with users and groups. The next phase is to start granting permissions to your users and groups, to determine which *objects* (devices, files, and folders) they can, and cannot, access.

Granting Permissions

You control access to various *objects* (the generic term for files, folders, and devices such as printers) by granting permissions to users and groups. As a rule, you're better off granting permissions to groups rather than individual users. Because that way, if a person gets promoted, you can just make that person a member of a different exiting group, instead of assigning new permissions to the individual on an object-by-object basis.

Tip

In Windows XP Home edition, you can assign permissions to shared resources only.

You can control permissions to individual objects through the standard Windows Explorer windows. Optionally, as discussed later, you can control permissions to shared objects through Computer Management. You'll find that approach easier because all the shared items are accessible from a single window — you don't need to navigate around through Explorer to find each shared object. For items that aren't shared, or haven't been shared yet, however, you need to grant permissions via Explorer. Here's how:

1. In Explorer, navigate to the icon for the object to which you want to control permissions.

2. Select the icon by pointing to it for a moment. Or, if you're using the classic double-click method to open icons, select the item by clicking it once.

3. Right-click the icon, or if you are choosing more than one icon, hold down the Ctrl key first, and then choose Properties.

You must right-click the actual icon for the object — a shortcut icon that points to the object won't do. You might need to navigate to the item through My Computer and Folder List in the Explorer window. In the case of a shared device, you might find it easier to get to security options through Computer Management, as discussed under "Managing Shares."

Once you've done this, the object's Properties dialog box will include a Security tab, which you can use to control permissions. The exact security options available vary from one object to another, but the techniques for granting and denying access is the same.

The top half of the dialog box lists users and groups who currently have some kind of access to the object. The bottom half of the dialog box shows permissions for whichever user or group is currently selected in the top half of the dialog box. In Figure 32-6, for example, the Administrators group is currently selected. The bottom half of the dialog box shows that this group has unlimited access to the file (by virtue of the fact that every Allow check box is selected).

Figure 32-6: The Security tab from a sample Shared folder

You can control access to the object by using the Add and Remove buttons to add and delete existing users and groups. For example, you could add the Accounting Admins group to the list to control access by members of that group. To allow and deny permissions, click that group name, and then make selections from the lower half of the dialog box.

Note   You can choose only combinations of permissions that make sense. For example, you can't allow Write access, but deny Read access, because one must be able to read a file in order to write to it!

Some Allow check boxes will have a dimmed appearance. These dimmed check boxes represent *inherited* permissions. An object inherits permissions from its parent object. Suppose, for example, that you're working with permissions for a folder that's contained within the Shared Documents folder. By virtue of the fact that the current folder is a child of Shared Documents, it inherits the Shared Documents folder's permissions for every use and group, and those permissions have the dimmed appearance.

As previously mentioned, different objects list different types of permissions. For example, a folder will include a List Folder Contents permission, which determines whether the selected user or group is allowed to view the contents of the folder. An individual file, on the other hand, does not offer that permission. In most cases, the permissions are self-explanatory. However, you can get more detailed by right-clicking the permissions list, choosing What's This?, and then choosing Permissions on Objects in the dialog box that pops up.

Tip   Here's another buzzword for you. The security settings you apply to an object are stored in its *access control list*, often abbreviated ACL. The list is actually part of every file and folder stored on an NTFS partition. Files stored on FAT32 partitions have no ACL, and hence advanced security options aren't available.

Clicking the Advanced button takes you to Advanced Security Settings dialog box for the object, as shown in Figure 32-7. This dialog box gives you much more information about current permissions, as well as an alternative way to control permissions. The Add button enables you to add a new user or group. The Edit and Remove buttons enable you to change or remove the currently selected user or group. (You cannot remove built-in users and groups, such as SYSTEM and Administrators, however, because they always have permission to access every object, by default.)

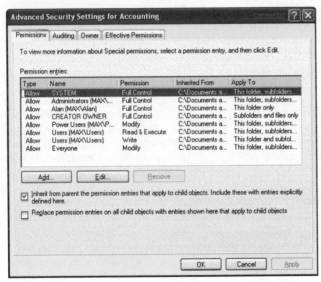

Figure 32-7: The Advanced Security Settings dialog box

When working at this level of detail, you'll notice a couple of users (their names in all uppercase letters) and a group named Everyone that weren't in your original list of users and groups. They are:

✦ **SYSTEM:** Refers to Windows itself. All objects need to grant Full Control to Windows.

✦ **CREATOR OWNER:** Refers to the person who created the object, unless the administrator has transferred ownership to herself or some other user.

✦ **Everyone:** As the name implies, basically everyone who can log on to the computer.

Note Unlike earlier versions of Windows, XP doesn't include members of the Anonymous Logon group to be members of the Everyone group.

You also can control inheritance from the Permissions tab of the Advanced Security Settings dialog box. By default, all objects inherit permissions from their parent object. But you can disable that by clearing the Inherit from parent the permissions check box. If you're changing the permissions of a folder and you want all child objects within that folder to inherit the new permissions, choose the Replace permissions entries on all child objects check box. Other tabs in the Advanced Security Settings dialog box are as follows:

✦ **Auditing:** Enables you to record successful and failed attempts to access the object.

✦ **Owner:** Displays the current owner of the object, and enables the administrator to change the current owner.

✦ **Effective Permissions:** Enables you to see what permissions will be granted to a user or group, before you actually add that user or group. In other words, this tab enables you to "test the waters" before actually adding the user or group.

Managing Shares

As you learned in Chapter 27, you can use the Sharing tab of an object's Properties dialog box to share file, folders, and devices with other computers in a local area network. The Computer Management tool offers a "centralized" way to manage shared resources (often called *shares*, for short). To get there, follow these steps:

1. Click the Start button and open Control Panel.

2. Open the Administrative Tools icon.

3. Open the Computer Management icon.

4. Under Shared Folders, click Shares.

The name Shared Folders is a little misleading, because all shared items are visible when you click Shares. In Figure 32-8, for example, the item named print$ under Shared Folders is actually a printer connected to that computer and shared across the network. The item named F$ is a shared volume that appears as drive F: in that computer's My Computer view.

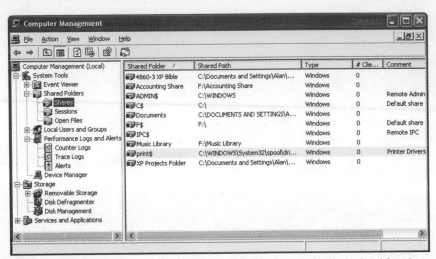

Figure 32-8: Shared items on this computer appear under Shared Folders in Computer Management.

The real beauty of the list of shares is that you can get to any item's security settings right from the list. To get to the basic security settings, double-click the item. The basic permissions are available on the Share Permissions tab of the Properties dialog box that opens. To get to the advanced security options, right-click the item and choose Properties. Then click the Security tab when the Properties dialog box opens.

Permission conflicts

It's important to understand that "allow" permissions are cumulative. Which is to say, the full set of "allow" permissions granted to a particular user is determined by all the groups to which that user belongs. Suppose, for example, that you have a folder named `Marketing` within the `Shared Documents` folder. You figure the accounting staff can look at the folder, but you don't want them to be putting any of their files in there. So you open the security settings for the `Marketing` folder, add the Accounting Staff group to its list, and Allow them to Read the folder, as in Figure 32-9.

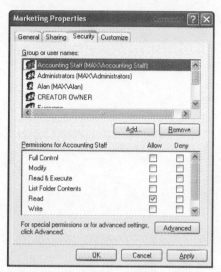

Figure 32-9: Members of the Accounting Staff group have Allow permissions to Read the Marketing folder.

To test things out, you log on as user Bobo, who is a member of the Accounting Staff group. You go to the Marketing folder and, lo and behold, you discover that Bobo has no problem writing to (creating files within) the Marketing folder. At first, this might seem to be some kind of bug, because you didn't grant write permission to the Accounting Staff group, of which Bobo is a member. So what's up?

Well, for one thing, Bobo is a member of several other groups by default, such as Everyone and Users. Assuming *those* groups have permission to write to the folder, Bobo has permission to write to the folder by virtue of his membership in those groups. Because you didn't specifically *deny* write permission to the Accounting Staff group, Bobo can write away to his heart's content.

To fix the problem, go back to the original object's security settings, choose the Accounting Staff group, and then specifically choose Deny for the Write permission, as in Figure 32-10. Deny permissions override the cumulative effects of other group memberships. So once you have made this change, members of the Accounting Staff group will no longer be able to write to the Marketing folder, regardless of which other groups a particular member belongs to.

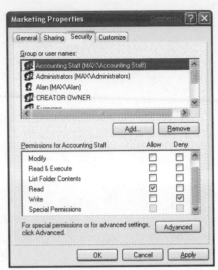

Figure 32-10: Members of the
Accounting Staff group have been denied
permission to write to the Marketing folder.

Caution   Be *very* careful with Deny permissions. For example, you wouldn't want to set a
Deny permission in the Everyone group, because doing so would deny everyone
permission — including yourself!

If you cannot seem to set the permissions you're trying to achieve in a particular
item, and things are getting confusing, you need to stop, back up, and think about
what's already going on behind the scenes. When setting permissions on a folder,
for example, you want to look at the permissions already provided to that folder via
the Everyone, Users, and whatever other groups are already listed for that item.
Remember that many of the existing permissions have been inherited from the parent object(s). So before you change any permissions, think whether you would be
better off changing the permissions at the parent level, or even higher.

In addition, don't forget that every user is potentially the member of several
groups. From time to time, you might need to go back to Local Users and Groups
and review a user's group membership, to refresh your memory. Also, remember
that the person who creates an item is automatically the owner of that item. Just
being the owner of the item automatically grants that person full control over the
item, unless the administrator goes in and changes ownership via the Owner tab in
the Advanced Security Settings dialog box.

Help with permissions

The whole security and permissions thing creates quite a web of interrelationships among users, groups, objects, and permissions. It's easy to get lost, and the generic help under Help and Support won't always give you the level of support you need to figure out all the relationships involved. You're probably better off using Help in the Computer Management tool. There are two ways to get help there. You can get immediate help with whatever item is selected in the console tree by clicking the Help button in the toolbar. Optionally, you can choose Help ➪ Help Topics from Computer Management's menu bar and use the Contents, Index, and Search tabs to locate the information you need.

Summary

Windows XP provides the features that corporate system administrators need to tightly control access to computer resources. Windows XP Professional inherits the concept of security groups, originally provided by the Windows NT/2000 product line. Here's a quick recap of the important points covered in this chapter:

✦ To uniquely identify each user who logs on to the system, the administrator can create user accounts, which give each user a name and a password.

✦ To simplify managing large numbers of users, Windows XP Professional provides for security groups.

✦ A user can belong to any number of groups.

✦ To control who has access to a specific object, the administrator can set permissions on the Security tab of the object's Properties dialog box.

✦ Advanced security options for files and folders are available only on NTFS volumes.

✦ Allow permissions are cumulative, in that a user's permissions are determined by all the groups to which the user belongs.

✦ Deny permissions override Allow permissions, and therefore need to be created with caution.

✦   ✦   ✦

Dealing with the Windows XP Registry

In this chapter, you will learn about the Windows XP Registry—what it is and how to use it. You also will learn how to use the Windows XP Registry Editor. The Registry Editor gives you the power to make changes to the Registry. You can fix problems or, if you're not careful, cause them. You can even remove all the information Windows XP needs to boot and run. This is why you also will learn how to save extra backup copies of the Registry and how to recover from Registry disasters. After learning how to manipulate the Registry, you will learn useful tricks for customizing your Windows XP environment—tricks you can perform only by manually editing the Registry.

What Is the Registry?

The Registry is a repository of information for Windows XP and its applications. What kind of information? Almost anything. For example, when you installed Windows XP, the setup program asked you for your name, and it stored this information in the Registry.

Windows XP also stores information about your hardware configuration in the Registry, such as settings for your modem, printers, video adapters, and so on.

Another example is Explorer, which uses the Registry for several purposes. In Explorer, every file has an icon. Windows XP uses the Registry to remember which icon goes with which file. When you open a file, Explorer looks up information about this file so that it can decide which application to launch. Where do you think Windows stores this information? That's right—in the Registry.

Most applications store additional information in the Registry, such as user preferences, configuration data, the files you edited most recently, and so on. Each application can store anything it wants.

Out with the old

You may be familiar with INI files. In Windows 3.1, an application typically stored its configuration data in a text file, such as `winword.ini`. You could find many of these files cluttering your Windows folder. Windows itself kept information in files, such as `win.ini` and `system.ini`. Windows 95 and 98 replaced these files with the Registry. When you upgraded to one of these versions, all the information in the INI files hanging around in your Windows folder was placed in the Registry. (The old INI files are still around just for applications designed for Windows 3.1 because these applications would not know how to look up settings in the Registry.)

Figure 33-1 shows an excerpt from `control.ini`, which stores information for the Control Panel. When you upgraded your computer to Windows XP, the setup program read `control.ini` and similar files and then copied this information into the Registry. Windows XP retrieves this information from the Registry rather than from `control.ini`. (If you look around on your drive, however, you might still find a `control.ini` file lurking somewhere. It's there for older programs that need to use it.)

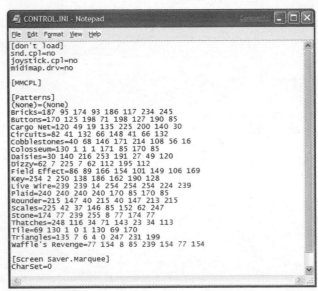

Figure 33-1: Windows 3.1 used `control.ini` to store Control Panel data.

Back when you installed a new application in Windows 3.1, the Setup program often created new INI files and modified existing ones. In some unfortunate situations, it asked you to manually edit one or more INI files, such as system.ini.

Some power users enjoyed working with INI files. The files are plain-text files, so you could use any text editor, such as Notepad, to examine or modify an INI file. Sometimes the only way to get out of a jam was to edit an INI file.

In with the new

In Windows 95, the plethora of INI files was replaced with a single database: the Registry. Windows 98 capitalized on the Registry, and this change also is present in Windows XP. Because the Registry is a single, centrally located database, it is easy to find the configuration data for a particular application. The Registry does away with the separate INI files and enables long names for its Registry entries, so you can find information much more easily than you could with INI files. Instead of trying to decipher eight-letter file names, you can search the Registry for a company name and then look for a full product name. This makes it easier to find information for a particular application.

Note

The original reason Microsoft created the Registry was to handle multiple users on a single system. The INI files could not easily identify different settings for different users. Since that original decision, however, Microsoft engineers have found many more uses for the Registry. Microsoft COM object technology, for example, depends heavily on the Registry. When you embed an Excel spreadsheet inside a Word document, Windows XP uses the Registry to determine how to store the Excel spreadsheet, what files to use when you edit the spreadsheet, and how to integrate Excel menus into Word.

What's in the Registry?

Because the Registry stores information for every application, it needs a way to organize this information. To keep one application's data from interfering with the data from another application, the Registry uses a tree-like arrangement, similar to the way files and folders reside on a disk drive.

Whereas a disk drive uses folders, however, the Registry uses keys. Just as a folder can contain other folders, a key can have its own subkeys. Instead of files, the Registry has values. For example, the Control Panel stores its information under the key, Control Panel. This key has subkeys for Appearance, Cursors, and so on. The Appearance subkey has its own subkey—Schemes—to record all the named color schemes you can define in the Appearance tab of the Control Panel's Display applet. Each named color scheme is a separate value, as in Figure 33-2.

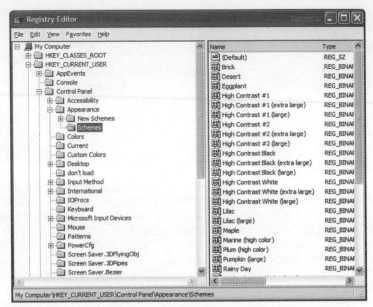

Figure 33-2: The Control Panel stores its Registry data in a tree under the Control Panel key.

In the Registry, a key has no relation to the keys on your keyboard, car keys, house keys, or any other key you are likely to encounter in real life. A key is one more bit of technojargon you need to learn. In computerese, a program uses a key to look up information. When you look up a word in a dictionary, for example, you are using the word as a key to search through the dictionary. A key in the Registry is similar — programs look up configuration data using keys and subkeys. The Registry stores the actual data (like the definitions in the dictionary) in a key's values.

Keys in the Registry are like relatives in a family tree. One key can be the parent of several child keys. All the child keys that share a parent are siblings.

The information for a key is its values. Every value has a name, a type, and data. For example, the Appearance key has a value — Current — that represents the name of the current color scheme. A value's type says whether the data are ordinary text, a number, or something else. To be specific, the Registry uses special names for these types. Table 33-1 lists the types you will see in the Registry.

Note The Windows XP Registry can hold several types of string values, including multi-string and expandable string values. Unless you know for certain that a value should be one of these types of strings, always select the plain old string value option when you add a string to the Registry.

DWORD is short for double word, which is another way of saying number. A word is a unit of computer storage. A double word is two adjacent words. But don't let this confuse you. Just remember, when the Registry says DWORD, it means number.

Table 33-1 Registry Value Types	
Type	*Registry Jargon*
Ordinary text	String
Numbers	DWORD
Everything else	Binary

To refer to a specific Registry key, use a path, which is analogous to a file path. A Registry path is a series of key names, separated by backslashes. Every Registry path starts with a root key, one of six special keys Windows XP defines. The root key is similar to a drive letter in file paths. For example, `HKEY_CURRENT_ USER\ Control Panel\Appearance\Schemes` is a Registry path that starts with the root key `HKEY_CURRENT_USER` and follows the keys Control Panel, Appearance, and Schemes.

That's enough theory. Now it's time to start getting your hands dirty. You can begin by learning how to back up your Registry before making changes (better safe than sorry).

Backing Up Your Registry

Before you make any changes to the Registry, you should make a backup copy. Some of the entries in the Registry are vital for Windows XP; therefore, if you accidentally delete the wrong key, you may be unable to start your computer.

Windows XP makes a backup copy of your Registry each time you restart your computer. Every time your computer starts, Windows XP's Registry Checker application automatically scans your Registry. If it finds a problem, it automatically replaces the Registry with the backup copy of the Registry it made from the last restart.

Windows XP does not change the current Registry backup to reflect any changes to the Registry that occur while Windows XP is running. This helps ensure that a valid backup of the Registry exists in case an application stores invalid information in the Registry and prevents Windows XP from running. You have a guarantee the Registry was valid when Windows XP created the backup files, so they are probably safe to use.

Sometimes, however, you want to make additional backups of the Registry. Suppose, for example, that you are about to make some manual changes to the Registry—perhaps you want to implement one of the ideas from the section "Useful Registry Tricks," which appears later in this chapter. You want to save the Registry in its current state, not the state it was in when you started Windows XP this morning (or yesterday, or last week, or whenever you booted your PC).

To make a manual backup of the Registry, follow these steps:

1. Click the Start button and choose All Programs ➪ Accessories ➪ System Tools ➪ Backup to open the Backup Utility Wizard.

2. Click Next to continue.

3. Make certain that the Perform a Backup option is selected and then click Next to continue.

4. Select the Only back up the System State data option as shown in Figure 33-3 and then click Next to continue.

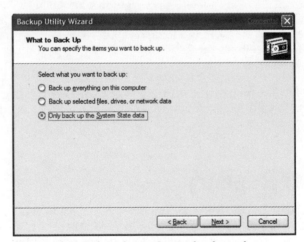

Figure 33-3: Select the option to back up the System State data.

5. Choose the destination for the backup and click Next to continue. You need fairly large medium for the backup, because the System State data can require hundreds of megabytes of disk space. You may want to use a CD-RW disc if you have this option available.

6. Click Finish to make the backup.

New Registry Backup Feature

Windows XP has a new Registry and system backup feature. Windows XP keeps multiple copies of your Registry on your hard drive. The Windows XP System Restore utility manages these backups. The System Restore program enables you to set system checkpoints whenever you want to make sure that you can return your system to a given state.

What is a checkpoint? Suppose you just visited the Windows Update site and installed all the latest upgrades for security. After you have finished installing, System Restore creates a checkpoint. Now if you go out and accidentally delete a file with a .dll extension from \Windows\System, you can recover that file by rolling back your computer to its state at the time the checkpoint was created. Data files and e-mails are not rolled back, but the Registry and installed programs are rolled back.

You can use System Restore to create manual checkpoints, in effect, to choose a reference point for backing up your system. This feature is handy for creating Registry backups before editing the Registry. It is also a good thing to use just before and just after you install new software. If the software screws up your system, you can always roll it back to the preinstallation state, fixing the problem.

To create a checkpoint, follow these steps:

1. Click the Start button and choose All Programs ⇨ Accessories ⇨ System Tools ⇨ System Restore.

2. Select Create a restore point using the option buttons. Click Next (see Figure 33-4).

3. Enter a description for the restore point in the text box.

4. Click Create to create the restore point.

Tip   Another useful way to back up your Registry is to select File ⇨ Export from the Registry Editor's menu. When the dialog box appears, make sure the All option button is selected and enter a file name. Clicking Save produces a text file with a .reg extension that contains all your Registry settings. If you need to restore your Registry, you can double-click this file. The default action for a REG file when double-clicked is to merge with the Registry. Even if you have to do a complete reinstall of Windows XP, you can get back most of your settings with a simple double-click. This technique saves reinstalling all your applications.

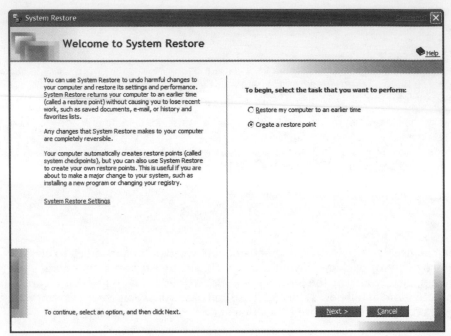

Figure 33-4: Select the option to create a restore point.

Using the Registry Editor

You can look at what's in the Registry by running the Registry Editor. From the Start menu, choose Run, type **regedit** and press Enter (or click the OK button). You will see a window similar to Figure 33-5.

As you read this chapter, you might find dragging the Regedit icon onto your desktop more convenient. You can find regedit.exe in the Windows folder.

The left pane shows several keys (HKEY_CLASSES_ROOT, and so on). You can expand each key to reveal subkeys, in much the same manner as Explorer. Click the little plus sign (+) to expand a key and view its subkeys. You also can press the plus sign on the numeric keypad to expand a key. Click the minus sign (−) to collapse the subkeys or press the minus sign on the numeric keypad.

When you select a Registry key, the Registry Editor displays the full path to this key in the status bar at the bottom of the window. If you cannot see the status bar, select View ➪ Status Bar from the menu bar.

The Registry always contains five standard, top-level keys. Every Registry path must start with one of these root keys, just as a complete file name starts with a drive letter. Table 33-2 lists the root keys in Windows XP.

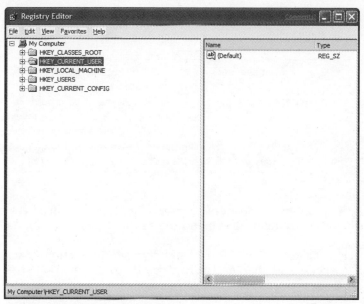

Figure 33-5: The Registry Editor

Table 33-2	
Standard Root Keys	
Key Name	**Description**
HKEY_CLASSES_ROOT	File associations (short for HKEY_LOCAL_MACHINE\ Software\Classes). Explorer uses this information to choose icons, respond to double-clicks, and display context menus.
HKEY_CURRENT_USER	Information for the current user (short for HKEY_USERS\ current user name). Applications store their preferences here.
HKEY_LOCAL_MACHINE	Information that applies system-wide. Windows XP stores information about hardware configurations here. Applications can also store information here that pertains to the computer rather than to users.
HKEY_USERS	Information for all users. If you configured Windows XP for multiple users, each user has a subkey under this key. When the user logs on, that user's subkey becomes HKEY_CURRENT_USER.

Continued

Table 33-2 *(continued)*	
Key Name	Description
HKEY_CURRENT_CONFIG	Current configuration of the local machine (short for HKEY_ LOCAL_MACHINE\Config\current configuration). When you boot Windows XP, it determines your hardware configuration and sets this key to the appropriate subkey of HKEY_LOCAL_ MACHINE\Config.This is important only if you use multiple configurations, such as a laptop computer that may or may not use a docking station.

You can use the Registry Editor to view, create, or modify Registry entries (keys and values). The following sections tell you how to use the Registry Editor.

Before you make any changes to the Registry, carefully read the section, "Backing Up Your Registry," earlier in this chapter. The Registry Editor has no Undo function. Always back up the Registry before modifying it.

Creating a new key

To create a new key, select the parent key and choose New ⇨ _Key from the short-cut menu or choose Edit ⇨ New ⇨ Key from the menu bar. The Registry Editor creates the key and gives it a name such as New Key #1. Change the name to the desired name and press Enter.

Notice the key automatically has a value, named (Default), but this value has no data. This is why the Registry Editor displays the data as (value not set).

Deleting a key

Select the key you want to delete and press Delete, choose Delete from the shortcut menu, or choose Edit ⇨ Delete from the menu bar. The Registry Editor confirms whether you want to delete the key.

Caution   When you delete a key, you also delete all its subkeys and values. The Registry Editor does not have an Undo feature. When you delete a key, that key is gone for good. Always make a backup copy of the Registry before you delete any keys.

Renaming a key

To change a key name, select that key, press F2 and type the new key name, followed by Enter. You also can choose Edit ⇨ Rename from the menu bar or choose

Rename from the shortcut menu. All the subkeys that share a common parent key must have different names. The Registry Editor will not enable you to assign a key name that is the same as a sibling key's name.

Values

When you select a key, the Registry Editor displays a list of values in the right pane. Notice the columns labeled Name and Data. A key can have any number of values, although most keys have none. The Registry Editor always displays one key, named (Default). For its data, you usually see (value not set), which is the Registry Editor's way of saying that this key does not really have a default value.

If you are a programmer, you should know the real name of the default value is an empty string. The Registry Editor displays the name as (Default) because this is easier to read. Think of it as the equivalent of "this value name intentionally left blank." You should never create a value with the name (Default) because this would be confusing to the operating system.

To see an example of a key with several values, expand HKEY_CURRENT_USER, expand the Control Panel, and select the Colors key. In the right pane of the Registry Editor, you can see a list of names and strings, where the strings contain mysterious-looking numbers. This is where Windows XP stores the color choices you make in the Display Control Panel applet.

Any changes you make in Windows XP update the Registry immediately, even if the Registry is open with Regedit. As you'll see in a moment, however, the opposite isn't always true. That is, changing the contents of the Registry with Regedit doesn't necessarily update all of Windows XP immediately.

Modifying a value

You can change any value in the Registry. Just double-click the name or select the value name and press Enter. The Registry Editor pops up a dialog box where you can type a new value.

The Registry stores information for Windows XP, but changing the information does not always cause an immediate change to Windows. For example, view the Control Panel\Desktop key and try changing a value by hand. For example, double-click the Wallpaper name and enter **C:\windows\clouds.bmp** (or another BMP file if your wallpaper is already clouds.bxmp) as the string data. Figure 33-6 shows you what this dialog box looks like. Press Enter or click OK. Notice the Registry Editor has the new values, but your desktop looks the same. It hasn't adopted the new background.

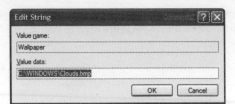

Figure 33-6: Double-click the Wallpaper name and type **C:\windows\clouds.bmp**. You need to restart Windows XP to see the effect of this change.

Exit and restart Windows XP. Now you can see the new background image. This is because when Windows XP starts, it reads the Registry to learn which background to make the desktop. After that, it doesn't check the Registry again until an application tells it the information has changed.

The moral of this story is that you can change values in the Registry Editor, but Windows XP may not act on the new values until you exit and restart Windows. Restarting Windows every time you make a minor change to the Registry would be tedious, so an application, such as a Control Panel applet, can inform Windows of a change to the Registry. In this case, Windows reads the new value from the Registry and redraws the background. This is how you can change the background image without restarting Windows.

For an example of editing a DWORD value, select the HKEY_CURRENT_USER\ Control Panel\Desktop key and double-click the SmoothScroll value. You can enter the new DWORD value as an ordinary number (decimal) or as a hexadecimal (base 16) value. Click Cancel or press the Esc key to exit the dialog box without making any changes. Figure 33-7 shows you the Edit DWORD Value dialog box.

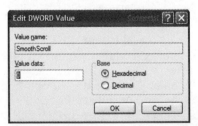

Figure 33-7: Enter a number in the Edit DWORD Value dialog box.

To see an example of the Edit Binary dialog box, select the Control Panel\ Appearance key and double-click the CustomColors value. Notice the data for CustomColors is a series of pairs of letters and numbers. Each pair represents one byte of data. When you edit the binary data, type to insert new bytes. Use the arrow keys to move around in the dialog box. The Delete key deletes the next byte, and the Backspace key removes the previous byte. You also can select many bytes at once and delete them or type to replace them with new data. Figure 33-8 shows you the Edit Binary Value dialog box.

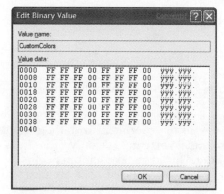

Figure 33-8: Edit binary data by inserting and deleting bytes in the Edit Binary Value dialog box.

Instead of double-clicking a value to modify it, you also can select the value name and press Enter. Alternatively, you can choose Edit ⇨ Modify from the menu bar or choose Modify from the shortcut menu. When you modify a value, make sure the new value is what you want. The Registry Editor does not have an Undo feature.

Adding a new value

Most of the changes you will make to the Registry will be modifications of existing values. Sometimes, however, you'll need to add a new value to a key. Choose Edit ⇨ New or choose New from the context menu. The cascading menu gives you the choice of creating a new String value, Binary value, DWORD value, Multi-String value, or Expandable String value. Choose the type of value you want to create, and the Registry Editor creates the value with default data and a name such as New Value #1. Type a new name for the value and press Enter.

The Registry Editor creates a String value with an empty string as the data. A DWORD value gets zero as the data and a new Binary value gets a zero-length value for its data. You can modify the default data, as described in the preceding section, "Modifying a value."

Deleting a value

To delete a value, select the value you want to delete (or select multiple values). Then press the Delete key. You also can choose Delete from the shortcut menu or from the Edit menu in the menu bar. The Registry Editor confirms whether you really want to delete the values.

Caution   The Registry Editor does not have an Undo feature. When you delete a value, that value is gone. If you make a mistake, you might damage your Registry in a way that prevents Windows XP from starting. Always make a backup copy of the Registry before you try editing it by hand.

Tip   Before deleting a value, it's a good idea to save the key using the File ⇨ Export command. Choose the Selected branch option to just save the currently selected branch.

Exporting and importing Registry entries

Instead of copying the entire Registry, you will often find saving a copy of only one key and its subkeys and values easier. If you want to experiment with the settings under `Control Panel\Appearance`, for example, you can save only those keys and values without copying the entire Registry. This can make undoing your changes easier. You can import the saved key to restore the original settings without out copying the entire Registry.

To export a key, its subkeys, and all their values, select the parent key and choose File ⇨ Export. The dialog box shows the Export range as the key you selected. Enter a file name and click OK. The exported file is not a Registry file, but a text file you can view or edit in any text editor.

If you are familiar with INI files, you will recognize the format of a Registry export file (`.reg`). The most striking difference is the section names in a REG file are complete key paths — for example, `[HKEY_CURRENT_USER\Software\Microsoft]`. Also, REG files can contain binary and DWORD values, such as `dword:0000016d`.

To import the entries from an export file, choose File ⇨ Import. Importing a Registry file merges the exported file with the entries already in the Registry. Figure 33-9 illustrates how values in the export file take precedence over values in the Registry, but any values or keys not present in the export file are unaffected by importing that file. (You also can open a REG file on the desktop, or anywhere else, and its contents will merge with the Registry.)

You also can save a copy of the entire Registry by exporting all its keys. Click the All button for the Export range to export the entire Registry.

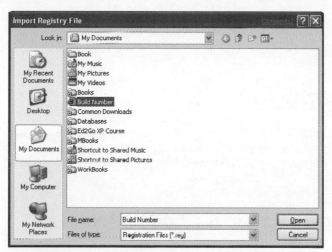

Figure 33-9: Import Registry tries to merge those entries with existing keys and values in the Registry.

How Applications Use the Registry

Applications typically use the Registry in one of two ways. The most common way is to store application-specific information, such as user preferences. The type of information that the applications stores depends on the application. Sometimes, you can learn about an application's Registry settings by reading the application's help files or other documentation. Usually, however, this information is not documented, and you should not try to manually edit the application's Registry entries.

If you are curious, you can use the Registry Editor to browse the Registry entries for an application. Look under the key HKEY_CURRENT_USER\Software. You will see a list of software companies, including Microsoft. The exact list depends on which software products you have installed on your computer. The subkeys under a company's key represent the company's products. For example, HKEY_CURRENT_USER\Software\Netscape may have a subkey for Netscape Navigator. Some products have subkeys for different versions of the product.

Try running the Registry Editor now. Look at the entries under HKEY_CURRENT_USER\Software to see which products have Registry entries. See whether you can find a match between the Registry entries and your preferences and options in an application.

Another kind of application presents a user interface to the Registry entries that other programs create and use. Several of the Control Panel applets work like this. These applications relieve you of the burden of editing the Registry manually by providing an easy-to-use interface. In addition to modifying Registry entries, these applications might also tell Windows XP about the new Registry entries, so you needn't restart Windows for the new settings to take effect.

Useful Registry Tricks

This section describes several ways you can use the Registry to customize your Windows XP environment. The are just a few situations when you need to edit the Registry manually, but sometimes you have no other choice. In the following situations, the Registry Editor is often your only choice.

Removing a program from the Add or Remove Programs list

Remember the program you deleted in your quest for more hard drive space? Know how it keeps showing up in the Control Panel's Add or Remove Programs folder, even though it's gone? The information Add or Remove Programs accesses is stored in the Registry, which means that you can edit the Registry and remove an entry manually from the list.

Caution You should back up your Registry before proceeding.

Open Regedit and find the key HKEY_LOCAL_MACHINE\SOFTWARE\Microsoft\ Windows\CurrentVersion\Uninstall (see Figure 33-10). This key contains a key for every application that can be uninstalled. Find the key with the name of the program you deleted and delete it. This operation can be performed for any number of programs. If you are unsure whether the key is the right one for the program, look at the DisplayName or QuietUninstallString string. The full name and version of the program it belongs to is usually contained in this string.

Moving an application

Sometimes you need to move an application from one folder to another — often from one drive to another. One way to do this is to uninstall the application and reinstall it to a new location. This means you lose all the preferences you have laboriously customized. Instead, you can move all the files by hand and then update the application's Registry entries by hand.

Suppose that you plan to move an application from C:\AppDir to D:\AppDir after buying a new hard drive. The first step is to move all the files. The next step is to update the application's Registry entries.

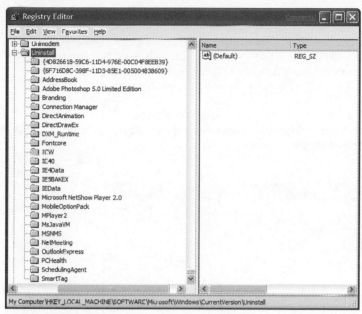

Figure 33-10: The keys for uninstalling programs that Add or Remove Programs uses to generate its list.

In the Registry Editor, choose Edit ➪ Find. Type **C:\AppDir** and press Enter. The Registry Editor searches for a Registry entry that contains "C:\AppDir" and selects the first one it finds. Press Enter to edit the value's data. Then type the new folder name (for instance, **D:\AppDir**) and press Enter.

Now press F3 to repeat the search. You can make this go faster by copying the new folder name to the Clipboard, which enables you to quickly paste it (by pressing Ctrl+V) when you change values.

Keep repeating this — F3, Enter, Ctrl+V, Enter — until the Registry Editor can no longer find any occurrences of the old application path. Congratulations! You have now moved the application without sacrificing your preferences. Some applications keep additional information in INI and other files. Consult your application's documentation for details. You might need to edit those files to change C:\AppDir to D:\AppDir the same way you changed the Registry.

If you find the repetition tedious, you can export the Registry to a temporary REG file and use a text editor to replace the file paths. Then import the edited REG file. Many text editors, such as WordPad, have powerful search and replace functions, which can make this task easier.

Before making any changes to the Registry, remember to make a backup copy. Exporting and importing the entire Registry opens the possibility of a major catastrophe, and you should be prepared.

File associations

You can easily create new file associations from Explorer by choosing Tools ➪ Folder Options and clicking the File Types tab, as discussed in Chapter 30. When you create a file association, Windows XP creates two or more entries in the Registry—one entry for the file type and one for each extension.

The (Default) value for the extension is the name of the key for the file type. This is how you can have several different extensions for the same file type. Figure 33-11 illustrates how file associations work.

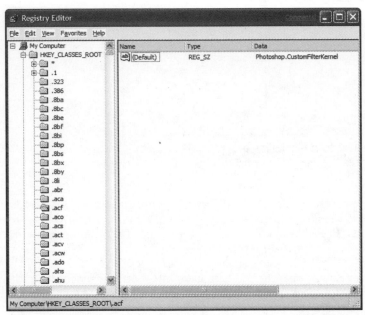

Figure 33-11: A file association links a file extension with a file type.

When you open a file, Explorer looks up the file extension under HKEY_CLASSES_ROOT. It uses the (Default) key to learn the file type, which it also looks up under HKEY_CLASSES_ROOT. From there, Explorer learns which command it must run to open this file. The file type can also specify an icon, a context menu, property sheet information, and so on.

When you use Tools ➪ Folder Options, Explorer automatically creates both kinds of Registry keys for you. But what happens if you change your mind and want to use different extensions for a file type? Explorer does not have a simple way to change the file name extensions it associates with a file type. For this, you must edit the Registry manually.

Suppose, for example, that you want to add a new extension (say, .text) to the existing extensions for plain-text files. First, you need to learn which Registry key Windows XP uses for text files. Open the Registry Editor and expand HKEY_CLASSES_ROOT. Look for an extension Windows XP currently uses for text files, such as .txt. The data for the (Default) value is the name of the file type key. As you can see in Figure 33-12, this key name is txtfile.

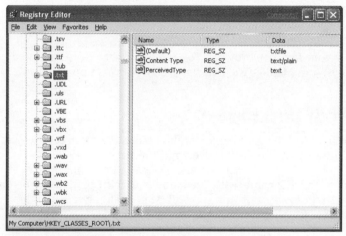

Figure 33-12: Add a new extension for a file type by creating a Registry entry under HKEY_CLASSES_ROOT.

Now you can create a new key for text files. Select HKEY_CLASSES_ROOT and choose Edit ➪ New ➪ Key. Type **.TEXT** and click OK to create the new key. In the value pane, double-click the (Default) name. In this case, the (Default) value is used to store a description of the file, so you can edit it safely. The Registry Editor prompts you for a new value. Type **txtfile** and click OK. You have now created a new Registry key and value.

Go to the Explorer window and choose Tools ➪ Folder Options. Look for Text Document, and notice that .text is now one of the extensions it lists. When you open a TEXT file, Explorer treats this file as a plain-text file and opens it using Notepad or another text editor you might have installed.

Bookmarks on floppy

Have you ever wanted to use your bookmark file on a different computer? Do you have it on a floppy? You're in luck!

If you use Netscape Navigator, telling Netscape where you want your bookmarks is not one of the configurable options, so this is where you can use the system Registry to your advantage.

First, open `regedit.exe` and find out where the values for the default bookmark destination are stored.

In my case, they are located at `HKEY_CURRENT_USER\Software\Netscape\ Netscape Navigator\Bookmark List`.

Depending on what version you use, however, you might have to look around. (Some versions, such as some Communicator versions, don't support it at all.) In the key File Location, just modify the value of the key, quit, restart Netscape, and you're done!

Do the same thing for your favorite browser. You might have to do some looking around to find the key, so remember Regedit's search feature if you get stuck.

Cleaning up your desktop

Not every user likes the Windows XP desktop and its icons. You can remove all the icons from your desktop in one swift move. Find the Registry key `HKEY_ CURRENT_USER\Software\Microsoft\Windows\CurrentVersion\Policies\ Explorer` and create a DWORD value, with the name NoDesktop. Change the data to 1. When you restart Windows, your desktop will be completely clean of icons. And you won't be able to drag files to the desktop.

If you ever want to revert to the original Windows XP desktop, change the NoDesktop value to zero (0) and restart Windows.

For the truly adventurous

If you have programs that don't want to run properly in Windows XP, there's an option you will want to know about. This option enables you to tweak Windows XP's behavior on a per-program basis. It makes Windows XP compatible with older programs.

A quick look at Figure 33-13 shows you how to select a compatibility mode for a program using the Run in compatibility mode options in the Properties dialog box. (Remember that you can display this dialog box by right-clicking and selecting Properties.)

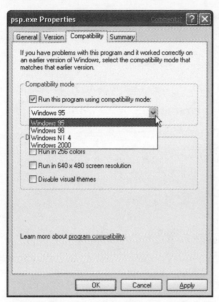

Figure 33-13: Compatibility mode enables you to help older programs run under Windows XP.

You should try this option under one circumstance only—when you have a program that you want to run and can't upgrade. How do you know which settings to apply? Generally, you guess based on the age of the program you're trying to run. It's usually best to try the newer Windows versions first, and if the program still won't run, try one of the older ones. Of course, what you are doing when you change compatibility mode settings is changing settings in the Registry. These are benign changes done on a per-executable file basis, so you need not fear destroying your system while trying to get an older program to run.

Summary

This information has become a bit technical. But, remember, most of you will probably never have to edit the Registry directly. Should the occasion arise, however, here are some important points to remember:

✦ The Registry is a collection of information about your Windows XP preferences and all the application programs on your PC.

✦ The Registry is automatically updated when you change preferences or install new programs, so a need to change the Registry yourself rarely occurs.

✦ The Registry replaces the initialization (INI) files used in Windows 3.1 and earlier.

✦ Information within the Registry is organized in a tree-like hierarchy, much like the way folders and files on a disk are organized.

✦ Always back up your Registry before making any changes to it manually.

✦ To edit the Registry, use the Regedit program that comes with Windows XP. To start Regedit, click the Start button, choose Run, type **regedit**, and then click OK.

✦   ✦   ✦

Special Features of Windows XP Professional

This chapter discusses features of Windows XP
Professional that aren't found in the Home/Personal edition. Some of these features, such as Dualview, Remote
Desktop Connection, Synchronization, and File Encryption,
are accessible to all users. Others are for professional system
and network administrators in corporate settings. An in-depth
treatment of the administrative topics is beyond the scope of
this book. This chapter does, however, point them out along
with resources for getting additional information.

Using Multiple Monitors

Windows XP Professional supports *Dualview* (a.k.a. multiple
monitors), a feature that enables you to connect multiple
monitors to a single computer. Each monitor becomes an
extension of your desktop. If you place the monitors side-by-
side and set each monitor to 800 x 600 resolution, for example, your actual desktop becomes 1600 x 600, as in Figure 34-1.
There, I have stretched an Excel worksheet across the two
monitors. There's still plenty of room for desktop icons off to
the left and an open Help window to the right.

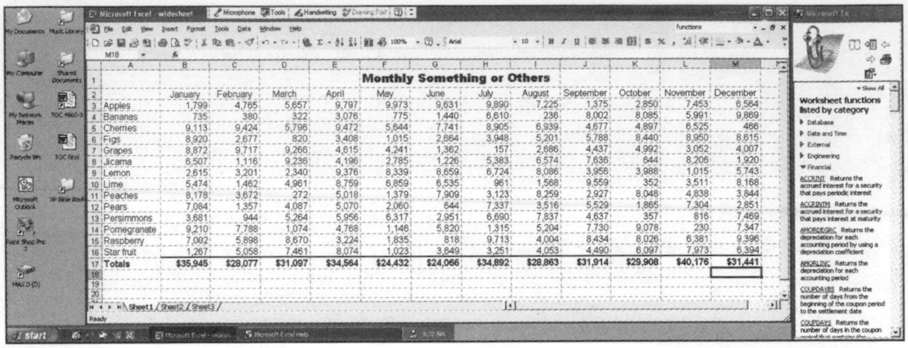

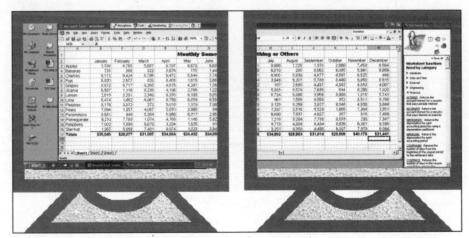

Figure 34-1: An Excel workbook stretched part way across a 1600 x 600 desktop

From your perspective, the desktop is split across the two monitors, as in Figure 34-2. The mouse and keyboard act as though they're one monitor. As you move or drag the mouse pointer off the edge of the monitor on the left, it instantly appears on the monitor on the right, as though it were a single monitor. You can drag items across monitors just as you drag them across one monitor.

Figure 34-2: What you actually see on the two monitors

There are a few ways to initiate multiple monitors. One way is to add a PCI or AGP graphics card for each monitor. You need to use graphics cards that are supported by Windows XP, as listed under the "Video" category in the hardware compatibility list (HCL) at www.microsoft.com/hcl.

A New Name

Dualview is the new name for the "multiple-monitor" capability found in previous versions of Windows. If you upgrade a computer that's already using multiple monitors, Windows XP Professional should be able to detect the graphics cards and install with multiple-monitor support intact. As to why they didn't add this capability to the Home/Personal edition of Windows XP, I can't say. There were a lot of complaints about this omission in the beta tester newsgroups. But so far, they've gone unheard.

 Caution   If the computer already has onboard video, it needs to be set to VGA mode for Dualview to work. The mode is set through the computer's BIOS Setup program, which you can usually get to by pressing Del or F2 as the computer is first starting up.

Another approach is to use a *dual-head* or *multi-head* graphics card. Currently, Windows XP Professional supports the following multi-head cards. However, you might want to check the current hardware compatibility list for updates.

- ✦ Appian Graphics Jeronimo Pro (PCI)
- ✦ Matrox Millennium G400 DualHead (AGP)
- ✦ Matrox Millennium G400 DualHead Max (AGP)
- ✦ Matrox Millennium G450 DualHead (AGP)
- ✦ Matrox Millennium G450 DualHead LE (AGP)
- ✦ Matrox Millennium G450 DualHead PCI (PCI)

Whichever approach you use, make sure you to shut down the computer and unplug it before changing or installing any cards. After the cards are installed, plug in and turn on the monitors and restart the computer. Windows should detect the new card(s) and install the drivers automatically. Don't be alarmed if the additional monitors don't work right away.

To activate additional monitors, as well as to control color depth, desktop area, and so forth on each monitor, use the Settings tab on the Display Properties dialog box. You can get there in one of two ways:

- ✦ Right-click the Windows desktop and choose Properties.
- ✦ Or, open the Display icon in Control Panel (Classic view).

The settings tab will show a "box" representing each monitor, as in Figure 34-3. To activate a monitor, click its box and choose the Extend my Windows desktop to this monitor check box. To see which monitor is which, click the Identify button, or point to either monitor box and hold down the primary (left) mouse button. A large number will appear on the monitor. You can arrange the monitors in the box to match the arrangement of your physical monitors. You can set the screen resolution and color depth of each monitor by first clicking the monitor's box or choosing a monitor from the Display drop-down list. The resolution and color-depth you choose affects only the current monitor.

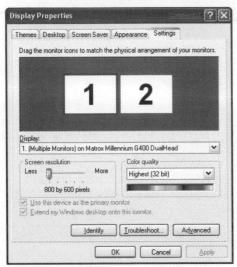

Figure 34-3: The Settings tab of Display Properties with two monitors attached to a dual-head graphics card

One monitor will act as the *primary monitor* that displays the logon screen and taskbar. You can make either monitor the primary monitor by selecting it and then choosing the "Use this device as the primary monitor" check box. If you have any problems getting multiple monitors to work, try the Troubleshooter. Just click the Troubleshoot button on the Settings tab in the Display Properties dialog box to get started.

Remote Desktop Connection

Windows XP Professional Edition offers Remote Desktop Connection, which allows you access to a Windows session that is running on some computer other than your own. For example, you could connect to your office computer from home and use all the resources of your company's network. In fact, you could just leave your office computer running, with any programs and documents you were working with open and on the desktop. When you get home and connect to the office computer, your home computer's screen will directly reflect the office computer's screen, exactly as you left it.

Remote Desktop in Home Edition

In Windows XP Home Edition, you can use the Remote Desktop Sharing capability of NetMeeting to perform most of the functions available in the Professional Edition. See Chapter 11, "Online Conferencing with NetMeeting," for more information.

The Home Edition also offers Remote Assistant, which allows another user to access your desktop to help you solve some problem. Or vice versa—someone can ask you for assistance and grant you control over her desktop. See "Using Remote Assistance" in Chapter 19 for more information.

You can use Remote Desktop in a variety of scenarios, such as accessing your office computer from a notebook. For the sake of example however, I'll refer to the computer that's being accessed remotely (from afar) as the office computer and the computer that's gaining access as the home computer. To use Remote Desktop, you need the following:

✦ The office computer must be running Windows XP Professional with the Remote Desktop feature enabled. That computer must also provide a network or Internet connection to which outside users can connect. The company system administrator also needs to set up appropriate accounts and privileges, as described later.

✦ The home computer can be any computer with Remote Desktop capability (including Windows XP Home edition). The home computer also needs to have access to the office computer through a modem, VPN, or other network connection.

Tip   Older operating systems can access the office computer using the Terminal Service Client. For specifics, search Windows XP Help and Support for *Remote Desktop*, and then view the "Obtain the client software" page.

Enabling Remote Desktop at the office

To set up the office computer to offer remote access, the computer administrator needs to follow these steps:

1. Click the Start button, open Control Panel, and open the System icon (in Classic view).

2. On the Remote tab, select Allow users to connect remotely to this computer.

3. Click the Select Remote Users button and add existing user names to the list of allowed users, as in the example shown in Figure 34-4.

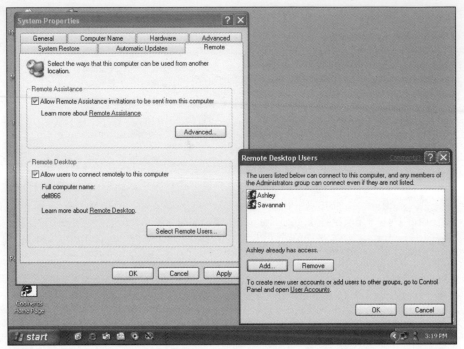

Figure 34-4: Enabling and specifying remote desktop users in Windows XP Professional on the office computer

Users are added to the group named Remote Desktop Users, which can also be managed from Local Users and Groups in Computer Management.

Cross-Reference   See Chapter 32 for more information on local users and groups.

That's about it for the administrator's duties. Next we'll look at it from the "consumer" side, the people who will be accessing the desktop remotely.

Using Remote Desktop at home

After the office computer has been configured to allow remote desktop users and you have been given an account, you need to do the following at your office computer, before you leave work. First, make sure you know your user name and password (if any) for logging on to the computer. (These are the same as when you log on locally, unless your administrator tells you otherwise.) Also, make sure you know the network name of the computer. If you're not sure, follow these steps:

1. Click the Start button and open Control Panel.

2. In Classic view, open the System icon.

3. Click the Computer Name. The name of the computer appears to the right of Full computer name on the tab.

4. Click OK or Cancel to close the dialog box. You also can close Control Panel.

Finally, leave the office computer running. You can log off if you want, leaving just the Welcome page visible on-screen.

Then, when you get home (assuming your computer there is using Windows XP Home edition or Professional), follow these steps:

1. Start up your computer normally and connect to the office network through your modem or Virtual Private Network icon through Network Connections.

2. Click the Start button and choose All Programs ➪ Accessories ➪ Communications ➪ Remote Desktop Connection.

3. In the dialog box that appears, enter your user name and the name of the computer to which you're connecting. Then click the Connect button.

4. In the next dialog box, enter your password and then click OK.

The desktop on your screen is actually the desktop on the office computer. This is to say, everything you do with your mouse and keyboard takes place on the office computer. When you want to return to your normal home desktop, log off from the remote computer by clicking the Start button and choosing Log Off ➪ Log Off.

After you're disconnected, Remote Desktop automatically locks the office computer so that nobody else can use it. If, upon your return to work, you find that the computer is still locked, press Ctrl+Alt+Del to unlock it.

Synchronization

Windows XP Professional offers Synchronization, which enables network users to automatically keep documents they work with offline in sync with documents stored on a network. For information on setting up Windows XP Professional to support Synchronization, see "Working Offline," in Chapter 24.

Encryption

Windows XP Professional also supports Encrypting File System (EFS), which you can use to protect files stored in NTFS volumes. It's especially useful on notebook computers because it prevents unauthorized users (that is, anyone who steals the computer) from viewing the contents of sensitive files. Once encryption is enabled, the process of encrypting and decrypting files is transparent. That is to say, any encrypted file is automatically decrypted when opened and encrypted when saved.

You can encrypt individual files, folders, as well as the files and subfolders within a folder. The procedure is simple. Just follow these steps:

1. Open My Documents and browse to the folder or files you want to encrypt.

2. Right-click the folder or file icon and choose Properties.

3. On the General tab, click the Advanced button.

4. Choose Encrypt contents to secure data, as in Figure 34-5.

5. Click the OK button.

6. If you encrypted a folder, choose whether you want to encrypt just the current folder or the contents of the folder as well.

7. Click OK.

Figure 34-5: Encrypting options available in the Advanced Attributes dialog box

Note   A compressed folder cannot be encrypted. If you encrypt a compressed folder, it decompresses automatically.

It might take a while to initially encrypt all the items. When encryption is in place, however, you can open and save documents normally, and they'll automatically be encrypted and decrypted as needed.

Local Security Policy

Windows XP Professional adds a Local Security Policy tool to Administrative Tools. As the name implies, this program enables a system administrator to control users' access to the local computer. To get to it, follow these steps:

1. Click the Start button and open Control Panel.

2. In Classic view, open Administrative Tools.

3. Open the Local Security Policy icon.

A Microsoft Management Console (MMC) opens, as in Figure 34-6. The left panel, called the console tree, lists categories of policies that can be created and maintained by the administrator. As usual, you can expand and contract categories by clicking the plus (+) and minus (–) symbols to the left of folders. Click any item to view its options in the right pane.

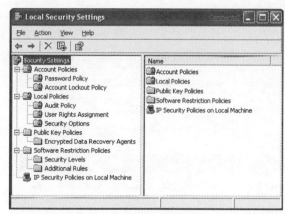

Figure 34-6: Local Security Policies in a Microsoft Management Console

These options are intended for experienced systems administrators and are beyond the scope of this book. (In fact, it would take a book half this size to go through all of the options!) If you are interested in learning more, everything is documented under Security Settings in the Microsoft Management Console Help. To get there, follow these steps:

1. Click the Help button in the toolbar or choose Help ➪ Help Topics from the menu bar.

2. Expand the Security Settings book in the left column.

There you'll find links to Best Practices, Concepts, Troubleshooting, and "How To's," as shown in Figure 34-7.

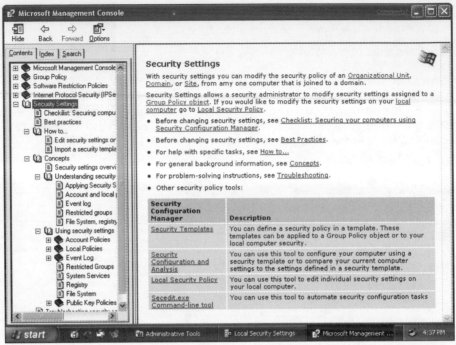

Figure 34-7: Help with Local Security Policies is available under Security Settings in MMC's Help.

Users and Groups

Both the Home (Personal) and Professional editions of Windows XP support the use of multiple users and user accounts. The User Accounts icon in Control Panel provides an easy tool for creating and managing user accounts. Windows XP Professional adds the concept of user *groups*, inherited from Windows 2000 and earlier versions of Windows NT. User groups can be managed via Local Users and Groups in the Computer Management tool. For more information, see Chapter 32.

Advanced Installation Options

The Windows XP Professional Resource Kit provides additional tools for performing installations across many computers in a corporate environment. For example, *unattended setup* enables an administrator to create predefined answers to questions imposed by the installation procedure, so that she doesn't need to sit at the computer during installation. *Cloning* (also called *disk imaging*) allows the same disk to be used to install Windows XP across several computers, even when their hardware characteristics don't match. For more information on the Resource Kit, check out www.microsoft.com/windowsxp.

Advanced Installation Scenarios

A network administrator can install Windows XP from a shared network folder that contains the Setup files. Optionally, you can use an MS-DOS or network installation that contains the network client software to connect to the network server.

If the computer on which Windows is being installed is currently running Windows 98, Windows Millennium Edition, or an earlier version of Windows NT, you can begin the installation from a command prompt by entering the path to the file Winnt32.exe on the shared volume. From this point on, the rest of the installation is the same as installing locally.

If you want to join a domain during the setup process, however, the procedure will differ a little from joining a workgroup. First, you need to have an account in the domain that you want to join. If you're upgrading from Windows NT, your existing computer account will be used. Otherwise, you need to create a new account before running Setup. Or, you need to have appropriate privileges to create a new account during the installation process.

More Tools for Administrators

Windows XP Professional offers some additional tools for experienced system and network administrations, including a deployment planning guide, support tools, Microsoft Active Directory Migration Tools, and more. You'll find them in the SUPPORT and VALUEADD folders on the Windows XP installation CD-ROM.

Summary

This chapter has covered some features found only in the Windows XP Professional. Some are features that any user can take advantage of. Others are designed for experienced corporate system and network administrators. Here's a quick recap of the important points covered in this chapter.

✦ Dualview (a.k.a. multiple monitors) enables you to stretch your Windows XP desktop across two or more monitors.

✦ Remote Desktop Connection enables remote users to access their office computers remotely by controlling that computer with the keyboard and mouse on their home computer.

✦ Encrypting File System (EFS) automatically encrypts and decrypts files and folders on NTFS volumes to protect sensitive data from prying eyes.

✦ Local Security Policies, found in Administrative Tools, enables system administrators to set security policies on the local computer.

✦ Additional tools for system administrators and other computer professionals are available in the SUPPORT and VALUEADD folders on the Windows XP Professional installation CD-ROM.

✦   ✦   ✦

Installing Windows XP

If you just purchased your PC and if it came with Windows XP preinstalled, you needn't do anything in this appendix—you can go straight to Chapter 1 and start enjoying the new Windows. If you're upgrading a previous version of Windows, or are installing Windows XP on a new hard drive, this appendix will help you with that.

System Requirements for Windows XP

To install Windows XP, your computer must meet certain minimal requirements. To simplify matters, Microsoft has designed the following "non-technical" system requirements:

+ Preinstalled with Microsoft Windows 2000 Professional or Microsoft Windows Millennium Edition operating system

+ Displays the Designed for Windows 2000 or Designed for Windows 2000/ME logo

More technically, your system needs to meet these requirements:

+ A minimum of 64 MB of RAM, although 128MB is much preferred. XP can handle a maximum of 4GB RAM.

+ 233 megahertz (MHz) Pentium or equivalent microprocessor.

+ A 2 GB or larger hard disk with at least 650 MB free space available.

+ VGA monitor.

+ Keyboard.

+ Mouse or compatible pointing device.

+ CD-ROM or DVD drive.

Those are the official specs as I write this. However, I've found on my systems that once installed, Windows XP eats up about 950 MB of hard disk space. It also seems to eat up more than 64MB of RAM most of the time. So I think the 64 MB lower limit on RAM is probably a bit too tight. These days, RAM is pretty inexpensive. Because too little RAM is often the culprit when a computer runs sluggishly, now might be a good time to consider beefing that up if you're using less than 128 MB.

If you're not sure whether your system is compatible with Windows XP, you'll find out when you start the installation. Windows XP automatically checks the system for incompatibilities before it changes anything on your hard disk and informs you of any potential problems. Before purchasing any new hardware, check the hardware compatibility list (HCL) at `www.microsoft.com/hcl` to make sure you purchase compatible hardware. Optionally, you can choose Perform Additional Tasks from the Welcome window once the installation starts. Then choose Check System Compatibility or Visit the Compatibility Web Site.

Preinstallation Housekeeping

If you've been using your PC for a while, now may be a good time to do a little spring cleaning and eliminate any old junk taking up space on your hard disk. Don't delete your existing version of Windows, however, and don't delete any programs you want to use after you install Windows XP. Delete only old projects you don't need anymore and any programs you no longer use. If you're upgrading from Windows Me or Windows 2000, you might want to use the Disk Cleanup feature in that program to clean off any unnecessary files.

Some other points to remember include the following:

+ If your computer has any timeout features, such as the suspend features used on portable PCs, disable those features now.

+ If you have an antivirus program handy, run it now to check for and delete dormant viruses that might still be lurking on your hard disk.

+ Make sure any external devices (modems, external CD-ROM drives, and so on) are connected and turned on, so Windows XP can detect them during installation.

+ To play it safe, back up the entire hard disk at this point.

+ If your PC is connected to a local area network (LAN), check to make sure you're connected to the LAN properly so that Windows XP can see your LAN during installation.

There are two main ways to install Windows XP. One is to do a "clean install," where you start with a blank hard disk. The other is to update your existing version of Windows to Windows XP.

Cross-Reference As discussed in Chapter 34, Windows XP Professional offers some additional installation options, including installing over a network.

Performing a "Clean Install"

A clean install is required when installing Windows XP to a brand new hard disk. However, a clean install is also good if you're looking to do some serious "house-keeping" and really start anew. The word *serious* is important here. Because in the process, you'll wipe your hard disk clean, which means you'll lose *everything*: programs, documents, Internet connection settings, passwords, favorites, names and addresses, and saved e-mail messages — everything that's "in your computer" so to speak. If you're not entirely sure what this means, don't do it! There is no changing your mind later; there is no "undo!"

If you do want to do a clean install, make sure you have a backup copy of everything you'll want to reinstall later. Remember that to reinstall any programs, you need the original CD as well as any CD keys or serial numbers that the installation requires. To reinstall anything you have downloaded, you need to make backup copies of the downloaded files, or you need to download new copies after the installation is complete.

If you can boot the computer from your current version of Windows, you can start a clean installation by following these steps:

1. Start your computer by running your current version of Windows, insert the Windows XP CD into your CD-ROM drive. Then. . . .

   - If your computer detects and starts the CD automatically, choose Install Windows.

   - If the Installation doesn't detect the CD automatically, click the Start button, choose Run, and enter **d:\i386\winnt.exe**. If your CD-ROM drive isn't drive D:, replace the *d* with the appropriate drive letter. Then press Enter.

2. When prompted to choose an installation type, select New Installation and then click Next.

After things get going, you can follow the instructions on the screen until you get to the "text setup" screen that enables you to choose a partition. Then skip to the following section, "Partitions and File Systems."

If you cannot boot the computer to an existing version of Windows, boot from your Windows XP CD-ROM. This can be tricky, because the settings for choosing boot devices are in the system BIOS. The only way to get to the BIOS settings is by pressing some key, usually F2 or Del, as the computer is booting up. Unfortunately, I can't help you with that because the exact keystroke required, as well as the BIOS Setup program that the key launches, varies from one computer to the next.

Within the BIOS settings, you also need to disable the Quick Boot and Quiet Boot options, if available, so that you can see what's going on as the computer is booting up. Set the first boot device to your CD-ROM drive, your second boot device to the floppy drive, and the third boot device to your hard disk. Put the Windows XP CD into the CD-ROM drive, save your BIOS settings to restart the boot process. You might see a prompt telling you to press a key to boot from the CD-ROM drive. Go ahead and do so to start the text-based setup program. (You need to use the keyboard for everything — the mouse won't work.) As you follow the instructions on-screen, you'll get to a screen that enables you to choose a partition on which to install, as discussed next.

Partitions and File Systems

When it comes time to choose a partition on which to install Windows, you can work with partitions on your hard disk. If the disk is already partitioned and you want to wipe the slate clean, use the D key, as instructed on the screen, to delete existing partitions. Then use the C key to create new partitions. You can create a single large partition, or divide the hard disk into smaller partitions. If you create two or more partitions, you can install Windows on one of them, and install other operating systems on the other partitions later. Or, you can treat each partition as a separate drive in Windows (for instance, C:, D:, and so forth).

Caution   Repartitioning your hard disk wipes out everything on the hard disk. This is your last chance to change your mind before losing everything on the drive. There is no "undo" or Recycle Bin from which you can restore deleted files later!

At this stage of the game, you need to create at least one partition for Windows XP. At the very least, you probably want this partition to be at least 2 GB in size to leave room for Windows XP and any programs you plan to install. If you're not planning on dividing the disk into multiple partitions, just use the maximum size allowable to create one partition.

After you finish, use the arrow keys on the keyboard to highlight the partition on which you want to install Windows XP (typically C: Partition 1) and press Enter to begin the installation. You'll be given options for formatting the partition as either a FAT or NTFS volume. NTFS is the preferred file system. If you plan to install some older version of Windows, or even DOS, on another partition, however, the other operating system(s) might not be able to access the NTFS volume. For more information on NTFS compatibility with other Microsoft operating systems, see Chapter 31.

Tip   Although the partition options don't specify FAT32, you can select that format after you choose the FAT option.

Tip

Most current distributions of Linux can access NTFS partitions. To be certain, however, check the documentation that came with your Linux distribution.

You can choose to perform a quick format or a regular format. I have tried the Quick format before, only the have the installation fail, causing me to start all over again. So I recommend just doing a regular format. It'll take a few minutes, but at least it works! After the partition has been formatted, Setup copies some files to the hard disk, and then the system reboots.

Caution

You only need to boot from the CD-ROM drive to get things started. After the installation program has started, do not boot from the CD again. Leave the CD in the CD-ROM drive, but just let the Press any key to boot from CD message go by!

Eventually, the computer will reboot to the graphical installation procedure, where you must enter your CD Key, choose language options, and so forth, as discussed under "Installation Options" later in this appendix. Don't forget that once the installation is complete, you can go back to your BIOS settings and re-enable Quick Boot, change the boot drives, and so forth.

Upgrading an Existing Version of Windows

To upgrade an existing version of Windows, start your computer normally. Then put the Windows XP CD in your CD-ROM drive and wait for the Welcome screen to open. If the CD won't boot automatically, follow these steps to get it going:

1. Open My Computer on your desktop.

2. Open the icon for your CD-ROM drive. If the Welcome screen opens, skip the next step.

3. Click (or double-click) the Setup (or setup.exe) file on the CD.

4. Choose the Install Microsoft Windows XP option.

5. Choose Upgrade from the Installation Type options and then click Next.

The installation procedure will begin. You might notice that the screen goes blank once in a while during the installation. Don't be alarmed; that's normal. If the screen goes blank for a long time, try moving the mouse around a bit to bring it back.

Installation Options

The exact procedure from this point on will vary a bit, depending on whether you're installing Windows XP Professional or the Home (Personal) edition. Also, the specific hardware connected to your computer determines the information that the setup procedure requests. Each request is largely self-explanatory, but here's a summary of the items you're likely to encounter along the way:

✦ **Regional and Language Options:** Choose your preferred location and keyboard layout.

✦ **Name and Organization:** Type your complete name and business name (if any).

✦ **Product Key:** Type in the CD Key. You should be able to find that on the sleeve in which the Windows XP CD-ROM was delivered.

✦ **Computer Name and Administrator Password:** (Professional) Enter any name you want to use to identify your computer and enter a password. You must the password twice to verify that you typed it as intended the first time.

✦ **Modem Dialing Information:** If your computer has a modem, choose the country you're in and enter the area code you're in now. If you're in an office that requires dialing some number to access an outside line, enter that number. If your system uses the older "pulse" dialing tone, as opposed to touch tone, choose Pulse dialing.

✦ **Date and Time Settings:** Set the date, current time, choose your time zone, and decide whether you want Windows to automatically adjust the time for daylight savings changes.

✦ **Network Settings:** Unless you're a network administrator who needs to customize networking capabilities on this computer, choose Typical Settings.

✦ **Workgroup or Computer Domain:** A *workgroup* is a collection of computers connected together in a local area network. If you've already set up a network and want this computer to be a member of an existing workgroup, choose No and enter the name of the workgroup to which this computer will belong. If this is a standalone computer, or you haven't set up a network yet, you can just select the suggested name, WORKGROUP. If this computer will be a member of a corporate *domain,* click Yes and enter the name of the domain to which this computer will belong.

The Setup Wizard

When the installation is complete, the computer reboots one more time, and you are taken to a final Setup Wizard. You'll be asked how you want to connect to the Internet. Your options are as follows:

✦ **DSL or Cable Modem:** Select this option if this computer is directly connected to a cable modem or DSL modem that provides access to the Internet.

✦ **Local Area Network:** Select this option if this computer is a member of a local area network, and some other computer on the network shares its Internet connection with other LAN members.

✦ **Telephone Modem:** Select this option if this computer has an internal modem or if it's directly connected to an external modem that provides Internet access through a standard (non-DSL) telephone line.

If you don't have an Internet connection at the moment but plan to get one, just choose whichever option best describes how you think you will connect. Don't worry; there's no big commitment here. You can make whatever kind of connection you want in the future.

If you connect through a LAN or broadband device (for instance, cable or DSL), you'll be asked about IP (Internet Protocol) and DNS (Domain Name Service) addresses. The settings you enter must match the settings provided by your Internet service provider. Many ISPs automatically assign IP and DNS settings. So if in doubt, you can select the check boxes that obtain that information automatically.

Activation

The wizard then asks that you activate your copy of Windows. If you have an Internet connection already on a modem that's connected to a phone line, you can choose Yes and activate now. Otherwise, select No to activate later.

Getting on the Internet

If your computer has a modem, you are given the option to set up your existing account information, as provided by your Internet service provider, or set up a new account from scratch.

Sharing the computer

If more than one person will be using the computer, you can choose to give each person his own account. That way, each user can have his own custom desktop settings, collection of favorites, and a private My Documents folder that other users can't get to. To set up multiple user accounts, click Yes and then give each user a name. You can use just each user's first name, such as Ashley, or an initial and last name, such as ASimpson. However, no two users can have the same name.

Done!

After you finish the final setup phase, click the Finish button. If you set up multiple user names, you come to a Welcome screen that lists each user name, plus a Guest account. Click your own user name to get to the Windows desktop. Windows XP is installed, and now you're ready to return to Chapter 1 in this book.

✦ ✦ ✦

What's New in Windows XP

This appendix summarizes new features in Windows XP, for both the Home and Professional editions. Of course, exactly how "new" a feature is depends on where you're coming from. For example, an upgrade from Windows 98 would be a bigger change than an upgrade from Windows 2000. So I apologize in advance if I alert you to any features that aren't so new in relation to where you're coming from.

New Visual Design

The whole look and feel of the Windows Interface has changed — providing a crisper, clearer display. The redesigned Start menu, shown in Figure B-1, automatically keeps track of recently used programs. The All Programs option on the menu offers the traditional Programs menu. You can easily customize the Start menu by right-clicking the Start button and choosing Properties. You also can drag items from the All Programs menu into the left side of the Start menu to "pin" them there so that they are always available.

Figure B-1: A fresh new design and Start menu

The taskbar, as well as the toolbars in many programs, can be locked, to prevent you from accidentally dragging them from their current locations. Once unlocked, you can customize the taskbar by right-clicking and choosing Properties.

Cross-Reference   Chapter 13 and Chapter 14 explore the many ways you can customize the desktop, Start menu, and taskbar to suit your own needs.

ClearType

Windows XP uses ClearType display technologies, which triples the horizontal resolution of LCD (Liquid Crystal Display) screens. The result is much sharper text on notebooks and flat monitors. To enable or disable ClearType, click the Effects button on the Appearance tab in Display Properties (Chapter 14). Select the Use the following method to smooth edges of screen fonts check box. Then select either Standard or ClearType from the drop-down list.

Multiple User Accounts

Both the Home and Professional editions now provide for multiple user accounts. Logging on and switching between users is simplified by the new Welcome screen (see Figure B-2). Each user can have her own private My Documents folder, favorites, desktop settings, and other items, without stepping on another user's toes. Items to be shared among users can be placed in the new Shared Documents, Shared Pictures, and Shared Music folders.

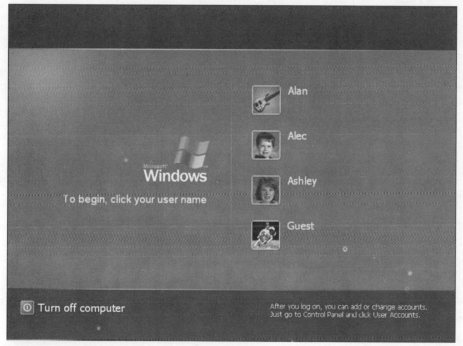

Figure B-2: Multiple user accounts are available in the Home and Professional editions.

Creating and managing user accounts is simple. Click the Start button, open Control Panel, and open the User Accounts icon. There you can limit users' access to the computer to protect against accidental sweeping changes, password-protect accounts for added privacy, change the picture associated with an account, and more.

 Cross-Reference See Chapter 20 for more information on user accounts.

Simplified File Management

Managing files and folders has never been easier. The new Explorer bar at the left side of the Windows Explorer program, visible in Figure B-3 through B-5, provides one-click access to common tasks and other places. A new Tiles view displays larger icons with descriptive text for easier identification of a file's contents. You can customize Details view to display whatever information you want about files in a folder.

 Cross-Reference   Chapter 2 introduces you to the new Windows Explorer.

Folders that contain pictures can be displayed in Thumbnails view, where each picture is shown as a small version of its contents, rather than some generic icon (see Figure B-3). The new Filmstrip view enables you to view both thumbnails of all pictures and a larger version of the currently selected picture (see Figure B-4). There's even a View as a Slide Show option that displays each picture full screen for a few seconds.

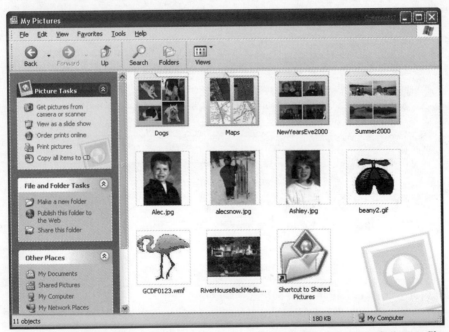

Figure B-3: The Thumbnails view enables you to view the contents of picture files, rather than generic icons.

Figure B-4: Filmstrip view enables you to view a larger version of any picture in a folder.

Cross-Reference See Chapter 22 and Chapter 23 for more information on working with pictures and photographs.

When you copy songs from audio CDs using Media Player 8, the songs are automatically organized by artist and album. If you have an Internet connection, a picture of the album cover is automatically placed on the folder that contains the CD songs, as shown in Figure B-5.

Figure B-5: Music copied from CDs is organized by CD, with a picture of the CD cover on the folder.

Cross-Reference Chapter 24 discusses ways to copy music from audio CDs and to create your own custom audio CDs.

Clicking the Search button in the toolbar opens the new Search Companion in the left pane of the Explorer window (see Figure 8-6). The assistant provides a single point of entry for searching your entire computer, Help and Support, and the Internet for virtually anything.

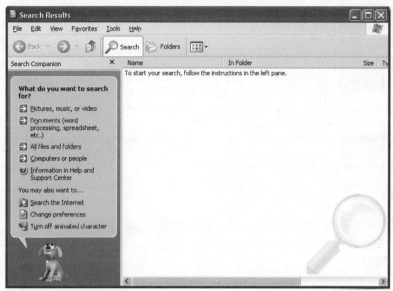

Figure B-6: The Search Companion in the left pane provides a centralized tool for all kinds of searches.

 "Searching for Lost Files" in Chapter 2 explains how to use the Search Companion.

Improved Multimedia

Windows XP brings many improvements to multimedia, including the following:

✦ **Windows Movie Maker:** Create your own custom video movies from your video camera. Add custom soundtracks, narration, and transition effects. The movies can then be viewed by anyone with Windows and Media Player. You also can copy music from LPs, TVs, VCRs — virtually any device you can connect to your computer — and save them to your hard disk (see Chapter 25).

✦ **Photo Printing Wizard:** Print photos and other pictures right from a folder, without using third-party programs. Or order prints from the Internet (see Chapter 23).

✦ **Improved support for cameras and scanners:** Copy pictures from supported digital cameras and scanners without using third-party software (see Chapter 23).

✦ **Web Publishing Wizard:** Publish your photos, movies, and audio clips to the Internet so that friends, family, and colleagues can view them from anywhere in the world (see Chapter 23).

✦ **Media Player 8:** Listen to audio CDs, create and organize custom multimedia libraries, create custom playlists (see Figure B-7), copy music from audio CDs to WMA or MP3 format, copy songs to supported portable digital music devices (MP3 players), burn custom audio CDs, listen to any of 3,000 radio stations worldwide, download music and video from the Web, all from within Media Player 8 (see Chapter 24).

✦ **DVD and video:** Watch and control DVDs and video in Media Player or full screen (see Chapter 24).

Figure B-7: Windows Media Player 8 with artists in the left pane and the custom playlist in the right

Built-in CD Burning

If you have a CD-R or CD-RW drive, you can burn files from your hard disk to a CD just by dragging and dropping, or by right-clicking and choosing Send To ➪ Writable CD. On a CD-R, files to be burned display in a "staging area" under Files to Add to the CD. On a CD-RW, files already on the disc display under Files Currently on the CD (see Figure B-8). In the Explorer bar, you can do the following:

✦ Click Write to CD to burn files from the staging area to the CD.

✦ Erase files from a CD-RW.

✦ Clear the staging area.

To burn audio CDs, just create the list of songs you want to copy in Media Player, and click the Copy to CD or Device button! It's that simple.

Cross-Reference See "Copying Files to a CD-R or CD-RW Disc" in Chapter 12 for information on burning to CD-R and CD-RW discs. See "Creating Custom Audio CDs" in Chapter 24 for burning audio CDs.

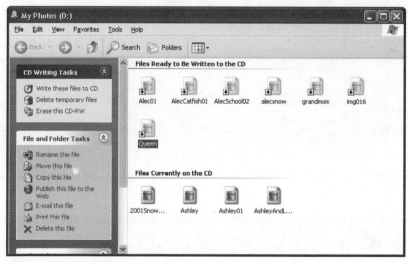

Figure B-8: Burn files to CD-R and CD-RW discs using simple drag-and-drop.

Built-in Handling of Zip Files

Compressed Zip files are treated as *compressed folders* in Windows XP. To add files to a compressed folder, select the files, right-click, and choose Send To ➪ Compressed (zipped) Folder (see Figure B-10). The Zip file appears as a manila file folder icon with a zipper on it. To copy and decompress files, right-click the compressed folder icon and choose Extract All.

 Caution   If you install a third-party Zip program, the "compressed folders" feature disappears. You'll need to use your third-party program to manage Zip files.

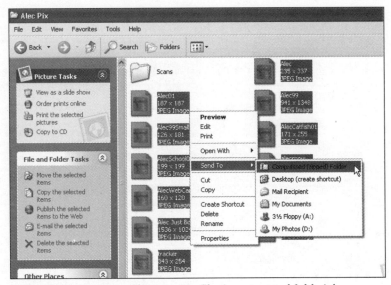

Figure B-9: Compress files to a Zip file (compressed folder) by selecting and right-clicking.

Speech and Handwriting Recognition

Speech recognition enables you to type text or choose menu commands by speaking into a microphone. Handwriting recognition can convert handwritten text to typed text. Although Windows XP itself doesn't provide for speech and handwriting recognition, it does enable you to centrally install speech and handwriting recognition *engines*. When you open a program that does support speech and/or handwriting, the Language bar appears, enabling you to dictate text, bark orders, or scribble on a tablet (see Figure B-10).

Figure B-10: The Language bar appears whenever you open a program that supports speech or handwriting recognition.

Versions 6 of Outlook Express and Internet Explorer, which come with Windows XP, both offer some speech and handwriting recognition. Programs in the Microsoft Office XP suite offer speech and recognition engines and also support recognition. See Chapter 15 for details.

Better Help and Support

The new Help and Support window provides simplified, centralized access to all types of help and support, including help files on the computer, troubleshooters, updates, and online support from a variety of sources (see Figure B-11). If you're connected to the Internet, the latest news displays automatically under "Did you know?" To get to Help and Support, click the Start button and choose Help and Support. Or, just press the Help (F1) key.

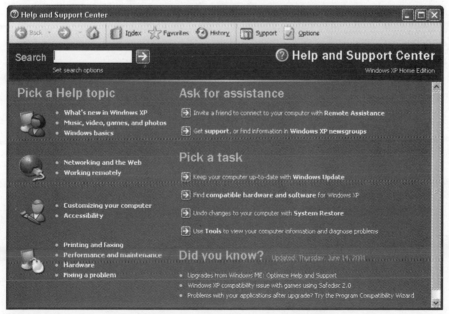

Figure B-11: The new centralized Help and Support window

Cross-Reference   See "You're Not Helpless" in Chapter 1 for more on Help and Support.

Remote Assistance

If you're connected to a network, you can turn control of your computer over to a friend or technician to allow that user to work on your computer from his own computer. You can type messages back and forth using Chat (see Figure B-12). For security purposes, you can take control of your PC at any time and require the assistant to enter a password. For more information on this feature, see "Using Remote Assistance" in Chapter 19.

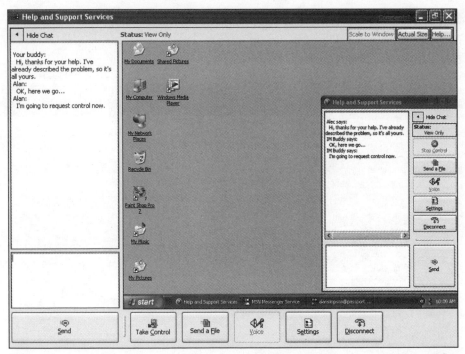

Figure B-12: Get live assistance from a trusted colleague right on your screen with Remote Assistance.

Files and Settings Transfer Wizard

The Files and Settings Transfer Wizard makes it easy to copy your personal preferences, favorites, taskbar options, Internet and e-mail settings, and personal documents from one computer to another. It's also a handy tool for backing up those items, in case you ever have a major system crash that causes all those items to be lost. There are two ways to get to the wizard:

✦ Click the Start button, and choose All Programs ➪ Accessories ➪ System Tools ➪ Files and Settings Transfer Wizard.

✦ Or, from the Welcome screen of the Installation Setup page, choose Perform Additional Tasks ➪ Transfer Files and Settings.

See "The Files and Settings Transfer Wizard" in Chapter 18 for details.

Personal Firewall

A firewall is a program that protects your computer from hackers and intruders who might otherwise be able to access your computer while you're connected to the Internet. Windows XP comes with the new Internet Connection Firewall (ICF) that you can use to protect a single computer or an entire network of computers that share a single Internet account and connection.

If you create a network that allows two or more computers to share a single Internet connection, the firewall is set up automatically. Creating a network and sharing an Internet connection is easy. Just purchase and install the appropriate hardware and run the Home Networking Wizard.

 Cross-Reference See Chapter 29 for more information on the personal firewall, and related network security topics.

Network Connections

All types of network connections, including dial-up, local area network, and VPN (virtual private networking), can be created and maintained within the single Networking Connections window shown in Figure B-13. The New Connection Wizard in that window takes you step-by-step through the process of creating any type of connection.

Figure B-13: The Network Connections window centralizes all your external connections, and provides an easy wizard for creating them.

You can access the Network Connections dialog box by using any of the following methods:

+ Open My Network Places and choose View Network Connection under Network Tasks.

+ Click the Start button and choose All Programs ⇨ Accessories ⇨ Communications ⇨ Network Connections.

+ Add a Network Connections option to your Start menu. Just right-click the Start button, choose Properties, click the Customize button, and choose Network Connections from the list of items on the Advanced tab.

System Restore

Whenever you're about to make a significant change to your system, such as installing some new hardware device, System Restore copies all your important system files to a folder on your hard disk. If your system doesn't work properly after the installation, you can use System Restore to get things back to the way they were before you installed. You also can manually set *restore points* at any time, in case you're concerned about some change you're about to make to the system.

Windows XP also adds additional protection by preventing program installations from overwriting important system files — one of the most common causes of system failures found in earlier versions of Windows.

Driver Signing and Rolling Back

Compatibility between the countless hardware devices that are available for the PC and all the different versions of Windows that have come and gone remains an issue for users, hardware manufacturers, and Microsoft. To help get this under control, Microsoft now offers *signed drivers*, which are guaranteed to work with Windows XP. These drivers are digitally signed to verify their quality and provide assurance that they've been tested to work with Windows XP.

When you install a device driver that hasn't been digitally signed, you'll see a warning to that effect. You can still install the driver, however. If the new driver is replacing an existing driver and if the new one seems to make matters worse, you can easily "roll back" to the preceding driver, without reinstalling anything. See Chapter 18 for details on System Restore and signed drivers.

Improved Performance, Reliability, and Compatibility

Windows XP is built on the fully protected 32-bit engine developed for Windows NT and Windows 2000. The old 16-bit DOS engine from Windows Me and its predecessors is gone for good! Compatibility has been approved, allowing hundreds of programs that wouldn't run on Windows 2000 to run without a hitch in Windows XP.

For those programs that still won't run, there's Compatibility mode, which allows a program to run in a Windows 95, 98, Me, NT 4.0 (Service Pack 5), or Windows 2000 environment.

Cross-Reference See "Dealing with Troublesome Programs" in Chapter 3 for more on compatibility.

Windows XP also supports all the latest hardware standards, including UDF 2.1 for DVDs, DVD-RAM drives, DirectX 8 for multimedia, Universal Serial Bus (USB), IEEE 1394 (FireWire) cards, and IrDA the Infrared Data Association standards.

✦   ✦   ✦

Special Folders and Shortcut Keys

This appendix provides a quick reference to special folders in Windows XP and to common shortcut keys. Everything in this appendix is optional. For example, you can rearrange items on the Start menu by dragging items to new locations within the menu. An alternative approach is to open your special Start Menu folder and rearrange icons there.

Tip If you drag items onto the Start menu, Windows XP will *pin* them into the area at the top of the menu. To remove them from this area, right-click the item and select Unpin from the Start menu. You can then drag the item off the top of the Start menu.

Similarly, you can do anything by clicking some item or option with the mouse. If your hands are currently on the keyboard and you don't want to lift them, however, you can use the shortcut key instead.

Special Folders

Your Windows XP program is actually a set of folders and files. Some of the folders play some special role on your screen. For example, all the shortcut icons on your Windows XP desktop are actually installed in a folder named `C:\Documents and Settings\`*username*`\Desktop`—where *username* is your user name. Even though these folders play special roles, they can still be manipulated, as can any other folder on your desktop. Table C-1 lists items accessible from the desktop that store their data in special folders.

Note   Each user has his own set of special folders, as shown in Table C-1. In addition, Windows XP has several folders with similar names that appear in the `C:\Documents and Settings\All Users` **and** `C:\Documents and Settings\All Users\Windows` folders. These folders hold items accessible to all users. When Windows XP displays the Start menu, it often combines items from the All Users folders with items from your personal folders in order to display the complete menu.

Table C-1
Windows XP Items That Store Data in Folders

Windows XP Feature	Gets Icons From
Autostart programs	`C:\ Documents and Settings\`*username*`\Start Menu\Programs\StartUp`
Desktop	`C:\ Documents and Settings\`*username*`\Desktop`
Documents menu	`C:\ Documents and Settings\`*username*`\My Recent Documents`
Favorites	`C:\ Documents and Settings\`*username*`\Favorites`
Fonts	`C:\Windows\Fonts`
History	`C:\ Documents and Settings\`*username*`\Local Settings\History`
Internet cache	`C:\ Documents and Settings\`*username*`\Local Settings\Temporary Internet Files`
Internet Explorer cookies	`C:\ Documents and Settings\`*username*`\Cookies`
Send To menu	`C:\ Documents and Settings\`*username*`\SendTo`
Start menu	`C:\ Documents and Settings\username\Start Menu`

Shortcut Keys

Windows XP offers many shortcut keys you can use in lieu of the mouse. These might come in handy when your fingers are on the keyboard and you don't want to remove them to click something. General shortcut keys applicable at (or before) the appearance of the Windows XP desktop are listed in Table C-2.

Table C-2
Shortcut Keys Used at the Desktop and During Bootup

Operation	Key(s)
Bypass CD-ROM autoplay	Hold down Shift while inserting the CD
Cancel dialog box	Esc
Cancel drag-and-drop	Esc
Capture screen to Windows Clipboard	Print Screen
Capture current window to Clipboard	Alt+Print Screen
Choose menu command/dialog box option	Alt+*underlined letter*
Close the current document window	Ctrl+F4
Close the current program window	Alt+F4
Diagnostic bootup	Press F8 at startup
Copy	Ctrl+C
Cut	Ctrl+X
Delete	Delete or Del
Delete immediately (no Recycle Bin)	Shift+Delete or Shift+Del
Find files or folders	F3
Help	F1
Paste	Ctrl+V
Properties of current item	Alt+Enter
Refresh window contents	F5
Rename	F2
Shortcut menu for current item	Shift+F10
Safe mode bootup	Press F8 after beep at bootup
Shut down	Alt+F4 (after all open windows are closed)
Start menu	Ctrl+Esc or Windows key
Switch to another open program	Alt+Tab
System menu for current document	Alt+hyphen (-)
System menu for current program	Alt+Spacebar
Undo	Ctrl+Z

Windows keyboards

Some keyboards, called *Windows keyboards*, have an extra Windows key and Application key, usually placed between the Ctrl and Alt keys. The Windows key usually has a little flying Windows logo on them. The Application key has a tiny window and mouse pointer icon on it. If your keyboard has those keys, you can use the shortcuts listed in Table C-3.

Tip   Windows keyboards also have a *context menu* key (usually next to the Ctrl key to the right of the Spacebar) that works just like right-clicking the mouse — it displays a context menu for the currently selected item.

Table C-3 Shortcut Keys Available on Special Windows Keyboards	
Operation	*Key(s)*
Cycle through buttons on the taskbar	Windows+Tab
Find files and folders	Windows+F
Find computers on the network	Ctrl+Windows+F
Help	Windows+F1
Lock the keyboard	Windows+L
Minimize or restore all windows	Windows+D
Right-click menu for current item	Application
Run	Windows+R
Start menu	Windows
System Properties dialog box	Windows+Break
Undo minimize all windows	Shift+Windows+M
Utility Manager	Windows+U
Windows Explorer	Windows+E

Drag-and-drop shortcuts

You can hold down a key while dragging an item or a selection of items, to force a move, or to copy or create a shortcut, as summarized in Table C-4. As an alternative to using any of those keys, you can drag using the right mouse button. When you drop (release the mouse button), a menu appears enabling you to choose what you want to do with the item(s).

Table C-4	
Shortcut Keys to Use During Drag-and-Drop Operations	
Operation	*Key(s) to Hold*
Cancel drag-and-drop	Esc
Copy file(s) being dragged	Ctrl+drag
Create shortcut to file being dragged	Ctrl+Shift+drag
Move files being dragged	Alt+drag

Accessibility shortcuts

If you activated Windows XP Accessibility features, use the keys listed in Table C-5 to activate/deactivate those features.

Table C-5	
Accessibility Features Shortcut Keys	
Operation	*Key(s)*
FilterKeys on/off	Hold down right Shift key for eight seconds
High Contrast on/off	Left Alt+Left Shift+Print Screen
MouseKeys on/off	Left Alt+Left Shift+Num Lock
StickyKeys on/off	Press Shift five times
Switch ToggleKeys on/off	Hold down Num Lock for five seconds
Utility Manager	Windows+U

Explorer

When browsing your system, you can use the keys listed in Table C-6 in lieu of mouse clicking.

Table C-6
Shortcut Keys You Can Use in Explorer

Operation	Key(s)
Close current folder and all its parent folders	Hold Shift while clicking Close (X) button
Close current window	Alt+F4
Collapse selected folder if expanded, or expand folder if it is collapsed	→
Collapse the current selection if it is expanded	←
Copy selected item(s)	Ctrl+C
Cut selected item(s)	Ctrl+X
Delete without copying to Recycle Bin	Shift+Delete
Expand all folders below current selection	* on numeric keypad
Expand the selected folder	+ on numeric keypad
Find all files	F3
Move backward to a previous view	Alt+←
Move forward to a previous view	Alt+→
Move to parent folder if current folder is not expanded	←
Paste	Ctrl+V
Refresh window contents	F5
Rename	F2
Select first subfolder if it is not collapsed	→
Switch between left and right panes; move to Address line	F6
View current item's properties	Shift+Enter or Shift+double-click
View the folder one level up	Backspace

Shortcut keys in most Windows programs

Many of the shortcut keys listed in preceding tables are universal in that they perform the same function within a Windows program as they perform at the desktop. Some shortcut keys are also universal to most Windows programs, even though no equivalent is at the desktop. The shortcut keys commonly used within programs are listed in Table C-7.

Table C-7
Universal Shortcut Keys Available in Most Windows Programs

Operation	Key(s)
Cancel menu, drag, or dialog box	Escape (Esc)
Close current document	Ctrl+F4
Close program	Alt+F4
Copy	Ctrl+C
Cut	Ctrl+X
Delete	Delete or Del
End of document	Ctrl+End
End of line	End
Find	Ctrl+F (or F3)
Help	F1
Menu (activate)	F10
New document	Ctrl+N
Open document	Ctrl+O
Paste	Ctrl+V
Print	Ctrl+P
Pull down specific menu	Alt+*underlined letter*
Replace	Ctrl+H
Save	Ctrl+S
Select All	Ctrl+A
Select item from open menu	*Underlined letter*
Start of line	Home
Top of document	Ctrl+Home
Undo	Ctrl+Z
What's This?	Shift+F1

Dialog box shortcut keys

Table C-8 lists shortcut keys that apply to most dialog boxes and the controls displayed within those dialog boxes. Keys that apply to specific controls work only when this type of control is selected (has the dotted border around it). To select a control, click it or press Tab or Shift+Tab until the border appears around the option you want to change.

Table C-8 Shortcuts Keys Available in Dialog Boxes	
Operation	*Key(s)*
Cancel without saving	Esc
Choose option	Alt+*underlined letter*
Clear/fill current check box or radio button	Spacebar
Click button (if selected)	Spacebar
Click default (dark-rimmed) button	Enter
Cursor to end of line	End
Cursor to start of line	Home
Drop-down list (view)	Alt+↓
Move backward through options	Shift+Tab
Move backward through tabs	Ctrl+Shift+Tab
Move forward through options	Tab
Move forward through tabs	Ctrl+Tab
Open a folder one level up in Save As or Open dialog box	Backspace
Open Save In or Look In from the Save As or Open dialog box	F4
Refresh the Save As or Open dialog box	F5
Scroll bar up/down	↑, ↓, Page Up, Page Down, mouse wheel
Slider left/right	←, →
Spin box up/down	↑, ↓

✦   ✦   ✦

Glossary

+ When used in *key+key*, this means hold down the first key, tap the second key, and then release the first key. For example, press Ctrl+A means hold down the Ctrl key, press and release the letter *A*, and then release the Ctrl key.

:-) Your basic *smiley* looks like a smiling face when flipped on its side. Often used in e-mail messages.

10BASE-T A type of cable used to connect computers together in a local area network (LAN). Typically plugs into an RJ-45 slot on a network adapter card and Ethernet hub. Transfers data at 10 megabits per second.

100BASE-T Same as 10BASE-T, but 10 times faster (100 megabits per second)

16-bit The chip architecture used for DOS and earlier Windows 3.*x* programs.

32-bit The more advanced chip architecture used in Windows 98, Me, NT, 2000, and XP.

access control The process of controlling access to files, folders, and devices by granting rights and permissions to users and groups.

ACL (access control list) A feature of NTFS files and folders that stores information about who can, and cannot, access the item.

ACPI (Advanced Configuration and Power Interface) A standard that provides for efficient use of power resources, Plug-and-Play devices, and hot docking.

Active Desktop The capability to put Internet-updateable HTML pages and objects onto the Windows desktop.

Active Directory A feature of recent Windows Server products that allows any object on a network to be tracked and easily found.

active window The window currently capable of accepting keyboard input. The active window can cover other windows on the desktop. Clicking anywhere on a window, or clicking its taskbar button, instantly makes that window active.

ADS Abbreviation for Active Directory Services.

AGP (Advanced Graphics Port) A special slot on the motherboard that provides high-performance graphics.

anonymous FTP A type of File Transfer Protocol used on the Internet that enables anyone to log on anonymously and download files.

AOL (America Online) A popular information service offering e-mail, special-interest groups, Internet access, and other services.

app Slang for application.

applet A small application program.

application Another word for program—software you purchase and use on your PC.

ASCII (American Standard Code for Information Interchange) A standard for describing characters that allows different makes and models of computers to communicate with one another. An ASCII file or ASCII text file is one containing only ASCII characters—no pictures or formatting codes.

associate To tie a file name extension to a program. For example, the .doc file name extension is usually associated with Microsoft Word. When you double-click a document with the .doc extension, Windows automatically opens Microsoft Word and opens the file displaying the document you clicked or double-clicked.

attributes Settings that can be applied to files and folders by right-clicking the item's icon and choosing Properties.

audio CD The regular kind of CD you buy in a music store to play on a stereo CD player.

auditing The process of recording various events that occur on a computer or network, and recording those events to an audit log.

authentication The process by which a system identifies a user's logon information by comparing the user's entry against a list of authorized users.

backward compatibility The capability to use documents, settings, and so forth from earlier products.

bandwidth The amount of information that can be transferred along a wire or other medium, such as a satellite, at any given time. A higher bandwidth means more information coming through the wire at a time and, therefore, faster interaction with whatever is on the other side of that connection.

baud The speed at which information is sent through a modem, equivalent to bits per second (bps). A higher baud rate means faster communications.

beta A version of a software product released to selected corporations and individuals for testing purposes prior to being released to the general public.

binding A process that establishes a communication channel between a network adapter card's driver and the driver for a network protocol.

BIOS The Basic Input/Output System that enables interaction between the computer and its input (mouse/keyboard) and output (screen, printer) devices. The brand name and version number of your computer's BIOS generally appear onscreen shortly after you first start your computer.

BIOS Settings A program that enables you to change BIOS settings on your computer. To get to it, you usually have to press the Del or F2 key shortly after first turning on the computer.

bit Short for *binary digit.* Represents a single switch that can be either on or off. A byte is a collection of eight bits.

bitmap A graphic file format in which each dot is actually represented by a bit. A vector image, on the other hand, stores graphics as mathematical data, which is then used to draw shapes.

boot The process of starting a computer. A *cold boot* is when you start the computer from scratch. A *warm boot* or *reboot* is when you reset the computer by clicking the Start button and choosing Turn Off Computer ⇨ Restart.

bps (bits per second) A measure of a modem's speed, also expressed as *baud*.

BRB Often used in online chats as an abbreviation for Be Right Back.

broadband A generic term for high-speed Internet access such as cable and DSL.

byte The amount of space required to store one character. For instance, the word *cat* requires three bytes of storage. The word *hello* uses five bytes.

cache Pronounced *cash*. A folder on the disk or some other resource used to store information, automatically, to speed up later operations.

capture To record to a video or other media to a file on a computer disk.

capture device An add-in card or other device that can record data from some external device into a file on a computer disk.

CD-R Recordable compact disc. A CD-R drive is one that enables you to burn (record) information to a CD-R disc.

CD-ROM (Compact Disc Read-Only Memory) A compact disk containing computer files rather than music. The Read-Only part comes from the fact that files can only be read from the disk. You cannot write to the disk or change its contents.

CD-RW Rewriteable compact disc. A compact disc that can be written to more that once.

certificate A document used for the secure exchange of files across a network.

character Any single letter, numeric digit, or punctuation mark. For example, the letter *C* is a character.

chat A program or Internet service that enables users to communicate with one another by typing messages back and forth.

Classic style An option that enables you to navigate Windows XP in a manner similar to Windows 95, in which you must double-click to open icons, click to select them.

clear To "unselect" a check box, or a toggle option on a menu, by clicking it.

ClearType A feature of Windows XP that triples horizontal resolution for better display on LCD (Liquid Crystal Display) screens.

click To rest the mouse pointer on some item onscreen and then press and release the primary mouse button.

client A computer in a network that can use shared resources.

clip A still picture or small chunk of video or audio used in a movie.

clipboard A place in the computer's memory where you can temporarily store text and pictures. Pressing Ctrl+C copies selected items to the clipboard. Pressing Ctrl+V pastes items from the clipboard to the current location.

close To remove an object from the screen so that it's no longer visible. Typically, closing an object removes it from memory (RAM) and saves it to the hard disk.

CMOS Memory maintained by a small battery within the PC. Often used to manage settings that come into play before the operating system is loaded.

codec A system to compress/decompress digital video and sound to minimize the amount of disk space required for storage.

compressed file A file that contains one more files shrunk down to their most effi-cient size to minimize storage requirements and transfer time across a network. Also called *compressed folders* in Windows XP. Files with the .zip extension are compressed.

compressed folder A compressed file. Called a compressed folder in Windows XP because its icon appears as a manila file folder with a zipper on it. If you install a third-party zip program, compressed folders display as the icon for that program.

computer name The name assigned to a computer in a network, visible in on the Computer Name tab of the System icon in Control Panel.

connectoid A collection of settings that defines how to connect to a network or other service. In Windows XP, they can be created and maintained in Network Connections.

content In the media biz, the text, pictures, and/or video that make up a presenta-tion or published work. Also called *source content*.

context-sensitive help Help relevant to whatever you're currently trying to do. Context-sensitive help is generally available when you click the Help button or press the Help (F1) key.

control Any button, list, or text box within a dialog box that enables you to control how the computer will behave.

Control Panel A collection of icons that enable you to manage and personalize Windows. Typically accessible from the Start menu. If not, right-click the Start but-ton, choose Properties, and click the Customize button. On the Advanced tab, choose Display as Link under Control Panel in the list of items to show in the menu.

cookie A small file placed on your hard disk by a Web site, usually to record infor-mation about your account so that you don't need to log on every time you visit.

Credential Manager A tool that enables users to enter a user name and password once, and then have that information automatically supplied to multiple domains without trust relationships.

Ctrl+click To hold down the Ctrl key while clicking an item.

Ctrl+point To hold down the Ctrl key while pointing to an item.

cut-and-paste A technique used to move or copy text or graphics from one docu-ment to another. After selecting the object to be moved or copied, pressing Ctrl+C copies the selection to the Windows Clipboard. Pressing Ctrl+X moves the selection to the Windows Clipboard. Pressing Ctrl+V pastes the Clipboard contents at the current cursor position. You also can choose Copy, Cut, or Paste from the Edit menu in most programs.

DCC (Direct Cable Connection) A means of connecting two computers with a cable, as opposed to Ethernet cards, hubs, or modems.

default A setting made for you when you don't make the selection yourself.

desktop The main Windows workspace that appears when you first start your PC. You can customize it by right-clicking the desktop and choosing Properties.

desktop icon (desktop shortcut) An icon that resides on the Windows desktop to provide easy access to some other location. You can choose some icons by right-clicking the desktop, choosing Properties, and clicking the Customize Desktop button on the Desktop tab. You also can drag icons to the desktop to create folders

desktop theme A combination of sounds, wallpaper, screen saver, and icons that give your entire desktop a particular appearance.

device A general term for any gizmo or gadget you put into a computer or attach to a computer with a cable.

device driver A small program that makes a hardware device work. To print, for example, you typically need a printer (hardware) and a driver (software) for that printer.

DHCP (Dynamic Host Configuration Protocol) A program that automatically assigns IP addresses to computers on a network so that they don't need to be addressed manually.

dialog box A window containing options from which you can choose. These options are generally settings — for color, size, speed, and so forth.

digital image A picture stored as a file on a computer disk.

directory A place on a disk where a group of files is stored. Also called a *folder*.

directory server A place on the Internet where people who want to communicate gather. Used in conjunction with a teleconferencing program such as Microsoft NetMeeting.

disk drive A physical device in the computer capable of storing information, even while the computer is turned off. Typically, the main hard disk is named C:. The floppy disk is A:. A CD-ROM drive might be D:, E:, or some higher letter.

DLL (dynamic link library) A file used by one or more application programs.

DNS (Domain Name System) A database used by Internet TCP/IP hosts to resolve host names and IP addresses. Enables users of remote computers to access one another by host names such as `www.whatever.com` rather than numeric IP addresses.

dock To attach a notebook computer to a docking station.

docking station Usually a piece of hardware that allows a laptop computer to connect to a normal-sized mouse, keyboard, monitor, and/or network.

document A file you create using some program. When you use a word processing program to type a letter, for example, that letter is a document.

domain A group of computers sharing a common domain database and security policy controlled by a Windows Server edition domain controller.

domain name On the Internet, the last part of an e-mail address. For example, in alan@coolnerds.com, the coolnerds.com part is the Internet domain name.

DOS (Disk Operating System) The first operating system for PCs.

double-click To point to an item and then click the primary mouse button twice in rapid succession.

download To copy a file from some remote computer on the Internet (or elsewhere) onto your own local PC.

drag To hold down the primary mouse button while moving the mouse.

drag-and-drop To move or copy an item by holding down the mouse button as you move the item to some new location. To drop the item, release the mouse button.

drive Short for disk drive.

drive letter The single-letter name assigned to a disk drive or network drive. For example, your floppy disk drive is probably named A:, your hard disk C:.

driver Short for *device driver*, a program used to control some device connected to your computer, such as a mouse.

drop To place an item on the desktop by releasing the mouse button after dragging.

drop-down list A text box with a down-arrow box attached. Enables you to choose an option from a list instead of typing in an option. To open the drop-down list, click the drop-down list arrow or press Alt+↓.

DSL (Digital Subscriber Line) A way of connecting to the Internet that allows high-speed access through traditional telephone lines.

DVD (Digital Video Disc) Stands for either digital video disc or digital versatile disc, depending on who you ask. DVD is a format that allows full-length motion pictures to be stored on a compact disc.

edit To change something, such as a letter you've written.

editor A program that enables you to change something, such as a letter you've written.

e-mail Electronic mail sent over the Internet or some other online service. Microsoft Outlook Express enables you to send and receive e-mail messages over the Internet.

e-mail address The address that uniquely identifies you on a network, much as your street address uniquely identifies the location of your home.

encryption A means of encoding the contents of a file to prevent unauthorized access to its contents.

engine The central core of an operating system that handles communications between programs and devices, and deals with errors and conflicts that arise.

error message Any little message that appears on the screen to describe some problem or error.

Ethernet A popular protocol for building a local area network from two or more PCs.

Ethernet cable The cable used to attach a PC's network adapter card to an Ethernet concentrator.

Ethernet hub The device to which cables in a network.

event Any activity from the mouse, keyboard, or a program the computer can detect. Mouse clicks and key presses are events.

expansion slot A slot on the computer's motherboard into which you can plug expansion cards, such as Ethernet cards, graphics display cards, and other internal devices.

extension The short part of a file name that comes after the period. In `myletter.doc`, for example, the filename extension is `.doc`. Filename extensions for known files are normally hidden in Windows. To bring the extension out of hiding, open the Folder Options icon in Control Panel. On the View tab, clear the Hide extensions for known file types check box.

extract To copy and decompress files from the compressed folder or Zip file so that they can be opened and edited normally.

FAQ (Frequently Asked Questions) A document you can browse on the Internet or download from a fax-back service answering common questions about a topic.

FAT/FAT 32 (file allocation table) The scheme that DOS and Windows use to keep track of files on a disk.

file The basic unit of storage on a disk. When you create and save a letter, for example, that letter is stored in a file. Each file within a folder has its own unique file name.

file name extension See *extension*.

file sharing Allowing multiple PCs on a local area network access to the same set of files on one PC.

file type The characteristics of a file that determine how it behaves when opened. Executable (EXE) files are programs that run when open. Document files open in whatever program is associated with that type of document. Windows identifies a file's type by the file's *extension*.

firewall Hardware or software at a connection device that prevents unauthorized attacks on a system.

FireWire Another name for high-speed IEEE 1394 connections, commonly used for digital video and other bandwidth-hungry connections.

flame To rant and rave on the Internet or another information service by sending obnoxious e-mail messages.

folder A place on a computer disk that holds one or more files. Also called a *directory*.

font A lettering style. Fonts can be installed by choosing File ⇨ Install New Font from the menu bar in the Fonts window. To get to that window, open Control Panel in Classic view, and open the Fonts icon.

FTP (File Transfer Protocol) An Internet service that can be used to upload and download files.

frame A single picture in a video or animation. Also a section of a Web browser screen that displays its own unique page.

G, GB, gig Abbreviation for gigabyte, roughly one billion bytes.

GIF (Graphics Interchange Format) A compact format for storing graphic images, allowing them to be transported over networks more quickly.

gigabyte Roughly one billion bytes.

graphics Pictures, as opposed to written text.

graphics accelerator A hardware device that speeds complex graphics rendering on-screen.

group In security, refers to a set of security options that can be applied to multiple users. Security groups are not available in Windows XP Home edition.

GUI (graphical user interface) Pronounced *gooey*, the icon-oriented interface offered by Windows XP and other modern operating systems.

handwriting recognition The capability to convert handwritten text to typed text.

hardware The physical components of a computer that you can see and touch.

hardware compression A feature available on some hardware devices that allows data to be compressed directly by the device.

Help key The key labeled F1 near the top of the keyboard, which you can press at any time for help.

hibernate A means of saving the system state to disk prior to shutting down the computer, and then reinstating that state automatically when the computer restarts.

home page The first page you come to when you visit a Web site on the Internet.

host Any computer you can access via the Internet or phone lines. In direct cable connection, the PC with the shared resources you want to access.

hot docking The capability to connect a portable computer to its docking station without powering down the portable PC.

hot swapping The ability to plug in a device, and remove it, without shutting down the computer.

HTML (Hypertext Markup Language) A set of tags used to define the format of a page presented over the World Wide Web.

HTTP (Hypertext Transfer Protocol) The protocol used in the World Wide Web to allow documents to call one another.

hub A device to which you can connect multiple cables.

hyperlink A clickable hot spot on a Web page or some other document that, when clicked, takes you to some new page or location on the Internet.

icon A little picture onscreen used to represent a disk drive, folder, or file. You can open an icon by clicking it, or by double-clicking if you're using Classic-style navigation.

ICS (Internet Connection Sharing) A feature of Windows XP that allows multiple computers in a network to share a single Internet connection and account.

IEEE 1394 A standard for high-speed transfer of data through a cable, also called *FireWire*.

image Also called a *digital image*. A picture that's stored on a computer disk as a file.

install To copy and set up a program so that it can be used on your computer.

Internet A huge collection of computers and networks from around the world. Popular services offered by the Internet include e-mail, World Wide Web, conferencing, chat, and FTP.

Internet Explorer (or Microsoft Internet Explorer) A program that enables you to explore and interact with the World Wide Web.

IP address A number that uniquely identifies a computer on a network. The format is usually *xxx.xxx.xxx.xxx* where *xxx* is any number from 0 to 255. On a local area network, each computer typically has an IP address that starts with 192.168.

IPX/SPX A network transport protocol used by Novell NetWare networks.

IR (infrared) Light that's outside the visible spectrum, which allows communication between devices without cables.

IRQ (Interrupt Request Line) The line a hardware device uses to get the attention of the processor.

ISDN (Integrated Services Digital Network) A high-performance telephone line available from most local phone companies. Mainly used to get faster access to the Internet.

ISP (Internet service provider) A company that provides people with access to the Internet.

JPEG (Joint Photographic Experts Group) A compact format for storing photo-quality graphic images, generally for use on the World Wide Web.

K or KB Abbreviation for kilobyte or 1,024 bytes.

kilobyte Roughly a thousand bytes (1,024 bytes to be exact).

known files Files that Windows knows how to handle. Document files are "known" when Windows has associated the file's extension with some program.

LAN (local area network) A group of computers connected together to share resources.

legacy A euphemism for old or obsolete. Refers to any hardware device that adheres to older, outdated standards.

local Everything stored in or directly connected to the computer at which you're sitting. Remote resources are items that can be accessed by the local computer through a network, Internet, or some other type of connection.

local computer On a network, the computer you're currently logged on to.

localization Adapting software to the language and formats of a specific country or culture.

logon The process of gaining access to a computer by entering a user name and (possibly) a password.

lurk To hang around and read messages in an Internet newsgroup without contributing to the group.

M, MB, meg Abbreviation for megabyte, roughly one million bytes.

MAC (Media Access Control) address A unique number tassigned to every network adapter at the time it's manufactured.

megabyte Roughly one million bytes.

memory Usually refers to the random access memory (RAM) component of a PC. Any documents you're currently working with are stored in RAM.

menu A list of options. Clicking the Start button displays the Start menu.

message The general term for any kind of correspondence, such as a note or letter, that takes place over computers.

message box Any box that appears onscreen to display a message.

MIDI (Musical Instrument Digital Interface) A standard for storing and playing music on a PC. Unlike recorded music, MIDI files just contain "musical notes," which are then played by the sound card or a MIDI device.

MIME (Multipurpose Internet Mail Extensions) Defines different types of data that can be transported over the Internet.

modem (modulator/demodulator) A device connecting your PC to a telephone line.

monitor The big TV-like component of a computer.

mouse button The primary mouse button, typically the mouse button on the left.

mouse pointer The little arrow that moves around the screen as you roll the mouse on your desktop.

MP3 A format used for storing CD-quality music on computer disks.

MPEG (Moving Picture Experts Group) A format used for storing video for presentation on a computer screen.

MS-DOS (Microsoft Disk Operating System) Another name for DOS, one of the earliest operating systems used in personal computers.

MSN (The Microsoft Network) An online service provided by Microsoft.

NDIS (Network Driver Interface Specification) The interface for network drivers. All transport drivers call the NDIS interface to access network adapters.

Net, or the Net Slang expression for the Internet.

NetBEUI (NetBIOS Extended User Interface) Pronounced *net buoy,* an older networking protocol used in early versions of Microsoft networking products.

netiquette Network etiquette, polite and proper conduct on the Internet.

netizen A citizen of a network or the Internet.

network Two or more computers connected to one. The Internet is the world's largest network.

network adapter card A hardware device that enables you to connect a PC to other PCs in a local area network. Also called a *network interface card* or *NIC.*

network administrator The person in charge of managing a local area network, including accounts, passwords, e-mail, and so on.

network bridge A simplified means of connecting heterogeneous networks together without the use of complex packet forwarding, routing, or complex devices.

Network Connections A feature of windows that enables you to create and manage connections to the Internet, a network, and other computers. Typically accessible from the Start menu. If not, right-click the Start button, choose Properties, and click the Customize button. On the Advanced tab, choose Network Connections from the list of items to show on the menu.

network drive A shared disk drive or folder on a LAN to which you mapped a drive letter so that you can access it from within My Computer.

network printer A shared printer physically connected to some other PC in the LAN. The opposite of a local printer.

network resource Any file, folder, or device that you can access through a network.

newbie Someone just learning to use a PC or the Internet.

newsgroup An electronic bulletin board on the Internet where people post messages to one another. You can use Microsoft Outlook Express to access Internet newsgroups.

NIC (network interface card) Also called a *network adapter card*. A piece of hardware required to connect a PC to a local area network.

NT The first "corporate" version of Windows, which eventually evolved into Windows 2000 and then into Windows XP.

NTFS A file system that provides larger files and improved security that the FAT system used in DOS and early versions of Windows.

Notification area The right side of the taskbar where the current time and small icons display.

object An individual chunk of data you can manipulate onscreen, which can be a chart, picture, sound, video, or chunk of text.

object-oriented An operating system that allows chunks of data to be manipulated as individual objects and easily moved/copied from one program to another.

offline Disconnected from a network (including the Internet).

online Connected to a network (including the Internet).

open To open a file to view or use its contents. You can open any icon by clicking, or double-clicking, it.

operating system A computer program that integrates a computer and all its peripheral devices (for instance, Windows, UNIX, Linux, and Mac OS).

option button A small, round button in a dialog box that generally enables you to select only one option of many. Also called *radio buttons* (because only one button can be pushed in at a time).

OS An abbreviation for operating system.

owner The person who creates a file or folder.

Passport Provides access to Passport-enabled services on the Internet with a single user name (your e-mail address) and password.

path The location of a folder described in terms of its drive, folder, and subfolder. For example, the path to the Shared Documents folder is C:\Documents and Settings\All Users\Documents.

PC card A credit-card-sized adapter card that fits into the PCMCIA slot of a portable or desktop PC.

PCI (Peripheral Component Interconnect) A slot for add-in cards, available on most modern Pentium PCs.

PCMCIA (Personal Computer Memory Card International Association) A standard defining how PC cards must be designed to work in the PCMCIA slot of a portable or desktop PC.

peer-to-peer network A way to connect several PCs into a local area network where any PC can act as either client or server.

playback device Any device that can play content that's been recorded and stored electronically. For example, a CD player or VCR.

PNP An abbreviation for Plug and Play, a standard that makes adding a hardware device to a PC relatively easy.

point To move the mouse so that the mouse pointer is touching some object onscreen. Also used as a unit of measurement in typography, where one point equals approximately 1/72 of an inch. In Web browsing, to point your Web browser to some Web site means to type that Web site's URL into the Address portion of your Web browser and then press Enter.

pointing device A mouse or trackball used to move the mouse pointer around on the screen.

pop-up menu The menu that appears when you right-click an object. Also called a *context menu* or a *shortcut menu*.

port A slot on the back of your PC into which you plug a cable that connects to some external device. Mice, keyboards, monitors, external modems, external CD-ROM drives, printers, and all other external devices plug into a port on a PC.

port replicator A compact-sized docking station for a portable computer that enables easy connection to a full-sized keyboard, mouse, monitor, and other devices.

primary mouse button The mouse button used for most activities, usually the button on the left.

privacy policy Settings that control your privacy by determining how much information about yourself you expose publicly over the Internet, and what types of e-mail messages are acceptable.

program Software you (generally) purchase and use on your PC.

properties Characteristics such as color, size, shape, and so forth. You can get to most items' properties by right-clicking their icon and choosing Properties from the menu that appears.

protocol An agreed-upon set of rules by which two computers can exchange information over a network.

public profile Information about yourself that you're willing to expose to the public on the Internet.

Quick Launch toolbar A set of icons, usually just to the right of the Start button, that provide quick access to frequently used programs. Can be hidden, displayed, moved, and sized.

RAM (random access memory) The part of the computer where only the stuff you're currently working on is stored. Things you aren't currently using are stored on the disk. Also called *memory* for short.

read-only A file that can be viewed, but not changed. Files copied from CD-ROMs are often set to read-only by default. To clear the read-only attribute, right-click the file's icon, choose Properties, and clear the Read-only check box.

reboot To restart the computer without shutting down. Click the Start button and choose Turn Off Computer ⇨ Restart.

registered file type A type of document file associated with a specific program, based on its file name extension. For example, all DOC files are registered to (associated with) the Microsoft Word for Windows program.

Registry A database on your hard disk that automatically keeps track of all your Windows XP settings.

remote Not a part of, nor directly connected to, the local computer.

resolution The general term for the number of pixels on the desktop (also called screen area). Common resolutions include 640 x 480, 800 x 600, and 1024 x 768. The higher the resolution, the more you can see on your screen. Can be changed by right-clicking the desktop and choosing Properties ⇨ Settings.

resource Anything offering a useful service or information.

rich text Text that contains special formatting like boldface and italics.

right-click To click an icon or other item using the secondary mouse button (typically the button on the right side of the mouse).

right-drag To hold down the secondary mouse button (typically the mouse button on the right) while dragging an object to some new location onscreen.

roll back To return to a previous state. Device driver rollback, for example, means the ability to return to a previous driver without reinstalling that driver from scratch.

root directory The topmost folder on a disk, usually named \. For example, C:\ represents the root directory of drive C:.

RTF (rich text format) Text containing special formatting such as boldface and italics.

Safe mode A means of starting the computer with the minimum settings and drivers, to help a user solve problems that are preventing normal startup.

scalable The ability to "upsize" without making dramatic changes to software.

scrap A picture or chunk of text dragged into a folder. The resulting scrap file can be copied into the Clipboard by right-clicking and choosing Copy.

SCSI (Small Computer System Interface) Pronounced *scuzzy*. An interface specification that enables multiple disk drives, CD-ROM drives, and other devices to be connected to one another and then connected to a single port on the PC.

search engine A special service on the World Wide Web that helps you find information on a particular topic. Alta Vista at www.altavista.com is a search engine.

secondary mouse button The button used for viewing options, rather than opening icons. In most cases, this is the mouse button on the right side of the mouse.

select Usually refers to the act of choosing one or more items to work with by dragging the mouse pointer through them.

selection An object (or objects) already selected and, hence, framed or highlighted in some manner.

server A computer that offers resources to other computers in a network.

share (shared resource) A file, folder, or device that's shared on a network so other computers in the network can have access.

shareware Software given to you free for a trial period so that you can try it before you buy.

Shift+click To hold down the Shift key while clicking some item.

Shift+point To hold down the Shift key while moving the mouse pointer to some item.

shortcut An icon on the desktop or in the folder that provides easy access to some file, folder, or device located elsewhere on the computer or the network. A *keyboard shortcut* refers to some key(s) you can press as an alternative to going through menus.

signed driver A device driver that's been "digitally signed" by Microsoft or other manufacturer, to verify its compatible with Windows XP.

SLIP (Serial Line Internet Protocol) A way to connect a PC to an Internet service provider. Point-to-Point Protocol (PPP) is preferred over SLIP when connecting to the Internet.

smart card A card that contains information that can be read by a computer or other device.

snail mail Standard postal service (paper) mail.

software The intangible instructions, stored on a computer disk, that tell the computer how to behave. All computer programs, including Windows XP, are software.

source content In the media biz, the text, pictures, and/or video that make up a presentation or published work. Also called just *content*.

spam Junk e-mail or any advertisement that's disguised as a message.

Start menu The menu that appears when you click the Start button in the lower-left corner of the Windows desktop.

standby A means of reducing the power consumption of a computer to the point where only enough electricity is consumed to keep RAM from going blank.

status bar The bar along the bottom of a program's window that provides information about the status of various options within that program.

streaming format Data that is sent and experienced as a continuous stream, as with TV.

string Textual, rather than numeric, data. For example, 123.45 is a number, whereas *My dog has fleas* is a string (of characters).

subfolder A folder contained within another folder. The containing folder is called the *parent folder*.

synchronization A means of keeping offline files in sync with their online counterparts.

System menu A menu you can open by clicking the icon in the upper-left corner of a window or by pressing Alt+Spacebar. Enables you to move and size a window using the keyboard rather than the mouse.

T1, T3 Special lines that provide high-speed, full-time access to the Internet.

taskbar The strip, usually along the bottom of the Windows desktop, that displays the Start button, a button for each open program, and the Notification area. When hidden, dragging the mouse pointer off the bottom of the screen brings it back into view.

TCP/IP (Transmission Control Protocol/Internet Protocol) The primary communications protocol used on the Internet.

text file A file containing only ASCII text codes such as letters, numbers, spaces, and punctuation—no hidden codes. Text files should be created and edited with text-only editors, such as Notepad available from the Accessories menu in Windows XP.

thread 1) A series of messages about a topic posted to an information service. 2) An executable chunk of program code that can run simultaneously with other threads in a microprocessor.

TIA Thanks In Advance, an acronym often used in e-mail or chat rooms.

title bar The colored area across the top of the window that shows the window's name and offers the Minimize, Maximize, and Close (X) buttons, and the System menu. To move a window, drag its title bar. You also can maximize or restore a window by double-clicking its title bar.

toggle A switch or option that can have only one of two possible settings: on or off.

toolbar A set of buttons and other controls that provide one-click access to frequently used menu commands.

ToolTip The little label that appears when you rest the mouse pointer on the toolbar button or other item.

Trojan horse A destructive program that appears innocent. Unlike a virus, a Trojan horse does not replicate itself across computers in a network.

UNC (Uniform Naming Convention) A method of identifying a resource by its computer name, followed by a resource name. The computer name is preceded by two backslashes; for example, \\Comm_Center\MyStuff represent a shared folder named MyStuff on a computer named Comm_Center.

upload To copy a file from your local PC to some remote computer on the Internet or elsewhere.

URL (Uniform Resource Locator) The address to some resource on the Internet, such as `http://www.coolnerds.com`.

USB (Universal Serial Bus) A connection that enables you to plug in a device without shutting down the computer. The Notification area informs you when the device has been detected and is ready for use.

Usenet A service on the Internet that enables people to communicate via newsgroups.

VESA (Video Electronic Standards Association) A group that defines standards for video displays.

VGA (Virtual Graphics Array) The type of display card and monitor that gives you rich color and graphics.

virtual driver A 32-bit device driver that can be loaded into upper memory via the Registry (as opposed to a Real-mode driver, which must be loaded into conventional or upper memory via `config.sys` or `autoexec.bat`).

virtual memory Disk space used as RAM when RAM runs out.

virus A computer program specifically designed to do damage on whatever PC it lands. High-tech vandalism.

VPN (virtual private networking) A means of connecting to private computers through the public Internet, providing security similar to that found in more expensive private connections.

WAN (wide area network) A group of computers that can share resources on a large scale. The Internet, for example, is one huge, global WAN.

WDM (Windows Driver Model) A program that allows hardware devices to work in Windows XP.

Web Short for World Wide Web, a service of the Internet.

Web browser A program, such as Microsoft Internet Explorer, used to browse the World Wide Web.

Web style An option (usually under Tools ⇨ Internet Options), which enables you to navigate Windows XP in a manner similar to the World Wide Web — by clicking rather than double-clicking underlined links.

Whiteboard A simple drawing program that can be used by several people at the same time. Microsoft NetMeeting comes with a Whiteboard.

window A frame onscreen that displays a single program or folder. Every window has a title bar across the top; Minimize, Maximize, and Close (X) buttons near the upper-right corner; and other features. A closed window appears as an icon onscreen.

WINS (Windows Internet Naming Service) A naming service that resolves Windows network computer names to Internet IP addresses.

workgroup A collection of computers in a LAN that all share the same workgroup name, and can share resources. Unlike *domains*, networks do not require a domain controller. Nor do they offer centralized user accounts and authentication.

workstation A PC with unusually high processing capabilities, often used for computer-aided design and similar calculation-intensive and graphics-intensive jobs.

World Wide Web A popular place on the Internet, where you can browse through documents that contain text, graphics, and even multimedia.

WWW Abbreviation for the World Wide Web, a service of the Internet.

X.25 A network transmission protocol that bypasses noisy telephone lines provided by X.25 dial-up carriers such as Sprintet and Infonet.

Zip file (zipped file) A file that's been compressed to speed transfer over a network. Appears as a compressed folder in Windows XP, unless some third-party Zip program is installed. All have the file name extension `.zip`.

zone (Internet zone) A means of categorizing Internet and network resources according to trust. For example, resources in the Restricted Sites zone are not allowed to store cookies on your computer.

Index

Continued

Continued

Continued

Continued

Continued

Continued